∿

Major Problems in the History of North American Borderlands

MAJOR PROBLEMS IN AMERICAN HISTORY SERIES

GENERAL EDITOR

THOMAS G. PATERSON

Major Problems in the History of North American Borderlands

Documents and Essays

PEKKA HÄMÄLÄINEN

Department of History
University of California, Santa Barbara

BENJAMIN H. JOHNSON

Department of History and Program in Global Studies
University of Wisconsin, Milwaukee

WADSWORTH
CENGAGE Learning·

Australia • Brazil • Japan • Korea • Mexico • Singapore • Spain • United Kingdom • United States

WADSWORTH
CENGAGE Learning

Major Problems in the History of North American Borderlands: Documents and Essays
Pekka Hämäläinen,
Benjamin H. Johnson

Senior Publisher: Suzanne Jeans

Acquisitions Editor: Jeffrey Greene

Development Editor: Terri Wise

Assistant Editor: Megan Chrisman

Editorial Assistant: Patricia Roach

Senior Media Editor: Lisa Ciccolo

Marketing Manager: Katherine Bates

Marketing Coordinator: Lorreen R. Towle

Marketing Communications Manager: Caitlin Green

Project Management: PreMediaGlobal

Senior Art Director: Cate Rickard Barr

Senior Print Buyer: Sandra Milewski

Senior Rights Acquisitions Specialist: Jennifer Meyer Dare

Cover Designer: Gary Ragaglia

Cover Image: Mexican women with her children and bundles on the edge of the Rio Grande River. Ca. 1910. © Everett Collection Inc/Alamy

Compositor: PreMediaGlobal

Back cover photograph of Benjamin Johnson courtesy of Michelle Nickerson

For product information and technology assistance, contact us at
Cengage Learning Customer & Sales Support, 1-800-354-9706

For permission to use material from this text or product, submit all requests online at **www.cengage.com/permissions**. Further permissions questions can be emailed to **permissionrequest@cengage.com**.

Library of Congress Control Number: 2011930735

ISBN-13: 978-0-495-91692-5

ISBN-10: 0-495-91692-7

Wadsworth
20 Channel Center Street
Boston, MA 02210
USA

Cengage Learning is a leading provider of customized learning solutions with office locations around the globe, including Singapore, the United Kingdom, Australia, Mexico, Brazil and Japan. Locate your local office at **international.cengage.com/region**.

Cengage Learning products are represented in Canada by Nelson Education, Ltd.

For your course and learning solutions, visit
www.cengage.com

Purchase any of our products at your local college store or at our preferred online store **www.cengagebrain.com**.

Instructors: Please visit **login.cengage.com** and log in to access instructor-specific resources.

Printed in the United States of America
1 2 3 4 5 6 7 15 14 13 12 11

Contents

PREFACE   xv

Chapter 1   What Is Borderlands History?   1

ESSAYS   2

Michiel Baud and Willem Van Schendel • A Comparative Approach to Borderlands   3

Jeremy Adelman and Stephen Aron • From Borderlands to Borders   14

Andrew Graybill and Benjamin Johnson • Telling North American Border Histories   26

FURTHER READING   39

Chapter 2   Early Borderlands: The Southwest   41

DOCUMENTS   42

1. Ginés de Herrera Horta Testifies on Spanish Treatment of Pueblo Indians, 1601   43

2. Pedro Naranjo (Keresan Pueblo) Explains the Pueblo Revolt, 1681   45

3. Bishop Benito Crespo Is Confounded by New Mexico, 1730   48

4. Father Francisco Casanas de Jesús Maria on How to Win the Allegiance of the Caddo Indians, 1691   49

5. Philibert Ory Urges Louisiana to Open Trade with Spaniards in Natchitoches, 1730   52

6. Captain Pierre Marie François de Pagès Reports on Texas, 1767   53

ESSAYS   54

Dedra S. MacDonald • Indians and Africans Collaborate in Colonial New Mexico   55

Juliana Barr • Captivity, Gender, and Social Control in the Texas-Louisiana Borderlands   68

FURTHER READING   81

Chapter 3   Middle Grounds, Borderlands, and Frontiers   83

DOCUMENTS   84

1. John Smith on the Powhatan Confederacy, 1624   87

2. Chief Powhatan Addresses John Smith, 1609   88

3. Father Jean de Brébeuf Instructs Jesuit Missionaries, 1637   89

4. Mary Jemison Looks Back on Her Capture by and Life Among Indians, 1824   91

5. The South Carolina Legislature Passes an Act for the Capture of Runaway Slaves, 1700   93

6. William Stephens Assesses the Prospects of Slavery in Georgia, 1742   94

7. Pierre Le Moyne d'Iberville Addresses Chickasaw and Choctaw Leaders, 1702   96

8. Governor Etienne de Périer Considers the Use of Black Slave Troops against Indians, 1730   97

9. Governor Etienne de Périer Appraises French-English-Chickasaw Relations, 1730   100

ESSAYS   101

James H. Merrell • Indian-English Frontiers of Cooperation and Conquest   103

Kathleen Duval • French Louisiana in the Native Ground   118

FURTHER READING   129

Chapter 4   Borderlands, Cultural Exchanges, and New Native Societies   132

DOCUMENTS   133

1. Maheo, All-Father Creator, Warns the Cheyennes about Life with Horses   134

2. Saukamappee (Cree) Recalls the Arrival of Horses, Guns, and Smallpox to the Northern Plains, 1787   135

3. The Marqués de Rubí Recommends the Extermination of the Apaches, 1768   138

4. Charles McKenzie Describes Horse and Gun Trade on the Northern Plains, 1805   140

5. Rudolph Friedrich Kurz on Gifts, Intermarriage, and the Fur Trade   142

6. Francis Chardon Records Relations between Fur Traders and Native Women and a Smallpox Epidemic in the Upper Missouri River, 1836–1839   143

ESSAYS   **146**

Sylvia Van Kirk • Intermarriage, Borderlands, and Power   147

Pekka Hämäläinen • Ecological Change and Indigenous Imperialism in the Southwest Borderlands   153

FURTHER FEADING   **165**

Chapter 5   Borderlands in Change: The View from Above   168

DOCUMENTS   **169**

1. Theodore de Croix Compares California to Older Spanish Colonies, 1781   170

2. Governor Alejandro O'Reilly Evaluates Louisiana's Position in Spain's Colonial Economy, 1769   171

3. Bernardo de Gálvez Outlines How to Achieve "Peace by Deceit," 1786   172

4. Pontiac Urges Ottawas, Potawatomis, and Hurons to Rise Up Against the British, 1763   174

5. Governor William Tryon Assesses the Potential of North Carolina Backcountry, 1765   176

6. George Washington Denounces the Royal Proclamation Line, 1767   177

ESSAYS   **178**

David J. Weber • New Spain and Its Borderlands   179

François Furstenberg • Anglo-America and Its Borderlands   189

FURTHER READING   **199**

Chapter 6   Borderlands in Change: The View from Below   201

DOCUMENTS   **202**

1. Athanese de Mézières Courts and Coerces Wichita Chiefs, 1770   203

2. John Sibley and a Comanche Chief Try to Impress One Another, 1807   205

3. Fernando de la Concha Laments the Corrupting Influence of Indians in the New Mexico Borderlands, 1794   206

4. Pedro Bautista Pino Assesses the Condition of New Mexico, 1812   207

5. Joseph Holt Ingraham Observes Indians and Slaves in Natchez, 1835   209

6. The Dohasan Calendar, 1832–1892   210

7. The First Census of Los Angeles, 1781   211

ESSAYS   212

Daniel H. Usner, Jr. • The Frontier Exchange Economy of the Lower Mississippi Valley   213

Steven W. Hackel • Surviving Mission Life in Alta California   218

FURTHER READING   229

Chapter 7   The Mexican North   231

DOCUMENTS   232

1. José María Sánchez Criticizes Tejanos and Anglo-American Immigrants in Texas, 1828   234

2. Tejano Leaders Give Their Opinion of Anglo-American Immigrants, 1832   236

3. Donaciano Vigil Mourns the Changing Relationships among New Mexicans, Anglo Americans, and Indians, 1846   238

4. Albino Chacón Describes Navajo Raiding and Mounting Discontent in New Mexico, 1837   239

5. New Mexico's Chimayó Rebels Denounce Mexico City's Plan for National Reform, 1837   241

6. Manuel Armijo Reports on the Suppression of the Chimayó Rebellion, 1837   241

7. Juan Bandini Envisions an International Future for California, 1830   243

ESSAYS   245

Andrés Reséndez • Markets, Persuasion, and Identity in the Southwest Borderlands   246

Albert L. Hurtado • Sex, Marriage, and Power in Mexican California   256

FURTHER READING   265

Chapter 8   Anglo–American Takeover of the Southwest Borderlands   266

DOCUMENTS   267

1. Texan Rebels Declare Independence, 1836   268
2. Stephen F. Austin's Map of Empresario Land Grants in Texas, 1835   271
3. Rufus Sage Condemns the Inhabitants of New Mexico, 1846   272
4. Thomas Catesby Jones Announces United States Takeover of California, 1842   274
5. Abraham Lincoln Condemns the War with Mexico, 1848   275
6. The Treaty of Guadalupe Hidalgo, 1848   278
7. Antonio Maria Pico and Others Criticize California's Land Policy, 1859   281

ESSAYS   283

Gregg Cantrell • Stephen F. Austin, Empresario and Borderlander   284

Brian Delay • How Indians Shaped the Era of the U.S.-Mexican War   291

FURTHER READING   302

Chapter 9   Negotiating National Borders   303

DOCUMENTS   304

1. Escaped Slave Describes Appeal of Canada, 1847   306
2. Frederick Law Olmsted on Slaves Escaping to Mexico, 1857   307
3. Mexican Government Complains of Laborers' Flight to the United States, 1873   309
4. U.S. Government Seeks Release from Treaty Obligation to Control Indian Raids into Mexico, 1851   311
5. Sitting Bull Crosses into Canada to Elude U.S. Authorities, 1877   312
6. General Crook Describes Difficulty of Capturing Geronimo, 1883   314
7. Juan Cortina Condemns Anglo Americans for Land Theft, 1859   316
8. Métis Defy Canadian Rule, 1869   319

ESSAYS   320

Sean Kelley • Slavery and the Texas-Mexico Border,
1810–1860   321

Gerhard J. Ens • The Border, the Buffalo, and the Métis
of Montana   329

Samuel Truett • Passages into the Sonora-Arizona
Borderlands   337

FURTHER READING   347

Chapter 10   Pacific Ties   349

DOCUMENTS   350

1. The United States Government Passes Chinese Exclusion,
   1882   351

2. Sonora Legislative Bans Mexican Chinese Marriage, 1923   355

3. British Columbia Labor Leader Warns of Dangers of Asian
   Migration, 1907   355

4. Journalist Julian Ralph Describes Human Smuggling in the
   Pacific Northwest, 1891   356

5. Clifford Perkins Describes Work as "Chinese Inspector" in
   Arizona, 1978   359

6. Frederick Remington Depicts Suffering of Chinese Migrant,
   1891   361

7. Cartoonist Points to Chinese use of Canadian and Mexican
   Borders to Enter the United States, 1880   362

ESSAYS   362

Patrick Ettinger • The Limits of Early U.S. Border
Enforcement   363

Erika Lee • The Impact of Exclusion on the Chinese in
America   373

FURTHER READING   380

Chapter 11   The Mexican Revolution   382

DOCUMENTS   383

1. Samuel Bryan Analyzes Increases in Mexican
   Immigration,1912   386

2. Flores de Andrade Recalls Her Revolutionary Activity as an
   Immigrant in El Paso, Texas, 1931   388

3. Mexican Migrant Describes Working Life in the United States,
   1927   391

4. South Texas Rebels Issue Manifesto, "The Plan of San Diego," 1915   393

5. President Woodrow Wilson Sends U.S. Army into Mexico, 1916   395

6. Sheriff Justifies Deporting Striking Miners from Arizona Town, 1917   396

7. U.S. Congress Imposes Restrictions on Migration, 1917   401

8. Mexican Migrants Protest Gasoline Baths, 1917   402

ESSAYS   **405**

Friedrich Katz • Mexico's Northern Border and the Coming of the Revolution   406

Benjamin Johnson • The Mexican Revolution and the Birth of the Mexican-American Civil Rights Movement   415

FURTHER READING   **427**

Chapter 12   Vice   428

DOCUMENTS   **429**

1. El Paso Reporter Recalls Lure of Juárez in 1920s, 1968   430

2. American Journalist Satirizes American Tourists in Juárez, 1925   432

3. Columnist C. D. Smith Lampoons American Tourists in Search of Drink in Canada, 1925   434

4. Ballad Praises Liquor Smugglers, 1920s   436

5. "Contrabando y tración" Marks Popularity of Narcocorrido, 1972   437

6. Writer Tom Miller Describes Smuggling Electronics into Mexico to Avoid Duties, 1981   438

7. Former Smuggler Don Henry Ford Jr. Describes Why Border Community Drawn to Smuggling Marijuana, 2005   440

ESSAYS   **442**

Stephen T. Moore • Canadians, Americans, and the Multiple Meanings of Border during Prohibition   443

Gabriela Recio • U.S. Prohibition and the Drug Trade in Mexico   451

FURTHER READING   **459**

Chapter 13   Migration, Race, and Border Enforcement   461

DOCUMENTS   462

1. U.S. Congressman John Box Warns of Dangers of Mexican Migration, 1928   464

2. Border Patrol Agent Clifford Perkins Recalls Early Challenges of the Organization, 1978   465

3. Philip Stevenson Describes the Deportation of Jesús Pallares, 1936   468

4. Report Examines Migrant Labor in South Texas, 1951   470

5. Bracero and Migrant Manuel Padilla Remembers Working Life in Borderlands, 1974   474

6. President Lyndon Johnson Signs New Immigration Law, 1965   477

7. Leslie Marmon Silko Condemns Border Enforcement from a Native American Perspective, 1994   479

ESSAYS   483

Mae Ngai • Deportation Policy and the Making and Unmaking of Illegal Aliens   484

Kelly Lytle Hernández • The Crimes and Consequences of Illegal Immigration: A Cross-Border Examination of Operation Wetback, 1943–1954   497

FURTHER READING   508

Chapter 14   Economic Integration and Mass Migration, 1994–Present   509

DOCUMENTS   511

1. U.S. President Bill Clinton Praises Free Trade Agreement, 1993   512

2. Environmental Groups Warn of Damage from NAFTA, 1993   516

3. Mexican President Defends Migrants   516

4. Minuteman Defense Corps Calls for Vigilante Border Enforcement, 2005   517

5. Reporter Questions Television Anchor's Anti-Immigration Crusade, 2007   518

6. Tribal Government Condemns Border Wall, 2008   521

7. Author Describes Death of Migrants in Arizona Desert, 2004   523

8. Journalist Reports on Killing of Women Maquiladora Workers in Juárez, 1997   525

9. Newspaper Describes Increasing Violence of Drug Trade, 2010   529

ESSAYS   **531**

Daniel Drache • Canada–U.S. Relations and the Impermeable Border Post 9/11: The Co-Management of North America   532

David Fitzgerald • The Stranger or the Prodigal Son?   536

FURTHER READING   **545**

Preface

History as a discipline is profoundly structured by the modern nation state. Most historians define themselves primarily by the country that they study; there are U.S. historians, French historians, Chinese historians, and the like, all with their own journals, annual conferences, and professional organizations. Even those who study time periods before their nation came into being—as, for example, specialists on American colonial history—have traditionally defined themselves in this way.

In recent years, however, historians have begun to rethink the connection between the study of the past and the nation-state. It has become a commonplace to observe that we live in an era of globalization, in which people, goods, capital, services, and fashions cross national borders with ease and frequency, in which information flows freely in cyberspace, when corporations operate on a transnational level, and various non-state actors like al-Qaeda and drug smuggling syndicates wield tremendous power. Because present-day circumstances always inform the questions we ask about the past, these dynamics have had a profound impact on how we understand history. As the world has become increasingly decentralized and intermingled, we have also started to see the past in similar terms. We have grown skeptical of the tight focus on the nation state— and its predecessor, the empire—as a proper unit for understanding life and history. We have learned to recognize and value historical phenomena that transcend imperial and national boundaries and we have learned to appreciate the messiness and open-endedness of human relations.

Borderlands have played a key role in this shift, and what is often called "borderlands history" is currently undergoing something of a renaissance. The word "borderland" itself has been in use in the historical profession for nearly a century. The renowned historian Herbert Eugene Bolton popularized the term in his short 1921 book *The Spanish Borderlands: A Chronicle of Old Florida and the Southwest*. For Bolton, borderlands were the Spanish colonial possessions in North America that eventually became part of the United States; his borderlands were a Hispanic counterweight to the Anglo-centric historiography of North America, in which a frontier dividing Euro-Americans from Indians was thought to have played a foundational role in creating the culture and institutions of what became the United States. This field, the original borderlands history, challenged U.S. historians to think of national historical origins and influences beyond the familiar world of the British Empire and the eastern seaboard of North America.

During the last three decades, the term "borderland" has taken on a wider set of meanings than it had for Bolton and his protégés. Students of Mexican-American history focused their attention on the marginalization and racialization of Mexican-descent people in the U.S. Southwest after 1848 even as they found the previous Spanish and Mexican periods relevant to their inquiries. Some scholars in this first wave of Mexican-American history were trained in part as Latin Americanists and recognized the continued ties between Mexican-American and Mexican history as an important factor in their accounts and as a challenge to U.S. historians ignorant of Latin American history. In the 1980s, the U.S. Southwest also drew the attention of "New Western" historians, who found the area—including its colonial past—to be fertile ground for the exploration of the themes of conquest, environmental destruction, and myth-making that were so central to their work.

Larger developments in the academy gave many of these scholars reason to call themselves, among other things, "borderlands" historians. The rise of the "new social history" in the 1960s and 1970s inspired scholars to rewrite history from the "bottom up," directing attention from high politics to mass experiences, from elites to common people, from capital to labor, from grand narratives of national development to the ways that race, class, and gender shaped social experience. The rise of post-modernism—which seeks to reveal the contradictions, incompleteness, and contingency of social categories and processes—changed the study of the Spanish or Mexican borderlands as much as it did any field. Whereas scholars once treated groups such as Spaniards, Indians, and mestizos as self-evident and distinct categories, they began to realize that the borders between them were quite porous and changed with circumstance and over time. Indeed, borders and border crossing have become general metaphors for cultural encounters. For most historians today, borderlands are socially charged meeting spaces where different peoples and ethnic groups collide, coexist, and redefine themselves in interaction. Borderlands are contact zones where no single group rules supreme, places that exist in between nation-states and non-state societies, literate and preliterate societies, colonial expansion and indigenous retreat. They are crossroads where people and their institutions and traditions come together, creating distinctive ways of organizing space and transforming the seemingly fixed edges of empires and nations into fluid transitional spaces.

Redefined, borderlands have, so to speak, left their cradle—New Spain's northern frontier—to become an analytical concept for illuminating not only what is the modern U.S.–Mexico border region, but contact zones across the continent. Courses on borderlands history are taught today across the United States—indeed across the world—and new borderlands studies are being published with accelerating rate. There is now a critical mass of studies to bring a sample of the best into a single volume. *Major Problems in the History of North American Borderlands* is the first collection of primary sources and essays aimed specifically for undergraduate classes. It is designed for undergraduate students in the subject, but it may also be assigned to provide alternative viewpoints to various introductory classes in North American history, American studies, and ethnic studies.

The organization of *Major Problems in the History of North American Borderlands* reflects the traditions and expanding scope of the field. The book is anchored in the American Southwest, the region of the United States where Spanish presence has been strongest and where Mexico and the U.S. now brush directly against one another. But the book also includes essays and documents that address borderlands dynamics in other regions, including connections between Indians, Africans, and Europeans in the Southeast; the rise of native equestrian cultures on the Great Plains; marriage and kinship ties forged between European traders and Indian peoples in what is now Canada; efforts to regulate native American and Asian crossings of the Canada-U.S. border; and more recent efforts to foster commerce and protect national security along both of the continent's international borders. In thematic terms, the coverage is similarly broad. Together the documents and essays address an array of topics, including the challenges, strategies, and limitations of European-Native American accommodation; settler-indigenous relations in the context of rapid environmental change; the presence of African people in predominantly Indian-European contact zones; different forms of slave trade and intermarriage on borderlands; identity formation in fluid multicultural environments; the impact of war and revolution on borders; efforts to regulate the flows of people and goods (including drugs and alcohol) across borders; and the ways in which various non-state actors have resisted, evaded, exploited, and suffered from the rise of national borders.

The book consists of fourteen chapters, each containing several essays, along with primary documents, that complement one another thematically and methodologically. After an introductory chapter that guides students into borderlands history, the chapters move chronologically to trace the emergence of North America's first borderlands. Chapter 2 examines the early Southwest from multiple viewpoints, and Chapter 3 turns to parallel and divergent developments in the eastern half of the continent. Chapter 4 adopts a more continental perspective and examines how new colonial frontiers unleashed forces that transformed indigenous societies across vast regions. The documents and essays in Chapter 5 take an even broader approach, including material on large sections of North, South, and Central America. Chapter 6 moves the focus closer to the ground and examines how late 18th-century borderlands functioned on a more intimate, face-to-face level. Chapters 7 and 8 bring us into the brief but formative Mexican period in North America. Chapter 7 analyzes the efforts of Mexico to incorporate its far north of Texas, New Mexico, and California, focusing on the experiences of Mexican and Native peoples. Chapter 8 details the failure of this effort with the Anglo-American takeover of the Southwest and the creation of the modern U.S-Mexico border.

The second half of the book treats the period since the mid-nineteenth century, when the contemporary map of a North America divided between the three nation-states of Canada, the United States, and Mexico emerged. Chapter 9 examines the ways in which people on the ground dealt with these new borders in the decades after their creation. Chapter 10 explores how the connections between these nations and east Asia, particularly the question of Asian migration, created early border enforcement. In Chapter 11, the focus is on the Mexican Revolution and its transformative impact on the U.S.-Mexico borderlands. The next three chapters pursue important themes in North American borders in the twentieth century. The ways in which "vice industries," such as liquor, prostitution, and drugs, were particularly prominent in border towns is the subject of Chapter 12. The subjects of migration, border enforcement, and race are the focus of Chapter 13. Finally, Chapter 14 tackles the ways that global free trade regimes and 9-11 have changed life and policy in North American borders in recent years.

The essays of this book use different definitions of the term "borderlands" and different understandings of what borderlands history is. Some authors view borderlands as permeable boundaries that both divide and connect, while others see them as borderless spaces. Some see borderlands as specific regions with distinct social forms, and others write about non-physical cultural frontiers. The essays also bring forward alternative concepts to borderlands. Some historians prefer a redefined "frontier" to depict spaces where cultures meet, while others approach borderlands history through the analytical lens of cores and peripheries. Some essays analyze what most historians easily identify as borderlands phenomena without ever mentioning the term.

If the terminology of borderland historians is varied, so too are their themes and theoretical approaches. Grounded in geography, borderlands history operates on various spatial registers—intimate, local, regional, national, global—and the essays of this book navigate those scales differently. Some authors write about borderlands to illuminate larger structures such as the rise of the Atlantic world or nationalism, while others are more interested in examining how large processes have played out on the local level. Some essays are explicitly theoretical, but others hide their conceptual frameworks behind stories and their human dimension. Yet similarities outweigh differences. There are several key themes—"major problems"—that appear throughout the book, inviting readers to identify parallels and continuities across places and periods and make comparisons among them. The themes that run through the volume include such traditional borderlands topics as race, identity formation, and cross-cultural exchange as well as newer ones, including class, gender, indigenous slavery, and the environment. Many of the book's essays explore the inherent unpredictability of borderland places and the ways in which borderlands history may help us move beyond essentializing views about the world and its peoples. The authors are interested in how in borderlands groups interact in ways that contradict usual assumptions about each group, and they show how seemingly straightforward activities and institutions—trade, marriage, captivity, kinship, violence, property—often assume multiple, surprising, and incompatible meanings.

The most central of the "major problems" is the question of power. Borderlands history is at its core about the negotiation of power, for borderlands are places where no single group can dictate the codes of proper behavior or the outcome of the encounter. For example, European colonialism may have brought enormous stress to native societies, but Europeans often had to accommodate themselves to Indian power; the contemporary United States may be the most powerful nation on the planet, but its government cannot simply do what it pleases with its long and permeable southern border. Dynamic tension is fundamental to borderlands, for although ethnic and cultural lines become blurred, they do not disappear altogether. Borderlands people are acutely aware of this hybridity and their interactions require constant negotiation and compromising. Borderlands are also sites where the reach of empires and nation states grows weaker but does not disappear entirely. As a result, there is constant uncertainty over the viability of the cross-cultural practices, for although distant, imperial or state power sporadically intervenes, destabilizing locally negotiated face-to-face relationships. This fluidity of power relations and the resulting anxiety is a recurring theme in the essays of this book. In one way or another, all the authors write about power, offering shifting perspectives on its distribution, expressions, contingencies, and meanings in borderlands settings. That does not mean that they agree: as with terminology, borderland historians sometimes disagree strongly on the questions of power and agency, and some of the essays here have provoked heated debates. We as editors welcome such debates as a sign of our field's vitality and have made no attempt to solve them. We leave that to future studies—and to our readers.

This book follows the general format of the *Major Problems in American History* series. Each chapter opens with a brief introduction that provides an overview of the problem under examination. Each chapter's essays and documents are introduced by a headnote that places the readings in historical and interpretive perspective. The documents and essays are selected to encourage students to evaluate different interpretations, tackle enigmatic sources, and reach their own conclusions. Each chapter closes with a bibliography of further readings so that students may read more about topics that intrigue them. Full sources are provided for each item in the chapter.

We would like to thank Juliana Barr, Katie Benton-Cohen, Sarah Cornell, Raymond Craib, Brian Delay, George T. Díaz, Andrew Graybill, Eric Meeks, Thomas Paterson, Brenden Rensink, Andres Reséndez, David Dorado Romo, Julía María Schiavone Camacho, Jeff Shepherd, and Sam Truett for their advice about particular documents and essays. The outside reviewers, Lawrence Culver, Utah State University; Grace Delgado, Pennsylvania State University; Daniel Murphree, University of Texas, Tyler; and Omar Valerio-Jiménez, University of Iowa; raised important issues about scope and coverage, in addition to making numerous thoughtful suggestions about essays and documents for possible inclusion. At Wadsworth/Cengage, Terri Wise and Jeff Greene offered sound advice and guidance. Rathi Thirumalai was fastidious and patient in the lengthy process of editing the manuscript copy.

Finally, the late David Weber was his typically erudite and modest self as he advised us on this volume's conceptualization. We are honored to dedicate it to his memory. *Que en paz descanse.*

B.H.J.

P.H.

CHAPTER 1

What Is Borderlands History?

What is borderlands history? In the broadest sense, North American borderlands history encompasses the interactions between different peoples, empires, and nations in the continent's past. Rather than focusing on the history of discrete nations, ethnic groups, or people, borderlands historians focus on places of encounter, whether the contemporary international borders of the United States, Mexico, and Canada, or such older meeting grounds as the Ohio River Valley or Missouri. They approach borderlands as contact zones where no single group rules supreme—places that exist in between colonial empires and indigenous territories, literate and nonliterate societies, nation-states and non–state societies. Borderlands are crossroads where people and their institutions and traditions come together, creating distinctive ways of organizing space and transforming the seemingly fixed edges of empires and nations into fluid spaces.

As a concept used by professional historians, "borderlands" dates back to the 1920s, when historian Herbert Eugene Bolton examined the Spanish colonial possessions in North America, from California to Florida, that eventually became part of the United States. Bolton challenged U.S. historians to think of national historical origins and influences beyond the familiar world of the British Empire and its colonies on the eastern seaboard of North America. In recent decades, historians have found the term borderland useful in understanding not only what became the current U.S.-Mexico border region but contact zones across the continent, as well. The interest in boundaries and their crossing—themes that are often obscured when historians focus too closely on nations and empires—helps us to understand the impact of the global movement of people, goods, capital, ideas, and fashions across borders today.

Major Problems in Borderlands History surveys the North American past from the point of view of its borderlands. The essays and documents discuss people and events likely to be familiar to you—the founding of early European colonies, U.S. independence, the War of 1812, the U.S.-Mexican War, Prohibition, and the like. But less widely known events and actors—expanding native peoples, the Bourbon reforms of the Spanish Empire, fleeing slaves and servants, border surveyors, the Mexican Revolution, key U.S. immigration legislation—also take center stage. In one sense, this volume is clearly a work of U.S. history, but it is also Canadian and Mexican and native history. And its overriding theme is that we must take into account the meetings of different peoples and nations if

1

we are to understand our past and present. We cannot simply read current boundaries back into the past as though they always existed and as though the present and its boundaries are the only possible outcomes of the past.

∿ ESSAYS

The three essays in this chapter introduce borderlands as a field of study. They reveal the kinds of questions that borderlands historians ask and how their approach is a departure from conventional nation-centered history. The authors discuss major developments in the history of the borderlands of North America and other places, but they are equally interested in how historians study this history: what kinds of questions they ask, what kinds of questions they should ask, what major historical turning points a borderlands approach suggests, what topics in borderlands history have been well-researched, and which ones remain relatively unexplored.

Michiel Baud and Willem Van Schendel call for historians to examine many world borders and to compare them over time. Rather than focusing on the central governments that created borders across the world, these two scholars emphasize the ways that border-making shaped the lives of borderlands residents and how borderlanders in turn made their own history. They emphasize that there are very different kinds of borderlands: Some are conflictual and perpetually violent, others noncontroversial and peaceful; some are characterized by strong cross-border cultural and economic ties, whereas others divide very different societies. In their account, the contemporary national borders of North America are not unique places onto themselves, but rather part of global processes and patterns.

Jeremy Adelman and Stephen Aron focus on the borderlands past of North America. Unlike Baud and Van Schendel, they emphasize the importance of European empires, rather than borderlands residents, in making this history. In places where European powers competed for control, Indians and other societies had broad autonomy and power. But in the nineteenth century, when European powers gave way to the nation-states of Canada, the United States, and Mexico, natives ended up as conquered people forced to live in the context of national, not borderlands, societies. National borders were much more constraining and less open than the porous borderlands of the colonial era. Historians, they argue, need to pay more attention to this major turning point and the break with the more open past that it represents.

Benjamin Johnson and Andrew Graybill trace the ways that historians have approached the U.S.-Mexico and U.S.-Canada borderlands. Although *borderlands* has traditionally been a term used to describe the parts of the contemporary United States previously held by Spain, in recent years the term has taken on a much wider set of meanings. Histories of the U.S.-Canada borderlands have increasingly addressed themes similar to those of the U.S.-Mexico borderlands, a trend that Johnson and Graybill applaud. Unlike Adelman and Aron, they emphasize continued exchange and influence across national borders.

These essays include a number of major concepts and debates in borderlands history. How do they help explain why historians are drawn to borderlands and borders? How have historians' approaches and the meaning of the term *borderlands* changed over time? How is the kind of history practiced in each article different from history centered on a particular country?

A Comparative Approach to Borderlands

MICHIEL BAUD AND WILLEM VAN SCHENDEL

National borders are political constructs, imagined projections of territorial power. Although they appear on maps in deceptively precise forms, they reflect, at least initially, merely the mental images of politicians, lawyers, and intellectuals. Their practical consequences are often quite different. No matter how clearly borders are drawn on official maps, how many customs officials are appointed, or how many watchtowers are built, people will ignore borders whenever it suits them. In doing so, they challenge the political status quo of which borders are the ultimate symbol. People also take advantage of borders in ways that are not intended or anticipated by their creators. Revolutionaries hide behind them, seeking the protection of another sovereignty; local inhabitants cross them whenever services or products are cheaper or more attractive on the other side; and traders are quick to take advantage of price and tax differentials. Because of such unintended and often subversive consequences, border regions have their own social dynamics and historical development.

Here, we are more interested in the historical effects of borders than in the politico-legal aspects of their creation. We look at the struggles and adaptations that the imposition of a border causes in the regions bisected by it, and we posit the need for comparative historical research into the history of *borderlands*. But we are also interested in the question of how the social dynamics of border regions affect the formation and territorialization of states. These questions should be studied systematically because they refer to important historical processes in the modern world.

Our point of departure is that we can properly understand the often unintended and unanticipated social consequences of national borders only by focusing on border regions and comparing them through time and space. Traditionally, border studies have adopted a view from the center; we argue for a view from the periphery. In this article we identify some of the central factors involved in the history of borderlands.

The historical analysis of borders is especially important in the case of the modern states in the eighteenth to twentieth centuries. In this period, borders all over the world became crucial elements in a new, increasingly global system of states.

Michiel Baud and Willem Van Schendel, "Toward a Comparative History of Borderlands," *Journal of World History* 8 (Fall 1997): 211–242.

Borders became markers in two ways. First, they revealed the territorial consolidation of states. Most states tried to curb regional autonomy and were no longer content with "rough edges." This was especially clear in the case of the colonial and postcolonial states in the so-called Third World. By taking possession of disputed or unclaimed areas, state elites tried to resolve the problem of loosely defined border regions to which two or even more states might lay claim. In this way, they drew sharper lines between citizens, invested with certain rights and duties, and "aliens" or "foreigners." If there is one thing that has been central to all borders, it has been the contest about these rules of inclusion and exclusion and the efforts of people to use, manipulate, or avoid the resulting border restrictions.

The mapping of modern borders, a process first perfected in Europe but soon applied all over the world, thus symbolized a collective attempt by state elites to establish a worldwide system of clear-cut territorial jurisdictions and to have their legal and political sovereignty confirmed cartographically. The mapping of borders tended to proceed in three stages: *establishment, demarcation,* and *control* of the border. As a result, conflicting territorial claims by neighboring states could no longer be ignored or played down: they had to be faced by means of negotiation, confrontation, or arbitration.

Second, borders became markers of the actual power that states wielded over their own societies. Leaders of the new states adopted the ambitious goal of making the state the dominant force in their societies, but to what extent could they really impose their jurisdiction on "the people"? Recent research has shown that these ambitions often failed because of the opposition of a stubborn society. The confrontation between "state" and "people" was especially clear in marginal areas such as borderlands. Even borders themselves were often a result of negotiations between regional society and the central state.

In this article the notion of *borderland* is of central importance. A borderland is usually understood as the region in one nation that is significantly affected by an international border. However, we favor a cross-border perspective, in which the region on *both* sides of a state border is taken as the unit of analysis. This approach allows us to take into account the paradoxical character of borderlands. Borders create political, social, and cultural distinctions, but simultaneously imply the existence of (new) networks and systems of interaction across them. The existence of a border is our point of departure, but at the same time we draw attention to the social networks that reach across that border.

Jorge Bustamante has argued that from the perspective of national centers of authority, the border between countries is a sharp line, an impenetrable barrier. But from the perspective of the border, borderlands are broad scenes of intense interactions in which people from both sides work out everyday accommodations based on face-to-face relationships. In this way, the study of border regions implies a critique of state-centered approaches that picture borders as unchanging, uncontested, and unproblematic. We argue that there is a definite heuristic and comparative value in studying the various ways in which people have manipulated and circumvented the constructed barriers that result from the territorialization of modern states.

The drawing of borderlines and the creation of borderlands are the outcome of the establishment of modern states all over the world. The wish for well-defined, fixed boundaries was a direct consequence of the idea of exclusive and uncontested territorial state power that emerged in the nineteenth century. This development was the belated result of the legal principle of *uti possidetis*, which implied flexible and often contested state boundaries. Many new states based the delimitation of their territory on this principle but in the process changed its meaning, often mixing it with arguments that sought to legitimize state borders in new legal, cultural, or racial terms. In this way, state elites removed the emphasis on the flexible nature of borders and used it to claim their eternal and irreversible sovereignty over a given territory.

Most modern borders were conceived in state capitals where they were negotiated in the corridors of power and made final on drawing boards. Their creation can often be pinpointed in time. Their precise location was marked on a map, which was then ratified by the states concerned, or else imposed by one state on its neighbor. Clearly, the state was always involved. State employees stationed in the borderland and their superiors in the provincial or state capitals could develop very different perspectives on their mission in the borderland. Customs officials might become involved in smuggling, schoolteachers might resist assimilatory language policy, and security forces might refuse to risk their lives against well-armed separatists.

In addition to the state and the regional elite, the "common people" of the borderland made its social history. Their relationship with the regional elites and the two states that claimed the borderland largely determined the social dynamics that unfolded in the region. How these peasants, nomadic herdsmen, traders, and so on (re)defined their territories in reaction to the creation of a border shaped subsequent events in the borderland. These definitions were an expression of local conceptions of the triangle of power relations between state, regional elite, and local people at the time. Once the definitions were formulated, they in turn began to exert a powerful influence on power relations.

The historical development of borderlands was determined simultaneously by the situation in two states, and by the social, economic, and political interactions between them. Such interactions vary enormously, and differences can be clearly reflected in the shared borderlands. Borders have long acted as ethnic or religious divides, although in modern history such differences have very often been state-induced rather than local phenomena. In the nineteenth and twentieth centuries, borders have served more prominently as political and economic divides. Colonial borders delineated the territorial claims of European superpowers in far-flung parts of their empires. During the Cold War, borders all over the world became markers of competing political projects, giving rise to imagery of iron and bamboo curtains.

One of our main points is that borders are too readily reified. Generally speaking, there has always been an enormous gap between the rhetoric of border maintenance and daily life in borderlands. In the vast majority of cases it was possible for borderland people to cross the border, legally or illegally. The interesting questions are when they did so and for what motives.

The creation of a border sets the scene for new power relations in the borderland, based on new local definitions of social and territorial boundaries, and new confrontations between social groups. This process has become more pronounced as a result of massive transnational migration, both "voluntary" (e.g., labor migrants) and "involuntary" (e.g., refugees), which has come to characterize many parts of the contemporary world. Such migration presents a new challenge to national states and diminishes and salience of national borders.

The social history of borderlands is determined first and foremost by the spatial dimension. Borderlands are geographically defined areas that can be drawn on a map like any other region. Traditional geography often thought in terms of two separate borderlands—one on each side of the border—but we argue that these should be seen as two parts of a single borderland. How far does the borderland extend "inland" from the border? At what point can we say that the influence of the border becomes so weak as to be no longer of importance to the lives of the people? This problem can best be approached by focusing on social networks in borderlands because these distinguish the borderland and determine the actual historical development of the region. We may roughly divide the border region into three geographical zones.

First, there is the *border heartland*, abutting on the border and dominated by its existence. Here, social networks are shaped directly by the border, depend on it for their survival, and have no option but to adapt continually to its vagaries. Often such regions were peripheral to the development of the central state, but nowadays they may be bustling industrial and urban regions: the Basle region where Germany meets Switzerland and France, the borderland between Singapore and Malaysia, and the U.S.-Mexican borderland (which nowadays boasts some of the fastest-growing cities of the American continent) are cases in point. Second, there is the *intermediate borderland*, the region that always feels the influence of the border but in intensities varying from moderate to weak. And finally there is the *outer borderland*, which only under specific circumstances feels the effects of the border. It is affected by the existence of the border in the same way that land protected by an embankment is affected by the sea. In daily life the border hardly plays a role at all, but there is always a hint of suspense, a slight tinge of uncertainty. Just as a tidal wave may sweep far into the interior, so a political storm may suddenly engulf this zone and involve it directly in border dynamics. In this way, borderlands may at times, though briefly, stretch to embrace entire countries.

This view of borderlands as changeable spatial units clashes with the visual representations of borders that we find on maps. Most of the time, these maps are of limited use for understanding the historical reality of borderlands because they are both too static and too simple. At the same time, they are indispensable as sources for the politics and ideologies of nation building, which in turn influence life in the borderlands. It is crucial to realize that the ideological and practical choices underlying the creation of maps shape our thinking about borders. The political significance of maps is so great that in many Latin American countries mapmaking is the monopoly of the military. It is remarkable that, in this age of satellite monitoring, India, Bangladesh, and other South Asian states continue to deny their own citizens access to maps of border regions, even out-dated ones. It is hard to miss the importance of this issue when, as in the case of Ecuador, national maps are manufactured that confer on the country almost twice the territory that it possesses in reality. But we hardly give a thought to the messages that mapmakers send when they mark the border with a bold dot-ted line and select different colors for the territories on either side of it. Likewise, we rarely reflect on the use of larger or smaller print to represent national, re-gional, and local units, or on the omission of old names for cross-border regions (e.g., Bengal) in favor of new, state-sponsored units of administration (Bangla-desh; West Bengal, India). The borderlands that we study, which extend on both sides of the border, are *never* shown on maps. For this reason alone, the spatial representations of border regions provided by maps ought to be part of the subject matter of border studies.

We now turn to what Lawrence Herzog has called "transboundary social formation," the extent to which political, economic, and cultural networks over-lap in the borderland. In this section we explore the political consequences of the changing "triangle of power relations" between state, regional elite, and local people in the borderland.

Borderlands are areas that are bisected by a state border. The actual bound-ary lines—demarcated by means of posts, stones, flags, fences, walls, or other landmarks, and highlighted by means of customhouses, border guards, and checkpoints—form their backbone. This display of statehood symbolizes the ef-fort of each state to maintain exclusive control of its half of the borderland, and in this respect the border is the ultimate symbol of its sovereignty. But this does not imply that the effort is ever wholly successful.

First, the power of the state is usually circumscribed by supra-state, interna-tional political networks that may be more or less formal, long-lived, and pow-erful. Among the more formal and long-lived are international alliances, colonial empires, the United Nations, and the European Community; among the less formal are international organizations based on ethnic allegiances, governments in exile, and the "long-distance nationalism" of emigrant groups. Such networks impinge on all regions of the state, including borderlands. Borderlands are not special in this regard, although supra-state political networks may affect border regions in specific ways.

Second, only in borderlands is the power of the state also circumscribed by local political networks that (continue to) connect the two sides and are there-fore international too. Cross-border political networks allow borderland politi-cians more leverage with regard to the state than their counterparts in interior regions, as well as access to the political resources of two state units. If cross-border political networks are strong, they may successfully defend "border inter-ests" in the two state capitals. The political project symbolized by the state bor-der is to eliminate such cross-border networks and to make borderland politicians resemble their counterparts in the interior. Structurally speaking, this is a shared interest of the two neighboring states, and they will often cooperate in stamping out cross-border political networks. When their relations are strained, however, states will use these networks to embarrass or subvert their neighbor. This is potentially dangerous line of action because it strengthens the borderland politi-cians against the state and may backfire, as in the case of Kashmir, where there was repeated, damaging war between India and Pakistan, as well as a movement for an independent Kashmir.

The Quiet Borderland. If state, regional elite, and local population are knit into a coherent power structure in which tension is relatively low, the border-land is likely to be peaceful. In these cases, territorial control by the state does not lead to major confrontations in the borderland, because the interests of the three actors are taken into account at every step. All three welcome, or at least accept, the creation and existence of the border, each for reasons of their own. We may call this the *harmonious* variant of the quiet borderland. A case in point is the Dutch/Belgian borderland after Belgium seceded from the Netherlands in 1830.

If state, regional elite, and local people are knit into a power structure in which the state clearly predominates, the creation of a borderland is also likely to be a relatively peaceful process. Here territorial redefinition can indeed lead to strong clashes of interest between the actors, but these will not be articulated in open confrontations. The interests of the state will prevail, as neither regional elite nor common people has the power to resist openly. We may call this the *enforced* variant of the quiet borderland. Border relations are in abeyance rather than peaceful. An example is the borderland between North and South Korea, after the Korean War ended in 1953.

The Unruly Borderland. When power structures are less coherent, border-lands are unlikely to be quiescent. The state may dominate, or have absorbed, a regional elite, but if neither state nor regional elite has established a com-manding position over the local population, the borderland will be difficult to control. Local society proves to be unruly, resisting the new social and ter-ritorial boundaries and the rules that come with them. In its attempt to enforce its sovereignty, the state is often exposed as weak because it oversteps the lim-its of its power and makes unrealistic claims to overlordship over civil society. The position of the regional elite weakens because it is exposed as an agent of the state rather than a protector of local rights and concerns. The usual policy in these cases is for the state to arm the regional elite and station troops in the borderland in an attempt to enforce state rule. If this policy of militarization is successful, the enforced variant of the quiet borderland ensues; if not, the bor-derland remains turbulent and disorderly despite the presence of an army of occupation, which may resort to a reign of terror. Northern Ireland is a case in point. Here in the late 1960s a Protestant elite backed up by the British state lost its ability to control a Catholic population. Neither British armed forces nor Protestant vigilantes could contain the armed insurrection of a sec-tion of the population that sought to merge the border region with the neigh-boring Republic of Ireland.

The Rebellious Borderland. In the case of a rebellious borderland, a regional elite sides with the local population against a state that seeks in vain to impose its authority on a border. The rebellion, led by the regional elite, challenges state control over the borderland, ignores the new border, and attempts to establish a regional counter-government. Such rebellions can be regionalist, separatist, or irredentist in their objectives. If the state is unable to crush the rebellion, the borderland can develop into a separate state with or without international recognition, or it can be annexed by a neighboring state. An example of a rebellious borderland is the Golden Triangle straddling the borders of China, Laos, Thailand, and Burma. Here various guerrilla groups (ethnic, left-wing, and drug-related) have been fighting state armies and each other for decades in attempts to establish separate states. Other current examples are Kurdistan (the rebellious borderlands of Iran, Iraq, and Turkey), the southern border region of Sudan, and the coca-producing regions of Colombia, Bolivia, and Peru.

Local communities along most international borders continue their cross-border economic links. In many cases they do not really have a choice because the government fails to integrate the border economy into the larger national economy. Cross-border economic and commercial activities are often based on preexisting networks of kinship, friendship, and entrepreneurial partnership that now span both sides of the border.

Much like the economies of other regions, cross-border economic networks are influenced by macroeconomic forces. Fluctuations in world market conditions may alter the productive structure of the borderland, change agricultural technology, introduce new crops, lead to new industrial activities, and so on. Unlike other regions, however, borderlands connect two economic systems. The economic policy of one state may create a scarcity or abundance of certain goods and services on one side of the border. Different national taxes may lead to sharply different prices and a reversal or intensification of existing commercial activity. For example, the policy of successive Nigerian governments to subsidize the consumer price of gasoline led to the illegal drain of this commodity to neighboring Benin where it was sold for higher prices. Such developments may motivate the state to impose strict border controls, making trade virtually impossible and provoking smuggling. Or the state may condone such trade in order to defuse the tensions that its economic policy causes, at least in the borderland. Finally, state officials themselves may actively engage in border trade for public or private gain.

Smuggling is a typical border activity in which the political and the economic come together. It develops whenever a state tries to impose restrictions on border trade that are not acceptable to (some of) those living in the borderland and that cannot be enforced.

Whenever a state applies restrictions on cross-border trade, it invites smuggling. Of course, smuggling is not confined to inhabitants of the borderland, nor does it involve all (or even most) of them. But it is most evident in the borderland, and this gives the entire border economy an air of stealth and subterfuge in the eyes of the state.

Border economies are always strongly influenced by political measures, and political processes on either side of the border do not normally coincide. Border economies react instantly to short-term policy changes, and constant adaptation lends them a speculative, restive character. This is one reason why it is so important to treat the region on both sides of the border as a single unit: changing economic policies on one side of the border lead to immediate adaptations on the other side as well.

Theorists of borderlands have tried to make a distinction between "natural" and "unnatural" borders, based on geographical parameters. Rivers, watersheds, and mountains are often considered perfect natural borders. Other theorists have tried to do the same with culture, ethnicity, or language. For them, a border is natural if it separates groups that differ clearly with respect to phenotype (race), language, or culture. The "naturalness" of such borders, however, is usually more apparent than real: evidently, differences in phenotype, language, and culture have often been manipulated in the service of a nationalist ideology that needed to legitimize existing borders by establishing, strengthening, or highlighting these differences after the fact.

After the United States conquered a large part of Mexico's northern territory in 1848, it strongly promoted the English language there. In the twentieth century, however, extensive immigration of Mexican workers into the United States made it increasingly difficult to maintain the artificial separation of Spanish and English. Nowadays Spanish is widely spoken in the entire borderland, and in daily life language is no longer a marker of the border.

There can be no doubt that borders that cut through a fairly homogeneous population should be distinguished from borders that coincide with cultural or ethnic divides. Where people from the other side of a border can be recognized easily by their physical appearance—clothing, language, or behavior—it is less easy for them to move back and forth across the border, and their position on the opposite side is less secure. Examples include the position of Haitians in the Dominican Republic or of Bolivians in Argentina. Where material or cultural differences are less obvious—as in the case of Bangladeshis in India or U.S. citizens in Canada—"passing" is much easier.

Despite attempts by central states to control their borderlanders and to impose a "national" culture on them, a fascinating aspect of many borderlands is the development of a "creole" or "syncretic" border culture. When two or more languages meet, a border lingua franca often comes into existence. Where different religions prevail on both sides of the border, people may visit each other's religious festivals, as well as festivities marking national holidays. Cross-border (and often interethnic) networks of friendship, courtship, and kinship are as much part of the border culture as cross-border economic and political partnerships. The existence of such border cultures is often resented by central governments. Government measures to suppress or deny these border cultures may take the form of attacking symbols of borderland unity—for example, by prohibiting the use of the local language in communications with state officials—and initiating a cultural offensive to replace border cultures by a more "civilized" national culture. State denial or suppression of borderland cultures has usually obscured these from the eyes of outsiders, including academics.

The study of borderlands invites us to look at states, concepts of social space, and local history from a different perspective. It helps us pose questions in a new form. There is an extensive literature on how states have dealt with their borderlands, but historians have paid much less attention to how borderlands have dealt with their states. As a result, borderlands have been represented as far more passive and reactive than is warranted. The study of borderlands assigns an active historical role to borderlands and their population. The purpose is to redress the imbalance of "state-centered" studies, and to discover which social impulses originated in the borderlands and what effects they had locally as well as beyond the borderland. We are interested in the cut-and-thrust of life as it was lived in thousands of borderlands all over the world and the ways in which local societies dealt with the appearance (and sometimes disappearance) of national borders in their territory.

The study of borderlands in Europe deals with a long process of trial and error in which the modern state developed more or less organically. Borders came to be generally accepted, and when violence between states broke out, disagreement about the location of borders usually was not the main cause. In the other continents, the modern state and its approach to borders usually arrived as one of the trappings of colonial rule. In each continent, it encountered a different situation. In Asia, for example, highly developed states existed with their own conceptions of territorial integrity and boundaries, which differed from the European model. As a result, in many parts of Asia precolonial statecraft exerted a powerful influence over colonial administration. Colonial borders were often superimposed on much older political and religious divides. After decolonization, Asia boasted strong and populous regional states that were able to engage in large-scale military campaigns to settle any border conflicts. These in turn brought in the major world powers as mediators, arms dealers, and combatants in border conflicts (for example, between China and India in 1962, Iran and Iraq in 1980–88, and Iraq and Kuwait in 1989–90). In the process, local border disputes were elevated to the level of major world events. The impact of Asian border wars on contemporary global politics underlines the importance of analyzing the long-term repercussions of encounters between well-developed local definitions of state boundaries and external, "colonial" definitions territoriality.

By contrast, in much of Africa and the Americas colonial rule was generally less restricted by precolonial state formation and local definitions of territoriality. Here colonial borders were more frequently drawn without any regard for local society and in places where no history of state border formation existed. In Latin America, the principal problem for the Spanish crown and the independent successor states of the nineteenth and twentieth centuries was how to physically occupy the immense territory. It was said in nineteenth-century Latin America that to govern was to populate, *gobernar es poblar*. This desire to control the marginal frontier areas was part of the "civilizing" policy that aimed at the incorporation or extermination of indigenous populations that were considered a symbol of "barbarism" and a threat to state formation and nationalism. This ideological content, combining political, economic, and moral objectives, may explain the fascination of Latin American politicians and historians with the "frontier" and the agricultural colonization of frontier regions.

With respect to political boundaries, the Spanish colonizers used the territorial boundaries of the Inca and Aztec empires to organize their colonial jurisdictions in Spanish America. But in many other regions they established borders with no regard for local territorial definitions. In a historical process that extended over three centuries, they created colonial borders that were sometimes superimposed on native borders but that often cut across them. Most of these colonial borders survived in the postcolonial period. In the nineteenth and twentieth centuries, border conflicts between the new states did occur, but they had nothing to do with the pre-Columbian political structures; rather, they were determined by the national ambitions of the new ruling elites. Only very recently have some pro-Indian politicians and intellectuals in the Andes started questioning the legitimacy of existing borders between Latin American countries, arguing that they ignore indigenous ethnic and spatial structures. In this they find inspiration in the arrangement on the U.S.–Canadian border, where Native American groups recognized as such by both governments are allowed to cross without any state interference.

[I]n a broader comparative perspective, the history of African borders is different in two ways. First, in most parts of the continent colonization occurred quite late and lasted only about sixty years. The borders that were drawn normally preceded nation building and state formation. Even the postcolonial states had relatively little time and inclination to come to grips with the resulting complicated situation. Although they accepted the colonial divisions for the postcolonial period during meetings of the Organization of African Unity in 1963 and 1964, they have not really been able to find a way out of the maze of ethnic boundaries, precolonial state borders, and colonial demarcations, as their serious falling-out over the status of the Western Sahara demonstrated. Cross-border ethnic, economic, and political ties have remained important, resulting in high levels of interaction between peoples and goods on either side of most African borders. This may be interpreted as the survival of ancient networks of regional trade and a form of protest against a predatory postcolonial state. It can also be seen as a result of the disintegration of old (trading) networks and the expansion of new export-oriented production. Intensive cross-border contact is a distinct characteristic of African borderlands. Ieuan Griffiths even suggests that African borders are specifically characterized by their permeability.

Clearly, there are broad regional differences in state formation and the imposition of national borders. But whether these different historical experiences warrant a distinction between three regional types of borderlands—Eurasian, African, and American—remains to be seen. The value of such models can be assessed only in their application. They may help us to better understand the complexity of the social history of any borderland. They may also allow us to gain a better insight into the structural similarities and contrasts of borderland dynamics and to make more systematic and meaningful comparisons.

National borders are political constructs that have exerted a remarkable influence on the minds of professional historians and the ways in which they have constructed historical narratives. People living in borderlands have often been rather less impressed by borders, as their attempts to create their own local history demonstrate.

We invite researchers to undertake the comparative history of borderlands. We have argued that the study of borders and borderlands has been unduly restricted by an emphasis on the geographical, legal, and political aspects of the creation and consequences of borders. This has led to a state-centered approach, in which researchers took the central state as their point of departure. Further, they have tended to focus their research on only one side of a certain border. In this way, they have grounded their research upon these artificial lines in social space and—often unwittingly and unwillingly—confirmed the nationalist claims that borders represent. By taking both sides of the border as a starting point for research, it will be easier to understand the social, cultural, and economic dynamics of borderlands and the particular historical transformations that they have experienced. It is necessary to invest borderlands, and their population, with a more active historical role. We should ask which social and political impulses originated in borderlands and what effect they had locally as well as beyond the borderland—particularly in relation to state building on both sides of the border. The crucial question is what borderlands can teach us about ways of conceptualizing social space and local identity, and the roles these have played in promoting or thwarting the development of modern states.

We began by emphasizing the artificial character of borders. They are prime examples of how mental constructs can become social realities. Once agreed upon in diplomatic meetings and neatly drawn on maps, borders become something real for the people living near them. To understand this process, it is necessary to explore new sources of information. Borderland historians may have to rely on oral history to reconstruct the historical self-images and perceptions of social groups in the borderland and the impact of these on people's political, economic, and cultural behavior. We feel that this is one of the most challenging tasks of borderland studies.

Whatever may be their real impact, borders become part of the perception and mental map of borderlanders. The paradox of how borders simultaneously separate and unite is the direct consequence of this mental mapmaking. Borders divide people living on both sides, who may have had a long history of cultural and social contact, but at the same time it unites them in the experience of closeness to the border and (partial) dependence on it. This paradoxical character of borders can be considered a metaphor of the ambiguities of nation building, which have recently provoked so much interest. This may be the strongest argument for the study of the mental, cultural, or ethnic consequences of borders. Research on the changing practice and meaning of borders can provide us with valuable clues as to the magnitude and limitations of the most powerful mental construction of the present-day world, the nation-state. Borderland studies offer a way of correcting the distortions inherent in state-centered national histories. They can be powerful exactly because they dispute the territoriality to which modern states lay claim. It is with this conviction that we propose the study of borderlands, not as another historical super-specialization but as an indispensable focus on the modern world.

From Borderlands to Borders

JEREMY ADELMAN AND STEPHEN ARON

The last decade has witnessed a sharp debate about the significance of the "frontier" in North American history. Among some self-proclaimed "new western historians," the word that Frederick Jackson Turner made synonymous with the study of American expansion has become a shibboleth, denoting a triumphalist and Anglocentric narrative of continental conquest. Even his defenders acknowledge the imperialist suppositions of Turner's thesis, yet some historians continue to assert the significance of a recast frontier. Reconstructed as a zone of intercultural penetration, the frontier has gained a new historiographic lease on life.

In many ways, this reformulation revives the notion of "borderlands" that was closely associated with Turner's protégé, Herbert Eugene Bolton. For Bolton, a historian of New Spain's northern territories, Turner's east-to-west model of American development shortchanged the divergent sources of European expansion. More so than Turner's Anglo-American frontier in which pioneer progress necessarily entailed Indian retreat, Bolton's concept of the Spanish borderlands appreciated the extended cohabitation between natives and newcomers that prevailed on the perimeters of European colonial empires. Picking up on this insight, recent historians have substituted "borderland" for all of North America's "frontiers" and, in doing so, have enriched our understanding of the complexity and contingency of intercultural relations. Instead of straightforward conquests, the history of North American borderland-frontiers has been rewritten to emphasize the accommodations between invaders and indigenes and the hybrid residuals of these encounters.

Yet the recent alignment of frontiers as borderlands has often buried an aspect of Bolton's story. For Bolton, northern New Spain was a different kind of frontier because it highlighted the friction between two Old World powers in the New: Spain and England. Too often, students of borderlands neglect the power politics of territorial hegemony. They overlook the essentially competitive nature of European imperialism and the ways in which these rivalries shaped transitions from colonies to nation-states in the eighteenth and nineteenth centuries. Absent the inter-imperial dimension of borderlands, the cross-cultural relations that defined frontiers take on a too simple face: "Europe" blurs into a single element, and "Indians" merge into a common front.

Moreover, by stressing the persistence of cross-cultural mixing, social fluidity, and the creation of syncretic formations, new work on borderlands-frontiers has downplayed profound changes in favor of continuity. In such work, a timeless legacy of cultural continuity shrouds the rise and fall of empires, the struggles between emerging independent nation-states, and the fate of increasingly dependent indigenous and métis/mestizo peoples. By contrast, Turner's

Jeremy Adelman and Stephen Aron, "From Borderlands to Borders: Empires, Nation-States, and the Peoples in Between in North American History," *American Historical Review* 104 (June 1999): 814–841.

frontier—warts and all—took into account the underlying transformations. Problematic as efforts to isolate apertures and closures have been, Tuner's frontier concept at least insisted on temporal boundaries.

In this essay, we seek to disentangle frontiers from borderlands to rescue the virtues of each construct. By frontier, we understand a meeting place of peoples in which geographic and cultural borders were not clearly defined. Consistent with recent studies of frontiers as *borderless* lands, we stress how intercultural relations produced mixing and accommodation as opposed to unambiguous triumph. Yet Bolton's original accent on the region as a site of imperial rivalry is no less important. Accordingly, we reserve the designation of borderlands for the contested boundaries between colonial domains. In a pairing of the intercolonial and intercultural dimensions, differences of European rationales and styles come to the fore, as do shifts in those rationales and styles. Equally important to the history of borderlands and frontiers were the ways in which Indians exploited these differences and compelled these shifts, partly to resists submission but mainly to negotiate intercultural relations on terms more to their liking. In this fashion, borderlands and frontiers together provide us with the vocabulary to describe the variegated nature of European imperialism and of indigenous reactions to colonial encroachments. This essay, in short, argues that the conflicts over borderlands shaped the peculiar and contingent character of frontier relations.

Nor, we insist, was this a timeless process across what Patricia Nelson Limerick has provocatively, if misleadingly, categorized as an "unbroken past." Like Turner's opening and closing frontier, borderlands also signifies an era with discrete turning points. Across the Atlantic in the late eighteenth and early nineteenth centuries, Old World empires imploded, yielding to new political configurations. In North America, as these dynasties ceded to nation-states, a new liberal cant came to govern international affairs. By no means was this a frictionless transition. Well into the nineteenth century, bellicose citizens of the United States coveted the lands of their neighbors—as Upper Canadians learned during the War of 1812 and northern Mexicans painfully discovered in the 1830s and especially in the 1840s. By the century's end, however, treaties recognized borders. The lexicon of mutual respect for boundaries inscribed in treaties crept into international diplomacy. What is more, with few exceptions, competition in trade and not territorial dominion was, by the end of the nineteenth century, the guiding framework of power politics. This shift from inter-imperial struggle to international coexistence turned borderlands into *bordered* lands. To the peoples for whom contested borderlands afforded room to maneuver and preserve some element of autonomy, this transition narrowed the scope for political independence. With states claiming exclusive dominions over all territories within their borders, Indians lost the ability to play off rivalries; they could no longer take advantage of occupying the lands "in between." Thus, as colonial borderlands gave way to national borders, fluid and "inclusive" intercultural frontiers yielded to hardened and more "exclusive" hierarchies.

We hope that reformulating the borderlands concept along these lines offers a framework for a more comparative and common "American" history. In the spirit of Bolton's "Epic of Greater America," this essay explores the transition from borderlands to borders in three North American theaters: the Great Lakes, the Lower Missouri Valley, and the Greater Rio Grande Basin. In the eighteenth century, each of these frontier regions was the site of intense imperial rivalry and of particularly fluid relations between indigenous peoples and European interlopers—in other words, these were borderlands. But, by the early nineteenth century, as empires were succeeded by incipient nation-states and imperial rivalries faded in North America, ethnic and social relations rigidified. From a borderland world in which ethnic mixing prevailed and in which still independent Indian and mestizo/métis peoples negotiated favorable terms of trade with competing colonial regimes, border fixing opened a new chapter in North American history in which property rights, citizenship, and population movements became the purview of state authorities.

We begin in the Great Lakes, where imperial rivalries allowed the greatest degree of Indian autonomy and where the bordered future first dawned. The Great Lakes region that now forms the boundary between the United States and Canada, what the French called the *pays d'en haut*, was contested territory before there was a United States, Canada, or even a New France. It was, however, Europeans' drive for the North American peltry that turned these woodlands into borderlands. Beginning in the seventeenth century, the fur trade molded the pattern of imperial competition and indigenous responses from one end of the Great Lakes to the other. In the middle of the eighteenth century, the focus of British-French rivalry had shifted to this region straddling the Great Lakes. Taking advantage of European dependence on Indian allies and traders, indigenes shaped the parameters of intercultural trade and military engagement. But, during the second half of the eighteenth century, the equation changed. If warfare brought these borderlands into existence, it also undid them: a series of wars—the Seven Years' War, the American Revolution, and the War of 1812—shattered the balance of forces and transformed the Great Lakes borderlands into a boundary between emerging nation-states. In the process, Indians lost first their power to determine the terms of exchange and, subsequently, were stripped of most of their lands.

European colonialism exacerbated existing enmities by altering the means and ends of intra-Indian conflicts. Across the breadth of the Great Lakes country, European microbes triggered epidemics in places where Europeans were barely known. In and around Iroquoia, populations declined by 50 percent. As in precolonial times, replenishing numbers by taking and then adopting captives remained a chief rationale for warfare. But the pressures were much greater than before, and, with Dutch-supplied firearms, the Iroquois had new means to wage combat. More important, they had new ends: where precolonial ways of war venerated symbolic demonstrations of courage while limiting actual bloodshed, seventeenth-century Iroquois raids aimed at gaining control of fur-bearing and fur-trading territories. A series of forays against Huron towns and later against Ohio and Illinois villages caused the disappearance of some peoples and the dislocation of others. Refugees scattered south, east, and especially west, recongregating in multi-ethnic communities around Lake Michigan and Lake Superior.

Traders led the French advance into the Great Lakes hinterland, followed by missionaries. From a base in the St. Lawrence, French traders fanned out into the interior, adopting aboriginal technologies for communication and transportation. During the seventeenth century, traders on both sides of the ethnic divide became skilled negotiators over the price and political significance of the exchange. Thus this intercultural trade quickly evolved into political allegiances, bringing Algonquian and Huron peoples, whose commercial links stretched as far as the upper Great Lakes, into alliance with the French.

French penetration and the advantage given to Indian groups north of the Great Lakes brought French allies into conflict with Iroquois to the south—who themselves were engaged in analogous relations first with the Dutch and later English through the Hudson River waterway. This rivalry over the Great Lakes would prove devastating, especially to Huronia, and set the tone for a persistent competition for the gateway to northern North America.

By the mid-seventeenth century, the rivalry began to congeal. As beaver stocks were depleted, Iroquois-Huron competition mounted, culminating in the destruction of Huronia in the 1640s. Coupled with the defection of the fur-trading firm of Groseillers and Raddison to the English and the creation of the Hudson's Bay Company in 1670, French traders rushed to reconstruct exchange networks, to rebuild the Huron intermediating roles, and to defend against other European traders. The pattern of diplomatic-commercial relations did not radically change with the evisceration of Huronia, but the mere coexistence that typified the French-Huron alliance yielded to more intimate bonds. In accord with Indian customs, nuptial alliances and *métissage* became the metaphor for political entente. Moreover, purely commercial calculations were subordinated to the mandates of intercultural diplomacy. So long as Indians were in the position to demand gifts as the price of alliance, the administrators of the French Empire had little choice but to sacrifice profits to presents.

Global imperial struggles heightened these political imperatives. After the War of the Spanish Succession (1701–14), the French moved to hem the English in along the Atlantic seaboard. Doing so required a more extensive presence in the interior, and the fur trade gained additional geo-political significance. The French deepened the central practice forged in the Huronia days—to combine indissolubly economic exchange relations with a network of political alliances.

Competition from the Hudson's Bay Company in the north Anglo-American traders to the south fueled the drive to consolidate the sprawling *postes du nord*. By the 1730s and 1740s, permanent posts were built as far as the Lower Saskatchewan River, checking the encroachment of the Hudson's Bay Company. These posts—with hubs at the present-day Straits of Mackinac and Detroit, Michigan—served as nodal points for formalized commercial-diplomatic relations. The French never proclaimed territorial sovereignty, merely the right of passage to posts, thus enabling Indians to shape considerably the terms of exchange. For the French, preserving the fealty of Indian allies involved greater attention to reciprocity and rising investments in "gifting." Herein flourished the political economy of what Richard White has called "the middle ground."

However, this tenuous common world forged by French men and Algonquian men and women—replete with ethnic mixing, syncretism, and cohabitation—rested on the contingencies of imperial rivalry. And these contingencies in turn depended on underlying shifts in metropolitan power balances. The growing population of the British colonies and English traders' increased presence in the traditional bailiwicks of New France destabilized the inclusive foundations of French-Algonquian relations. For the four decades after the Treaty of Utrecht (1713), New England and New France lived in tense, competitive peace, interrupted by an inconclusive war in 1744, and ultimately brought to a close by the events of 1759, with the fall of Quebec and Niagara. Ironically, France was winning the battle for control of the fur trade; Albany could not meet the Montreal challenge so long as the French were prepared to forsake profits in favor of presents. Gift giving and alliances had their costs: so long as the peltry trade dominated the economic concerns of merchant capitalists in Montreal and policy makers in France, population growth through arable agricultural settlement was at best a secondary goal. For the French, continental sprawl did not translate into large-scale permanent settlement of the frontier or a particular interest in the commodification of Indians' primary resource: subsistence lands.

British encroachment and French defensiveness presented Indians in between with possibilities—and perils. Many Indians favored English goods and drove harder and more expensive bargains with their French allies. Nor were the military bonds quite as solid as the French hoped; Indians were content to refer to the French as "fathers" to reinforce French obligations, but this did not imply deference to ethnic hierarchies.

Warfare jeopardized this borderland balance. Once its strength, French reliance on Indian allies became a debility. The thin reach of the French in North America made its hinterland the weak point of empire, and it was here—not in Europe—that the British chose to strike its decisive blows in the Seven Years' War (1756–63). Hemmed in, the British began changing borderland rules. Intercultural diplomacy gave way to a spirit of outright conquest. Territorial colonization replaced exchange. To be sure, at the very edges of their domain, especially in the Ohio Valley, the British partially respected borderland ways. Only with the French gone and imperial rivalry eclipsed did the British, with Jeffrey Amherst as commander-in-chief and governor-general leading the way, attempt to impose unilateral commercial rules. Thus, in North America, the British sphere became the first to host the transition from borderland to frontier colonies.

This was the first chapter in the waning of these borderlands. If Amherst aimed to accelerate the obliteration of borderland ways to emphasize the unrivaled presence of the British, his plans inspired a series of loosely coordinated uprisings among the Indians of the Great Lakes country from 1763 to 1764. Here, the British saw the lurking French hand. Indeed, the Indians fought to restore, if not the French presence, then the borderland legacy. In the wake of the Indian revolt, the British recoiled from ushering in a phase of full-throated, unmediated frontier dominion.

The next phase in the demise came with the American Revolution. Like the British after the Seven Years' War, American authorities picked up on Amherst's aborted designs. They, too, attempted to dictate the terms of intercourse. Furthermore, the national independence of the American republic removed the restraining influence that British policy had attempted to exert on the expansion of colonial settlement. In the wake of the revolution, swarms of westering settlers pursuing personal independence through private land ownership poured into the Ohio Valley. As never before, the lands of Great Lakes Indians became the targets for European occupation. This was a decisive moment in the shift from borderlands to bordered lands.

The northern borders of New Spain were for Bolton the classic, indeed only, borderlands. Yet, ironically, the greater Rio Grande was the last region to become a true borderland. Well into the eighteenth century, Spain continued to deal with Indian peoples as subjects and not partners. Only belatedly, in response to threats from colonial rivals, did Iberian authorities turn to the diplomacy of gift-alliances and commercial exchange. Their heirs in the Mexican Republic, however, could not solidify these tentative borderland arrangements. Thus it was that in northern Mexico the United States deployed manifest destiny to mount a war of conquest, attempting first to eviscerate the borderlands and then to push the border between the United States and the Republic of Mexico south to the Rio Grande.

Having discovered major silver deposits in the region of Zacatecas in the 1540s, Spanish conquerors spread their domain further north and established in 1563 the vast northern province of Nueva Vizcaya, embracing the frontier region from southern Chihuahua to Saltillo, from which all expeditions into New Mexico and the Mississippi would be staged. Until the late seventeenth century, the north was of little interest, for tribute payment was difficult, the population too dispersed to serve as effective sources of mining labor, and the establishment of *encomiendas* a discredited option for incorporating new territories (especially after the New Laws of 1542, designed to protect Indians from Spanish exploitation). After Juan de Oñate's ill-fated New Mexican venture, the northern frontier became a "military-missionary venture." A combination of missions, mainly Franciscans and later Jesuits, and presidios—military outposts—staked out the Spanish claim. Pioneered by the vanguards of military conquest and religious conversions, Spanish civilians never migrated en masse to this region, nor for that matter to Spain's other northern provinces.

If Bolton conceived of frontier missions as one-way vectors to strip aboriginals of their native cultures, he left half the story out: Indians resisted much of Catholic penetration or used friars as buffers against civilian Spanish exploitation. The long-term effect was as varied as the people the friars encountered. On the whole, they did better among sedentary villagers, such as the Yaquis, than semi-nomads such as the Apaches. Indeed, settlements of mission converts (*reducciones*) made easy prey for predators. The combination of the Spanish spreading from the south and natives fleeing from the north and east compressed the subsistence base, especially of nomads, forcing them into sustenance by plunder. Undaunted, missionaries continued to carry out their purposes.

Military outposts also dotted the land. In the wake of the 1680 Pueblo Revolt, Spanish officials called for greater investment of manpower, resources, and a comprehensive pacification of Indians. As it was, frontier Indians were increasingly forced to rely on the defenses of Spanish presidios as Apache nations proved a greater menace to their livelihoods than Spanish acculturation. From the beginning of the eighteenth century, military outposts existed largely to ward off Apaches—other Indians were willing to accept the Spanish protective umbrella.

What made this increasingly violent frontier region into a borderland was the arrival of the French at the mouth of the Mississippi in the 1680s. This accentuated the vulnerability of New Spain's northern frontier. The Spanish governor, fearing Indian alliances with the French intruders and more alarmed at the prospect of a French overland threat to Mexican silver (previously, European rivals restricted their attack on the Spanish silver supply to high-seas plunder and maritime contraband), ordered military expeditions to drive the French back up the Mississippi as far as the Missouri. But France's threat was clear: in coming down from the Great Lakes to seal off the English and seeking overland access to New Spain's silver, they encroached on the porous northern frontier and posed a direct challenge to Spanish sovereignty. No longer a Spanish-Indian frontier, this had become an imperial borderland.

Confrontation with France drew Spanish interest to Texas, hitherto a backwater of Iberian concern so long as the silver wealth of central and northern Mexico faced no overland threat. In 1691, Texas was officially created as a frontier province to buffer the "silver provinces." After the War of the Spanish Succession, Spanish officials, with the help of a renegade French trader, Louis Juchereau de Saint-Denis, struggled to reoccupy Texas. The linchpin of borderland policy involved a profound mutation of Spanish approaches to Indian populations. Rather than create vassal subjects through conquest, eighteenth-century Iberian envoys went north with instructions to imitate the French and English patterns of signing treaties with Indians, implying a mutual relationship between autonomous peoples and abandoning the principle of paternalistic pacification.

Imperial warfare was, once again, a watershed. The Seven Years' War forced Spain to adopt more consciously a borderland-style approach to the frontier. This was paradoxical: French defeat in 1762 might have brought relief to northern Mexican outposts: gone were the French trading parties plying their contraband through the silver provinces, gone was the French military threat from Louisiana. Viceregal authorities breathed a premature sigh of relief. They did not account for the defensive agency of Indians themselves, for Comanche-Apache conflict only intensified. Reinforcement and reform did little to alleviate the damage. By the 1770s, these borderlands were becoming a dark and bloody ground. Apache raids struck deep into the heart of Nueva Vizcaya, leaving behind charred remains in the Valle de San Bartolomé, Parras, Saltillo, and the royal mines of Guarisamey. These were not pre-political acts of banditry: many raiding parties were made up of multi-ethnic peoples, Indians, Africans, Europeans, and mestizos, with complex internal hierarchies and elaborate espionage networks. Nor did they sabotage commodity flows: raiding parties systematically sold their loot to rival European buyers.

To such mayhem, the Spanish responded by abandoning all local pretense of paternalistic pacification in favor of a policy of calculated deceit though negotiation. Some Spanish authorities, most notably Viceroy Bernardo de Gálvez, urged the adoption of "the French model," by which he meant that Spain should trade guns with, rather than aim them at, Indians.

Thus, by the 1790s, Spain was inching away from paternalistic pacification and adopting a borderland stance of accommodation and reciprocal exchange with Indian peoples. The inter-imperial truce after the Seven Years' War provided only short-lived respite from European interloping. Spain lost Florida but kept Cuba; it acquired Louisiana by default, thereby extending silver's buffer into the Mississippi Basin. But U.S. independence in 1783 posed a new problem for Mexico. Just as Spain embraced borderland tactics, the Iberian flank faced the emerging territorial threat of the United States.

Belatedly and ineffectually, Spain turned to the commercial-diplomatic option, the hallmark of a more fully borderland-style approach to Euro-Indian affairs. Presidios became the home for protected Apache families (among many others) who tilled lots and raised livestock that they sold on local markets. Spanish outposts also furnished food and trading goods to allies.

The belated and half-hearted shift from a frontier policy of pacification to borderland accommodation meant that, over the course of a generation, Spain and then independent Mexico lost all its claims from the Ohio to the Rio Grande. First came the French Revolution, whose bellicose fallout hammered the fiscal base of the Iberian war machine on both sides of the Atlantic. In desperation, the Spanish Bourbons opted for diplomatic conniving to thwart competitors swarming from the heartland of North America. The Treaty of San Lorenzo del Escorial (1795) ceded all Spanish claims to the Ohio Valley and granted American traders free navigation of the Mississippi. This calculation, however, had the combined effect of allowing the spread of U.S. goods into the Spanish borderlands, and left Spain's hitherto allies, the Creeks, Choctaws, and Chickasaws, all within the territory of the United States, thereby losing the confederation of southeast tribes as a buffer against American expansionism. In desperation, fearing both a French invasion of the peninsula and American marauding of the borderlands, Godoy was persuaded by Napoleon to cede Louisiana back to France in the Treaty of San Ildefonso (1800). (To be fair to the otherwise venal minister, the treaty did stipulate that the territory not be transferred to a third party.)

This, the minister hoped, would restore the buffer between the greater Rio Grande and the swarming North American heartland. The gamble backfired: Napoleon, in an effort to galvanize American support (or neutrality) in his rivalry with Great Britain, sold the sprawling province to Jefferson in 1803. New Spain was thrust back into the defensive position it had in 1762. But the menace of American expansion eclipsed anything posed by the French or British in an earlier day.

Transatlantic warfare forced Spain into an increasingly borderland-style policy, but the depth of the imperial rivalry over Spain's precious dominions made them prey to interlopers' thirst to claim these possessions as their own. In due course, the borderlands became a bordered land between a hobbled republic to the south and an expanding regime to the north. Bereft of central authority, Mexico City's grip on the northern borderland slipped. To compound matters, the consolidation of the North American heartland as the site of territorial occupation pushed borderland Indians south and west. The Osages jostled with the Cherokees for shrinking hunting grounds, culminating in fierce raiding and counter-raiding in 1818 and 1819. By 1820, East Texas was dotted with hamlets of Cherokee refugees. To their west, semi-sedentary Wacos, Tawakanis, and Taouayas struggled to defend compressed homelands whose own western flank lay open to mobile and ever more armed Comanches. Indian appeals for Mexican treaties, gifts, and territorial guarantees to stabilize the borderlands fell on the fiscally deafened ears of Mexico City rulers. If the region still seemed like a borderland, it was only because one colonial rival was too weak to stake territorial claims, while the other was too busy inducting the Missouri borderland into its frontier designs.

This was more of a borderland by default than by arrangement. Indians defended their dwindling independence with renewed vehemence. Comanche and Lipan Apaches stepped up their raiding—to which the Cherokees replied with offers to Mexican authorities to help stymie nomad assaults if the Americans could be kept out of Cherokee lands. When Mexico wavered, the Cherokees and Comanches even dallied with the idea of a common alliance against all white authority, to no avail. Eventually, the Comanches went their own way and honed their skills in guerrilla warfare. This was not recidivist war. Comanches used their ability to criss-cross the border for profit. They plundered and stole cattle, selling their booty to the other side. Apaches did the same. The Mexican government countered with an even more gruesome form of commodification: offering pecuniary rewards for Indian *piezas*, bits of indigenous bodies, like ears, scalps, and heads. The Mexican state created incentives for large private possess and armies to chase down armed borderlanders. The "scalp market" thrived.

Borderland warfare gave way to war over the border. Fearing Anglo-American penetration, northern Mexican authorities invited new occupants, hoping they would become reliable Mexicans and stabilize these unruly provinces. In effect, Mexico City abandoned the remnants of borderland policies in an effort to consolidate Texan allegiance to the south. It backfired, quite like Spain's former gamble in Missouri. Newcomers turned against their political hosts. The Missouri *empresario* Moses Austin (father of Stephen) set out for San Antonio bearing a proposal to the Texan government (which was still loyal to the fissiparous regime) to settle 300 families in the region. After much wrangling, the Mexican government approved the plan in early 1821. Moses died that year, but Stephen Austin carried out his father's plan. By 1823, settlers were flooding in—to the alarm of local Indians. Cherokees complained to the mayor of Nacogdoches of "illegal" American occupation of their lands. Still, some saw the Cherokees as potential allies against raiding. Stephen, for one, relied on brokers like Richard Fields to secure some measure of Cherokee loyalty. But settler numbers mounted, eviscerating any hope of borderland accommodation. Indian raiding increased; Mexican authority plunged into civil war. Anglo-American, and even sparse Hispanic dwellers, could not count on protection from the south. It was not long before a local settler chorus rose for switching fealty from Mexico to Washington.

The stage was set first for Texan secession in 1836 and subsequently New Mexico, Arizona, California, Colorado, Utah, and Nevada's annexation to the United States in 1848. An impoverished Mexican state could not secure Indian allies, defend local settlers, or thwart American aggrandizing aims. Texan-American traders like Charles Stillman of Brownsville extended their reach from Matamoros as far as Saltillo and San Luis Potosí, nursing dreams of making the Rio Grande into a great riverine conduit for commerce. Grandiose plans never materialized, but businessmen-cum-frontier consolidators were happy to back a war to incorporate definitively much of the borderland region into the territorial reach of the American republic. In early 1848, the Treaty of Guadalupe Hidalgo inscribed the Rio Grande as a border. Within the U.S. side of this line, former Indian lands were given over to occupation and Hispanic ranchos yielded to the surveyors of and claimants to private property. In turn, albeit later during the regime of dictator Porfirio Díaz, the *porfiriato* (1876–1911), Mexico, too, brought the intra-border region into the domain of an enclosed proprietary structure for capitalist occupation. This did not put an end to the relatively unobstructed border crossings of Indians and Mexicans, but they did so most often in search of a wage rather than to escape commercial colonialism—and they did so precisely because border fixing allowed an entirely different commercial rationale to prevail over the erstwhile borderlands. Either way, border peace brought trans-border collusion among nation-states to curb the mobility and autonomy of borderlanders. For many borderlanders on the Mexican side, public armies and private head hunters waged little less than a war of extermination.

This exploration of the transition in North American history from borderlands to borders has emphasized the connections between imperial competition and intercultural relations. Stated simply, where the former flourished, the latter more likely featured inclusive frontiers. Where European colonial domains brushed up against one another, Indian peoples deflected imperial powers from their original purposes and fashioned economic, diplomatic, and personal relations that rested, if not entirely on Indian ground, at least on more common ground. During the eighteenth century, the Spanish, the French, and the British would not have survived their North American rivalries without Indian allies. As the French struggled to restrict British colonists to the east of the Appalachians, as the Spanish sought to slow the drainage of specie to French and British traders, and as the British worked to enlarge their share of North American resources, each empire had to come to terms with Indian peoples. The French learned the art of intercultural mediation, the Spanish abandoned their longstanding policy of paternalistic pacification, and the British, most ironically, on the eve of the American Revolution, showed signs of mastering the diplomacy of the middle ground. To varying degrees in the borderlands that were the Great Lakes, the lower Missouri Valley, and the Greater Rio Grande, intermarriages and gift exchanges cemented political alliances.

But borderlands born of imperial rivalry and cross-cultural mixing became borders when the costs of ethnic alliances surpassed their benefits and when European empires decayed. The demise of the Great Lakes fur trade and the territorial expansion south of the lakes forced the custodians of the old *pays d'en haut* to abandon their existing diplomatic commitment to Indian partners in favor of a new diplomatic commitment to the peaceable coexistence of states on either side of an international border. Deprived of imperial rivalry, Indians of the Great Lakes struggled on in a futile effort to defend remaining homelands and to preserve the fraying ligaments of cross-cultural exchange. The same held true for the peoples of the Rio Grande. If the Spanish came late to borderland ways of alliance making, nomadic and pueblo Indians did try to manipulate Bourbon frailty to their advantage—although it was this very weakness of Spanish and later Mexican territorial control that led to annexation by the United States.

Thus Indian agency posed contingencies with which European powers had to contend, forcing them to adapt their expansionist ways. Cross-cultural brokering and conflict shaped but did not determine the patterns of coexistence. In the end, Old World conflicts and eighteenth-century warfare provided the decisive markers for hinterland processes. The crucial turning point in the above narratives came with the age of "democratic revolutions"—a process that sundered all three empires of North America and gave way to liberal statemaking. The American and French revolutions shattered the delicate equipoise of borderland adaptations and put Indian peoples on the permanent defensive. The fate of the Missouri Valley exemplified this aboutface most dramatically. The American Revolution and the Jeffersonian ascendance that followed wrecked generations of syncretic and symbiotic Indian-European arrangements by unleashing a virulent model of homestead property. In Missouri, two rival regimes of occupation converged: one based on slave labor, the other on free, and both had unlimited appetites for land. Thus did Missouri change from borderland to border state. But the conflict between free and slave labor, which for Americans proved to be the biggest difference (and culminated in the carnage of the 1860s), made little difference to Indians, who were displaced by both forms of exclusive occupation.

The Age of Revolution and the ensuing Napoleonic Wars also remapped the borderlands in the Great Lakes and Rio Grande regions. Heightened military conflict not only shattered the French and Spanish regimes in North America and initiated Britain's gradual withdrawal, it also laid waste the rival commercial and intercultural links of the borderlands. As the continental wars spread to North America, culminating in the War of 1812, they wrote the final chapter in the Great Lakes evolution from borderlands to border. Thereafter, border fixing gave way to the birth pangs of Canadian statehood and the coming of age of the American republic.

To be sure, borders formalized but did not foreclose the flow of people, capital, and goods. Even if the eclipse of imperial rivalries afforded less space for

Indian and métis/mestizo autonomy, the prolonged weakness of nation-states left some room to maneuver. International boundaries remained dotted lines that took a generation to solidify. Up to the 1880s, Apaches flaunted the conventions of border crossing—that is, until General Díaz consolidated Mexico City's hold over the nation's north, and General George Crook managed to contain Geronimo and his followers. Almost simultaneously, the Canadian–United States border solidified. For the Canadian Métis, the surviving extension of the Great Lakes middle ground, border drawing narrowed the range of movement, imperiling their folkways and ultimately setting the stage for the uprising of Louis Riel (1869–70, 1885). Lest readers see Apache resistance or Métis freedom as unique, borders and the consolidation of nation-states spelled the end of autonomy for Yaquis, Comanches, Sioux, Blackfoot, and countless other peoples who once occupied these North American borderlands. Hereafter, the states of North America enjoyed unrivaled authority to confer or deny rights to peoples within their borders.

If borders appeared juridically to divide North American people, they also inscribed in notions of citizenship new and *exclusivist* meanings. They defined not only external sovereignty but also internal membership in the political communities of North America. Defended by treaties, borders separated new nation-states; they also helped harden the lines separating members from non-members within states. The rights of citizens—never apportioned equally—were now allocated by the force of law monopolized by ever more consolidated and centralized public authority.

For those included, this unleashed new eras of freedom and autonomy; for the excluded, life within nation-states more often meant precisely the opposite— the loss of political, social, and personal status. Furthermore, ossified borders reduced the freedom of "exit," at a minimum the ability to leave and at best the power to play off rival rulers. With the consolidation of the state form of political communities, borderland peoples began the long political sojourn of survival within unrivaled polities.

Over the long run, excluded or marginal former borderlanders began to reconcile themselves to accommodation, and eventually assertion within multi-ethnic or even multinational states (especially in Canada). In the parlance of census takers and apostles of national integration, borderlanders became "ethnics"—minorities distinguished by phenotype or language from the "national" majority. It took some remarkable political dexterity to transform this particularizing and separating category into a basis for challenging the unitary claims of North American national-statists. Of late, the idiom of self-determination has enabled borderlanders to champion the idea of community sovereignty with rights that even transcend nation-states. This, however, is a recent phenomenon, and should not be projected backward onto peoples who, a century ago, cared little for states and less for nations. Whatever lands Indian and métis/mestizo peoples may reclaim will be won as much in national courts as in their own councils. These triumphs, however, will hardly restore the power and autonomy once enjoyed by the peoples in between.

Telling North American Border Histories

ANDREW GRAYBILL AND BENJAMIN JOHNSON

In March 2005 George W. Bush welcomed Mexican president Vicente Fox and Canadian prime minister Paul Martin to his ranch in Crawford, Texas. Their meeting was unusual, if only because the last official U.S. gathering of the three continental heads of state had taken place more than twelve years earlier, for the initialing of the North American Free Trade Agreement. In contrast to the comity of that 1992 visit, this summit revealed significant fissures dividing the nations, including the simmering dispute between Ottawa and Washington over the trade in softwood lumber, and growing vigilantism directed at illegal Mexican immigrants in the American Southwest. But on one thing Bush, Fox, and Martin could readily agree: namely, that the fates of all three countries are knitted together. As Martin put it: "Our safe borders secure our people not only against terrorism, but they make possible a speedy flow of goods, services and people and information among our three nations."

By comparison, historians of North America have been far more hesitant to explore the interconnectedness of Canada, the United States, and Mexico. Doubters need only consult the map section of most books on any one of the three countries; almost invariably, the drawings end abruptly at either the 49th parallel or the Rio Grande, as if weather patterns, topography, or even human beings naturally observe such boundaries. There are several reasons that may explain this persistent habit, but the most significant is the simple fact that the nation-state has come to serve as the basic unit of analysis in the modern practice of historical scholarship. As such, many historians tend to color entirely "within the lines," telling stories, often very good ones, that stop arbitrarily at the boundaries—between North Dakota and Saskatchewan, for example, or between Arizona and Sonora—and that ignore the land and the people just on the other side, as well as the line in between. They also often succumb to the temptation to superimpose these lines on earlier historical periods, when they did not yet exist, thereby assuming the inevitability of the modern map.

Precisely because the nation-state has become the dominant form of political organization in the modern world, we often look at modern maps and the borders that divide nations without questioning or even recognizing these assumptions. By the mid-twentieth century, nation-states has divided up most of the earth's territory, population, and economic life among them, having supplanted, incorporated, or conquered all non-national societies. But rather than unquestioningly accepting the existence of such national borders, we might instead treat them as interesting inrellectual problems, and ask some historical questions about them: How did they come to be, and how and why did they take on their current configurations? With what other ways of organizing people and space did they come into conflict, and how were these struggles resolved? What kinds of goods and which sorts of people did national governments want to cross these borders easily, and which ones not at all? And how many of these items and individuals have actually crossed? Did borders mean the same things to local residents of border areas as they did to national policymakers? How have borders and the issues that they raise been represented in film and literature, and how have these depictions changed expectations about border policies and border crossings? And how have the answers to these sorts of questions changed over time, and why?

By posing these sorts of queries, we seek to uncover the meaning and significance of our national borders, rather than taking them for granted. Like other kinds of transnational and comparative history, our approach offers one productive way of telling stories that transcends both the geographic and conceptual limits imposed by national boundaries, a task to which the historical profession is now turning with great vigor. Nations still matter in these stories—indeed, their governments are often the most powerful actors, and they created the very borders under examination. But as Vicente Fox, George Bush, and Paul Martin all recognized, each nation acts in relation to other nations and to political and economic realities that they cannot always control.

Historians of North America have been posing questions about borders for some time. Recent works on the Canada-U.S. and Mexico-U.S. borders ask similar questions, often feature parallel historical actors, and push accounts of national development to acknowledge wider historical circumstances. Yet scholars of both border regions generally work in personal and intellectual isolation from one another. Indeed, until quite recently, the term "borderlands" served as a sort of shorthand to refer to the present-day U.S. Southwest and the Mexican North, with little thought to the border dividing Canada from the United States. Innovative methodologies and approaches applied to the study of one border have not necessarily been brought to bear on investigations of the other, despite the fact that a range of groups—among them, U.S. government officials, Asian migrants, and smugglers—have adapted the knowledge gained in one borderlands to the challenges posed by its northern or southern counterpart.

A generation ago, "borderlands" referred to the northernmost reaches of the Spanish colonial project, an area that encompasses the present-day U.S. states of California, Arizona, New Mexico, Texas, Louisiana, Alabama, Georgia, and Florida. This borderlands history was originally articulated by Herbert Eugene Bolton in the early 1920s, and continued by his protégé John Francis Bannon as a kind of answer, or at least a Hispanic counterpart, to Frederick Jackson Turner's famous and influential thesis that the frontier experience had shaped a distinctive American character as well as democratic institutions and habits of mind. This field, the original "borderlands" history, challenged U.S. historians to think of national historical origins and influences as having developed beyond the familiar world of the British Empire and the eastern seaboard of North America. Although practitioners of Boltonian borderlands history sought to make a mark on the wider study of U.S. history, for the most part they were unsuccessful. U.S. historians continued to focus on the British roots of American culture and institutions, and historians of Latin America found borderlands scholarship similarly marginal to their enterprise. At the same time, historians of the American Southwest were as uninterested in crossing the 1848 temporal boundary as were Boltonian scholars in pursuing their studies after the Mexican-American War remade their region.

By the 1970s, the Boltonian school of Borderlands Studies had expanded to include scholars with different agendas and approaches to the study of this region. Students of Mexican American history focused their attention on the marginalization and racialization of people of Mexican descent in the U.S. Southwest after 1848, even as they found the earlier Spanish and Mexican periods relevant to their inquiries. Some scholars in this first wave of Mexican American history had been trained in part as Latin Americanists. They appreciated the continuity between Mexican history and Mexican American history, and recognized the challenge that writing such accounts posed to U.S. historians ignorant of the Latin American past. One of them, Oscar J. Martínez, expanded upon his early work on the twin border towns of El Paso and Juárez to encompass a broader examination of the border itself. At about the same time, scholars of Native American history found much of interest in the areas colonized by New Spain, particularly because the region's Native peoples had endured for nearly four centuries under different forms of colonialism—Spanish, Mexican, and then American—yet had managed to retain their distinct group identity, along with substantial portions of their pre-Columbian territories. In the 1980s, the U.S. Southwest also drew the attention of the "New Western" historians, who found the area—including its colonial past—to be fertile ground for exploration of the themes of conquest, environmental destruction, and myth-making that were so central to their work. Both Patricia Nelson Limerick and Richard White, for example, examined the deep ties between Mexico and the U.S. West in their surveys of the region's history. Limerick even argued for adopting the idea of the *"frontera,"* a term derived from studies of the U.S.-Mexico borderlands, which she said offered "a realistic view of this nation's position in the hemisphere and in the world," one that the concept of the "frontier" did not, because of the latter term's fostering of an "illusion of vacancy" and "triumphal conclusions." But, for both authors, "border" meant Mexico, and as with the New Western history in general, they almost entirely neglected Canada, its West, and the border that links Canada to the United States.

At about the same time, the Mexican North began attracting greater attention from historians of Mexico. Prompted in part by a broader revitalization of that nation's regional history, these scholars analyzed the relationship of the northern Mexican states with the centers of national power, emphasizing in particular the states' roles in the Mexican Revolution (1911–20). Their work generally treated the North as a set of regions (Baja California and Sonora, Chihuahua, and the Monterrey-dominated Northeast) rather than a unified border zone. Nevertheless, in their accounts, the border with the United States was seen as a major force in the politics, society, and economy of each of these regions.

Broader developments within the academy gave many of these scholars good reason to call themselves, among other things, "borderlands" historians. As it did for many disciplines, the rise of postmodernism—which seeks to reveal the contradictions, incompleteness, and contingencies of social categories and processes—changed the study of the Spanish or Mexican borderlands. Whereas scholars once viewed "Spaniards," "Indians," and "mestizos" as self-evident and distinct categories, they now began to realize that the boundaries between these groups were in fact quite porous, and changed with circumstance and over time. In nineteenth-century New Mexico, for example, a person who began life as a subject of the Spanish crown, might subsequently have claimed membership in a Pueblo Indian community, or assumed an active political role as a Mexican citizen, or become a U.S. citizen—all within the course of three or four decades. The ideas of "borders" and "border-crossing" seemed well-suited to grapple with such complexity. The simultaneous connections and distinctions that the term "border" implies—particularly in the case of such seemingly different nations as Mexico and the United States—spoke directly to the core concerns of postmodernism. Indeed, "borders" and "border-crossing" have become leading metaphors for the postmodern condition, and works that study the U.S.-Mexican borderlands are widely cited by scholars of the history and literature of other regions.

The growing interest in transnational history in the 1990s and early 2000s also drew historians to the study of borders in general, including the U.S.-Mexican borderlands. History as a discipline is still structured to a considerable degree around nation-states, whose territoriality and understandings of their antecedents provide historians with the demarcations of their subjects and time frames. Most historians, particularly of the modern world, are trained and hired as historians of a particular nation. Recently, however, a rising chorus of historians has questioned the tight focus on nationalist historiographies, arguing that such an orientation minimizes transnational and non-national developments and obscures the extent to which nations themselves are shaped by larger dynamics—such as migration, commerce, technology, and ideas—that may be underestimated or ignored by versions of the past yoked too firmly to nation-based inquiry. These historians continue to find nations and national histories important subjects and frames for their work, but they also write stories centered on regions, like the Atlantic and Pacific worlds, or on processes, like migration or global economic networks, or on intellectual and cultural worlds that cut across national boundaries. Accounts of border areas can similarly illuminate the contingency of national histories and provide opportunities for creating stories about the past that transcend both the geographic and conceptual limits imposed by national boundaries.

Contemporary developments along the U.S.-Mexico border have also heightened scholarly interest in the region's history. Population on both sides of the border has been growing rapidly for two generations, an enormous number of manufacturing and assembly plants have been built on the Mexican side, and Mexican immigration to the United States is transforming the social fabric of both nations even as it generates ongoing controversy. By 2000, the border had become the focus of two Mexican scholarly journals, *Frontera Norte* and *Estudios Fronterizos*, published respectively by the border universities El Colegio de la

Frontera Norte and La Universidad Autónoma de Baja California. Although the work of historians from Mexico, the United States, and other countries appear in both journals, the preponderance of the articles they publish are contributed by anthropologists, sociologists, demographers, economists, and policy analysts, with a heavy emphasis on contemporary issues and very recent developments. North of the line, it is estimated that by 2050 one-quarter of the U.S. population may claim Latino—mostly Mexican—ancestry, so the boundary between the United States and Mexico has never seemed so relevant to the U.S. academy as in recent years. And clearly the connections that this border has fostered are as important as the divisions it has ostensibly maintained.

By the first decade of the twenty-first century, then, for an academic to label his or her work as "borderlands" scholarship could mean any number of things: a focus on the northern reaches of New Spain, or on the regional histories of the northern states of Mexico, or on those of the U.S. Southwest; or a concentration on Mexican American history, or Mexican migration, or the region's ethnohistory; or even an interest in cultural hybridity and identity-formation in the area now bisected by the U.S.-Mexico border. Increasingly, however, historians based in the United States who label themselves as "borderlands historians" have emphasized the key role that the border itself has played in shaping this borderlands: its creation as the result of long processes of colonialism and encounter; the way it has reflected the national projects of Mexico and the United States; and its shifting meanings and implications for the diverse groups who cross the border and call the region their home.

Recent studies have demonstrated the productivity of examining border-making and its impacts on both sides of the line. For example, we now know that the international boundary created in 1848, in the wake of the Mexican-American War, altered class relations in much of the Mexican North. Regional economic elites and the central state no longer needed the services of the subaltern class to act as a military check to Apache and Comanche raids, and so felt free to trample on this group's rights to land. At the same time, in the Mexican Northeast, the ease of crossing into Texas for work led to the collapse of debt peonage and to generally milder treatment of peasants by hacienda owners, even as large numbers of slaves in Texas fled south across the Rio Grande to Mexico, where slavery had been abolished decades earlier. The policing of the new border probably had the greatest effect on Native peoples, with the Mexican and U.S. governments cooperating in efforts to end the migration and raiding that had been so essential to continued Native independence. The long-standing efforts of ethnic Mexican borderlands communities to maintain their autonomy vis-à-vis the power of the central government persisted throughout the nineteenth century, often through the continuation of cross-border political and economic ties, and sometimes through armed uprisings. The border also became a site where national notions of race and citizenship were forged; by the twentieth century, U.S. immigration restrictions had led to the active policing of the border against migrants—though not Mexican migrants, as most would assume today, but rather Asians, who had been banned from entry into the United States by the 1882 Chinese Exclusion Act and the 1907 Gentleman's Agreement with

Japan. By the 1910s, this border also exhibited a certain vitality in the realm of cultural production, as its dividing river, fences, and markers now became symbols of national and racial difference, disseminated across Mexico and the United States in travel accounts, postcards, novels, and films. Often meant to evoke distance, division, and dread, invocations of the border could also provoke yearning, fascination, and desire. Long before the age of NAFTA, then, the U.S.-Mexico border loomed large in the development of both nations.

Much of this new borderlands history is explicitly and proudly transnational, and many of its proponents tout it as part of the effort to transcend what they see as the limiting focus of historians—particularly U.S. scholars—on the nation-state. As Samuel Truett and Elliott Young have argued in an influential historiographic review and critique of the new incarnation of borderlands history, "Studying the U.S.-Mexico border-lands allows one to engage … hidden stories [those that escape nation-centered accounts] while reflecting critically on the process of territorialization that coincided with the rise of nation-states." For many borderlands scholars, telling these sorts of stories is also a way to contribute to political projects and movements that are critical of nationalism—particularly U.S. nationalism—in an era of remarkable American power.

Nevertheless, scholars of this new borderlands school remain more rooted in the universities, territory, archives, and historiography of the United States than their transnational rhetoric might lead one to believe. Historians of Mexico, particularly Mexican nationals, have not shown nearly the enthusiasm of U.S. historians (almost all of them American nationals) for embracing a rubric of "borderlands" to frame their work. Despite the strong orientation of Mexican historians to the study of that nation's center of population and political power, there is also a long tradition of writing about the Mexican North. Most scholars of Mexico's North characterize the border as a zone of conflict between two discrete and highly unequal nation-states, paying scant attention to the cultural hybridity that exists there and overlooking the critique of nation-centered history that characterizes so much of the U.S. literature. When asked by a U.S. historian about Mexican sovereignty, the Mexican historian and diplomat Carlos Rico Ferrat articulated the reasons behind the resistance of some Mexican scholars to the post-national turn. "We have been historically more adamant in asserting our legalistic perspective on legal sovereignty," he explained, "not only because our law is a major defense against a much stronger nation, but also because that nation is on our border."

Compared with the long history and great diversity of scholarship on the U.S.-Mexico borderlands, there has been far less academic attention directed at the Canada-U.S. borderlands. Several factors may help to explain this discrepancy. For one thing, Canada and the United States, as advanced liberal capitalist democracies populated mostly by descendents of European settlers, appear to have more in common with one another than they do with Mexico. Accordingly, for most Americans and some Canadians—at least until the emergence of terrorism as a perceived threat to American national security—the international boundary separating the two countries has seemed largely inconsequential, as suggested by the familiar refrain that Canada and the United States share the longest undefended border in the world. Contrast that with the writer Gloria Anzaldúa's description of the U.S-Mexico border as "*una herida abierta* [an open wound], where the Third World grates against the first and bleeds." Whereas armies and insurrectionists have splashed their way across the Rio Grande on numerous occasions, since the War of 1812 the northern border has experienced much less international conflict. Even the most contentious issue in the history of the northern borderlands—the dispute over the Oregon boundary—was resolved through diplomatic channels (at almost the same moment that the United States invaded Mexico to conquer what later became the American Southwest). Moreover, the border-related issues that usually divide Washington and Ottawa tend to be of a milder nature (concerns about American cattle possibly transmitting mad cow disease to Canadian livestock, for example) than those (like the intractable matter of illegal immigration) that estrange federal officials in the United States from their Mexican counterparts.

Although there is no body of work on the northern borderlands equivalent to that of the Boltonian school, some Canadian historians did probed the significance of their boundary with the United States. Writing in the late 1920s and 1930s, at roughly the apex of Bolton's career, Walter Sage showed that immigrants in the North American West had repeatedly crossed the border in search of available land and economic opportunities, and that Canada's western provinces were more socially and economically integrated with adjacent U.S. states than they were with Canada's economic and population centers farther to the east. John Bartlet Brebner, a Toronto-born scholar who spent his career at Columbia University in New York, took a similarly continental approach. George F. G. Stanley, on the other hand, placed more emphasis on the importance of the border itself; according to Elizabeth Jameson and Jeremy Mouat, for Stanley, "the border separated American violence, lawlessness, and greed from Canadian civility, order, and managed development." Like the much more influential Boltonians, then, these early Canadian scholars formulated historical narratives that placed their nation within a larger, continental framework.

It was not until the period after the Second World War that other writers picked up these lines of inquiry. When they did, their interpretations tended to emphasize the 49th parallel as a clear marker of national difference, confirming the findings of Stanley rather than Sage. In 1955, Wallace Stegner published *Wolf Willow*, a memoir of the six years he spent as a boy on his family's homestead not far from Eastend, Saskatchewan in the early twentieth century. In his youth, the Iowa-born Stegner had been acutely aware of the existence of the international border with the United States, which passed just south of his parents' farm and whose bifurcating presence saturates the book. Indeed, in one passage from *Wolf Willow*, Stegner noted that the 49th parallel "ran directly through my childhood, dividing me in two." This schism shaped his life in subtle ways: the textbooks he read in school were published in Toronto rather than New York; the signature national holiday he celebrated was Canada Day and not the Fourth of July; his family received mail-order catalogs from Eaton's as opposed to Sears. But even in his childhood, Stegner recognized that the line did more than merely differentiate social norms. As he writes, "the 49th parallel was an agreement, a rule, a limitation, a fiction perhaps but a legal one, acknowledged by both sides."

Surprisingly—considering the relative inattention to the northern borderlands at the time—another book about the region appeared that very same year. Unlike Stegner's volume, however, *Whoop-Up Country* was the work of an academic historian, Paul F. Sharp, and it was concerned less with the fact of the border than with how the boundary had come to be in the first place. Sharp discovered that Canadian and U.S. officials had trained their gaze on the region at roughly the same moment in the late nineteenth century, and for similar reasons: to abolish the area's illicit whiskey trade and to assert control over its indigenous peoples, all in preparation for the arrival of white settlers. Sharp argued that those efforts were so successful that by 1885 the once unified Alberta-Montana borderlands had been divided and then absorbed by their respective nations. It was this reordered landscape that the young Wallace Stegner recalled from his youth. Though Sharp had approached the 49th parallel through archival collections in the United States and Canada, rather than lived experience, like Stegner he saw the border as a fault line, a marker of fundamental national difference.

Whoop-up Country offered a possible model for the trans-border study of the region, and initially seemed to make a wide impact. In the United States, it was broadly and favorably reviewed.... Canadian historians, by contrast, were much less taken with Sharp's account of the border. *Whoop-Up Country* and Sharp's earlier publications remained important works for scholars of the North American West, but Canadian historians roundly criticized him for emphasizing the regional unity of the northern Great Plains. The dominant school of Canadian history at the time, represented by the political economist Harold Innis, stressed the economic links between the eastern core of the nation and its western hinterlands, leaving little room for north-south connections and making it easy for Sharp's more politically oriented account to be treated as a regional, and not national, story. Moreover, the emphasis by Innis and other leading Canadian scholars on Canadian distinctiveness blunted the effect of Sharp's work in Canada. As Thomas Isern and Bruce Shepard have argued, "The reason for Sharp's minimal impact in Canada has been the nationalist orientation of the Canadian historical tradition." Thus, much as in the Mexican academy, Canadian historians resisted integrating their history with that of the United States, and so, again as in Mexico, no cohesive school of border studies emerged in Canada.

In the mid-1970s, however, a fresh generation of historians—mostly from Canada—shifted their attention to the northern borderlands, primarily to the region lying between the Great Lakes and the Pacific Ocean. While these newcomers continued to investigate the area through the prism of real and perceived national divergence, just as Sharp (and Stegner) had, they also infused their work with a heightened sense of Canadian patriotism. Such sentiment was on the rise in Canadian academic circles at that time, fueled by discontent with the ongoing U.S. war in Vietnam, but also by a renewed resistance to the use of American models as explanations for historical development in Canada. Of particular concern to Canadian scholars was Turner's frontier thesis. Though Turner made no particular claims for the relevance of his thesis to Canada, historians north of the border were keen to prove its inapplicability to their nation's past, and to thus assert the significance of the 49th parallel.

Some of these pieces tackled the Turnerian question head on, arguing that while the United States may have acquired and preserved its unique characteristics through constant westward migration, Canada had looked to the east—to the Old World—for its identity, even as the Dominion expanded onto the western prairies and across the Rocky Mountains. How else to explain the rigid Victorian class structure of Alberta's range cattle industry, especially by comparison to its lawless but (supposedly) leveling American counterpart? And what about that most Canadian of all institutions, the North-West Mounted Police, which took its inspiration from the Royal Irish Constabulary and thus developed in precisely the imperial context that Ottawa planned to replicate in its own hinterlands? Such studies identified a distinct Canadian metropolitanism that stood in contrast, even opposition, to Turner's (American) frontier. And the collective message of these contributions was clear enough: the border marked the northward limit of one country, and the beginning of another, presumably better one.

By the late 1970s, however, some scholars had resumed questioning the definitiveness of the 49th parallel as a continental fault line between the United States and Canada, as Walter Sage had done a half century before. Like Sage, most of these scholars adopted a regional rather than a national perspective on the northern borderlands, one that emphasized the social and environmental connections that created trans-border and geographically discrete areas such as the Pacific Northwest or the Great Plains. Their attention was drawn to the western portion of the border, particularly the Plains, perhaps because this region had been the focus of intense Canadian and U.S. efforts to finalize their borders, whereas east of the Great Lakes the boundary had long been taken for granted. In their research, these authors discovered that various groups—from homesteaders to industrial workers—had more in common with their counterparts directly across the international boundary than they did with their respective Canadian and American countrymen in the distant East. Other historians identified ideas and practices, such as anti-black racism or settlement boosterism, that crossed the line and thus came to characterize life and experience on both sides of the 49th parallel. Taken together, such works called for less emphasis on U.S.-Canadian divergence, and more attention to overlap and interplay. The Canada-U.S. border, in these accounts, was important precisely for its failure to create or mark fundamental national difference. A regionalist approach also characterized a cluster of works on the New England-Eastern Canada borderlands that came out of an institute at the University of Maine in the late 1980s and early 1990s.

Until quite recently, scholarly examination of the northern borderlands gravitated toward one of these two poles. Most investigations focused doggedly on the notion of the 49th parallel as a deep fissure dividing U.S. and Canadian society, politics, and culture; a smaller collection of works, meanwhile, identified pockets of regional unity that supersede the boundary line. Both of these approaches have been enormously important in fostering our understanding of the area and its complex development. But the early years of the twenty-first century have seen a surge of renewed interest in the northern borderlands, and historians have begun to examine the significance of the 49th parallel from new perspectives. Like most of the earlier work, this scholarship has a strongly western cast, for reasons that are difficult to parse but may have something to do with the centrality of conquest and colonialism to the history of the western border. Or perhaps such explanations are more deeply rooted—the phrase "the 49th parallel," for example, often serves as a shorthand for the entire border, despite the fact that from Lake of the Woods eastward the line does not run along the geographic parallel. These scholars are prompted, at least in part, by the same developments that have piqued interest in the U.S.-Mexico border—the heightened visibility of international commerce, migration, and the critique of nation-centered history. Their studies move beyond the stark dichotomy of similarity and difference and have pushed the field in promising new directions. Most of the work falls into four broad groups.

The first category includes works that interrogate the implications of border-making for indigenous peoples, who had been largely overlooked by earlier writers. As North America's empires and nations attempted to demarcate and absorb their peripheries, Indian groups witnessed the swift and arbitrary division of their homelands. Such circumstances imposed severe limitations, to be sure, including the rupturing of kinship networks, the reduction of hunting grounds, and a more general loss of geographic mobility. But at times, the drawing of borders opened up new and unforeseen possibilities as well. For instance, Aboriginal inhabitants all along the boundary between the United States and Canada, from the colonial period to the late nineteenth century, used the border to their advantage by pitting rival trading companies against one another in their quest for Indian assistance in the fur trade, or by finding sanctuary from their enemies (white and Native) across the line.

The second group focuses on the cross-border migrations of non-Aboriginal peoples. In general, these volumes emphasize the exceptional permeability of the U.S.-Canadian boundary, noting how—for much of the twentieth century—white movement across the line was effectively unimpeded, especially (though not exclusively) in the West. These scholars have noted the varied reasons that led people to move north or south of the border, but most agree that economic opportunity was of paramount importance. Unlike most of the scholarship focusing on the northern borderlands, migration studies encompass the full length of the border, reflecting the heavy impact of cross-border migration in eastern as well as western portions of the borderlands. And yet, despite their numbers, these newcomers seem to have garnered much less notice from residents and federal officials than did arrivals from Europe and Asia. This trend, no doubt, stemmed from the real and perceived similarities between Anglo-Americans and their Canadian counterparts, a notion recently picked up by a number of historians who have emphasized the social continuities found in trans-border regions such as the Great Lakes and Prairie-Plains.

A third group of works examines the relationship of the border to the natural world that it bisects, a division no less capricious to ecosystems than to human populations. After all, with few topographical features west of the Great Lakes to define it, the boundary between the United States and Canada was marked simply by piles of stones and mounds of dirt for much of the nineteenth century. Given its practical invisibility, it stands to reason that the 49th parallel did little to shape how borderland residents understood their relationship to the land, and indeed some scholars have found that the peculiar and distinct conditions of the region engendered a shared sense of identity rooted firmly in place, one that largely transcended state, provincial, and even national boundaries. Other historians have discovered that the border, in fact, mattered very much, especially for fish and wildlife populations that traversed the line in the course of their migrations. Just as with people, there were animals that states wanted to easily cross borders and those whose mobility it tried to restrict. It took concerted action on the part of government officials in Ottawa and Washington (and beyond) to regulate predation and enforce conservation measures.

A fourth and final collection of studies analyzes the impact of the border on the formation of national identity. In so doing, they revisit some of the observations first made by Paul Sharp in *Whoop-Up County*, particularly the notion that federal officials in the United States and especially in Canada strove to enforce their shared international boundary beginning in the late nineteenth century. These newer works probe the influence of Washington and Ottawa in amplifying the reality as well as the symbolism of the border, while assessing the long-term success of these efforts. For example, some historians have suggested that the northern borderlands were the object in a continental endgame of national expansion, where federal officials in both capitals projected their newfound or resurgent economic and political power into a region once thought too remote for incorporation. And yet, according to other scholars, these grandiose attempts to divide, conquer, and integrate the hinterlands into their respective nations were, in the main, incomplete, as the 49th parallel seems no more significant in creating or marking national difference today than it did more than a century ago, when it was first enforced.

As the previous historiographic discussion suggests, there has been a convergence in the kinds of questions asked by historians of North America's two borders. Yet scholars of these places still work in isolation from one another, reading different bodies of literature, working at different institutions, and publishing with different presses.

First, this book points to the value of comparative accounts of border-making. On the most general level, comparison can help to destabilize normative or exceptionalist explanations, while casting light on similarities as well as structural and contingent differences. Given the isolated state of the two fields, comparison might also inspire the importation of questions salient in one field but not yet applied to the other. For example, the racialization of those crossing from Mexico into the Unites States by medical inspections has been the subject of sustained scholarly scrutiny, and similar questions might be asked about migrants moving from Canada into the United States, especially French Canadians. Furthermore, a comparative approach to border formation might well help scholars provide more compelling answers to their shared questions about the ways that boundaries have re-made, and failed to re-make, identities congruent with the claim of modern nation-states to territorial exclusivity. The longer history and greater quantity of literature on the southern border has led many to deploy the U.S.-Mexico border as paradigmatic of borders in general, including the northern border of the United States. The greatly unequal balance of power between Mexico and the United States, and the frequency with which U.S. observers have thought of this in racial terms, however, may make this border more distinctive than diagnostic. Have Canadians and Mexicans and their governments used their borders with the United States in parallel ways, or have the great differences between Canada and Mexico sharply differentiated their border-making projects?

A similar set of questions might be asked with respect to Native peoples and how they dealt with those borders whose creation abrogated some groups' territoriality and sovereignty but offered others the chance to play settler-nations off against one another. For example, the modern national myths of both Canada and Mexico feature celebrations of racial hybridity between European settlers and Indians. To what extent did these racial formations offer political and cultural space for Indian peoples not permitted by the United States' more exclusionist and assimilationist understanding of Indians' place within modernity? More broadly, if some Native peoples were able to navigate a bordered world more successfully than others, was that because of the differing nature of the state-building projects that they faced, or because of their own divisions, heterogeneity, resources, and decisions?

These questions point to more-encompassing comparative inquiries. In a more general sense, do the histories of these two borders teach us similar or different lessons about the ability of modern states to enforce their claims to territorial exclusivity on the ground, and about the impact of those claims on the lives of those living on borders?

Second, some questions about borders cry out not just for comparison, but for integrated accounts. Many historical actors in fact engaged both borders, and recapturing their experiences requires historians to follow in their footsteps. Consider the case of Asian migrants to North America. Canada, the United States, and Mexico all share the Pacific Rim with Japan and China, and starting in the mid-nineteenth century Asians migrated to all three nations, forming interconnected diasporic communities, and encountering nativist movements that articulated notions of nationhood in opposition to them and the networks that had brought them to North America. Asian migrants crossed both borders in pursuit of economic, family, and political goals, and, the differences in the three nations' immigration laws to secure rights of transit otherwise unavailable to them. Yet we miss these stories if we focus on just one nation, or even two nations and their shared border. Other important stories similarly encompass both borders: U.S. bureaucrats and law enforcement officials moved from one American border to the other, presumably taking their understandings and expectations with them as they implemented immigration, customs, and medical procedures on two sometimes very different frontiers. The cultural production surrounding borders has also often encompassed them both, as suggested by the similarities in the lure of border town cantinas and speakeasies during Prohibition.

Third, if borderlands scholars might profit from broadening their frame to continental dimensions, this book suggests that they would also benefit from narrowing their scope to acknowledge the continued particularities of place. Transnational history can be local history, but some historians writing after the transnational turn emphasize large-scale perspectives that can obscure local and regional distinctiveness. It would be unfortunate if the framing of border histories as transnational studies were to lead scholars to ignore the extent to which border places and border lives have been different from one another, reflective of local and regional histories, geographies, economies, and politics as much as of national and international dynamics. Borders may be international spaces, but border communities are also local spaces whose distinctiveness should be accounted for rather than obscured by the transnational turn in border studies.

Fourth, the approaches to borders taken in this volume open the way for more-nuanced treatments of the relationship between borderlands communities and national states. Contemporary borderlands scholarship portrays the modern state in almost entirely negative terms, as an outside, coercive force whose arrival ends the autonomy and freedom enjoyed by Natives and other peoples who once lived beyond its control. Indeed, the most influential treatment of the emergence of national borders, Jeremy Adelman and Stephen Aron's "From Borderlands to Borders," depicts the rise of national borders as the end of the more-fluid territoriality and identities allowed for by the earlier borderlands between empires and Native peoples. This is with good reason: North America's borders were far removed from the centers of national power and population at the moment of their creation, and the central state was in fact a distant entity controlled by and serving the interests of people far from the border. The United States in particular projected its power more through violence—forcibly opening its new peripheries to national markets and imposing its more-fixed and hierarchical racial categories—than by capturing the imaginations and loyalties of borderlanders themselves.

But this isn't the full picture of the state. Borderlanders, also used national states and their boundaries for their own purposes and sought to forge nations that reflected their own identities. Various groups in all three countries demanded border policies that served their own interests—to provide or control labor, to protect themselves from human and livestock epidemics, and to defend themselves from enemies, to name a few. Others pressed central states to let goods and people pass unhindered, as when Mexican entrepreneurs lobbied for a duty-free zone on their half of the border with the United States, or when Mexican Americans in South Texas agitated for the rights of their families to move between neighboring border cities without encumbrance, or when Métis refuges who had fled Canada during the 1885 Northwest Rebellion sought to return from their cross-border exile in the United States. These examples reflect the continued importance of non-national imagined communities and territoriality, as well as the ways that these projects could be pursued through the methods of state power as much as in contradiction to them. The state ended up as much an invited guest in the borderlands as it did an armed stranger. The lure of de-centering national histories, an impulse that has given border studies so much of their prominence in the U.S. academy, need not become a brief for anti-nationalist politics or for historical inquiry centered on the nation-state. As the Canadian literary scholar Bryce Traister has insisted in his trenchant critique of U.S. scholarship on the Mexican border, "We have lost our ability to understand the liberal nation-state as a positive and still intriguing contributor rather than impediment to meaningful and even politically progressive identity."

Fifth, this book suggests that borders are simultaneously places and ideas, and should be studied through the lenses of cultural and intellectual—as well as social and political—history. Images and accounts of borders circulated by dime nov-elists, tourism boosters, journalists, filmmakers, and historians made North American borders resonant well beyond the border regions themselves, engaging the same issues of national territoriality, national and racial difference, and state violence that shaped life in the borderlands. The national differences implied by borders could be used to celebrate (and sell) cultural difference. At other times, depictions of borderlands minimized the starkness of national boundaries, sug-gesting commonality or solidarity rather than evoking difference or engendering fear. Historians are also producers and consumers of ideas about borders, if often unconsciously. Much North American historical scholarship has read national boundaries backwards into the period before their existence, obscuring non-national forms of territoriality and community that did not simply vanish with the drawing of national boundaries. Exploring the relationship between borders as places and borders as ideas and symbols—tasks that are now split between so-cial and political historians, on the one hand, and cultural historians and literary scholars, on the other—ought to be one of the primary tasks of border scholars.

FURTHER READING

Anzaldúa, Gloria, and Sonia Saldívar-Hull. *Borderlands/La Frontera* (1999).

Bannon, John Francis. *The Spanish Borderlands Frontier, 1513–1821* (1974).

Bolton, Herbert E. *The Spanish Borderlands: A Chronicle of Old Florida and the Southwest* (1921).

———. "The Epic of Greater America." *American Historical Review* 38 (April 1933): 448–474.

Brown, Jennifer S. H., and Elizabeth Vibert, eds. *Reading Beyond Words: Contexts for Native History* (2003).

Diener, Alexander, and Joshua Hagen, eds. *Borderlines in Borderlands: Political Oddities at the Edge of the Nation-State* (2010).

Hall, Thomas D. *Social Change in the Southwest, 1350–1880* (1989).

Hurtado, Albert L. "Herbert E. Bolton, Racism, and American History." *Pacific Historical Review* 62 (May 1993): 127–142.

Johnson, Benjamin, and Andrew Grayibill, eds. *Bridging National Borders in North America: Transnational and Comparative Histories* (2009).

Klein, Kerwin. *Frontiers of Historical Imagination: Narrating the European Conquest of Native America, 1890–1990* (1997).

Maier, Charles. "Consigning the Twentieth Century to History: Alternative Narratives for the Modern Era." *American Historical Review* 105 (June 2000): 807–831.

Sahlins, Peter. *Boundaries: The Making of France and Spain in the Pyrenees* (1989).

Scott, James C. *The Art of Not Being Governed: An Anarchist History of Upland Southeast Asia* (2009).

Smith, Linda Tuhiwai. *Decolonizing Methodologies: Research and Indigenous Peoples* (1999).

Spicer, Edward H. *Cycles of Conquest: The Impact of Spain, Mexico and the United States on the Indians of the Southwest, 1533–1960* (1962).

Torpey, John. *The Invention of the Passport: Surveillance, Citizenship, and the State* (2000).

Truett, Samuel, and Elliott Young, eds. *Continental Crossroads: Remapping U.S.-Mexico Borderlands History* (2004).

Turner, Frederick Jackson. "The Significance of the Frontier in American History." Presented at the American Historical Association Annual Meeting in Chicago in 1893. Printed in the *Proceedings of the State Historical Society of Wisconsin*, December 14, 1893. Reprinted in *Rereading Frederick Jackson Turner: "The Significance of the Frontier in American History" and Other Essays*, ed. John Mack Faragher, pp. 31–60 (1998).

Usner, Daniel H. Jr., "Borderlands." In *A Companion to Colonial America*, ed. Daniel Vickers, 408–424 (2003).

Weber, David J. *The Mexican Frontier, 1821–1846: The American Southwest Under Mexico* (1982).

———. "Turner, the Boltonians, and the Borderlands." *American Historical Review* 91 (February 1986): 66–81.

———. *The Spanish Frontier in North America* (1992).

White, Richard, and Patricia Limerick. *The Frontier in American Culture* (1994).

CHAPTER 2

∿

Early Borderlands

The Southwest

Indigenous-European encounters in North America began in the early sixteenth century, when Spanish, French, and English explorers, traders, missionaries, and soldiers began to probe the continent. Distinctive borderlands of sustained cultural interpenetration emerged in the seventeenth century, when imperial bridgeheads consolidated into colonial societies, and when those societies had to come to terms with powerful indigenous groups on their fragile borders. This chapter explores the emergence of early borderlands in the North American Southwest, where Spanish and French colonists clashed, contended, and eventually compromised with indigenous realities.

Spanish conquistadors pushed into the Southwest in the early sixteenth century, hoping to replicate the lucrative conquests of the Aztec and Inca empires in Mexico and Peru in the 1520s and 1530s. But North America yielded few immediate riches, and conquistadors gave way to priests, farmers, and soldiers; Spanish colonialism in the far North became largely a missionary enterprise backed by military force and systematic exploitation of native labor. In 1598, Don Juan de Oñate founded New Mexico in the upper Rio Grande valley, and over the following decades the region's many Pueblo Indian societies were bound to the Spanish colonial system through forced conversion and labor drafts. Spain was the only European power in the Southwest until the late seventeenth and early eighteenth centuries, when France established a string of small communities along the Mississippi valley in an effort to secure a foothold on the Gulf Coast and dominate Indian trade in the interior. The Spanish Crown saw these outposts as threats to its silver mines in Mexico and founded the colony of Texas to block French advances to the west. Seen from Mexico City, Texas was a defensive borderland that would protect the empire's vital areas from foreign intrusion.

These various colonization projects extended the Spanish and French empires into the Southwest and implanted a distinctive colonial community on its landscape: isolated, economically fragile, male-dominated, and multiracial. They also marked the beginning of a new era for the hundreds of indigenous societies living in the Southwest. Native peoples encountered lethal microbes, hostile settlers, eager traders, and indomitable missionaries, and they suffered vast losses of lives, land, culture, and autonomy. But nowhere were Indians powerless, passive victims of European colonization. European newcomers expected quick and complete native submission within colonial realms, but they frequently faced fierce resistance that sometimes erupted into rebellion. Independent native peoples living outside of colonial realms were also drawn into close relations with Europeans through war, diplomacy, and commerce, and their lives changed irrevocably through the introduction of new diseases, technologies, ideas, and markets. Some native groups struggled to find a place in the rapidly changing borderlands world, but others grew increasingly powerful, marginalizing rival native groups while forcing Europeans to adjust to their ways of doing things. These expanding Indian groups had learned how to make the presence of European colonists on their borders to serve their interests. For a very long time, the balance of power in the borderlands tended to favor them over the European newcomers.

∿ DOCUMENTS

In 1680, after decades of Spanish rule and exploitation, the Pueblo Indians in New Mexico began a concerted rebellion under the leadership of the charismatic Popé. The Pueblo Revolt was the most successful indigenous uprising against colonial rule in North America, and it kept the Spaniards away from New Mexico for over a decade. Document 1 is the testimony of Ginés de Herrera Horta, an auditor and legal assessor, on the effects of Spanish rule on the Pueblo Indians of New Mexico in 1601, three years after Don Juan de Oñate had led the first colonist to the upper Rio Grande Valley. Appearing at a hearing in Mexico City, Horta discusses the abuses, punishments, and tribute payments that fueled resentment among the Pueblo people. In the second document, Pedro Naranjo, a Keresan Pueblo, offers his view of the rebellion and its causes in 1693. Recorded a year after the Spanish reconquest of New Mexico, Naranjo's account helps illuminate several key questions about the revolt and its causes. What role did religion play in the revolt? Pueblo Indians killed several hundred Spanish colonists during the rebellion; how does Naranjo explain this violence? Document 3 is from the report of Bishop Benito Crespo, who inspected New Mexico in 1730, thirty-four years after the suppression of another, much smaller, Pueblo revolt in 1696. In the aftermath of the second rebellion, Spanish officials abolished the *encomienda* system in New Mexico and took measures to protect Indian lands and legal rights, and Franciscans adopted a more tolerant stance toward traditional Pueblo religious ceremonies. Crespo found in New Mexico a socially charged world marked by deep cultural divides and distrust, and he struggled to understand the social life in the colony that defied many of his expectations.

Document 4 is the report of Franciscan Father Francisco Casanas de Jesús Maria on Spanish efforts to win the allegiance of the Caddo Indians, who lived in the region between French Louisiana and Spanish Texas and New Mexico. Both Spanish and French colonists strove to extend their presence among the strategically located Caddos, and both had to adhere to Caddo customs to do so. Casanas's account, written in 1691, reveals the cultural differences, misunderstandings, and disputes that shaped the relationships between Caddos and

Spaniards. Document 5 illustrates how, in distant borderlands on empires' edges, colonists from rival nations often found it more beneficial to work with, rather than against, their enemies. In 1721, Spaniards built Los Adaes, a small fort that served as the capital of Spanish Texas until 1773, near a French post of Natchitoches, hoping to weaken French influence among the Indians and block French intrusions toward Spanish settlements. The document shows how Philibert Ory, the controller general of finances in the French court, viewed the situation in the borderlands and how he wished Louisiana to respond to the challenge posed by Los Adaes.

Document 6 is from the account of the French captain Pierre Marie François de Pagès, who toured Spanish Texas and the Texas-Louisiana borderlands in 1767, five years after France had ceded Louisiana to Spain. Pagès describes the pastoral ranching economy of Texas and the Indian-European relations on the borderlands, reporting on continual Indian raids and discussing why Spaniards failed to contain the Apaches. He also notes the complex ethnic composition of the borderlands: Although Nacogdoches was a Spanish town, it hosted many French traders who had stayed behind after Louisiana was transferred to Spain in 1762.

1. Ginés de Herrera Horta Testifies on Spanish Treatment of Pueblo Indians, 1601

In Mexico, July 30, 1601, Factor Don Francisco de Valverde called as witness the bachiller, Ginés de Herrera Horta, a resident of this city, who took his oath in due legal manner and promised to tell the truth. On being questioned the witness stated that he went to the provinces of New Mexico about a year and a half ago, more or less, as chief auditor and legal assessor to Don Juan de Oñate, governor of the said provinces....

Asked what good and bad experiences the Spaniards had encountered, what opposition, what modes of offense or defense the Indians had offered from the time the governor arrived in the province ... this witness states that, in discussing the conditions of the country with the leading persons, both friars and laymen, they told him in detail what had happened to the Indians of a pueblo named Acoma, which is situated on a high rock.

The maese de campo at that time was Don Juan de Zaldívar, nephew of the governor. He had gone with twelve or fourteen men to explore and seek new things not yet known. This witness was told that unless they found something worthwhile, he intended to return to New Spain with his men. While they were on this exploration, they came to the pueblo of Acoma, where they asked the Indians for provisions. The natives furnished them some, and the Spaniards proceeded on their journey about two leagues beyond the pueblo.

Then the maese de campo, Captain Escalante, Diego Núñez, and other men turned back to ask again for provisions, fowl, and blankets, and even to take

George P. Hammond and Agapito Rey, eds., *Don Juan de Oñate: Colonizer of New Mexico 1595–1628* (Albuquerque: University of New Mexico Press, 1953), 6: 643–657.

them by force. When the Indians saw this, they began to resist and to defend themselves. This witness was told that the Spaniards had killed one or two Indians. Then the Indians killed the maese de campo and Diego Núñez and the others with rocks and slabs of stone. When the governor learned of this, he declared war by fire and sword against the Indians of the pueblo and named Sargento Mayor Vicente de Zaldívar, his nephew, and brother of the slain maese de campo, as chief of the punitive army. He set out with seventy soldiers to punish the aforesaid Indians. Afraid of what the Spaniards might do, the natives refused to surrender, but defended themselves.

Thus the punishment began, lasting almost two days, during which many Indians were killed. Finally, overcome and exhausted from the struggle, the Indians gave up, offering blankets and fowl to the sargento mayor and his soldiers, who refused to accept them. Instead, the sargento mayor had the Indians arrested and placed in an estufa [kiva]. Then he ordered them taken out one by one, and an Indian he had along stabbed them to death and hurled them down the rock. When other Indian men and women, who had taken shelter in other estufas, saw what was going on, they fortified themselves and refused to come out. In view of this, the sargento mayor ordered that wood be brought and fires started and from the smoke many Indian men, women, and children suffocated. This witness was told that some were even burned alive. All of the men, women, and children who survived were brought to the camp as prisoners. The governor ordered the children placed in the care of individuals. The men and women from eighteen to nineteen years of age were declared slaves for twenty years. Others were maimed by having their feet cut off; this witness saw some of them at the said camp. He was told that most of the slaves had run away, that they had tried to reëstablish the pueblo, and that the governor neither authorized nor prevented this, but dissimulated, although this witness heard that he wanted to send someone or go himself to see the said pueblo.

The reason why the commissary charged this witness on his conscience to tell this story was because he considered the punishment and enslavement of the Indians unjust and that the viceroy should order the prisoners liberated.

Asked whether the governor had levied any tribute or personal service on the friendly and peaceful Indians under his jurisdiction to work the fields, harvest the crops, or do other necessary labors in his camp, the witness said that all he knows is that every month the soldiers go out by order of the governor to all the pueblos to procure maize. The soldiers go in groups of two or three and come back with the maize for their own sustenance. The Indians part with it with much feeling and weeping and give it of necessity rather than of their own accord, as the soldiers themselves told this witness. If any kernels fall on the ground, the Indians follow and pick them up, one by one. This witness has seen this happen many times. Some of the Indians, men and women, who formerly lived at this pueblo where the camp now is, remained there and bring wood and water for the Spaniards, so that the latter would give them some maize. This witness has seen it himself. He was told that the Indians store their maize for three and four years to provide against the sterility of the land, for it rains very seldom, although there is much snow, which helps to moisten the ground so that they may harvest what they plant.

The tribute which the governor has levied on the Indians requires that each resident give a cotton blanket per year. Those who have no blankets give tanned deerskins and buffalo hides, dressed in their usual manner. The lack of blankets is due to the scarcity of cotton grown there. This witness has seen the cotton next to the maize fields of the Indians. He was assured that, in the pueblos where the soldiers went, if the natives said that they had no blankets to give, the soldiers took them from the backs of the Indian women and left them naked.

As for personal services, this witness does not know that they have been imposed on the natives, except that when there is need to repair a house the Spaniards ask the governor's permission to bring some Indian women to repair it, for, as he has stated, the women are the ones who do this. The Spaniards also employ Indians to help plant the vegetables and cultivate the soil. This witness has seen Spaniards plowing all by themselves, without the assistance of Indians. He has heard that wheat does very well, and that this is because at the camp there is water for irrigation, which is not found elsewhere, and so wheat is grown only there. He does not know nor has he heard that it is planted anywhere else.

Asked whether the Indians of those provinces were of such habits that they could be brought to our holy Catholic faith by the normal diligence of the friars, the witness said that the reason the Indians did not associate with the Spaniards was because they were afraid of them. This witness believes that if they were well treated and attracted, their conversion would be easy, because they are extremely quiet, gentle, and friendly, not known to possess any vices. This witness considers these people of better habits and nature than the people of New Spain.

The people are also troubled by the sterility of the land, so they will lack provisions for some time to come, and also because the Indians are few and the pueblos more than eighty leagues apart, including those that are said to have more people, as they are at that distance from the camp. For these reasons, this witness does not think that the people could be maintained without great cost to his majesty in provisions, clothing, and other things. Even if this majesty should incur much expense to help them, this witness believes that if the people were free to choose they would prefer to abandon the land and seek their livelihood around here. He never heard a single one say that he was there of his own will, but through force and compulsion. What his excellency, the viceroy of New Spain, should know and remedy is that the orders he transmits to those regions are neither obeyed nor carried out.

2. Pedro Naranjo (Keresan Pueblo) Explains the Pueblo Revolt, 1681

In the said plaza de armas on the said day, month, and year [December 19, 1681], for the prosecution of the judicial proceedings of this case his lordship caused to appear before him an Indian prisoner named Pedro Naranjo, a native

Charles Wilson Hackett, ed., *Revolt of the Pueblo Indians of New Mexico and Otermin's Attempted Reconquest, 1680–1682*, trans., Charmion C. Shelby (Albuquerque: University of New Mexico, 1942), 2: 245–249.

of the pueblo of San Felipe, of the Queres nation, who was captured in the advance and attack upon the pueblo of La Isleta. He makes himself understood very well in the Castilian language and speaks his mother tongue and the Tegua. He took the oath in due legal form in the name of God, our Lord, and a sign of the cross, under charge of which he promised to tell the truth concerning what he knows and as he might be questioned.

Asked whether he knows the reason or motives which the Indians of this kingdom had for rebelling, forsaking the law of God and obedience to his Majesty, and committing such grave and atrocious crimes, and who were the leaders and principal movers, and by whom and how it was ordered; and why they burned the images, temples, crosses, rosaries, and things of divine worship, committing such atrocities as killing priests, Spaniards, women, and children, and the rest that he might know touching the question, he said that since the government of Señor General Hernando Ugarte y la Concha they have planned to rebel on various occasions through conspiracies of the Indian sorcerers, and that although in some pueblos the messages were accepted, in other parts they would not agree to it; and that it is true that during the government of the said señor general seven or eight Indians were hanged for this same cause, whereupon the unrest subsided. Some time thereafter they [the conspirators] sent from the pueblo of Los Taos two deerskins with some pictures on them signifying conspiracy after their manner, in order to convoke the people to a new rebellion, and the said deerskins passed to the province of Moqui, where they refused to accept them. The pact which they had been forming ceased for the time being, but they always kept in their hearts the desire to carry it out, so as to live as they are living to-day. Finally, in the past years, at the summons of an Indian named Popé who is said to have communication with the devil, it happened that in an estufa [kiva] of the pueblo of Los Taos there appeared to the said Popé three figures of Indians who never came out of the estufa. They gave the said Popé to understand that they were going underground to the lake of Copala. He saw these figures emit fire from all the extremities of their bodies, and that one of them was called Caudi, another Tilini, and the other Tleume; and these three beings spoke to the said Popé who was in hiding from the secretary, Francisco Xavier, who wished to punish him as a sorcerer. They told him to make a cord of maguey fiber and tie some knots in it which would signify the number of days that they must wait before the rebellion. He said that the cord was passed through all the pueblos of the kingdom so that the ones which agreed to it [the rebellion] might untie one knot in sign of obedience, and by the other knots they would know the days which were lacking; and this was to be done on pain of death to those who refused to agree to it. As a sign of agreement and notice of having concurred in the treason and perfidy they were to send up smoke signals to that effect in each one of the pueblos singly. The said cord was taken from pueblo to pueblo by the swiftest youths under the penalty of death if they revealed the secret. Everything being thus arranged, two days before the time set for its execution, because his lordship had learned of it and had imprisoned two Indian accomplices from the pueblo of Tesuque, it was carried out prematurely that night, because it seemed to them that they were now discovered; and they killed religious, Spaniards, women, and children. This being done, it was proclaimed in all the pueblos that everyone in common should obey the commands of their father whom they did not know, which would be given through El Caydi or El Popé. This was heard by Alonso Catití, who came to the pueblo of this declarant to say that everyone must unite to go to the villa to kill the governor and the Spaniards who had remained with him, and that he who did not obey would, on their return, be beheaded; and in fear of this they agreed to it. Finally the señor governor and those who were with him escaped from the siege, and later this declarant saw that as soon as the Spaniards had left the kingdom an order came from the said Indian, Popé, in which he commanded all the Indians to break the lands and enlarge their cultivated fields, saying that now they were as they had been in ancient times, free from the labor they had performed for the religious and the Spaniards, who could not now be alive. He said that this is the legitimate cause and the reason they had for rebelling, because they had always desired to live as they had when they came out of the lake of Copala. Thus he replies to the question.

Asked for what reason they so blindly burned the images, temples, crosses, and other things of divine worship, he stated that the said Indian, Popé, came down in person, and with him El Saca and El Chato from the pueblo of Los Taos, and other captains and leaders and many people who were in his train, and he ordered in all the pueblos through which he passed that they instantly break up and burn the images of the holy Christ, the Virgin Mary and the other saints, the crosses, and everything pertaining to Christianity, and that they burn the temples, break up the bells, and separate from the wives whom God had given them in marriage and take those whom they desired. In order to take away their baptismal names, the water, and the holy oils, they were to plunge into the rivers and wash themselves with amole, which is a root native to the country, washing even their clothing, with the understanding that there would thus be taken from them the character of the holy sacraments. They did this, and also many other things which he does not recall, given to understand that this mandate had come from the Caydi and the other two who emitted fire from their extremities in the said estufa of Taos, and that they thereby returned to the state of their antiquity, as when they came from the lake of Copala; that this was the better life and the one they desired, because the God of the Spaniards was worth nothing and theirs was very strong, the Spaniard's God being rotten wood. These things were observed and obeyed by all except some who, moved by the zeal of Christians, opposed it, and such persons the said Popé caused to be killed immediately. He saw to it that they at once erected and rebuilt their houses of idolatry which they call estufas, and made very ugly masks in imitation of the devil in order to dance the dance of the cacina [kachina, or spirit]; and he said likewise that the devil had given them to understand that living thus in accordance with the law of their ancestors, they would harvest a great deal of maize, many beans, a great abundance of cotton, calabashes, and very large watermelons and cantaloupes; and that they could erect their houses and enjoy abundant health and leisure. As he has said, the people were very much pleased, living at their ease in this life of their antiquity, which was the chief cause of their falling into such laxity. Following what has already been stated, in order to terrorize them further and cause them to observe the diabolical commands, there came to them a pronouncement from the three demons already described, and from El Popé, to the effect that he who might still keep in his heart a regard for the priests, the governor, and the Spaniards would be known from his unclean face and clothes, and would be punished. And he stated that the said four persons stopped at nothing to have their commands obeyed. Thus he replies to the question.

Asked what arrangements and plans they had made for the contingency of the Spaniards' return, he said that what he knows concerning the question is that they were always saying they would have to fight to the death, for they do not wish to live in any other way than they are living at present; and the demons in the estufa of Taos had given them to understand that as soon as the Spaniards began to move toward this kingdom they would warn them so that they might unite, and none of them would be caught. He having been questioned further and repeatedly touching the case, he said that he has nothing more to say except that they should be always on the alert, because the said Indians were continually planning to follow the Spaniards and fight with them by night, in order to drive off the horses and catch them afoot, although they might have to follow them for many leagues.

3. Bishop Benito Crespo Is Confounded by New Mexico, 1730

I have seen, understood, and heard in all the pueblos that the precept prescribing annual confession and communion is not fulfilled in any one of them, because there has not been, and is not, any minister who understands the language of the Indians. And the latter do not confess except at the point of death because they do not want to confess through an interpreter. They told me before I reached the said [province] that they [the interpreters] made their sins public. And because I was ignorant of this, whenever I preached I exhorted and especially the Indians through an interpreter, telling them that the confessors, even though they might be killed for it, could tell nothing. The latter thanked me for it. But afterwards I learned the reason [for the Indians' reluctance], which is that they make said confessions through an interpreter belonging to the same Indians. And since the final conquest, which took place in the year 1696, there is no case when there has been a minister who knows the language of the Indians, which must [cause wonder?]. And as a unique thing, they tell of two, Fray Antonio Miranda and Fray Francisco Irazabal, who know the language, not in general but only that of the Zuñi Indians. [Irazabal] is at present minister of Spaniards at the aforesaid capital of Santa Fe, and he is now in this pueblo [of El Paso]. Fray Antonio Miranda is [the minister] of the Keres Indians, whose tribe consists of the pueblo of Acoma, [where] he has been about twenty years. And at present he is blind, as is evident from his statement about the place of Moqui. And with regard to the rest, for there are many who have been in residence eighteen or twenty years, not one has dedicated himself, and they are as alien as if they had had no dealings with the said Indians. I have seen learned this, and I have heard that the same thing has been going on since time immemorial.

For this reason not many of the pagans on the borders are converted. They are bartering and trading with them every day, as I have seen. And all the pueblos of said missions remain in their paganism and idolatry, as the fathers themselves affirm, and they apostatize daily. It is the common opinion that this has been the origin of the uprisings that have occurred in said province. And the reason why they have not revolted since the last conquest has been the royal presidio which is in the said capital. And the reciprocal lack of love, both of the father ministers for the Indians and of the latter for the said fathers, arises from this, and especially when the languages are not so difficult that they cannot be comprehended in a short period of friendly intercourse and communication; because in those I heard, I found ease of pronunciation, which is not the case with many others of this diocese. All the Indians in general complain of this, telling me that they are Christians and that for this reason they lack what is most important; as well as asking how they are to believe what is preached to them if they see the contrary done by the very father ministers in general, since scarcely four out of them all are exceptions, and two of these, newcomers to said missions.

4. Father Francisco Casanas de Jesús Maria on How to Win the Allegiance of the Caddo Indians, 1691

I trust that by the grace of the Most High, through the protection of our Most Holy Mother and the good wishes of our Catholic Majesty and of your Excellency, all these tribes will be subdued. This will be true if those who come from Spain to this country to live will furnish a good example. This done, and the spirit of the evangelical ministers being joined therewith, it is inevitable that much glory and fruit for the two Majesties can be expected.

The dissatisfaction of all the Indians is great when the Spaniards live among them without their wives. I say also from what I have experienced that, if it be possible, it would be to our interest if no man came without his wife. However, I realize that, on account of what little there is in the mission, it is impossible unless the Indian patches are robbed. Before I left the mission of Santiago, a letter was written me giving the information of the people that were on their way to Texas, and of the flocks they were bringing. I read this letter to the captains and nobles who were alltogether in a council. The first thing they noticed in the letter was that the men were coming without their wives, and they knew that

Mattie Austin Hatcher, trans., "Descriptions of Tejas and Asinai Indians, 1691–1722," *Southwestern Historical Quarterly Online* 30 (April 1927): 287–290, 294–295, 300–301, 303. URL http://www.tshaonline.org/shqonline/apager.php?vol=030&pag=287 (Accessed 25-01-2010)

there would [necessarily] be additional men to guard the stock. If objections be made to these few, how much greater objection will be raised, your Excellency, if a great number come into this country to stay. Every day these Indians ask me whether the Spaniards are going to bring their wives with them when they come back. I tell them yes. But in spite of everything they do not give me any credence. They tell me that I must write to Your Excellency, their great captain, and tell you in this missive that they want to be friends, but if the Spaniards want to live among them it must be under such conditions that no harm will be done the Indians by the Spaniards if they do come without their wives; but, if the Spaniards bring their wives, the Indians will be satisfied.

I must say that the demand of these Indians is just and reasonable. And it has already been agreed to. I know from experience gained upon two occasions when duty to the church called me to the work of conversion that this will be wise; and it will be well to leave for my protection three or four unmarried men. I have been much distressed and feared to lose all the fruit that might be produced; and, therefore, prostrate at your feet, I beg of Your Excellency to look with favor upon this work which is so pleasing to the Lord, that it should not be lost. And do not send criminals taken from the prisons, or bachelors, or vagabonds, who, when they are here, away from home where there are no Christians, would commit great atrocities, and, by their depraved lives and bad example, counteract the efforts of the ministers, depriving them of the fruit of these souls of the Indians. It would be better for that class of men to be sent somewhere else where they can be kept down with lash in hand.

In this way, and in no other, may their souls be saved. For, God knows, souls cannot be saved by one who does not regard his own soul; by one who does not believe in human justice nor acknowledge the justice of God. What a pity.

It is to be feared that these poor things will bewail their souls in Hell because of [their] superstitions.... The demon put it into their heads that we had brought the epidemic into the country; and, when they saw that during the scourge which the Lord sent upon them in the year 1691 some three or four hundred persons—more or less—had died in that province during the month of March, they maintained their superstition even more firmly, saying that we had killed them. Some of them tried to kill us. When I found this out, I went to the house of the governer. I found that he was in conclave with the old men. The first thing they all said to me was the above. I asked them if they had killed Father Fray Miguel Font Cuberta and the soldier who had died soon after arriving in their country. They all said no. I answered that they had spoken well, and that they were quite right, as it was God who killed him; and that whenever He wishes He will kill us but that neither I nor anyone knows why it is done. I told them that we must all die, but as to how, when, and from what cause not even the great captain of the Spaniards knew, nor did I know; but that I did know that as sure as the sun sets my hour would come—while to some of those present it might come at dawn. I told them that all who love God must submit to His holy will; and that when He wishes to do so, He will kill the Spaniards as He was now killing them; and that, therefore, whatever God does we must believe is done for the best.

I gave them these and other arguments which made such a great impression upon them that nobody disputed me.

I trust by the Grace of God that, as soon as the ministers are able to speak the language perfectly and when we have the protection and watchful care of the Spaniards, we will uproot all the discord which the mortal enemy of our souls has sown in this county and that the faith will be planted with greater perfection than in other sections: especially as we enjoy the protection of our Catholic king and of Your Excellency who tries to encourage this work with so much zeal and order by sending ministers and by doing everything else which you may think necessary, since it is for the service of God, our Lord, without which all that has already been done will be lost, if God does not intervene.

The Lord knows that in this whole matter I am inspired only by the desire I have that not a single soul shall be lost and that these poor miserable people may die only after receiving the holy baptism. It would certainly be a great misfortune if they should perish for want of encouragement because it has not yet been ascertained, nor is it not known, whether there are other unconverted tribes who are more civilized and settled than these Indians and their more immediate neighbors; for all of them cultivate their fields. They do not lack for food. They never abandon their houses nor their country, although they do go to war with their enemies.

They are an industrious people and apply themselves to all kind of work. Indeed, if during the year and three months I have been among them if I had had some bells, some small clasp knives, some glass beads, and some blue cloth—which they greatly prize,—some blankets, and other little things to exchange with these Indians, I could have started a convent with the articles it would have been possible to make from the best materials that are abundant here. I, therefore, declare that it will be well for the ministers to have some of these things—not that one person only should have them—because the Indians are of such a nature that they have no love save for the person who gives them something. So strong is this characteristic that only the person who gives them something is good while all others are bad. They do not even want to receive the holy sacrament of baptism except from some person who has given them a great many things. Even the ministers are not able to persuade them, nor will it ever be possible to develop the mission without these presents. During my stay of one year and three months in this country and during the ten months since I started this, Your Excellency's mission, under the name of Santíssima Nombre de María, I have not had a scrap or anything else. I have born even my bittered garments up to give to some Indian for helping me. The governor of this mission of yours can vouch for this.

I have information that the *Cadauhacho* have hopes that the French will return, because they promised when leaving the country that they would return when the cold season again set in, and that a great many of them would have to come in order in occupy the country completely. This is nothing but Indian gossip, though for several reasons it is to be feared that they speak as they are instructed to speak. The French may also be compelled to return on account of their companions whom they left here. I know nothing more of this matter than that in the month of February there were nine or ten Frenchmen at a feast which the Indians had in a neighboring province, about thirty leagues from us called the province of *Nacaos*.

Most Excellent Sir, I know well that much of what I have related does not concern me, but I have had no motive in so doing save the desire I have of bringing souls to the Lord. Although there are many of the tribes who have died, there is no lack of material for conversion for all the ministers who may come. In the name of our Saviour and that of the blessed Mary, prostrate at their feet, I pray for aid and protection and that His Divine Majesty may grant you good health in order that Your Excellency may be the patron of a work which is so pleasing to God.

5. Philibert Ory Urges Louisiana to Open Trade with Spaniards in Natchitoches, 1730

I pass on to the commerce with the Spaniards … you ought to fix your sights in the direction of the land, where I should think commerce easier or at least more secret, and it is at the Natchitoches that I should like to make an establishment, that is to say merely to put that post in a state of defense with its garrison and warehouses in which in the future there would be a good quantity of merchandise suitable for trade. The post of the Adais [Adaes] belongs to the Spaniards. They also have a mission there. It is only fifteen leagues distant. It does not appear to me difficult to enter into trade by means of the missionaries, governor, or other persons of that sort whom it will be necessary to interest by promising them a certain percentage of all the money that they would cause to be obtained for our merchandise in the places upon which we would agree with them. Mexico in the direction of New Mexico and still more New Mexico are not guarded at all. The governors, [who are] not at all strict and usually without opportunities to enrich themselves, will eagerly grasp the means that will be presented to them to do so, so I do not foresee that the missionaries, who besides have great influence with the Spaniards, will have much difficulty in winning over the governors, especially when all will find their profit in it. If you add to that the excessive prices at which goods coming from Old Mexico are priced when they have arrived in New [Mexico], you will see that everything ought to contribute to success.

I think, then, that Sieur Macmahon, to whom you will communicate what I am writing you on the subject of the Spanish commerce, ought to have an agent go to the Natchitoches with a considerable quantity of merchandise, especially chosen, and give him instructions for attempting to open up commerce through the Adais. He must see to it that this agent understands and speaks the Spanish language sufficiently not to need an interpreter, because ordinarily people do not like to have a third person present at such negotiations. I do not put any limit at all to what you are to promise the missionary or to the gratuity to

Patricia Kay Galloway, Dunbar Rowland, and Albert G. Sanders, eds. and trans., *Mississippi Provincial Archives: French Dominion* (Baton Rouge: Baton Rouge Louisiana State Historical Society, 1984), 4: 49–50. Reprinted by permission.

the agent, leaving you and Sieur Macmahon the authority to act according to the situations and circumstances that you find. You will call Sieur Macmahon's attention to the fact that he must fix the prices of the merchandise that he will have taken to the Natchitoches on a higher level than that which is established at New Orleans and to make them proportionate to those of the merchandise in New Mexico, being watchful, however, to establish them in such a way as to make them distinctly attractive to the Spaniards in order to induce them to resort to this direction.

6. Captain Pierre Marie François de Pagès Reports on Texas, 1767

We arrived at the river Guadeloupe [Guadalupe], the last of any consequence on the road to San Antonio: and here the same tedious and irksome method of passing on paths was repeated in four days more we came to plantations of Indian corn, from the appearance of which I could easily perceive that the inhabitants of this settlement are not so miserably idle as those of Adaés. The crops are large and beautiful, and interspersed with meadow ground, upon which are reared herds and flocks of almost every denomination.

At this post [San Antonio], the second in the same direction belonging to the Spaniards, I met with the new governor of the province, whom I had just seen at Adaés. In the countries bordering on those rivers reside the savage tribes named Tegas and Apaches, the last of which entertain an implacable enmity against the Spaniards. The Apaches, after driving them from a settlement in those parts, called San Xavier, were repelled in their turn, and obliged to seek habitations in more northern regions. Although the population of savage nations is not expected to be very considerable, yet from the province of Louisiana to San Pedro we passed their villages at intervals of twenty-five and thirty leagues, and sometimes at a shorter distance. But that vast country situated on this side of the San Pedro villages, and which stretches all the way to Rio Grande, is totally destitute of inhabitants. It is true, those regions are still frequented by savages; but they have no other object in view than to make war upon the Spaniards, to drive off their cattle, to hunt the buffalo, and to gather *plaquemines* [persimmons] and chestnuts, with which they retire to their villages in the north. Owing to their very frequent incursions, however, they have been improperly represented as wandering tribes.

Whilst I remained at this settlement, the savages through whose boundaries we had passed at San Pedro, incensed against the governor on account of his prohibition of their trade with the French of Naquadoch [Nacogdoches], made an irruption into the country, and carried off four hundred horses from San Antonio. The alarm being given, the garrison beat to arms, and mounting their horses, pursued to the distance of a hundred leagues, with being able to come up

Marilyn McAdams Sibley, ed., "Across Texas in 1767: The Travels of Captain Pagès," *Southwestern Historical Quarterly Online* 70 (April 1967): 593–622. URL http://www. tshaonline.org/shqonline/apager.php?vol070&pag=601 (Accessed 25-01-2010)

with the enemy. The Spaniards were on their return home, and had reached the river Guadeloupe, when another party of the same nation rushed from the woods, and made a smart fire upon them. The garrison, after making a vigorous resistance for the space of three hours, at last yielded to superior numbers, and lost on this occasion, besides other property, a hundred and fifty horses. A few days after the garrison was insulted again by a detachment of the same tribe; and the governor began to see the necessity of putting the fort in a better state of defense.

Fort San Antonio stands in a valley of an oblong form, one side of which fronts an angle of a small river in its vicinty. The different avenues leading to the settlement are defended by large pallisadoes, while the houses built upon its circumference serve the purpose of walls: but being of very considerable extent, and as many of the houses are in ruins, it is but weakly fortified, and has much occasion for a stronger garrison. It is besides much incumbered from without by several miserable villages, which give encouragement to the incursions of the enemy. The space too inclosed by the angle of the river is crowded by a multitude of huts, which are occupied by a number of emigrants from the Canary Isles.

In the settlement of San Antonio we find a Spanish colony from the Canary Isles; whilst all their other stations consist merely of soldiers, and a few Indians who have been seduced from the innocence of savage life. Their principal employment is to rear horses, mules, cows, and sheep. Their cattle, commonly allowed to roam at large in the woods, are once in two months driven into fields adjoining to the houses of their owners, where every means is used to render them tame and tractable. After having been subjected to hunger and confinement, they receive their liberty, and are succeeded by others, which experience in their turn a similar course of discipline. Such of the inhabitants as are at pains to prevent their herds from running entirely wild, are found to possess five or six thousand head of cattle.

They have likewise the use of tame animals, which, besides being serviceable to them in milk, supply them with fat and dried flesh for their extensive peregrinations. Their horses and mules are no sooner a little broken in, than they are offered to sale; but here the marked price is so extremely low, as indeed may be imagined, that I have seen a good horse sold for a pair of shoes. Having only one or two keepers for all the cattle of the settlement, even their domestic animals run day and night in the woods.

~ ESSAYS

The Spanish colony of New Mexico has traditionally been viewed as a hybrid biracial society where Spaniards and Pueblo Indians clashed, intermingled, and for over two centuries, coexisted. In the first essay, Dedra S. MacDonald, lecturer in history at Hillsdale College in Hillsdale, Michigan, adds nuance to this picture by unearthing a forgotten thread in the history of Spanish New Mexico: the presence of African peoples in the province. MacDonald shows how Indians and Africans found commonalities under the Spanish rule that marginalized and disempowered both and how they came together to resist colonial exploitation. Indians and

Africans intermarried, had children, built small *zambo* communities, and formed anti-Spanish criminal alliances. MacDonald also sheds new light on the pivotal event in the history of Southwest borderlands, the Pueblo Revolt, by emphasizing the central role of mulattoes in the uprising. In her telling, the revolt emerges as a broad multiracial rebellion of oppressed people who had found a common cause in their position at the bottom of a colonial society. MacDonald makes a case for a Black history of colonial New Mexico, and she concludes her essay by asking why that history has been so neglected. She argues that a key reason can be found in growing class-consciousness in late eighteenth-century New Mexico, where elites—both Spanish and Indian—became preoccupied with ideas of racial purity and strove to erase the memory of Black ancestors.

The second essay shifts the focus from cross-cultural contestation within colonial realms to Indian-European interactions in fluid borderland places where independent powers contended with one anther. Juliana Barr, professor of history at the University of Florida, examines a long-neglected but central borderlands institution: Indian slave trade. The origins, expansion, and eradication of chattel slavery in the American South has long captured the attention of historians, who only recently have begun to explore the many different slave systems that have existed in North America. For over three centuries, native peoples across the continent participated in various slave systems that defy easy racial categorization: Indians themselves captured, sold, bought, and enslaved Indians, as too did Spanish, French, and English colonists. Indian slavery fueled violence and warfare and dismantled entire societies, but it could also bring stability: Exchanges of slaves between rival groups could lubricate diplomacy and cement alliances. Barr illuminates such paradoxes of Indian slavery as they unfolded in eighteenth-century Louisiana-Texas borderlands, where Spaniards, French, and various Native Americans competed for power, wealth, and space. She shows how some native groups benefited from the traffic in Indian slaves, while others grew increasingly weak. She also shows how female captives became pawns in a male-dominated international diplomacy that, in the closing years of the eighteenth century, brought peace to this war-ridden borderland world. Like the California missions discussed in Chapter 5, Indian slave trade emerges here as a site of both indigenous exploitation and indigenous survival.

Indians and Africans Collaborate in Colonial New Mexico

DEDRA S. MACDONALD

In 1539, Esteban de Dorantes of Azamor, an enslaved Black Moor, ventured into Pueblo Indian territory in the vanguard of Fray Marcos de Niza's expedition to the unexplored north. Esteban had traveled in the northern reaches of New

Dedra S. MacDonald, "Intimacy and Empire: Indian-African Interaction in Spanish New Mexico, 1500–1800," in *Confounding the Color Line: The Indian-Black Experience in North America*, ed. James F. Brooks, pp. 21–46 (Lincoln: University of Nebraska Press, 2002). Reprinted by permission of the University of Nebraska Press. Copyright 2002 by the University of Nebraska Press.

Spain before—he, along with three Spaniards including the famed Álvar Núñez Cabeza de Vaca, had survived Pánfilo de Narváez's disastrous attempt to colonize Florida. Cabeza de Vaca's tales of the group's eight years of wanderings though present-day Texas and northern Mexico piqued Spanish interest in the "Northern Mystery." Although the survivors repeatedly claimed to have seen no signs of exploitable wealth in the north, New Spain's viceroy, Antonio Mendoza, and others hoping to find an "otro México" planned an expedition. Cabeza de Vaca, however, refused to return to the north, and Mexican officials could not allow a slave to lead this expedition. Hence, Viceroy Mendoza purchased Esteban and selected Franciscan Fray Marcos de Niza to head the journey northward, to be accompanied by Esteban.

Ranging several days ahead of Fray Marcos with a group of Christianized Pimas (who had followed Cabeza be Vaca to Mexico) and Mexican Indians (Tlaxcalans), Esteban reached the Zuni settlement of Hawikuh. He was the first non–Native to visit Pueblo lands, an event made more significant by his African, rather than European, heritage. During his travels north to Zuni, Indians had treated Esteban as a "black god," regaling him with gifts of turquoise and women. Although no one knows for sure what transpired when Esteban entered Hawikuh, legend has it that his arrogance led him to expect similar privileges and to make demands for gifts and women. This angered the Zunis, who killed him. Another twist to the legend involves a gourd rattle Esteban carried as part of his "black god" persona. The gourd rattle offended the Zunis, thereby leading to the slave's death. Additionally, some scholars have postulated that Esteban interrupted Zuni ceremonials, thereby angering them to the point of murder.

Zuni oral tradition corroborates the tale of Esteban's demise related in Spanish documents. While living at Zuni during the late nineteenth century, Smithsonian ethnologist Frank Hamilton Cushing heard stories of a murdered Black Mexican. In a lecture given to the American Geographical Society in 1885, Cushing admitted that when he first heard the "Zuni legend of the Black Mexican with the thick lips," he had no knowledge of Fray Marcos de Niza's 1539 northern expedition. Cushing described the story to archaeologist Adolph Bandelier, who matched it to events described in Spanish documents. In Bandelier's account of the events in Hawikuh, "The Zunis definitely informed Mr. Cushing, after he had become … adept by initiation into the esoteric fraternity of warriors, that a 'black Mexican' had once come to O'aquima [Hawikuh] and had been hospitably received there. He, however, very soon incurred mortal hatred by his rude behavior toward the women and girls of the pueblo, on account of which the men at last killed him." Hence, both Zuni oral tradition and Spanish written documents recorded the ill-fated encounter between Native Americans and the advance guard of the Spanish conquerors. As Bandelier noted, "A short time after that the first white Mexicans, as the Indians call all white men whose mother-tongue is Spanish, came to the country and overcame the natives in war."

What transpired at Hawikuh between the Zunis and Esteban resulted in a black kachina known as Chakwaina, or monster kachina, throughout the Pueblo world. Esteban served as a harbinger of the Spanish conquest, which permanently altered Pueblo life. Thus, Chakwaina kachina emerged as a tangible symbol of Pueblo interpretations of the Spanish conquest. According to anthropologist Frederick Dockstader, legendary accounts attribute the impetus for Chakwaina to Esteban. Dockstader notes that "the appearance of this kachina and the fact that Chakwaina is known in all the pueblos as a horrible ogre, support this legend. Esteban would be remembered because of the color of his skin, because he was the first non-Indian seen in Cibola, and because of the circumstances surrounding his fate." Anthropologist E. Charles Adams argued that in modern western Pueblo societies, kachinas in the form of ogres and whippers fill the role of disciplinarians and overseers of communal work groups. As the impetus for the ogre kachina Chakwaina, Esteban lives on, reminding us of changes wrought in the Pueblo world by the aggressive presence of White and Black outsiders. Although they effectively defused the threat posed by Esteban, the Zunis could not so easily evade the Spaniards who followed. Scarcely a year passed before explorer Francisco Vásquez de Coronado and his entourage of several thousand Spaniards and Mexican Indians appeared in Zuni lands, occupying Hawikuh from July to November of 1540.

This less-than-auspicious beginning for African-Indian relations in today's American Southwest, however, did not keep the two groups apart. Sometimes at odds with one another, other times brought together in the most intimate of relations, sexual liaisons sometimes resulting in formal marriage—African descendants and Native Americans in northern New Spain interacted throughout the Spanish colonial era. These interactions formed a web in which one group's actions affected the other group, resulting, for example, in the Pueblo kachina Chakwaina or, in the case of the Black Seminoles, in ethnogenesis, the formation of a new group of people. Children of African and Native American sexual unions, known throughout the early colonial period as mulattoes and later as *zambos,* at particular times and places formed new, third groups, such as the Black Caribs or the Black Seminoles. In New Mexico, however, a third group never emerged. The small African population—at the very least 2.5 percent, according to one scholar—was partially responsible for this failure. The close connection between the absence of mixed-blood group formation and exploitation, however, provides a better explanation for the absence of a New Mexico version of Black Indians.

Despite the relatively small African population in colonial New Mexico, the Spanish system of racial stratification and coerced labor placed Africans and Indians in a context of deep intercultural contact.... This essay will examine interactions between Indians and persons of African descent in New Mexico, the northernmost outpost of New Spain, focusing on the seventeenth and eighteenth centuries. First, the essay will briefly survey the history of Spanish American slavery and initial relations between Africans and Indians....

Next I will discuss specific intercultural contacts, particularly episodes in which Africans and Indians worked together—episodes that emanate from the marginalization and disempowerment the two groups faced.... [H]owever, Native Americans and Africans did not automatically become allies. Indeed, the Spanish government frequently sought to keep the two groups apart, implementing "divide and conquer" policies in an attempt to prevent episodes like the Pueblo Revolt. Additionally ... Africans at times emulated Spaniards, exploiting Indians through their higher status as artisans and supervisors of native agricultural workers.

Third, this essay will examine sexual liaisons and intermarriages, the ultimate deep intercultural contact, and the cultural discussions surrounding the creation of new bloodlines, such as the mulatto and the *zambo*, as illustrated in a popular eighteenth-century genre of paintings known as *las castas*.

Finally, this study will draw some conclusions responding to the central question raised by Esteban's reincarnation as the Chakwaina kachina and by Indian and Black collaboration in Spanish colonial New Mexico: What is the nature of interaction between Blacks and Indians in New Mexico, and what do those interactions suggest about the relationship between the absence of mixed-blood group formation and imperial exploitation?

Africans accompanied the earliest Spanish explorers in the Americas and thereby made contact with Native Americans from the beginning of the Spanish conquest.... By the middle of the sixteenth century, as many as 18,500 Africans and their descendants populated New Spain (Mexico).

Because Indians and Africans both were considered laborers, if not outright slaves, the first extensive relations between the two groups centered around their mutual enslavement.... Interracial unions likely occurred first in the West Indies, particularly due to the highly imbalanced sex ratio among Africans brought to the New World.... Another motivation for African men to intermarry with Indian women centered on the Spanish law of the womb; that is, a child's freedom rested on that of its mother. This motivation became even more salient after 1542, when many Native Americans gained liberation from formal slavery. After that year, Indian women, at least theoretically, could not be enslaved. For their part, Indian women may have found motivation for intermarriage in the sexual imbalance in their villages.

Given the above incentives, the population of free "Red-Black people" rose steadily throughout the sixteenth century. [Historian Jack] Forbes maintained that "this free population, freed not by individual Spaniards but by its native mothers' status, represented a threat especially whenever [that population] existed near hostile native groups or communities of Red-Black. Sixteenth-century Spanish authorities issued numerous laws and decrees in often futile attempts to control Indian-African alliances and offspring. A 1527 law required that Blacks only marry other Blacks. In a similar vein, a 1541 decree required slaves to marry legally, in reaction to reports that African slaves frequently kept "great numbers of Indian women, some of them voluntarily, others against their wishes." A decree (*cédula*) issued in 1551 and reissued in 1584 note "that many negros have Indian females as *mancebas* (concubines) or treat them badly and oppress them." In 1572, authorities issued a law requiring children of African men and Indian women to pay tribute "like the rest of the Indians [although] it is pretended that they are not [Indians]." King Philip II in 1595 ordered that unmarried non-Natives living among Natives be expelled from Indian villages. These shifting laws governing the status of African descendants reveal the Spanish colonial state's ambivalence over the racial/ethnic identity of this group.

Another branch of decrees and laws focused on revolts and communities of runaway slaves. A 1540 decree allowed for *cimarrónes* to be pardoned only once. A decree issued the same year stated that *cimarrónes* should not be castrated as punishment for having run away. Two years later, laws appeared that placed limitations on Black mobility. As of 1542, Blacks were not permitted to wander through the streets at night. Additionally, in 1551, Africans could no longer serve Indians and neither free nor enslaved Blacks or *lobos* (offspring of Indians and mulattoes) could carry weapons. In a further limitation of African freedom, a 1571 law forbade free and enslaved-Black and mulatto women from wearing gold, pearls, and silk. An exception could be made, however, for free *mulatas* married to Spaniards, who had the right to wear gold earrings and pearl necklaces.

New Mexico's status as a province of New Spain meant that the above laws applied to Indians and Africans living on the far northern frontier. The Spanish Archives of New Mexico include copies of decrees and declarations of kings and viceroys that clarified or changed earlier rulings. For example, a 1706 order compelled African descendants to attend church. In 1785, New Mexico governor Joseph Antonio Rengel received a letter advising that the custom of branding Africans on the cheek and shoulder had been abolished. A 1790 viceregal order granted freedom to slaves escaping into Spanish territory. In the interests of agriculture, in 1804 King Carlos IV renewed the privilege held by Spaniards and foreigners of importing African slaves into specified Spanish American ports. A related 1804 *cédula* renewed the privilege of free importation of African slaves. Finally, in 1817, King Fernando VII abolished the African slave trade. Hence, extant documents in New Mexico archives trace the gradual abolition of African slavery. These same archives, however, contain no evidence of continued attempts to exert Spanish authority over African-Indian relations.

Beginning with their initial contact, Native Americans and Africans collaborated in committing armed resistance against Spanish exploiters ... On the 1594 Leyva y Bonilla expedition, which wandered as far as Wichita tribal lands in present-day Kansas, soldier Antonio Gutiérrez de Humaña murdered Leyva y Bonilla and then took over the expedition. At Quivira, Wichitas killed the entire entourage, except for one Spanish boy, Alonso Sanchez, and a mulatto woman who was half-burned. A 1601 expedition led by New Mexico colonist Juan de Oñate learned that the boy and the woman still lived and endeavored to locate them. Oñate, in fact, brought to New Mexico in 1598 several African slaves. Given the proximity of the initial Spanish settlement at San Gabriel to San Juan Pueblo, it is probable that Oñate's slaves frequently intermeshed with the San Juans.

In the decades leading up to the Pueblo Revolt of 1680, intense church and state rivalry for jurisdiction over the Pueblos, among other things, split the less than two hundred *vecinos* (citizens, including Spaniards, mestizos, and African descendants) into two vitriolic factions. In 1643, Governor [Alonso] Pacheco [de Heredío] executed eight leading citizens of Santa Fe. Incensed Franciscan friars claimed he could not have done so without the support of strangers, a Portuguese man, mestizos, *zambahigos* (sons of Indian men and African women), and mulattoes. This charge suggests the existence of a "racial cleavage in New Mexico, with the persons of non–Spanish ancestry supporting the secular side of the dispute."

Such venomous disputes between New Mexico's civil and religious authorities showed Puebloans the weaknesses in the Spanish governing structure.

On the other hand, marginalization and intolerance by Spanish colonials also threw [Indians and Africans] together in attempts to oust their oppressors. Rumors surrounding the Pueblo Revolt illustrate this type of cooperation. In 1967, Fray Angelico Chavez published an article on the successful 1680 revolt, arguing that it was not led by the Puebloans themselves, but by a mulatto. Employing a racist argument in which he questioned the intelligence and ability of Pueblo Indians to pull off a successful rebellion, Chavez sought to give credit for the organization and leadership of the entire uprising to Naranjo, a big Black man with yellow eyes mentioned in Indian testimonies about the revolt. Comparing Puebloans and Africans in words reflective of racist assumptions of the 1950s and 1960s, Chavez claimed that the revolt was "not the first time that an African spoiled the best-laid plans of the Spaniard in American colonial times, but it was the most dramatic. More active and restless by nature than the more passive and stolid Indian, he was more apt to muddle up some serious Hispanic enterprise." Using records of Indian testimonies, Chavez argued that Naranjo, a mulatto of Mexican Indian roots who called himself the representative of Pueblo god Pose-yemu, directed the course of the Pueblo Revolt from his hiding place in a Taos kiva. Some twenty-three years later, in 1990, historian Stefanie Beninato challenged Chavez's controversial argument, interpreting the same documents but using a wider cultural framework. She agreed that a mulatto worked with the Puebloans as a tactical leader but postulated that a non-Pueblo man could not have been a leader in the revolt. Hence, she suggested that Naranjo's roots were Puebloan rather Mexican Indian.

Both Chavez and Beninato, however, overlooked the significance of the mulatto Naranjo's involvement in an event that epitomized Indian resistance to Spanish colonial rule. According to Jack Forbes, the Pueblo rebels included "mestizos and mulattoes and people who speak Spanish." Since the early sixteenth century, Spaniards had feared just such an alliance, and with good reason. The Pueblo Revolt had been preceded by numerous similar alliances throughout Spanish America. Forbes argued that slavery and general labor oppression created an atmosphere of resistance among marginalized peoples, making conditions favorable for the establishment of intimate relationships between African descendants and Native Americans.

Reports by New Mexico governor Antonio de Otermín and his military officers demonstrate that African-Indian interaction in the province led to what Spaniards perceived as a frustrating and threatening alliance. In a document dated 9 August 1680, the day Puebloans launched their attack on the Spaniards, Otermín related events reported by captured Indians. "There had come to them from very far away toward the north a letter from an Indian lieutenant of Po he yemu to the effect that all of them in general should rebel, and that any pueblo that would not agree to it they would destroy, killing all the people. It was reported that this Indian lieutenant of Po he yemu was very tall, black and had very large yellow eyes, and that everyone feared him greatly." Encouraged by the successful example set by the Puebloans, neighboring tribes also planned revolts. Worried Spaniards recorded these rumors in reports and letters as they tried to ascertain the extent of the threat. On 29 August 1680, Andrés López de Gracia wrote to don Bartolomé de Estrada concerning a Suma plot. Similar to the 1667 Concho and Suma rebellion discussed above, this revolt resulted from a mulatto servant's abuse of Indians. López de Gracia reported that the Suma actions were "instigated by only a few Indians, who do not number more than eight.... According to the information I have, the cause of it all is a mulatto who is the Río de los Janos, a servant of ... Father Juan Martínez, because of what he did to an Indian, whose ears he cut off." In hopes of defusing the Suma rebellion, López de Gracia ordered the mulatto servant arrested. Mistreatment from any source incurred Indian retaliation.

Rebel Indians also formed alliances with other mistreated groups, making the Pueblo Revolt even more widespread and threatening to Spaniards. Otermín on several occasions noted his frustration with such alliances. In order to counteract a rear action conducted by mounted Pueblo and Apache Indians and led by Picuris leader Luís Tupatú, the ousted New Mexico governor retreated downriver toward his Isleta stronghold. In his report of this action, Otermín described a much-feared alliance formed by Tupatú's followers and "the confident coyotes, mestizos, and mulattoes, all of whom are skillful horsemen and know how to manage harquebuses and lances, together with the main body and column of the rest of the people of all the nations." Several days later, in a report regarding the pacification of Isleta Pueblo, Otermín castigated the Pueblos and their allies:

> Obstinate and rebellious, they have left their pueblo houses, the grain upon which they subsist, and other things, taking their families, and fleeing with them to the roughest of the sierras, joining together to resist and willing to lose their lives rather than submit. Many mestizos, mulattoes, and people who speak Spanish have followed them, who are skillful on horseback and who can manage firearms as well as any Spaniard. These persons incited them to disobedience and boldness in excess of their natural iniquity.

The importance of these alliances to Pueblo strategy remains unknown, but Spaniards forced to abandon New Mexico viewed *casta* (mixed blood) cooperation with Indians as a disloyal and threatening act, particularly in that such alliances symbolized the rejection of Spanish civilization. Although scholarship and extant documents surrounding the revolt do not reveal whether the Indian-*casta* alliance continued after 1682, it is likely that allied mestizos and mulattoes intermarried with Puebloans during the revolt years (through 1696). Native Americans and *castas* shared a marginal status in Spanish New Mexican society, in which pretensions to power required at least the illusion of *limpieza de sangre*. Both groups stood to gain from rebellion against Spanish authority. By joining Pueblo rebels, New Mexico *castas* constructed a group identity as "not-Spanish," which meant they would no longer acquiesce, at least for the revolt years, to Spanish domination over Puebloans and *castas* alike.

Witchcraft provided another means for the two groups to work together toward a specific end. In one such case, mulatto Juana Sanches, wife of Captain Juan Gomes, obtained herbs from a Tewa Indian woman living at San Juan Pueblo. Juana Sanches wanted to make her husband stop treating her badly. She claimed that he beat her and that he was engaged in a "bad friendship" with a concubine. The Indian woman gave Sanches two yellow roots and two grains of blue corn with points of white hearts inside. She chewed the corn and anointed her husband's chest with it and repeated the exercise with the herbs. Sanches added to her 1631 testimony to New Mexico's agent of the Inquisition that ten or twelve years prior, Hispanicized (*ladino*) Mexican Indian Beatris de los Angeles, wife of the *alférez* Juan de la Cruz, visited her. Finding Juana Sanches to be sad from her husband's mistreatment, Beatris de los Angeles counseled her to take a few worms that live in excrement and toast them, then put them in her husband's food. With this, he would love her very much and stop beating her. Sanches did this, but to no avail. The potion did not alleviate her situation.

Sanches also implicated her sister, Juana de los Reyes, also a mulatto, in committing similar activities. Sanches declared that five or six years before, her sister claimed to know something about herbs and roots, which she had given to her husband, mulatto Alavaro Garcia, so that he would stop visiting concubines. An Indian woman supplied Reyes with the herbs and roots to anoint her husband's chest. Juana de los Reyes made her own declaration, stating that she had been very sad because her husband was sleeping around and not staying in the house with her. So, she asked her sister, Juana Sanches, for help. Sanches said that she had an herb, given to her by an Indian woman, that was good for such occasions. She gave Reyes three or four grains of corn, and Reyes gave this potion to her husband in his food twice and also made an ointment for his chest. With this potion, her husband loved her very much and forgot his vices. She gave him the potion another time in his food and anointed his chest once more, with the result that he woke up, threw off her hand, and left her. Because the potion now had no effect, she left the situation in God's hands. Juana de los Reyes also described another remedy told to her by the Indian woman: Suck on your two big fingers and give the saliva from the sucked fingers to your spouse in his food and he will love you well and stop seeing concubines. Reyes declared that she tried this once and did not want to try it again because it made her nauseous and it had no effect on her husband. Finally, at the same time that the above testimonies were made, Beatris de la Pedraza also made a declaration. She claimed to be the Indian woman who gave advice and herbs to Sanches and Reyes.

[An] interesting question surrounds the two *mulata* women's close working relationship with Indian *curanderas*. How they made connections with Indian women and why they did not implicate medicine women by name in their depositions remain unanswerable questions. Perhaps gender concerns brought Native American and African women together. Additionally … in early Spanish colonial usage, *mulato* frequently referred to a person of Indian and African heritage rather than its later usage as a referent for the offspring of African and European unions. Given this insight, it is possible that Juana Sanches and her sister, Juana de los Reyes, sprang from African and Indian parentage. If so, they may have long held knowledge of Indian and African *curanderas* and the types of situations that could be remedied with herbal potions. Additionally, Sanches and Reyes used their connections with Indian medicine women in desperate attempts to control their husband's abusive behavior. In order to gain control, the women relied on female knowledge and cross-cultural community.

Despite imperial efforts to keep Africans and Indians apart, social and economic disempowerment sometimes led those at the bottom of the Spanish empire's racial hierarchy to join forces against exploitive *ricos* (elites) and middling Hispanos. On 23 June 1762 in Santa Fe, testimony began in the criminal case against mulatto Luis Flores and *genízaro* (detribalized Indian) Miguel Reaño for the robbery of a cow. Santa Fe officials surveyed the houses of all citizens living on the edges of the mountains on the outskirts of town, searching for signs of a recently butchered beef cow. They found what they were looking for at the home of Luis Flores. He had indeed butchered the cow, and Miguel Reaño had brought the animal to Flores's home. New Mexico governor Tomás Velez Cachupín ordered that the beef be distributed among Santa Fe's widows and other poor men and women and that the two suspects be imprisoned.

The testimonies that follow reveal a confused situation in which middling Hispanos seem to have taken advantage of their poorer and hungrier neighbors. Miguel Reaño testified that Antonio Sandobal owned the cow and that his son, Juan Sandobal, had sold the cow to him in exchange for a horse. In his declaration, Flores claimed that he planned to cut the brand from the cow and give it to Antonio Sandobal, the owner of the cow, and that he and Reaño would share the meat. Juan Sandobal, however, declared that he had not sold a cow to Reaño and that he had not left his house at all, much less to barter with Reaño. Two witnesses verified that Sandobal had not left his house except to look for a horse to ride to mass, so he could not have engineered the sale of a cow.

In light of these testimonies, Governor Velez Cachupín declared Flores and Reaño guilty as charged for the robbery of a cow and condemned the "criminals" to pay for the animal. Because Reaño had no personal effects other than his labor, Velez Cachupín ordered him to serve Antonio Sandobal until he had earned one-half the cost of the cow. Luis Flores, for pain of his sin and for setting a bad example for the Indian Miguel Reaño, was sentenced to repair Santa Fe's royal adobe buildings. The bureaucratic language that Spanish interrogators and scribes employed makes it difficult for readers two and a half centuries later to determine guilt. It does seem, however, that Luis Flores and Miguel Reaño, as members of the lowest rung in Spanish society, never stood a chance. In all likelihood, the Sandobals passed off a rejected cow on the unsuspecting duo, gaining a monetary return, a horse, and free labor to boot. The town of Santa Fe benefited as well, gaining food for its poor as well as free refurbishing work on royal buildings. Flores and Reaño stood as the only losers. More important, this case illustrates the ease with which Native Americans and African Americans interacted.

Spanish colonial censuses and marriage registers contain records of numerous legal unions between Native Americans and African Americans—unions regulated under the same "divide and conquer" strategy that guided colonial officials' thinking in matters of crime and legal slavery. Social laws forbade marriages between elite Spaniards and mixed bloods. Many unions between these groups took place, however, despite efforts to maintain social honor and "pure" bloodlines.

Intermarriages between the two groups involved people in a variety of circumstances: Indian and African slaves; free people of color in the Americas; Africans who fled to Indian nations and were initially enslaved but later became members of the group through marriage and adoption; Africans who escaped slavery to form *quilombos* or *cimarrón* (runaway) communities; and individual African runaways. Thus, especially in New Mexico, frontier areas served as a "cultural merging ground and a marrying ground." In historian Gary Nash's pithy words, "Nobody left the frontier cultural encounters unchanged."

Marriage records in the Archives of the Archdiocese of Santa Fe show the extent to which New Mexico fit the above description. Although pre-1680 ecclesiastical documents disappeared in the Pueblo Revolt, many of the records from the 1690s forward have survived. Marriage investigations (*diligencias matrimoniales*) and entries in Roman Catholic matrimonial books (*libros de casamientos*) record significant numbers of marital unions between persons of African descent and Native Americans throughout New Mexico's colonial period. Moreover, *diligencias* often provide information beyond the names and racial or ethnic identities of betrothed couples. Details about personal histories, such as work or residential mobility, are mentioned in these documents. Pieced together, *diligencias* and other sacramental records depict a landscape of interaction between Indians and African descendants on the intimate level of marriage, as well as in society and the economy.

From 1697 to 1711, several mixed couples residing in New Mexico initiated marital proceedings. In 1697, mulatto widower José Gaitín, native of San Luis Potosí, married Indian widow Geronima de la Cruz, native of San Felipe, Chihuahua. Likewise, in 1711, mulatto Fabián Naranjo married Tewa Indian Micaela de la Cruz. Both spouses were New Mexico Natives. Similar unions took place in El Paso del Norte, which was a part of New Mexico throughout the colonial period. María Persingula, Indian from Ysleta del Sur Pueblo, married free mulatto Cayeano de la Rosa, native of Santa Fe, in 1736. Two other marriages between mulatto men and Indian women took place that same year. The following year, Apache Indian María Ysidora, who had previously been married to a mulatto slave, united in matrimony with another Apache, Salvador María. In 1738, another Apache woman, Antonia Rosa, married free mulatto Juan Pedro Vanegas. Yet another Apache-African union occurred in 1760, between Black slave and Congo native Joseph Antonio and Apache Indian servant Marzela. A similar marriage took place in 1764. Finally, two 1779 unions featured Indian grooms and free mulatto brides.

While frontier fluidity facilitated cross-cultural unions, it also fostered a chaotic atmosphere in which bigamy flourished. In one such case, occurring in 1634, two traveling soldiers discovered that mulatto Juan Anton, a recent arrival in New Mexico from Nueva Vizcaya, had two wives. He had married a Mexican Indian named Ana María in Santa Fe. The soldiers met Juan Anton's first wife, an African slave woman, in Cuencamé, Nueva Vizcaya, while en route to Mexico City. The first wife had four or five children, all fathered by Juan Anton.

When he heard that denunciations had been made against him for the crime of bigamy, he disappeared. Juan Anton's choice of wives—first a Black slave and then a free Mexican Indian—comprises a striking element of this case. He may well have chosen his second wife in order to facilitate the birth of free rather than enslaved offspring, as the status of children followed that of the mother. Additionally, his marriages illustrate the ease with which *castas* and Indians intermarried. Indeed, New Mexico Inquisitor Fray Estevan de Perea declared in 1631 that New Mexico's population consisted of mestizos, mulattoes, and *zambohijos* (offspring of Indians and mulattoes).

Similarly, the 1750 Albuquerque census well illustrates the deep intercultural contacts precipitated by frontier demographics and dynamics. Out of 191 families, 18 households included both Native Americans and African descendants. Some of these households, like that of mulatto couple Juan Samora and Ynes Candelaria, included Indian servants. In this case, nine-year-old María served Samora, Candelaria, and their four children, who ranged in age from two years to nine years. In other households, Indians and mulattoes lived together as husbands and wives. For example, mulatto Chrisanto Torres, age thirty, and his forty-year-old wife, Indian Luisa Candelaria, lived with their four daughters, who ranged in age from two to ten years. Out of the eighteen mixed households, however, fifteen featured Indians in service roles, although in some cases Indians served alongside mulatto or Black servants. Clearly, by 1750, some mulatto families achieved socioeconomic distinction over the Native Americans with whom they had once been equally marginalized.

Other Indian and mulatto families, however, joined forces in land grant ventures. In 1751, Governor Velez Cachupín issued the Las Trampas grant as part of New Mexico's Indian defense policy. The grant location would serve as a barrier to nomadic raiders and would increase the amount of agricultural land available to Santa Fe's poor. Las Trampas petitioners hailed from the Barrio de Analco region of Santa Fe, whose residents were primarily presidio soldiers, Mexican Indian servants, and *genízaros*. Additionally, Las Trampas settlers included African descendant Melchor Rodríguez, his son, and his daughter. Hence, Las Trampas settlers represented mixed *genízaro,* Tlaxcalan, African, and Spanish bloodlines. As in the *genízaro* settlements of Abiquiu and San Miguel del Bado, "the task of holding frontier outposts against Indian attack fell primarily to other Indians and mixed-blood Spaniards."

Additionally, after 1750 only one marriage between Indians and African descendants gained mention in the marriage record books for Albuquerque, the 1763 union of mulatto Gabriel Barrera and Apache Indian María. This lack of marriage records could be attributed to a change in the way priests recorded marriages: As the eighteenth century progressed, priests recorded ethnicity less and less frequently. Or the lack of evidence for marriages between African Americans and Native Americans may signal that class and racial distinctions became far more salient in the late colonial period. Indeed, historian Ramón Gutiérrez argues that increasing numbers of *castas* in New Mexico frightened *ricos,* "who expressed concern over the pollution of their blood lines and the loss of honor." In an attempt to control these racial demographic changes,

New Mexico elites turned to a legal skin color-based categories, borrowing heavily from schema adhered to in central New Spain.

A genre of paintings known as *las castas* appeared in New Spain in the mid to late colonial period. While these paintings depicted the complex mixtures of people in Spanish America, they also underscored the colony's strict social hierarchy, based largely on skin pigmentation. Mexican scholar Nicolás Leon's 1924 pamphlet, *Las castas del méxico colonial o nueva españa*, detailed this genre of paintings. According to Leon, the *castas* distinction arose from a societal understanding that the products of intermarriages could not be considered of equal category and importance before society. Therefore, the distinction of castes emerged, "each one with a special name according to the class of the original primitive element that formed it."

Caste paintings simultaneously illustrated awareness of racial distinctions and the widespread nature of racial mingling. They showed husband, wife, and their mixed-blood child, usually with a label describing the process. For example, a *casta* painting by Ignacio Castro, now housed in Paris, proclaims, *"De indio y negra, nace lobo"* (of a male Indian and a female Black a lobo is born). In this portrait, the Black woman is young, gracious, and operates an open-air food stand. Her husband, the Indian, extends his hand to receive a plate of chiles, which the little lobo hands to him with a look of curiosity. In sum, this caste painting embodies a scene of domestic tranquillity.

On the other hand, caste paintings also carried overt messages regarding the vices of the lower classes—vices that interracial unions exacerbated.... Inscriptions on caste paintings ensured that audiences would understand the artist's message about dangerous racial mixtures. Yet, one wonders if *casta* artists captured the mood of Spanish colonial society with such portraits or if they served a more didactic purpose, providing yet another means through which colonial officials attempted to "divide and conquer" the lower classes.

Another interesting element of caste paintings concerns their implicit encouragement of interracial relationships between Spaniards and other groups. Some paintings suggested that domestic tranquillity increased in direct proportion to amounts of Spanish blood, or *limpieza de sangre*. Inscriptions even went so far as to credit success and intelligence to the presence of European blood. For example, one family portrait announces that "the pride and sharp wits of the mulatto are instilled by his white father and black mother." In contrast, the *cambujo* (child of a lobo father and Indian mother) "is usually slow, lazy, and cumbersome."

One type of caste painting featured a chart of racial mixtures, beginning with the highest level of Spanish blood and ending with the lowest level. Even the names given to offspring of the latter intermarriages indicated societal disdain. For instance, the product of a union between a *calpan mulata* and a *sambaygo* carried the name *tente en el aire* (grope in the air). The next lower rung, the child of a *tente en el aire* and a *mulata,* was called *no te entiendo* (I don't understand you). Finally, the offspring of *no te entiendo* and an Indian woman became known as *hay te estas* (stay where you are). Hence, the upper rungs of Spanish colonial society, or at least the artists, did not oppose interracial marriages as such. They did, however, associate danger and violence with unions between the most marginalized and disempowered groups. The marriage records cited above indicate that intimate relations between Native Americans and African Americans continued, albeit at a reduced rate, in late-eighteenth-century New Mexico, despite class-based assumptions about lower-class intermarriages. Indeed, it is likely that racist assumptions embedded in caste paintings had little impact on the very groups depicted. Caste paintings served to buttress upper-class attempts to distinguish themselves from lower classes rather than to discourage interracial marriages.

In addition, caste paintings symbolized elite attempts to revise New Mexico's racial heritage. Father Juan Agustín de Morfi penned an *Account of Disorders* in 1778, in which he delineated the myriad problems facing New Mexico. One area of great concern to Morfi centered on the exploitation of Indian Puebloans by other *castas*. The priest lamented that laws prohibiting Spaniards, mulattoes, mestizos, and Blacks from living in Indian pueblos were not enforced. "And," Morfi added, "it is difficult to judge if the resulting intermingling of races is useful or harmful to the Indians themselves and to the State." For their part, Morfi continued, Spaniards and *castas* find life in Indian pueblos much preferable to farming their own lands, and all too often "they shrewdly take advantage of the natural indifference of those miserable people to heap upon them new obligations." These obligations include domestic service and the elections of mulattoes and coyotes as Indian pueblo governors. According to the priest, "this rascal's treatment of the Indian is guided by hatred and arrogance." Morfi recommended that all outsiders be expelled from Indian pueblos, and non-Indian partners in mixed marriages should not hold public office in the pueblo. Interestingly, Morfi had nothing but scorn for non-Indian *castas,* particularly mulattoes, whom he viewed as exploiters of victimized Puebloans. While he certainly disapproved of *casta* pretensions, Morfi by no means ignored their presence. His *Account* stands as one of the latest documents to include African descendants and to link them in interactions with Indians.

Writing some thirty-four years later, New Mexico *rico* don Pedro Baptista Pino, in his *Exposition on the Province of New Mexico, 1812*, declared that "in New Mexico there are no *castas* of African origin. My province is probably the only one with this prerogative in all of Spanish America. At no time has any *casta* of people of African origin been known there." In making this claim, Pino deliberately revised New Mexico's racial history, denying the existence of a small yet visible group of Africans and their descendants, many of whom held Indian heritage as well. Pino's denial symbolized an overt attempt by elites to obliterate a history of racial mixtures and alliances born of resistance to dominate group exploitation. As Pino's comments suggest, constructions of racial identity in New Mexico increasingly moved toward a fantasy "White" heritage decades before Anglo-Americans arrived on the scene. Such racial reification all but obliterated African descendants and their interactions with Native Americans from the historical record.

Captivity, Gender, and Social Control in the Texas-Louisiana Borderlands

JULIANA BARR

Increasing attention to the enslavement of Indians has pushed United States historians beyond identifications of North American slavery as primarily an African American experience and of North American captivity as primarily a white experience.... [S]cholars also are beginning to focus attention on women as the victims of that slave trade. Their scholarship is deepening understandings of the roles of Indian women in their peoples' interactions with Europeans. Women often stood in unique positions to learn languages, to act as translators and emissaries in cross-cultural communications, and to create ties between cultures. Though scholars have recognized that the conflicting European and native systems of power in which native women operated constrained the women's opportunities, an emphasis on women's agency has obscured the more coercive traffics in women that were equally central to Indian-European relations. In seeking to redeem the humanity of such women and to recognize their important roles in trade and diplomacy, scholars have often equated agency with choice, independent will, or resistance and de-emphasized the powerlessness, objectification, and suffering that defined the lives of many. Perhaps the best-known example of this trend in American history and popular culture is Sacagawea, whose capture at the hands of raiding Hidatsas turned into enslavement when she was purchased by the French Canadian trader Toussaint Charbonneau —bondage that continued through her time with the Lewis and Clark expedition. The violence and coercion that reduced her to the status of a slave among Euro-Americans has been lost as popular preference casts her as Charbonneau's "wife" and a celebrated mediator of Indian-European diplomacy.

The scholarly focus on mediation and accommodation as women's characteristic activity in Indian-European relations often leads us to overlook the importance of women in political economies of war and imperial rivalry. Multiple coercive traffics in women became essential to European-Indian interaction long before Sacagawea fell into the hands of her captors. Recognition of the diversity of trafficking not only enriches our understanding of the gender dynamics of European-Indian diplomacy and conflict but also enables us to move beyond the homogeneous conception of slavery suggested by using only African American enslavement, specifically, racial chattel slavery (defined here as a form of property and system of compulsory labor entailing permanent and hereditary status) to explore bondage and unfreedom in America. In fact, the very heterogeneity of Indian bondage suggests comparisons with range of slave practices in Africa, Asia, the Mediterranean, and other parts of the world where at different times and places persons, primarily women, were held and used as

Juliana Barr, "From Captives to Slaves: Commodifying Indian Women in the Borderlands," *Journal of American History* 92 (June 2005): 19–46.

not only economic but also social and political capital—comparisons that resonate with growing scholarly discussions of slavery in a global perspective.

The confluence of Spanish, French, and Indian peoples in the areas later known as Comanchería, Apachería, Spanish Texas, and French Louisiana makes them an ideal venue for exploring the forms that traffic in women might take and the kinds of currency that women might represent to Indian and European men who exchanged them. Distinct systems of captivity, bondage, and enslavement developed in a matrix of expanding Indian territories, French mercantilism, and Spanish defensive needs during the eighteenth century. At the end of the seventeenth century, steadily increasing numbers of Spaniards coming north from Mexico and Frenchmen coming south from Illinois and Canada began to invade the region and establish neighboring, competing provinces. At the same time, the territories of bands of Apaches and later Comanches and Wichitas were shifting to include increasingly large areas of present-day north and north-central Texas. As those groups converged in the eighteenth century, European and Indian men—as captors, brokers, and buyers—used captured and enslaved women to craft relationships of trade and reciprocity with one another. A key difference between such exchanges and those involving intermarriage was that the women whom men captured and enslaved were strangers or enemies to their kinship systems. When Indian bands brokered marital unions in the service of diplomacy, a woman's own family or band leaders usually negotiated on her behalf, as in the fur trade of Canada, the Great lakes region, and the American Southeast. In contrast to such women, who may have expanded their existing social and economic authority through intermarriage, enslaved Indian women in Texas and Louisiana remained outside the kin relations of the households that made them objects of exchange. Not only did Indians of another group suffer the loss of their women when their enemies sought to build trade ties with Europeans through captive women and children. If efforts to cement diplomatic and economic ties did not succeed—as often happened between Indians and Spaniards—military and state officials made punitive war, seeking out captives and hostages in retribution for failed negotiations. Thus hostility as much as accommodation was the context for the traffic in women. The political and commercial aspects of the exchanges also set them apart from most Indian practices of captivity and from European systems of enslavement: Indians did not take the women to avenge or replace the dead, as they took most captives; nor did Europeans intend to use them as a servile labor force, as they used most slaves. Instead, the exchanges interwove the categories of captivity and slavery and thereby transformed Indian women into valuable commodities of cross-cultural war, diplomacy, and power.

In the hands of Spanish and French buyers and enslavers, women faced fates from sexual servitude to consignment to labor camps to use as political capital in attempts to win or impose alliances or to signal the failure of those efforts. The multiplicity of experiences reflected not only differences of culture or race but also different understandings of how to govern, how to express power, and how to seek and build political relationships with other men and the nations they represented, whether native or European. This, then, is the story I would like to explore: the ways Spanish, French, and Indian men sought to forge or coerce bonds of obligation through a trade in female pawns. The diverse conditions to which such women were reduced reveal new ways of understanding bondage and unfreedom.

Our story begins with French-Indian captive trade across the Plains and along the Texas-Louisiana border. Initial European observations at the end of the seventeenth century suggest that natives in the southern Plains and the Red River valley did not maintain captives as a source of labor. Instead, Indian peoples took a few captives in warfare only for ritualized ceremonies of revenge or, less often, for adoption. Men rarely allowed themselves to be captured, preferring death on the battlefield; those captured most often were destined for torture, which furnished the opportunity for the honorable warrior's death denied them in battle (the honor acquired by enduring pain). In contrast, captors deemed women and children easier to incorporate into their communities. Outside the realm of war, exchanges of women and children more often took a peaceful form, particularly in the service of diplomatic alliance. Intermarriage often united bands in political and economic relationships, such as the Hasinai, Natchitoches, and Kadohadacho confederacies created by the alliance of various Caddo bands by the end of the seventeenth century. Children might also be exchanged among Wichita and Caddoan bands and adopted into their communities as signs of alliance and insurance of peace.

After the French province of Louisiana was established in 1699, French officials decided to orient their trade interests to the west and north. In 1706 the Spanish expedition leader Juan de Ulibarri reported to New Mexican officials that Wichitas in the southern Plains had begun to sell captive Apache women and children to the French. Attempts to find routes to New Mexico put the French in contact with Indian bands whose reactions to the French newcomers further signaled their spreading reputation as slave raiders.

Frenchmen next attempted to open trade with Apaches, the very people who were losing relatives to French enslavement. In 1724 Etienne de Bourgmont sent a twenty-two-year-old woman and a teenage boy of sixteen whom he had purchased from Kansas Indians back to their village among Plains Apaches. Three months later, he traveled there and tried to build on this gesture in seeking trade relations with Apache leaders. Standing in the midst of trade goods he had carefully laid out for display—rifles, sabers, pickaxes, gunpowder, bullets, red cloth, blue cloth, mirrors, knives, shirts, scissors, combs, gunflints, vermilion, awls, needles, kettles, bells, beads, brass wire, and rings—Bourgmont both symbolically and rhetorically made the case that the Apaches would derive advantage from trade with Frenchmen. Apache leaders, though, saw quite a different gain to be had and quickly grabbed the opportunity. "We will go to visit the French, and we will bring horses to trade with them," an Apache chief first informed Bourgmont. The next day, as negotiations continued, he neatly and publicly committed the French to supplying much more than the goods so carefully advertised by Bourgmont. Standing before more than two hundred warriors and an equal number of women and children who served as audience to the ceremonial meetings, the Apache leader announced: "You see here the

Frenchman whom the Great Spirit has sent to our village to make peace with us.... Henceforth we shall be able to hunt in peace.... They will return to us our women and children whom they have taken from us and who are slaves in their country in exchange for horses that we will give them. The great French chief has promised this to us." But both men's machinations would be in vain.

Despite Bourgmont's peaceful intentions and the Apache chief's persuasive rhetoric, French posts in western Louisiana had already become, and would remain throughout the eighteenth century, nuclei of a slave trade in Apache captives brought by Caddos, Wichitas, and later Comanches.

The Indian peoples with whom Frenchmen sought trade enjoyed powerful positions in the region, and almost all of them used the European presence to maintain and even strengthen those positions. Caddo, Wichita, and Comanche willingness to trade war captives to Frenchmen in exchange for European material goods indicates that the three groups—displaying a range of socioeconomic systems—did not secure captives with the intention of keeping them in their own communities for labor or other purposes. Caddoan peoples maintained three affiliated confederacies spread thickly over hundreds of square miles in present-day Louisiana, Texas, Arkansas, and Oklahoma. The multiple communities in those confederacies rested economically on steadily intensifying agricultural production and a far-reaching commercial exchange system, involving trade in hides, salt, turquoise, copper, marine shells, bows, and pottery with New Mexico, the Gulf Coast, and the Great Lakes. By the end of the seventeenth century, Wichita-speaking peoples had moved into the lower southern Plains to establish fifteen to twenty consolidated, often palisaded, villages scattered across the northern regions of present-day Texas, most in fertile lands along rivers where they could successfully farm without jeopardizing their defensive capabilities. The trade connections Wichitas then developed over the first half of the eighteenth century with Frenchmen and Caddos to the east and newly allied Comanches to the west secured a steady supply of guns and horses as well as critical alliances needed to defend their populous and productive communities against Osage and Apache raids. Like Wichitas, Comanches had moved onto the southern Plains by the early eighteenth century, operating as independent, bison-hunting groups loosely tied to one another in defensive and economic alliances. By midcentury Comanche, Wichita, and Caddo bands had formed mutually beneficial trade relationships that brought European material goods, Plains hides, and Spanish horses together for exchange. All three also shared common enemies—multiple bands of Apaches living in mobile encampments across central Texas and western New Mexico—and all three took increasing numbers of Apache captives for trade in Louisiana.

The economic visions of Frenchmen in Louisiana dovetailed with those of native groups, as the French extended their involvement in the native trade networks that crisscrossed the southern Plains and lower Mississippi Valley. Though plantation agriculture increasingly garnered the attention of Frenchmen in south and central Louisiana, the Indian hide trade remained an important component of the province's economy to the end of the eighteenth century. Thus, a satellite system of trading posts gradually began to line the western and northern reaches of the French province with a mandate to establish and maintain the economic and diplomatic relations that underwrote that trade. The Frenchmen of the outlying posts did not have the numbers or force to subjugate Indians or dispossess them of their lands, nor did they wish to. Rather, they sought to establish profitable exchange, and as a result, they entered into egalitarian relations with dominant Caddo, Wichita, and, by extension, Comanche peoples. Frenchmen offered European trade goods that the Spaniards in Texas would not, thus stealing a march on their rivals to the west. French demographic and settlement patterns further contributed to their success as traders. In the Louisiana hinterlands, French social and familial intermixing with Indians was widespread, as the French built their trading and military posts in or near native villages and consequently joined with Indians not only for trade but also for subsistence, family building, and daily life. Community ties, in turn, brought Frenchmen into the heart of Indian political economies and offered foundations for long-lasting alliances.

As such ties developed, bands of Caddos, Wichitas, and Comanches found female Indian captives to be as valuable as hides and horses in French markets in Natchitoches and other western Louisiana posts. In exchange, French trade offered native groups guns and ammunition essential not only for hunting but also for defense in the context of increasing competition and militarization among the region's native peoples. To its Indian participants, the developing slave trade represented two sides of native conventions of reciprocity. Caddos, Comanches, and Wichitas obtained their trade goods from a range of sources: the hides from hunting, the horses from raids on Spanish settlements in Texas, and the captives from warfare with native enemies (primarily Apaches). One aspect of native conventions dictated that the three groups took captives only from those they designated enemies or "strangers" to systems of kinship and political alliance—thus they took captives only in the context of war. On the flip side, once captive women became desirable commodities in Louisiana, they also served as tools Comanche, Wichita, and Caddo men could use to build trade relations with Frenchmen. In the eighteenth century, therefore, the French markets gave new value to an old by-product of warfare.

The trade in women following their capture resulted in more than individual benefit or profit, however. Like diplomatic exchanges, the Indian slave trade brought together men of French and Indian nations in an exchange that served both utilitarian and prestige purposes. Reciprocal relations both required and created kinship affiliation. Participation in exchanges made groups less likely to engage in confrontation and violence and brought them into metaphorical, if not real, relations of kinship. Caddo, Comanche, and Wichita men cast trade alliances in terms of fictive kinship categories of "brotherhood" and male sodalities. The women who were the objects of the exchange did not create or constitute the tie of personal or economic obligation. The exchange process itself created relationships, binding men to each other in the act of giving and receiving. Practices of intermarriage, adoption, and symbolic kinship relations among different Indian peoples and among Europeans and Indians meant that "kinship" expanded to include relations beyond those of only familial (biological) descent.

Economic ties could not be separated from political ones, and trading partners were also military and political allies. Quite simply, one did not fight with brothers, just as one did not trade with enemies.

Though the relations formed by the trade were between men, the female sex of the majority of enslaved Indians determined the supply, the demand, and thus the very existence of the trade network. Women were what Frenchmen wanted, and women were what Indian warriors had for exchange. Caddo, Comanche, and Wichita men traded only captive Indian women and children to Frenchmen (captive men were tortured and killed). In turn, the French market for female captives was not merely a response to the availability of such commodities in native societies but represented the needs of soldiers and traders in such French frontier settlements as Natchitoches. Unlike settlers in the British colonies and New France (Canada), those in French Louisiana made little systematic attempt to exploit enslaved Indians as a labor force. The minimal use of Indian slaves in the establishment of French plantation agriculture and the French preference for enslaved African Americans as a servile labor force indicated that the continuing *Indian* slave trade held importance primarily for male domestic demands in the hinterlands of French settlement.

French settlers and traders by and large came from Canada rather than France and brought with them a social and cultural heritage of intimate association with Indian peoples. Intimate unions with women of allied nations and later with female slaves acquired for sexual exploitation were thus not new to the Frenchmen who emigrated to Louisiana. Because single male traders and agents, who often lived among their native trading partners, originally predominated in the French occupation of Louisiana, Frenchmen needed to intermarry if they were to have wives and families. Abbé Guillaume-Thomas-François de Raynal, writing in the 1770s and looking back over the century, argued that the French had brought to Louisiana "the custom of living with the savages, which they had adopted in Canada" and which often involved marrying Indian women with the "happiest results." "There was never observed the least coolness in the friendship between these two so diverse nations whom matrimony had united," Raynal continued, because "they have lived in this intercourse and reciprocity of mutual good-will, which made up for the vicissitudes of events brought by the passage of time."

In this spirit, Frenchmen at posts such as Fort St. Jean Baptiste aux Natchitoches formed marital unions with their Caddo trading partners and sexual unions with the captive Apache women who were the objects of French-Caddo trade. Sexual and marital relations solidified French relationships with Caddoan peoples as demonstrable acts of permanence and commitment. The slave trade played a crucial role in supplementing the female population at Natchitoches throughout the eighteenth century. French colonial officials linked the Indian slave trade directly with a "licentious" mode of living that they considered a challenge to the colonization and development of Louisiana. Despite such concerns at the imperial and provincial levels of church and state, however, the number of Apache women among enslaved populations and in Louisiana households steadily increased as trade networks in hides, horses, and captives grew between the French and Caddos and, through Caddos, extended to Wichitas and Comanches.

On the other side of the Texas-Louisiana border, Indian enslavement exerted quite a different influence on the early invasion and settlement of the Spanish province of Texas. The advance of the Spanish frontier northward over the sixteenth and seventeenth centuries into the regions claimed as the provinces of Nueva Vizcaya, Coahuila, and Nuevo León (south of what became the province of Texas) had brought with it the spread of European diseases and the intrusion of slave-raiding expeditions seeking forced labor for Spanish mines and ranches—inexorable forces that preceded much of the colonization of those regions. Epidemics that began in the 1550s had, by the 1700s, scythed 90 percent of the native population of those northern regions of Mexico. Under law, moreover, the Crown might assign to Spaniards the labor and tribute of a specific Indian community in an arrangement termed an *encomienda*. Consequent Spanish demands for labor on farms and ranches and in mines brought their own brand of annihilation. By 1600 trafficking in enslaved Indians had become an established way of life in Nuevo León. Once the Spaniards there had killed off all the nearby Indian peoples by congregating them in crowded, unsanitary work camps where disease or overwork devastated their numbers, they extended the relentless reach of their slave raids ever northward. A 1672 royal cedula reiterated the royal prohibitions against the enslavement of Indians first expressed in the New Laws in 1542—reconfirmed in the 1680 Recompilation of the Laws of the Indies—and required their Christian conversion instead. But Spaniards in the region merely renamed their *encomiendas*, calling them *congregaciones* (Indian communities nominally congregated for acculturation and religious instruction) and continued their raids into the mid-eighteenth century in search of Indian bodies for labor, not souls for salvation.

Just as Indian groups had done when they encountered the early French traders on the Plains, Indians in Texas quickly learned what would be of value to the Spaniards whose expeditions had targeted the region even before permanent Spanish settlement was attempted in the 1690s. For some time rumors and evidence had been reaching them that the Europeans from Mexico and New Mexico were both buyers and actual enslavers of Indians.

Others sought their own advantage in Spanish labor systems and thereby pulled native peoples from the southern Plains into an increasingly commercialized exchange system to the west in New Mexico. Many eastern Apache groups, who had been victims of Spanish slave raiding in New Mexico, began to bring their own captives to New Mexican markets. As early as the 1650s, the Franciscan missionary Alonso de Posada reported that in addition to hides and chamois skins, some Apaches now sought "to sell for horses some Indian men and women, girls and boys" taken from Wichita bands from the lands of Francisco Vásquez de Coronado's fabled Quivira (the southern Plains). Such Wichita women and children became members of a population of detribalized and enslaved Indians known as *genízaros* that grew to be a significant element in the New Mexico settlements. *Genízaros* aided the expansion and defense of New Mexico's borders as members of slave militias and frontier communities.

To the east, as Spaniards sought a toehold in Texas in the 1710s, they focused on building a cordon of mission-presidio complexes as bulwark to protect the silver mines of New Spain's northern provinces against French aggressors. Throughout the eighteenth century, however, the Spanish government faced serious problems attracting settlers, soldiers, and native converts to populate colonial centers so far north. The Spanish population of the Texas province at its height in 1790 was only 3,169. Spanish colonial development also remained rigidly hemmed in by far more populous and powerful Indian nations—both indigenous to the region (such as Caddos) and newly arrived (such as Lipan Apaches and later Comanches and Wichitas). Spaniards thus found that even in the limited areas claimed by Spanish settlement, their imperial policies regarding Indians involved, not imposing rule on others, but defending themselves against superior native rivals.

Of the four native powers, Lipan Apaches were the first to challenge the Spanish presence in Texas; as a result Spanish-Indian relations there took a different path than did the relations enjoyed by the French to the east, and the path led to a different form of bondage—one defined by punitive war. Though now less well-known than their western relatives, Lipan Apaches represented a widespread and formidable power throughout the eighteenth century. Eastern Apaches living in what is now Texas had gained an early advantage among Indians there with horses acquired in the seventeenth century through trading and raiding in New Mexico. By the 1740s, "Lipan" had become the designation used by Spaniards to refer to the easternmost Plains Apache groups. Their economy centered on hunting and raiding for bison and horses, which did not allow permanent settlement, though they did practice semicultivation. Social units farmed and hunted in rancherías (a Spanish term for Indian encampments) that might cluster together for defense and ceremonial ritual. No central leadership existed, and group leaders made decisions in consultation with extended-family headmen, but unity of language, dress, and customs maintained collective identity and internal peace.

Apache economies came under attack in the early eighteenth century, however, as Comanches and Wichitas migrated south to challenge Apache bands for the rich bison territories of northern and north-central Texas. Hostilities quickly erupted that pitted Apaches against Comanches and Wichitas as well as Spaniards, and the treble embattlement gradually weakened Apaches' defenses, making them increasingly vulnerable to all three opponents. Apache women and children thus became the focus not only of raids by Comanche and Wichita warriors seeking captives for French markets in Louisiana but also of Spanish military campaigns seeking prisoners whom Spaniards could use to coerce or punish their Apache foes. Throughout the 1720s, 1730s, and 1740s, Lipan Apaches mounted raids on the horse herds of San Antonio de Béxar missions, civilian ranches, and presidio to sustain a supply of horses crucial to the mobility and defense of their family bands amid mounting conflicts. In turn, Spanish fear and frustration escalated when presidial forces proved unable to stop the warriors' attacks and led to desperate bids by Spaniards to stem the raids. Spanish officials, making war to achieve peace, ordered Apache women and children to be taken captive to force diplomacy, arguing that the best way to manipulate native groups was through their captive kinsmen or, more accurately, kinswomen. Sometimes Spaniards went so far as to single out as political hostages the wives, daughters, sisters, and mothers of leading chiefs and warriors.

Spanish captive policy devastated many Lipan Apache bands by preying on their women and children. Indian captive taking involved small numbers of individuals; Spaniards introduced captive taking on a scale unimaginable to most Indian nations. To use captives for political coercion may have seemed a logical tactic to Spanish officials, who could refer to long traditions of prisoner and hostage exchange in European warfare. Yet, when Spanish forces attacked Apache rancherías, took captives, and then tried to force peace with the bands they had attacked, they sought to forge alliance through an act of hostility. Moreover, even by Spanish terms of hostage exchange, their captive policy was fundamentally unequal because it never represented an exchange of Indian women for Spanish women. Unlike the Comanche warriors in New Mexico who took Spanish women and children as well as horses as the booty of their raids, Apache men in Texas focused their raiding on horse herds.

Not surprisingly, Spanish actions brought only more hostilities with Apaches. For the Apache women and children held prisoner in San Antonio de Béxar, the situation worsened. As captivities lengthened from months into years, officials distributed the Apache women and children as "servants" among soldiers and civilians in Texas and other provinces to the south. Spaniards, who had long found ways around the Crown's legal prohibitions against the enslavement of Indians, now rationalized their decision to keep such women and children in bondage by claiming the necessities of defense. By sleight of interpretation, they deemed the only *cautivos* in New Spain's northern provinces to be Spaniards captured by Indians—Apache women and children captured by Spanish forces were *prisioneros* (prisoners of war). Critics, however, clearly saw that officials and civilians alike sought profit rather than peace through such enslavement.

Some of the Apache women distributed by Spanish authorities may have remained as slaves in Spanish communities and households, but unlike Indian women in French trading posts, they were not often involved in intimate unions with their captors. Although, like the French in Louisiana, Spaniards needed to increase their settler population, there is no indication that they intermarried with either the native peoples they sought as allies or the native captives whom they manipulated in the service of peace. Intermarriage with Indians was not uncommon in Spanish America, but by the eighteenth century it was no longer used as a means of diplomacy and alliance with *independent* Indian nations. Rather, Spanish-Indian sexual relations and intermarriage took place only within Spanish society, involving Indian individuals who had been incorporated into that society as subjects of the Spanish church and state.

Having proclaimed defensive needs as their *carte blanche* for wartime enslavements, [Spanish] militia groups made up of soldiers and civilians devastated Apache family bands, causing repeated loss of kinswomen and children, and nearly brought on their own destruction at the hands of infuriated Apache leaders and warriors until a peace treaty in 1749 ended hostilities for twenty years. During those twenty years, Apache leaders would strive without success to regain family members lost in the 1730s and 1740s. By the 1760s, intensifying Comanche and Wichita pressures on both Apaches and Spaniards brought their brief experiment with peace to an end. By then, Spanish officials had decided to ditch Apaches as allies, preferring their more powerful Comanche and Wichita enemies.

It is at this point, in the late 1760s, that our two stories (and the two slave networks) come together. French trade relations with powerful Caddo, Wichita, and Comanche bands—relations underwritten by the traffic in women—had been all too clear to watchful Spanish eyes since the beginning of the century. For as long as French traders had been operating in the region, Spanish missionaries and military officials in Texas had been trying to effect alliances of their own in the hope of offsetting the influence of their French rivals. Throughout the first half of the century, however, such efforts had met with abject failure even as the Spaniards watched Indian-French ties steadily strengthen. Reports filtered in from all across the Plains and New Mexico detailing how Frenchmen had expanded their native alliances and their slave trade. Imperial Spanish officials feared that growing trade relations signaled military alliance and the potential for a united French-Indian attack on Spanish territories. Such laments remained focal points of Spanish rhetoric as they watched first Caddos, then Comanches and Wichitas, build economic ties to the French colony. The ever-increasing military power of Comanche and Wichita nations soon became far more daunting than that of the French, however. The armaments acquired through French trade had equipped Comanche and Wichita bands better for the raids that from the 1740s on plundered Spanish horse herds in civil and mission settlements in both Texas and New Mexico. By 1758 officials in Mexico City feared Comanche *invasion* of the Spanish provinces south of the Rio Grande.

Yet without the finances to offer competitive trade of their own or the military power to stop French-Indian alliances by force, Spaniards in Texas found they could do little to offset French advantage. It was not until the 1760s that the cession of Louisiana from French to Spanish rule following the Seven Years' War opened up new possibilities for Spanish officials. Spanish law officially prohibited the enslavement and sale of Indians, and Alejandro O'Reilly, then serving as governor of Louisiana, extended that prohibition to the province with the formal assumption of Spanish power in 1769. Spanish officials saw an opportunity to cut off the trade that put guns into the hands of native groups deemed "hostile" to the Spanish government. Local imperatives ensured the enforcement of the ban in the Red River valley along the Texas-Louisiana border, particularly among Wichitas and Comanches. Spanish officials finally had the means to sever the commercial ties that had allied native bands in Texas and the southern Plains with Frenchmen. Thus in response to O'Reilly's edict, officials in Natchitoches forbade the trade in horses, mules, and slaves from those Indian nations, and they recalled from their subposts or homes among "hostile" Indians all licensed traders, hunters, and illicit "vagabonds"—many of whom the Natchitoches commander Athanase de Mézières described in 1770 as men "who pass their scandalous lives in public concubinage with the captive Indian women whom for this purpose they purchase among the heathen, loaning those of whom they tire to others of less power, that they may labor in their service, giving them no other wage than the promise of quieting their lascivious passion."

Once at Natchitoches, the traders and hunters had to answer questions about their native trade relationships and to register their Indian slaves. In fear of losing their slaves, some Frenchmen sought to secure the women by whatever means possible. Though government officials recognized provisional ownership pending a royal decision on the status of enslaved Indians in the province, some men clearly chose not to let their fate rest on the vagaries of a royal decree. Many married their slaves or promised freedom if the women swore to remain with them as servants or consorts. Intimate relations thereby became a means of prolonging women's servitude.

Meanwhile, reports from Natchitoches indicate that despite the new trade prohibitions on the books, the slave traffic along the Texas-Louisiana border kept up a steady, if illicit, flow of women from west to east on the ground. As late as the 1780s, peltries (primarily deerskins) still made up a significant portion of Louisiana's exports, indicating the continued importance of Indian trade and the extensive network of trading posts that supported European-Indian exchange. Marriage and baptism records in Natchitoches were testament to the continued role of enslaved Apache women as consorts, wives, and mothers through the end of the eighteenth century. Maria Modesta, the "natural" daughter of Marie Magdalena, an Apache slave of Jean Louis le Court, grew up to marry Jean Laurent Bodin and have a son, while Therese Lecompte, the natural daughter of an enslaved Apache woman also named Therese, married Louis Metoyer, a free man of color. Another Apache woman named Marie Rosalie married Louis Guillori, an Opelousa Indian. The unions of the two Louises indicate that French traders were not the only men in the market for Indian wives. Unlike the black population in urban New Orleans, the black residents of Natchitoches, both slave and free, were predominantly male, leaving them with fewer potential consorts among enslaved or free women—a demographic factor that may have encouraged their intermarriage with Indian women. Official censuses only hinted at the numbers, and sacramental records—listing almost two hundred enslaved Indian women and children in the Natchitoches area over the century—also offer only a partial accounting. Nevertheless, by 1803 almost one-quarter of the native-born European population in northwest Louisiana counted Indian slaves in their ancestry, and 60 percent of that number claimed descent directly from an enslaved Indian parent or grandparent.

Most enslaved women appear in records only as the subjects of baptism at their French owners' behest or as mothers of natural children whose fathers usually, but not always, went unnamed in sacramental registers. Thus the lives of most enslaved Indian women rested on the whims of their owners, and a woman might find her world turned suddenly upside down if she were used to pay medical bills, exchanged for horses, seized for debt, or enumerated in a will. The experiences of these women began in war, when they were torn from their communities by brutal force, and culminated in their sale into sexual and labor relations defined by coercion.

The position of power enjoyed by Comanches and Wichitas stood in stark contrast to that of Apaches, as the Comanche and Wichita women who fell prey

to Spanish bondage were few and Comanche and Wichita men more easily re-
gained those who did.

Spanish officials increasingly chose to negotiate truce and alliance with
Comanche and Wichita warriors by ransoming from them any enemy captives
they took in war. In the process, Spaniards also attained for themselves, by commercial rather than violent means, captive Indian women to use in diplomatic
relations with the women's families and peoples. Most commonly, they purchased Apache captives from Comanche and Wichita men. Native captive raiding may have risen in response to Spanish attempts to broker deals with victims'
family members. Fray Juan Domingo Arricivita asserted that while Apaches
might take captives in war to sell to other nations, they equally took them "to
exchange them for some of their relatives who have been made prisoners."
Spanish diplomatic traffic in women was not limited to transactions with
Comanches and Wichitas. For instance, when eighty Apache warriors led by
seven chiefs captured a woman, one girl, and two boys in a revenge raid on a
Tonkawa ranchería in 1779, Texas governor Domingo Cabello offered eight
horses for the captives. He claimed to want the children because they "could
become Christians by virtue of their youth," but his desire for the woman was
purely political, since she could be restored to a Tonkawa band as "proof of
friendship." Interestingly, the Apache men refused to give him any of the captives, not because eight horses was an unfair price, but because they saw little
political gain to be had from the Spanish governor at that time. Further proof
of the Apache men's careful assessment of where their interests lay came when
chief El Joyoso chose instead to give one of the children, a ten-year-old Mayeye
girl, to his "good friend Don Luis Menchaca," a Spanish merchant in San
Antonio who had long traded with Apache peoples and shown them good
faith (sometimes against the wishes of the provincial government).

Caddos and Wichitas also found remuneration by ransoming Spanish
women whom they had acquired from Comanches who had captured them in
New Mexico. The payment received by Taovayas (Wichitas) from the trader
José Guillermo Esperanza for a New Mexican woman, Ana María Baca, and her
six-year-old son spoke to the possible profits. For Ana María Baca, Taovayas
received: "three muskets, three netted cloths, two blankets, four axes, three
hoes, two *castetes* with pipe, one pound of vermilion, two pounds of beads, ten
knives, twenty-five gunflints, eight steels for striking flints, six ramrods, six awls,
four fathoms of wool sash, and three hundred bullets with necessary powder."
For Baca's son, Esperanza gave Taovayas: "one otter hide, one hundred bullets
with necessary powder, one ax, three *castetes* with pipe, one and one-half quarter
pounds of vermilion, one netted cloth, one blanket, and one musket." Notably,
in this exchange Taovayas were not the only ones who planned to profit from
Ana María Baca's captivity. The Nacogdoches lieutenant Christóbel Hilario de
Córdoba, to whom Esperanza had related his purchase, reported with outrage
that Esperanza went on to say that he planned to take the woman and sell her
in Natchitoches "where there could not but be plenty of Frenchmen to purchase
her and bother her, as is their custom, since she still is attractive." Córdoba forestalled the woman's sale into concubinage by taking her and her son into

protective custody. Córdoba's intervention (which Spanish officials vehemently supported) made clear how aberrant it was that Ana María Baca's Spanish identity had not excluded her from the category of women whom Esperanza felt he might acceptably sell into the sex trade.

Although Spanish officials spent much time bemoaning the loss of Spanish women to Indian captivity, the charge remained rhetorical in eighteenth-century Texas. Spanish captives were few in number, and the new Spanish-Indian traffic in "redeemed" captives remained primarily one of Indian women. The rhetoric about Spanish female captives in Indian hands was meant to appeal to government superiors in Mexico and thereby to gain more military men and supplies with which to defend the province against indomitable Comanche and Wichita forces, but that tactic often failed. In response to complaints from the commandant of the Interior Provinces that Texas officials had failed to contribute to the alms that Spanish law demanded all settlements in the provinces collect for the ransoming of Christian captives held by Indians, Cabello explained that no captives from Texas had been taken, thus little local imperative to give to such a fund existed in Texas. In Texas, then, fictitious Spanish women were objects of persuasion and real Indian women were the objects of exchange—whether in French trade markets or in Spanish diplomatic negotiations.

The gradual stabilization of relations among Spaniards, Comanches, and Wichitas in the waning years of the century meant only ill for Apaches, as the maintenance of the three groups' peace agreements often involved the enslavement of Apaches still deemed enemies by them all. Whether captured by Spanish presidial forces or ransomed to them by Comanche or Wichita warriors in diplomatic exchange, Apache women and children continued to fall victim to punitive Spanish policies that sent younger children to missions for conversion and all other to labor camps or prisons in Mexico City and, beginning in the 1780s, in the Caribbean. Many died in transit to Mexico. Most never saw their homes again. Despite the impossibility of return, back home their husbands and fathers received promises of the women's return if they agreed to treaty negotiations. Thus when, in one instance, Apache men arrived at a meeting site and did not find their wives among the women brought for exchange, officials responded by offering them their pick of other women captured elsewhere. For those Spanish officers, Apache women had become so commodified that they were interchangeable. Spanish records rarely detail the suffering of women themselves, but a handful of incidents give mute testimony to it, none more powerfully than the stories of women who tried to take their own lives rather than remain captive. The Comanche woman who tried to kill herself upon recapture after she escaped from the San Antonio mission in 1772 was not alone in preferring death to enslavement. Jean Louis Berlandier recorded that another Comanche woman captured early in the nineteenth century "asked for a knife to remove a thorn she said was hurting her foot, but when they gave it to her she plunged it into her heart." The fate of these captive and enslaved Indian women signified irremediable moments of Spanish-Indian interchange in eighteenth-century Texas. Theirs is the story that remains to be written.

Beyond telling of warfare and its spoils, the stories of enslaved Apache women and children document the ways European and Indian men used them as social and political capital in efforts to coerce and accommodate one another. Looking at how bands and empires or traders and diplomats transformed women into currency allows one to see multiple sources and forms of bondage: from pre-Columbian indigenous warfare that created captivity as an alternative to battlefield deaths, to captive raiding and commercial trade that created human commodities, to hostage taking and deportation that created prison labor. Pressed into service, women became objects for sex, familial reproduction, and reciprocal trade relations; gifts that made peaceful coexistence possible for their captors; or victims who paid the price for their captors' hostility. This diversity of slaveries unfolded from the confrontations and collusions of European and native political systems that structured economic behavior, battlefield enmity, and diplomatic maneuvering. Putting standardized categories of slavery and unfreedom to the test in complicated borderlands where two imperial powers sought to negotiate multiple configurations of Indian social and political organization shows how wanting those categories can be. Slavery in North America has been cast as a monolithic, chattel-oriented system of coerced labor, thus making it a distinctive and anomalous model when compared to forms of bondage instituted in other times and places. Meanwhile the forms of captivity and exchanges of women involved in European-Indian relations in the Americas have fallen into categories often perceived to be more benign. If bondage could prove such an infinitely variable institution in just one region of colonial North America, imagine what we may find as we piece together experiences across the entire continent.

Explicating such diversity will bring American practices of slavery into better global perspective and more fruitful comparison with colonial geopolitics and cultural geographies around the world.

FURTHER READING

Adler, Michael A., and Herbert W. Dick, eds. *Picuris Pueblo through Time: Eight Centuries of Change at a Northern Rio Grande Pueblo* (1999).

Albers, Patricia C. "Symbiosis, Merger, and War: Contrasting Forms of Intertribal Relationship among Historical Plains Indians." In *Political Economy of North American Indians*, ed. John H. Moore, pp. 93–132 (1993).

Anderson, Gary Clayton. *The Indian Southwest, 1580–1830: Ethnogenesis and Reinvention* (1999).

Bailey, L. R. *Indian Slave Trade in the Southwest: A Study of Slavetaking and the Traffic of Indian Captives* (1966).

Bannon, John Francis. *The Spanish Borderlands Frontier, 1513–1821* (1970).

Barr, Juliana. *Peace Came in the Form of a Woman: Indians and Spaniards in the Texas Borderlands* (2007).

Blackhawk, Ned. *Violence over the Land: Indians and Empires in the Early American West* (2006).

Brooks, James F., ed. *Confounding the Color Line: The Indian-Black Experience in North America* (2002).

———. *Captives and Cousins: Slavery, Kinship, and Community in the Southwest Borderlands* (2002).

Burton, Sophie H., and F. Todd Smith. *Colonial Natchitoches: A Creole Community on the Louisiana-Texas Frontier* (2008).

Carter, William B. *Indian Alliances and the Spanish in the Southwest, 750–1750* (2009).

Chipman, Donald E., and Harriett Denise Joseph. *Spanish Texas, 1519–1821* (2010).

Forbes, Jack D. *Apache, Navajo, and Spaniard* (1960; reprint, 1994).

———. *Black Africans and Native Americans: Color, Race, and Caste in the Evolution of Red-Black Peoples* (1988).

Gutiérrez, Ramón A. *When Jesus Came, the Corn Mothers Went Away: Marriage, Sexuality, and Power in New Mexico, 1500–1846* (1991).

Hall, Thomas D. *Social Change in the Southwest, 1350–1880* (1989).

Hickerson, Nancy P. *The Jumanos: Hunters and Traders of the South Plains* (1994).

John, Elizabeth A. H. *Storms Brewed in Other Men's Worlds: The Confrontation of Indians, Spanish, and French in the Southwest, 1640–1795* (1975).

Jones, Oakah L. Jr. *Los Paisanos: Spanish Settlers on the Northern Frontier of New Spain* (1979).

Kenner, Charles L. *The Comanchero Frontier: A History of New Mexican-Plains Indian Relations* (1969; reprint, 1994).

Kessell, John L. *Kiva, Cross, and Crown: The Pecos Indians and New Mexico, 1540–1840* (1979).

———. *Spain in the Southwest: A Narrative History of Colonial New Mexico, Arizona, Texas, and California* (2002).

Knaut, Andrew L. *The Pueblo Revolt of 1680: Conquest and Resistance in Seventeenth-Century New Mexico* (1995).

Mapp, Paul W. *The Elusive West and the Contest for Empire, 1713–1763* (2011).

Officer, James E. *Hispanic Arizona, 1536–1856* (1988).

Reff, Daniel T. "The 'Predicament of Culture' and Spanish Missionary Accounts of the Tepehuan and Pueblo Revolts." *Ethnohistory* 42 (Winter 1995): 63–90.

———. *The Kachina and the Cross: Indians and Spaniards in the Early Southwest* (1999).

Riley, Carroll L. *Rio del Norte: People of the Upper Rio Grande from Earliest Times to the Pueblo Revolt* (1995).

Simmons, Marc. *Spanish Pathways: Readings in the History of Hispanic New Mexico* (2001).

Snyder, Christina. *Slavery in Indian Country: The Changing Face of Captivity in Early America* (2010).

Weber, David J. *The Spanish Frontier in North America* (1992).

———, ed. *What Caused the Pueblo Revolt of 1680?* (1999).

CHAPTER 3

Middle Grounds, Borderlands, and Frontiers

The early borderlands of North America were born of mutual weakness. European colonists lacked the numbers and the military strength to subdue neighboring native societies, and the Indians were either unable or unwilling to drive the newcomers away from their borders. Indians and Europeans also possessed things that the other needed—food, furs, technology, information, sexual partners, allies—and that were easier to obtain through persuasion than force. Such a blend of wants and weakness spawned a long history of mutual conciliation that saw European settlers and administrators becoming gradually drawn into native social and economic networks, even as Indians themselves adjusted their traditions to European expectations. Well into the eighteenth century, European colonial ventures in North America reflected grand metropolitan designs only to a degree. They were also, and perhaps primarily, locally driven negotiated systems with Native Americans who, in a sense, forced the Europeans to leave the relative safety of their colonial enclaves for the untested terrain of mutual accommodation.

The most notable of such realms of mutual accommodation existed in the seventeenth- and eighteenth-century Great Lakes region, where French colonists met and mingled with various indigenous societies. Here both the natives and the newcomers failed to impose their will by force and therefore had to accommodate one another in mutually beneficial ways. This "middle ground" of coexistence and compromise, as historian Richard White has called the new intercultural arrangements, rested on practices and rhetoric that were neither entirely Indian nor entirely European, but a fusion of both. The middle ground was a world where conciliation achieved more than coercion and where diverse peoples tried to reach their goals not by clinging to their own principles but by appealing to what they thought to be the cultural premises of others. Indians and French frequently, and often deliberately, misunderstood one another, yet that did not thwart conciliation between them because out of their misunderstandings arose new meanings and practices—the meanings and practices of the middle ground. Listening to one another, misunderstanding one another, appealing to one another, and eventually reinventing one another, the French and the Indians forged a vast array of mutual accommodations—economic, political, diplomatic, legal, sexual—that became the bedrock of their long coexistence.

The Great Lakes middle ground was a creation of local actors—traders, chiefs, petty colonial officials, missionaries, and native women—who found their traditional practices inadequate for navigating the new and confusing intercultural world. But the middle ground was also a product of large historical forces and of a specific geopolitical context. In the Great Lakes region, both the French and the Indians felt threatened by the more powerful English and Iroquois in the East, a position of vulnerability that not only drew them to seek protection in an alliance but also pushed them to make the necessary cultural compromises that underwrote the alliance. The Great Lakes middle ground, then, emerged not only from mutual weakness, from an inability of the French and Indians to dictate to one another. It also grew out of a shared sense of vulnerability that compelled both to overcome their deep reluctance to readjust their behaviors, compromise their standards, and alter their customs.

By revealing the layered texture and the often paradoxical nature of cross-cultural encounters, White's book galvanized the study of Indian-European relations and borderlands in North America. It has also engaged historians in a prolonged debate: Was the middle ground a unique historical phenomenon specific to the Great Lakes region, or is it possible to identify other middle grounds elsewhere in the Americas? This chapter focuses on two broad North American contact zones that bore both similarities to and differences from the Great Lakes middle ground: seventeenth- and eighteenth-century eastern North America, where westward-moving English colonists brushed against the many native societies in the interior, and eighteenth-century Louisiana, where French newcomers faced numerous native societies on both sides of the lower Mississippi Valley. The two areas lend themselves to several comparisons, both with one another and with the Great Lakes region. The English colonies and French Louisiana both sought mediation with the native peoples on their borders, but their efforts did not result in anything like the Great Lakes middle ground. Why the difference? Why did the French-Indian middle ground not extend from the Great Lakes region down to the lower Mississippi Valley into French Louisiana? And why did the English settlers push their border with Indian country gradually westward during the seventeenth and eighteenth centuries, while the French settlement remained anchored in the shores of the Great Lakes and the St. Lawrence and Mississippi rivers? Why, in other words, did the English engender an aggressively expanding settlement frontier, whereas the French did not? Demography leaps to mind—English colonists far outnumbered French colonists in North America—but did other factors play a role?

∿ DOCUMENTS

The first three documents illustrate how Indians and Europeans struggled to understand one another in the early stages of colonization. Jamestown, the first permanent English colony in North America, was founded in 1607 in the Chesapeake Bay, a region dominated by the powerful Powhatan Indian Confederacy, which was held together by marital and kinship ties that centered around Chief Powhatan. The first document is a description of the Powhatans, written by John Smith, Jamestown's principal liaison with the Powhatans, and published in 1624. (Smith also wrote an account claiming that he had been captured by the Powhatans and then rescued by Pocahontas, the daughter of Powhatan, the paramount chief of the confederacy. That event, if it actually took place, was probably a ritualized adoption ceremony intended to turn Smith into a subordinate chieftain under the Powhatans.) The second document is a speech Chief Powhatan reportedly delivered to Smith in 1609, when Powhatan-English relations had collapsed to violence. The speech is open to interpretation. Was the chief trying to forge a zone of coexistence based on peace and trade, was he submitting himself to the English, or was he trying to incorporate them as fictive, adopted kin?

The third document presents the instructions of Father Jean de Brébeuf, written in 1637, for Jesuit missionaries among the Huron Indians. Brébeuf's focus on the external dimensions of behavior may appear superficial, but it does not mean that his manual for cross-cultural communication was not effective. Early North American contact zones were highly ritualized places where small gestures, expressions, and utterances mattered a great deal. They mattered so much precisely because the relationships between Indians and Europeans—peoples separated by a vast cultural gap—were so fragile.

Early Indian-European borderlands were sites of cross-cultural negotiation and coexistence, but because they brought together people from vastly different cultures, clashes were inevitable. One of the most dramatic sources and expressions of conflict was captive raiding, which complicated native-newcomer relations across the Americas. Document 4 presents extracts from the autobiography of Mary Jemison, a white woman who was captured in 1757, at the age of fifteen, by a Shawnee-French raiding party on the Pennsylvania frontier. She was adopted by the Seneca Indians, renamed Dehgewanus (Dickewamis in the document), and married to a Delaware Indian man. Jemison lived out her days among the Senecas. In 1823, she told her story to James Seaver, who the next year published *The Life and Times of Mrs. Mary Jemison*, one of the most famous captive narratives. Jemison's autobiography reveals the shock of being incorporated into the Seneca society that, despite more than a century of sustained interactions between Iroquois and English, remained alien and terrifying. But Jemison's account also suggests how captive raiding could foster understanding between cultures and narrow the crevasse between them.

In the late seventeenth century, the southeastern corner of North America became a contested international borderland, where Indians, Spaniards, and English vied for power, formed alliances, and reluctantly adjusted to each other's presence. Spanish Franciscans had maintained a string of missions in Florida since the early seventeenth century, imposing their religious and civil institutions on native communities, but the establishment of a new English colony in South Carolina in 1670 opened a new, turbulent era in the region. South Carolina grew rapidly in numbers, sending colonists south and west, and the borderland between Florida and South Carolina became a site of fierce contestation. Slavery was at the heart of this rivalry. South Carolina became a center of a burgeoning Indian slave trade, which extended across the South, keeping some native groups on the English orbit, while alienating the victims of the traffic. In 1693, in an effort to undermine the plantation economy in the English colonies, Spanish King Carlos II decreed that fugitive slaves from Carolina be granted asylum and freedom in Florida if they converted to Catholicism. That policy was later extended to runaway slaves from Georgia, which was established in 1732. The next two documents illuminate these borderland ties and rivalries from different angles. Document 5 is a part of the act that the South Carolina legislature passed in 1700 concerning runaway slaves and their apprehension. Fearful that Indians and Africans might unite against them, Carolinians hoped to foment mutual hostility between the two groups. This act served that objective by encouraging Indians to serve as a police force for the colony, but it also helped enforce a sharp racial hierarchy among Europeans, Indians, and Africans. Document 6 is a letter of William Stephens, president of the colony of Georgia, written in 1742 when the War of Jenkins's Ear raged in the Florida-Georgia borderlands. Stephens assesses the prospects of African slavery in Georgia, complicated by the colony's proximity to Spanish Florida.

The last three documents focus on French-English-Indian relations in the Southeast borderlands. Since its founding, South Carolina engaged in active trade in Indian slaves with its native neighbors, extending its commercial influence as far west as the Mississippi Valley. The French responded by extending its own Indian alliance eastward from Louisiana, and the result was a protracted borderlands rivalry with fluid and shifting demarcations: The French and English competed for native loyalties, and the powerful Indian nations—the Chickasaws, Choctaws, Natchez, and others—played the two colonial rivals against one another. Document 7 is an excerpt from the journal of Pierre Le Moyne d'Iberville, who established French presence at the mouth of the Mississippi River in 1699. Threatened by South Carolina's growing influence among the southeastern Indians, especially the powerful Chickasaws, Iberville in 1702 invited the Chickasaws and Choctaws to a meeting where he hoped to forge a unified French-Indian front against English incursions. Mixing offers of gifts and mediation with threats, he goaded the Chickasaws to accept peace with the French and the Choctaws. Political stability in the Southeast borderlands remained elusive, and the continuing French-English-Indian rivalries put the thinly populated and internally heterogeneous Louisiana—approximately two-thirds of its nearly six thousand inhabitants were slaves—in a vulnerable position. The seriousness of the situation became evident in late 1729, when the Natchez Indians rose against the French. The Natchez approached other native nations and Louisiana's African slaves, inviting them to join the war. Document 8 is a letter by Etienne de Périer, the governor of Louisiana, to Jean-Frédéric Phélypeaux, Count of Maurepas, the secretary of state for the Navy, written a month after the outbreak of the war. It captures the fear that gripped French Louisiana and the governor's ambivalence over arming and using African slaves against the Indians. Document 9 is a letter by Périer to Philibert Ory, the controller general of finances in the French court, written eight months into the Natchez War, and it reveals the opportunism and daunting complexity of the borderlands diplomacy Périer had to employ to save his colony.

1. John Smith on the Powhatan Confederacy, 1624

ALthough the Country people [Powhatans] be very barbarous, yet have they amongst them such government, as that their Magistrates for good command-ing, and their people for due subjection, and obeying, excell many places that would be counted very civill. The forme of their Common-wealth is a Monarchiall government, one as Emperour ruleth over many Kings or Governours. Their chiefe ruler is called Powhatan, and taketh his name of his principall place of dwelling called Powhatan. But his proper name is Wahunsonacock. Some Countries he hath which have beene his ancestors, and came unto him by inheritance, as the Country called Powhatan, Arrohateck, Appamatuck, Pamaunkee, Youghtanund, and Mattapanient. All the rest of his Territories expressed in the Mappe, they report have beene his severall Conquests. In all his ancient inheritances, he hath houses built after their manner like arbours, some 30. some 40. yards long, and at every house provision for his entertainement according to the time. At Werowcomoco on the Northside of the river Pamaunkee, was his residence, when I was delivered him prisoner, some 14 myles from James Towne, where for the most part, he was resident, but at last he tooke so little pleasure in our neare neighbourhood, that he retired himselfe to Orapakes, in the desert betwixt Chickahamanta and Youghtanund. He is of personage a tall well proportioned man, with a sower looke, his head somwhat gray, his beard so thinne, that it seemeth none at all, his age neare sixtie; of a very able and hardy body to endure any labour. About his person ordinarily attendeth a guard of 40 or 50 of the tallest men his Countrey doth afford. Every night upon the foure quarters of his house are foure Sentinels, each from other a flight shoot, and at every halfe houre one from the Corps du guard doth hollow, shaking his lips with his finger betweene them; unto whom every Sentinell doth answer round from his stand: if any faile, they presently send forth an officer that beateth him extreamely.

A myle from Orapakes in a thicket of wood, he hath a house in which he keepeth his kinde of Treasure, as skinnes, copper, pearle, and beads, which he storeth up against the time of his death and buriall. Here also is his store of red paint for oyntment, bowes and arrowes, Targets and clubs. This house is fiftie or sixtie yards in length, frequented onely by Priests. At the foure corners of this house stand foure Images as Sentinels, one of a Dragon, another a Beare, the third like a Leopard, and the fourth like a giantlike man, all made evill favouredly, according to their best workemanship.

He hath as many women as he will, whereof when he lieth on his bed, one sitteth at his head, and another at his feet, but when he sitteth, one sitteth on his right hand and another on his left. As he is weary of his women, he bestoweth them on those that best deserve them at his hands. When he dineth or suppeth, one of his women before and after meat, bringeth him water in a wooden platter

John Smith, *The Generall Historie of Virginia, New-England and the Summer Isles: Together with the True Travels, Adventures and Observations, and A Sea Grammar* (New York: Macmillan, 1907), 1: 77–79.

to wash his hands. Another waiteth with a bunch of feathers to wipe them in stead of a Towell, and the feathers when he hath wiped are dryed againe. His kingdomes descend not to his sonnes nor children, but first to his brethren, whereof he hath 3. namely, Opitchapan, Opechancanough, and Catataugh, and after their decease to his sisters. First to the eldest sister, then to the rest, and after them to the heires male or female of the eldest sister, but never to the heires of the males.

He nor any of his people understand any letters, whereby to write or reade, onely the lawes whereby he ruleth is custome. Yet when he listeth his will is a law and must be obeyed: not onely as a King, but as halfe a God they esteeme him. His inferiour Kings whom they call Werowances, are tyed to rule by customes, and have power of life and death at their command in that nature. But this word Werowance, which we call and construe for a King, is a common word, whereby they call all commanders: for they have but few words in their language, and but few occasions to use any officers more then one commander, which commonly they call Werowance, or Caucorouse, which is Captaine. They all know their severall lands, and habitations, and limits, to fish, foule, or hunt in, but they hold all of their great Werrowance Powhatan, unto whom they pay tribute of skinnes, beads, copper, pearle, deere, turkies, wild beasts, and corne. What he commandeth they dare not disobey in the least thing. It is strange to see with what great feare and adoration, all these people doe obey this Powhatan. For at his feet they present whatsoever he commandeth, and at the least frowne of his brow, their greatest spirits will tremble with feare: and no marvell, for he is very terrible & tyrannous in punishing such as offend him.

2. Chief Powhatan Addresses John Smith, 1609

Captaine Smith you may understand, that I, having seene the death of all my people thrice, and not one living of those 3 generations, but my selfe, I knowe the difference of peace and warre, better then any in my Countrie. But now I am old, and ere long must die, my brethren, namely Opichapam, Opechanka-nough, and Kekataugh, my two sisters, and their two daughters, are distinctly each others successours, I wish their experiences no lesse then mine, and your love to them, no lesse then mine to you; but this brute from Nansamund that you are come to destroy my Countrie, so much affrighteth all my people, as they dare not visit you; what will it availe you, to take that perforce, you may quietly have with love, or to destroy them that provide you food? what can you get by war, when we can hide our provision and flie to the woodes, whereby you must famish by wronging us your friends; and whie are you thus jealous of our loves, seeing us unarmed, and both doe, and are willing still to feed you with that you

Philip L. Barbour, ed., *The Complete Works of Captain John Smith, 1580–1631* (Chapel Hill: University of North Carolina Press, 1986), 1: 247–248. Published for the Omohundro Institute of Early American History and Culture. Copyright © 1986 by the University of North Carolina Press. Used by permission of the publisher.

cannot get but by our labours? think you I am so simple not to knowe, it is better to eate good meate, lie well, and sleepe quietly with my women and children, laugh and be merrie with you, have copper, hatchets, or what I want, being your friend; then bee forced to flie from al, to lie cold in the woods, feed upon acorns, roots, and such trash, and be so hunted by you, that I can neither rest, eat, not sleepe; but my tired men must watch, and if a twig but breake, everie one crie there comes Captaine Smith, then must I flie I knowe not whether, and thus with miserable feare end my miserable life; leaving my pleasures to such youths as you, which through you rash unadvisednesse, may quickly as miserably ende, for want of that you never knowe how to find? Let this therefore assure you of our loves and everie yeare our friendly trade shall furnish you with corne, and now also if you would come in friendly manner to see us, and not thus with your gunnes and swords, as to invade your foes.

3. Father Jean de Brébeuf Instructs Jesuit Missionaries, 1637

The Fathers and Brethren whom God shall call to the Holy Mission of the Hurons ought to exercise careful foresight in regard to all the hardships, annoyances, and perils that must be encountered in making this journey, in order to be prepared betimes for all emergencies that may arise.

You must have sincere affection for the Savages,—looking upon them as ransomed by the blood of the son of God, and as our brethren, with whom we are to pass the rest of our lives.

To conciliate the Savages, you must be careful never to make them wait for you in embarking.

You must provide yourself with a tinder box or with a burning mirror, or with both, to furnish them fire in the daytime to light their pipes, and in the evening when they have to encamp; these little services win their hearts.

You should try to eat their sagamité or salmagundi in the way they prepare it, although it may be dirty, half-cooked, and very tasteless. As to the other numerous things which may be unpleasant, they must be endured for the love of God, without saying anything or appearing to notice them.

It is well at first to take everything they offer, although you may not be able to eat it all; for, when one becomes somewhat accustomed to it, there is not too much.

You must try and eat at daybreak unless you can take your meal with you in the canoe; for the day is very long, if you have to pass it without eating. The Barbarians eat only at Sunrise and Sunset, when they are on their journeys.

You must be prompt in embarking and disembarking; and tuck up your gowns so that they will not get wet, and so that you will not carry either water or sand into the canoe. To be properly dressed, you must have your feet and legs bare; while crossing the rapids, you can wear your shoes, and, in the long portages, even your leggings.

Reuben G. Thwaites, ed., *The Jesuit Relations and Allied Documents: Travels and Explorations of the Jesuit Missionaries in New France* (Cleveland: Burrows Brothers, 1896–1910), 12: 117, 119, 121, 123.

You must so conduct yourself as not to be at all troublesome to even one of these Barbarians.

It is not well to ask many questions, nor should you yield to your desire to learn the language and to make observations on the way; this may be carried too far. You must relieve those in your canoe of this annoyance, especially as you cannot profit much by it during the work. Silence is a good equipment at such a time.

You must bear with their imperfections without saying a word, yes, even without seeming to notice them. Even if it be necessary to criticise anything, it must be done modestly, and with words and signs which evince love and not aversion. In short, you must try to be, and to appear, always cheerful.

Each one should be provided with half a gross of awls, two or three dozen little knives called jambettes [pocket-knives], a hundred fishhooks, with some beads of plain and colored glass, with which to buy fish or other articles when the tribes meet each other, so as to feast the Savages; and it would be well to say to them in the beginning, "Here is something with which to buy fish." Each one will try, at the portages, to carry some little thing, according to his strength; however little one carries, it greatly pleases the Savages, if it be only a kettle.

You must not be ceremonious with the Savages, but accept the comforts they offer you, such as a good place in the cabin. The greatest conveniences are attended with very great inconvenience, and these ceremonies offend them.

Be careful not to annoy any one in the canoe with your hat; it would be better to take your nightcap. There is no impropriety among the Savages.

Do not undertake anything unless you desire to continue it; for example, do not begin to paddle unless you are inclined to continue paddling. Take from the start the place in the canoe that you wish to keep; do not lend them your garments, unless you are willing to surrender them during the whole journey. It is easier to refuse at first than to ask them back, to change, or to desist afterwards.

Finally, understand that the Savages will retain the same opinion of you in their own country that they will have formed on the way; and one who has passed for an irritable and troublesome person will have considerable difficulty afterwards in removing this opinion. You have to do not only with those of your own canoe, but also (if it must be so stated) with all those of the country; you meet some to-day and others to-morrow, who do not fail to inquire, from those who brought you, what sort of man you are. It is almost incredible, how they observe and remember even the slightest fault. When you meet Savages on the way, as you cannot yet greet them with kind words, at least show them a cheerful face, and thus prove that you endure gayly the fatigues of the voyage. You will thus have put to good use the hardships of the way, and have already advanced considerably in gaining the affection of the Savages.

This is a lesson which is easy enough to learn, but very difficult to put into practice; for, leaving a highly civilized community, you fall into the hands of barbarous people who care but little for your Philosophy or your Theology. All the fine qualities which might make you loved and respected in France are like pearls trampled under the feet of swine, or rather of mules, which utterly despise you when they see that you are not as good pack animals as they are. If you could go naked, and carry the load of a horse upon you back, as they do, then you would be wise according to their doctrine, and would be recognized as a great man, otherwise not. Jesus Christ is our true greatness; it is he alone and his cross that should be sought in running after these people, for, if you strive for anything else, you will find naught but bodily and spiritual affliction. But having found Jesus Christ in his cross, you have found the roses in the thorns, sweetness in bitterness, all in nothing.

4. Mary Jemison Looks Back on Her Capture by and Life Among Indians, 1824

The Indians by whom I was taken were a party of Shawanees, if I remember right, that lived, when at home, a long distance down the Ohio.

My former Indian masters, and the two squaws, were soon ready to leave the fort, and accordingly embarked; the Indians in a large canoe, and the two squaws and myself in a small one, and went down the Ohio.

On our way we passed a Shawanee town, where I saw a number of heads, arms, legs, and other fragments of the bodies of some white people who had just been burnt. The parts that remained were hanging on a pole which was supported at each end by a crotch stuck in the ground, and were roasted or burnt black as a coal.

At night we arrived at a small Seneca Indian town, at the mouth of a small river, that was called by the Indians, in the Seneca language, She-nan-jee, where the two Squaws to whom I belonged resided. There we landed, and the Indians went on; which was the last I ever saw of them.

Having made fast to the shore, the Squaws left me in the canoe while they went to their wigwam or house in the town, and returned with a suit of Indian clothing, all new, and very clean and nice. My clothes, though whole and good when I was taken, were now torn in pieces, so that I was almost naked. They first undressed me and threw my rags into the river; then washed me clean and dressed me in the new suit they had just brought, in complete Indian style; and then led me home and seated me in the center of their wigwam.

I had been in that situation but a few minutes, before all the Squaws in the town came in to see me. I was soon surrounded by them, and they immediately set up a most dismal howling, crying bitterly, and wringing their hands in all the agonies of grief for a deceased relative.

Their tears flowed freely, and they exhibited all the signs of real mourning. At the commencement of this scene, one of their number began, in a voice somewhat between speaking and singing, to recite some words to the following purport, and continued the recitation till the ceremony was ended; the company at the same time varying the appearance of their countenances, gestures and tone of voice, so as to correspond with the sentiments expressed by their leader:

"Oh our brother! Alas! He is dead—he has gone; he will never return! Friendless he died on the field of the slain, where his bones are yet lying unburied! Oh, who will not mourn his sad fate?

James E. Seaver, *A Narrative Life of Mrs. Mary Jemison* (Norman: University of Oklahoma Press, 1992), 75–79, 81–83, 85. Reprinted by permission.

And why do we mourn? Though he fell on the field of the slain, with glory he fell, and his spirit went up to the land of his fathers in war! Then why do we mourn? With transports of joy they received him, and fed him, and clothed him, and welcomed him there! Oh friends, he is happy; then dry up your tears! His spirit has seen our distress, and sent us a helper whom with pleasure we greet. Dickewamis has come: then let us receive her with joy! She is handsome and pleasant! Oh! she is our sister, and gladly we welcome her here. In the place of our brother she stands in our tribe. With care we will guard her from trouble; and may she be happy till her spirit shall leave us."

In the course of that ceremony, from mourning they became serene—joy sparkled in their countenances, and they seemed to rejoice over me as over a long lost child. I was made welcome amongst them as a sister to the two Squaws before mentioned, and was called Dickewamis; which being interpreted, signifies a pretty girl, a handsome girl, or a pleasant, good thing. That is the name by which I have ever since been called by the Indians.

I afterwards learned that the ceremony I at that time passed through, was that of adoption. The two squaws had lost a brother in Washington's war, sometime in the year before, and in consequence of his death went up to Fort Pitt, on the day on which I arrived there, in order to receive a prisoner or an enemy scalp, to supply their loss.

It is a custom of the Indians, when one of their number is slain or taken prisoner in battle, to give to the nearest relative to the dead or absent, a prisoner, if they have chanced to take one, and if not, to give him the scalp of an enemy. On the return of the Indians from conquest, which is always announced by peculiar shoutings, demonstrations of joy, and the exhibition of some trophy of victory, the mourners come forward and make their claims. If they receive a prisoner, it is at their option either to satiate their vengeance by taking his life in the most cruel manner they can conceive of; or, to receive and adopt him into the family, in the place of him whom they have lost. All the prisoners that are taken in battle and carried to the encampment or town by the Indians, are given to the bereaved families, till their number is made good. But if their mental wound is fresh, their loss so great that they deem it irreparable, or if their prisoner or prisoners do not meet their approbation, no torture, let it be ever so cruel, seems sufficient to make them satisfaction. It is family, and not national, sacrifices amongst the Indians, that has given them an indelible stamp as barbarians, and identified their character with the idea which is generally formed of unfeeling ferocity, and the most abandoned cruelty.

It was my happy lot to be accepted for adoption; and at the time of the ceremony I was received by the two squaws, to supply the place of their brother in the family; and I was ever considered and treated by them as a real sister, the same as though I has been born of their mother.

My sisters were diligent in teaching me their language; and to their great satisfaction I soon learned so that I could understand it readily, and speak it fluently. I was very fortunate in falling into their hands; for they were kind good natured women; peaceable and mild in their dispositions; temperate and decent in their habits, and very tender and gentle towards me. I have great reason to respect them, though they have been dead a great number of years.

Not long after the Delawares came to live with us, at Wiishto, my sisters told me that I must go and live with one of them, whose name was She-nin-jee. Not daring to cross them, or disobey their commands, with a great degree of reluctance I went; and Sheninjee and I were married according to Indian custom.

Sheninjee was a noble man; large in stature; elegant in his appearance; generous in his conduct; courageous in war; a friend to peace, and a great lover of justice. He supported a degree of dignity far above his rank, and merited and received the confidence and friendship of all the tribes with whom he was acquainted. Yet, Sheninjee was an Indian. The idea of spending my days with him, at first seemed perfectly irreconcilable to my feelings: but his good nature, generosity, tenderness, and friendship towards me, soon gained my affection; and, strange as it may seem, I loved him!—To me he was ever kind in sickness, and always treated me with gentleness; in fact, he was an agreeable husband, and a comfortable companion.

I had then been with the Indians four summers and four winters, and had become so far accustomed to their mode of living, habits and dispositions, that my anxiety to get away, to be set at liberty, and leave them, had almost subsided. With them was my home; my family was there, and there I had many friends to whom I was warmly attached in consideration of the favors, affection and friendship with which they had uniformly treated me, from the time of my adoption.

One thing only marred my happiness, while I lived with them on the Ohio; and that was the recollection that I had once had tender parents and a home that I loved. Aside from that consideration, or, if I had been taken in infancy, I should have been contented in my situation. Notwithstanding all that has been said against the Indians, in consequence of their cruelties to their enemies—cruelties that I have witnessed, and had abundant proof of—it is a fact that they are naturally kind, tender and peaceable towards their friends, and strictly honest; and that those cruelties have been practiced, only upon their enemies, according to their idea of justice.

5. The South Carolina Legislature Passes an Act for the Capture of Runaway Slaves, 1700

IV. That if any Indian or Indians shall apprehend or take or shall be assisting in apprehending or takeing any Runnaway as aforesaid, and the same shall bring back, shall have all the armes and ammunition that shall be taken in the possession of the person or persons so apprehended and taken, and such further reward as by the Governor shall be thought fitt, not exceeding twenty shillings to every Indian that shall be assisting in apprehending and takeing the said Runnaways.

V. And every white man that shall apprehend or take or shall be assisting in apprehending or takeing such Runnaways as aforesaid, shall have and receive out of the publick treasury for every such Runnaway so apprehended or taken, by an order under the hand of the Governor, not exceeding five pounds, and such order to the Receiver shall be his discharge.

Thomas Cooper, ed., *The Statutes at Large of South Carolina* (Columbia, S.C.: A. S. Johnston, 1837), 2: 181.

VI. And for the better security of all such persons that shall endeavour to take any Runnaways, it is hereby declared lawful for any white person, or Indian in whose company there is a white person, to beat, maime or assault any person aforesaid resisting, and if such Runnaway aforesaid cannot otherwise be taken, to kill, he makeing resistance to avoid being apprehended or taken as aforesaid.

6. William Stephens Assesses the Prospects of Slavery in Georgia, 1742

S'r, ... I do not conceive that from what you are pleased to write in your last, concerning Negros, it is expected I should enter into the Argument of their utility comparatively with white men, and take upon me to give reasons why the honble. Trust[ees] have not thought it hitherto expedient to allow the use of 'em in this Colony; since I find That already done so judiciously, and with such clear Strength of Reason publish'd to the World in the Year 1741; That I think it unanswerable: but for as much as I observe from what you write, that several Gentlemen of Eminence in Trade had given to the Trust[ees] their Opinion in favour of Negros, under proper Regulations and Restrictions; what they are pleased to expect from me now (I think) is, my opinion how Negros can be admitted here consistently with the safety of the Province: which therefore is the Point I am to stick to.

If tis meant without exception as to time, I apprehend the answer is so obvious, and past all controversy, that twill admit of no disquisition: for during the War we have with the Spaniards, and Augustine remaining in their hands, it is impracticable with Safety to make use of Negros in Georgia; which is a Frontier of such a nature, that I conceive it impossible, even for the General, to prevent their escape to the Enemy; tho' his whole Regiment were appointed to keep a Guard for that purpose; as his Excellence has at this time, divers Troops of Rangers appointed by him, to watch and examine persons of all kinds, passing to, and fro' wherever they are found: nevertheless Negros, seeking for liberty, were they now among us, would soon find means, by untrodden paths thro' a Wilderness of thick Woods, to flee to Augustine so near us as tis; more especially when they will not only obtain their promised freedome, but also have Arms put into their hands, and become a part of their Army to fight against us.

Presuming what I have so far said, to be undeniable; it is next to be considered with what safety they can be admitted in time of Peace. As I have always professed my own natural Aversion to keeping Slaves; and still (were it in my choice) would rather prefer keeping of white Servants, if they might be had for moderate Wages; perhaps I may be looked on as prejudiced in my opinion: but since it has fullyly appeared, that there is little or no likelyhood of supplying this Colony wth a competent number of those, to make such improvement in Cultivation of Land as is to be wishd, and at this very time most of our ablest young

Elizabeth Donnan, ed., *Documents Illustrative of the History of the Slave Trade to America* (New York: Octagon Books, 1965), 4: 603–606.

people, have rather chosen to go into the Publick Service, (either in Scout boats, or as Rangers etc.) than labour in clearing and improving of Land, which too many of 'em shew an aversion to. For these reasons, if the Use of Negros is admitted after the War; tis natural that I should (among others) be dealing for a few also: and in such case I am to offer such regulations and restrictions as occur to me necessary to be observed, for the future preservation and advantage of the Colony: which I shall endeavour, with due deference to better Judgments, and with a perfect impartiality.

1. If Augustine remains in the Spaniards hands at the conclusion of this War (the contrary of which must be wished for, by all good Englishmen, who have experienced already too much what a Thorn they are in our side in times of Peace) it ought not to be supposed but that due care would be taken in a Treaty of Peace, effectually to prevent any runaway Negros from being received or entertained by the Spaniards, either at Augustine, or in any other of their Settlements on Florida: wherein too much care can not be had to prevent their eluding such an Article again, as has been formerly practiced, and which they are very fond of. But in case of any future Rupture betwixt the two Nations, and Augustine still in the hands of the Spaniards; what the consequence then might be, of the negro's revolting to the Enemy, who by that time might probably be some thousands in Number; I must leave to the consideration of those, whose capacitys reach far beyond mine.

2. As to the proportion necessary for the safety of the Colony, how many Negros may be allowed towards carrying on Plantation Work; I conceive that any number not exceeding 4 at most will require one white man, of Growth and Strength sufficient for bearing Arms in defence of his King and Country, always to attend; and either work with 'em, or at least constantly inspect 'em: as well to see them properly employd in the Day time, as to secure them at nights: for which reason such white man must make his abode on the Plantation: and in that case, if the Owner himself shall at any time chuse to continue on his Plantation, to see his own Work carried on, he may be understood to be such a White man as here meant; otherwise he must employ one for that purpose: and whether he himself or a Servant under him be so employd; strickt care should be taken, that Arms of all kinds be kept out of the power of Negros coming at them.

3. Whereas the reason given for the use of Negros has been principally, if not wholly, an Impossibility of clearing land to any degree, and cultivating it without 'em: it tacitly implys, that they are not wanted on any other occasion: which indeed I think: and therefore they ought not to be allowed in Towns, or any where, but on Plantation work: under which term it is to be understood, that rowing in a Boat on his Masters Service, or going to and from one Town or place to another, on the same, is included; since it may conduce to the improvemt of his Plantation: for a greater liberty would be a great discouragement to labouring white people coming to live among us; who by such means would find little Room to work; as many of our Deserters to Carolina have sadly experienced, contrary to their Expectations: where Negros take off all occasion of white men being hired: and if the case is so, with respect to Day labourers only; much more then ought there to be here a total prohibition of Negro's

occupying or learning any trade; which must inevitably contribute to the unpeo-
pling of this Colony. Nor should the Master of such Negros be permitted to let
them out to hire for wages which would confirm the practice of converting
them to no other use, that putting so much money in his pocket, wherewith
to live idle, and voluptuously; as tis most notorious was the case of too many
among us formerly who were the first, that upon their Servts. times expiring,
and that Fond failing began to be clamorous, and to perswade the World to believe, they were driven hence thro' fear of starving.

7. Pierre Le Moyne d'Iberville Addresses Chickasaw and Choctaw Leaders, 1702

At eight o'clock in the morning I had the presents laid out that I desired to give
these two nations: to each, 200 livres of powder, 200 livres of bullets, 200 livres
of game-shot, 12 guns, 100 axes, 150 knives, some kettles, glass beads, gun flints,
awls, and other hardware, which made a considerable present indeed. After this I
had them assembled. My brother De Bienville acting as interpreter, I said to
them: "I rejoice to see you disposed to live in peace with each other and with
all the nations of the region"—after I had made them perceive the advantages to
be had from good relations rather than from destroying each other, which they
had been doing. I said: "The Chicacha [Chickasaw] have foolishly followed the
advice of the English, who have no other objective than to work their destruction by inciting the Chicacha and the Chaqueta [Choctaws] to make war on
each other so that the English can get slaves, whom they send away to other
countries to be sold. One proof that the English are not your friends, but are
seeking only to destroy you is, as you well know, that your enemies have taken
Chicacha prisoners, whom the English of St. Georges bought, as they bought the
Chaqueta, and whom they sent off to the islands to be sold—far from sending
them back home, as they should have done. You Chichacha can observe that
during the last eight to ten years when you have been at war with the Chaqueta
at the instigation of the English, who gave you ammunition and thirty guns for
that purpose, you have taken more than 500 prisoners and killed more than
1,800 Chaqueta. Those prisoners were sold; but taking those prisoners cost you
more than 800 men, slain on various war parties, who would be living at this
moment if it had not been for the English. The Chaqueta see it well—and the
Chicacha ought to see it, too,—that the Englishman is to blame for the loss of your
dead brothers. And the ultimate plan of the Englishman, after weakening you by
means of wars, is to come and seize you in your villages and then send you to be
sold somewhere else, in faraway countries from which you can never return, as the
English have treated others, as you know. To prevent all these calamities, you must
no longer listen to the Englishman.

"And, if you do not drive him from your villages, the French and you cannot be friends with one another, and I shall engage in no trading with you.

Richebourg Gaillard McWilliams, trans. and ed., *Iberville's Gulf Journals* (Tuscaloosa:
University of Alabama Press, 1981), 171–173. Reprinted by permission.

I shall arm with guns all the Chaqueta, the Mobilians, and the Tohomés as I have already begun to arm the Nadchés and the other nations that are our allies. Far indeed from preventing the Illinois from making war on you, I shall incite them to it. Certainly you see that you will be in no condition to hold out against so many nations; you will suffer the sorrow of seeing yourselves killed at the gates of your villages, along with your women and children.

"But, if you drive the Englishman from your villages, who likes nothing except blood and slaves, I will have a village built between the Chicacha and the Chaqueta, as you want it, where you will find all kinds of goods to be bartered for skins of buffalo, deer, and bear—those are the slaves I want. You will feed yourselves and all your families on the meat of the animals you kill. To get them will not cost you your lives."

I had them told, after their manner of speaking, several other things that aimed solely at driving the English out and ruining them in the minds of the Chicacha. They promised me to drive the Englishman out provided I would engage in trading with them, about which we came to an agreement over prices. Then I gave a gun, a blanket, a hooded cloak, an ax, two knives, some powder, and bullets to a Chicacha as payment for the Chaqueta slave he had taken away from the Englishman and given to M. de Tonty. I armed with guns all the chiefs of the two nations and their men and gave each a hooded cloak, a shirt, and additional trifles. Next I gave them the presents for their nations. I promised the Chicacha to warn at once all the nations, our allies, to go in war no more among the Chicacha and promised to send some of my men with the Chicacha to escort them safely to their country, from which my men would go on to the Illinois and bring back their men held as prisoners by the Illinois and have the Illinois make peace. For their part, the Chicacha would induce the Conchaques and the Alabamon[s] to make peace with the Chaqueta, the Tohomés, and the Mobilians, to come to the French fort, and to listen to the English no more. If they did not do so, they could assure themselves that our friends the Apalaches— whose tomahawks I controlled—would make cruel war against them, which I had so far prevented. All these Indians seemed to me quite satisfied and disposed to live in peace.

8. Governor Etienne de Périer Considers the Use of Black Slave Troops against Indians, 1730

On the second of December I learned from Sieur Lunel, inspector of tobacco, and from Mr. Charpentier who had been appointed captain at the Natchez that on the 28th the Indian nation of that place had attacked between nine and ten o'clock in the morning all the French of that post and those who were in that district. In order to succeed in it with certainty it had taken the following measures.

Dunbar Rowland and Albert G. Sanders, eds. and trans., *Mississippi Provincial Archives: French Dominion* (Jackson, Miss., 1932), 3: 61–65.

They were all armed and equipped as if they had wished to go hunting, and as they passed by the houses of the colonists whom they knew best they borrowed their guns with the promise to bring them venison in abundance. To remove all suspicion they brought what they owed in grain, in oil and other produce, while one party went with two calumets to the house of Sieur de Chépart who was in command, to whom they carried some chickens to keep him in the state of confidence in which he was that the Indians were speaking no evil against the French, as they had taken pains to assure him the day before in regard to several rumors that had spread abroad that the Natchez were going to assassinate the French. The confidence of this officer had gone to the extent of having put in irons seven colonists who had asked to assemble to forestall the disaster with which they were menaced. This very confidence had allowed him to see without [a sense of] danger about thirty Indians in the fort and as many in his house and in the neighborhood, while the rest of this nation were scattered in all the houses of our colonists and even in the workshops of our workmen which were two or three leagues away in the cypress-groves above and below the Natchez. When this arrangement had been made and the hour had come the general assassination of our French was the signal for the affair; so short it was that a single discharge ended it, with the exception of the house of Sieur de La Loire Desursins, in which there were eight men, of whom six were killed and the two others escaped in the night without the Indians having been able to capture them during the day.

Sieur de La Loire was on horseback when the attack began, not having been able to return to his house. He defended himself until death, having killed four Indians. His house killed eight of them. So it cost the Natchez only twelve men to destroy two hundred and fifty of ours; through the fault of the officer who would have deserved alone the evil fate which so many unfortunate people have shared with him and which it was easy with the information and the people that he had to turn back upon our enemies, a loss which has brought this colony within two finger-breadths of ruin as you are going to see. These barbarians before undertaking this massacre had made certain of several negroes, among others those of the White Earth at the head of whom were the two foremen who gave the other negroes to understand that they would be free with the Indians, which was in fact the case during the time that they remained with them; and that our wives and our children would be their slaves; that on the same day on which they would destroy us at the Natchez the other nations would strike in all the French quarters, which would have been carried out if I had not diverted the storm by summoning here in the month of last October the Choctaw chiefs who I knew were in conferences with our neighbors of the East who were to enter this nation with one hundred and twenty horses loaded with merchandise which was to be the compensation for our destruction with which we have long been threatened in this province; which we regarded as a rumor of the Indians who are ordinarily liars.

On the same day on which I learned of the destruction of the post of the Natchez I sent the Sieur de Merveilleux, a Captain of Infantry, in a pirogue with a detachment to warn all our colonists on both sides of the river to keep themselves on their guard and to make themselves fortifications at intervals in order to put their slaves and cattle in them in case of attack, which was promptly carried out on both sides of the river so that now only men would be lacking to be in security, the forts being made and in a state of defense. I ordered also Sieur de Merveilleux to examine closely the small nations that are on the river and not to give them arms until I should be sure of their fidelity. I sent out on the same day a courier to carry a letter for me to the Choctaws and to notify two chiefs of that nation who were hunting on Lake Pontchartrain to come and talk to me.

On the third of December there arrived a pirogue coming from the Illinois in which there was a Choctaw who had made the journey, who asked the interpreter for a private conversation with me. I had him come at once. After having paid me his compliments he said to me: "I am very sorry about the death of our brothers. I should even have been able to prevent it if I had not regarded as a lie what the Chickasaws told me when I was up the river, but now I see that they did not lie to me. That is why you must be on your guard. They then told me that the Indians were to attack all the French quarters and assassinate them all; that even our nation was in the conspiracy, which had made me regard the thing as false, because of the friendship that we have for our brothers the French. So let me go to our nation so that I may see what is happening there. I shall carry a letter to the French officer who is there and I shall bring back to Mobile news of what he has done."

I had no sooner left this Indian than others of the small neighboring nations came to warn me that we had reason to fear the Choctaws; that it was even said that they had already attacked Mobile. In fact we had had one man killed and one wounded in the Mobile River without having been able to find out by whom. This bad news which I was seeking to hide spread as quickly as the terror. It was then that I saw with great sorrow that people were less French in Louisiana than elsewhere. Fear had so powerfully taken the upper hand that even the Chaouchas who were a nation of thirty men below New Orleans made our colonists tremble, which made me decide to have them destroyed by our negroes, which they executed with as much promptness as secrecy. This example carried out by our negroes has kept the other little nations up the river in a respectful attitude. If I had been willing to use our negro volunteers I should have destroyed all these little nations which are of no use to us, and which might on the contrary cause our negroes to revolt as we see by the example of the Natchez, but I had considerations to observe, and in the situation in which I was I could not rely however little on the Frenchmen whom I had; which caused me to have them all assembled in order to arm those who were not armed. I have divided those of the city into four companies which are composed of about one hundred and fifty men. At the head of each I have put a councillor and some employees as officers. I have also put the principal colonists at the head of those that I have had formed on the river, and I then had negroes come to work on an entrenchment around our city which I shall have continued this autumn.

9. Governor Etienne de Périer Appraises French–English–Chickasaw Relations, 1730

Since my letters of the eighteenth of last March ... the Illinois chiefs whom I had summoned have come to see me. I have spoken to each one separately about the activities of the Chickasaws, the friends of the English, who are the ones who led the last conspiracy. They confirmed for me the information that some Indians had given me two days after the defeat of the [post of the] Natchez, which was that the Indians were to attack all the French quarters on the same day. I have treated this conspiracy as a wild idea in order to reassure our colonists, who for nine months have been seized by such a great terror that the least rumor makes them rush to the woods like hares. They make us pay them dearly, especially the Choctaws, who do not cease to murmur although they are the best treated. There is every probability that this nation will be divided unless the English cease their active solicitations, which they express with an infinite number of presents that they give both to the chiefs of these nations and to the ordinary warriors, assuring them that they would always sell them their goods more cheaply by half than would the French. These solicitations, which are so urgent, make me believe that the English will carry out badly the agreements that will be made both on the subject of the boundaries and about the nations that will be considered allies. The colony will continually be by depending upon the caprice of the Indians, whose inconstancy is unequaled and who think that we use them only because we are not capable of making war. That is the idea we have given them of us by using them in our defense. The least little nation thinks itself our protector in the situation in which we are, whereas if we had forces to sustain ourselves by our own efforts the greatest nations would respect us and would very carefully seek an alliance with us, which would be as honorable as it would be useful for them. It would be necessary to be strong in troops for only five or six years, after which they would be reduced from year to year to a number sufficient to guard the forts. The best colonists here are those who have been soldiers, and in all the colonies it is the same, especially in the beginning. They will also carry out more surely and more promptly the things with which they are charged. I have had the time in the last ten months to test what I am suggesting. Since the Natchez have been on the other side of the river I have sent out five different parties of Indians to destroy the grain and the crops of our enemies. Not one has executed my orders about that. The first killed about ten men; the second killed four; the third brought me nine prisoners, four of whom they burned here; the two others returned without doing anything under different pretexts; so that one may draw the conclusion that the Indians are not suitable for really making war, but to serve as greyhounds to chase fugitives, and not at all to hold firm or to do anything that calls for patience and order.

Patricia Kay Galloway, Dunbar Rowland, and Albert G. Sanders, eds. and trans., *Mississippi Provincial Archives: French Dominion* (Baton Rouge: Louisiana State Historical Society, 1984), 4: 39–42, 44–45.

If I had received the assistance that I was led to expect, I would already have set out to complete the destruction of the Natchez, which is absolutely necessary in order to serve as an example to the other nations. That of the Chickasaws will be no less necessary at the proper time. That is a nation that we must never trust. It is too closely bound to the English. In addition to that, it is situated in the midst of our nations. It is the one that has been sending the goods of the English into our nations to induce them to slaughter all the French. The thing is certain and proved; so that there is no circumspection to be used with this nation except that which is necessary in order not to lose track of them and to destroy them without fail—but that must not be done until the Natchez are destroyed—and to do it in such a way as not to use the Choctaws, in order to show them that we do not need them and that if we treat them with respect it is only because of pure friendship. That is what I shall give them to understand at Mobile, where I shall go in the month of October to give them their presents and to learn from them themselves the sources of their causes of dissatisfaction, since I have not wished to reproach them with having entered in part the conspiracy that the Chickasaw nation organized at the solicitation of the English. The only thing of which they complained last year is that goods were sold to them too dearly. Thereupon the Administrative Council withdrew the trade from M. Diron, who would not sell them the goods at the prices that we had agreed upon with them. This led M. Diron to write me the most offensive and the least restrained letter in the world. I entreat your Lordship, my lord, to put an end to all these missives that are hindering and causing the ruin of this colony. They are enough to discourage the most zealous man in the world. Nothing is so hard as to establish a country. A thousand difficulties follow, one after another.

I am sending your Lordship the map for which M. Le Pelletier had asked me in order to establish the boundaries between the English and us. The line that I have marked in red is what it is advisable that we should have as boundaries. I have indicated with a "P" all the nations that are our allies and that receive presents from us, and with two "P"s those that receive presents from the English and from us. Whatever may be done, I do not think that the English will carry out in good faith what they will promise in the matter of the boundaries. There will be perpetual quibbling. The only good that that can do will be to delay them in the plan that they have of approaching Mexico. The expenditures that they have been making for three years to bring about the success of this plan are astonishing. They sell their goods at a very low price to all the Indians, with the promise to sell to them at an even better rate if they will aid them to establish themselves on the river.

∿ ESSAYS

Much of the borderlands scholarship focuses on events and activities that are most visible in the historical record: battles, raids, epidemics, rituals, treaties, trade, missionary overtures. But people in encounter also did many other things that at first glance might seem mundane, even forgettable. They exchanged gifts and shared meals; they learned—or, pointedly, refused to learn—each other's languages; and they laughed with, but mostly at, one another. These were ordinary things often done by ordinary people, but they were not insignificant, argues James H. Merrell, professor of history at Vassar College, in his essay on Indian-English relations in eastern North America during the colonial era. Wars, diseases, and demographics largely determined the balance of power between natives and newcomers, but we cannot fully understand their shared history without exploring the endless face-to-face dealings, for the human drama of contact was played out in those intimate encounters. It mattered, Merrell writes, who was laughed at and whose language was spoken in intercultural settings, because such outcomes reveal who was likely to be in charge of the situation. Merrell traces how native rules usually prevailed in early contacts and how they gradually yielded as English settlements pushed westward and the line separating—and linking—Indian and English worlds moved deeper into the interior. Merrell calls that shifting line a frontier, but his frontier is not the frontier Frederick Jackson Turner made famous in 1893: a divide between civilization and savagery, the past and progress. Merrell's frontier is a contact zone where Indian and European realms brushed against and partially blended into one another. Such frontiers of cultural interpenetration rose and fell across the East over several generations until, by the late eighteenth century, the colonial world engulfed the indigenous one. Merrell concludes his essay with an overview of the struggles the Indians faced and the survival strategies they employed once the passing frontier had delivered them into an Anglo-American world.

The English-Indian borderlands were in many ways a study in contrasts with French Louisiana and its borderlands, the subject of the second essay. English-Indian contact zones were shifting and short-lived, moving constantly across space over time, whereas the French-Indian borderlands in Louisiana were firmly anchored in the lower Mississippi valley. English colonial agents rarely involved themselves with the day-to-day affairs of contact zones, but in Louisiana French officials strove to manage all aspects of the colony's Indian relations. And in Louisiana's borderlands Indians remained much more powerful than in the East, where English settlers kept pushing westward, rendering any cross-cultural arrangements temporary at best. Indeed, of the many peoples living in eighteenth-century Louisiana and its borderlands, the French were the least authoritative and least independent, argues Kathleen Duval, professor of history at the University of North Carolina at Chapel Hill, in her essay. French colonists and their African slaves did establish themselves on both sides of the lower Mississippi Valley, but they did so in native terms and under native control. The French, Duval concludes, never became more than marginal players in a complex borderlands world where indigenous norms remained dominant. But if Indians held such an advantage in power over the French, how then did French Louisiana survive in the Mississippi Valley until the end of French tenure in North America in 1763?

Indian-English Frontiers of Cooperation and Conquest

JAMES H. MERRELL

It was 1634, Maryland's first year, and already there was trouble on the colony's northern border. At William Claiborne's Chesapeake Bay trading outpost on Kent Island a Susquehannock Indian had injured a Wicomiss while both were doing business there, and some of Claiborne's men thought it funny. Soon five Susquehannocks and three of Claiborne's people lay dead, ambushed by angry Wicomiss warriors. Now, two months later, the Wicomisses sent a messenger to Governor Leonard Calvert with word that they wanted to make amends for the actions of their young men. "What will give you content," the envoy asked Calvert. The governor's answer was simple: turn over the culprits "unto me, to do with them as I shall thinke fit."

There was "a little pause." Then the Wicomiss spokesman tried to set the governor straight. "It is the manner amongst us Indians," he said, "that if any such like accident happen, wee doe redeeme the life of a man that is so slaine, with a 100. armes length of *Roanoke* ... and since that you are heere strangers, and come into our Countrey, you should rather conforme your selves to the Customes of our Countrey, then impose yours upon us." If Calvert understood, he did not let on. "It seemes you come not sufficiently instructed in the businesse which wee have with the Wicomesses," he replied; "therefore tell them what I have said; and that I expect a speedy answere; and so dismist him."

Calvert's conversation with the Wicomiss was part of a continuing debate in colonial times as native Americans and Anglo-Americans tried to establish whose country this was and whose customs ought to hold sway. Their exchange was more explicit than most, however, because in 1634 both natives and new-comers could at least claim to rule the Chesapeake. Elsewhere the issue was not in doubt, and conformity was not up for debate. When John Lawson left Charleston, South Carolina, in 1700 to head inland through "a Country inhabited by none but Savages," for example, he was careful to behave in a manner "acceptable to those sort of Creatures." He relied on Indian guides, said nothing when his Keyauwee hosts served such delicacies as "Fawns, taken out of the Doe's Bellies, and boil'd in the same slimy Bags Nature had plac'd them in," and sat patiently through the night in a Waxhaw council house as old men sang and young people danced.

Compare this with Dr. Alexander Hamilton's journey from Maryland to Maine and back again more than forty years later. Hamilton, too, met many native Americans in his travels, enjoyed the hospitality of a local headman, and sat with Indians at a sacred ceremony. Yet here any resemblance to Lawson's

James H. Merrell, "The Customes of Our Country': Indians and Colonists in Early America," in *Strangers within the Realm: Cultural Margins of the First British Empire*, ed. Bernard Bailyn and Philip D. Morgan, pp. 117–156 (Chapel Hill: University of North Carolina Press, 1991). Published for the Omohundro Institute of Early American History and Culture. Copyright © 1991 by the University of North Carolina Press. Used by permission of the publisher. www.uncpress.unc.edu.

journey ends, for Hamilton never left the familiar Anglo-American confines of taverns and clubs, concerts and churches, enthusiastic New Lights and impertinent social upstarts. Along the coast colonists were many, natives few, and it was Indians who had to fit in. Instead of fawns, Hamilton's Indian host (who "lives after the English mode") served him a glass of excellent wine. Instead of joining the "confused Rabble" in the Waxhaw council house, Hamilton took a pew near some Indians during a service in a Boston church.

Between Hamilton's journey and Lawson's lay a barrier that scholars has labeled a frontier, a cultural divide, or a marchland. On one side of this line native Americans set the conditions under which intercultural encounters occurred; on the other, colonists did. Frederick Jackson Turner's Eurocentric version of the American frontier has given the concept a bad name, but there can be no doubt that a frontier existed in colonial times. Certainly English colonists had no doubts. "Wee are here att the end of the world," wrote William Byrd I in 1690 from his plantation at the falls of the James River. And Byrd was right: it was the end of his world, the English world, and the beginning of another—called "Indian Country"—where different rules applied.

Different sorts of Indian peoples lived on opposite sides of this frontier. Nonetheless, this spectrum of native cultures broke down into two basic types: those inhabiting Byrd's world and those from Indian Country.

The invisible barrier between [native and non-native worlds] was crucial in shaping the life of an Indian people. A tribe's population, its economy, and its political life—indeed, its entire culture—depended less on whether it lived in New England, New York, or North Carolina than on whether it was located among the English. Thus "plantation Indians" in Massachusetts and Virginia had more in common with one another than with some "back nation" nearby. North or south, their numbers were small, their subsistence routine disrupted, their political autonomy compromised, their customs under indirect influence from colonial neighbors if not direct attack from Christian missionaries.

Not the least of the differences between resident and inland groups was the way they interacted with the English. While hardly a precise gauge, laughter helps draw this distinction, because in intercultural contacts whoever made fun of the other generally was in control of the situation. In Indian Country the joke was on the colonist. Lawson's hosts often "laugh'd their Sides sore" at his antics, and he was not alone. Natives made fun of the Anglo-American because his fingernails were too short and his spoons too small. They laughed at his attempts to speak their language, laughed at his prayers, laughed at his beard. Where a man like Hamilton felt at home, on the other hand, Indians tended to be the butt of the jokes. When the "queen" of a local tribe performed a ceremonial dance in Williamsburg in 1702, the audience burst out laughing, and the laughter never stopped. Colonists mocked Indian efforts to speak English or ride a horse, dress in English clothing or understand English law.

"Above all things," wrote one colonist of the Massachusett Indians, they "loved not to be laughed at." The Massachusetts—and, eventually, Indians throughout the East—would have to get used to it. When English colonists first arrived in America, virtually all of the land between the Atlantic and the Mississippi was Indian Country; by the end of the colonial era virtually none of it was.

The history of Indian–English relations in early America is the story of how this dramatic change in the country and its "Customes" came about. It is no laughing matter, but listening for laughter is one way of retracing the steps that led from "remoter Indians" to "neighbour-Indians," from "wild" to "domestic."

The place to begin is with that border between Anglo-America and Indian America, a border as difficult to pinpoint on a map as it was real. Sometimes its location was obvious. In 1524, when Abenakis on the Maine coast refused even to allow Giovannie de Verrazano's exploring party to come ashore, it reached right down to the water's edge. Plotting its position thereafter can be more complicated. For one thing, there was no inexorable advance across the continent; the English push into the interior could quickly reverse itself when Indians fought back. During King Philip's War of 1675–1676, for example, native warriors destroyed thirteen New England towns, and it was 1700 before colonists reoccupied the lands they had held at the war's beginning. Even when the boundary did move west, its progress was uneven. Much depended on when the English arrived in a particular area: Carolinians in 1670 (not to mention Georgians in 1732) were clinging to the beaches at a time when their fellow colonists to the north had conquered the entire coastal plain. To complicate matters further, navigable rivers helped some colonists get ahead in the race for land. Thus the Connecticut River valley boasted a thriving English population one hundred miles from the coast at a time when most towns were little more than a day's walk from Boston or Plymouth, and this pattern of settlement was followed later along the Hudson, the Potomac, and the Savannah.

Whatever its twists and turns, its distortions and detours on the way west, the frontier did move across the continent, and the principal forces behind it were warfare, disease, and colonial settlement. Each was crucial in tipping the scales from what John Winthrop called a land "full of Indians" to one dominated by European immigrants.... violence along the edges of the colonial world was endemic, and untold numbers of natives perished in forgotten skirmishes.

The casualties suffered in wars with Anglo-America were certainly appalling; the Indians' losses from exposure to alien diseases—conservatively estimated at 75 percent in New England alone—almost defy comprehension. Yet noting that demographic disaster formed a grim backdrop to all of colonial history is one thing, coming up with reliable population estimates for Indians quite another. A best guess for the number of natives east of the Mississippi River on the eve of permanent English settlement might be close to 1,000,000; a century earlier the total would have been higher still, for by the time the English set foot on these shores, Indians were well acquainted with imported diseases. Whatever the earlier figures, after Anglo-Americans arrived native numbers plummeted with frightening speed. In 1674, inquiries among New England tribes elicited similar answers: from 4,000 warriors to 300, from 5,000 to 1,000, from 3,000 to 300, from 3,000 to 250, on and on the roll call of death went as memory called forth the world Indians had lost. Some thirty years later another curious colonist took a census of natives in Virginia, and again the response was a litany of loss: "much decreased of late"; "reduc'd to very few Men"; "a small number yet living"; "almost wasted"; "Wasting"; "but three men living, which yet keep up their Kingdom, and retain their Fashion."

English colonists considered the Indians' catastrophic losses a sign of God's favor. It was, wrote one colonial governor, "as if Heaven designed by the Diminuition of these Indian Neighbours, to make room for our growing Settlements," and indeed disease often did clear the way for colonial farmers. But the farmers helped. Natives still around when the English moved into an area found that their new neighbors were "like pidgeons": "where one of those people settled, ... a thousand more would settle." A generation or so after the first pioneers arrived, the colonial population would reach a critical mass, the pressure on Indians would increase, and many tribes would retreat. Within twenty years of Pennsylvania's founding, Indians near Philadelphia talked of heading into the hinterlands, and near Charleston in 1710 local native groups had "gone further up in the Country Thro' badd usage they received from some of Our People." In 1755 Edmond Atkin, soon to be the crown's superintendent of Indian affairs for the Southern Department, blamed it less on "badd usuage" than a simple "difference of manners and way of life" between Indian and English. Whatever the reason, history taught him that "the Indians generally chuse to withdraw, as white People draw near to them." "Will not it be impossible for Indians and White people to live together?" wondered a Pennsylvanian. "Will not there be ... a perpetual Scene of quarreling?" The answer, throughout England's mainland provinces, was often yes.

War, disease, settlement—these three horsemen of the Indian apocalypse are essential to an understanding of English contacts with native America. But they are more the story's beginning than its end, for they cannot capture the substance and subtlety of the American encounter. The conquest of the continent was not as swift as the emphasis on depopulation and displacement implies; Indians did not surrender or disappear overnight. Without belittling the devastation wrought by smallpox, militias, or settlers, we need to remember that Indians survived. While some abandoned traditional burial rituals in the aftermath of an epidemic, most continued to inter their dead in customary fashion. While warfare or sickness utterly destroyed some groups, others constructed new societies from fragments of the old. While many did retreat when faced with the prospect of being hemmed in by farms and fences, many others did not.

To understand how the Indians lost America and the English won it, we must look past the grand events—warfare, epidemics, the frontier's advance—to examine the less celebrated but no less important meetings between peoples. The real (and still largely untold) story is less dramatic than invasions and battles, less drastic than sickness and settlement; more intimate, more human in scale, it is also harder to uncover. These long-forgotten encounters lie in scraps of evidence, mere snatches of conversations that took place in several different contact arenas—linguistic, economic, diplomatic, legal, and religious—where Indian met colonist. The conversations, taken together, speak of a shift in patterns of interaction as face-to-face contacts slowly became more Anglo-American than native American, more like Alexander Hamilton's journey than John Lawson's. If that shift, that frontier, is often hard to pin down precisely, the overall trend is unmistakable: Indians slowly gave way and colonists slowly took over, until the line between one world and another was not Verrazano's shore or Byrd's plantation but the Appalachians and then beyond.

American Indians and English colonists brought to their encounter considerable experience with exotic peoples. For native Americans the English were only the latest in a series of European intruders, while those English colonists had a fund of knowledge about alien cultures derived from books about America and contacts with Ireland. Yet if neither were novices in dealing with foreigners, they had a hard time making sense of one another once sustained interaction began at the end of the sixteenth century. Indians in New England called "every thing which they cannot comprehend" *Manitóo,* and they used the term frequently when talking among themselves about the English. Indians, whose cultures emphasized personal restraint, were appalled by the colonists' "excited chattering, … the haste and rashness to do something," and some wondered aloud why, if "the *Europeans* are always rangling and uneasy, … they do not go out of this World, since they are so uneasy and discontented in it." Colonists were no better at comprehending natives. "Uncivil and stupid as garden poles," noted one. "A very strange kind of People," wrote another. "An odd sort of People," agreed a third. "Their way of Living is so contrary to ours," concluded John Lawson in 1709, after studying Carolina Indians for eight years, "that neither we nor they can fathom one anothers Designs and Methods."

True understanding of the other would remain elusive. But the quest for that elusive goal started immediately, with a search for some way to cross the linguistic barrier. Thus began a tug-of-war between English and Indian as each tried to impose its modes of communication on the other. Natives expected colonists to follow local custom, which dictated that "the most Powerful Nation of these Savages scorns to treat or trade with any others (of fewer Numbers and less Power) in any other Tongue but their own." The English agreed in principle, but insisted that they, not Indians, had the numbers and the power. Moreover, colonists felt that the English language should prevail not only because England *should* rule; it would actually *help* England rule, because "changing of the language of a barbarous people, into the speech of a more civil and potent nation" was a way "to reduce such a people unto the civility and religion of the prevailing nation."

Colonists expecting Indians to welcome the chance to learn "the treasure of our tongue" were disappointed. The intruders did eventually win the war of words, but it was a long struggle, waged against stiff opposition. At first an elaborate pantomime was probably the most common means of conversing, no doubt accompanied by wild swinging of arms, exaggerated facial expressions, and whatever sounds might help get the gist of the message across. Crude, perhaps, but it worked. It was not hard to guess that Indians waving furs on the end of a stick at a passing ship were interested in trade or that an Englishman piling beads into an Indian's canoe wanted to make friends. Nor was it easy to mistake the meaning behind "stern-look'd Countenances" or a "scornefull posture."

[T]he need to discuss more complex matters encouraged the two cultures to break through the language barrier. The first halting steps were probably secondary to the sign language in common currency: a verbal exchange between the explorer William Hilton and a tribe of Carolina Indians, for example, consisted of many gestures but only two words, "Bonny" and "Skerry." Far more useful were pidgin languages—English as well as several different Indian versions—that developed. Impatient colonists, who called these inventions "a broken language," "a made-up, childish language," were always trying to learn more, but Indians held back. In New Netherland, where the linguistic battle has been studied most thoroughly, natives clearly sought to establish and then maintain the upper hand. One frustrated colonial student claimed "that they rather try to conceal their language from us than to properly communicate it, except in things that have to do with everyday trade, saying that it is sufficient for us to understand them to this extent." The Indians' purpose was obvious: "Even those [colonists] who can best of all speak with the savages, and get along well in trade, are nevertheless altogether in the dark and as bewildered, when they hear the savages talking among themselves." Another "Indian grammarian" trying to crack this code became hopelessly confused by the different tenses and pronunciations: "I stand oftentimes and look, but do not know how to put it down." His efforts to sort out the confusion failed, for Indians, he concluded, were "very stupid" and his fellow colonists ignorant. One supposed expert, consulted about variable pronunciations, explained the mystery by claiming that local tribes altered their entire language every few years.

The "Indian grammarians" did not give up easily. Their persistence, coupled with the growing need to communicate as contacts became more frequent, overcame the Indians' reluctance to train capable linguists. Most early interpreters were colonists who mastered a native language, not Indians speaking English, for despite claims that some natives were delighted to learn and then show off their English, most colonists agreed that the local tribe's speech "is the first thing to be employed with them." Over time, however, Indians were the ones expected to learn a foreign language. Not surprisingly, neighboring groups were the first to face this language requirement; indeed, a pledge to learn English could be part of formal submission to colonial rule.

Even as they lost linguistic predominance, Indians resisted by refusing whenever possible to speak an alien tongue. "If you ask them a question," one Virginian complained of the tributary Indians in the 1680s, "unlesse they be made three parts drunk they will not answer, tho they can speake English." "Notwithstanding some of them could speak good English," reported another visitor to the colony's tributaries three decades later, "yet when they treat of any thing that concerns their nation, they will not treat but in their own language, ... nor will not answer to any question made to them without it be in their own tongue." Such stubbornness only slowed the spread of linguistic imperialism, however. In 1734, "seeing the tributary Indians understand and can speak the English language very well," Virginia removed the natives' facade of superiority by discharging its official interpreters.

Natives themselves helped hasten the spread of writing. Awed by this new means of conversing and eager to capture its power, Indians copied the figures John Lawson jotted down, asked that their initials be carved into a tree alongside those of colonial explorers in order to "be an Englishman," and pestered Roger Williams, "Make me a paper." Even native diplomats who protested against "that Pen and Ink work" began demanding copies of the treaties to take home.

Indian and English forms coexisted well into the eighteenth century. In 1758, messengers sent from Philadelphia to the Ohio country carried belts of wampum that were keyed to a written speech, so that the talk could be read and the belts delivered simultaneously. To Indians this marked a real improvement, for it "was like two tongues": the letter "confirmed what the Messenger said to them" through the belts. Even so, the direction—from the rattle of wampum beads to the scratch of pen on paper—was clear. A few Indians learned to read and write, either in English or in their own language. But the vast majority remained illiterate, inhabitants of a symbolic universe they were unable to decipher.

Much of the impetus for communication between peoples—that march from gesture through jargon to fluency—came from a shared eagerness for trade. It was trade that prompted Indians to hoist furs on sticks, trade that gave birth to the pidgin languages, trade that trained most interpreters. The lists of Indian words colonists compiled reveal how closely talking was tied to trading. Each phrase book had Indian equivalents for all sorts of merchandise, numbers for counting these items, and handy phrases every enterprising salesman should know, like "How d'ye do," "Have you got anthing to eat," "Englishman is thirsty," "What price," "I will sell you Goods very cheap," "I will pay you well," "My money is very good," and "It is worth it."

The colonists' concern with price serves as a reminder that, while Indian and English were both experienced traders and each had products the other wanted, they were schooled in different classrooms. Hence handing over one object in return for another was not as simple or as easy as it looked. Among Indians, exchange was embedded in a ceremonial code designed to cement relations between peoples; in these rituals the giving itself was as important as the gift. Colonists, on the other hand, tended to think more of prices and profits. Intercultural trade in colonial America combined both traditions at first; eventually, however, commerce went the way of speech, and natives ended up living by the economic rules of the Atlantic world.

Indians unacquainted with European ways were a colonial trader's favorite customers. These people, still operating within the context of aboriginal exchange, cared little about sampling the entire range of trade goods and less about prices. They sought wares that fitted established norms—glass instead of shell beads, for instance, or mirrors that substituted for crystal—and in return they gave whatever the colonist considered fair. It did not take Indians long to catch on, however. In New England they had "already" in 1634 "learned much subtiltie and cunning by bargaining with the *English*," and Roger Williams agreed that "they are marvellous subtle in their Bargaines." Experience made natives discriminating consumers: instead of accepting whatever was offered, they began to shop more carefully. "The Indians wilbe very long and teadeous in viewing" a trader's merchandise, complained one colonist, "and doe tumble it and tosse it and mingle it a hundred times over." They were looking not just for beads or mirrors but cloth, tools, and weapons. Moreover, that cloth had to be "a sad colour," that iron hoe a certain weight, that gun a light flintlock instead of a cumbersome matchlock. And all—cloth, hoe, gun—had to be for sale at a fair price, for the more Indians traded with colonists, the fewer qualms they had about haggling over rates of exchange.

Indians, though soon enough "wise in trade and traffic" with colonists, did not immediately become slaves to European habits of exchange or pawns in the Atlantic economic system. In fact, during the early years of intercultural trade the colonist who hoped to succeed tried to meet his customers' needs and obey their rules. In putting together a cargo he selected the right color, the right weight, and the right price. Upon arriving in a village he gave gifts to the proper people and accepted their offer of adoption, even marriage, into a kin-ship network. Once the bargaining began, he said nothing about the Indians' preference for bartering, "not by any certeyne measure or by our English waightes and measures," but by an arm's length instead of a yard and a mouth-ful instead of a pint. He went along because competition for Indian customers was fierce—not only between England and France but between Pennsylvania and New York, Albany and Schenectady, even within (especially within) Albany itself—and Indians could afford to be selective. "If any traders will not suffer the Indians soe to doe [examine the goods for sale]," one colonist la-mented, "they wilbe distasted with the said trades and fall out with them and refuse to have any trade."

As time went on, however, few Indians could simply refuse to trade. While natives did not become dependent on European wares overnight, within a gen-eration or two of their entry into regular trade relations they did become depen-dent. The early shift from comity to competition and from passive acceptance to active haggling was only the beginning. The next stage removed the production of goods from its traditional context. Deer once put to many different uses were now left to rot as the hunter stripped the skin from the carcass and moved on. Prisoners of war once adopted to replace dead kinfolk or tortured to assuage a mourner's grief were now sold. Wampum once restricted to persons of high sta-tus was now mass-produced by coastal communities that interrupted their sea-sonal subsistence routine to concentrate on the shells. The final step was more obvious, as people less able to remember and to replicate traditional craft skills found they simply could not get along without European commodities.

Settlement Indians were the first to pass through these three stages. But even peoples well removed from colonial settlements found that a generation or so of colonial trade had taken its toll and "they cannot live without the assistance of the English." "What are we red People?" a Cherokee asked in 1753. "The Cloaths we wear, we cannot make ourselves, they are made to us.... We cannot make our Guns, they are made to us. Every necessary Thing in Life we must have from the white People." Lest any Indians forget this harsh truth, colonists reminded them: "We can live without you, but you cannot live without us." "'Tis in vain for you to stand out [against us]," a South Carolinian informed the Creeks in 1728. "What can you do without the English?"

Following the native Americans' entry into an alien economic system ob-scures how far trade remained what it had been in aboriginal America, an arm of diplomacy. Certainly Indians and colonists were aware that swapping mer-chandise was more than a way to make a living. Natives often spoke of peace and trade as one and the same thing, and colonists were quick to agree. In 1736, after giving some of the credit to God and the king, the South Carolina legislature asserted that the colony's "Security and Welfare ... hath been owing to nothing more than the Regulations ... with regard to the Trade and Commerce carried on from hence with the several Nations of Indians almost surrounding us.... [I]t is by these means alone that We have been able to preserve a general Peace and Friendship with them." For trade to serve as a vital cog in any diplomatic machine, however, that machine had to be built; learning to communicate and working out rules of exchange were essential to successful diplomacy, but without a mutually agreed-upon body of protocol for conducting a formal conversation they were just talking and trading.

Confusion reigned at first, in part because many early colonial leaders—Ralph Lane at Roanoke, John Smith in Virginia, Miles Standish of Plymouth—were by training and temperament about as far from diplomats as they could be. The conquistador was their model, and they came to America fresh from service among alien peoples where the sword was the first rather than the last resort. But even colonists who put more stock in negotiation often fared little better. Faced with a political world that bore little resemblance to their own, they tried to conjure up emperors, kings, and nations that were not there. In fact, most eastern Indian chiefs led by persuasion and example, custom and council. Whatever authority a headman did wield generally was limited to a narrow sphere of face-to-face relations; few ruled an extensive territory. Reality inevitably intruded, leaving many English diplomats feeling as Carolina authorities did in 1682 as they cast about for an alliance with a people "whose Government is lesse Anarchicall" than the colony's current friends.

Experience taught colonists the limitations of kingly power and the narrow definition of nationhood in native America.

Colonists sorting out Indian political reality also had to undergo a crash course in native diplomacy, for, once diplomatic relations opened, Indian rules prevailed. The Covenant Chain, forged in the late seventeenth century to connect the Iroquois and other Indians with New York and other colonies, was only the most famous example of how native diplomacy shaped formal intercultural contacts. From Creeks and Cherokees to Delawares and Shawnees, natives set the tempo and tenor of diplomatic encounters. They came when they pleased, and in delegations larger than cost-conscious crown officials liked. They insisted on preliminary rituals ("the usual Salutation of Shaking of hands" in the Southeast, "the usual Salutation of Shaking of hands" in the Southeast, "the usual Compliments of Condolence" in Iroquoia) and punctuated their talks with wampum belts and gifts. The talks themselves sounded strange to colonial ears, for native ambassadors spoke in a rich, metaphorical language of elder brothers and nephews, paths clear or bloody, hatchets taken up or thrown down, a language that invested kinship terms and everyday objects with deeper meaning.

Anglo-American diplomats went along initially because they had to: their pretensions to conquest aside, the English simply lacked the power to dictate forms, much less terms. But they continued to play the diplomatic game by Indian rules, because treaty protocol became a tool for exerting influence.

Wherever the fall in native numbers and the Indians' dependence on trade tipped the balance of power toward the English, native diplomatic formulas became a means of wielding that power. Skillfully employed, diplomacy was a vehicle not only for contracting alliances and settling differences but also for issuing threats, acquiring land, and, as one governor phrased it, putting "a Bridle in the Mouths of our Indians." It is true that for the Five Nations treaty councils were "a species of drama in which the Iroquois were the playwrights, the directors and the teaching actors"; but with Indians along the coast in the seventeenth century, Anglo-Americans had begun to direct the play themselves, and, before 1800, more distant groups also found that the path between peoples was becoming a one-way street, the chain was becoming fetters.

Once the fetters were in place, colonial officials demonstrated the depth of their commitment to native treaty forms by abandoning them. For Catawbas, the shock came shortly after the smallpox epidemic of 1759 cut to one hundred the number of warriors they could muster and threats from Cherokees and the French subsided. South Carolina saw little point in placating its old allies any longer, and a Catawba delegation visiting Charleston in September 1761 found its efforts to follow "the usual" rituals brusquely turned aside. Officials complained that the Indians had come, complained about the size of the delegation, complained about the presents requested, and bluntly informed the Indians not to return unless summoned. The chill in the air was perceptible, and later delegations found it still colder. By the end of the American Revolution Catawbas rarely approached the South Carolina capital, and even the once-mighty Iroquois faced diplomats who believed that "instead of conforming to Indian political behavior We should force them to adopt ours—dispense with belts, etc."

Anglo-America could afford to treat Catawbas and Iroquois so casually because they were joining Pamunkeys, Narragansetts, and the many other tribes that long since had been surrounded by settlers. Among some of these neighboring peoples the diplomatic niceties might still be observed for a time— negotiations continued, treaties were signed—but they were now at best a mere shadow of their former grandeur, at worst a caricature. Native delegations accustomed to arriving when it suited them now came once a year at a time set by the colony. The ceremonial exchange of gifts turned into a public display of subjection, with Indians handing over a few pelts or arrows as token tribute and officials responding with a present or two that was more charity than bribery. In such encounters it is safe to assume that native formal expression went the way of large delegations, elaborate presents, and official interpreters, forcing headmen to conform to English speech and English practice.

With even the pretense of equality stripped away, function followed form; diplomatic relations became less negotiation than protection and, finally, less protection than subjection. The time devoted to hearing a tributary's complaints and the energy spent redressing grievances dwindled with the years, and enforcement of treaty rights, never very rigorous, fell still lower on the public agenda. In the end, diplomacy was a way to build a paper prison. Treaties stipulated that the selection of headmen be supervised, contacts with other native groups curtailed, and the tribe confined to certain lands.

For most native Americans, judges took up where diplomats left off, and the courtroom, not the council chamber, regulated intercultural relations. Unlike diplomacy, trade, or language, however, when it came to questions of law English colonists never considered submitting to native forms. The reason was simple: by English standards Indians had no law to speak of. There was no written code, no institution to interpret and enforce that code, in short nothing recognizable in English terms. Indian law consisted of rules upheld by ostracism, shaming, compensation, and—between clans or tribes—retaliation. Colonists, who missed the power of ridicule and looked upon revenge as savagery, had no misgivings about imposing their own legal framework upon the native. From the very outset they promised to punish any colonist committing a crime against an Indian but insisted that, if the situation were reversed, the Indian must submit to English law.

English assertions of legal imperialism had little impact on tribes far from colonial capitals. As Leonard Calvert had learned from the Wicomisses in 1634, claiming jurisdiction was one thing, exercising it quite another. Some distant Indians might sign a treaty in which they agreed to surrender a native suspected of committing a crime against Anglo-America. But, treaty or no treaty, natives beyond the frontier commonly dealt with an unruly colonist in their own way and ignored pleas to give up any Indians wanted for trial. The best that Anglo-Americans could hope for was that diplomatic pressure might persuade these Indians to do the job themselves. In 1748, South Carolina informed the Cherokees that, if they executed an Indian who had killed a colonist, the province would build a long-promised fort in the Cherokee country; if not, the colony's traders would withdraw. After the Cherokees complied, Governor James Glen proclaimed it "a great step towards civilizing savage and barbarous Nations when they can be brought to doe Publick acts of Justice upon their Criminals." Certainly the Cherokees' acquiescence testified to the power of trade, but it was still a long way from getting the wrongdoer into a colonial court. That would have to wait until distant Indians became neighbors.

Once that change had taken place, an Indian committing a crime was far more likely to wind up in court. Civil disputes still might be handled by negotiation and provincial magistrates might overlook crimes among Indians, but a native who killed, robbed, or otherwise harmed a colonist was going to come before the bench.

The erosion of native legal rights was most evident in New England, where those rights had been most advanced. During the first decades of colonization some Indians were active participants in the judicial system, sitting on juries, giving testimony, serving as constables, even running their own courts. This was hardly equality: native jurors were balanced if not outnumbered by settlers, and restricted to cases involving Indians; native courts operated under the watchful eye of a supervisor who could overturn decisions. But it was more justice than they had after Kind Philip's War, when even this limited say in judicial affairs crumbled swiftly. Colonial officials, claiming that natives could not handle the responsibility, dismantled Indian courts and replaced them with "guardians" or "overseers," men appointed by the executive whose powers over their native charges reached beyond the courtroom. During the same period the number of statutes discriminating against Indians expanded dramatically. To the old laws aimed at keeping kegs and muskets out of native hands were added curfews and restrictions on assembly and travel; even carrying a cane could land an Indian in trouble.

The Indians' treatment at the hands of colonial law cannot obscure the more fundamental legal issue at stake here: whose rules were law. While Anglo-American leaders may have sought justice as they construed it, Indians saw things differently. To them, crimes were being defined in alien terms and dealt with in alien ways. The gap between the colonial ideal of justice for all and the native view of proper treatment was evident in Virginia in 1729, when an intoxicated Saponi headman killed a colonist. The Saponis considered this an unfortunate accident that should be forgotten, since by native custom those under the influence of alcohol were not responsible for their actions. Virginia's governor, William Gooch, thought otherwise, and unlike Leonard Calvert a century earlier he was in a position to do something about it. He sent word to the Indians to give the culprit up and ordered them to Williamsburg to witness the proceedings. During the ensuing trial and execution Gooch took great pains to explain to the assembled natives "that the proceedings in the Court against Him were the same as in the like Case, they would be against a white Man, and indeed as it hap'ned, ... there was one tryed and executed with him."

Colonist and Indian, swinging side by side from the gallows: what could be more fair? The Saponis, Gooch concluded happily, sat through it all "without any sign of resentment." Appearances were deceiving, however. Even as Gooch closed the books on the case, Saponis were leaving the colony in search of more civilized patrons. Small wonder that as the noose of alien law tightened, many neighboring Indians—in New York, South Carolina, Virginia, and elsewhere—still tried to go through diplomatic channels when disputes arose or crimes were committed, preferring to take their chances with governor and council rather than with judge and jury.

The legal controls that Saponis and other tribes tried to escape went hand in hand with the work of English missionaries. It was a fundamental tenet of the faith English Colonists brought to America that belief and behavior were two sides of the same coin, that civilization must accompany—indeed, it must precede—Christianity. The law could not dictate belief, but it could do something about behavior. In 1646, a week after skeptical Indians heckled a Puritan minister during a sermon, Massachusetts Bay passed a law against blasphemy by anyone, Christian or pagan. Six years later, Plymouth legislators forbade Indians from working on the Sabbath, and in 1675 Connecticut went even further, not only insisting that natives honor the Sabbath but requiring their "ready and comely attendance" whenever preachers held services for them. Once the law had stopped Indians from working or heckling and got them to pay attention, it was up to missionaries to do the rest.

The missionary's ability to win an Indian audience for Christ depended largely on where that audience was. Tribes beyond the frontier were for the most part indifferent to the Christian message as translated by the English, in part because English clergymen, unlike the Jesuits operating in New France, rarely visited Indian Country to spread the word. In New England, every minister was tied to a particular congregation and therefore could not venture too far away in search of converts. But even men recruited to do the Lord's work among remote tribes tended to hug the coast. Clergymen sent to South Carolina in the early eighteenth century by the Society for the Propagation of the Gospel in Foreign Parts to "propagate Christianity ... among the wild Indians in the woods" found some excuse—rumblings of war among those distant peoples, plenty of pagans close at hand among the colonial population—to postpone their mission. Few went beyond asking traders about the best tribes to approach and having the Lord's Prayer translated into Yamasee or Shawnee for future use. In Virginia the story was much the same. "The missionaries that are now sent," reported the Anglican cleric Hugh Jones in 1724, "generally keep among the English, and rarely see an Indian."

Reluctance to head into the interior may have stemmed from a lack of nerve, but it also could have arisen from a sense that Indians there were not very fertile soil for sowing the English version of Christianity. Jesuits with a tolerance for native ways, a gift for languages, and a religion rich in symbol and ritual enjoyed considerable success. English Protestants, on the other hand, usually lacked the delicate touch needed to convert distant Indians. They "know but little how to manage them [Indians]," Jones remarked; "for you may as well talk reason, philosophy, or divinity to a block, as to them, unless you perfectly understand their temper, and know how to humour them." If a missionary did make the effort, he discovered that natives beyond the frontier were uninterested in the gospel according to the English, especially when they found out that conversion entailed political subjection and cultural suicide. Some reacted with open scorn, laughing or going so far as "flatly to say, that our Lord God was not God, since hee suffered us to sustaine much hunger, and also to be killed of the Renapoaks." Others listened politely and walked away. Still others were ready to grant that Christianity was fine for the English but not for Indians, who preferred a different way. "We are Indians," they would say when pressed, "and don't wish to be transformed into white men. ... As little as we desire the preacher to become Indian, so little ought he to desire the Indians to become preachers."

Settlement Indians were more susceptible to the missionary's message. Confidence in their own cultural traditions had been badly shaken by demographic disaster; who could doubt the power of the Englishman's God when Indians mysteriously died by the score and colonists did not even become ill? The awe an epidemic could inspire was clear from the very beginning of the English colonial venture. At Roanoke, where disease visited every native town that opposed the English beachhead and "the people began to die very fast," colonists reported that survivors were "perswaded that it was the worke of our God through our meanes, and that wee by him might kil and slai whom wee would without weapons and not come neere them." Once the colonists' more conventional weapons had defeated Indians in battle, the newcomers further sapped native commitment to ancient deities and added to the growing evidence of the Christian God's power.

Those neighboring Indians who *were* offered the chance to convert sometimes turned it down. Narragansetts, Mohegans, and other groups defeated in

King Philip's War wanted nothing to do with the religion of the victors, and well into the eighteenth century they spurned missionary overtures. In South Carolina, clergymen in coastal parishes conversed regularly with "Neighbouring Indians," but found these remnant groups unlikely candidates for conversion. They "are a moving People," one reported, "often changing their place of habitation so that I can give no account of their Number"—much less the state of their souls. Prodding them did no good, for they seemed "wholy addicted to their own barbarous and Sloathful Customs and will only give a laugh w[he]n pleased or a grin w[he]n displeas'd for an Answer." "It must be the work of time and power that must have any happy Influence upon em," one would-be savior concluded glumly.

After more than a century, the missionary campaign had enjoyed mixed results. On the one hand, signs of progress were clear: in New England at one time or another more than a score of Indian churches had been built, nearly one hundred praying towns or reservations organized, and even more natives had become teachers or preachers. On the other hand, however, those bent on wiping out every stain of paganism were disappointed. Too many Indians remained outside the fold, and those within it had entered on their own terms, shaping the new religion to serve their spiritual and cultural needs. Far from making Indians English, the new faith (where natives embraced it) proved to be a powerful revitalizing force, helping people to cope with defeat and dispossession, to rebuild their aboriginal communities on a new foundation.

In the end it proved easier to kill Indians than convert them, easier to make them speak English than make them listen to a sermon, easier to get them into a courtroom than into a church, easier to bring them to acknowledge the English king than the English God. The missionary's failure to see his dreams become reality is a useful reminder that natives were neither the "Indian dust" one early New Englander envisioned nor the "soft Wax, ready to take any Impression" that a Virginian described. Far from crumbling and being swept aside or passively receiving everything the English handed them, Indians learned to conform to the new "Customes of the Countrey" without surrendering unconditionally to the country's new rulers.

It was not easy. Some tribes fought, some fled. Others stayed behind and protested the invasion of America in their own way, stealing a colonial school's Latin and Greek books or burning a planter's fences, acts some have termed "purely whimsical" but that may have had symbolic significance. Still others made their feelings known by refusing to abide by colonial customs. The problem in the Massachusetts praying town of Natick was as simple as saying "Hello." Waban, the community's first headman and one of John Eliot's converts, won praise for greeting colonists "with English salutations." But some inhabitants of Natick would not follow Waban's lead. In 1680 they were "refusing to take notice of an Englishman if they meet him in the street," and decades later one holdout, Hannah Pittimee, still "past by ... with a great deal of scorn ... with her face turned right from us."

Pittimee and every other Settlement Indian had reason to be scornful, for those natives living behind the frontier faced a future of poverty and oppression.

As their resources disappeared and their skills eroded, natives searched desperately for ways to put food in their mouths and a roof over their heads. The search sometimes led to an ancestor's grave, which Indians ransacked for the valuable wampum it contained. Not everyone was driven to such lengths, but almost all struggled to scrape together the necessities of life, and they did so amid the insults, the laughter, the abuses spawned by the conquerors' hatred. Sometimes that hatred was disclosed only by a slip of the pen: a clerk in a Massachusetts court referred to an Indian as "it," and a Philadelphia scribe wrote that the spectators at a council consisted of "many other People and Indians." More often the colonists' feelings were easier to detect. Young Indian apprentices discovered that "their fellow Prentices viz. English Boys will dispise them and treat them as Slaves." The colonial youths picked up this attitude from their parents, who openly doubted that anything besides "Powder and Ball" would convert the natives, and, acting on that belief, placed only "a Bullet and Flynt" in a missionary's collection plate. Even colonists with good intentions inflicted their own kind of pain. When the evangelist George Whitefield's colleague Benjamin Ingham built a schoolhouse for Indians atop an ancient temple mount near Savannah, Georgia, he dismissed the local Creeks' spiritual attachment to the site and insisted that it now serve a different deity.

But if neighboring Indians did not prosper, they did survive. One secret of their survival was the ability they had to make themselves inconspicuous. When drinking, for example, they aped their English neighbors. "It rent my heart as well as ears," wrote one Virginian in the 1680s, "when once passing by a company of Indians in James City, that drinking in a ring were deplorably drunk ... one cried to another swear swear, you be Englishman swear, w[i]th that he made a horrid yelling, imperfectly vomited up oaths, whereupon the other cryd, oh! now your [*sic*] be Englishman."

Natives learning to drink and curse like an Englishman were also learning to dress like one, and this camouflage, too, was crucial to their survival. Simply putting on English clothes was not enough; one had to know how to wear them.

As important as this mimetic talent was the ability to retain a distinctly Indian identity. Natives imitating colonists still stood out in subtle ways in every sphere of contact. For most, English was a second language, imperfectly mastered and used only for talking with colonists and slaves. In the mid-eighteenth century, one Rhode Island native woman's English vocabulary consisted of a single word—"broom"—and in Massachusetts confused colonists learned that the Braintree Indians' English disguise held up only "till you come to converse with them." In material culture and economic pursuits, too, their conversion was less than complete. Many led a peripatetic life modeled on traditional habits of seasonal migration. From Etiwans in South Carolina to Naticks in Massachusetts, they were "strangely disposed and addicted to wander from place to place." If they did come to lead what colonists considered a settled existence, Indians still might depart from colonial norms. One built an English frame house but no chimney, preferring to rely on an open fire; others put brick fireplaces into their wigwams; still others bought tea tables, dressers, chairs, and other articles commonly found in colonial households, then placed the furniture in the domed dwellings they made out of bark and saplings.

The same habit of blending into the landscape of English America without becoming wholly invisible can be seen in diplomacy, law, and religion. Though native enclaves might be "little Tribes," tribes they were, not mere aggregates of individuals or a vaguely defined ethnic group. However unequal the terms of diplomacy had become, Indians with their own corporate identity and cadre of leaders were equipped to deal with colonial politicians on a diplomatic footing. They were also in a position to police themselves, and many continued to settle their own disputes. In 1704, some Settlement Indians in New England were "Govern'd by Law's of their own making." "If the natives committ any crime on their own precincts among themselves, the English takes no Cognezens of it," and the same was true of South Carolina's Indians more than a century later. Finally, and perhaps most important, the Christianity that some remnant groups used as the new foundation for an ancient identity remained distinct from its English progenitor. The sharing of tobacco during services on Martha's Vineyard incorporated old rituals into a new ceremonial context, and in Rhode Island the Narragansetts' August Meeting—several days of services, feasts, and dances—harked back to a traditional harvest festival. In all of these ways, Indians managed to pacify the powerful without losing all sense of a unique past—and a separate future.

This adaptive talent was present from the first. In 1634—the very year Clavert and the Wicomiss were meeting along the Chesapeake—it was already on display in New England, where William Wood and two companions got lost on the way to Plymouth, "being deluded by a misleading path." It was, the travelers thought, too wide to be an Indian trail, but they were wrong. They had been fooled because "the dayly concourse of *Indians* from the *Naragansets* who traded for shooes, wearing them homewards had made this *Indian* tract like an *English* walke, and had rear'd up great stickes against the trees, and marked the rest with their hatchets in the *English* fashion, which begat in us a security of our wrong way to be right." Like Narragansetts, Indians throughout the East who might look English were in fact following, indeed carving, paths that took them toward another destination. Learning to survive as a conquered people by combining European and aboriginal ways: this was the fate in store for every native group as the English and other migrants from the Old World pushed deeper into the heart of the American continent.

French Louisiana in the Native Ground

KATHLEEN DUVAL

In 1750, after more than half a century of colonization, the French governor of Louisiana declared in exasperation, "we can do nothing by ourselves." While the French called Louisiana their colony, in reality, as Governor [Pierre François de

Kathleen Duval, "Interconnectedness and Diversity in 'French Louisiana,'" in *Powhatan's Mantle: Indians in the Colonial Southeast*, ed. Gregory A. Waselkov, Peter H. Wood, and Tom Hatley, pp. 133–162 (Lincoln: University of Nebraska Press, 2006). Reprinted by permission of the University of Nebraska Press. Copyright 1989, 2006 by the Board of Regents of the University of Nebraska.

Rigaud, Marquis de] Vaudreuil, knew, officials, explorers, priests, merchants, traders, and slaves became small parts of the large, complex neighborhood of the Mississippi valley. One narrative of the late seventeenth and eighteenth centuries stars French colonial officials such as Vaudreuil forging (and losing) Louisiana, where they sought to profit and to challenge France's European rivals. But countless other intertwined narratives run through this place and time, centering on Choctaws, Natchez, Chickasaws, Tunicas, Osages, Quapaws, Bambaras, Mobilians, Caddoans, Britons, Spaniards, and other groups and individuals within them.

This is not to say that the French has no effect on Louisiana. On the contrary, European diseases and goods changed the region's history. Indians became entangled in the world economies that colonialism created, and ultimately the arrival of the French proved one of the most important events of the late seventeenth-century Mississippi valley. But emphasizing change that occurred after Europeans arrived can create the impression that Europeans *directed* change. In reality, the French had little power, and the Mississippi valley remained largely an Indian-defined and Indian-controlled place through the end of the eighteenth century.

Native peoples chose how to deal with and interpret the new dangers and opportunities that resulted from foreign incursions. Most Mississippi valley people's priorities did not center on Europeans. To Indians, who constituted the vast majority of Louisiana's population, Indian rivalries, alliances, military strategies, trade networks, and ways of conducting foreign relations generally bore more relevance than Europeans. Indians sought European alliances and trade in order to gain an advantage in their rivalries with other Indians or to draw Indians into alliance by offering desired goods. Even most of the colonial population operated with little regard for French colonial interests. Seeking converts and trading partners, priests and traders focused on Indians. Runaway slaves and deserting soldiers by definition worked against the colonial establishment.

All people living in the place that Europeans called colonial Louisiana found themselves entangled in foreign relations. Any of them could have complained of their inability to do anything "by ourselves." But the ambitions of the colonial project made the French particularly dependent on others. Because they wanted a colony to rival the Spanish and English and because they sought to rule Louisiana despite lacking a large army, they had to pay attention to Indian priorities. Of the scores of diverse and intertwined peoples who populated Louisiana, the French proved one of the least independent and least successful in manipulating others.

By the late seventeenth century, most North American Indians saw reciprocal gift-giving and marital or fictive kinship ties as the means to establish and maintain good relations between peoples. When the French arrived, Indians greeted them with the same ceremonies they used to transform any foreigners into friends and allies—calumet (peace pipe) dances and songs, speeches of welcome, and feasts to demonstrate generosity and friendship.

Indians courted the French because the French had something that Indians wanted. Facing threats from others newly armed with Spanish and English weapons, Indians throughout the Mississippi valley needed French guns and ammunition. By 1700 Chickasaw bands were raiding old enemies, and making new ones, to acquire slaves to trade to the English at Charlestown for guns, ammunition, and horses. In the northeast, Iroquoian peoples monopolized Dutch and British trade and regularly attacked Illinois Indians and others east of the Mississippi. In the west, Apache and Comanche bands soon blocked Spanish trade.

Despite their immediate popularity, the French were one of the weakest groups in a land full of people struggling to strengthen their positions in the wake of sixteenth-century changes. Although colonial officials regularly requested more soldiers and arms to "intimidate the Indians," tight budgets, desertions, and recurrent French war against other European nations kept Louisiana's forces small and unstable. At times, fewer than two hundred soldiers were assigned to the entire colony, on both sides of the Mississippi. In the mid-1720s Louisiana had some 2,500 French, plus 1,500 slaves. In contrast, Louisiana Indians numbered well over 35,000. While many Indian groups were tiny, the Choctaws, Chickasaws, Natchez, Osages, and Caddoans all had populations greater than the French, and many others rivaled the French population. No one people had the power to rule the others, and all found themselves entangled in webs of foreign relations and obligations.

Size was not everything. Although the largest group, Choctaws found that regional and ethnic loyalties often outweighed national interests. Some smaller groups such as the Quapaws used their relative unity to wield an influence beyond their numbers. Even more fragmented than the Choctaws, the French arrived in North America as diverse people with various goals and methods, which only occasionally combined into serving the colonial project. French men and women came to the region for many reasons besides the advancement of the colony—converting Indians to Christianity, making individual profits, escaping trouble at home, and forced removal from the streets of Paris and Marseilles.

The presence of powerful native peoples weakened French officials' control over the colonial population by broadening opportunities. The *voyageurs* (independent traders) who traversed the land held more allegiance to their own interests and often to their Indian trading partners than they did to French officials, as the French hierarchy was well aware. Etienne de Périer, Louisiana governor in 1729, petitioned his superior to strengthen the Louisiana government in order to "subdue the inhabitants of this area who are just *voyageurs* and *coureurs de bois* who work that trade only because they want to be their own masters and who would easily withdraw from their obedience to the King if we were not prepared to repress them." Like the Chickasaws at Kaskaskia, these Frenchmen sought trade from multiple sources, which could help them "be their own masters." Even French soldiers did not always serve colonial interests. Desertion was a constant problem as the fur trade lured scores of soldiers away from the dangers and deprivations of the colonial army. The Quapaws recruited French deserters to settle nearby in order to strengthen their own numbers on a contested Indian borderland. At times the Quapaws successfully protected and incorporated runaway slaves and soldiers accused of treason, desertion, and even murder.

The extreme fragmentation of the colonial population put the French in a unique position. In some ways being fragmented made them more influential because they spread across the countryside, encountering a wider variety of people than most Indians met and offering goods the native peoples wanted. But being fragmented also meant that the French were more influenced by native peoples than they might otherwise have been. Various French people's goals and methods often conflicted, and their decentralized nature attenuated them, giving more centralized, established, and knowledgeable people opportunities to influence the newcomers. French officials quickly learned that their low numbers and fragmentation precluded dominating Indians.

In fact, Indian power and French weakness forced the French to do the opposite—attempt to persuade Indians to fight French battles. But more often than not French officials found themselves conducting foreign policy according to their Indian allies' interests. In 1730 Périer informed his superiors that using Indian allies was the least efficient way to run the colony. As he explained, he had to spend so much on gifts to allies that "it will cost the Company more to make the Indians act when they are needed" than to support the same number of troops. To make matters worse for the governor, paying Indians by no means guaranteed that they would do his bidding. As Périer put it, "the least little nation thinks itself our protector" and "that we use them only because we are not capable of making war"—which of course was true. Indians knew how much the French depended on them.

How various Indians used this knowledge depended on their own history, their beliefs about themselves and the world, their current relations with neighbors, what they needed or wanted from Europeans, as well as what kind and how many Europeans they met and how often. As the French attempted to make Indians serve colonial purposes, Indians worked to shape the French into useful allies and neighbors. All Indian allies demanded French compliance with the dictates of reciprocity. As early as 1717, the Commissary General of Louisiana, Marc Antoine Hubert, could report that "all the chiefs of the Indians, even those remote from these posts," regularly traveled "to see the commandants, with the expectation of receiving some presents." Within the rubric of reciprocity, these gifts served as the obligation of those wealthy in exotic goods but short on practicalities to those able to provide guides, interpreters, warriors, food, and land. Often in fact short on goods, French officials thought of these demands as tribute.

French officials had no choice but to comply. There was no other way to counter the English and Spanish. In fact, Indians' desire for French weapons to counter enemies armed by Spanish and especially English trade harmonized with French imperial objectives. French-Indian negotiations developed a standard vocabulary that drew on the presence of other Europeans. Indians complained of attacks by European-armed foes, and French officials promised not only weapons but also a friendship more in line with Indian ideals of reciprocity and obligation than other Europeans would provide.

Native peoples in turn used their knowledge of European rivalries to instruct Europeans in how they should act. Louisiana Indians sought trade with as many Europeans as possible, and most traded at least sporadically with the English from at least 1700. Despite French, English, and Spanish admonitions that trading relationships were exclusive to one European power, their Indian partners did not agree. In 1745 Quapaw leaders warned their local commandant that if supplies did not improve they would "see the English again." They knew that mentioning the English would always agitate the French official, who quickly wrote to the governor requesting more merchandise.

At times people used an alliance with one nation to attract others. The Choctaw delegates who met Iberville in 1702 surely hoped to use French trade to draw their troublesome Chickasaw neighbors into a peaceful alliance, as the Quapaws and Osages had unsuccessfully attempted at Kaskaskia twenty years before. Chickasaw and Creek raids were enslaving and killing thousands of Choctaws. The same month, other Choctaws and Chickasaws were using French officer Henri de Tonti as a mediator. Similarly the Chickasaws used English trade goods to entice Indians into trading relations.

Events surrounding the Natchez war, which began in 1729, illuminate this unstable world of alliances and rivalries. Triggered by Natchez–French conflict, war spread through the complicated alliances of the Mississippi valley.

[D]istrust [had] mounted between Natchez and French leaders, as each attempted to dominate the other. To the Natchez allowing French settlements made these French into subordinates, like previous Indian settlers. When French traders and officials proved less pliable than the Natchez expected, some began to consider that pillaging French goods and recruiting English trade might be a more reliable way to maintain Natchez security than continuing this unstable and unpredictable relationship.

On several occasions beginning in the 1710s Natchez killed and raided French parties when they violated Natchez propriety. In the 1720s the Natchez's White Apple village found itself at the center of conflict. In the winter of 1723 a dispute over debt led to the death of one of that village's men. When the French commandant only reprimanded the murderer, warriors from the White Apple village attacked nearby French settlements.... Louisiana Lieutenant Governor Jean-Baptiste Le Moyne, Sieur de Bienville, led an army the following winter to punish the White Apple village. Pressured by French violence and probably the insistence of other villages, the White Apple village surrendered the chief whom Bienville demanded as recompense for the previous winter's violence. In the peace terms the Natchez agreed to build a fort on their lands that the French would staff and supply, granting the Natchez steadier access to trade and a means for settling future disputes with French traders and settlers.

Despite the tension more French settlers came to farm tobacco on Natchez lands. In the 1720s these settlements grew to 200 Frenchmen, 80 Frenchwomen, 150 French children, and 280 black slaves. Although the Natchez had originally welcomed settlers, they seemed to be growing out of Natchez control. Indeed, in the 1723 conflict White Apple village warriors had attacked the symbols of French settlements, livestock and slaves, as well as the settlers themselves. Although the Natchez had assigned the previous land grants, in late November of 1729, the commandant of the French post, the Sieur de Chépart, ordered the White Apple village to evacuate so that French settlers could farm their land.

More accustomed to giving than taking orders, the Natchez decided to get rid of these interlopers once and for all. At the urging of the White Apple village's chiefs, the Natchez again sent representatives to meet with potential allies, including Yazoos, Koroas, Illinois, Chickasaws, and Choctaws. Changing tactics this time, they also reached out to African slaves held on the plantations near Natchez. According to a later report, the Natchez invited all slaves to join the Natchez side and thereby gain their freedom. But they warned that those who refused would be sold to the Chickasaws and the English when the Natchez prevailed. At eight in the morning of November 28, Natchez warriors knocked at the door of each French house and asked to borrow guns for a hunting expedition. Then they turned the guns on their owners, killing nearly all the Frenchmen, including the commandant and the Jesuit priest. The Natchez captured the slaves and most of the French women and children and burned the houses and sheds, destroying thousands of pounds of tobacco. Thus they cast out the disrespectful newcomers who would not play by Natchez rules.

The Natchez attack decisively placed the French on the opposite side of this conflict. But lining up the sides did not determine how the French should react. Many desired vengeance, but fear was the dominant reaction among the French population. As Governor Périer reported in 1730 of his colonists, "the least rumor makes them rush to the woods like hares." Local Indians stoked these fears with reports that the powerful Chickasaws and Choctaws had joined the conspiracy and were going to kill all the French throughout the colony. With frightened and outnumbered colonists, French officials knew that they would have to persuade their allies to reject Natchez overtures and instead assist the French in getting revenge.

The crisis of 1729 brought alliances into the open, forcing people who preferred to cultivate friendship broadly now to choose sides. In the conflict all Natchez neighbors felt pulled by the demands of allies, and all attempted to enforce their own notions of alliance obligations on others. Generally having the least power, Africans took opportunities when they came. Slaves at Natchez did not kill any French that November, but some apparently joined the Natchez defense later. In January of 1730 captured slaves fought off a Choctaw attack long enough to allow the Natchez to regroup within their forts. More often, Africans' wartime opportunities came in fighting for the French or laboring for the French military. Although officials feared armed slaves, they continued to use them (in small numbers) because, as Governor Périer put it, slaves seemed to fight considerably better than the French soldiers, "who seem expressly made for Louisiana, they are so bad." In addition, Périer hoped that pitting slaves against native enemies would prevent Indian-African collaboration.

Most Indians' reactions to the crisis depended more on relationships with other Indians than with Europeans. The Yazoos and Koroas agreed to join the Natchez effort. Their familial and alliance ties to the Natchez and the devastation they had experienced from European disease joined to pull their loyalties to the Natchez side. Following the Natchez example the Yazoos and Koroas killed their Jesuit missionary, the French who were in their post, and several ill-fated traders who happened to pass along the Mississippi. Koroa women, who apparently had the authority to determine the fate of captives, decreed that five French women and four children be taken to the Chickasaws and sold rather than killed. With their decision to attack the French in November of 1729, the Yazoos and Koroas found their destinies linked with the Natchez.

The Quapaws' choice was as clear as the Yazoos' and Kiroas'. Since the Quapaws' move west, they had resisted these Missisppian descendants, who contested the Quapaws' right to settle on the Mississippi River. The Quapaws eagerly joined the fight against their enemies, declaring that "while there was an [Quapaw] in the world, the Natchez and the Yazoos would not be without an enemy." Throughout the 1730s they conducted successful raids against the Natchez, Yazoos, and Koroas. Rather than fighting *for* the French, as historians often describe Indian-European military alliances, the Quapaws were delighted to have an agitated ally who would provide troops, supplies, and encouragement.

The Quapaws' good relations with the French also contributed to their decision. In contrast to the Natchez the Quapaws built a strong friendship with their French neighbors. One reason was the smaller numbers of French—fewer than fifty—living in their midst. And these French and the Quapaws both had reasons to be more adaptable than did their French and Natchez counterparts. Not only outnumbered in a strange land hundreds of miles from Louisiana's French capital, non-Indians on the Arkansas also had not come as settlers determined to build plantations. They were voyageurs, *engagés* (indentured servants) freed and stranded by John Law's 1720 financial debacle, and deserters. For the Quapaws' part, their status as newcomers on a contested land seems to have given them a flexibility that the long-powerful Natchez chiefs lacked as well as a greater desire to get along with the most recent newcomers. The French farmed fields and lived in a town surrounded by Quapaw fields and towns, and under their supervision. The French settlers provided mutual protection in a dangerous place and traded furs, food, and other material goods. Their needs coincided with those of the Quapaws, and Quapaw rituals transformed neighbors into family. Having successfully incorporated French men and women, largely on local terms, the Quapaws seized the opportunity to ally with the French against old enemies.

Although not enemies of the Natchez, Yazoos, or Koroas, the Choctaws had no particular affinity for them and hoped to profit from the captives, spoils, and French supplies that would come from the war. French officials very much hoped to have this powerful people on their side, whose participation would be infinitely more valuable than the Louisiana army. In January of 1730, French soldiers established a siege on Natchez. But when the Natchez charged out of the fort to fight, the French soldiers fled "without firing a single shot," as Governor Périer despondently informed his superior. To the governor's and the Natchez's surprise, five hundred Choctaws attacked Natchez two days later. In the battle, they killed at least one hundred Natchez and recovered fifty French women and children and between fifty and one hundred African slaves. The French governor's delight was dimmed a bit by a rumor that the Choctaws had attacked rapidly because they wanted to retrieve the captives before the French or any other Indians got to them.

When the French politely asked for the captives' return, the Choctaws demanded ransoms for each, in part to make up for the hunting their warriors had forfeited in order to fight. They declared their willingness to sell the African captives to the English if they gave better prices. The French claim that the slaves belonged to them carried little weight. The Choctaws considered them justly acquired in battle. While the French might have a claim to the return of their families, they had held the Africans in bondage and had no right to prevent the Choctaws or English from doing the same. Alibamon Mingo, a Choctaw chief from the town of Concha, listed the price for each black slave: "a coat, a gun, a white blanket, four ells of limburg cloth," plus presents for each town and for individual chiefs. One Choctaw chief told French officer Régis du Roullet that his men were keeping the slaves that they had captured to serve them and that "the French ought to be content with those who had been returned to them." Without Choctaw assistance, the chief pointed out, the French "would have got nothing at all" because they "did not have enough courage to take them."

The Tunicas' history with the Natchez made them more ambivalent than the Yazoos, Koroas, Quapaws, or Choctaws. They apparently had allied with the Natchez in the past, but conflict had erupted in 1723 when Tunicas killed three Natchez. In early 1730 the Tunicas swore to fight the Natchez and their allies. They scouted for the French, although it is not clear that they actually engaged in battle. Whatever their earlier designs, in June of 1730 the Tunicas made a mistake. One hundred Natchez men plus women and children who had fled after the Choctaw attack sought refuge among the Tunicas. They asked for Tunica mediation to make peace with the French. Whether sincerely or in hopes of capturing the Natchez to deliver to the French, the Tunicas invited the Natchez refugees to settle among them. When the Tunicas asked the Natchez men to hand over their arms, the men answered that they wanted to but they needed to hold onto them "to reassure their wives," who were naturally apprehensive about entering the town of their former enemy. Acceding to the sensibility of the women's fear, the Tunicas hosted the Natchez with a calumet ceremony and feast that lasted well into the night. After the Tunicas went to sleep, the Natchez guests killed twenty of them and drove off the rest long enough to escape with the Tunicas' guns and ammunition, of which they had a large supply due to recent French recruitment. This betrayal placed the Tunicas firmly on the anti-Natchez side. They routed Natchez refugees along both sides of the Mississippi through the early 1740s, demanding provisions and armaments from the French to supply their missions.

According to one account the Natchez were assisted at the Tunicas by Koroa and Chickasaw warriors who had hidden outside the town during the feasting. Traditionally allies of the Natchez, Yazoos, and Koroas, the Chickasaws at first hoped to play both sides in the conflict. The French had failed to defeat them in the "First Chickasaw War" of the early 1720s, but most Chickasaws seemed to prefer neutrality to overt war. They apparently knew of Natchez plans in 1729 but did not join in the violence. However, when refugees from the three nations sought protection in Chickasaw country after the Choctaws drove them from their homes in early 1730, the Chickasaws could not remain neutral. The demands and plight of the Natchez pulled the Chickasaws toward war. In the summer of 1730 they sent emissaries to the Quapaws, Choctaws, Cherokees,

Miamis, and several Illinois peoples proposing that they all join against the French with the Natchez, Yazoos, and Koroas, armed with English weapons supplied by the Chickasaws. Apparently at least one former French slave who had been captured by the Natchez simultaneously traveled to New Orleans to tell slaves that "they would get their liberty" if they revolted against the French.

By early 1731, after some debate, the Chickasaws escorted Natchez refuges onto Chickasaw lands, allowing them to settle near their clustered towns to act as a barrier from Choctaw raids. Although Chickasaw–Natchez relations would occasionally become strained, the Chickasaws generally fulfilled their alliance obligations. When Governor Périer demanded that the Chickasaws surrender these refugees, the Chickasaws answered that they "had not gone to get them in order to hand them over." As they committed themselves to the Natchez coalition in the 1730s the Chickasaws continued to attempt to recruit the Choctaws, Tunicas, and Quapaws, and the French determined to pursue a second Chickasaw war.

Despite occasional disagreements the French, Choctaws, Quapaws, and Tunicas generally agreed to fight the Natchez, Yazoos, and Koroas.

Fighting the Natchez fit Quapaw, Tunica, and Choctaw alliance obligations as well as interests. Not only were the Natchez old aggressors, their attacks on the French and the Tunicas did seem to break the rules. Even a Chickasaw chief reportedly told a Natchez delegation in 1730 that the French had a right to defend themselves and avenge the killings at the Natchez post. For most Indians, fighting Chickasaws was harder to justify. While often enemies of the Quapaws and Choctaws, their main offense here was harboring fugitives. More importantly, the Chickasaws were more populous and better armed, and starting a war against them would decisively cut off the English trade that they brokered.

Much of the debate surrounded the nature of alliance. To all, alliances entailed obligations, within limits. As Patricia Galloway has demonstrated, Europeans and Indians often interpreted one another's vocabularies and symbols of alliance differently, a misinterpretation useful in first encounters but that could cause difficulties in determining responsibilities in times of crisis. Reciprocal by nature, the alliances were under no one people's control. Having the same enemy did not necessarily make two peoples into allies. In the spring of 1734, 150 Quapaws going to fight the Natchez came across a band of Tunicas on the same mission. They instead began to argue, reviving their old animosity. Just before their warriors came to blows the Tunicas turned home, and the Quapaws did the same, both abandoning their war plans. At least out in the field their old rivalry trumped their opposition to common enemies and their common alliance with the French. French officials instructed their allies to destroy the Chickasaws, but the Quapaws, Tunicas, and Choctaws fought according to their own method and goals.

Choctaws had varying reactions to this French-Chickasaw war. The divided nature of the Choctaw polity meant that different divisions maintained ties with different neighbors, and the Choctaw western towns had in recent years found themselves drawn into Chickasaw offers of trade. The history of Chickasaw and English violence against the Choctaws proved a vivid enough memory to prevent the Choctaws from joining the Chickasaws' coalition, but a unified anti-Chickasaw policy proved elusive.

On other occasions French-Choctaw war parties split over strategy, and Choctaw reasoning generally prevailed. In contrast to their essential and decisive participation in the Natchez war, Choctaw warriors preferred small skirmishes intended to obtain spoils but not alienate English traders or Choctaws opposed to the war. For example, in the 1730s, Red Shoe, who had trading and familial ties with certain Chickasaw towns, raided other Chickasaw towns in the late fall or early spring, just in time to reap rewards at the annual French present ceremonies, while trading with the English throughout much of the year.

Tensions over alliance methods heightened when the French attempted to assemble their allies to defeat the Chickasaws in one decisive conflict. The war party was to include 1,000 French soldiers led by Bienville, more than 300 African slaves, Choctaws, Quapaws, Indians and French civilians from the Illinois country, and an Iroquois contingent, which the Quapaws supposedly had recruited. At first the allies heartily backed such a decisive plan. In the fall of 1737 Quapaw guides led a French party to explore the route from the Mississippi to the Chickasaw towns. Quapaws and several parties of Illinois Indians helped to build forts on both sides of the Mississippi to house the coming troops and supplies for an assault in the fall of 1739. But Bienville repeatedly postponed the attack because of delays and lack of communication among New Orleans, the forces assembled on the Mississippi, the reinforcements supposedly coming from the Illinois country, and the promised Iroquois. In addition, French officials vacillated between including the Choctaws and keeping them out of the battle for fear they would demand high prices for their services.

Frustration mounted. For months the assembled warriors urged Bienville to commence the fight. But Bienville wanted everything to be ready first, including roads built to the Chickasaw towns for his heavy artillery. His war strategy must have seemed absurd to people who believed that the best military tactic was surprise attack. Building a road to the enemy's town certainly spoiled the surprise. French soldiers were no happier with the delay and exposure to potential Chickasaw assaults and grew more mutinous as provisions ran out and illness decreased their ranks. In January of 1740 a contingent of French soldiers, acting without orders, sent a message to the Chickasaws saying that, if they surrendered the Natchez refugees and cast out the English, the French would make peace. The Indian allies began to disband, and Bienville had to accept a Chickasaw peace plan, which lasted only long enough for the Chickasaws to ascertain that the war party had dispersed.

When the peace proved short-lived and Chickasaws began to inflict heavy damage on French convoys, the Quapaws persuaded the French to accept an alternative war plan for protecting the Mississippi River. The Quapaws fought the Chickasaws when they wished, in parties of 30 to 50 warriors who could strike quickly and escape without major casualties. The French contributed by paying the Quapaws for Chickasaw scalps. Nor did they interfere when Quapaw attacks occasionally hit the Choctaws. Louisiana's governor in the 1740s, Vaudreuil, told his superiors that he had "engaged" the Quapaws to raid the Chickasaws; however, it is clear that the Quapaws were now in charge of their effort and that their methods were more effective.

In contrast, Choctaw unity dissolved as the war dragged on. Unable to remain neutral, Choctaws disagreed over their Chickasaw, English, and French policies, arguments that devolved into violent civil strife in the 1740s. Many historians have labeled the Choctaw divisions in this civil war as "pro-English" (usually the western towns) and "pro-French" (the eastern). But European relations were less central to Choctaw decision-making than these labels imply. The conflict centered on how Choctaws as a society would decide how to handle the demands and inducements of their neighbors, including the Chickasaws, English, French, and other nations.

By the 1740s many Choctaws had wearied of the Chickasaw war. If the French had met the Choctaws' pecuniary demands, they might have simply skirmished occasionally against the Chickasaws, as Red Shoe did in the 1730s and the Quapaws and Tunicas continued to do. But the persistent temptations of trade that the Chickasaws offered prompted some Choctaws to desire a Chickasaw alliance. When rumors spread that the French were trading and allying with the Chickasaws behind Choctaw backs, many Choctaws felt they had been duped into depriving themselves of Chickasaw trade. These desires and grievances pulled against both the eastern Choctaw towns' continued reliance on French trade and the Choctaws' history of alliance with the French versus the Chickasaws and English. A movement arose to make a publicized peace with all. In 1738 Red Shoe declared in front of French and Chickasaw listeners, "I have made peace with the Chickasaws whom I regard as my brothers. For too long a time the French have been causing the blood of the Indians to be shed." Over the next few years more Choctaws came to agree with Red Shoe, while others resolutely opposed him. In the 1740s violence escalated and became more chaotic as groups of Choctaws, French, and Chickasaws raided and counterraided one another, some Choctaws attacked English traders, and ultimately various Choctaw factions committed violence against one another.

Old alliances and animosities had expanded the Natchez-French conflict into regional, and in one case civil, war. When the Natchez used extreme violence against the French invaders, they forced their neighbors to make choices, informed by their relations with others. Pushed by their allegiance to the Natchez and conflict with the French, Choctaws, and Quapaws, the Yazoos and Koroas supported the Natchez. By the summer of 1732 most of them were dead, enslaved and shipped to the Caribbean, or refugees among the Chickasaws, Creeks, and Cherokees. While some African captives fought with the Natchez, most found themselves treated like booty, captured in Choctaw and Chickasaw raids and counterraids. At least twenty returned to French slavery. Others were sold to the English or died in captivity, and a few escaped to build lives lost to the records. The Natchez war had repercussions for other Africans, too. Participation on the French side resulted in permanent free black participation in Louisiana militia. And the Natchez war may have inspired an attempted slave revolt. In the summer of 1731, French officials in New Orleans uncovered an apparent plot to kill the masters returning from mass. Even if the French exaggerated the conspiracy, clearly some New Orleans men and women had considered following the Natchez example, or at least taking advantage of the troops' preoccupation to the north, and some were executed for the possibility. The Choctaws, Tunicas, and Quapaws sought moderate policies, which led the Tunicas to expose themselves to Natchez deception and the Choctaws to internal discord. Still, all remained influential groups into the nineteenth century and beyond. Despite their decision to support the Natchez, so too did the Chickasaws, whom the French by no means succeeded in destroying.

Europeans and Africans carved out what spaces they could in this native world. Rather than being colonized, Indians drew these newcomers into local alliances, rivalries, and ways of conducting diplomacy, trade, and war, which held sway even as they adapted to changing circumstances. By molding colonialism to fit Indian desires and demands, French officials maintained a presence in Louisiana for nearly a century, but the colonial project of extracting natural resources for profit failed, and Louisiana's economy remained more Indian than colonial. This is not to say that any particular Indians ruled Louisiana, or that their world did not change. Rather, groups and individuals used Europeans and Africans to forward their own priorities in the intricate and changing relationships of the Mississippi valley.

FURTHER READING

Anderson, Gary Clayton. *Kinsmen of Another Kind: Dakota-White Relations in the Upper Mississippi Valley, 1650–1862* (1984; reprint, 1997).

Axtell, James. *The Invasion Within: The Contest of Cultures in Colonial North America* (1985).

Brown, Kathleen M. *Good Wives, Nasty Wenches, and Anxious Patriarchs: Gender, Race and Power in Colonial Virginia* (1996).

Bushnell, Amy Turner. *Situado and Sabana: Spain's Support System for the Presidio and Mission Provinces of Florida* (1994).

Calloway, Colin G. *New Worlds for All: Indians, Europeans, and the Remaking of Early America* (1997).

———. *One Vast Winter Count: The Native American West before Lewis and Clark* (2003).

Cayton, Andrew R. L., and Fredrika J. Teute, eds. *Contact Points: American Frontiers from the Mohawk Valley to the Mississippi, 1750–1830* (1998).

Chaplin, Joyce E. *Subject Matter: Technology, the Body, and Science on the Anglo-American Frontier, 1500–1676* (2001).

Cronon, William. *Changes in the Land: Indians, Colonists, and the Ecology of New England* (1983; rev. ed., 2003).

Daunton, Martin, and Rick Halpern, eds. *Empire and Others: British Encounters with Indigenous Peoples, 1600–1850* (1999).

Demos, John. *The Unredeemed Captive: A Family Story from Early America* (1994).

Dennis, Matthew. *Cultivating a Landscape of Peace: Iroquois-European Encounters in Seventeenth-Century America* (1993).

DuVal, Kathleen. *The Native Ground: Indians and Colonists in the Heart of the Continent* (2006).

————. "Indian Intermarriage and Métissage in Colonial Louisiana." *William and Mary Quarterly* 65 (April 2008): 265–304.

Eccles, W. J. *The Canadian Frontier, 1534–1760* (1983).

Edmunds, David R., and Joseph L. Peyser. *The Fox Wars: The Mesquakie Challenge to New France* (1993).

Galgano, Robert. *Feast of Souls: Indians and Spaniards in the Seventeenth-Century Missions of Florida and New Mexico* (1995).

Gallay, Alan. *The Indian Slave Trade: The Rise of the English Empire in the American South, 1670–1717* (2002).

Greer, Allan. *Mohawk Saint: Catherine Tekakwitha and the Jesuits* (2005).

Haefeli, Evan, and Kevin Sweeney. *Captors and Captives: The 1704 French and Indian Raid on Deerfield* (2003).

Havard, Gilles, and Cécile Vidal. *Histoire de l'Amérique française* (2003; rev. ed., 2006).

Hinderaker, Eric. *Elusive Empires: Constructing Colonialism in the Ohio Valley, 1673–1800* (1997).

Hinderaker, Eric, and Peter C. Mancall. *At the Edge of Empire: The Backcountry in British North America* (2003).

Kaptizke, Robert L. *Religion, Power, and Politics in Colonial St. Augustine* (2001).

Kupperman, Karen Ordahl. *Indians and English: Facing Off in Early America* (2000).

Landers, Jane. *Black Society in Spanish Florida* (1999).

Lepore, Jill. *The Name of War: King Philip's War and the Origins of American Identity* (1998).

Mandell, Daniel R. *Tribe, Race, History: Native Americans in Southern New England, 1780–1880* (2008).

McConnell, Michael N. *A Country Between: The Upper Ohio Valley and Its Peoples, 1724–1774* (1992).

Merrell, James H. *The Indians' New World: Catawbas and Their Neighbors from European Contact through the Era of Removal* (1989).

————. *Into the American Woods: Negotiators on the Pennsylvania Fronteir* (1999).

Merritt, Jane T. *At the Crossroads: Indians and Empires on a Mid-Atlantic Frontier, 1700–1763* (2003).

Merwick, Donna. *The Shame and the Sorrow: Dutch-Amerindian Encounters in New Netherland* (2006).

Milanich, Jerald T. *Florida Indians and the Invasion from Europe* (1995).

Norton, Mary Beth. *In the Devil's Snare: The Salem Witchcraft Crisis of 1692* (2002).

Oatis, Steven J. *A Colonial Complex: South Carolina's Frontiers in the Era of the Yamasee War, 1680–1730* (2004).

Parmenter, Jon. *The Edge of the Woods: Iroquoia, 1534–1701* (2010).

Preston, David L. *The Texture of Contact: European and Indian Settler Communities on the Frontiers of Iroquoia, 1667–1783* (2009).

Richter, Daniel. K. *The Ordeal of the Longhouse: The Peoples of the Iroquois League in the Era of European Colonization* (1991).

————. *Facing East from Indian Country: A Native History of Early America* (2001).

————. *Before the Revolution: America's Ancient Pasts* (2011).

Rushforth, Brett. "'A Little Flesh We Offer You': The Origins of Indian Slavery in New France." *William and Mary Quarterly* 60 (Oct. 2003): 777–808.

Salisbury, Neil. *Manitou and Providence: Indians, Europeans, and the Making of New England, 1500–1643* (1982).

Shoemaker, Nancy. *A Strange Likeness: Becoming Red and White in Eighteenth-Century North America* (2004).

Silver, Peter. *Our Savage Neighbors: How Indian War Transformed Early America* (2007).

Silverman, David J. *Faith and Boundaries: Colonists, Christianity, and Community Among the Wampanoag Indians of Martha's Vineyard, 1600–1871* (2005).

———. *Red Brethren: The Brothertown and Stockbridge Indians and the Problem of Race in Early America* (2010).

Trigger, Bruce G. *Natives and Newcomers: Canada's "Heroic Age" Reconsidered* (1986).

Townsend, Camilla. *Pocahontas and the Powhatan Dilemma* (2004).

Waselkov, Gregory A., Peter H. Wood, and Tom Hatley, eds. *Powhantan's Mantle: Indians in the Colonial Southeast* (2006).

White, Richard. *The Roots of Dependency: Subsistence, Environment, and Social Change among the Choctaws, Pawnees, and Navajos* (1983).

———. *The Middle Ground: Indians, Empires, and Republics in the Great Lakes Region, 1650–1815* (1991).

Wood, Peter H. *Black Majority: Negroes in Colonial South Carolina from 1670 through the Stono Rebellion* (1974; reissue, 1996).

CHAPTER 4

Borderlands, Cultural Exchanges, and New Native Societies

Borderlands history came into being as an effort to see the world anew. In a sense, it shows us how to squint, how to deflect the blinding light of empires and nations as embodiments of history in order to see what lies hidden behind them. Borderlands history looks at how ordinary peoples have defied, negotiated, and eluded the attempts of larger entities to control their lives and how they have carved out distinct social spaces amidst empires and nations—or across imperial or national boundaries. Borderlands history is therefore inherently concerned with the intimate and culturally specific dimensions of human interactions. It tends to look at history through a local lens, focusing on the actions and experiences of individuals and small groups, fringe peoples at the edges of empires, nations, and cultures.

Yet borderlands history is not just about face-to-face relationships and local dynamics. Because in borderlands central powers exert limited control over human interactions, borderlands often become sites for unexpected alliances, political innovation, and cultural reinvention, the repercussions of which can reverberate far and wide. Examples of borderlands spawning far-reaching historical changes abound. The momentous shift in New Spain's Indian policy in the 1760s and 1770s towards the "French model" of conciliation, exchange, and gifting has often been seen as the result of the ambitious reforms emanating from the Royal Palace in Madrid, but the policy shift was pioneered and tested by innovative frontier officials in New Mexico and elsewhere a generation before the crown institutionalized it. The Seven Years' War (1754–63) began at the contested borderlands of the Ohio Valley, where the French, British, and Indians had vied for power for generations, and from there it spread over three continents, becoming the first global war. Borderland conflicts could become international conflicts, but the pacification of borderlands could be equally consequential. When peace brought diverse peoples into closer contact through trade, diplomacy, and intermarriage, it created propitious conditions for viruses to jump hosts and trigger epidemics that could devastate previously unexposed native societies across vast distances. And borderlands also influenced the birth of other borderlands. When people moved to new locations, they carried with them their accumulated knowledge of intercultural dialogue, and when they encountered new peoples in new environments, they tried to apply the practices that had worked before. North American borderlands were rarely created afresh; they were built on prior experiences and expectations.

In early America, hard colonial frontiers often softened into porous borderlands of cross-cultural exchange and accommodation where imperial authority was sometimes eclipsed by indigenous power. Yet throughout North America colonial outposts profoundly transformed native societies by introducing new diseases, technologies, markets, and ideas. This chapter examines the various ways in which European contact reshaped native cultures, focusing on technological and biological exchanges (especially horses and firearms) and intermarriage. But the chapter also turns the lens around by asking how the new native societies influenced colonial outposts.

◯ DOCUMENTS

The first document is a traditional Cheyenne story of the moment when foreign traders first brought horses to Cheyenne villages. Deeply impressed by the animals, Cheyennes asked Maheo, All-Father Creator, for horses of their own. Maheo granted their wish but also warned that their lives would be changed forever. Maheo's warning reveals some of the complexities of horse adoption and offers clues about how Cheyennes came to regard their choice. In the second document, Saukamappee, an elderly Cree Indian living among the Piegan Blackfoot Indians, relates the Blackfeet's first encounter with horses, guns, and smallpox around 1730. The account, recorded in 1787 by fur trader David Thompson, illuminates how Indians reacted to new technology and diseases and how their prior experience with dogs may have facilitated the adoption of horses. The account also suggests how the introduction of horses and guns changed native warfare.

Documents 3 and 4 illuminate the changes in Native American power relations that came with the rise of equestrianism. In Document 3, the Marqués de Rubí, a Spanish officer who toured New Spain's northern provinces in 1766–68, recommends a new Indian policy for the Texas and New Mexico borderlands. For decades, Spain had maintained an on-and-off alliance with the various Apache groups of the southern Plains against the expanding Comanche Indians, but Rubí advocated an alliance with the Comanches and possible extermination of the Apaches. His rationale for the policy change reveals how Spaniards tried to protect the borderlands and sheds light on Spanish attitudes toward Indians and alliances with Indians. The next document reveals what happened when two expanding frontiers of European technology intersected. While native trade networks shuffled horses northward across the Great Plains, other indigenous channels moved guns southward from Canadian trading posts in the plains-woodlands borderlands. The two technological frontiers converged in the upper Missouri Valley in the late eighteenth century, plunging the region into wars over trading privileges. Some native groups were marginalized, while others came to dominate multiple trade channels and won secure access to both guns and horses. Charles McKenzie, a Canadian fur trader in the service of the North West Company, visited the upper Missouri River in 1805. In Document 4, McKenzie describes the dynamics that turned the Mandan and Hidatsa Indian villages into great trading bazaars. His account also illuminates the challenges European fur traders faced when trying to enter into native-controlled exchange networks.

In the late eighteenth and early nineteenth centuries, the northern Great Plains emerged as the focal point of the North American fur trade as both British Canadian and U.S. companies extended their operations there. The Hudson's Bay Company, the American Fur Company, and others maintained numerous trading posts along the region's major river valleys, incorporating several native societies into the fur trade. The last two documents—excerpts from the diaries of fur traders Rudolph Friedrich Kurz and Francis Chardon—shed light on cross-cultural accommodations, gender relations, and the roles of native women in the context of the northern plains fur trade. Together, the documents describe how intermarriage between native women and fur traders supported trade relations and how native women became involved in nearly all facets of the fur trade as mediators, cultural transmitters, producers, consumers, and companions. They offer glimpses into the intimate domestic dynamics of fur trade marriages and show how native women carved out personal social places in the male-dominated trading posts. The documents also illuminate how Euro-American traders struggled to understand, navigate, and modify native customs, and they bespeak of the difficulties of cross-cultural communication. Chardon's journal also contains references to the devastating 1837–38 smallpox epidemic that spread across the northern plains, killing thousands of Indians and changing the chemistry of Indian-Euro-American relations in the region.

1. Maheo, All-Father Creator, Warns the Cheyennes about Life with Horses

Maheo was the one who made the world and the people and animals and wind and stars. He was the one who brought the light and divided night from day. Maheo, the All Spirit, watched over his people, the Cheyenne, and taught them everything.

One day the Comanches came to see the Cheyennes. The Comanches were riding on horses. "Wah! That is wonderful," said the Cheyennes. "Where do you get them?"

"From the Pueblos," the Comanches said. "They have lots of horses."

"What do you trade for them?" asked the Cheyennes. Their own women made many pretty things, decorated with earth paints and porcupine quills that they dyed with the earth colors and berry juices, but they knew the Comanches did not do that kind of work.

"Trade for them!" said the Comanches, laughing. "We don't trade for them. We just go and take them."

"Don't the Pueblos get angry?" asked the Cheyennes.

Alice Marriott and Carol K. Rachlin, *Plains Indian Mythology* (New York: Thomas Y. Crowell, 1975), 96–97.

"Oh, they don't like it very much, but they're too afraid to go out of their houses to come and get them back."

"We never heard of horses," said one Cheyenne priest. "Perhaps Maheo wouldn't like for us to have them."

"Why don't you ask him?" a Comanche said. "We'll trade with you, if you're too afraid to go and get them."

The Cheyennes knew that was true because the Comanches enjoyed taking great risks. They were gamblers, who were always looking for things to put at stake in their lives or their games.

The Cheyenne priests all gathered in the largest house in the village, which was the medicine lodge, and they sat and smoked and prayed to Maheo, fasting, for four days. At last Maheo took pity on them, and spoke to them through the oldest priest.

"You may have horses," Maheo said. "You may even go with the Comanches and take them. But remember this: If you have horses everything will be changed for you forever.

"You will have to move around a lot to find pasture for your horses. You will have to give up gardening and live by hunting and gathering, like the Comanches. And you will have to come out of your earth houses and live in tents. I will tell your women how to make them, and how to decorate them.

And there will be other changes. You will have to have fights with other tribes, who will want your pasture land or the places where you hunt. You will have to have real soldiers, who can protect the people. Think, before you decide."

The priests sat and smoked and thought another four days. Then the oldest one said, "Maheo, we think we can learn the things you can teach us and our women. We will take the horses, and with your guidance we will learn the new life."

"So be it," said Maheo. "But you must never forget where you came from or who you are. Once a year you must make a lodge in the shape of an earth lodge, and in it you must pray and dance and smoke and sing. It will be your offering of your own flesh and blood in my honor."

All the priests agreed. Then Maheo said, "I will give the power of this dance to the oldest of you, and he can pass it on. But because women are the mothers of life, as I am the father of everything, it must be passed through a woman. On the third night of the dance, the priest must take the wife of a man who is making offering into a special tipi, set aside, and lie with her. Then she will lie with her husband, and the power will be passed through her body to his."

2. Saukamappee (Cree) Recalls the Arrival of Horses, Guns, and Smallpox to the Northern Plains, 1787

The Peeagans [Piegans] were always the frontier Tribe, and upon whom the Snake [Shoshone] Indians made their attacks, these latter were very numerous,

J. B. Tyrrell, *David Thompson's Narrative of His Explorations in Western America, 1784–1812* (Toronto: Champlain Society, 1916), 328–338.

even without their allies; and the Peeagans had to send messengers among us to procure help. Two of them came to the camp of my father, and I was then about his age (pointing to a Lad of about sixteen years) he promised to come and bring some of his people, the Nahathaways with him, for I am myself of that people, and not of those with whom I am [living now]. My father brought about twenty warriors with him. There were a few guns amongst us, but very little ammunition, and they were left to hunt for the families; Our weapons was a Lance, mostly pointed with iron, some few of stone, A Bow and a quiver of Arrows; the Bows were of Larch, the length came to the chin; the quiver had about fifty arrows, of which ten had iron points, the others were headed with stone. He carried his knife on his breast and his axe in his belt. Such was my fathers weapons, and those with him had much the same weapons. I had a Bow and Arrows and a knife, of which I was very proud. We came to the Peeagans and their allies. They were camped in the Plains on the left bank of the River (the north side) and were a great many. We were feasted, a great War Tent was made, and a few days passed in speeches, feasting and dances. A war chief was elected by the chiefs, and we got ready to march. When we had crossed and numbered our men, we were about 350 warriors (this he showed by counting every finger to be ten, and holding up both hands three times and then one hand) they had their scouts out, and came to meet us. Both parties made a great show of their numbers, and I thought that they were more numerous than ourselves.

After some singing and dancing, they sat down on the ground, and placed their large shields before them, which covered them: We did the same, but our shields were not so many, and some of our shields had to shelter two men. Theirs were all placed touching each other; their Bows were not so long as ours, but of better wood, and the back covered with the sinews of the Bisons which made them very elastic, and their arrows went a long way and whizzed about us as balls do from guns. They were all headed with a sharp, smooth, black stone (flint) which broke when it struck anything. Our iron headed arrows did not go through their shields, but stuck in them; On both sides several were wounded, but none lay on the ground; and night put an end to the battle, without a scalp being taken on either side, and in those days such was the result, unless one party was more numerous than the other.... I grew to be a man, became a skilfull and fortunate hunter, and my relations procured me a Wife. She was young and handsome and we were fond of each other. We had passed a winter together, when Messengers came from our allies to claim assistance.

By this time the affairs of both parties had much changed; we had more guns and iron headed arrows than before; but our enemies the Snake Indians and their allies had Misstutim (Big Dogs, that is Horses) on which they rode, swift as the Deer, on which they dashed at the Peeagans, and with their stone Pukamoggan knocked them on the head, and they had thus lost several of their best men. This news we did not well comprehend and it alarmed us, for we had no idea of Horses and could not make out what they were. When we came to our allies, the great War Tent [was made] with speeches, feasting and dances as before; and when the War Chief had viewed us all it was found between us and the Stone Indians we had ten guns and each of us about thirty balls, and powder for the war, and we were considered the strength of the battle. After a few days march our scouts brought us word that the enemy was near in a large war party, but had no Horses with them, for at that time they had very few of them. When we came to meet each other, as usual, each displayed their numbers, weapons and shiel[d]s, in all which they were superior to us, except our guns which were not shown, but kept in their leathern cases, and if we had shown [them], they would have taken them for long clubs.

The War Chief was close to us, anxious to see the effect of our guns. The lines were too far asunder for us to make a sure shot, and we requested him to close the line to about sixty yards, which was gradually done, and lying flat on the ground behind the shields, we watched our opportunity when they drew their bows to shoot at us, their bodies were then exposed and each of us, as opportunity offered, fired with deadly aim, and either killed, or severely wounded, every one we aimed at.

The next morning the War Chief made a speech, praising their bravery, and telling them to make a large War Tent to commemorate their victory, to which they directly set to work and by noon it was finished.

After all the war ceremonies were over, we pitched away in large camps with the woman and children on the frontier of the Snake Indian country, hunting the Bison and Red Deer which were numerous, and we were anxious to see a horse of which we had heard so much. At last, as the leaves were falling we heard that one was killed by an arrow shot into his belly, but the Snake Indian that rode him, got away; numbers of us went to see him, and we all admired him, he put us in mind of a Stag that had lost his horns; and we did not know what name to give him. But as he was a slave to Man, like the dog, which carried our things; he was named the Big Dog.

The terror of that battle and of our guns has prevented any more general battles, and our wars have since been carried by ambuscade and surprise, of small camps, in which we have greatly the advantage, from the Guns, arrow shods of iron, long knives, flat bayonets and axes from the Traders.

While we have these weapons, the Snake Indians have none, but what few they sometimes take from one of our small camps which they have destroyed, and they have no Traders among them. We continued to advance through the fine plains to the Stag [Red Deer] River when death came over us all, and swept away more than half of us by the Small pox, of which we knew nothing until it brought death among us. We caught it from the Snake Indians. Our Scouts were out for our security, when some returned and informed us of a considerable camp which was too large to attack and something very suspicious about it; from a high knowl they had a good view of the camp, but saw none of the men hunting, or going about; there were a few Horses, but no one came to them, and a herd of Bisons [were] feeding close to the camp with other herds near. Next morning at the dawn of day, we attacked the Tents, and with our sharp flat daggers and knives, cut through the tents and entered for the fight; but our war whoop instantly stopt, our eyes were appalled with terror; there was no one to fight with but the dead and the dying, each a mass of corruption. We did not touch them, but left the tents, and held a council on what was to be done. We all thought the Bad Spirit had made himself master of the camp and destroyed them. It was agreed to take some of the best of the tents, and any other plunder that was clean and good, which we did, and also took away the few Horses they had, and returned to our camp.

The second day after this dreadful disease broke out in our camp, and spread from one tent to another as if the Bad Spirit carried it. We had no belief that one Man could give it to another, any more than a wounded Man could give his wound to another. We did not suffer so much as those that were near the river, into which they rushed and died. We had only a little brook, and about one third of us died, but in some of the other camps there were tents in which every one died. When at length it left us, and we moved about to find our people, it was no longer with the song and the dance; but with tears, shrieks, and howlings of despair for those who would never return to us. What little we could spare we offered to the Bad Spirit to let us alone and go to our enemies. To the Good Spirit we offered feathers, branches of trees, and sweet smelling grass. Our hearts were low and dejected, and we shall never be again the same people.

3. The Marqués de Rubí Recommends the Extermination of the Apaches, 1768

The enemies who present themselves at this location [Rio Grande Valley] are now of a very different character, and the terrain is of a better nature for the cavalry of our presidios. We should consider as our frontier neighbors and transborder counterparts from here on, as far as the point set on the coast of the Gulf of Mexico, only the perfidious Lipan Apaches, who have been emboldened by our own credulity and the shameful indulgence with which we have treated their frequent attempts [at mischief] and insults.

Of these [Lipanes], those who live toward the Santa Rosa Range, on the upper bank of the Río del Norte, generally join together with the Natagés [Apache] for their incursions into Vizcaya and the haciendas of Coahuila. They are well acquainted with the country because of the liberty with which they are allowed to enter it under the pretext of their apparent peace with this government. Those who are next to them, downstream on both banks of the river, at San Vicente, San Rodrigo, San Marcos, and several other extended banks where springs are found in greater or lesser abundance, overrun the scarce population and the encampments near the new town of San Fernando de Austria. Nor do they pardon the abundant haciendas of Sardinas, Cuatro Ciénegas, and others, penetrating to the interior toward the Sabinas and perhaps the Nadadores Rivers.

Always following the course of this river, more or less close to its banks, extend many other villages of this same nation and language, with the various names of

Jack Jackson, ed., *Imaginary Kingdom: Texas Seen by the Rivera and Rubí Military Expeditions, 1727 and 1767* (Austin: Texas State Historical Association, 1995), 179–183.

their leaders and petty chiefs such as Boruca, Zapato Bordado (Embroidered Shoe), Casaca Colorada (Red Jacket), Cavezón (Big Head), Canos, and others that change as new chiefs come to power. The profession of thieves constitutes the character of this depraved nation—which subsists on the flesh of horses and mules, preferring this over all other foods—and has made them likewise abhorrent to all the others, who have continued pressing in on them, fighting them, and destroying them, from the most unknown distances of the North. There is a tradition of the Lipanes once having lived in the North, and a little later in the Fort that the Taguayás [Taovayas] now occupy, two hundred leagues from the vicinity they now inhabit on the Rio Grande. From here, under the shadow of our inconvenient mercy, and the shelter of the presidios constructed in their sight, they have sheltered themselves from the pursuit of their innumerable enemies.

Yet, they have not for that reason stopped laying waste, like housebreakers, to our own possession of San Antonio de Béxar and its most opulent missions, those of the Rio Grande, the encampments of Laredo, and as much as exists in their vicinity. They have occasioned also the much graver danger of drawing to our frontiers—attracted by their irreconcilable hate for them—the northern nations: the Comanches, Iscanis, Taguacanas, Taguayas, etc., innumerable, war-like, armed with rifles, and until now little known. Now these nations not only daily attack San Sabá, irritated by our unfortunate alliance with the Lipanes, but also the imaginary mission of El Cañón, the town of San Antonio, and much farther into the interior. They have established their villages and encampments with daring confidence on the Alarcón, Guadalupe, Janes, Trancas, and San Sabá Rivers, bordering on our settlements, which are weak, ill-placed, and incapable—because of their internal discord—of making opposition to a torrent of enemies who in reality are appreciable in strength and in number.

This brief sketch of the damages and expenses which, both by themselves and indirectly, the infidel Lipanes have caused to the possessions and treasury of the King, spoon-feeding us with their deceitful friendship and supposed desire to be reduced and made into a never-realized congregation, makes me take into consideration the remediation of such an urgent danger. I may well be deceived by the desire for their chastening and punishment. It is, surely, the only means of attracting them to any side—be it to religion or to the state—but I confess that to me what I am now proposing seems simple and sure.

With this vile nation—incapable of resisting our presidios in an open war—walled in between our frontier and their enemy Nations of the North, it will suffer a war before and behind it, which it cannot sustain; and the [war] parties will find themselves forced to allow that which their illustrious evil will make inevitably known to them. While the Comanches and their allies finish them off, which will not be difficult for them, it is probable that they [the Lipanes] will seek asylum in our missions and presidios; but this should not be conceded to them except at the cost of moving them far to the interior and dividing them, extinguishing or confusing them (as has occurred with several other nations whose [barbarous] legacy has perished from memory), [for they are] a nation whose sagacity, rapacity, and industry will be always unfortunate and indecorous to the progress of the arms of the King and to the tranquility of his possessions.

We shall have, it is undeniable, one day the Nations of the North as neighbors; they already are approaching us now. But these, whose generosity and bravery make them quite worthy of being our enemies, perhaps will not be [our enemies], as those of our new colony of Louisiana are not, nor those of our present Presidio of Los Adaes, who have more proximity. [Those] of San Xavier were not [our enemies], nor do they show themselves as such in New Mexico, where they come annually to the Valley of Taos to celebrate their feasts with us. Capable of some formality in their dealings, they have what is necessary to know how to observe [amicable relations]. Removed from the proximity of the hated Lipanes, who plunder them as they do us, they shall live (thus I judge it) tranquilly in their true dominions—without crossing over to our frontiers— and shall enjoy their peaceful possession of the bison hunt, which is their whole sustenance, cultivation, and ambition.

These advantages (with which I do not know how to stop enchanting myself) make me consider as necessary the total extermination of the Lipanes, or at least their complete reduction in terms which would make impossible the effects, so many times experienced, of their constant fickleness—dealing at the same time with the location of the presidio which is next to that of Santa Rosa, namely San Juan Bautista de Río Grande. Even if one wanted to transfer [the latter] more toward the bank of this river, to a spot where it would uncover and dominate to a greater extent its many routes and fordable passes, the transfer would not amount to even one league from its present location, which is at the corresponding latitude.

4. Charles McKenzie Describes Horse and Gun Trade on the Northern Plains, 1805

About the middle of June the Rocky Mountain Indians [Crows] made their appearance. They consisted of more than three hundred Tents, and presented the handsomest sight that one could imagine—all on horseback. Children of small size were lashed to the Saddles, and those above the age of six could manage a horse—the women had wooden Saddles—most of the men had none. There were a great many horses for the baggage, and the whole exceeding two thousand covered a large space of ground and had the appearance of an army; they halted on a rising ground behind the Village; formed into a circle—when the Chief addressed them, they then descended full speed—rode through the Village, exhibiting their dexterity in horsemanship in a thousand shapes—I was astonished to see their agility and address:—and I could believe they were the best riders in the world. They were dressed in leather, looked clean and neat— Some wore beads and rings as ornaments. Their arms were Bows and arrows, Lances, and round stones enclosed in leather and slung to a shank in the form of a whip. They make use of shields, and they have a few Guns.—

W. Raymond Wood and Thomas D. Thiessen, eds., *Early Fur Trade on the Northern Plains: Canadian Traders among the Mandan and Hidatsa Indians, 1738–1818* (Norman: University of Oklahoma Press, 1985), 245–247. Reprinted by permission.

On the following day the Mississouri Indians [Mandans and Hidatsas] dressed in their best fineries returned the compliment by a similar exhibition. These having the advantage of residing in the vicinity of trading Establishments were better provided with necessaries and consequently had a more warlike appearance; but they were inferior in the management of their horses.—

In the mean time *Le Borgne* [Mandan chief] sent for us in order to introduce Mr. La Roque to the Rocky Mountain Chief, whose name in *Nakesinia* or Red Calf. When we offered to shake hands with this great man, he did not understand the intention, and stood motionless until he was informed that shaking hands was the sign of friendship among white men:—then he stretched forth both his hands to receive ours. *Le Borgne* said a great deal in favor of the North West Company, but he did not praise the Americans.

Mr. La Roque's great pipe was handed round as a precious offering and each took a few whiffs—then Mr. La Roque presented to the Red Calf a Flag; a Stem, with some mercantile articles; and the Chief to testify his Sense of the obligation adopted Mr. La Roque as Father, and promised to respect and consider him as such for ever after.

Les Gros Ventres [Hidatsas] made the Corbeaux [Crows] (for so the Rocky Mountain tribe was called) Smoke the pipe of friendship, and at the same time laid before them a present consisting of two hundred guns, with one hundred rounds of ammunition for each, a hundred bushels of Indian Corn, a certain quantity of mercantile articles, such as Kettles, axes, Cloths &c. The Corbeaux in return brought two hundred and fifty horses, large parcels of Buffalo Robes, Leather Leggins, Shirts &c.

This exchange of trading civilities took place dancing—when the dancing was over, the presents were distributed among the Individuals in proportion to the value of the articles respectively furnished—this dance therefore is a rule of traffic. The Mandane Villages exchanged similar civilities with the Same Tribe. It is incredible the great quantity of merchandize which the Missouri Indians have accumulated by intercourse with Indians that visit them from the vicinity of Commercial Establishments.—

This unpleasant disagreement [over La Roque's intention to visit the Crow Indians] caused a bustle in the Camp, and most of the Indians collected around us—finding this a favourable opportunity, the Great Chief, our friend *Le Borgne,* addressed the Indians and his adopted Son the Red Calf as follows:—

"My Son and my friends, rejoice—White men are to visit your Land and you will feel easy in their company—but we shall regret their absence. White men are curious—they came from far—they know much and wish to learn more. Three only form their party; Your party consist of a thousand and more—you see their skin, it is white—their hearts are as white as their skin— they are good and will do you no harm. Give them plenty to eat; let them have the best, and be the first served—let your women be kind to them— never ask anything from them: they are generous, and they will pay you for your kindness—White men love Beaver and they are continually in search of Beaver for its Skin—What use they make of the Skin I know not:—but they give us good things in return—they exchange it for Guns, Ammunitions &c.

Our Fathers were not acquainted with White men—We live better than our Fathers lived.

5. Rudolph Friedrich Kurz on Gifts, Intermarriage, and the Fur Trade

Cree are said to be most valiant warriors, excellent marksmen with the rifle, but very cautious and pertinacious in trade. Assiniboin excel in shooting with bow and arrow (but it must be taken into consideration that they get fewer good rifles from Americans than the former receive from the English). "Indians at this post place little value on us whites," says the bourgeois [Denig].

They maintain that we are capable of doing just anything for the sake of getting buffalo robes—we lie, we cheat, we work in the dirt even, just as their wives do. We are poor people who could not exist without them, because we must have buffalo robes or we should perish from cold. To impress them, therefore, on our part, we think it best to assume a proud, reserved attitude, to act as though we take no notice of them, and refuse to imitate them either in dress or manner. The instant we should seek them, treat them in an intimate free-handed manner, they would only believe that we were courting their friendship for the sake of protection, and accordingly would give them a more exalted idea of their importance and a more significant proof of our own helplessness. In that event we should have to pay dearly for their friendship and their so-called defense, for there would be no limit to their demands. Among themselves, Indians value liberality, "largesse," very highly as a virtue; in consequence every gift is designated, even as a "coup," on the buffalo robe. But generosity on the part of a paleface wins neither their friendship nor their respect. They do not look upon a white person as one of themselves or as a recognized friend; his liberality shows his dependence; he seeks protection. The paleface owns no land; he is obliged to get permission to found his fort, to trade with the native race; and he is required to pay formal tribute for the privilege. Accordingly, if one presented an Indian with a gift every day in the year—this morning, a horse; tomorrow, a gun; the day after tomorrow, a blanket; the next day, a knife; and so on until the last day in the year—and then might forget or simply neglect to give him anything at all on the 365th day, he would be all the more angry on account of the omission. The same is true of an Indian woman; the more one gives her to win her good will, all the more convinced is she that the donor is in her power. She does not respect him, much less love him; only treats him kindly for the sake of the gifts. An Indian woman must fear her husband; she then esteems him for his manliness. She desires a warrior—no good-natured pantaloon. Therefore several sound lashings or other rough treatment is necessary from time to time to keep alive her respect and affection. Besides, an Indian woman loves her white husband only for what he possesses—because she works less hard, eats better food, is

J. N. B. Hewitt, ed., Myrtis Jarrrell, trans., *Journal of Rudolph Friedrich Kurz* (Washington, D.C.: Government Printing Office, 1937), 154–156.

allowed to dress and adorn herself in a better way—of real love there is no question. After the third or fourth child, when they are getting too old for their Indian dandies, they begin to devote themselves entirely to the father of their children. If an Indian woman runs away, one is not to pay the least attention to her nor to show the least grief; one is to forget her. To go after her, to beg her to return, is beneath the dignity of a brave—is not considered to be worth while.

Men in charge of trading posts like to marry into prominent Indian families when they are able to do so; by such a connection they increase their adherents, their patronage is extended, and they make correspondingly larger profits. Their Indian relatives remain loyal and trade with no other company. They have the further advantage of being constantly informed through their association with the former as to the demands of trade and the villiage or even the tent where they can immediately find buffalo robes stored away. For a clerk a woman of rank is too expensive and brings him no advantage, for the reason that he is employed at a fixed salary and receives no further profit. If he falls into debt he is brought under obligation to the company.

6. Francis Chardon Records Relations between Fur Traders and Native Women and a Smallpox Epidemic in the Upper Missouri River, 1836–1839

[May 5, 1835]—Started out at Day-light to hunt Buffaloe—Discovered a bande at 10 A.M—Run them at 12—Killed three, started for Home at 3 P.M.—and arrived at 9—found my family increased to one more Boy—the Mandans started out to dry Meat—

[July 15, 1835]—Went to the Medicine dance last Night—Came back late and got a whipping from my Wife for my bad behaviour—

[Aug. 30, 1836]—Set the Men a chopping fire wood—The Cerimony for crying, and cutting, for the *Dead,* was performed at the Village to day—Men, Women and Children, bellowing like so many Bedlamites, the Mandans arrived with fresh Meat—Committed fortification to day and got a Whipping from my beloved *Wife,* for my trouble—Oh poor Me—the Cerimony at the Village continued all day—

[Aug. 31, 1836]—As for Durant he is a poor *Devil,* Make the best of him, as he cannot for his life leave his *squaw*—for fear of some one running away with her

[Sep. 16, 1836]—The Saons [Cheynnes] left here early this Morning for their Camp—Sent with them a Yancton woman that I bought from the Gros-Ventres, Council with the Rees [Arikaras] gave them a small present of Powder, Ball and tobacco—in the name of the Agent—Sent Bullé up to the Gros-Ventres after Robes—Durant started out Beaver hunting—

Annie Heloise Abel, ed., *Chardon's Journal at Fort Clark, 1834–1839* (1932; reprint, Freeport, N.Y.: Books for Libraries, 1970), 31, 37, 78, 80, 96, 98, 109, 123–125, 131, 154, 160, 164–165, 170, 173–175, 182–183, 186.

[Jan. 27, 1837]—Pleasant day, the Mandans discovered the tracks of enemies on the opposite side, supposed to be about twenty, to day a young Mandan came, either with the intent to Kill or scare Me. I left him approach in graspe length, when I disarmed him of his gun and Tomahawk, and sent him back to the Village with his tail between his legs. My Woman and her child being at the Village (at a dance) Prevented me from strikeing him to the earth. No doubt it is better as it is.

[May 8, 1837]—My hunters arrived late last Night without Meat, haveing been pillaged by the Assinneboines of four horses, they were attacked early in the morning of the 6th by a War party of fourty, Who fired on them (Mistaken them for Mandans,) and unfortunately Killed N. Durant—a free hunter Who has been in his Country several Years, his wife left the Fort this Morning, to take up her quarters in the Village. She appears to not care much about it. What affectionate Wives We all have in this Country!

[April 24, 1837]—The Mandans that crossed the River the 20th inst arrived to day with plenty of Meat—report cattle far off, and scarce. My Childrens Mother died this day at 11 OClock—Sent her down in a canoe, to be entered at Fort Pierre, in the Lands of her Parents—Pressed Packs 15—Trade going on slow—

[July 26, 1837]—The Rees and Mandans all arrived to day well loaded with Meat, Mitchel also arrived with 150 pieces. The 4 Bears (Mandan) has caught the small pox, and got crazy and has disappeared from camp—he arrived here in the afternoon—The Indians of the Little Village all arrived in the evening well loaded with dried Meat—the small pox has broke out among them, several has died,

> Speech of the 4 Bears a Mandan Warrior
> to the Arricarees and Mandans, 30th July 1837—

My Friends one and all, Listen to what I have to say—Ever since I can remember, I have loved the Whites, I have lived With them ever since I was a Boy, and to the best of my Knowledge, I have never Wronged a White Man, on the Contrary, I have always Protected them from the insults of Others, Which they cannot deny. The 4 Bears never saw a White Man hungry, but what he gave him to eat, Drink, and a Buffaloe skin to sleep on, in time of Need. I was always ready to die for them, Which they cannot deny. I have done every thing that a red Skin could do for them, and how have they repaid it! With ingratitude! I have Never Called a White Man a Dog, but to day, I do Pronounce them to be a set of Black harted Dogs, they have deceived Me, them that I always considered as Brothers, has turned Out to be My Worst enemies. I have been in Many Battles, and often Wounded, but the Wounds of My enemies I exhalt in, but to day I am Wounded, and by Whom, by those same White Dogs that I have always Considered, and treated as Brothers. I do not fear *Death* my friends. You Know it, but to *die* with my face rotten, that even the Wolves will shrink with horror at seeing Me, and say to themselves, that is the 4 Bears the Friend of the Whites—

Listen well what I have to say, as it will be the last time you will hear Me. think of your Wives, Children, Brothers, Sisters, Friends, and in fact all that you hold dear, are all Dead, or Dying, with their faces all rotten, caused by those dogs the whites, think of all that My friends, and rise all together and Not leave one of them alive. The 4 Bears will act his Part—

[Aug. 22, 1837]—Cool pleasant weather. The disease still Keeps ahead 8 and 10 die off daily, Thirty five Mandans [Men] have died, the Women and children I Keep no account of—Several Mandans have came back to remain in the Village. One of my Soldiers—(Ree) died to day—Two young Mandans shot themselves this Morning—News from the Little Village, that the disease is getting worse and worse every day, it is now two months that it broke out—A Ree that has the small pox, and thinking that he was going to die, approached near his wife, a young woman of 19—and struck her in the head with his tomahawk, with the intent to Kill her, that she might go with him in the Other World—she is badly wounded, a few Minutes after he cut his throat, a report is in Circulation, that they intend to fire the Fort—Stationed guards in the Bastion.

[March 24, 1838]—Trade brisk to day—the water fell several feet. Garreau turned his Wife off for infidelity, poor thing—

[May 18, 1838]—Last Night just after I had got to bed, I herd an alarm, of to Arms, to Arms, and all the Indians of the Village a Yelling and shouting. I seized My gun and rushed out, the Night being dark we could Not discover our enemies, who had fled, after fireing in one of the Lodges, and Killing one of the principal cheifs (The long Horn)—and Wounding an other in two places—A large piece of ice passed in the river—Separated from My dear Ree Wife, after a Marriage of one Year.

[June 15, 1838] haveing lived for two Months a single life, and could not stand it any longer, I concluded to day, to buy myself a Wife, a young Virgin of 15—which cost $150—

[June 25, 1838] after an absence of 39 Days My Absent Wife thought that she fared better at the Fort, made her appearance, after a few reproaches on both sides, harmony was restored.

[Aug. 3, 1838]—Left camp early and arrived at the Fort at 10 A.M—found all Well, except my beloved Ree wife, who has deserted my bed & board, the Indians all left Yesterday, to Make dried Meat. Finished hauleing hay at the little river 30 loads.

[Oct. 27, 1838] Old Charboneau, an old Man of 80, took to himself and *others* a young Wife, a young Assinneboine of 14, a Prisoner that was taken in the fight of this summer, and bought by me of the Rees, the young Men of the Fort, and tow *rees,* gave to the Old Man a splendid *Chàrivèree,* the Drums, pans, Kittles &c Beating; guns fireing &c. The Old gentleman gave a feast to the Men, and a glass of grog—and went to bed with his young wife, with the intention of doing his best—The two Indians who had never saw the like before, were under the apprehension that we were for Killing of them, and sneaked off—

[Oct. 30, 1838]—Started up to the Gros Ventre Camp, about four Miles above the Rees. I was well received by them also, had a talk with the Principal Cheifs and Warriors, they have all promised to behave well. They presented me with a quantity of fresh and dried Meat, and told me that their Harts were all good, and friendly disposed towards the Whites, that this time last year, they were all fools, and talked bad, that they had lost a great Many of their tribe by the small Pox, and that it was the Whites that gave them the disease, but since that time they have Killed a great many of their enemies, and that their harts were good, & that they would show by their future Conduct that they would do their best to please me. I slept at their Camp that Night—

[Nov. 17, 1838]—Gave a good Whipping to my young Wife, the first since our union, as I am united to one, that I stole from my Friend, J. Halsey, on my visit to Fort Pierre last summer—

[Jan. 24, 1839]—One Fox and one wolf Started out to run a band of Cows on the hill. Killed one fat Cow—Gave a whipping to my beloved wife, for not mending my Moccassins

[Feb. 28, 1839] I have traded since the departure of the Steam Boat last summer 2500 Buffalo Robes, Beaver, Otter, Wolf and Fox—and stole a young Wife, which you have been apprised of before. As yet we agree very well together. I suppose on account of haveing no young Bucks near the Fort. However, spring is advancing and Numbers will flock in before long and then, Poor White Man, take care of your *Ribs!*

Killed 41 Rats this Month—3479
20 Wolves
14 Foxes

〰 ESSAYS

These essays examine cultural exchanges in borderlands and explore how new ideas and innovations can spread, transforming societies and cultures far beyond their points of introduction. The first essay, by Sylvia Van Kirk, professor emerita of history at the University of Toronto, explores a central borderlands institution: interracial marriage. Van Kirk offers a panoramic overview of marriages between Indians and Europeans in colonial Canada over two centuries. She traces how the French and the Indians forged the practice in the seventeenth century, how that practice became a crucial component of the fur trade, and how it changed after New France was absorbed into the British Empire in 1763. Intermarriage, she shows, transformed native societies, facilitated cross-cultural interactions, and, eventually, paved the way for the expansion of European markets and colonialism. Besides illuminating how intermarriage sustained larger processes of cross-cultural collaboration, Van Kirk's essay also raises important questions about the role of native women in the making—and unmaking—of cross-cultural arrangements. Were native women mere tools in a male-dominated world, or did they have agency of their own? Is it possible that they were at once victimized and empowered by the institution of intermarriage? How did intermarriage shape European views of native women—and men—and how did those views change over time?

In the second essay, Pekka Hämäläinen, professor of history at the University of California at Santa Barbara, shows how the introduction of Spanish horses to the Southwest borderlands transformed native societies and their relationships with colonial powers. Spanish horses triggered an equestrian revolution that swept across the Great Plains and spawned an indigenous empire that eventually turned the tables on European colonialism in the Southwest. Like Kathleen DuVal in the previous chapter, Hämäläinen depicts an Indian–European borderland in which the balance of power was tipped in the favor of the Indians. Maneuvering independently of European designs, Indians often controlled international politics and exchange in both the lower Mississippi Valley and the Southwest borderlands. But differences between the two borderlands may have been even more striking than their similarities. Consider, for example, the contrast in the distribution of power among societies, the forms and purposes of intercultural violence, and the role of the environment in shaping cross-cultural relations.

Intermarriage, Borderlands, and Power

SYLVIA VAN KIRK

Although considerable work has been done on the nature of intermarriage in fur trade society there has been little attempt to fit these patterns into the larger colonial context or to examine their legacy for settler/Aboriginal relations. This article offers a broader analytical framework and raises some of the fundamental questions that need to be asked. It argues that over the course of the colonial period, from the early seventeenth to the late nineteenth centuries, the practice of Aboriginal/non-Aboriginal marriage shifts from "marrying-in" to "marrying-out." I deliberately use the term "marrying-in" to focus on the host Aboriginal societies whose homelands at the time of European contact later became Canadian territory. Especially in the fur trade context, a major impetus for such unions came from Aboriginal groups themselves. The idea was to create a socioeconomic bond that would draw the Euro-Canadian male into Native kinship networks. However, by the end of the colonial period, intermarriage had been transformed by settler society into "marrying-out." Aboriginal women lost their Indian status if they married nonstatus males. Aboriginal groups were deprived of any say in the matter and their kinship structures were ignored.

Charting the course of how this happened over several centuries raises challenging questions and demonstrates how such a study must be nuanced in terms of the intersection of race and gender. Historically much concern was expressed by colonizers over such unions because of their cultural and racial implications. The marital union of European and Aboriginal was perceived as problematic because it symbolized the mixing of irreconcilable dichotomies: civilized versus

Sylvia Van Kirk, "From 'Marrying-In' to 'Marrying-Out': Changing Patterns of Aboriginal/Non-Aboriginal Marriage in Colonial Canada," *Frontiers: A Journal of Women Studies* 23, 3 (2002): 1–11. Rreproduced with permission from the University of Nebraska Press. Copyright 2003 by Frontiers Editorial Collective.

primitive and Christian versus heathen. It must be remembered that even though such notions are discredited today, Europeans in the past were quite apprehensive about mixing with those they categorized as being of a different and lesser race and whose "degenerate" qualities they thought could be transmitted by blood. In the context of colonial Canada it also becomes apparent that the phenomenon of intermarriage was not gender neutral. In the majority of cases the union was between a Euro-Canadian *man* and an Aboriginal *woman*. This pattern has been accepted as a given while the racial and gender hierarchies that are embedded in this dynamic have not been subject to much analysis. This is starkly revealed in the rarity of the reverse union (that is, Aboriginal man married to a Euro-Canadian woman) and the negative reaction to such an occurrence.

Given the complexities of cross-cultural sexual and marital practices it is nec-essary to explain how I am defining "marriage" throughout this study. European commentators, especially religious ones, were quite certain that only *their* marital practices had legitimacy and were adamant that Aboriginal people adopt them. Aboriginal people, of course, thought otherwise; for them, polygamy and divorce were widely accepted concepts. In the Canadian fur trade one finds European men willing to accept or tolerate Aboriginal marital practices to an unusual extent. This becomes quite a complicated social and legal context, but it is significant that a fascinating Canadian court case in 1867 highlighted the essential components of a marital union that were adhered to in *both* Aboriginal and Euro-Canadian societies: a marriage was defined as being openly recognized and characterized by mutual consent, cohabitation, and public repute as husband and wife.

In Canada the widespread and long-lasting phenomenon of the fur trade assumes great importance in accounting for the frequency of Aboriginal/ non-Aboriginal marriage. This is in contrast to contexts where a settler agenda is more explicit, such as in New England for example. In Acadia and New France, fur trade and military concerns were intertwined with small-scale settlement projects, which contributes to the perception that intermarriage was more commonplace than it actually was. There is a general impression that intermarriage was widespread in New France and that Frenchmen had a natural predilection for Aboriginal women. Upon closer scrutiny, however, the French Canadian experience can be differentiated in terms of context: the settler colony along the St. Lawrence was ultimately far less enthusiastic about intermarriage than were fur traders in the hinterland. At the beginning of the colonization of New France during the early seventeenth century, it appears that intermarriage might have been a key component of French colonization policy. This stems from Champlain's famous remark, "Our young men will marry your daughters and we shall be one people," but far too much can be made of this. By the time a Crown Colony was established in 1663, it was acknowledged that intermarriage had failed to produce a stable demographic base. The new approach was to begin state-supported importation of French women, the *filles du roi*.

One of the reasons that intermarriage had failed was that French colonizers had explicitly different motives in promoting it than did their Aboriginal allies. This becomes clear in a fascinating debate about the terms of intermarriage between French Jesuits and a delegation of Huron chiefs in 1637. The Hurons declared themselves to be favorably disposed toward intermarriage because the French traders were proving to be quite good Hurons, but they had some temporal concerns that focused on questions such as bride price and the woman's right to property and divorce. The Jesuits were shocked by these views; the Hurons had to be made to understand that the purpose of these marriages was to work in the opposite direction: "to make them like us, to give them the knowledge of the true God, ... and that the marriages ... were to be stable and perpetual." To the extent that intermarriage was to be encouraged, it was to be a vehicle for missionization and Frenchification. Only Aboriginal women who had been Christianized and introduced to a gender-role similar to that of French peasant women would make acceptable wives for French settlers. As one colonial administrator emphasized, the introduction of a new gender role was as important as religion: "One must teach them to live like villagers in France, meaning to teach them to spin, sew, knit and take care of animals." But in spite of the efforts of the Ursuline nuns, only a small number of Native women were exposed to this kind of acculturation program, and not many were interested or successfully converted. In any event, Aboriginal women would not likely have been accepted as the "founding mothers of New France." Inherent in the settler project was cultural replication: women of another culture were not really deemed appropriate to play the vital female social and reproductive roles necessary for this. Indeed, the lack of French women signals the beginning of a refrain that will be repeated on several Canadian frontiers—that *white* women are vital to a colony's demographic stability and cultural success. It does seem, however, that in this early period Aboriginal women were found unsuitable as settler's wives more on cultural grounds rather than on racial or biological grounds. If contemplated at all settler society only conceptualized intermarriage as a vehicle of "marrying-out," but such unions really did not advance the settlers' agenda or destabilize their Eurocentric conventions. From the early days of New France, it can be argued, settler society was deeply ambivalent about whether this practice should be encouraged at all.

This was not so in the fur trade, however, where very different motives were at play. One of the reasons that French colonial officials came to discourage intermarriage was that they were alarmed at the propensity of Frenchmen to "go Native." The success of the fur trade (unlike settlement) depended on intricate social and economic interactions with Aboriginal people and intermarriage very much facilitated this process. From the Aboriginal point of view, cross-cultural unions were way of integrating the Euro-Canadian stranger into Native kinship networks and enmeshing him in the reciprocal responsibilities that this entailed. The Native woman's gender role was also complementary; indeed, her work was vital to the functioning of the trade as she supplied indigenous clothing, food, and means of transportation. For well over a century, intermarriage in the vast domains of what is today Western Canada was subject to regulation by Aboriginal custom and fur trade company policies alone. Initially the Hudson's Bay Company (HBC), which was founded in 1670, had tried to forbid intermarriage with Native women, but this policy soon proved unenforceable. In contrast, during the late eighteenth century the North West Company, with its headquarters in Montreal, inherited the French traders' appreciation of the benefits of intermarriage.

It was within the context of the Northwest fur trade that the indigenous (indeed, unique) marital rite known as marriage "after the custom of the country" reached its height. Only its main elements need to be summarized here. Initially fur trade marriages were most influenced by Native attitudes and customs, which included payment of a bride price and did not necessarily entail a lifetime commitment. Some HBC officers even went so far as to adopt the Aboriginal custom of polygamy, which was seen as a mark of prestige for a husband. This is not to say that all traders appreciated the reciprocal obligations they had incurred or were above exploiting what appeared to be a more open Native sexuality, but marriage "after the fashion of the country" was *the fundamental social relationship* through which a fur trade society developed. As fur trade society became more endogamous, marriage rites evolved more toward European custom. During the era of the HBC's monopoly after 1821, the company actually introduced marriage contracts that emphasized the husband's financial responsibility and the monogamous bond. But fur trade society was not autonomous. Within this specific social context, Euro-Canadian males had proved themselves adaptable to Aboriginal custom, but many felt ambivalent, and the pull of their own cultural norms remained strong. When they retreated from this fur trade world, their unions, which had not been sealed by European religious ceremony—and, by extension, their wives and families—were vulnerable to the differing attitudes of settler society, where retiring traders might renege on their commitments.

This is why the court case alluded to earlier is so intriguing. The validity of marriage "after the fashion of the country" was tested in the Canadian courts in 1867 after the death of Chief Factor William Connolly, who, upon retiring to Montreal in 1830, had repudiated his Cree wife of nearly thirty years and married a cousin according to Catholic rite. After Connolly's death the children by his Cree wife sued for what they believed was their legitimate inheritance. The transcript of the Connolly case is a fascinating source of firsthand testimony as to what constituted "the custom of the country." In a remarkably balanced judgment, Chief Justice Coram Monk ruled that William Connolly's union with the Cree Suzanne constituted a valid marriage in both cultures—on the one hand because Suzanne had been married according to the customs and usages of her own people and, on the other, because the consent of both parties, the essential element of "civilized" marriage, had been proved by twenty-eight years of repute, public acknowledgement, and cohabitation as man and wife.

Given the widespread and long-lasting nature of the fur trade in the history of Canada, one might speculate that it should have had more of an impact on settler society. The mutual interdependence inherent in fur trade relations might have provided an alternative to conflict-ridden settler/Aboriginal relations. But there is no evidence that this was so. In spite of the progressive cultural relativity shown by the chief justice, this was not the prevailing norm in the settler colonies that developed in Eastern Canada. In Upper Canada, in spite of the importance of Aboriginal allies in the early years of the colony, intermarriage does not appear to have ever been articulated by any colonial official as a useful means of securing good relations with the Indians or enhancing the demographic base of the colony. By the early nineteenth century, intermarriage was reported to be quite rare. Isolated comments suggest that miscegenation was only a symptom of the widespread degradation of Native population, which, although relegated to the margins of colonial society, was nevertheless becoming an expensive burden for colonial administration. As a result the prospect of transferring economic responsibility from the state to a white husband became one of the few reasons advanced for sanctioning the marriage of an Aboriginal woman outside her band. The Bagot Commission, which investigated Indian affairs in the Canadas in the 1840s, noted approvingly: "The principle has been lately sanctioned by the Governor General, who has directed that no Indian woman, living, married or otherwise, with a white man shall receive presents." Both the desire to save money with regard to treaty obligations and the desire to assimilate Native people were consolidated in subsequent Indian Acts. By the Indian Act of 1869, an Indian was defined in patriarchal terms as "as any male person of Indian blood reputed to belong to a particular band"; a wife's status was determined solely by that of her husband's. An Indian woman who married a non-status male legally ceased to be an Indian and lost all rights related to Indian status, as did her children. Thus, by the mid-nineteenth century, the process of intermarriage had become effectively colonized. Intermarriage was seen as a vehicle for removing Aboriginal women from their own cultures.

The patriarchal assumptions inherent in the Indian Act, however, contained a peculiar irony. Should an Euro-Canadian woman marry a status Indian, she would become an Indian! One might ask why, given their Eurocentric assumptions, settler society would permit its own women to sink to the status of Aboriginal. It seems that the likelihood of this happening was too appalling to contemplate; there is no evidence that this corollary was even discussed, much less sanctioned. Intermarriage, as we have seen, had been shaped by its own gender dynamics: there was no symmetry in the pattern of these relationships. In the process of colonization, males of the dominant society might form sexual and marital unions with subordinated females, but such men revealed little tolerance for the possibility of their own race and gender hierarchies being challenged.

It is significant that there were very few examples of an Aboriginal man marrying a Euro-Canadian woman in colonial Canada. This was not just because of demographics. Two cases from Upper Canada underscore the fact that, although the men in question were Christian and held positions of prestige, the very idea that *red* men should marry *white* women was anathema to colonial society. The first case was the marriage of Mississauga leader Peter Jones to a middle-class British woman, Eliza Field. Jones, who was also a Methodist preacher, had met his future wife when he was on a fund-raising trip to England in the early 1830s. The couple was forced to overcome severe criticism from her relatives, but they persisted, as their touching correspondence reveals, and they finally married when Field came out via New York in 1833. But instead of congratulations, they were faced with humiliating public condemnation. A scurrilous account published in the *New York Spectator* portrayed Jones as a conniving savage who had somehow managed to dupe an innocent Englishwoman, who could have had no idea of the fate that awaited her. The author decried the way in which an Indian man had transgressed racial boundaries: "We heard the Indian and herself pronounced man and wife! It was the first time we ever heard the words ...

sound hatefully.... The idea is very unpleasant with us, of such ill-sorted mixtures of colors." To Jones's great distress, the article was circulated widely in the papers in Upper Canada and, although some supporters attempted to refute these accusations, he continued to be the target of criticism and plagued by rumors that the marriage had foundered.

Similar criticism was expressed in the second case in 1859, when George Johnson, a prominent Mohawk chief of the Six Nations, married the Euro-Canadian Emily Howells. Her brother-in-law, who was an Anglican clergyman, declared, "I'll have no Indian come here after my wife's sister," and refused to acknowledge the couple for many years. While the Johnsons apparently did find some sympathetic support, it is important to probe the sense of outrage that accompanied the actions of these Aboriginal men, who were both community leaders. In these cases the fear that civilized white women would be returning to the primitive was not at issue. Both of these women were marrying into a highly acculturated Aboriginal elite. Emily Howells actually improved her living conditions; her home, "Chiefswood," on the Six Nations reserve was a Victorian mansion much superior to many Upper Canadian settlers' homes. Nor were these women's prescribed gender roles as bearers of European civilization challenged; indeed, Eliza Field was to assist her husband in his missionizing endeavors. Such marriages might have been promoted as a way of furthering assimilation, but the colonial reaction illuminates deeply-rooted anxieties about the potential threat to white male dominance in these transplanted societies. Both the Aboriginal man and the Euro-Canadian woman were deemed to be behaving inappropriately. Aboriginal men were seen to be usurping Euro-Canadian male prerogatives; and it was not acceptable for a white woman to be subordinate to an Aboriginal man. On the other hand, "whiteness" could not prevail in the person of a woman; for any man to be subordinate to a woman was unthinkable. These cases bear out the findings of historians analyzing the intersection of race and gender in other contexts. In colonizing patriarchal societies exclusive control of women goes hand in hand with the subordination of the "racial" Other, both male and female.

Nevertheless, Euro-Canadian hegemony could not be taken for granted; it had to be built. As settler society spread west, the reification of racial and gender hierarchies was used to gain control, throwing all patterns of miscegenation into disrepute. In British Columbia, the fur trade frontier was rapidly transformed into a settler colony as a result of the gold rush in the late 1850s. Given the demographic imbalance incoming white men continued to have sexual relations with Native women, although these appear to have been more transient and exploitative than they were previously during fur trade society ... the colonial discourse was virulently hostile to Aboriginal people and race-mixing. Miscegenation was denounced as a "vice," and the old refrain—harkening back to the days of New France—about the necessity of importing marriageable white women was given new urgency. However, due partly to the legacy of the fur trade, which meant that several HBC/Native families were prominent in the early colonial elite, British Columbia never went as far as the new states south of the border in passing antimiscegenation laws.

In the prairie West racism and prejudice against intermarriage had been growing since the latter days of the fur trade, with the intrusion of agents of settler society in the persons of the missionary and the Euro–Canadian woman. For the new homestead west of the prairies, with its renewed emphasis on replicating Euro–Canadian family structures, Sarah Carter has effectively shown how the Aboriginal woman was constructed as the sexually permissive Other: someone with whom Euro–Canadian males might have clandestine sex, but definitely not someone to marry. Symbolic of this hardening of colonial attitudes is another court case in 1886 that negates the judgment of the original Connolly case. In adjudication another test of marriage "after the fashion of the country," an eastern Canadian court ruled that it could *not* accept that "the cohabitation of a civilized man and a savage woman, even for a long period of time, gives rise to the presumption that they consented to be married in our sense of marriage." This represents the consolidation of the Eurocentric privileging of who gets to define what constitutes marriage. It is no accident that this coincides with the rise of racist attitudes that focus more explicitly on the degenerate consequences that were supposed to result from "the mixing of blood."

The physical legacy of fur trade intermarriage, which had produced the métis people of Western Canada, was further discredited by the North West Rebellion, which had been ruthlessly crushed by the Canadian government in 1885. Increasingly racist rhetoric condemned the product of miscegenation as degenerate. Even the highly acculturated mixed-race families of the colonial North West found their progenitors' choice of marriage partners disparaged. In the first official history of the Pacific Northwest the American historian Hubert Howe Bancroft denounced miscegenation as "the fur trader's curse." He lamented that the distinguished officers of the Hudson's Bay Company had stooped to marrying Indian and "half-breed" women, for, by doing so, "their own old Scotch, Irish and English blood would … be greatly debased."

By the end of the colonial period the legacy of fur trade intermarriage had effectively been negated, and the place of Aboriginal/non-Aboriginal marriage in Canadian society had undergone a major transformation. Because of the importance and longevity of the fur trade in the Canadian experience, it had at one time been a widespread and vital phenomenon, but settler society had always been ambivalent about its desirability, and, as Euro–Canadian patterns of settlement were solidified, intermarriage was increasingly denigrated and marginalized.

Ecological Change and Indigenous Imperialism in the Southwest Borderlands

PEKKA HÄMÄLÄINEN

The Europeans who conquered the New World liked to credit their astonishing successes to their god and their own ingenuity, but modern broad-gauge bio-histories suggest that all the conquerors often had to do was to show up and

Pekka Hämäläinen, "The Politics of Grass: European Expansion, Ecological Change, and Indigenous Power in the Southwest Borderlands," *William and Mary Quarterly* 67 (April 2010): 173–208. Reprinted by permission.

somehow stay alive; their microbes did the rest. Arriving with oceangoing ships, steel, and horses, Europeans held a decisive military edge over the Indians, yet the conquest of the Americas would have been neither as fast nor as complete without Europe's biological advantages. The biological thrust of colonization has been recognized since smallpox toppled the Aztecs—the conquistadors knew they were advancing in the wake of infectious diseases even if they spoke of divine rather than epidemiological interventions—but it was not until scholars coined such arresting macrohistorical concepts as the Columbian Exchange and ecological imperialism that biological interpretations entered the mainstream. The result was that might be called a biological turn of American colonial history. Suddenly the conquest of Native America seemed a product not so much of Europe's techno-organizational superiority as of blind biogeographic luck.

Grand, large-scale biohistories have reoriented the story of America's Europeanization, but precisely because they compress complex processes into digestible formulas, they can obscure as much as they reveal. Preoccupied with global patterns, they often distort the realities on the ground, where Europeans did not expand as a monolith and Indians did not die in the aggregate. Abstract by design, the big-picture ecohistorical models tend to suffuse history with biological determinism: European colonization becomes a mere corollary of an undeclared biological warfare, and Indians, their immunologically naive bodies but soft fodder for aggressive Old World pathogens, seem naturally selected for dispossession. History is reduced to a Darwinian process where biological encounters inexorably lead to colonial conquests, undisturbed by instances where European biota—animals, plants, pathogens—did not trigger immediate aboriginal decline and where Europeans were not the primary beneficiaries of transoceanic exchages.

Such deterministic, flattening tendencies of macroscale biohistories have come under increasing criticism, or been sidelined, as historians have produced more complex and nuanced narratives that show how indigenous decline in the face of Europe's biological onslaught was neither immediate nor inevitable. This shift in focus has reconfigured environmental history, but it does not mean that, in efforts to avoid sweeping and deterministic generalizations, historians ought to consign environmental history to local case studies. A nascent historiographical middle ground is emerging that moves among local, regional, continental, and transoceanic perspectives and focuses on the interplay among political, economic, cultural, and biological forces. By blending environmental history, transatlantic history, borderlands history, ethnohistory, and colonial studies, historians question ossified assumptions about the potency of state power, the contours of indigenous agency, the cultural specificity of human-environment relationships, and the arrows of environmental and historical change. Just such an approach, applied to the Comanche Indians, a hunter-gatherer group of modest origins, reveals an unforeseen imperial expansion sustained by an equally unexpected ecological undercurrent.

In the eighteenth-century American Southwest and Great Plains, an imposing Comanche imperial structure arose amid European colonial outposts and in an environment that was rapidly being remade by Europe's biological exports.

Initially unsettled by European intrusions, Comanches learned to protect their bodies and homelands against dangerous Old World organisms while adopting what was useful in Europe's export package, and theirs is a story of a domineering indigenous power exploiting European exports to exploit European colonists in a world that was new for all. But to stay in power—to survive their ascendancy—Comanches had to reenvision their relationship with the natural world. They had to forge strategies to offset the ecological burdens of their political and economic expansion and, when those strategies could no longer absorb the burdens of growth in their Great Plains niche, find ways to transport these costs elsewhere. The colonial Southwest and northern Mexico were gradually drawn into the expanding Comanche sphere as raiding domains and ecological safety valves.

The rise of this Comanche-centric order and its ecological underpinnings illuminate the complex and unexpected ways in which transoceanic exchanges, biological encounters, and human ambition could intertwine to shape power relationships in early America. They form a counternarrative to conventional colonial histories by revealing a world where Indians benefited from Europe's biological expansion, safeguarded their homelands by displacing ecological burdens on colonial realms, and debilitated European imperialism with imperial aspirations of their own. It is a counternarrative that expands the scope of indigenous agency from the social to the biological sphere because it shows how Indians could determine not only the human parameters of colonial encounters but also the ecological ones. As such it is a story that may help bridge the gap that separates the declensionist narratives of American Indian environmental history from the works that emphasize the resilience of indigenous polities and cultural forms. Native survival in colonial America was often a race against ecological degradation and the loss of land and its resources. As the rise of the Comanches shows, however, the outcomes of that contest could remain undertermined for a long time.

Like many now-renowned Native American societies, the Comanches were born out of creative responses to the dangers and opportunities unleashed by European contact. In the seventeenth century, Comanches did not exist as an ethnic entity. Their parent group, the Uto-Aztecan-speaking Shoshones, lived on the central Great Plains of North America, having migrated from the Great Basin in the mid-1500s, when the plains bison proliferated under the cool and wet conditions of the Little Ice Age. Their location deep in the continent's core sheltered the Shoshones from European influences, but eventually that centrality turned their homelands into a confluence of Columbian exchanges. In the late seventeenth century, an unknown disease, possibly smallpox, reached them with devastating results: people died, kinship networks fractured, and the Shoshones split in two. One faction, carrying the name Shoshone with it, gravitated toward the dense bison populations of the northern plains … The other faction pushed hundreds of miles to the south, emerging in New Mexican records as Comanches. Disease may have put these proto-Comanches on the move—Indians often abandoned places infested with dangerous, unexplainable forces—yet it was another biological frontier that pulled them south. In 1680 allied Pueblo Indians banished their Spanish overlords from New Mexico, only to fall victim to escalating raids by surrounding nomads who covered the horses that the fleeing Spaniards had left behind. The nomads traded a portion of the stolen animals to their allies, propelling the horse frontier deep into the interior where the Comanches encountered it, securing enough beasts to envision the possibilities of the equestrian way of life. Tracing the equine flow back to its source, Comanches arrived in New Mexico's borderlands sometime in the 1690s, just as the Spaniards arrived from the south to recapture the colony.

Comanches entered this world of possibility and peril cautiously. They forged an alliance with the Utes, another Uto-Aztecan group living in New Mexico's borderlands, and, guided by their new partners, added guns and metal tools to their inventory of European technology. Though embracing Spanish innovations, Comanches kept their distance from Spaniards themselves. They used Spanish horses and guns to raid neighboring Spanish and native communities for livestock and captives and then entered New Mexico's urban centers under temporary truces to barter meat and slaves for corn and horses. Interlaced with violence, such visits were by necessity brief and sporadic cross-border plunges that yielded European technology without extended exposure to European microbes. By the 1710s Comanches were raiding slaves deep on the southern plains, where their probing migration transformed into a sweeping colonization project, at the heart of which was a bitter war of attrition with the formidable Apaches.

The wars continued until mid-century, when the Comanches gained the upper hand over both the Apaches and their Spanish allies. Fully mounted, well equipped with European weaponry, and apparently untouched by major epidemics since the late seventeenth century, they were growing rapidly in numbers, their population probably nearing fifteen thousand by 1750. Meanwhile the Apaches, especially the Jicarillas, Mescaleros, and Lipans who had gradually moved toward Spanish settlement in New Mexico and Texas, faced the grim side of Columbian encounters. Spanish officials not only denied them European technology but also tried to pressure them to give up hunting and accept Christianity in the Franciscan fold even as other Spaniards conducted unrelenting slave raids into Apache villages. Pinched between the aggressively encroaching Comanche frontier and the aggressively absorptive Spanish frontier, Apaches began retreating to the desert lands near the Rio Grande. By the 1760s all Apache groups had abandoned the plains for the desert lands in southern Texas and New Mexico and northern Chihuahua.

The success of Spanish colonialism hinged on its agents' ability to prevent nonsedentary natives from accessing European weaponry, but in the far north Spaniards clashed with Comanches who rode Spanish animals to pillage Spanish animals, pierced coats of mail with iron-tipped arrows, and killed from the safety of distance with state-of-the-art flintlock muskets. Guns and metal weapons in Comanche hands shocked the colonists, yet it was horses, and the way the Comanches used them to make war, that tipped the balance of power in the Spaniards' disfavor. Comanches never engaged in pitched battles if they could avoid it and eschewed large cavalry tactics for small hit-and-run attacks, thus neutralizing the Spaniards' crucial advantage over Native Americans—their ability and willingness to pin down enemies and kill them en masse. The contest over military dominance in the Southwest borderlands would be determined piecemeal, in incessant small-scale skirmishes rather than in climatic battles, which gave the Comanches an enduring advantage.

The mid-eighteenth-century Comanches had experienced an astounding ascent, but as their territorial expansion slowed down, the factors that had made them so powerful began to render them vulnerable. Comanchería's massive size sustained a rapid economic growth, yet its vastness also left the Comanches exposed: their homeland was encircled by dozens of native powers, several of them clamoring for its immense natural resources, some harboring deep resentment for having been marginalized.

Another key advantage that over time turned into a liability was Comanches' willingness to rearrange their existence around foreign innovations. Their expansion was propelled by a steady, partially coerced inflow of horses, guns, metal, and carbohydrates, and its culmination brought a somber realization: to retain what they had seized, Comanches needed unhindered access to imported food and technology.

The problem was that Comanchería, a geopolitical backwater, was also a commercial frontier. Major long-distance trade routes still skirted or ended on its borders, forcing Comanches to search for commercial openings in the surrounding urban centers.

The trade journeys to border fairs were also biologically hazardous, exposing Comanches to the teeming microbe pools of densely packed trading villages.

Out of Comanches' efforts to protect their lives, land, and autonomy sprang the second stage of their ascent. Secluded and vulnerable in their new homeland, they designed and improvised in the late eighteenth and early nineteenth centuries a series of geopolitical arrangements that molded the bordering regions—New Mexico, Texas, and northern Mexico—into a configuration that could sustain their fragile existence.

Once again, the horse was the catalyst. If the prospects and exigencies of equestrianism had powered Comanches' territorial conquest, their postterritorial ascent rested on their ability to use horse wealth to connect, pacify, and manipulate adjacent societies. As the lords of the southern plains, Comanches had enviable access to the rich animal reservoirs in the Spanish Southwest, an advantage they exploited to the full. They alternately purchased and plundered horses from Texas and New Mexico, accumulating reserves of tens of thousands of tradable surplus animals, which was enough to pull most of the Plains Indians into their commercial orbit, to support several variously successful indigenous horse cultures on the continental grasslands, to equip New Orleans and other eastern colonial centers with draft animals, and to support the westward expansion of America's settlement frontier in the Deep South.

In return for supplying a good portion of the continent with equine power, Comanches won access to several colonial and indigenous markets and two vital imports: guns and food. They soon surpassed Spanish colonists in firepower, thus further accelerating their ascent on the competitive technological ladder that rested on Columbian exchanges, and the technological balance of power in the borderlands remained titled in their favor well into the nineteenth century.

If the bustling trading empire furnished the Comanches with the necessary technology to dominate the Southwest, it also helped them support the necessary numbers to do so. With a steady inflow of corn, beans, squash, sunflower seeds, and even baked bread from neighboring farming societies, they built a diet that many modern nutritionists would consider almost ideal: moderate or high in protein, iron, and vitamin B-12; moderate in complex carbohydrates; and low in saturated fat, cholesterol, and sodium.

For European microbes, moreover, the Comanche trade network was a thoroughly frustrating entity. Such was its drawing power that Comanches, one of history's most mobile societies, largely stopped traveling for trade. Instead of visiting surrounding, germ-filled urban centers for commerce, they simply waited in their camps deep in Comanchería for foreign trade convoys to arrive, an immeasurable advantage in the new post-Columbian disease environment. Comanchería was vast and, because the sick rarely traveled far, the visiting trading parties that made the distance were consistently healthy. It appears that smallpox reached epidemic levels only four times in Comanchería before the mid-1840s—a strikingly small number given its geopolitical centrality and numerous commercial ties—and the well-nourished Comanches quickly rebounded after each outbreak. The Comanche population hovered from twenty to thirty thousand until the mid-nineteenth century, making them by far the most populous indigenous society in the colonial Southwest.

Prosperous, populous, and connected, Comanchería emerged by the dawn of the nineteenth century as the kinetic center of the lower mid-continent, a seat of power that possessed a strong political, economic, and cultural hold over the surrounding native and European societies. It was a startling power asymmetry that flowed—through human agency—from a compelling environmental asymmetry. On the Great Plains north of Comanchería, winters became increasingly longer and growing seasons shorter, thwarting animal husbandry. Living in one of the world's great natural equine habitats, the ecologically privileged Comanches could maintain large horse herds with relative ease and export surplus animals to perennial deficit regions, where their native customers grew increasingly dependent on Comanchería's commercial services. By controlling the south-to-north flow of animal wealth in mid-America, Comanches held the key to the economic and military success of numerous societies, a position of daunting geographic power that transformed into seductive soft power. Dazzled by Comanchería's dynamic horse culture and dwarfed by its economic reach, native societies across the plains attached themselves to the Comanche orbit as political allies, making Comanchería one of the most tranquil places in early America. They mimicked Comanche customs, learned Comanche language, and accepted Comanche norms of proper behavior, turning economic dependency into cultural intimacy. Eventually, many immigrated to Comanchería, enticed by its material wealth and political security, and became, in contemporary language, the "subordinates" or "vassals" of the Comanches, who "teach them their own martial habits and help to improve their condition," "finally amalgamating them into their nation."

Viewed from the north and east, Comanchería was a massive trade pump that siphoned Eurasian livestock into North American trade arteries, growing increasingly wealthy and powerful from the arrangement. Facing the Spanish colonies in the south and west, Comanches displayed a different variation of indigenous imperialism, one embedded in coercion and exploitation. The two facets were linked. To maintain their commercial hegemony, Comanches needed secure access to Spanish animal reserves, which in turn made it necessary for them to have a particular kind of New Mexico and Texas on their borders: militarily weak, politically submissive, yet economically viable. This imperative explains why scholars find the Comanches raiding across the Southwest, decade after decade, for domesticated, ready-to-sell horses even while parleying, trading, and collecting gifts under the threat of violence at certain frontier outposts. Comanches, in other words, blended organized pillaging, tribute extraction, and coerced exchange into a complex economy of violence that eventually reduced much of the Spanish far north to an exploited periphery.... The Comanches' composite foreign policy gradually fragmented Spain's already dis-jointed northern frontier after its own image. Eastern New Mexico, Spanish offi-cials feared, was being corrupted by the long shadow of Comanche influence, its citizens gravitating toward Comanchería's markets and prestige, desiring to live "in a complete liberty, *in imitation of the wild tribes which they see nearby,*" even as the rest of the Spanish frontier was being subjected to wholesale Comanche raiding. By the 1810s Comanches were treating the Spanish Southwest like a colonial possession.

Comanches bent others to their will because they wanted what most hege-monic people want—security, prosperity, respect—but to fully understand their expansionist drive historians must move closer to the ground and examine the pol-itics of grass. For all the geopolitical, economic, and cultural incentives, the over-riding impulse that pushed the Comanches to expand was a need to maximize grasslands holdings on which their survival and their power ultimately rested.

Grass mattered so much because Comanches had become pastoralists. Dur-ing the eighteenth century, they converted their foraging economy into a hybrid economy of hunting and herding, thereby entering an uncharted realm of eco-nomic possibilities and ecological constraints. Comanchería, a luscious patchwork of buffalo, grama, and bluestem grasses, hardly seems a setting where animal her-ders would feel confined, but the impression of limitless natural bounty conceals a volatile environment whose gifts were at once abundant and unpredictable. The seemingly bottomless forage supply of normal years dwindled as much as 90 percent during dry spells that frequently scourged the southern plains. When the rains failed, grasses went underground, storing nutrients in their sprawling root structures and beyond animals' reach. Pastures also fluctuated seasonally as dry winter currents suppressed the rains, leaving grasses starved and stunted. During those nutri-tional crunches, there was not enough grass to go around for all. The main rivals were horses and bison, two ecologically incompatible species with an 80 percent dietary overlap and nearly identical survival strategies.

Viewed abstractly, the late-eighteenth-century Comanches were heading toward an ecological impasse out of which there were two immediate paths, both of them bad. Comanches could have continued their delicate balancing between herd maximization and overgrazing within the existing material parameters, yet that ran the risk of ruining their nutritional mainstay. They also could have curbed the size of their domesticated herds—or, alternatively, their own numbers—to alleviate the pressure on the bison, but that would have undercut their commercial pull and military power, rendering them vulnerable to colonial and indigenous rivals. And so, instead of adjusting to existing ecological limits, Comanches crafted, in stages and over several decades, a multilayered land-use strategy that rested on creative exploitation of not only Comanchería's resources but also those of the neighboring regions. It was a strategy that would eventually extend the Comanche resource base deep into Mexico, yet it began as a simple bid to preserve what was readily available at home.

The new resource strategy revolved around a complex annual cycle of activities that helped allocate life's essentials for prey and domesticated animals. Like the bison, Comanches shifted in winters toward the riverine lowlands and their life-sustaining offerings of tall grasses, timber, water, and shelter. For more than four months, they led a largely sedentary life, moving their villages up and down the bottomlands only when grasses failed or camp refuse became unmanageable. They dwelled close enough to the buffalo to conduct small-scale hunts but far enough to secure their horses foraging areas not already exhausted by bison.

Comanches did not reenter the nomadic phase until late spring, when short grasses sprouted on the highlands. Large winter villages broke into numerous small bands to maximize grazing areas, and Comanchería transformed into a pastoral beehive, where dozens of scattered bands moved constantly, seeking fresh forage to bulk up their horses and carefully synchronizing their movements to avoid overlapping grazing areas. As in winters Comanches kept their horses and the bison segregated.

The distinctive annual cycle was a complex adaptation that helped ease the ecological contradictions at the heart of the new Comanche economy that married subsistence hunting to intensive market-driven pastoralism. But Comanches changed not just the way they used the land; they changed the land itself. The pastoral Comanchería was an anthropogenic landscape that had been altered biologically to meet the needs of expanding animal husbandry. Comanches burned patches of grass to encourage new growth for forage, harvested massive amounts of cottonwood for supplemental winter fodder, and turned vast sections of riverine habitats into veritable equine sanctuaries by crowding out other animal species. And yet, in the end, such adaptations could carry them only so far. Sometime in the late eighteenth century, the pastoral growth reached a threshold at which Comanches had to either reduce their herding economy or find ways to channel its ecological burdens out of Comanchería. The first alternative was all but unthinkable—not only the nation's collective power but also its members' personal status depended on horse wealth—and so Comanches embraced the latter option, with momentous repercussions for themselves and the peoples around them.

One early experiment with ecological cost management involved transhumance, seasonal movement of people and their livestock to new pastures. In the 1770s, apparently prompted by an exceptionally intense drought, Comanches began migrating between lowland plains valleys in winters and cool mountain pastures in summers. These vertical migrations moved a portion of Comanche horse herds—along with the accompanying ecological burdens of animal foraging—from Comanchería to Spanish borderlands in New Mexico and Ute territory in the Colorado plateau. Regardless of destination the westbound migrations coincided with violent raids—in New Mexico on Spanish outposts and in the plateau on the Utes, whose alliance with the Comanches had unraveled—underscoring the extent to which grass had become a political object.

Episodically expanding Comanchería beyond its plains base, seasonal transborder migrations remained a vital drought-combating strategy into the late nineteenth century, but they were not enough to stabilize Comanchería's burgeoning pastoral economy. Around 1800 the growing horse herds began to cut deep into Comanchería's increased carrying capacity even under normal climatic conditions, forcing Comanches to expand their archive of land-use strategies. They found a solution, undoubtedly through trial and error, in an age-old borderlands institution that at first glance has little to do with ecological management: frontier raiding.

By pillaging colonial settlements for domesticated horses, Comanches implemented an unequal division of labor and ecological exchange in the borderlands. They focused on the high-profit activities of livestock raiding and trading and, through border raiding, forced New Mexican and Texan settlers to absorb the bulk of the labor and ecological costs of animal husbandry. Settlers invested enormous amounts of energy, grass, and grain in raising horses, only to repeatedly lose significant portions of their herds to Comanche raiders who, in a sense, used the twin colonies as an animal factory and an ecological relief valve. When Comanches raided New Mexico and Texas for horses, they appropriated not only marketable animals but also foreign natural resources to conserve their own. With each pilfered horse, they got more than the animal itself. They also extracted the years of labor and the millions of calories that went into bringing that animal to maturity, all of which meant crucial savings of human and natural resources in Comanchería.

Raiding thus served to externalize the environmental costs of market-oriented pastoralism, an advantage Comanches amplified by keeping separate clusters of animals for different economic and cultural purposes. As one contemporary discovered, they "could scarcely be induced to sell" their domestically raised animals, which had been trained for various tasks from pulling travois to bison hunting. The stolen animals, in contrast, were promptly channeled into trading circuits. Thoroughly commodified, they were often sold within weeks or months of being pilfered—Comanches raided and traded almost year-round, constantly shifting between the two activities—which meant that they left a relatively light ecological hoofprint on Comanchería's natural setting.

By the time Spanish rule yielded to Mexico in 1821, generations of unremitting raiding had finally crippled the Texas ranching economy, making it difficult for Comanches to conduct profitable raids in the colony. From the mid-1820s, moreover, Texas was flooded by well-armed Anglo-American settlers, whose presence in the colony made raiding a risky proposition. New Mexico, too, lost its appeal to Comanche raiders. Mexican officials attached the province to Comanchería through a thinly veiled tribute relationship that shielded it from violence, and New Mexicans specialized increasingly in sheepherding, having less than one thousand horses in the late 1820s. Needing a new source of horses to keep their market-oriented economy running, Comanches pushed below the Rio Grande in such intensity that several northern Mexican departments organized their meager resources for war.

Mexico yielded not only horses but also the laborers to manage them, and most Comanche raiding parties brought home human captives as well as animals. Scouring northern Mexico for human loot, they transformed themselves into large-scale slaveholders in roughly a generation. By the 1830s the slave component of their population probably exceeded 10 percent. Slaves thus boosted the Comanche population, yet their bodies also carried a hidden gift. Studies suggest that Native Americans were so vulnerable to Old World diseases not because their immune systems were weaker but because they were strikingly homogenous: once adapted to their relatively uniform immune systems, infections may have taken a greater toll than in more heterogeneous populations. Since Comanches drew most of their slaves from a different gene pool—a large portion of them were mestizos—the slavery-marriage-motherhood continuum may have given their communities some measure of protection through immune system diversity.

Contemporaries understood that the expansion below the Rio Grande was first and last an economic endeavor that sustained the vast Comanche trading empire north of the great river. The plains-based commercial network, its limbs reaching toward the Canadian Plains and the U.S. South, formed with the Mexican raiding hinterland the economic foundation of a transregional power complex that kept numerous peoples on the Comanche orbit through overlapping bonds of violence, exchange, extortion, and dependency. What has been less clear is that the push into Mexico was also a biological necessity. During the first third of the nineteenth century, Comanches experienced three momentous changes that boosted their political and economic might while placing unforeseen pressure on their natural resources. Possibly prompted by the 1799–1816 smallpox epidemics, they incorporated several Arapahoe and Wichita bands and the entire Kiowa and Naishan nations into their increasingly multiethnic realm, where newcomers exchanged varying degrees of their autonomy for access to Comanchería's wealth and safety. Then, diffusing potential conflict with commerce, Comanches forged exchange relationships with the encroaching immigrant tribes of Indian Territory—the Cherokees, Chickasaws, Choctaws, Creeks, and others—who began conducting regular trade journeys into Comanchería, subsisting on its bison as they traversed across it. Finally, spurred by the establishment of Bent's Fort and other Anglo-American trading posts on their borders, Comanches embarked on a mass-scale production of bison hides, converting their commissary into an animal of enterprise. It was not long before Comanchería's bison started to show signs of overexploitation. Strains started to appear in the 1810s, and by the 1830s the herds had become visibly diminished.

The Mexico-bound incursions were, in part, a response to the bison's troubles. War bands brought back massive numbers of horses that were promptly exchanged for food and manufactured goods at Anglo-American posts or, increasingly, eaten. Early-nineteenth-century Comanches consumed increasing amounts of horseflesh—some sources call it their favorite food—which reduced pressure on the bison. But if large-scale raiding helped the bison by furnishing an alternative food source, it also helped by simply carrying humans away. The deeper into Mexico the Comanches pushed, the longer they stayed there, and the larger their war bands, the less human pressure there was on Comanchería's distressed bison. As the burden on Comanchería's bison ecology increased, so did the size and frequency of Comanche raiding expeditions, which in the 1840s routinely featured hundreds of warriors. Pushing deep into Durango, Zacatecas, and San Luis Potosí, the massive war bands spent months on foreign soil, living off the land while sacking ranches, villages, towns, and mining communities. They butchered cattle, pigs, sheep, and goats for food across the countryside and extracted gifts of meat and bread in urban centers. They let their oversize horse herds forage on the abundant grama grasses of the Mexican plateau, where killing frosts came rarely, and they took their herds to graze in the dampish mountain forests of Coahuila and Nuevo León. After successful raids they sometimes allowed their animals to feed on Mexican grain stores. Their war trails and campsites were littered with animal bones, rotting carcasses, trampled fields, and drained food caches, all markers of a new environmental strategy that allowed them to displace environmental loads to the south to sustain their power far in the north.

Strategy? Such an argument for intentionality might seem anachronistic, registering as too Western, too openly in conflict with accepted truths about indigenous environmental ethics that are embedded in a spiritual matrix, but that is not necessarily the case. There is, first of all, the sheer scale of Comanche operations to consider. In the course of the 1830s, Comanche raids into Mexico escalated into cyclical migrations. War bands started to travel with entire families and stay below the Rio Grande for months and sometimes years. The Bolsón de Mapimí, a vast mountain-nestled desert plateau in the heart of northern Mexico and the chief crossroads of Comanche war trails, began to take the shape of a permanent, self-sustaining settlement colony. The Bolsón was a neo-Comanchería in the making, a transformed territory where Comanches lived as they did in Comanchería proper, hunting game and gathering wild plants for subsistence and slowly migrating from one camping ground to another. They lined their favorite Bolsón campsites with parapets and crowded river bottoms with their massive herds, and their horses scarred the landscape with their hooves, pervading the region with an aura of a colonized landscape.

All these developments—the hundreds-strong war bands, the multiseasonal expeditions, the Bolsón colony—appear excessive for the purposes of livestock raiding, suggesting that another motive was involved. That motive, it seems, was ecological: the massive invasion of foreign territories helped stabilize Comanchería's battered bison ecology that was collapsing under the weight of an imperial economy. Yet listing the ecological benefits of large-scale long-distance raiding only suggests causality; it does not reveal intention. To access Comanche motives, it is necessary to have Comanche words. In 1872 at Fort Sill Agency in Indian Territory, U.S. government agents met with prominent Comanche chiefs, trying to convince them to become farmers and give up hunting and raiding. When told that the bison would soon disappear—the United States' industrial assault on the herds was already under way—a Comanche speaker retorted that "there were yet millions of buffalo, and there was no danger on that hand." But "lest they might fail," he continued, "they, the Comanches, had determined to hunt buffalo only next winter, then they would allow them to breed a year or two without molestation, and they would rely on Texas cattle for subsistence meantime." This startling declaration laid bare the dual character of Comanche imperialism that had dominated the history of the American Southwest for more than a century: it was a geopolitical endeavor of projecting power outward and a biological endeavor of dispatching environmental burdens of expansion elsewhere.

An economic colossus resting on a relatively delicate ecological foundation, the Comanche power complex was an inherently unstable entity. Comanches' massive horse herds, the source and symbol of their power, also rendered them vulnerable to ecological damage and external aggression. Comanches managed to head off the looming implosion by shifting environmental costs to adjacent regions, but the onset of a twenty-year dry spell in the mid-1840s brought on a full-scale crisis, then collapse.

Even with many of their bands in Mexico, Comanches and their horses crowded Comanchería's few riparian habitats where forage and water remained available, denying the bison access to the life-sustaining drought refuges. Half of Comanchería's seven million bison may have perished, leaving the Comanches reeling. Famine left them exposed to disease, and they were struck by cholera in 1849 and smallpox in 1848, 1851, and 1861. By the early 1860s, the Comanches had lost more than half their numbers and, with that, their power to command. They surrendered their raiding domains, gave up tribute extraction, and witnessed their commercial pull dissipate to almost nothing.

Yet it was not inevitable that this crisis would lead to collapse. Comanches had repeatedly recovered from drought- and disease-induced crises during their imperial tenure, and they may well have done so this time as well. Indeed, as the drought passed in the mid-1860s, Comanches resumed large-scale raiding, their war bands ranging across debilitated, post–Civil War Texas, stealing livestock, taking captives, and subsisting on stolen cattle. The Comanches of the late 1860s seemed to have found a new ecological balance in their home territory, and they were becoming a domineering force in the borderlands once again.

And then it ended, not because large biohistorical dynamics had suddenly turned against them but because a new player entered the scene. The United States had extended its southwestern boundary to the Rio Grande in the

Mexican-American War, boxing in the Comanches, whose devastating raids across Mexico had inadvertently helped the Americans win the war, yet the expansionist republic did not become a major disruptive force in Comanche history until the late 1860s. For nearly two decades after the Mexican-American War, the U.S. pressure on Comanchería came in pieces—in the the the form of overland trails, new military forts at the Texas frontier, and Anglo-Texan settlers—but the end of the Civil War brought the deluge: agribusiness, ranching industry, and railroads ushered in a new order of free-labor capitalism in which there was no place for independent slave-raiding Indians. In 1871 the U.S. Army launched a total war in Comanchería, targeting horses, bison, and food caches as much as people. Still a shadow of their former imperial selves, the recovering Comanches were powerless against the onslaught, and their last, half-starved bands moved to Indian Territory in 1875.

FURTHER READING

Anderson, Gary Clayton. *The Indian Southwest, 1580–1830: Ethnogenesis and Reinvention* (1999).

Anderson, Karen. *Chain Her by One Foot: The Subjugation of Native Women in Seventeeth-Century New France* (1991).

Aron, Stephen. *How the West Was Lost: The Transformation of Kentucky from Daniel Boone to Henry Clay* (1996).

———. *American Confluence: The Missouri Frontier from Borderland to Border State* (2006).

Barbour, Barton H. *Fort Union and the Upper Missouri Fur Trade* (2001).

Barr, Juliana. *Peace Came in the Form of a Woman: Indians and Spaniards in the Texas Borderlands* (2007).

Binnema, Theodore. *Common and Contested Ground: A Human and Environmental History of the Northwestern Plains* (2001).

Blackhawk, Ned. *Violence over the Land: Indians and Empires in the Early American West* (2006).

Brooks, James F. *Captives and Cousins: Slavery, Kinship, and Community in the Southwest Borderlands* (2002).

Brown, Jennifer S. H. *Strangers in Blood: Fur Trade Company Families in Indian Country* (1980).

Cronon, William. *Changes in the Land: Indians, Colonists, and the Ecology of New England* (1983; rev. ed., 2003).

Crosby, Alfred W. *The Columbian Exchange: Biological and Cultural Consequences of 1492* (1972).

———. *Ecological Imperialism: The Biological Expansion of Europe, 900–1900* (1986).

DeJohn Anderson, Virginia. *Creatures of Empire: How Domestic Animals Transformed Early America* (2004).

Ewers, John C. *The Horse in Blackfoot Indian Culture: With Comparative Material from Other Western Tribes* (1955).

Flores, Dan. "Bison Ecology and Bison Diplomacy: The Southern Plains from 1800 to 1850." *Journal of American History* 78 (Sep. 1991): 464–485.

Gunlög, Fur. *A Nation of Women: Gender and Colonial Encounters among the Delaware Indians* (2009).

Gutiérrez, Ramón A. *When Jesus Came, the Corn Mothers Went Away: Marriage, Sexuality, and Power in New Mexico, 1500–1846* (1991).

Hackel, Steven W. *Children of Coyote, Missionaries of Saint Francis: Indian-Spanish Relations in Colonial California, 1769–1850* (2005).

Hämäläinen, Pekka. "The Rise and Fall of Plains Indian Horse Cultures." *Journal of American History* 90 (Dec. 2003): 833–862.

———. *The Comanche Empire* (2008).

Harrod, Howard L. *The Animals Came Dancing: Native American Sacred Ecology and Animal Kinship* (2000).

Hoxie, Frederick E. *Parading through History: The Making of the Crow Nation in America, 1805–1935* (1995).

Isenberg, Andrew C. *The Destruction of the Bison: An Environmental History, 1750–1920* (2000).

Jackson, John C. *Children of the Fur Trade: Forgotten Métis of the Pacific Northwest* (1995).

John, Elizabeth A. H. *Storms Brewed in Other Men's Worlds: The Confrontation of Indians, Spanish, and French in the Southwest, 1640–1795* (1975).

Kelton, Paul. *Epidemics and Enslavement: Biological Catastrophe in the Native Southwest, 1492–1715* (2007).

Krech, Shepard III. *The Ecological Indian: Myth and History* (1999).

Lansing, Michael J. "Plains Indian Women and Interracial Marriage in the Upper Missouri Trade, 1804–1868." *Western Historical Quarterly* 31 (Winter 2000): 413–433.

Mancall, Peter C. *Deadly Medicine: Indians and Alcohol in Early America* (1995).

Martin, Calvin. *Keepers of the Game: Indian-Animal Relationship and the Fur Trade* (1978).

Morgan, Jennifer L. *Laboring Women: Reproduction and Gender in New World Slavery* (2004).

Perdue, Theda. *Cherokee Women: Gender and Culture Change, 1700–1835* (1998).

Plane, Ann Marie. *Colonial Intimacies: Indian Marriage in Early New England* (2000).

Radding, Cynthia. *Wandering Peoples: Colonialism, Ethnic Spaces, and Ecological Frontiers in Northwestern Mexico, 1700–1850* (1997).

Ray, Arthur J. *Indians in the Fur Trade: Their Role as Trappers, Hunters, and Middlemen in the Lands Southwest of Hudson Bay, 1660–1870* (1974).

Seeman, Erik R. *Death in the New World: Cross-Cultural Encounters, 1492–1800* (2010).

Silver, Timothy. *A New Face on the Countryside: Indians, Colonists, and Slaves in the South Atlantic Forests, 1500–1800* (1900).

Sleeper-Smith, Susan. *Indian Women and French Men: Rethinking Cultural Encounter in the Western Great Lakes* (2004).

————. *Rethinking the Fur Trade: Cultures of Exchange in an Atlantic World* (2009).

Spear, Jennifer M. *Race, Sex, and Social Order in Early New Orleans* (2009).

Thorne, Tanis C. *The Many Hands of My Relations: French and Indians on the Lower Missouri* (1996).

Van Kirk, Sylvia. *Many Tender Ties: Women in Fur-Trade Society, 1670–1870* (1983).

Weisiger, Marsha. *Dreaming of Sheep in Navajo Country* (2009).

West, Elliott. *The Contested Plains: Indians, Goldseekers, and the Rush to Colorado* (1998).

White, Richard. *The Roots of Dependency: Subsistence, Environment, and Social Change among the Choctaws, Pawnees, and Navajos* (1983).

————. *The Middle Ground: Indians, Empires, and Republics in the Great Lakes Region, 1650–1815* (1991).

Wishart, David J. *The Fur Trade of the American West: A Geographical Synthesis* (1979).

CHAPTER 5

Borderlands in Change

The View from Above

*In 1763, the great powers of Europe assembled in Paris to end the protracted Seven Years'
War that had pitted Britain, Prussia, and Portugal against a coalition of France, Austria,
Russia, Spain, Sweden, and Saxony. The war had destabilized colonial arrangements in
three continents; now peace instated a new world order. France, subdued by crushing defeats
in Europe and North America, ceded all its American possessions except for outposts in
Newfoundland, the Caribbean, and Guyana. Spain, France's ally, lost the strategically
critical Florida to Britain, but it had received New Orleans and the Louisiana territory
from France in a secret treaty a year earlier. Britain was the great victor in Paris. Triumphant in war from Montreal to the Philippines, it won Grenada, Senegal, Canada, and
Florida, emerging as the world's dominant colonial empire.*

*The Treaty of Paris redrew the imperial map of North America. The complex collage
of colonial possessions and claims was replaced by a symmetrical division into British East
and Spanish West along the Mississippi Valley. But this was only one in a series of tre-
mors that rocked the North America of the late eighteenth century. In 1763, as the British
made a bid to turn their new paper claims into real control, several native nations launched
a virulent borderlands rebellion, Pontiac's War, that inflamed different parts of eastern
North America for three years. The consequences of Pontiac's War—increased tax burden
in British America, the 1763 Proclamation Line that excluded settlers from the trans–
Appalachian West—fueled resentment in the thirteen colonies and helped spawn an independent republic that quickly came to possess enough power to remold human relationships
on a continental scale. Meanwhile, in the lands west of the Mississippi Valley, more subtle
shifts animated the borderlands. Alarmed by Spain's waning global power and inspired by
the Enlightenment movement, the Bourbon monarchs implemented a series of reforms to
modernize New Spain's administrative and economic structures and pacify its extensive
frontiers. The Bourbon Reforms played a particularly strong role in places where the empire
was weakest and most vulnerable: the borderlands.*

*This and the next chapter take a broadly comparative look into these sweeping changes
by exploring how they altered the relationships among colonial empires and between*

Europeans and Indians across the hemisphere. What did the division of North America into British and Spanish spheres mean to the native societies that controlled the lands that had been reduced to diplomatic chips in European capitals? How did the rearrangement of colonial claims affect the autonomy and strategic options of Indian societies? How did the big geopolitical convulsions play out on the local level? Were borderlands peoples mere bystanders of the macroscale changes, or did they play an active role in shaping events and outcomes? Did some of them benefit from the changes?

〰 DOCUMENTS

The first two documents focus on Alta (Upper) California and Louisiana, which became part of the Spanish Empire in the late eighteenth century. In the first document, written in 1781, Theodore de Croix, the chief officer of New Spain's northern provinces, assesses the progress of Alta California's colonization until then and compares the new colony to the older colonies in Coahuila, Sonora, Texas, and New Mexico. The next document shifts the focus to Louisiana. France had ceded the colony in 1762, but Spain did not assume formal possession until 1769. In Document 2, Alexandro O'Reilly, the first Spanish governor to actually exercise power in Louisiana, assesses Louisiana's economic position in the Spanish Empire. Louisiana had been a financial drain for France, and O'Reilly proposes measures to reverse that situation under Spanish rule. But O'Reilly is also alarmed by the international, multiethnic character of New Orleans, which he portrays as a polyglot hub teeming with foreign merchants.

In 1776, the Spanish Crown created a new administrative unit, the Commandancy General of the Interior Provinces of the North, to increase the autonomy and effectiveness of the northern provinces of the Viceroyalty of New Spain. The new arrangement recognized New Mexico and Texas as vitally important buffer colonies for Mexico's silver mining districts and brought them unforeseen administrative attention. Document 3 is an excerpt from the 1786 *Instructions for Governing the Interior Provinces of New Spain*, in which Viceroy Bernardo de Gálvez provided practical guidelines for the administration of the northern provinces. The excerpt focuses on the subjugation of independent Indians through what Gálvez called "peace by deceit."

In the 1763 Treaty of Paris, France surrendered its remaining North American possessions (except in Newfoundland) to Great Britain, but the Indians who lived on the ceded lands fiercely resisted the transfer, insisting that the French had no right to give away territories controlled by native nations. Document 4 is an excerpt from a journal, probably kept by the French soldier Robert Navarre during Pontiac's War. The excerpt contains parts of speeches that the Ottawa leader Pontiac delivered to Ottawa, Potawatomi, and Huron Indian audiences in the spring of 1763. Pontiac evokes Indian grievances against the British—lack of respect, lack of gifts, restrictions on trade—and he spreads the message of Neolin (Wolf in the document), a Delaware prophet, who urged Indians to reassess their relationships with Europeans, reject the old practices of cross-cultural coexistence, and form a pan-Indian confederacy against the British. The excerpt contains many voices: that of Pontiac himself, as transcribed by Navarre; that of Neolin, as channeled by Pontiac; and that of Navarre, inserting his interpretations into the narrative.

One of the consequences of Pontiac's War was the formation of the Royal Proclamation Line, which established the Appalachian Mountains as a boundary between Indian lands and colonial settlements and thus recognized native rights to unceded lands in British North America. The Proclamation Line stemmed from royal officials' desire for regulated, clearly defined imperial frontiers, and it reflected their belief that segregation, not interaction, should define Indian-European relations in North America. The next two documents look at how elite British colonists viewed the Proclamation Line and the new order it heralded. Document 5 is a letter by William Tryon, the royal governor of North Carolina, describing the prospects for life in the North Carolina backcountry. The sixth document is a letter that George Washington, then a private citizen, sent to Captain William Crawford in 1767, concerning the prospect of enlarging his estate.

1. Theodore de Croix Compares California to Older Spanish Colonies, 1781

It appears to me, most excellent señor, that my measures with relation to California have been efficacious and diligent, and that from them ought to be expected the increase of its population, the security of its defenses, the union and free communication of the old possession and the new ones by the important establishment of the presidio of the Santa Bárbara Canal, its three inchoate missions, and pueblos of Guadalupe and Porciuncula. These successes have been achieved with a minimum of expense, and those promised by a regulation, made up of methodical points of easy and simple practice, will lessen some part of the expenditures of the annual allotments.

It is increasing the number of officers, troops, and settlers; sets up for them the observance of the particular good rules of government and discipline; assures the pure management of their interest; redeems the royal treasury in this region from bankruptcies, losses, damages, and waste; facilitates, though in small amount, the circulating of money; and creates the pleasing prospect of permanency and increase of the military and colonizing establishment. Finally, with the most minute points clarified, the door is opened wide to the erection of new missions for propagating the voice of the Gospel and reducing docilely the numerous small bands of barbarians that are vagrant in the territory and on the coasts of California as far as the boundaries of the province of Sonora and New Mexico.

Most excellent señor, may all the provinces have the happy aspect of that of the Californias! However, your Excellency already sees that Texas is surrounded by a numerous heathenism that it cannot resist without uniting its weak forces,

Alfred Barnaby Thomas, trans., *Teodoro de Croix and the Northern Frontier of New Spain, 1776–1783* (Norman: University of Oklahoma Press, 1941), 241–243. Reprinted by permission.

dispersed settlements, and few and dissident settlers; that Coahuila, experiencing the suffering of Texas, produces its own because of its friendship with the Lipan Apache whom it protects in its bosom without being able to protect itself from their devastation of a territory that would be opulent in agricultural resources, mineral riches, and advantageous sites for settlement. The well-known riches of New Vizcaya would be destroyed shortly by the incessant hostility of the Apache that it resists, were not the Apache forestalled by my efficient measures of covering the extensive frontiers of the province with the number of troops that I have at my orders, by increasing the provincials, and by operations which make possible its defense and conservation. New Mexico, because of its distance and because of the proximity of all the barbarous enemy nations, will always offer grave cares. The unfortunate province of Sonora, afflicted notably with the cruel plagues of war, pestilence, and hunger, is beginning to breathe in alleviation from its sorrows and in the hope of their remedy. I am devoting myself to all, aiding, succoring them as far as forces and resources reach, and maintaining vigilance by seeking all exact means for establishing the zeal that animates me in my profound loyalty to the king and my humble gratitude to your Excellency, who I beg may be pleased to place me at the royal feet of his Majesty.

2. Governor Alejandro O'Reilly Evaluates Louisiana's Position in Spain's Colonial Economy, 1769

My Very Dear Sir: Your Excellency is well aware that this province cannot live without commerce. It needs flour, wine, oil, tools, arms, munitions, and all kinds of cloth to make clothing, and can obtain them only by exporting its products.

These are wood, indigo, cotton, peltries, and a little corn and rice. There would be no outlet in Spain for the wood, which is one of the most important products for these people. Of our colonies, Havana is the only one where it would have a sale. I consider its importation there profitable for both the King and that island. It would be advantageous to the King because it would conserve, for the construction of his ships, the cedars now being used for sugar chests, and planks from here would cost His Majesty less for sheathing vessels and other works in which they could be employed.

This lumber would be profitable for that island, because it would make the sugar chests cheaper, as well as other works carried on by the people of Havana.

By permitting this province to engage in the free commerce with Spain and to carry it on with Havana, as Florida formerly did, these inhabitants would find in Havana itself an outlet for all their products, and obtain there most of the things they need. Thereby the King would obtain the duties which those goods pay in Spain, and the excise which they pay on being landed in the island of Cuba. The sugar mills would develop greatly with an outlet for the rum which is now useless and lost. Its consumption here would be very considerable, and

Lawrence Kinnaird, ed., *Spain in the Mississippi Valley, 1765–94: Translations of Materials from the Spanish Archives in the Bancroft Library* (Washington, D.C.: Government Printing Office, 1946), 1: 103–105.

each barrel would pay the two pesos duty which is placed on it in Havana. But in order for this commerce to develop and be mutually useful, it seems to me advisable and necessary that the wood, peltries, indigo, cotton, corn, and rice of this province should not pay import duties at Havana and that, on goods from there shipped to this province, no new excise or export duty be demanded.

From Catalonia vessels would come with red wine. They would load wood and other things here for Havana, and get sugar there. I think that this arrangement would assure an outlet for the products of this colony and a supply of what it needs, and I do not think it possible to establish it more securely or more advantageously to the interests of our commerce.

I found the English entirely in possession of the commerce of this colony. They had merchants among the Germans and stores in this city, and I can assure you that they got nine-tenths of all the ready money spent here. The commerce of France accepted the products of the colony in payment for goods, but the English, selling more cheaply, got all the silver. I made the English merchants and other citizens of that nation whom I found in this city depart, and I shall henceforth admit none of their vessels into this port.

May Our Lord guard and bless Your Excellency's life many years.

3. Bernardo de Gálvez Outlines How to Achieve "Peace by Deceit," 1786

I am certain that the vanquishment of the heathen consists in obliging them to destroy one another. They are not capable under their present system of being reduced to the true religion or to vassalage, without a miracle of the Almighty, or of preserving constant faith in their armistices; but I also understand that in the state in which they keep our provinces a bad peace with all the tribes which ask for it would be more fruitful than the gains of a successful war.

The enemy Indians upon our frontiers well know how to surprise and destroy our troops in the mountains and on the plains. They are not ignorant of the use and power of our arms; they manage their own with dexterity; and they are as good or better horsemen than the Spaniards. And having no towns, castles, or temples to defend, they may be attacked only in their dispersed and movable rancherías.

In this region the methods of the conquerors of Mexico are not applicable, excepting that of granting peace to the Indians and using them in their mutual destruction. For this purpose, the king's alien colonies could still be used to prevent hostilities. And it is the only method for subduing those who devastate these provinces.

Peace is founded, as everything else, on private interests, and the Indians, in general, have not been able to have advantages in peace treaties which they have enjoyed up to now. They live by hunting and warfare. These are not enough to

---

Bernardo de Gálvez, *Instructions Governing the Interior Provinces of New Spain 1786*, ed. and trans., Donald E. Worcester (Berkeley: Quivira Society, 1951), 37–42, 47–49.

supply the prime necessities of existence. And so, if they do not rob, they perish of hunger and misery.

This is the motivating cause by which we might have peace by deceit, and it actually comes to this. For our grants are not sufficient to maintain them, nor can other assistance, which is absolutely necessary for their existence, be lent.

We shall benefit by satisfying their desires. It will cost the king less than what is now spent in considerable and useless reinforcements of troops. The Indians cannot live without our aid. They will go to war against one another in our behalf and from their own warlike inclinations, or they may possibly improve their customs by following our good example, voluntarily embracing our religion and vassalage. And by these means they will keep faith in their truces.

The interest in commerce binds and narrows the desires of man; and it is my wish to establish trade with the Indians in these provinces, admitting them to peace wherever they ask for it.

One should also foment skillfully the discord and hostility between the factions of the same tribe and the irreconcilable hatred of the Nations of the North for the Apaches.

In the voluntary or forced submission of the Apaches, or in their total extermination, lies the happiness of the Provincias Internas; because they are the ones who have destroyed these provinces, live on their frontiers, and cause the apostatism and unrest of the reduced Indians.

I do not believe that the Apaches will submit voluntarily (God alone could work this miracle), but we may contribute to the means of attracting the different factions of this tribe, making them realize the advantages of rational life, which should please them. They should be made accustomed to the use of our foods, drinks, arms, and clothing, and they should become greedy for the possession of land.

After all, the supplying of drink to the Indians will be a means of gaining their goodwill, discovering their secrets, calming them so that they will think less often of conceiving and executing their hostilities, and creating for them a new necessity which will oblige them to recognize their dependence upon us more directly.

Firearms will be advantageous to them in their hunting, as I have already said, and in the warfare of the heathen tribes with one another, but not in their hostility to us; for if the Indians should abandon the arrow for the firearm, they would give us all the advantages.

Guns for trade should be long, because these the Indians appreciate, and thus they would sell, with barrels, stocks, and weak bolts without the best temper, and with superficial adornments which delight the sight of ignorant persons.

Their size will make them awkward for long rides on horseback, resulting in continual damages and repeated need for mending or replacement. The use of the guns and the maladjustment of the bolts produce the same effect.

Powder should be supplied with regular abundance, in order that the Indians put the use of the firearm before that of the arrow and begin to lose their skill in handling the bow; for in this case we will have the certain advantage (assuming that they make war on us) of their lack of ammunition. Consequently, they would be forced to seek our friendship and aid.

4. Pontiac Urges Ottawas, Potawatomis, and Hurons to Rise Up Against the British, 1763

After the Indian [Neolin] was seated the Lord said to him: "I am the Master of Life, and since I know what thou desirest to know, and to whom thou wishest to speak, listen well to what I am going to say to thee and to all the Indians:

"I am He who hath created the heavens and the earth, the trees, lakes, rivers, all men, and all that thou seest and hast seen upon the earth. Because I love you, ye must do what I say and love, and not do what I hate. I do not love that ye should drink to the point of madness, as ye do; and I do not like that ye should fight one another. Ye take two wives, or run after the wives of others; ye do not well, and I hate that. Ye ought to have but one wife, and keep her till death. When ye wish to go to war, ye conjure and resort to the medicine dance, believing that ye speak to me; ye are mistaken,—it is to Manitou that ye speak, an evil spirit who prompts you to nothing but wrong, and who listens to you out of ignorance of me.

"This land where ye dwell I have made for you and not for others. Whence comes it that ye permit the Whites upon your lands? Can ye not live without them? I know that those whom ye call the children of your Great Father supply your needs, but if ye were not evil, as ye are, ye could surely do without them. Ye could live as ye did live before knowing them,—before those whom ye call your brothers had come upon your lands. Did ye not live by the bow and arrow? Ye had no need of gun or powder, or anything else, and nevertheless ye caught animals to live upon and to dress yourselves with their skins. But when I saw that ye were given up to evil, I led the wild animals to the depths of the forests so that ye had to depend upon your brothers to feed and shelter you. Ye have only to become good again and do what I wish, and I will send back the animals for your food. I do not forbid you to permit among you the children of your Father; I love them. They know me and pray to me, and I supply their wants and all they give you. But as to those who come to trouble your lands,—drive them out, make war upon them. I do not love them at all; they know me not, and are my enemies, and the enemies of your brothers. Send them back to the lands which I have created for them and let them stay there. Here is a prayer which I give thee in writing to learn by heart and to teach to the Indians and their children."

The Wolf replied that he did not know how to read. He was told that when he should have returned to earth he would have only to give the prayer to the chief of his village who would read it and teach him and all the Indians to know it by heart; and he must say it night and morning without fail, and do what he has just been told to do; and he was to tell all the Indians for and in the name of the Master of Life:

M. Agnes Burton, ed., *Journal of Pontiac's Conspiracy, 1763* (Detroit: Published by Clarence Monroe Burton under the auspices of the Michigan Society of the Colonial Wars, 1912), 28, 30, 32, 36, 40.

"Do not drink more than once, or at most twice in a day; have only one wife and do not run after the wives of others nor after the girls; do not fight among yourselves; do not 'make medicine,' but pray, because in 'making medicine' one talks with the evil spirit; drive off your lands those dogs clothed in red who will do you nothing but harm. And when ye shall have need of anything address yourselves to me; and as to your brothers, I shall give to you as to them; do not sell to your brothers what I have put on earth for food. In short, become good and ye shall receive your needs. When ye meet one another exchange greeting and proffer the left hand which is nearest the heart.

"In all things I command thee to repeat every morning and night the prayer which I have given thee."

The Wolf promised to do faithfully what the Master of Life told him, and that he would recommend it well to the Indians, and that the Master of Life would be pleased with them. Then the same man who had led him by the hand came to get him and conducted him to the foot of the mountain where he told him to take his outfit again and return to his village. The Wolf did this, and upon his arrival the members of his tribe and village were greatly surprised, for they did not know what had become of him, and they asked where he had been. As he was enjoined not to speak to anybody before he had talked with the chief of his village, he made a sign with his hand that he had come from on high. Upon entering the village he went straight to the cabin of the chief to whom he gave what had been given to him,—namely, the prayer and the law which the Master of Life had given him.

This adventure was soon noised about among the people of the whole village who came to hear the message of the Master of Life, and then went to carry it to the neighboring villages. The members of these villages came to see the pretended traveler, and the news was spread from village to village and finally reached Pontiac. He believed all this, as we believe an article of faith, and instilled it into the minds of all those in his council. They listened to him as to an oracle, and told him that he had only to speak and they were all ready to do what he demanded of them.

Pontiac ... sent runners the following day, Monday, the 2nd of May, to each of the Huron and Pottawattamy villages to discover the real feeling of each of these two nations, for he feared to be crossed in his plans. These emissaries had orders to notify these nations for him that Thursday, the 5th of May, at mid-day, a grand council would be held in the Pottawattamy village which was situated between two and three miles below the Fort toward the southwest, and that the three nations should meet there and that no woman should be allowed to attend for fear of betraying their plans.

Pontiac ordered sentinels to be placed around the village in order not to be disturbed in their council. When all these precautions had been taken each Indian seated himself in the circle according to rank, and Pontiac at the head, as great chief of all, began to speak. He said:

"It is important for us, my brothers, that we exterminate from our lands this nation which seeks only to destroy us. You see as well as I that we can no longer supply our needs, as we have done, from our brothers, the French.

The English sell us goods twice as dear as the French do, and their goods do not last. Scarcely have we bought a blanket or something else to cover ourselves with before we must think of getting another; and when we wish to set out for our winter camps they do not want to give us any credit as our brothers, the French, do.

"When I go to see the English commander and say to him that some of our comrades are dead, instead of bewailing their death, as our French brothers do, he laughs at me and at you. If I ask anything for our sick, he refuses with the reply that he has no use for us. From all this you can well see that they are seeking our ruin. Therefore, my brothers, we must all swear their destruction and wait no longer. Nothing prevents us; they are few in numbers, and we can accomplish it. All the nations who are our brothers attack them,—why should we not attack? Are we not men like them? Have I not shown you the wampum belts which I received from our Great Father, the Frenchman? He tells us to strike them,—why do we not listen to his words? What do we fear? It is time. Do we fear that our brothers, the French, who are here among us will prevent us? They do not know our plans, and they could not hinder anyway, if they would. You all know as well as I that when the English came upon our lands to drive out our Father, [François Marie Picotè de] Belestre [the last French commander at Detroit], they took away all the Frenchmen's guns and that they now have no arms to protect themselves with. Therefore, it is time for us to strike. If there are any French who side with them, let us strike them as well as the English. Remember what the Master of Life told our brother, the Wolf, to do. That concerns us all as well as others. I have sent wampum belts and messengers to our brothers, the Chippewas of Saginaw, and to our brothers, the Ottawas of Michillimackinac, and to those of the Thames River to join us. They will not be slow in coming, but while we wait let us strike anyway. There is no more time to lose. When the English are defeated we shall then see what there is left to do, and we shall stop up the ways hither so that they may never come again upon our lands."

5. Governor William Tryon Assesses the Potential of North Carolina Backcountry, 1765

We are in want of nothing but Industry & skill, to bring every Vegetable to a greater perfection in this Province. Indian Corn, Rice, and American Beans (Species of the Kidney Bean) are the grain that is Cultivated within a hundred and fifty Miles of the Sea Board at which distance to the Westward you begin to perceive you are approaching high ground, and fifty Miles farther you may get on tolerable high Hills. The Blue Mountains that Cross our Province I imagine lay three Hundred Miles from the Sea. Our Settlements are carried within one Hundred Miles of them. In less than twenty years or perhaps in half the time inhabitants may Settle at the foot of these Mountains. In the Back or

This document is available in Karen Ordahl Kupperman, *Major Problems in American Colonial History: Documents and Essays*, 2nd Edition.

Western Counties, more industry is observed than to the Eastward, the White People there to, are more numerous than the Negroes. The Calculation of the Inhabitants in this Province is one hundred and twenty Thousand White & Black, of which there is a great Majority of White People. The Negroes are very numerous I suppose five to one White Person in the Maritime Counties, but as you penetrate into the Country few Blacks are employed, merely for this Simple reason, that the poorer Settlers coming from the Northward Colonies sat themselves down in the back Counties where the land is the best but who have not more than a sufficiency to erect a Log House for their families and procure a few Tools to get a little Corn into the ground. This Poverty prevents their purchasing of Slaves, and before they can get into Sufficient affluence to buy Negroes their own Children are often grown to an age to work in the Field. Not but numbers of families in the back Counties have Slaves some from three to ten, Whereas in the Counties on the Sea Coast Planters have from fifty to 250 Slaves. A Plantation with Seventy Slaves on it, is esteemed a good property. When a man marries his Daughters he never talks of the fortune in Money but 20 30 or 40 Slaves is her Portion and possibly and agreement to deliver at stated Periods, a Certain Number of Tarr or Turpentine Barrels, which serves towards exonerating the charges of the Wedding which are not grievous here.

6. George Washington Denounces the Royal Proclamation Line, 1767

GEORGE WASHINGTON TO WILLIAM CRAWFORD

Mount Vernon, *September* 21, 1767

I then desired the favor of you (as I understood rights might now be had for the lands which have fallen within the Pennsylvania line,) to look me out a tract of about fifteen hundred, two thousand, or more acres somewhere in your neighborhood, meaning only by this, that it may be as contiguous to your own settlement as such a body of good land can be found. It will be easy for you to conceive that ordinary or even middling lands would never answer my purpose or expectation, so far from navigation, and under such a load of expenses as these lands are incumbered with. No; a tract to please me must be rich (of which no person can be a better judge than yourself), and, if possible, level. Could such a piece of land be found, you would do me a singular favor in falling upon some method of securing it immediately from the attempts of others, as nothing is more certain than that the lands can not remain long ungranted, when once it is known that rights are to be had.

C. W. Butterfield, ed., *The Washington-Crawford Letters: Being the Correspondence between George Washington and William Crawford, from 1767 to 1781, Concerning the Western Lands* (Cincinnati: Robert Clarke & Co. 1877), 1–4.

The mode of proceeding I am at a loss to point out to you; but, as your own lands are under the same circumstances, self-interest will naturally lead you to an inquiry.

I offered in my last to join you in attempting to secure some of the most valuable lands in the King's part, which I think may be accomplished after awhile, notwithstanding the proclamation that restrains it at present, and prohibits the settling of them at all; for I can never look upon that proclamation in any other light (but this I say between ourselves) than as a temporary expedient to quiet the minds of the Indians. It must fall, of course, in a few years, especially when those Indians consent to our occupying the lands. Any person, therefore, who neglects the present opportunity of hunting out good lands, and in some measure marking and distinguishing them for his own, in order to keep others from settling them, will never regain it. If you will be at the trouble of seeking out the lands, I will take upon me the part of securing them, as soon as there is a possibility of doing it, and will, moreover, be at all the cost and charges of surveying and patenting the same. You shall then have such a reasonable proportion of the whole as we may fix upon at our first meeting; as I shall find it necessary, for the better furthering of the design, to let some of my friends be concerned in the scheme, who must also partake of the advantages.

By this time it may be easy for you to discover that my plan is to secure a good deal of land.

I recommend, that you keep this whole matter a secret, or trust it only to those in whom you can confide; and who can assist you in bringing it to bear by their discoveries of land. This advice proceeds from several very good reasons, and, in the first place, because I might be censured for the opinion I have given in respect to the King's proclamation, and then, if the scheme I am now proposing to you were known, it might give the alarm to others, and, by putting them upon a plan of the same nature, before we could lay, a proper foundation for success ourselves, set the different interests clashing, and, probably, in the end, overturn the whole.

~ ESSAYS

The essay by late David J. Weber, professor of history at Southern Methodist University, is framed with a startling fact: In the late eighteenth century one half of the Western Hemisphere was still under the control of independent Indians. This posed a particularly serious challenge to the Spanish Empire, whose boundaries were contested by numerous autonomous native groups and, after 1783 along the Mississippi River, the United States. The essay explores how the Spanish Empire responded to these external threats by modernizing its borderlands and implementing a new Indian policy. Lacking the numbers and military force to seal off the empire's ragged edges, Spanish administrators set out to protect them through alliances with independent Indians who, they hoped, would help keep rival empires at bay. Influenced by Enlightenment-era ideas of rationality and tolerance, they tried to achieve this not by force but by persuasion: Gifts, trade, and treaties, not coercion would have to bring "wild Indians" into the Spanish fold. At the heart of Weber's essay is a gap between ideals and practice, between metropolitan dreams and borderlands reality. To what extend was Spain's new Indian policy successful? What were its achievements, failures, and contradictions? Weber's panoramic essay invites comparison with the findings of the more geographically focused essays. For example, what does Hämäläinen's argument of expanding Comanche power in the Southwest borderlands in Chapter 3 suggest about the goals and rationale of Spain's new Indian policy?

In the second essay, historian François Furstenberg of the University of Montreal examines the struggles for power and territory in the trans-Appalachian West, the region between the Appalachian Mountains and the Mississippi River. Furstenberg focuses on the period between 1754 and 1815, picking up the story where James Merrell's essay left it in Chapter 3. But where Merrell concentrated on Indian-English relationships, Furstenberg looks at the larger geopolitical rivalries that shook and shaped the region. He provides a wide-angle view of the turbulent era, showing how several Native American powers and four imperial players—Britain, France, Spain, and the United States—fought over the control of the region in what he calls a "Long War for the West." Furstenberg's essay is not traditional diplomatic history, in which native peoples are reduced to bit players in a European-driven drama. Furstenberg sees imperial centers as powerful historical agents, but he also emphasizes the importance of local actors and borderland spaces in the shifting, multistage geopolitical rivalry that eventually delivered the trans-Appalachian West to the United States. Furstenberg highlights the contingency of historical change and rejects the teleological view that the Anglo-American takeover of the trans-Appalachian West was inevitable. But why was the United States ultimately triumphant? Furstenberg provides a nuanced, open-ended explanation in which mountain ranges, wind currents, colonial officials, borderland inhabitants, and Napoleon all play a part.

New Spain and Its Borderlands

DAVID J. WEBER

In the mid-eighteenth century, two centuries after the Spanish conquest of Mexico and Peru, independent Indians controlled over *half* of the land mass that we think of today as Spanish America. Clearly, Spain had not completed the conquest of America in the Age of Conquest. Independent Indians still held much of the tropical forests and drylands—northern Mexico, the Central-American lowlands and the Gulf of Darién, the Amazon and Orinoco basins, the Gran Chaco, the pampas, Patagonia, and Tierra del Fuego. From Hispanic perspectives, independent Indians occupied the frontiers of Spain's New World

David J. Weber, "Bourbons and Bárbaros: Center and Periphery in the Reshaping of Spanish Indian Policy," in *Negotiated Empires: Centers and Peripheries in the New World, 1500–1800*, ed. Christine Daniels and Michael V. Kennedy, pp. 79–103 (New York: Routledge, 2002).

empire and the lands beyond; from the perspectives of independent Indians, Hispanics occupied the frontiers of Indian-controlled lands, and the territory beyond.

In the last half of the eighteenth century, Bourbon officials moved with renewed vigor to win the allegiance of the independent Indians who lived along and beyond the peripheries of the empire. Those officials, products of the Age of Enlightenment, brought new values and sensibilities to the task of controlling "savages," who themselves had acquired new values, skills, and technologies for coping with Spaniards. Out of the dialectic between the program that emanated from the Bourbon centers and the strategies of peoples who lived on Spain's American peripheries, came new ways for Spaniards and "savages" to relate to one another.

For the Habsburgs who ruled Spain until 1700, the benefits of extending the conquest of the mainland beyond the highlands of Mexico, Central America, and South America had not, in the main, seemed worth the cost. With notable exceptions (such as the cacao-producing area of Venezuela, the Cauca and Magdalena River Valleys in present Colombia, parts of Paraguay, and central Chile south to the Biobío River), the climate, accessibility, and an apparent lack of valuable resources in the lowlands had discouraged Spaniards from making them their own. These impediments continued to discourage Bourbon administrators, who replaced the Habsburgs in the eighteenth century. As a viceroy of Peru explained in the mid-1700s, "The unconquered country is jungle and mountains, difficult to traverse, and plains that are humid, swampy, and hot, and so cannot support Spaniards." Native opposition in these regions also deterred Spaniards from permanently occupying them. In general, Spaniards chose to conquer highland farming peoples whose labor they could exploit and whose hierarchical governments they could control rather than waging prolonged wars against nomads or seminomads who tended to live in the lowlands.

By the mid-eighteenth century, it became more difficult for Bourbon officials to ignore the Indian country that bordered the empire. Out of those lands came Indians who, more boldly and adeptly than ever before, raided Spanish farms and ranches, destroyed Spanish property, took Spanish lives, and blocked the arteries of commerce that kept empire alive. Spaniards knew these independent Indians by their local names, but referred to them generically as "savages" (*indios bárbaros* or *salvajes*), as "wild Indians" (*indios bravos*), as heathens (*gentiles*), or as "Indians who had not submitted" (*indios no sometidos*), and so distinguished them from Christian Indians, or Indians who recognized Spanish authority—*indios sometidos, reducidos, domésticos, or tributarios.*

Throughout the world in the modern era, state societies in general have found it difficult to control tribal societies, especially nomadic and seminomadic peoples. For Spaniards in America, the difficulty seemed to increase as "savages" made themselves more effective adversaries.

Throughout the hemisphere, indios bárbaros had studied the fighting techniques of Spaniards, learned to defend themselves against them, adopted Spanish horses and weapons, and reorganized themselves into new polities or societies.

Spaniards had begun to feel the effects of those transformations in the sixteenth century, most famously in the effective resistance of Araucanians in southern Chile, Chichimecas in northern New Spain, and Chiriguanos in southern Peru. Those borderlands where Spaniards encountered "indomitable" Indians had grown more extensive as Spaniards and Indians alike moved onto new frontiers, and as Indians obtained ammunition and firearms from Spain's European rivals.

By the mid-eighteenth century, Spanish policymakers also had to worry that indios bárbaros might ally themselves with Spain's chief European rival, England, and facilitate English expansion into lands long claimed but never occupied by Spain.

Along the margins of the empire, independent Indians also threatened the commercial viability of Spain's colonies. Allied with Englishmen or other foreigners, independent Indians could facilitate the introduction of contraband and retard the growth of Spanish trade. Conversely, independent Indians could trade stolen Spanish property to English merchants in exchange for guns and ammunition, then use their greater firepower to steal still more goods from their Spanish neighbors.

Independent Indians seemed poised to weaken the margins of the empire at the same time that Bourbon reformers hoped to strengthen them. Eager to draw more revenue from America in order to reverse what they saw as Spain's economic decline, the Bourbons sought to streamline public administration, raise productivity and trade, and increase security in America. That project, begun early in the century, reached fruition in the reign of Carlos III (1759-88), the most dynamic, innovative, and America-oriented of Spain's eighteenth-century monarchs. As he and his enlightened advisors, such as [Pedro Rodríguez de] Campomanes, looked beyond the empire's profitable cores to the development of its vulnerable but potentially profitable peripheries, it became apparent that they had to bring the "savages," who occupied those peripheries, under control.

The ways that Bourbon administrators sought to achieve that control tell us much about the formulation of policy by the absolutist Bourbon regime, which has seemed to some historians to part from the Habsburg tradition of compromise and to govern instead through "non-negotiable demands" or a "hard line." If Bourbon policies toward indios bárbaros can be taken as exemplary, Bourbon officials compromised as readily as had their Habsburg predecessors.

For Bourbon administrators in search of ways to control indios bravos along the empire's peripheries, Spanish tradition offered two obvious solutions: send fighting men to conquer recalcitrant natives by force or missionaries to conquer them through persuasion. But armed Indians on horseback did not succumb readily to the blandishments of missionaries, whose successes seemed to diminish in the eighteenth century. Similarly, private armies led by *encomenderos* or would-be encomenderos, upon whom Spain had previously relied to advance its frontiers, no longer filled the bill against increasingly mobile bands of Indian raiders.

Enlightened thought and British and French examples, however, offered the Bourbons another strategy: control Indians through commerce rather than by physical or spiritual conquest. Nowhere in Spanish thought was this idea articulated more clearly than in the well-known *Nuevo sistema de gobierno econó-mico para la América*, a master plan for the economic development of Spain's colonies.

The author of the *Nuevo sistema* lamented that Spain had wasted millions of pesos in making war against Indians who, "if treated with tact and friendship, would be of infinite use to us." In the early sixteenth century, he reasoned, Spaniards in America had no alternative to military force "for there were few Spaniards in America and millions of Indians to subject." But Spain made the mistake of "preserving the spirit of conquest beyond its time, and preferring do-minion over the advantages and utility of commerce and friendly trade with the savage nations."

Even as the wildest beast can be tamed by kind treatment, the *Nuevo sistema* analogized, "there is no savage who cannot be dominated by industry and made sociable by a ready supply of all the things he likes." Establishing trade with "wild Indians" would take "time, skill, and patience, but it is not impossible." Other nations had already done so.

Spaniards, however, had a handicap: They had earned "the hatred of neigh-boring Indian nations." But if Spain's missionaries could enter the lands of those Indians by treating them with kindness, he argued, so could Spain's merchants. Indeed, the *Nuevo sistema* suggested that merchants would have an easier time of it. Unlike missionaries who "threaten [Indians] with hell if they become drunk or take more than one woman, harshly condemning all of the vices to which they are naturally very inclined," he said, merchants treat Indians kindly, give them goods that they need and alcohol (*aguardiente*) "that they so esteem" while making no demands on them.

In this enlightened formulation, Indians would become the foundation of Spain's commercial and economic revival in America rather than enemies, and they would play their role in a new way. Where Spaniards of the Renaissance had expected Indians to adopt the Christian faith when missionaries revealed it to them, the *Nuevo sistema* expected Indians to behave like rational European consumers when merchants displayed their wares. Where Spaniards traditionally viewed Indians as vicious or lazy by nature, needing to be forced to work for their own good, the *Nuevo sistema* argued that Indians would respond to profits and self-interest and voluntarily become producers and consumers.

José de Gálvez, the powerful and dynamic minister of the Indies from 1776 to 1787 ... had his own sources of intelligence, including a nephew and protégé whom he had appointed acting governor of Louisiana in 1776. Drawing from his observations in Louisiana, as well as previous experience fighting Apaches, Bernardo de Gálvez had urged his uncle to rely on trade to control Indians rather than fight costly and ineffective wars. Through trade, he argued, "the King would keep [Indians] very contented for ten years with what he now spends in one year in making war upon them."

Apparently persuaded by this argument, and strapped for resources as he prepared for war with Great Britain, José de Gálvez ordered a policy of "kind-ness, good treatment, and benevolence" toward Indians in Provincias Internas of New Spain in 1779. He instructed his officers to take defensive action only, to avoid bloodshed, and to make Indians dependent on Spaniards for merchandise, including luxury goods and guns, so that "they will not be able to live without our help." The king, he said, preferred a slow and peaceful conquest. Three years later, however, Gálvez ordered a return to offensive warfare when Apaches refused to substitute trading for raiding, and when powerful oligarchs angrily demanded a more aggressive military policy that would protect their dwindling herds from Indian predators.

In 1786, when Bernardo de Gálvez benefited from his uncle's penchant for nepotism to become viceroy of New Spain, he ordered officials in the Provincias Internas to return to the kind of policy that his uncle had enunciated in 1779. Although he placed greater emphasis on offensive action against Apaches than his uncle had, Bernardo de Gálvez still hoped for the same result: to force Apaches to appeal for peace and to enter into trade with Spaniards. "With time," he suggested in his well-known *Instrucción* of 1786, "trade may make them dependent on us."

With various modifications and embellishments, Gálvez's policy, as articulated in his *Instrucción* of 1786, prevailed in the Provincias Internas of New Spain. Spain's ablest officers followed his dictum and offered independent Indians access to trade fairs, gifts, cooperation against mutual enemies, and more equitable and consistent treatment than they had in the past. Conciliation and negotiation, previously subordinate to force, became the hallmark of Bourbon Indian policy in northern New Spain in the late 1780s.

This conciliatory Indian policy included reservations for Apaches who appealed for peace. On these reservations, some Spanish policymakers hoped to turn Apaches into town-dwelling Spanish Catholics who farmed, ranched, and practiced familiar trades. Since the Bourbons needed to populate the empire's vulnerable frontiers with loyal subjects but lacked sufficient colonists to achieve that goal, it made sense to try to turn Apaches into Spaniards. Spain had relied heavily on missionaries to achieve this kind of transformation on earlier frontiers and, despite withering criticism by some enlightened Bourbon administrators, they would continue to do so in places where Indians seemed "docile," as in Alta California. But among peoples whom missionaries had failed to convert, soldiers became the preferred agents of paternalistic cultural change on the late-eighteenth-century reservations in northern New Spain. Bernardo de Gálvez's plan ignored missionaries, whose political and economic power had diminished in northern New Spain during the reign of Carlos III.

For Spain, a conciliatory Indian policy promised more than economic and strategic advantages. It also offered a soothing balm for enlightened Spaniards stung by their forebears' reputation for cruel oppression of Indians during and after the conquest of America. "Humanity is the greatest characteristic of civilization. All the sciences and arts have no value if they serve only to make us cruel and haughty," wrote one Spanish botanist in America, José Mariano Moziño, as he lamented the brutal way that some of his less enlightened countrymen treated independent Indians. Indeed, some Spanish army officers close to the scene also extolled the new Indian policies as humane as well as effective. Writing at El Paso in 1796, for example, Lt. Col. Antonio Cordero y Bustamante, a veteran frontier soldier, noted that the "wise measures" of the Spanish government were bringing the war to a close. Spain did "not aspire to the destruction or slavery of these savages," he noted with pride. Rather, Spain sought "their happiness ... leaving them in peaceful possession of their homes," while at the same time getting them to recognize "our justice and our power to sustain it" so they would cease raiding Spanish settlements.

The more humane policy that Cordero applauded could not work, however, if Apaches were demonized. Frontier officers like Cordero, Bernardo de Gálvez, and José Cortés needed a new discourse if they were to redeem Apaches—and they found one. These enlightened officers depicted Apaches as fierce, courageous, and skilled warriors, but not as innately indolent, untrustworthy, and thieving, as the previous generation of officers, intent on exterminating Apaches, tended to do. Enlightened officers sought to explain Apaches' behavior as responses to external forces, rather than as innate characteristics. If Apaches possessed "extraordinary robustness" it was because they lived outdoors and ate basic foods; if they moved with a great agility, speed, and endurance it was because of daily exercise and the conditioning of a nomadic life. If Apaches waged "cruel and bloody war" against Spaniards, the cause could be found in the Spaniards' own "trespasses, excesses and avarice," as Cordero put it. If Apaches treated Spaniards cruelly, it was, Gálvez observed, "because he owes us no kindness, and that if he avenges himself it is for just satisfaction of his grievances." "The truth is," Gálvez wrote, "that they are as much grateful as vengeful, and that this latter [quality of vengeance] we ought to forgive in a nation that has not learned philosophy with which to master a natural feeling...."

These were ideas whose time had come, defended on pragmatic grounds and shared by enlightened officials who faced "savages" throughout the frontiers of the hemisphere. In Chile, for example, Ambrosio Higgins, an Irish-born Spanish officer, argued that Spain could not defend its vast Pacific coast from foreigners without the goodwill of Indians. Indians would not support Spaniards, he said, "while we are at every opportunity irritating and beating Indians along the frontiers, making them internal enemies." Alienated from Spain, they would ally themselves with Spain's opportunistic European rivals.

Frontier imperatives, then, forced the Bourbon state to find peaceful ways to win the allegiance of independent Indians and, in the words of one historian, turn them into "frontier soldiers of the Crown." That policy was consistent with Bourbon efforts to draw other native-born Americans, criollos and mestizos, into its defensive system after the loss of Havana in the Seven Years' War revealed how badly Spain could be outmanned in one of its own colonies.

During the Bourbon era officials came increasingly to see the practical benefits of recognizing that some Indians had the right to live autonomously beyond the bounds of the empire—a recognition that occurred, ironically, at the same time that the Bourbons extended the effective boundaries of the empire. In the 1700s, Spain's recognition of Indians' rights to autonomy increasingly took the form of written treaties that rose out of formal discussions. In North America, for example, Spanish officers entered into a series of treaties with independent Indians, following Spain's acquisition of Louisiana from France in 1762. In

1784 alone, officials in Mobile signed written agreements with representatives of Alabamas, Chickasaws, and Choctaws, and officials in Pensacola signed an agreement with Creeks. In 1785 and 1786, respectively, the Spanish governors of Texas and New Mexico signed treaties of alliance with Comanches; in 1786, the New Mexico governor also signed a treaty of alliance with Navajos. In 1793, Spanish officials in Louisiana signed a treaty of mutual assistance with Alabamas, Cherokees, Chickasaws, Choctaws, and Creeks, all of whom, on paper if not in fact, had formed a confederation.

In these agreements, Spaniards referred to Indian peoples as "nations" and recognized Indian polities as distinct from their own. Both parties agreed to peace, to make war against common enemies, and to establish commerce. In signing these treaties, Indians usually accepted the "protection" of the Crown, as did Ecueracapa, the leader of the western Comanches in 1786, and the tribes bordering on Louisiana and Florida in 1793. These natives did not, however, become "vassals or subjects" of the Crown, surrender autonomy, or accept missionaries. Nor did Spanish leaders ask these things of them. Rather than attempt to tax these Indians, Spanish officials regularly presented gifts to their leaders, as the French and English had done before. By 1794, gifts to Indians amounted to 10 percent of Spain's cost of supporting Louisiana and west Florida suggesting that, where Spaniards failed to tax Indians, Indians had succeeded in taxing Spaniards.

In the Southeast, Spaniards came to recognize a native "nation" as more than a people of common origin (an ordinary usage of *nation* in that era), but as a sovereign nation–state—inferior, to be sure, but a nation–state nonetheless. Manuel Gayoso de Lemos, governor of Spanish Louisiana's Natchez district, offered that view explicitly in regard to Creeks, Chickasaws, and Choctaws, when he wrote in 1792 that those Indians "are free and independent nations; although they are under His Majesty's protection, we cannot forcibly prevent them from signing a treaty with the United States." United States Secretary of War Henry Knox had argued similarly in 1789 that "the independent nations and tribes of Indians ought to be considered as foreign nations, not as the subjects of any particular State." The idea that Indians could maintain their sovereignty while under Spanish protection conformed to the usage of the day. "Mere alliances of protection, tribute or vassalage, which a state may contract with another, do not hinder it from continuing perfectly sovereign," one jurist noted in 1788.

By the late eighteenth century, Spanish Indian policy in the Southeast had come to resemble French and British policy, as the *Nuevo sistema* had urged. Traders or interpreters on the Spanish payroll, many of them mestizos who understood Indian languages and customs, with names like Brashears and Thompson, lived among the Indian nations to maintain their friendship and trade, as provided for in the treaties with southeastern tribes (as had a 1786 treaty with Navajos in the Southwest). In this way, Spain tried to control Indians indirectly through trade without exercising dominion.

Circumstances in southeastern North America in particular gave Spain no other practical alternative. As Campomanes warned in 1792, if Spain tried to assert direct control over the "savage Indians" along the Gulf of Mexico or build settlements among them, the Indians would "lose confidence [in us] and ... call the Americans to their defense." Even as the benevolently despotic Bourbon monarchy reduced the power of its own subjects—Spanish aristocrats, American criollos, and indios domésticos—it paradoxically loosened its claims to dominion over some of North America's independent Indians.

Spanish officials' reliance on written documents that recognized Indian autonomy in North America represented an innovation. In the past, Spaniards had treated with Indians throughout the hemisphere, but usually to specify the terms of the Indians' surrender and to require that Indians put themselves at the service of the Crown. Previously, as one historian has aptly put it, "Spaniards understood Indian peoples to be royal subjects, ready for Christianization and exploitation, but inappropriate for the kinds of bargaining and negotiation that might have resulted in [written] treaties."

The Bourbons' employment of written treaties, however, had precedents in South America that reached back to the Habsburg era. In Chile, Spanish officials had held formal negotiations, or *parlamentos*, with Araucanians as early as 1606 and 1612, and by 1641 Aracanians had forced Spaniards to recognize the Biobío River as a permanent boundary. According to one version of the treaty, the Araucanians agreed in 1641 to recognize their "vassalage" to the Spanish Crown and to permit missionaries to come among them. Nonetheless, well into the late eighteenth century Spaniards *implicitly* recognized that Araucanian lands, the Estado de Arauco, enjoyed autonomy. Beginning in 1774, Araucanians even sent ambassadors to represent them in the Spanish capital.

In the late eighteenth century, influenced by their Chilean counterparts, officials in the Río de la Plata also began to employ capitanes de amigos, and written treaties became commonplace, too, on the pampas and the Gran Chaco. In contrast to those late-eighteenth-century treaties in North America that recognized full Indian autonomy, written treaties in South America usually required Indians to accept missionaries, settle in specified areas, recognize their vassalage to the Crown, and obey royal officials. In the Araucanía, the Chaco, and the pampas, Indians lacked the immediate threat of powerful foreign allies that enabled their North American counterparts to gain greater concessions by playing one side against the other.

South American precedents appear to have had little if any influence on the Spanish policy that evolved in North America in the 1780s and 1790s. Rather, the impetus for change in North America seems to have come from Indians themselves, who demanded the kind of treatment they had received from the French and English, and from officials on the scene like Bernardo de Gálvez, who recognized that Spain needed Indian allies to hold its borders against Americans in the Southeast and Apaches in the Southwest even if it meant taking the radical step of giving Indian allies arms and ammunition. In North America, then, recommendations for change seemed to flow less from the metropolis to the frontiers than from the frontiers to the metropolis, where they met a ready reception by Bourbons schooled in enlightened thought.

In the late eighteenth century Spain continued to import colonists and to found new towns in strategic areas that it wished to maintain but had not occupied previously, such as Patagonia, the Miskito coast, Louisiana, and California. And Carlos III, in particular, sent a wave of Spanish scientists to America, who intellectually appropriated peripheral territories—along with their flora and fauna, natural resources, and inhabitants—as an integral part of taking actual possession of them in the Age of Enlightenment. Yet amid this continuing expansion and reconnaissance, the idea of pressing Spanish claims to areas that lacked strategic value came to be regarded as anachronistic by some enlightened officials. Theirs was an eminently "rational" response to the reality that Spain could not defend or colonize all of the space that it claimed. In military terms alone, it seemed prudent, as one army officer put it, to try to control only those regions that Spaniards actually occupied—"what should be called the dominion and true possessions of the King."

Some enlightened thinkers went a step further and argued against military expenditures to defend even Spain's "true possessions," when the cost exceeded the benefits. [The Spanish savant and mariner, Alejandro] Malaspina, who thought it foolhardy to occupy the California coast, argued that Spain should abandon its effort to defend northern New Spain with soldiers and forts: "a border that consumes a million pesos to defend property worth 100,000 pesos should be avoided." In economic terms, Malaspina seems to have been attracted to the views of philosophes who argued that "in these distant climates, one must trade not conquer." Campomanes and the mysterious author of the *Nuevo sistema* would have agreed, although they probably would not have carried the argument to the extreme that the Conde de Aranda did in famously advising the Crown in 1783 that, with the exception of some ports of call or bases for trade on islands like Cuba and Puerto Rico, "you Majesty should rid himself of all his dominions on the continent of both Americas."

Those Spanish policymakers in administrative centers of the empire who sought to limit Spain's claims to dominion and to emphasize domination through commerce, redefined the use of power on the frontiers of the empire. Their new definition of Spain's relationship to those American lands it had not settled or firmly controlled provided a theoretical and legal rationale for recognizing the autonomy of Indians (who were, of course, autonomous in fact). The new policy also provided ideological space for Spaniards to build relationships with independent Indians based on the law of nations, rather than require Indians to submit as vassals or suffer the consequences of war or "pacification."

Whatever ideas informed their actions, Bourbon officials in the colonial centers and on the frontiers responded pragmatically to local circumstances as their Habsburg predecessors had done. Spanish officials made substantial concessions to Indians who forced them to recognize that conquest would cost more than peace, and to Indians who could turn to foreigners for support. In places such as southeastern North America, the Miskito coast, and the Araucania, Spanish officials, like Europeans on similar frontiers, paid tribute to natives and recognized their autonomy.

Conversely, when Spain expanded into California beginning in 1769, officials saw no need to sign treaties or enter into alliances with small groups of seminomads who lacked horses, firearms, the political organization to offer effective resistance, and had little prospect of aid from foreign powers. In California, as in other remote areas like Tierra del Fuego, or the llanos of today's Colombia, where Indians offered only modest resistance, Bourbons relied on missionaries and small mission guards to establish dominion, much as the Habsburgs had done.

Between these two extremes were places where Spaniards succeeded in isolating Indians from weapons and allies, defeated them, and forced them to surrender. Some Apache prisoners, whom Spaniards regarded as incorrigible, were be put in chains and sent into virtual slavery—a time-honored practice. Others were confined to reservations around military posts, through the formal treaties that Bourbon officers came to rely upon. On May 17, 1787, for example, Spaniards obliged the leaders of two small, bedraggled groups of Mescalero Apaches to enter into an eleven-part agreement at Presidio del Norte. Rather than guarantee their independence, the treaty required the Mescalero bands to live near the fort, not to leave without obtaining a license.

At the level of the individual, Bourbon policies toward indios bárbaros were subverted by "Spaniards" and "savages" who chose to ignore established categories. Individuals from each group moved across the porous boundaries that separated them and resided within the society of the other. Some did so by choice and others as captives. Some moved back and forth with the seasons. "Wild" Indians, for example, entered the Hispanic world to work temporarily in missions or for wages in haciendas, just as Hispanic traders in pursuit of profit ventured into Indian territory and lived among "wild" Indians. Some marginalized individuals—Hispanics, Indians, and mixed bloods—lived together in multiethnic outlaw bands as outcasts from both societies. In such ways, individuals on the frontiers of the empire looked after their own interests, usually preferring commerce and negotiation over war, a preference that they came to independent of the policies or philosophies of enlightened Bourbon officials.

In the Bourbon era, then, policy was not consistent or consistently applied. Directives that originated in the core of the absolutist Spanish state often took local conditions into account, and peripheral peoples—native and European alike—shaped and reshaped royal directives according to their own needs, perceptions, and power. New Indian policies emerged out of the interplay between core and periphery, tradition and innovation, pragmatism and ideology, and venality and idealism. In this respect, then, Spain resembled other early modern empires where, as historian Jack Greene has noted, authority did not merely flow "by imposition from the top down or from the center out but through an elaborate process of negotiation among the parties involved"—even in situations where relationships of power were unequal.

The various ways that Spaniards engaged independent Indians in the late colonial period would seem unremarkable were it not for the tendency of North American scholars to regard Spanish policy toward independent Indians as homogeneous and timeless, fixed in the sixteenth century, and to reduce Spain's multifaceted and pragmatic practices to caricature. Familiar oversimplifications resonate throughout our literature: the idea that the Indian policy of England and France "was based on trade ... and Spain's was based on the vain hope of mass conversion to Catholicism," the generalization that all Indians who resisted conquest "were defined [by Spaniards] as barbarians, as natural beings to be conquered and tamed by their betters," the argument that "placelessness" of nomads and seminomads "deprived them of any autonomous right to a frontier territory," the notion that "there were no Spanish-Indian treaties, the common-place distinction that, "While the French sought a consensual 'alliance' with the natives, Spaniards sought submission. Even the most benevolent methods of enacting Spanish authority *never* sought consent from natives...."

Never say never.

Anglo-America and Its Borderlands

FRANÇOIS FURSTENBERG

The Appalachian Mountains may have been the continent's single most important feature. Separating the eastern seaboard from the Mississippi Valley, the Iroquois in the uplands from the Algonquian peoples along the coasts and valleys, the British from the French colonies, the ocean-facing coast from the western-oriented backcountry, the Appalachian Mountains were responsible for the great problem of North American, and perhaps even Atlantic, history from 1754 to 1815: the fate of the trans-Appalachian West.

By drawing on the arguments and sensibility of an older diplomatic historiography, and connecting that to the methodological and historical insights of a newer ethnological and social history of the frontier and more recent scholarship on empire, we gain new insights on North American history from 1754 to 1815. In particular, certain continuities emerge over more familiar ruptures—including, in the U.S context, the all-important division between "colonial" and "early national" periods. Taking an Atlantic perspective on the continental interior, it appears that the Seven Years' War, which ostensibly ended in North America in 1760 and in Europe in 1763, in fact continued with only brief interruptions to 1815—in the form of the American Revolution of the 1770s, the Indian Wars of the 1780s and 1790s, and the War of 1812. Call it a Long War for the West. During this Long War, as the action shifted among various "hot spots" across the trans-Appalachian West, the great issue animating Native, imperial, and settler actors alike revolved around the fate of the region: Would it become a permanent Native American country? Would it fall to some distant European power? Or, perhaps the most unlikely scenario of all, would it join with the United States? Only in the wake of the British defeat in the War of 1812 was the region's fate as part of the expanding United States settled once and for all.

François Furstenberg, "The Significance of the Trans-Appalachian Frontier in Atlantic History," *American Historical Review* 113 (June 2008): 647–677. Permission granted by University of Chicago Press.

Facing East, as it were, from Native America, the years from 1754 to 1815 most clearly emerge as a single, coherent period of extended struggle to maintain Native control of the trans-Appalachian West. As historians now largely accept, where Native military power encountered the distant reaches of European empire, and none could claim supremacy, Euro-American interaction most often resulted from negotiation born of "mutual weakness." European empires in the West existed—as they later would in other forms of non-settler colonialism—not through military or demographic domination, but by fostering various forms of consent or "persuasion" among local allies; European imperialism drew settlers and colonial administrators into Native "diplomatic, economic, judicial, and family ways" as often as it did the reverse. The result was a complex system of shifting alliances continually beset by diverging Native and European interests.

This system began to collapse in the Ohio Valley—the "hot spot" of the trans-Appalachian West in the mid-eighteenth century, where the Long War for the West began. It was there that Native control over hunting grounds and trade routes was most contested. It was there that the British Empire confronted the French over issues of territorial sovereignty.

From the perspective of France's Native American allies, the French imperial collapse in the Seven Years' War was an ambiguous event. On the one hand, the territorial cessions being drawn on maps in Paris bore little connection to realities in the trans-Appalachian West, where Native American nations—unlike their French allies—remained undefeated.... On the other hand, the 1763 Treaty of Paris, which ended the war, radically transformed North America's geopolitical landscape, upending the imperial balance of power and with it longstanding patterns of Native-European interaction. France's defeat marked the beginning of a unipolar North America. Native Americans throughout the West discerned a sinister British design to seize their land and render them impotent.

Eager to restore a balance of power, some western [Native] nations urged the French to reconsider their capitulation.... Alas, these and other overtures were rebuffed. Exhausted by war, its navy in tatters and its treasury drained, France was not about to renew hostilities.

And so the western Indians fought on, with even some Iroquois nations abandoning their former allegiance to resist Britain's new imperial power. Their objectives essentially carried forward previous French imperial policy: to contain British settlement between the Appalachians and the Atlantic. The hot spot of the trans-Appalachian West now shifted from the Ohio Valley to the forts and frontier settlements along the Appalachains and the Great Lakes, where Native nations allid under the Ottawa chief Pontiac launched a series of devastating assaults on British settlements. If Pontiac's War of 1763–1764 failed to push the British into the Atlantic, it succeeded in restoring some autonomy to Native Americans in the West.... Britain agreed to limit colonial settlement in the trans-Appalachian West, reserving the area as an autonomous Native American territory—an objective that would persist in various forms over the next several decades.

The British imperial crisis of the 1770s and 1780s began, like the French crisis before it, on the imperial periphery: at the crest of the Appalachians, where imperial authorities found themselves squeezed between the conflicting demands of the rebellious Native and settler populations. This will come as little surprise to those who have followed recent scholarship on eighteenth-century empires, which has largely turned away from the perspective of older diplomatic historians—imperial conflict as seen from European capitals—to focus instead on imperial edges, emphasizing local forces in what are variously called frontiers, borderlands, or marchlands. Shifting its sights from traditional state actors, this newer historiography focuses on local agents—missionaries, fur traders, petty colonial officers, land speculators, settlers, and of course Native Americans—people who navigate native grounds, middle grounds, or divided grounds.... Local actors were the driving force ... rather than imperial capitals imposing their will on populations of distant peripheries, the actors on those peripheries impose *their* will on policymakers in the center. The tail in effect wags the dog. With so much emphasis placed on imperial margins, however, the metropole often drops out of such studies, and it might be asked whether the pendulum has swung too far—whether an older imperial perspective can be integrated into this new narrative by setting metropole and periphery in dialogue with each other.

From the perspective of London, the vast territory acquired by Britain in the Seven Years' War created daunting new challenges. The scope of its victory, the territoriality of an empire that had theretofore defined itself as maritime, the multitude of new peoples and ethnicities now under British dominion, all led to a fundamental rethinking of the nature of empire, and ultimately to the greatest crisis the British Empire had yet seen. In seeking to accommodate the objectives of their new American subjects—Native American and Catholic—imperial policymakers ran headlong into the ambitions of their older subjects.

The first conflict emerged in the wake of Pontiac's War, when the government enacted the Royal Proclamation of 1763, forbidding colonists from "making any Purchases or Settlements whatever, or taking Possession of any of the Lands," and ordering those who had settled there "forthwith to remove themselves." Even as it eased Native tensions, the proclamation infuriated local settler populations, who, seeing their hard-won western land claims denied, began to look suspiciously on the distant imperial authority. Settlers' fears of losing control of the West were reignited a decade later by the Québec Act of 1774, which granted religious and legal rights to the *habitants* in the Saint Laurence Valley. By detaching the Ohio Valley from the seaboard colonies and attaching it to the new province of Québec—restoring, in effect, the configuration of New France as the French had insisted it was in 1754, and as the British had sworn it could never be—the Québec Act further alienated British settlers.

These and other attempts to rationalize imperial governance led the settlers, like Native Americans before them, to discern a sinister design to seize their land and render them impotent. Like the Native Americans before them, they feared being made into "slaves" and having their property taken from them at pleasure. And so they, like the Native Americans before them, rebelled.

The end of war in 1783 did not settle the fate of the trans-Appalachian West, however. Once again, the Ohio Valley lay at the center of the geopolitical conflict. Britain ceded the region to the United States hoping to divide the Americans from their French allies. Whatever goodwill was achieved by the gesture, however, was immediately extinguished by British postwar diplomacy. Militarily, Britain's Native American allies, fiercely opposed to U.S. power, remained dominant in the region. Diplomatically, the British government was in an even stronger position to claim the Ohio Valley for its Native allies, for here was an issue on which Britain and its enemies agreed: Britain, Spain, and France all united in hoping to see the region between the Appalachians and the Mississippi dominated by Native American power, a buffer zone to stall U.S. expansion at the Appalachians. Had the British negotiated the peace of 1783 in combination with European and Native powers—granting concession to the indigenous rather than settler populations—U.S. borders might well have remained permanently fixed at the Appalachians.

If British-native alliances seemed poised to keep American settlers from the Northwest, Spanish-Native alliances were designed to do the same in the South. Although Spain had taken possession of Louisiana after the Seven Years' War, imperial authorities valued Louisiana not per se, but rather as what the Spanish minister Conde de Aranda called a "recognizable barrier" to protect its invaluable Mexican possessions.

Spanish imperial policy in the trans-Appalachian West had two primary objectives: to protect Mexico from British/American expansion, and to ensure Spanish dominance in the Gulf of Mexico. These aims determined the Spanish response to the American rebellion in the 1770s. Despite their reluctance to support the colonial rebellion … Spanish authorities eventually bent to French pressure and entered the war, providing the United States with crucial military assistance. In return, they demanded a reacquisition of the Floridas in the immediate term, and the restriction of American settlers from the trans-Appalachian West in the long term.

After 1783, the Southwest in general—and New Orleans in particular—emerged as the hot spot of the trans-Appalachian West. In order to preserve control over the Gulf of Mexico and shore up its Louisiana buffer, Spanish officials pursued a two-pronged strategy to keep Americans from the Southwest: frustrate trade along the Mississippi, and offer logistical and material support to Native allies. Spanish officials refused to grant Americans trading rights through New Orleans, hoping, as a 1782 French government report put it, to close "the Missisipi [sic] to the Americans, and to disgust them from making establishments on that river." Thanks to these efforts—and to the feeble U.S. response—the Spanish Empire seemed poised not just to block American expansion, but even to pluck away U.S. territories south of the Ohio River.

From the perspective of Paris, it was unclear that France had been permanently chased from North America in 1763. Only in retrospect does the year emerge as a defining moment, and even then it can appear as one of those turning points at which history failed to turn. In certain respects, "France" remained in

North America: French settlers continued to populate the West, French officers continued to conduct Spanish diplomacy in Louisiana, and French diplomatic *moeurs* continued to shape Native relations with both the Spanish and the British. Most important, perhaps, French policymakers continued to harbor ambitions—and sponsor attempts—to reestablish their North American empire. This continuing French presence in the trans-Appalachian West—demographic, diplomatic, cultural, and imperial—decisively influenced the Long War for the West.

French imperial planners retained a keen interest in North America for two reasons: to counter the ambitions of Great Britain, France's principal rival for global hegemony; and to protect its all-important Caribbean colonies, especially Saint Domingue, which now lacked a mainland base for provisions and military operations.... Postwar French policy thus aimed to ensure the permanent estrangement of Great Britain and its former colonies, ideally with the United States as a French client state.

As for the United States, its primary objective after the Revolution was to become an independent nation-state; and as many at the time recognized, the greatest obstacles to that ambition lay in the trans-Appalachian West. From 1783 through the end of the eighteenth century and beyond, it remained possible that the region would become a neutral Native American territory, or that it would fall to some distant European power. U.S. sovereignty in the trans-Appalachian West would be ensured only by overcoming three challenges: the geography of North America, and of the Appalachian Mountains in particular; Native American resistance; and the ambiguous loyalties of western colonists.

If the maps drawn in London in 1783, and by Jefferson and others in the years that followed—maps still used in history surveys today—extended U.S. sovereignty to the Mississippi River, such cartographic imagining was hardly in accord with the realities on the ground, where vexing geographic obstacles could not be so easily erased, Native Americans remained dominant, and settlers remained little swayed by feelings of national loyalty.

In seeking to control both sides of the Appalachians, U.S. policymakers were attempting something that no political entity, Native or European, had ever accomplished without rapidly disintegrating. Unlike the Atlantic Ocean, which served as both barrier and bridge between Europe and America, the Appalachian Mountains were an unambiguous obstacle dividing the East from the West. Also unlike the Atlantic, the Appalachians could be crossed at only a few points. The two most important passages lay along the Mohawk River in New York—dominated by the Iroquois, which helps explains their strategic importance—and, some seven hundred miles of rugged terrain to the southwest, through the Cumberland Gap, the old Indian trial that had been converted into a wagon road.

The separation was not simply one of distance; it was more fundamentally one of orientation, founded in the diverging paths of North American waterways. In the original thirteen states, where most settlement lay within fifty miles of the tidewater, the economy and society naturally faced out toward the Atlantic. "The inhabitants of the Atlantic coast give [to the West] the name *Back-Country*," a French traveler once observed, "indicating by this term their moral attitude, constantly turned towards Europe." Not so in the western settlements: "Scarcely had I crossed the Alleghanys [sic], before I heard [the residents] ... call the Atlantic coast the *Back-Country;* which proved that their geographic situation has given their views and their interests a new direction, in conformity with that of the waters that serve as roads and doors toward the Gulf of Mexico." Waterways were indeed the key. Through them, nature had decreed that the trans-Appalachian West would be more connected to New Orleans, and even to the Caribbean, than to Philadelphia, New York, or Boston. For it was not from any eastern port, but down the Mississippi, via New Orleans and through the Caribbean, that all commerce from the vast region must eventually pass.

These geographical forces made the Southwest in general, and New Orleans in particular, the hot spot of the trans-Appalachian West after 1783. Without control of New Orleans, no part of the region was safely American. Barges and boats from distant reaches of the Ohio Valley floated goods to New Orleans, and thence into international markets.

The second great challenge to U.S. sovereignty in the West was Native American power. If the American War of Independence was what scholars call a settler rebellion, it had the particularity of occurring amid an indigenous rebellion that began with the Seven Years' War and extended into the nineteenth century. In many respects, the ultimate success of the settler rebellion—long-term national sovereignty—would hinge on the outcome of the indigenous one; one had to fail for the other to succeed. The Long War for the West thus continued through the 1780s and into the 1790s, as the United States sought to establish its military supremacy in the Mississippi Valley, where Native Americans, as historian Eric Hinderaker remarks, refused to "accept the principle that the lands abandoned during the war had been forfeited by the Indians or won by the United States."

If Native Americans posed an immediate military threat to U.S. sovereignty in the West, the tenuous loyalties of the region's settlers posed a longer-term existential threat. Given past and present connections between westerners and the British Empire, the bonds tying western settlers to Britain "were potentially much stronger" than those tying them to the eastern states. There were many good reasons to suspect that western settlers might break away from the United States to make a separate peace with Spain or Great Britain.

It was precisely this fault line between eastern elites and western settlers that the international situation exacerbated. Nothing inflamed the resentment of settlers more than the Spanish policy of harassing commerce along the Mississippi River, and many feared that their welfare would be sacrificed on the altar of eastern interests. "The right to unrestricted access of the Mississippi was the *sine qua non* of western loyalty," observes Andrew Cayton. "And many frontiersmen, particularly residents of Kentucky, were convinced that the United States was not interested in obtaining it." As American settlers poured into western lands, provoking Native reprisals, it was becoming imperative for the U.S. government to assert its sovereignty—or risk losing the region entirely.

Securing the loyalties of trans-Appalachian settlers—keeping them from "an apostate and unnatural connection with any foreign power"—was, in short, a matter of existential importance to the young nation. No one really knew whether the semi–United States could survive as a little strip of settlements huddled along the Atlantic coast and hemmed in by the Appalachian Mountains. At the very least, they would have become what both French and British policymakers were trying to make them: the client states of a great power.

The year 1789 stands as an important date in this story of the trans-Appalachian West. It saw the inauguration of a new U.S. government, which moved quickly to secure the West—with military force against the Ohio Valley Indians, and with diplomatic overtures to open the Southwest. Despite the more robust military commitment, however, the new government would have, in its first years, no more success than the previous one in defeating Native Americans, who, as long as the British and Spanish maintained a western presence, found ready support to resist U.S. expansion.

But 1789 marks a turning point for a second reason: that year, some ten weeks after Washington's inauguration, revolution exploded in France. Its reverberations would be felt throughout Europe, across the Caribbean, and deep into the North American interior. Although the impact of the French Revolution on the United States has generated much scholarship, historians usually attend to its partisan and ideological implications along the East Coast, obscuring its other legacy: the sectional tensions it fomented between eastern elites and western settlers. As frontier regions across the United States seethed with unrest during the 1790s, local political conflicts repeatedly merged with transatlantic geopolitics.

Nowhere did sectional tensions merge with partisan conflict more dramatically than in the Whiskey Rebellion of 1794, which saw insurgents in western Pennsylvania call on other westerners to join the insurrection as "citizen[s] of the western country." Settlers across the Ohio Valley responded, and for a time the events seemed to portend a settler rebellion like that of 1776. "We are too distant from the grand seat of information," charged one angry Kentuckian. As the frontier disturbances spread from Pennsylvania, Maryland, and Virginia across the Ohio Valley to Kentucky and Ohio, some Kentuckians proclaimed their willingness to "renounc[e] the allegiance to the United States and annex themselves to the British."

French officials were well aware of these sectional tensions, of the open talk of disunion among westerners, and of western Republicans' sympathy for France—sometimes at the expense of their loyalty to the United States.

In light of all this ... Jay's Treaty of 1794 emerges as a diplomatic triumph. Today the treaty is best remembered for the partisan war it unleashed—a perspective, however, that ignores the more important sectional peace it ensured. Jay's Treaty secured Britain's evacuation of the long-disputed western posts, isolating the Ohio Valley Indians, crippling their resistance to U.S. expansion, and setting the stage for the Treaty of Grenville, which saw Native leaders abandon their longstanding demand for an Ohio River boundary between Native American country and the United States. By defusing a crisis with Britain, it strengthened the United States' negotiating position with Spain so much that Spanish officials soon acceded to longstanding settler demands to open Mississippi River trade in the 1795 Treaty of San Lorenzo. Even as Jay's Treaty reduced Spanish,

British, and Native American threats in the trans-Appalachian West, however, it created a new and even more ominous French menace.

It is ironic that France's defeat in the Seven Years' War, by forcing it to retrench in the Caribbean, inaugurated what might be called the golden age of the French Atlantic. The development had major implications for the trans-Appalachian West, whose waterways fed into the Gulf of Mexico and thence to the Caribbean; and it explains why, from 1794 to 1803, Saint Domingue emerged as the hot spot with the greatest impact on the trans-Appalachian West.

It is hard to exaggerate the importance of Saint Domingue in this period. Over the course of the eighteenth century, the French colony—one-half of a single Caribbean island, with an area one-sixth the size of Virginia—had experienced an economic boom without precedent, and by 1789 it was the richest, most productive colony not just of the French Empire, but of any empire.... And in 1791 it all came crashing down, in a revolution that quickly fused with the bitter imperial conflict between revolutionary France and Great Britain in the Caribbean.

The United States would soon be drawn into these Caribbean events.... As the crisis deepened, the abolition of slavery in Saint Domingue was ratified in the name of the French republic, and a force never before seen in the modern era— of slaves become citizens—was mobilized to crush France's enemies. With the British navy crippling French shipping, France was forced to open its colonies to unrestricted trade with the United States in 1793.... "The force of events hands the French colonies over to us," a smug Thomas Jefferson told French minister Fauchet in 1795. "France enjoys sovereignty and we, profits." Rather than make the United States into its client state, as France had hoped after American independence, France was now becoming dependent on the upstart nation.

By the mid-1790s, then, French policymakers came to realize that they could no longer depend on their fickle ally; they would need a more secure continental foothold. And so they turned their sights to Louisiana.... It was a prospect that many Americans feared above all others. A French Louisiana, warned a New York newspaper in 1802, could "hold forth every allurement to the inhabitants of the Trans-Alleghany settlements ... and inveigle them by degrees into the idea of forming a separate empire." Equally ominous was the impact that a French Louisiana might have on American slavery; the specter of France's transracial Caribbean armies loomed large. "A few French Troops with ... arms put into the hands of the Negroes," Mississippi's territorial governor warned in 1798, "would be to us formidable indeed."

"Before Bonaparte could reach Louisiana," Henry Adams once remarked, "he was obliged to crush the power of Toussaint ... If he and his blacks should succumb easily to their fate, the wave of French empire would roll on to Louisiana and sweep far up the Mississippi; if St. Domingo should resist, and succeed in resistance ... America would be left to pursue her democratic [sic] destiny in peace."

The road to Louisiana, in other words, ran through Saint Domingue—not just metaphorically but also geographically. By giving France control of the

Windward Passage between Cuba and Saint Domingue, which separates the Atlantic Ocean from the Caribbean Sea, the island secured French access into the Caribbean and to the Gulf of Mexico. With navigation dependent on winds and currents, ships headed for the Caribbean or the Gulf of Mexico passed almost of necessity through the Windward Passage.

And so in 1802 Napoleon sent his brother-in-law, General Charles Victor Emmanuel Leclerc, along with a force that would eventually total more than 80,000, to conquer Saint Domingue. If a commitment to preserving the plantation order explains why the British navy let Leclerc's force cross the Atlantic, American support for the French mission is harder to fathom. Certainly Jefferson, now president, had no wish to see France installed in Louisiana. "There is on the globe one single spot, the possessor of which is our natural and habitual enemy," said Jefferson in 1801. "It is New Orleans." No amount of lingering attachment to France could alter this view. "France, placing herself in that door, assumes to us the attitude of defiance." To be sure, the alternative to a French recapture of the island was profoundly troubling to Jefferson, whose terror—not to say hysteria—at the prospect of a republic of former slaves in the Caribbean is well known. The thought of an independent Saint Domingue inspired nightmares of "the Cannibals of the terrible republic" pulling into American ports, sending "black crews, supercargoes & missionaries thence into the Southern states," and fomenting insurrection throughout the nation.

In the end … Napoleon's fatal insistence on fighting Toussaint led to the collapse of his American ambitions. Jefferson played the diplomatic game perfectly, luring the French into Saint Domingue with promises of assistance before abandoning them in the quagmire. The game was up. France had lost its last doorway into the North American interior, and it was obvious that Louisiana could not be held.

But Napoleon had one last matter to clear up as he withdrew from America. "It was left to him," wrote [François] Barbé-Marbois [Napoleon's finance minister], "only to prevent France's loss from becoming Britain's advantage." And so Napoleon hastened to turn the colony over to the Americans and grab whatever cash he could. Although the purchase was financed in the London capital markets—raising money for France to wage war against Great Britain—the British government did not object because it believed that an American Louisiana was less threatening than a French Louisiana.

The long war for the West did not end with this second French loss of Louisiana. The dynamic that had shaped events in the trans-Appalachian West since 1754 continued, European imperial competition joining with enduring Native/settler conflict to keep the region's fate uncertain. A simmering warfare persisted in the years after 1803, as American settlers pushed west and up the Mississippi River into Native lands…. British-Native military mobilization, building on years of village politics in Indian country, stirred up the embers of western settler unrest, which burst into flame in 1812, a war that in retrospect emerges as the last battle of the Long War for the West.

If the United States and Great Britain fought a war in the East and on the Atlantic over questions of maritime rights and impressment, American settlers and

Native Americans in the Mississippi Valley fought a far more consequential war whose objectives were, on the one side, continued U.S. expansion into Native and British land, and, on the other, the preservation of the West as an Indian country forever protected from American settlement. If this seems familiar, that is because these objectives echoed those for which France had gone to war in 1754, for which Pontiac had fought in 1763, and which the British had pursued since 1783: the restriction of American settlement from the trans-Appalachian West, and the creation of a buffer between the United States and British and Spanish territory. Like previous wars, the War of 1812 saw the emergence of pan-Indian unity and ideology: where in the past it had been led by Neolin and Pontiac, now it was led by the Shawnee leader Tecumseh and his brother Tenskwatawa. As previous wars had seen Native leaders urging a return of the French to counterbalance British power, this war saw Native leaders in the North and Southwest reach out to the British and Spanish to balance U.S. power.

This western war … ended with the Treaty of Ghent in 1815, which once again left Native Americans empty-handed. British diplomats began the negotiations in Ghent insisting as "a *sine qua non* for peace" that the Native nations be included in the treaty negotiations, and that a 250,000-square-mile area in the Northwest between the United States and Canada—equivalent to roughly 15 percent of the U.S.—be set aside for Native Americans, which the United States would be forever barred from purchasing. It was a prospect that the British almost certainly could have accomplished in 1783, with the help of Spanish and French diplomats, who would have proven supportive. By 1815, however, it was too late: American negotiators contemptuously dismissed the cession of what they considered to be their territory as "injurious and degrading." Too many American settlers had poured into the Mississippi Valley, their American loyalties now cemented by the searing experience of war and the increased political power they exerted in Washington, where Kentuckian Henry Clay served as speaker of the House of Representatives, and where the presidency would soon pass to Andrew Jackson of Tennessee. The French, defeated once and for all at Waterloo, no longer threatened Britain's global hegemony. The Spanish, now isolated in the West and under pressure from settler independence movements across the Americas—many of them modeled on the United States—were no longer in a position to challenge U.S. territorial claims, which they finally ceded in the Adams-Onís Treaty of 1820. Most important of all, Native nations across the trans-Appalachian West were now bereft of international military support. The Long War for the West was finally over. It was a decisive victory for the United States and a final defeat for Native nations of the trans-Appalachian West, who could never again hope to make their lands into an autonomous Indian country.

To whom does the trans-Appalachian West belong? That was the great question animating imperial, Native, and settler actors alike during the Long War for the West, as each group battled alone and in shifting alliances to retain a hold on the region. But on a different, historiographical, register, the question remains as pressing today as it did in the eighteenth and nineteenth centuries: Does the region belong to U.S. history, imperial history, Native American history, frontier history, Atlantic history, or some combination of them all in a confused, even entangled, form? ... The history of the trans-Appalachian West shaped the destinies not just of Native America, nor of Mexico, Canada, and the United States, nor even of the most powerful global empires of the nineteenth century, but by extension of modern world history itself.

With the trans-Appalachian West thus set in its fullest context, we are ultimately poised to return to U.S. history, and there to better recognize the sweeping forces of imperialism and global warfare that buffeted a young and fragile United States, decisively shaping its history as well as its geography. Of course, few at the time could have seen the irony of the U.S. victory in the Long War for the West, which, by opening the Mississippi Valley to a contested U.S. expansion, half slave and half free, would eventually generate sectional conflicts so severe that the country would be confronted with the greatest existential crisis of its history. To the victor went the spoils. In the near term, however, the U.S. victory resolved the fate of the trans-Appalachian West. Never more would tenuous western loyalties, Native American resistance, or European imperialism threaten U.S. sovereignty east of the Mississippi.

FURTHER READING

Anderson, Fred. *The Crucible of War: The Seven Years' War and the Fate of Empire in British North America, 1754–1766* (2000).

Anderson, Fred, and Andrew Cayton. *The Dominion of War: Empire and Liberty in North America, 1500–2000* (2005).

Bailyn, Bernard, and Philip D. Morgan, eds. *Strangers within the Realm: Cultural Margins of the First British Empire* (1991).

Billington, Ray Allen. *Westward Expansion: A History of the American Frontier* (1949; 5th ed., 1982).

Bolton, Herbert E. "The Epic of Greater America." *American Historical Review* 38 (April 1933): 448–474.

Calloway, Colin G. *The Scratch of a Pen: 1763 and the Transformation of North America* (2006).

Cohen, Paul. "Was There an Amerindian Atlantic? Reflections on the Limits of a Historiographical Concept." *History of European Ideas* 34 (Dec. 2008): 388–410.

Countryman, Edward. *Americans: A Collision of Histories* (1996).

Dowd, Gregory Evans. *A Spirited Resistance: The North American Indian Struggle for Unity, 1745–1815* (1992).

———. *War under Heaven: Pontiac, the Indian Nations, and the British Empire* (2002).

Elliott, J. H. *Empires of the Atlantic World: Britain and Spain in America, 1492–1830* (2006).

Greene, Jack P., and Philip D. Morgan, eds. *Atlantic History: A Critical Appraisal* (2009).

Guy, Donna J., and Thomas E. Sheridan, eds. *Contested Ground: Comparative Frontiers on the Northern and Southern Edges of the Spanish Empire* (1998).

Guyatt, Nicholas. "'The Outskirts of Our Happiness': Race and the Lure of Colonization in the Early Republic." *Journal of American History* 95 (March 2009): 986–1011.

Hine, Robert V., and John Mack Faragher. *The American West: A New Interpretive History* (2001).

Hu–DeHart, Evelyn. *Missionaries, Miners, and Indians: History of Spanish Contact with the Yaqui Indians of Northwestern New Spain, 1533–1830* (1981).

Lewis, James E. *The American Union and the Problem of Neighborhood: The United States and the Collapse of the Spanish Empire, 1783–1829* (1998).

Meinig, D. W. *The Shaping of America: A Geographic Perspective on 500 Years of History.* Vol. 1 (1986).

Nasatir, Abraham. *Borderland in Retreat: From Spanish Louisiana to the Far Southwest* (1976).

Nobles, Gregory H. *American Frontiers: Cultural Encounters and Continental Conquest* (1997).

Richter, Daniel K. *Before the Revolution: America's Ancient Pasts* (2011).

Rohrbough, Malcolm J. *Trans-Appalachian Frontier: People, Societies, and Institutions, 1775–1850* (1978; 3rd ed., 2008).

Stagg, J. C. A. *Borderlines in Borderlands: James Madison and the Spanish-American Frontier, 1776–1821* (2009).

Taylor, Alan. *American Colonies: The Settling of North America* (2001).

Wallace, Anthony F. C. *Jefferson and the Indians: The Tragic Fate of the First Americans* (1999).

Weber, David J. *The Spanish Frontier in North America* (1992).

———. *Bárbaros: Spaniards and Their Savages in the Age of Enlightenment* (2005).

CHAPTER 6

⌇

Borderlands in Change
The View from Below

The great imperial changes of the late eighteenth century had a profound impact on inter-cultural relations across the Americas. In eastern North America, the fall of New France deprived Indians of the chance to play rival European powers off one another and tipped the balance of power in the favor of Anglo Americans. Long-enduring borderlands of cultural accommodation gave way to frontiers of expansion and exclusion. The Great Lakes middle ground crumbled. In western North America, Spain acquired Louisiana from France, established a new colonial realm in California, and revised its policy with independent Indians. Spanish California was built around missions, but elsewhere Spanish authorities replaced the policy of isolating Indians into missions with the policy of incorporating them into Hispanic society. Across Spain's far-flung frontiers, war, coercion, and conversion gave way to diplomacy, trade, and accommodation.

These were dramatic changes that altered the broad geopolitical context in which Indians, Europeans, and rival empires negotiated their conflicts and coexistence. But the late eighteenth century also witnessed more subtle changes in how people from different cultures related to one another in everyday settings. These relationships were not immune to the imperial reorganization and macro-level changes discussed in the previous chapter, but often they followed their own distinct logic and rhythm. This chapter probes how these quotidian changes and continuities manifested themselves in such intimate borderlands spheres as food trade, slavery, and gender relations.

The previous chapter looked at borderlands from above, from a bird's-eye perspective, and it examined how empires, states, great wars, and high diplomacy shaped the history of cross-cultural relations in the Americas. This chapter looks at borderlands from below, from the perspective of ordinary people, small communities, and those on the social margins. The two chapters complement one another, providing together a multilevel view of North American borderlands in the late eighteenth century. They also illuminate the paradoxical nature of borderlands, that they are at once resilient and rigid, that they both spur and thwart historical change. The previous chapter showed how borderlands actors can adapt their strategies to external challenges; this chapter focuses on the persistence of long-evolved intercultural practices, which can defy massive geopolitical changes, imperial interventions, and state control. It explores how borderlands people, by creatively preserving their traditions, can deflect outside attempts to subjugate, remold, and categorize them. It illuminates how borderlands can endure against daunting odds.

∿ DOCUMENTS

In the first document, Athanase de Mézières, a French career officer who moved into Spanish service with the transfer of Louisiana to Spain, addresses Wichita Indians in a meeting at a Kadodacho Caddo village on the lower Red River in 1770. Mézières tried to impress upon the Wichitas that the shift from French to Spanish rule was real and permanent and that the Wichitas must recognize the Spanish king as their sovereign; to put force behind his words, Mézières had already persuaded the Caddos to put the Wichitas in a trading boycott. But Mézières's message was not all threats. As an inducement, he offered to the Wichitas a protective alliance and trade, the cornerstones of the French Indian policy that often had outdone the Spanish policy in securing native allegiances. Mézières concluded treaties with several native groups, but the geostrategic chemistry of the Texas borderlands changed when the United States acquired Louisiana in 1803. The second document depicts a meeting between John Sibley, the U.S. Indian agent for the Orleans territory, and Comanche chiefs at Natchitoches in 1807. Assigned to bring the southwestern Indians into U.S. orbit, Sibley cajoled Comanche representatives with gifts and ceremonies. He also delivered a speech in which he presented a kind of version of American history that he thought would appeal to his native audience. A Comanche chief's response leaves it open how impressed he was by Sibley's performance of borderlands diplomacy, but by the next decade Comanches were trading regularly with itinerant American traders, selling them horses stolen from Spanish Texas.

The next two documents focus on the multiracial borderlands of Spanish New Mexico, which seem to have been little affected by the Bourbon Reforms and their modernizing pressure: Spanish dreams of secure borders, regulated commerce, and political centralization seem to have crashed head on against local borderland realities. In Document 3, written in 1794, Fernando de la Concha, the governor of New Mexico, reports on the activities and attitudes of the province's eastern villagers. He is appalled by their autonomous inclination and suspicious of their loyalties, fearing that they were being corrupted by the Comanches and other Plains Indians. In the fourth document, Pedro Bautista Pino, New Mexico's representative in the Spanish parliament, describes the province in 1812, finding a wide gap between the projections of Bourbon reformers and the reality of the far northern borderlands. Pino analyzes the province's economy, ecclesiastical government, and educational and medicinal system, finding them all lacking, and insists that the province needed to be reinforced to counter the growing influence of the United States in the Southwest borderlands. When assessing Pino's report, it is necessary to keep in mind that it was written with the objective of securing more financial support for New Mexico from the Spanish government.

Document 5 captures the surprise of Joseph Holt Ingraham, an American writer and a professor, when he visited the town of Natchez in the southwestern corner of Mississippi in 1835. Natchez had been part of the United States since the Treaty of San Lorenzo in 1795, but Ingraham found it still mired in its borderlands past. Indians not only seemed to be a natural part of the urban scene: they even carried guns. Black slaves behaved in ways that seem to have violated Ingraham's expectations of slave conduct. And many white residents spoke French or Spanish or both. Ingraham's account bespeaks of how borderland traditions can endure long after the borderlands themselves have been incorporated into nation-states. Document 6 reveals different kinds of borderland continuities. It is a copy of the Dohasan Calendar, a pictorial Kiowa calendar kept by a Kiowa Indian named Dohasan and his nephew, also named Dohasan, between 1832 and 1892. The calendar begins at the lower left corner and spirals toward the center, each pictograph marking a major event of each year. Although the Kiowas were deeply involved in the cross-cultural life of the Southwest borderlands, the things they recorded are often quite different from those found in Euro-American historical records. For example, the first symbol depicts a deadly encounter with a party of Americans, the second refers to a raid by Osages who beheaded their Kiowa victims, and the third to a meteor shower, which in Kiowa culture signifies the beginning of a new era. The last symbol in the center of the calendar represents a measles epidemic in 1892.

The last document focuses on the colonization of Alta California, which began in 1769, when Spaniards began to establish missions and presidios on the California coast. Document 7 is the first census of Los Angeles, taken in 1781, and it underscores the centrality of *mestizaje*, the intermixing of races, in Spanish California. In California, as elsewhere in New Spain's northern borderlands, Spaniards, that is, people of pure Spanish descent, were a minority amid mixed-race people who were divided into different ethnic and social categories, or *castas*. The Spanish social and legal hierarchy recognized hundreds of *castas*, and their definitions and meanings varied from region to region. The Los Angeles census includes Indians, Negros (people of full African descent), mulattoes (people with black and white parents), mestizoes (people with Spanish and Indian parents), *coyotes* (people with Indian and mestizo parents), and *chinos* (people with Indian and mulatto parents).

1. Athanese de Mézières Courts and Coerces Wichita Chiefs, 1770

The harangue which I made to these [Indians] was essentially as follows:

That at last had come the much-wished-for day when I was permitted to tell them by word of mouth of the matters which I had already communicated by means of the friendly tribes; that for this purpose I gladly came at the command of the captain-general of Luiziana, my chief, father and protector of the Indians; that it was his wish to be fully informed of their

Herbert Eugene Bolton, ed. and trans., *Athanase de Mézières and the Louisiana-Texas Frontier, 1768–1780* (Cleveland: Arthur H. Clark, 1914), 1: 209–213.

disposition and that, if this seemed to me good, I had orders to assure them of his benevolence; that they could not doubt, in view of that respectable flag which they saw hoisted, that we had become naturalized as Spaniards; that our new and beloved monarch was the most powerful in the world, and emperor of the Indies; that, notwithstanding the fact that they had gained the indignation of so high a prince—the illustrious chief whom I represented and for whom I spoke in this small portion of his extensive dominions—he would grant them the peace which they had come to seek if they would but show themselves constantly deserving of such a boon; that the clemency and the magnanimity of the Catholic king equalled his immense power; that those of his subjects on whom he looked with the most love and compassion were the natives; that he pitied their helplessness and wished to remedy it; that the wish of this illustrious sovereign was that in the future none of them should be slaves of his other subjects, but their brothers instead; that they should profit by the good example and inviolable fidelity of the friendly Cadodachos [Caddos], whose hands, far from having been stained with our blood, had been dedicated, at the cost of their own, to the defense of our lives; that they should look to the north, at the Osages; to the west, at the Comanches; to the south, at the Apaches; and to the east, at the Spaniards of Luisiana, all their enemies; that they were placed in the midst of four fires, which, raising their horrible flames, would reduce them to ashes as easily as the voracious fire consumes the dry grass of the meadows; that they should inform me of the decision they had made in so obvious and so frightful a situation; that they should, above all, refrain from moving their lips to invent excuses which sooner or later their deeds would belie; and finally, that they should rest assured that there was no hope for aid except under the conditions above expressed, since the very name of Frenchman had been erased and forgotten; that we were Spaniards, and, as such, as sensitive to the outrages committed as we would be interested in avenging them as soon as they might be resumed.

Then I arose and, cordially and affectionately taking the hand of each one of the surrounding Spaniards, I tried by this demonstration to make more evident the close and sacred pact which binds us.

Then, when it was their [Wichitas'] turn to respond, after having consulted at length with one another, the one who was skilled in the Cadodacho language gravely, without confusion, and with calm countenance raised his voice and said:

That their discord with the Spaniards arose from the fact that, with the recent founding of the presidio and mission of San Saba, the Spaniards had treated as guests and given aid to their enemies, the Apaches; that they truly desire and ask for peace; that their punctual obedience in coming to secure it has been very disastrous to them, because the Comanches, who were formerly among their allies, having been irritated by this decision, are now waging a most cruel war against them, but that not on that account will they waver in their promises; that they deserve the greatest compassion; and that they implore with confidence that of the French, their ancient protectors.

I again took up the discussion and said:

> Do not forget that there are now no Frenchmen in these lands, and that we are all Spaniards. I have and will keep in mind your promises in order to report them to my chief, to whom they will undoubtedly be pleasing, and he will receive you into the number of his children and of the happy subjects of our monarch. But meanwhile it is fitting, since you have committed so many insults, robberies, and homicides in San Antonio de Vexar and vicinity, that without loss of time you should journey to that city, with the interpreter whom I shall provide for you and two Spaniards who will accompany you, carrying a flag to protect you. There you will humble yourselves in the presence of a chief of greatest power who resides there.

2. John Sibley and a Comanche Chief Try to Impress One Another, 1807

As the Hietans [Comanches] were about taking their departure after receiving their presents, the Principal Chief produced a Spanish Flag and Lay'd it down at my feet, and desired the Interpreter to tell me, "that he receiv'd that Flag from Govr Cordero of St Antonio, & wish'd now to exchange it for a flag of the United States, that it might be known in their Nation.

I told him we were not at War with Spain and had no disposition to offend them, Otherwise I should have Anticipated his request by Presenting him with a United States flag before, but it might offend the Spanish Gov^t and be in the end disadvantageous to them; he said "they were very desirous of having Our Flag and it was the Same to them whether Spain was pleas'd or displeas'd and if I would give him One it Should wave through all the Hietan Nation, and they would all die in defence of it before they would part with it.

I regretted that it was not in my power to have taken a Vocabulary of their Language, there were so many different Nations here at the Same time I was Incessantly Occupied Amongst them.

I delivered to them the following talk.—Brothers,

By Arrangements with France and Spain two Nations beyond the great Water we the people of the United States have become your Neighbours, and all the great Country Called Louissana as formerly Claim'd by France now belongs to us, the President of the United States the great friend & father of all the Red people Assures you he is your friend and will Continue to be so, so long as you are his friends, & friends to the People of the United States. It is now so long since our Ancestors came from beyond the great Water that we have no remembrance of it, we ourselves are Natives of the Same land that you are, in other words white Indians, we therefore Should feel & live together like brothers & Good Neighbours, we Should do no harm to One Another but all the good in our power.

John Sibley, *A Report from Natchitoches in 1807*, ed. Annie Heloise Abel (New York: Museum of the American Indian, 1922), 54–58, 61–63.

Brothers, the boundaries between Our Country and Spain are not yet fixed, we therefore do not know how far towards the Setting Sun Our Limits will extend; but you may rest Assured that whether the Country that you inhabit falls within Our Boundaries or not, it will always be Our wish to be at peace & friendship with you; we are not at war with Spain, we therefore do not wish, or Ask you to be less their friends for being Ours, the World is wide enough for us all, and we Ought all of us to live in it like brothers,

Brothers, I think I ought to Caution you Against Opening Your Ears to the bad talks of Any people whatever who may Wish to make us enemies; but be always perswaded that we have not Come to this Country to do harm to Any of our Red brethren, but to do them good.

It is the wish of your great & good Father the President of the United States, that all his red Children should live together in peace And Amity with one Another, that all their paths may be Clean, that there may be no more wars between them, that their Children may Multiphy, & their women no more fear the Tommehawk of an enemy.

An Hietan Said "their best Speaker was absent he went out to where their Horses were put, & had not return'd.

"From the Moment (said he) we heard of the Americans being Arriv'd at this place we were determined to come & see them our New Neighbours; and we are now all of us highly pleas'd that we have Come, on Our way we fell in with Some of Our friends who came Along to Accompany us, we are in want of Merchandize and Shall be Always Glad to trade with you on friendly terms, and now we have found the way & see that you have every thing we want we Shall probably visit you again.

3. Fernando de la Concha Laments the Corrupting Influence of Indians in the New Mexico Borderlands, 1794

Nothing is so difficult as knowing man, and only the practice of observing his conduct closely provided on occasions helps form some idea of his character. The knowledge which experience has given me in general of the inhabitants of the Province of New Mexico (excepting the Indians of the towns) is of little value. Under a simulated appearance of ignorance or rusticity they conceal the most refined malice. He is a rare one in whom the vices of robbing and lying do not occur together. Because of the dispersion of their settlements, the bad upbringing resulting from this, the proximity and trade of the barbarous tribes in which they are involved, the removal of more than two thousand laborers to another area would be very useful to society and the state. It is the environment that remains and every day propagates similar vices. These cannot be checked except under a new set of regulations and by means of a complete change in the actual system of control.

The people have made repeated unfounded accusations against them [Spanish colonial officials]. All of these I have examined with the greatest care, and they

Fernando de la Concha, "Advice on Governing New Mexico, 1794," ed. and trans. Donald E. Worcester, *New Mexico Historical Review* 24 (July 1949): 243–244, 249–250.

have never been able to prove those which have been made. Seeking the source of these I have discovered easily that they do not spring from anything but the lack of obedience, wilfulness, and desire to live without subjection and in a complete liberty, in imitation of the wild tribes which they see nearby.

The new Governor must apply his entire attention to effecting the complete consolidation of the capital city. In the year 1789 an executive order from the higher authorities was passed to me in order that I should put it into effect without delay or without listening to petitions. Knowing the difficulties which attended it in that time, I stated the methods which to me appeared opportune for accomplishing it without serious damage on the part of the inhabitants, which was adopting the prudent means of not permitting rebuilding, repairing, or mending of the establishments which are widely dispersed. The chief officers approved, and in consequence I issued an edict which expounded this prohibition, under pain of the infractors incurring the penalty noted in it. From these measures already it has been given a regular form, but the work will never be completed if the least negligence is permitted, and if you are not vigilant and do not sustain the measure which is the dominant factor. The inhabitants are indolent. They love distance which makes them independent; and if they recognize the advantages of union, they pretend not to understand them, in order to adapt the liberty and slovenliness which they see and note in their neighbors the wild Indians.

4. Pedro Bautista Pino Assesses the Condition of New Mexico, 1812

It has never been possible to consider levying municipal taxes. Even though one proposed to collect them in kind, no outside market is available and the products consequently would rot in warehouses or it would cost the community as much to export as to produce them. Nor has there ever been a body authorized to promote the establishment of a treasury, or provincial sub-treasuries, or to report on behalf of the New Mexicans whatever might be deemed conducive to prosperity.

The foresight of the sovereign congress has supplied a remedy for this evil. Title 6 of our constitution … places in the hands of the settlers everything relating to the happiness of the settlements. However, it is useless to organize ayuntamientos in New Mexico if the people are not accorded the circulation of money, or if they are not aided by provisions which may stimulate commerce.

The twenty-six Indian pueblos and the 102 settlements of Spaniards, which constitute the population of the province of New Mexico, are under the spiritual supervision of the diocese of Durango. These pueblos and settlements are served by twenty-two missionaries of the order of Saint Francis from the province of Mexico. In only one pueblo of the district of El Paso and in the capital are the parish priests secular clergymen. All of the missionaries and the priests receive an income

H. Bailey Carroll and J. Villasana Haggard, trans., *Three New Mexico Chronicles: The Exposición of Don Pedro Bautista Pino 1812; the Ojeada of Lic. Antonio Barreiro; and the Additions by Don José Agustín de Escudero, 1849* (Albuquerque: Quivira Society, 1942), 44–45, 50–51, 59, 94–95.

from the treasury, excepting those of the villas of Alburquerque, Santa Cruz de la Cañada, and the capital, who have no income other than the offerings at the altar.

It is noteworthy that the distance from the pueblos, in which the missionaries reside, to the Spanish settlements range from eight to ten leagues. In view of such long distances, therefore, not all the parishioners can go to one town to hear mass, nor can the parish priests say mass in two towns on the same day; it is also impossible to have vicariates, because the income or allotment assigned the missionaries for the spiritual administration of those towns is itself insufficient. The present allotments were made at an early date without considering the 102 settlements which have been established since the year 1780 for the preservation of the province.

For more than fifty years no one has known that there was a bishop; nor has a bishop been seen in the province during this time. Consequently, the sovereign provisions and the instructions of ecclesiastical discipline have not been fulfilled. The misfortunes suffered by those settlers are infinite because of the lack of a primate. Persons who have been born during these fifty years have not been confirmed. The poor people who wish, by means of a dispensation, to get married to relatives cannot do so because of the great cost of traveling a distance of more than 400 leagues to Durango. Consequently, many people, compelled by love, live and rear families in adultery. The zeal of the ministers of the church is unable to prevent this and many other abuses which are suffered because of the aforesaid lack of ministers. It is truly grievous that in spite of the fact that from 9,000 to 10,000 duros are paid by that province in tithes, for fifty years the people have not had an opportunity to see the face of their bishop. I, an old man, did not know how bishops dressed until I came to Cádiz [Spain].

[Improvements requested by New Mexicans] will prove their physical and moral needs; and they will make a place in the charitable heart of your majesty in order that the state of neglect and disregard in which the settlers have lived up to the present, because of the indolence of the government, may be changed. *Lastly, these official instructions will prove to your majesty the imminent danger of these provinces' falling prey to our neighbors, thus leaving the other provinces to the same fate, one after another.* I trust your majesty may become aware of this fact, because the *purchase of Louisiana by the Uniuted States has opened the way for the Americans to arm and incite the wild Indians against us; also the way is open for the Americans to invade the province.* Once this territory is lost, it will be impossible to recover it. Since there is still time to prevent this disaster, your majesty should take advantage of this warning, which incidentally has been brought over by me, because a delay in furnishing remedial relief may permit the development of the evils which are feared by the one who has the honor of making them known to your majesty.

The province of New Mexico does not have among its public institutions any of those found in other provinces of Spain. So backward is it in this matter that the names of such institutions are not even known. The benefit of primary letters is given only to the children of those who are able to contribute to the salary of the school teacher. Even in the capital it has been impossible to engage a teacher and to furnish education for everyone.

Of course there are no colleges of any kind. This condition gives rise to expressions of discouragement by many people who notice the latent scientific ability of the children in this province. For a period of more than two hundred years since the conquest, the province has made no provision for any one of them in any of the literary careers, or as a priest, something which is ordinarily done in other provinces of America.

There are no physicians, no surgeons, and no pharmacies. I repeat, in the entire province there is only one surgeon, and he is supported by the 121 soldiers whose salaries are paid by the treasury. Whenever this surgeon makes medical visits to other towns, he has to be paid for them by the person who calls him. If he falls sick, one is obliged to try to find another doctor 300 leagues away. Imagine the condition of a person, gravely wounded, by the time the doctor arrives. The settlers who engage in campaigns at their own expense do not have even the comfort of a doctor to dress the wounds they received in action. And how is it possible for one man to take care of the needs of all the people in a territory consisting of 3,500 square leagues? I am leaving this matter to the consideration of your majesty.

5. Joseph Holt Ingraham Observes Indians and Slaves in Natchez, 1835

As I was crossing from the bluff to the entrance of one of the principal streets—a beautiful avenue bordered with the luxuriant China tree, whose dark rich foliage, nearly meeting above, formed a continued arcade as far as the eye could penetrate—my attention was arrested by an extraordinary group, reclining in various attitudes under the grateful shade of the ornamental trees which lined the way. With his back firmly planted against a tree, as though there existed a sympathetic affinity between the two, sat an athletic Indian with the neck of a black bottle thrust down his throat, while the opposite extremity pointed to the heavens. Between his left forefinger and thumb he held a corncob, as a substitute for a stopper. By his side, his blanket hanging in easy folds from his shoulders, stood a tall, fine-looking youth, probably his son, his raven hair falling in masses over his back, with his black eyes fixed upon the elder Indian, as a faithful dog will watch each movement of his intemperate master. One hand supported a rifle, while another was carelessly suspended over his shoulder. There was no change in this group while I remained in sight; they were as immoveable as statues. A little in the rear, lay several "warriors" fast locked in the arms of Bacchus or Somnus, (probably both,) their rifles lying beside them. Near them a knot of embryo chiefs were gamboling in all the glorious freedom of "*sans culottes.*" At a little distance, half concealed by huge baskets apparently just unstrapped from their backs, filled with the motley paraphernalia of an Indian lady's wardrobe, sat, cross-legged, a score of dark-eyed, brown-skinned girls and women, laughing and talking in their soft, childish language, as merrily as any ladies would have done, whose "lords" lay thus supine at their feet. Half a score of miserable, starved wretches, "mongrel, whelp and hound," which it were an insult to the

Joseph Holt Ingraham, *The South-west, by a Yankee* (New York: Harper and Brothers, 1835), 2: 24–26.

noble species to term dogs, wandering about like unburied ghosts "seeking what they might devour," completed the novel and picturesque *ensemble* of the scene.

On the opposite side of the way was another of a different character, but not less interesting. Seated in a circle around their bread and cheese, were half a dozen as rough, rude, honest-looking countrymen from the back part of the state, as you could find in the nursery of New-England's yeomanry. They are small farmers—own a few negroes—cultivate a small tract of land, and raise a few bales of cotton, which they bring to market themselves. Their carts are drawn around them forming a barricade to their camp, for here, as is customary among them, instead of putting up at taverns, they have encamped since their arrival. Between them and their carts are their negroes, who assume a "cheek by jowl" familiarity with their masters, while jokes, to season their homely fare, accompanied by astounding horse-laughs, from ivory-lined mouths that might convey a very tolerable idea of the crater of Etna, pass from one group to the other, with perfect good will and a mutual contempt for the nicer distinctions of colour.

6. The Dohasan Calendar, 1832–1892

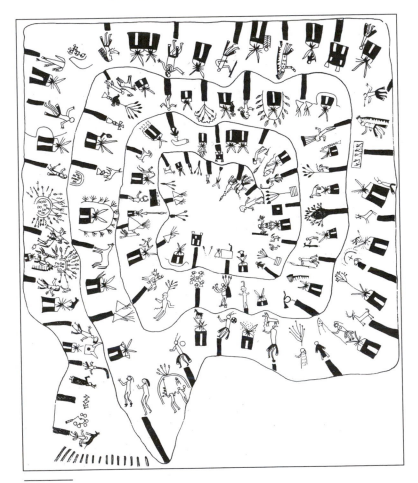

Phoebe A. Hearst Museum of Anthropology, Berkeley, CA.

7. The First Census of Los Angeles, 1781

Census of the population of the City of the Queen of the Angels, founded September 4th, 1781, on the banks of Porciúncula River, distant 45 leagues from the Presidio of San Diego, 27 leagues from the site selected for the establishment of the presidio of Santa Barbara, and about a league and a half from the San Gabriel Mission; including the names and ages of the residents, their wives and children. Also an account of the number of animals and their kind, as distributed; with a note describing those to be held in common as sires of the different kinds, farming implements, forges, and tools for carpenter and cast work, and other things as received.

(1) Lara, Josef de, Spaniard,	50
Maria Antonio Campos, india Sabina,	23,
Josef Julian,	4,
Juana de Jesus,	6,
Maria Faustina,	2.
(2) Navarro, Josef Antonio, mestizo,	42,
Maria Rufina Dorotea, mulata,	47,
Josef Maria,	10,
Josef Clemente,	9,
Maria Josefa,	4.
(3) Rosas, Basillio, indian	67,
Maria Manuela Calixtra, mulata,	43,
Jose Maximo,	15,
Carlos,	12,
Antonio Rosalino,	7,
Josef Marcelino,	4,
Juan Esteban,	2,
Maria Josefa,	8.
(4) Mesa, Antonio, negro	38,
Ana Gertrudis Lopez, mulata,	27,
Antonio Maria,	8,
Maria Paula,	10.
(5) Villavicencio, Antonio, Spaniard,	30,
Maria de los Santos Seferina, indian,	26,
Maria Antonio Josefa,	8.
(6) Vanegas, Josef, indian	28,
Maria Maxima Aguilar, indian,	20,
Cosme Damien,	1.

David J. Weber, ed., *Foreigners in Their Native Land: Historical Roots of the Mexican Americans* (Albuquerque: University of New Mexico Press, 1973), 33–35.

(7) Rosas, Alejandro, indian	19,
Juana Rodriguez, coyote indian	20.
(8) Rodriguez, Pablo, indian,	25,
Maria Rosalia Noriega, indian,	26,
Maria Antonia,	1.
(9) Camero, Manuel, mulato,	30,
Maria Tomasa, mulata,	24.
(10) Quintero, Luis, negro,	55,
Maria Petra Rubio, mulata	40,
Josef Clemente,	3,
Maria Gertrudis,	16,
Maria Concepcion,	9,
Tomasa,	7,
Rafaela,	6.
(11) Moreno, Jose, mulato,	22,
Maria Guadalupe Gertrudis,	19.
(12) Rodriguez, Antonio Miranda, chino,	50,
Juana Maria,	11.

〜 ESSAYS

The first essay, by Daniel H. Usner Jr., professor of history at Vanderbilt University, explores the common world that Indians, Europeans, and Africans built along the lower Mississippi Valley in the eighteenth century. This flexible borderland, built around intercultural trade in basic necessities, was based on intimate face-to-face interactions that took precedence over the market-driven forces of the expanding transatlantic economy. In North America, the term frontier has traditionally been understood as an advancing edge of empires or states, as a line that separates one people, polity, or culture from another. Usner, however, places the frontier at the *center* of a regional world that followed its own rules and rhythm. Here the frontier connects. Wars, regime changes, and slavery stirred the eighteenth-century lower Mississippi Valley, but the frontier exchange economy endured, sometimes surreptitiously, sometimes in plain sight. Debilitating change came to this borderland late, and its collapse illuminates the conditions under which borderlands worlds flourish and fail. Usner emphasizes the roles of sugar and rice cultivation as key forces; why were they incompatible with the older frontier exchange economy? It is important to remember that crops and farms do not create and destroy social systems; human choices do.

Alta California, the subject of the second essay, was in many ways unique among Spain's imperial projects. Its colonization began late, in 1769, and it was pronouncedly a missionary endeavor at a time when the mission system was in steep decline throughout the Spanish Empire: the reform-minded Bourbon kings promoted military forts over missions and local economic development over prose-lytization, and by the mid-eighteenth century most missions had been turned into parishes. Yet, in Alta California, Spanish colonialism was anchored to missions, and its success hinged on Franciscan friars' ability to draw Indians in, convert them to Catholicism, and put them to work. To achieve this, Franciscans employed a variety of methods that ranged from persuasion to humiliation and violence, from reli-gious indoctrination to painstaking monitoring of neophyte behavior. Despite its breadth and force, the Franciscan program was far from an unqualified success for the Franciscans, for the Indian converts fought passionately and creatively to protect their privacy and practices within the missions. Rather than sites of one-way cultural engineering, California missions became sites of cross-cultural negoti-ation; they were contact zones where both Indians and Spaniards adapted their plans and actions to the demands and expectations of the other. Steven W. Hackel, professor of history at the University of California at Riverside, examines these mutual accommodations through the lens of Indian leadership in the mis-sions. Like colonists across the Americas, Franciscans tried to exert control over native societies by co-opting their leaders, only to learn time and again how the Indian elite continued to maneuver independently, using their strategic position to both implement and alleviate colonial control. Hackel also highlights a central thread in the history of Spanish California: the disputes between missionaries and secular leaders over the treatment of Indians. Hackel's essay can be compared with the Pueblo Revolt discussed in Chapter 2: How did the roles, objectives, and strategies of California and Pueblo Indian leaders differ from one another?

The Frontier Exchange Economy of the Lower Mississippi Valley

DANIEL H. USNER, JR.

It is an old fact and far from a new observation that the lower Mississippi Valley has been generally relegated to the margins of early American historiography. The re-gion has been borderland territory for historians as it once was for the English colo-nies of the Atlantic coast, and its people have been largely ignored or casually dismissed as mere bit-players in the drama of American development—colorful, no doubt, but peripheral and unimportant.... The lands along the Mississippi River have remained an amorphous area "dimly realizing westward" ... and waiting to be occupied by Anglo-Americans and their Afro-American slaves. This West, in a word, has been only dimly realized by historians as a place with a history of its own and a people whose tale is worth telling in its own right.

Even the most devoted historians of Louisiana are quick to point out that the colony in the Mississippi Valley constitutes "a study in failure" or "a holding action" in comparison with the English colonies along the Atlantic seaboard.

Daniel H. Usner, Jr., "The Frontier Exchange Economy of the Lower Mississippi Valley in the Eighteenth Century," *William and Mary Quarterly* 44 (April 1987): 166–192. Reprinted by permission.

Louisiana suffered from a low priority in the mercantile designs of both France and Spain. Immigration and population growth proceeded slowly, exportation of staple products to Europe fluctuated, and subsistence agriculture predominated over production of cash crops. But Louisiana's sparse populace and tentative transatlantic commerce can actually be used to the historian's advantage, allowing one to turn more attentively to dimensions of economic life that have been neglected in the lower Mississippi Valley as well as in other colonial regions of North America. Studies of economic change in North American colonies concentrated for a long time on linkages with home countries and with each other through the exportation of staple commodities. Historians are now turning to economic relationships that developed within regions, with greater attention to activities not totally dependent upon production for the Atlantic market.

Here I will examine the formation of a regional economy that connected Indian villagers across the lower Mississippi Valley with European settlers and African slaves along the Gulf Coast and lower banks of the Mississippi. The term *frontier exchange* is meant to capture the form and content of economic interactions among these groups, with a view to replacing the notion of frontier as an interracial boundary with that of a cross-cultural network. For this conceptualization of an interethnic web of economic relations I am indebted to anthropologists and historians who give as much emphasis to the prosaic features of livelihood as to the institutional structures of commerce. Small-scale, face-to-face marketing must be taken seriously, especially for understanding how peoples of different cultures related to and influenced each other in daily life.

A decade of immigration and slave trading to Louisiana, attended by death for hundreds of Europeans and Africans, resulted by 1732 in a population of only about 2,000 settlers and soldiers with some 3,800 slaves, at a time when the number of Indians of the lower Mississippi Valley, though rapidly declining from disease and war, was still in the range of 30,000. Large-scale immigration from Europe stopped by the mid-1720s, and only about 400 black slaves reached the colony between 1732 and the 1760. This slow growth of population—to approximately 5,000 slaves, 4,000 settlers, and 100 free people of color—meant minimal encroachment on Indian lands: most settlers and slaves lived along the Gulf Coast and the Mississippi River below its junction with the Red River. Trade relations with the Indians developed more freely because, for a time at least, the region's tribes were not markedly agitated by French pressure on their territory.

At first, given the scanty and erratic supply of trade goods from France, Louisiana officials relied on distribution of merchandise among Indian leaders in the form of annual gifts. In doing so, they accommodated by necessity to Indian protocols of trade and diplomacy. For the Indians, exchanges of material goods represented political reciprocity between autonomous groups, while absence of trade was synonymous with a state of war. Because commerce could not operate independently from ritual expressions of allegiance, such formal ceremonies as gift giving and smoking the calumet had to accompany economic transactions between Indians and Europeans. Conformity to these conventions recognized the leverage of such large tribes as the Choctaws and Caddoes on Louisiana's commerce and defense. They were essential to the initiation of the network of trade for deerskins and food—both items important to the success of Louisiana—against the threat of English competition from South Carolina and Georgia.

Demographic and geopolitical changes that began in the 1760s, however, portended greater challenges to the trade-alliance network. Immigration into the lower Mississippi Valley resumed after Great Britain drove French settlers from Nova Scotia in 1755. By 1767, seven years after Spain obtained Louisiana from France, more than a thousand of these Acadian refugees reached the colony, forming new settlements along the Mississippi about seventy miles above New Orleans and at Atakapas and Opelousas on Bayou Teche. From 1778 to 1780, two thousand "Islenos" migrated from the Canary Islands and established their own communities, along the Mississippi and Bayou Lafourche below New Orleans. In 1785 seven ships carried another 1,600 Acadians from France to Louisiana. Meanwhile Great Britain was accelerating colonization on the eastern side of the river, having acquired West Florida by the Treaty of Paris in 1763. Settlers from the Atlantic seaboard, many with slaves, increased the colonial population of West Florida to nearly 4,000 whites and 1,500 blacks by 1774. An even larger influx occurred after the outbreak of the American Revolution as loyalist refugees sought asylum in the Florida colony and settled mainly in the Natchez area. By 1783, when Spain gained sovereignty over West Florida and control over both sides of the Mississippi, the colonial population of the lower Mississippi Valley approached 16,000 Negro slaves, 13,000 whites, and over 1,000 free people of color.

By the 1780s, the Indian population in the region was, for the first time, becoming outnumbered by colonial inhabitants, while the colonial economy shifted toward greater dependence upon expanding commercial agriculture. Consequently, Louisiana officials exerted tighter political control over interethnic exchange in order to concentrate slave labor on cash crops and to reduce the mobility of Indian villagers. The frontier exchange economy did not fade from the lower Mississippi Valley, however, for efforts continued to be made into the nineteenth century by many old and new inhabitants to perpetuate small-scale trade across heightening racial divides.

Before 1783 the deerskin trade had encouraged widespread participation in a network of diffuse exchange from Indian villages to colonial port towns. Indian customs and French commercial weaknesses, … required a formal sphere of trade-alliance relations, but many people across the region also relied upon informal and intimate forms of cross-cultural trade.

Many settlers and even slaves exchanged something for deerskins once in a while, and innumerable colonists passed in and out of the deerskin trade as a temporary means of livelihood. Others made a lifetime occupation from seasonally trading imported merchandise for peltry and other native products.

After 1762 the number of traders operating in Indian villages increased with the growth of the colonial population, and their ethnic composition became more English. By the mid-1780s, Spanish officials estimated that five hundred traders, employees, and transients were living in and around Choctaw and Chickasaw towns, while nearly three hundred more operated in Creek towns. Considered "vagabonds and villains" by colonial administrators interested in orderly commerce, many of these men married Indian women and became affiliated with specific villages. The children born to this generation of traders and their Indian wives belonged to the clans of their mothers, and some became important tribal leaders by the beginning of the nineteenth century.

Most deerskin traders learned to speak the language of the tribe with whom they dealt.... Many traders probably spoke Mobilian, a trade language or lingua franca, instead of or in addition to distinct tribal languages: "when one knows it," noted Lt. Jean François Benjamin Dumont de Montigny, "one can travel through all this province without needing an interpreter." ... Mobilian was a convenient second language for many settlers and slaves as well as traders to use among Indians, and through the nineteenth century it continued to be spoken by Indians, Negroes, and whites in southern Louisiana and eastern Texas.

Deerskin traders and other peddlers played a dynamic role in the frontier exchange economy. While immediately helping distribute the produce of Indians, slaves, and settlers, they performed a long-term economic function. Indian hunters required an advance in goods before they pursued the winter season's thickly furred animals, forcing traders to wait until spring for their pay. In response to this seasonal pattern, traders acquired goods on credit from town merchants and obliged themselves to pay with interest within a year. By extending larger amounts of credit to more inhabitants of the area and by dealing more frequently in dry goods and export commodities, itinerant traders contributed to the commercialization of marketing in the lower Mississippi Valley.

The frontier exchange economy also involved trade in foodstuffs. Colonists in Louisiana, though ill supplied from home, were at first reluctant to labor to feed themselves by growing crops; fortunately for them, Indians were able to produce more than they needed for their own use. Thus there developed a lively trade, though one less visible to historians even than the diffuse trade in deerskins. While sailors and soldiers from France, with some Canadian coureurs de bois, were constructing the colony's first fort at Biloxi Bay, the Pascagoulas, Mobilians, and other coastal Indians eagerly swapped surpluses of corn, beans, and meat for axes, beads, and other useful items of European manufacture. During the first decade of the eighteenth century, colonial officials regularly sent parties up the Mobile and Mississippi rivers to purchase maize from Indians. In order to facilitate their trade with the French, some villages relocated closer to the coast and planted larger volumes of grain.

Many *habitants* of Louisiana preferred direct exchange with Indians for their subsistence, which proved easier than learning how to produce their own food from the soil and wildlife of an unfamiliar land. Trade with Indians for food also allowed a degree of freedom from the pressures inherent in colonial agriculture, causing alarm among colonial officials and merchants who hoped to build a colony that would export some profitable staple. [One] observer found in France's feeble commitment to colonizing the lower Mississippi Valley the reason why inhabitants had for two decades "done nothing else than try to get a little trading merchandise to obtain from the savages their sustenance, consisting of Indian corn, beans, pumpkins, or small round pumpkins, game and bear grease." The

Indian trade, by deflecting colonists from agriculture, thus helped frustrate early efforts to integrate the region into the world market for the benefit of both the colony and the mother country. What looked to officials like laziness was really a testimony to the vitality of the exchange economy.

Many of the several thousand African slaves shipped to Louisiana during the 1720s to expand commercial agriculture turned to small-scale cultivating and marketing of foodstuffs. As in other plantation colonies, the autonomous production and distribution of foodstuffs by slaves resulted from more than the economic interests of slaveowners. In addition to producing such export staples as tobacco, indigo, and timber, black Louisianians on both small and large grants of land, called *concessions,* grew food crops for their own consumption and occasionally for their owners to sell to other colonists. On their own time slaves attended to their personal subsistence needs and eating tastes.

Afro-Americans became aggressive traders in the food market of Louisiana. Many slaves were sent from plantations to the towns of Mobile, New Orleans, Natchez, and Natchitoches to sell poultry, meats, vegetables, and milk on their owners' behalf. They also sold foodstuffs and other items independently of their owners whenever and wherever possible. Although the colonial government intermittently enforced regulations upon slave peddlers, requiring them by 1751 to carry written permits from their owners, the open marketing of goods by slaves benefited too many people to be forcibly prohibited during the first half of the eighteenth century. The limited self-determination for slaves that stemmed from the production and trading of food had several advantages. It helped owners to maintain their slaves at a level of subsistence minimizing hardship, death, and rebellion; it provided consumers with a larger quantity and wider array of foods than would otherwise have been available; and it gained for slaves some means of autonomy from their masters. From these circumstances in the marketplace, not to mention those in colonial kitchens, came the heavy African influence upon Louisiana's famous creole cuisine.

The participation of Indian villagers, black slaves, and white colonists in fur and food marketing discloses closer interaction and greater cultural exchange among them than historians of colonial regions have generally portrayed. Clearly, Indians did not just hunt, blacks did not just grow crops for export, and whites did not merely choose to become either subsistence farmers or staple planters. However, a complex of forces circumscribed economic and ethnic relations and minimized the leveling potential of frontier exchange. The institution of slavery, European class divisions, racism, colonial policy, and violent conflict all contributed to the building of racial barriers in Louisiana and West Florida, especially after the demographic scale tipped unfavorably for Indians. The transformation of the lower Mississippi Valley into an agricultural export economy, which accelerated during the last quarter of the eighteenth century, further intensified the hierarchical stratification of both race and class.

Accelerated commercialization of the frontier exchange economy inexorably upset its traditional customs and patterns. Most notably, traders carried ever-larger quantities of rum into Indian villages, the distribution of gifts occurred less often, and the tribes fell into chronic debt to merchant houses and thereby became more vulnerable to pressure against their land.

By the end of the eighteenth century, the frontier exchange network was rapidly being superseded by the commercial production of cotton and sugar. Even so, people living in the region did not wholly relinquish older forms of economic exchange. Even after the large tribes of the deep South were removed, Indians continued to peddle foodstuffs and other goods along the Mississippi and in Mobile, Natchez, and New Orleans. Hundreds of Louisiana Indians—Choctaws, Houmas, Chitima-chas, Tunicas, and others—camped on the outskirts of New Orleans, usually during the late winter, and peddled in the city an array of foods and food-related items.

Afro-Americans resorted to surreptitious forms of exchange to compensate for their deteriorating trade opportunities. In violation of ordinances adopted in the early nineteenth century by the Orleans and Mississippi territories, many residents continued to exchange goods with slaves as well as Indians. Some of the very middlemen whose appearance marked the marginalization of slaves in the food market were willing to buy items from them. Peddlers called *caboteurs,* who traveled the waterways in pirogues and bought all kinds of produce for the New Orleans market, became infamous for their illicit trade with slaves. They were frequently accused of encouraging Negroes to steal from their owners, but pilferage by slaves had long been part of their resistance and survival under bondage.

Economic life in the lower Mississippi Valley during the eighteenth century, in which many later subsistence activities and adaptive strategies were rooted, evades historians who seek only strong commercial institutions and growing export values for their evidence. Within an extensive network of coastal towns and interior posts stretching from the Alabama River to the Red River, the region's inhabitants participated in a cross-cultural web of economic relations. When one follows the movement of deerskins and foodstuffs through this net-work, the importance of small-scale trade among diverse groups of people comes into focus. Louisiana was indeed an extraordinary North American colony, imposing even less demographic and commercial pressure upon the continent than did French Canada. But the backcountry of England's Atlantic seaboard provinces, as well as Canada and New Mexico, also passed through a long period of frontier exchange. The form and content of interethnic relations discussed here, and made more visible by Louisiana's history, can be profitably explored at the obscure crossroads and marketplaces of other colonial regions.

Surviving Mission Life in Alta California

STEVEN W. HACKEL

In 1769, Spain set out to defend the Pacific Coast against settlement by other European powers by developing a series of colonial outposts that eventually

Steven W. Hackel, "The Staff of Leadership: Indian Authority in the Missions of Alta California," *William and Mary Quarterly* 54 (April 1997): 347–376. Reprinted by permission.

stretched from San Diego to San Francisco. In this region, known to Europeans as Alta California, Spain depended on religious missions more than military fortifications or civilian towns to solidify its control. During the second half of the eighteenth century, missions had declined in importance in the rest of northern New Spain. In 1767, the crown expelled the Jesuits from Spain and its colonies and gradually converted most surviving missions in Arizona, New Mexico, and Texas to parishes overseen by secular priests. But in Alta California, Franciscan missions steadily increased in number and power as the most important centers of interaction between Indians and Spaniards. By 1821, when Spanish rule gave way to Mexican independence, roughly 70,000 Indians had been baptized in the region's twenty missions. Even after more than five decades of demographic disaster brought on by the ravages of disease, mission Indians still outnumbered Spanish settlers and soldiers 21,750 to 3,400; missions outnumbered military garrisons by a ratio of five to one and civilian settlements by six to one.

The Franciscans' strategies to convert and control Indians in Alta California have sparked an intense debate that has recently involved the general public as well as scholars. Public interest has focused on the canonization of Fray Junípero Serra, founding father of the California missions, and more generally of Indian-Spanish relations in those missions. Promoters of the Spanish colonial past portray the Franciscans as saving childlike Indians from savagism; detractors depict the missions as brutal labor camps, committed to cultural genocide. Although participants in this dispute have generated a considerable number of articles and books, the involvement of Indian leaders in the running of the California missions remains largely unexplored. Neither side has sufficiently examined the extent to which the missions depended on the persistence of Indian leadership, nor has either explored how Indian authority was created and legitimated within the missions.

Most Alta California missions counted between 500 and 1,000 Indian residents, two missionaries, and a military guard of four of five soldiers. Because their numbers were few and their resources limited, Spaniards looked to Indian leaders to help organize and regulate the missions' life and work. To this end, they instituted and directed annual elections in which the mission community chose its own officials, thereby enabling Spanish religious and military authorities to rule Indians through Indians. This system, though hierarchical in form, was flexible in operation. Indian officials not only served the needs of Spanish overlords, but they also protected the interests of the Indian community and, in some cases, ultimately rebelled against the Spanish order.

Recent studies of Indian communities in colonial America have noted the importance of Indian leaders and the challenges of their position. Colonists frequently tried to advance their objectives by co-opting Indian leaders, on whom they attempted to impose European forms of leadership. This practice involved a risk, for Indian leaders could subvert as well as implement colonial objectives. They, too, had much to gain though even more to lose in these encounters, for by participating in European systems of governance, they could foster or hinder their own autonomy as well as that of their communities. Indians, therefore, responded in a variety of ways to imposed forms of governance, and Europeans accommodated those forms to the communities they sought to control. These responses and accommodations are crucial to the ethnohistory of all of colonial America from the sixteenth century through the nineteenth, from New France to New England to New Spain.

In California, Spaniards encountered the most linguistically diverse and densely settled native population in all North America. Estimating that 310,000 Indians lived within the boundaries of the present state on the eve of Spanish colonization, scholars have classified these Indians into six culture areas and at least ninety distinct languages. Spanish settlement was concentrated in the coastal region between San Diego and San Francisco, where Indians probably numbered around 60,000 in 1769.

Despite this great linguistic and cultural diversity, Indians in Alta California pursued a common subsistence strategy. They were hunter-gatherers who used burning, irrigation, and pruning to maximize food sources. Women collected and processed the acorns, seeds, roots, and berries that constituted the mainstay of the diet; men fished and hunted game, birds, and sea mammals. Crafts were also divided by sex: women wove baskets, clothes, and household articles; men made tools and weapons.

Social organization in precontact California is poorly understood, but recent studies suggest that villages—the principal unit of organization—were stratified into a ruling elite, commoners, and an underclass. The elite was treated with respect, awe, and caution by commoners, who had no rank, and the underclass, who had no formal ties to an intact lineage. Social status was ascribed and authority was distributed hierarchically: elite males inherited political, religious, and economic power through their fathers' lines. Access to power and control of ritual knowledge distinguished the elite, who also wore the finest clothes, inhabited the largest houses, and avoided manual labor. The community owned the village land, but the elite determined its use. At the top of the village hierarchy stood a chief, who oversaw the production, allocation, and trade of the community's food and material goods. This was the complex and stratified Indian world Spain sought to control after 1769.

In California, soldiers and friars drew on policies, developed during the Reconquest of the Iberian peninsula and refined trough two and a half centuries of colonization in New Spain, that promoted the incorporation of frontier peoples and regions into the expanding Spanish realm. In the Reconquest, the *municipio* (township) emerged as the principal vehicle through which new territories were settled and secured, and in the New World it became the primary form of local political organization. In areas settled by Spain, formal attachment to a municipality was not an option but a legal requirement and one of the preconditions for a productive and civilized life.

To eighteenth-century Spaniards, the California Indians' small huts and scattered villages were a sure indication of a savage and undisciplined existence. Like their predecessors elsewhere in New Spain, the Franciscans took as their first goal the resettlement of Indians into compact villages. In Alta California, as in Baja California and Sonora, where Indian settlements were dispersed, missionaries combined coercion and incentives to create new, large, Indian communities.

Furthermore, disease reduced that Indian population, undercut the native economy, and prompted Indians to relocate to the missions. As a result, Indians from
different villages, who had had only occasional contact in trade or war, began to
live, work, and pray together.

Officials in New Spain used the Castilian *cabildo* (town council) as a model
for the political organization of these new Indian communities as well as of their
own. In Spain, most towns were governed by a council composed of six to
twelve *regidores* (councilmen). Regidores usually represented the economic interests of the most important families, and they served long tenures, sometimes for
life. Two *alcaldes* (judges) served ex officio on the town council, but unlike
regidores, who were their social superiors, they rotated off the cabildo after a
single year in office. A *corregidor,* a crown-appointed outsider who represented
both the town and the central government, presided over the cabildo. True to
this model, most Spanish towns in the Americas were administered by a cabildo
composed of four to eight regidores, two elected alcaldes, and various minor
officials, all governing in concert with an *adelantado* or a governor. These New
World cabildos, whose members were usually *encomenderos* or Spaniards with
aristocratic pretensions, had authority over the basics of urban life: they drafted
ordinances, punished wrongdoing, and regulated the local economy.

As conquered peoples, Indians rarely served on Spanish cabildos, but they
retained a measure of control over their communities through annually elected
cabildos of their own. Known collectively as the "Republic of Indians," these
councils by the late seventeenth century were regulated by the *Recopilación de
leyes de los reynos de las Indias,* which prescribed the frequency of elections and
the number of officials. Most Indian cabildos in New Spain were composed of
a governor, several regidores and alcaldes, and various lesser officials, in numbers
proportional to the population of the settlement.

In establishing Indian cabildos in New Spain, Spaniards accommodated and
to a certain extent institutionalized Indian forms of social and political organization. In central Mexico, newly appointed Indian governors continued the roles
of preconquest dynastic rules: they had judicial and financial responsibilities and
oversaw the use of land.

In addition to the governor, alcaldes, and regidores, most Indian cabildos had
a religious official known as a *fiscal.* Because there were so few missionaries in New
Spain, *fiscales* frequently held wide-ranging responsibilities. Elected or appointed
annually, they managed local church finances, rang bells for mass, and gathered
parishioners for religious celebrations. At a minimum, fiscales were "church constables" who punished villagers for violating Catholic teachings, but usually they
were full members of the cabildo; most had previously served as regidores or
alcaldes. All together, the officials of the cabildo formed an elite that controlled
many of the most important aspects of Indian community life in New Spain.

As the seventeenth century drew to a close, Spanish settlement in northern
New Spain took different forms than in central Mexico. *Presidios* (military garrisons) and missions became the primary means for extending Spanish control into
the region and for protecting the silver mines and the roads linking them to central Mexico.

As governor of Alta California, [Felipe de] Neve implemented the national policy of assimilating Indians into the conquerors' political system. In Neve's words: "With the elections and the appointment of a new Republic, the will of His Majesty will be fulfilled in this region, and under our direction, in the course of time, He will obtain in these Indians useful vassals for our religion and state." Neve and his successors believed that extending to Indians the rudiments of Spanish municipal government would teach them a civics lesson that was at least equal in importance to the Franciscans' catechism.

The governor's inclusive political vision was challenged by the Franciscans' restrictive religious agenda. The friars wanted absolute control over the missions and the Indians who lived in them, and they believed that Indians so recently subjugated to the church and the crown could not possibly be ready for a measure of self-government, no matter how elementary its form. Moreover, they did not want the Indians to understand that the Spanish governor had civil and judicial authority over Indians, and the Franciscans feared that Indian officials would use their status to pursue their own goals. The Franciscans formally based their opposition to Indian elections on a legal technicality. The *Recopilación* specified that in each Indian town and *reducción* Indians were to elect officials and that *curas* (local priests) should supervise these elections. The Franciscans argued that they themselves were apostolic missionaries, not parish priests; therefore, the *Recopilación* did not apply, and the governor's order had no foundation in law.

At San Diego, where in 1775 the Tipai and Ipai had signaled their rejection of Spanish authority by destroying the mission and killing one Franciscan and two Spaniards, the governor's insistence in 1779 on elections in the rebuilt mission prompted the Franciscans to threaten resignation. Fray Junípero Serra called on the governor to suspend the elections in all the designated missions. The conflict came to a climax just before mass on Palm Sunday in 1779 when Governor Neve and Father Serra exchanged bitter words. Later that evening, overcome with agitation and unable to rest, Serra cried out: "¿Qué es esto Señor?" ("What is the meaning of it, Lord?") Serra was calmed by a voice from within that repeated one of Christ's admonitions to the Apostles: "Be prudent as serpents and simple as doves." Reassured, Serra decided to go along with the governor's orders but only in ways that would not "cause the least change among the Indians or in the mode of governing" that the Franciscans had established. Serra believed that, with God's help, he could join the simplicity of the dove with the cunning of the serpent and thus outmaneuver the governor and prevent the elections from decreasing Franciscan authority. After the early 1780s, elections of Indian officials usually occurred annually in the largest and oldest missions.

As Serra intended, the Franciscans quickly gained a large degree of control over the elections. Even though Neve sought to extend the crown's power into the missions, the Franciscans convinced him that only with their guidance would Indians and Spaniards profit from the elections. At several of the missions, according to Serra, Indian officials had committed crimes or behaved arrogantly, as if they were "gentlemen." By January 1780, when the second annual elections were to take place, several of the officials had abandoned their missions, while others were too ill to vote. Consistent with Spanish law, Neve specified that only former Indian officials could vote, but he increased the missionaries' role in the elections, telling them to supply "direction" when necessary. The Franciscans usually supplied direction by controlling the nomination of candidates.

By narrowing the field of candidates, the Franciscans guaranteed the election of men whom they expected to facilitate their control of the mission.

In addition to securing for the missionaries a large measure of control over the elections, Serra tried to prevent Indian officials from learning that the military constituted a powerful secular counterpart to Franciscan authority. Serra instructed his trusted subordinate at San Diego, Fray Fermín Francisco de Lasuén, to speak to the presidio officer whose responsibility it was to confirm the Indians in office: "Ask him to carry out this function so that, without failing in the slightest degree in his duty toward his superior officer, the Indians may not be given a less exalted opinion of the fathers than they have had until now." Furthermore, Serra preferred that the Indian officials remain ignorant of the responsibilities with which the military charged them. "The document that is used in conferring these offices on them," Serra advised Lasuén, "may be as powerful as they wish, provided Your Reverences are the only ones to receive it and read it." Even after these precautions, the Franciscans resisted sending newly elected Indians to the presidios for installation. An inquiry in the mid-1790s by Governor Diego de Borica revealed that none of the current presidio commanders had ever been called on to give Indians their oaths of office.

The Indian cabildos elected in the California missions—like those in the missions of Sonora, Texas, and New Mexico—had fewer officials, smaller responsibilities, and less autonomy than those in the Indian *pueblos* and parishes of central Mexico at the same time. Rarely did a California mission have more than two alcaldes and two regidores. Nor was an Indian governor appointed. Throughout the missions of northern New Spain, the duties of ecclesiastical and civil Indian officials overlapped, but in Alta California, perhaps to a greater extent than elsewhere in the Spanish borderlands, Indian alcaldes and regidores served as assistants to the missionaries, much like the fiscales of central Mexico.

The subordination of Indian officials to the Franciscans was noted in 1787 by Governor [Pedro] Fages: "Although these authorities are granted some powers, they are necessarily dependednt on the missionaries, without whose direction they would not be able to exercise them." Franciscans treated Indian officials with the same heavy-handed paternalism that characterized all their interactions with Indians. Officials were subject to corporal punishment at Franciscan hands, and they were not permitted to bring charges against the missionaries. This disability set them apart from their counterparts in central Mexico, who frequently used legal channels to claim that their curates manipulated elections, misappropriated communal funds, and imposed excessive labor demands. In New Spain, to be left without the right to seek protection or redress through the law rendered one virtually defenseless.

Under Franciscan supervision, Indian officials in California nevertheless had wide-ranging authority over other mission Indians. According to the *Recopilación,* they were charged with ensuring that Indians attended mass and remained sober. They were to "keep guard" around the mission village at night and to "lead the people to prayer and to work."

The Franciscans, emphasizing religious indoctrination, used catechisms to ready Indians for baptism and confessional manuals to prepare them for penance and communion. Whether Indian officials helped translate these handbooks into local languages is not clear, but the records show that they were among the few Indians who participated in the sacraments of baptism and marriage as godparents and witnesses. On these occasions, the Franciscans relied on Indian officials to translate Catholic rites into terms that were comprehensible to their people. We do not know the content of these unrecorded translations, but in trying to explain Catholic rituals, officials may well have invoked concepts that gave the rituals an Indian meaning.

Never content simply to instruct Indians, the Franciscans tried to control their lives, especially their sexual behavior. To that end, most missions had single-sex dormitories for the unmarried, and Indian officials were charged with keeping unmarried men and women from having illicit contact. In 1797, Mission Santa Cruz even had one alcalde for men and another for women. In this area of responsibility, many alcaldes showed more regard for the desires of other Indians than for the demands of the Franciscans. In 1821, Modesto, an alcalde at Mission San Juan Bautista, took advantage of the illness of one of the friars and "delivered" the single women to the men. He was quickly suspended from office and replaced by Francisco Sevilla, a former alcalde who had "taken good care of the single women."

Franciscans also attempted to remake the Indians' daily routines, primarily through a rigid labor regime; here, too, Indian officials often played a crucial role. [Pablo] Tac recounted how alcaldes circulated through the villages telling people when and where to report for work: "Tomorrow the sowing begins and so the laborers go to the chicken yard and assemble there." When their calls went unheeded, officials punished those who they or the Franciscans believed were shirking. In 1797, Claudio, an Indian baptized at Mission san Francisco who later absconded, declared that one of the reasons he had run away was that the alcalde Valeriano "made him go to work" when he was sick. Homobono, who also fled, declared that Valeriano "hit him with a heavy cane for having gone to look for mussels at the beach," an outing that most likely took him away from his work at the mission. Not all Indian officials could be counted on to enforce the Franciscans' labor regime. In 1814, the *padres* at Mission San Francisco lamented that, when they asked the alcaldes to supervise work in and around the mission, "not infrequently the alcaldes and the men spend their time in play and remain away [from the mission] for another day despite the fact that their task is an urgent one."

Franciscans also looked to Indian officials to administer a share of the corporal punishment they considered necessary for the Indians' souls. Foreign visitors and Anglo-American immigrants emphasized that Indians "did a great deal of chastisement, both by and without [Franciscan] orders." However severe, corporal punishments by Indian officials did not take the place of beatings dealt directly by the Franciscans. Viewing themselves as the spiritual fathers of the Indians, Franciscans maintained that it was their responsibility to chastise them; they flogged Indians for repeatedly running away, for practicing native religious beliefs, and for performing a host of other acts considered disrespectful or sinful.

When Indians remained incorrigible after several floggings, the friars sent them to the presidio for more beatings and hard labor.

In addition to being the intelligible voice and strong arm of the Franciscans, Indian officials were meant to be the military's eyes and ears at the missions. Military officials expected Indian alcaldes to investigate and report crimes that occurred at the missions. When a man at Mission San Juan Capistrano killed his wife, it was Bruno, the mission alcalde, who heard the murderer's first admission of guilt and carried the news to Spanish officials. Indian officials, however, rarely cooperated as readily as Bruno; in fact, alcaldes exposed very few of the crimes committed at the missions. In 1808, after several Indians at Mission San José brawled and fled the mission, an alcalde failed to notify the Spanish authorities, a dereliction of duty that led the governor to brand him a criminal accomplice. More often than not, when Indian officials were called on to explain murders or robberies at their missions, their testimony proved unremarkable, merely echoing accounts offered by others.

Some actions of Indian officials, such as administering punishment, may have had no precedent in pre-mission village leadership, but many of their duties and responsibilities resembled those of earlier native leaders. Village leaders oversaw the production of the community's food while remaining exempt from basic manual labor; similarly, alcaldes participated in the productive life of the mission as coordinators, not laborers. Village captains made crucial decisions concerning the distribution of food; alcaldes, too, decided how to allocate the mission's food resources.

The alcaldes' perquisites of office resembled the advantages that had distinguished village captains from the rest of the Indian community. The elite had constituted a self-perpetuating oligarchy; similarly, in the early years of the elections, only Indian officials cast votes for their successors. Village captains, like Indian officials, were supported by the labor of the community. Both sets of leaders wore distinctive clothing and lived in special houses. And according to Julio César, an Indian baptized at Mission San Luis Rey, alcaldes were among the few Indians allowed to ride horseback, a privileged act in Spanish California. Despite these advantages, Indian officials—like village captains—enjoyed only a slight material advantage over their people, and that advantage was never secure, dependent as all Indians were on a fragile mission economy.

As intermediaries between cultures, Indian officials were often caught between the conflicting demands of the Indian community and the Franciscans. Indians such as Homobono and Claudio at San Francisco—and surely others who do not appear in the historical record—resisted the labor regime the alcaldes reinforced and so resented the alcaldes' use of their authority that they left the missions. Conversely, officials' conformity to Indian expectations often invited Franciscan condemnation. Baltazar, one of the first alcaldes at San Carlos Borromeo, ran afoul of Serra when he fathered a child by his wife's sister. Serra's god demanded that his people be monogamous, whereas Indians expected their leaders to be polygamous. The Indian community probably saw Baltazar's sororal polygyny as an emblem of his status; the Franciscans considered it proof of his depravity. They hounded him out of the mission, branded him a deserter, and tried to sever his connection to his people. Serra then accused Baltazar of "sending messages to the people here, meeting personally with those who leave here with permission, and thereby trying to swell the numbers of his band from the mountains by new desertions of the natives of this mission."

Resistance by some alcaldes, such as Modesto and Baltazar, to Franciscan notions of marriage and sexuality and acquiescence by others, such as Francisco Sevilla and Valeriano, to their directives suggest the ambiguities of the alcalde's role and rule. Even though their behavior at times appeared unpredictable—even unacceptable—to Indians or Spaniards, Indian officials occupied a privileged space in the Spanish system as interpreters, mediators, and enforcers of the new colonial order. The influence of Indian officials within the Indian community, however, depended not only on the authority Spaniards invested in them but also on the legitimacy these men brought to their leadership positions. Based on kinship and lineage networks, this legitimacy, in turn, helps explain the ability of Spanish officials to orchestrate social, religious, economic, and political change within native communities and the ability of native officials on occasion to keep such initiatives at bay.

The historical record speaks far more directly about what Indian officials did than about who they were—an imbalance that is mirrored in the scholarship. Fortunately, records created by colonial administrators allow investigation of the place of Indian leaders in the complex web of kinship and lineage that defined the Indian community. Franciscans notified presidio commanders of election results and occasionally mentioned Indian officials in baptismal, marriage, and burial records. By combining these reports—fragmentary as they are—with information on family relations, village affiliations, and vital statistics contained in sacramental registers, we can sketch a composite portrait of the mission staff of leadership.

Mission San Carlos Borromeo presents the most complete materials for a case study. Its sacramental registers are intact and thorough, and more reports of its annual elections have survived than for any other California mission. Established in June 1770 as the second mission in Alta California and the first on the central coast, San Carlos Borromeo served as the early residence of the father president, who set policy for the region. Located about three miles from the Monterey presidio, the headquarters of the region's governor, Mission San Carlos was overseen by Franciscans until its secularization by the Mexican government in 1834. The record keeping of the Franciscans and the efficiency of the microcomputer enable one to identify and situate within the native community forty-six alcaldes and regidores who served at San Carlos Borromeo from 1779 to 1831, probably about half the officials during those five decades. References by Franciscans at San Carlos Borromeo to fiscales cease at roughly the same time that elections for alcaldes and regidores begin. The Franciscans may have continued to appoint fiscales, but in all likelihood they relied on alcaldes and regidores instead.

Typically diverse, the Indian community at the mission comprised Indians from the Costanoan and Esselen linguistic families who came from at least ten different villages. At the time the mission was founded, the population of the Monterey region seems to have numbered around 2,800. In almost every year, because disease was endemic, the Franciscans recorded more burials than births; only the baptisms of Indians from the surrounding area allowed the mission's population to reach a peak of around 875 in the mid-1790s. The mission population subsequently declined, and after 1808, when the friars recorded the baptisms of the last Indians they recruited from the surrounding area, went into free fall. Disease continued to take a heavy toll, and by 1825, the mission had only about 300 Indians.

At San Carlos Borromeo, Indian officials were always baptized men who were married or widowed. They were usually older and had been baptized earlier than other men from their villages. Thirteen out of fourteen, for example, who served during the period 1779–1798 fit this pattern. Of those who served in 1792, Hilario José was one of the first adult Esselen men baptized, Atanasio José was older and had been in the mission longer than most Costanoan men, and Sancio Francisco and Nicomedes were older than most of the men from their communities.

During the mission's early recruiting years, Indian officials were likely to have been village captains or their close associates. For example, the sacramental registers identify Sancio Francisco and Abrahan—officials in the 1790s—as former village leaders. The baptismal record of Nicomedes, also an official in the 1790s, describes him as the "principal confidant" of the village captain Aristeo José. Later, the mission community tended to produce its own leadership. After the early 1790s, fewer captains came to the mission; those who did were not elected to leadership positions. As the mission population matured, it developed a cadre of men who spoke Spanish and were familiar with the Franciscan regime—qualifications that supplanted previous experience as village captains.

In native California, political leadership customarily descended from father to son. This practice carried over to San Carlos Borromeo, although it was disrupted by persistently high mortality. Of the thirty-seven baptized sons of village captains identified in the mission's records, only eight lived to their mid-thirties. Four of these gained positions of responsibility, three as officials, one as an interpreter. The high death rate among the young made it very hard for elite families to maintain a direct line of influence. Yet the son of a village leader who lived to adulthood had a far better chance of becoming a mission official than others his age. Officials who did not have blood ties to former village captains were frequently related to other leading Indians: two were the sons of officials, three pairs were brothers, ten pairs were brothers-in-law, and eleven officials had close ties to mission interpreters. In addition, many alcaldes were related by marriage to soldiers. For example, Atanasio José, an alcalde for many years, had a daughter whose first and second husbands were soldiers at the Monterey presidio. Other officials were related to privileged Indians from Baja California who worked closely with the Franciscans during the first years of the mission. Extended leadership families such as these suggest that in the face of high death rates, marriage provided a means for surviving members of powerful Indian families to maintain leadership status in the mission.

Spanish laws regulating cabildos promoted turnover in officeholding, but at San Carlos Borromeo, as elsewhere in New Spain, these laws proved ineffective, because they conflicted with the native practice of long-term rule and the Spanish desire to support cooperative local leaders. A common strategy to assure continuity of leadership was to rotate alcaldes and regidores in office each year. At Mission San Carlos, Oresio Antonio was regidor in 1810, 1812, and 1814 and alcalde in 1811, 1813, and 1815. Other officials sat out a year or two and then returned to office. As the rotational system suggests, differences between the responsibilities of alcaldes and of regidores faded over time. Important and cooperative Indians, provided they could stay alive, were thus never far from office; some served continuously for up to six years, and others rotated in and out over more than fifteen years.

Indian officials reflected the ethnic and linguistic diversity of the mission community, as the mission's two language families and four largest village groups could each frequently claim one of the officials. After 1776, when Esselen villagers first came to the mission, San Carlos was composed of both Costanoan- and Esselen-speakers, the former enjoying numerical superiority over the latter throughout the mission's life. The Franciscans carefully noted the village affiliation of all Indians at baptism and monitored the changing composition of the population. If late eighteenth-century guidelines for the Franciscan missionaries at Mission Nuestra Señora de la Purísima Concepción in San Antonio, Texas, are typical of Franciscan electoral management in northern New Spain—and there is no reason to suppose otherwise—the Franciscans at San Carlos Borromeo worked hard to ensure that officials were drawn from the mission's largest groups. The San Antonio instructions, probably written in 1787 or 1788 by Fray José García, urged the missionaries to "remind" voters that the positions of governor and alcalde alternated annually between the most populous groups at the mission, the Pajalache and the Tacame. This correlation between the ethnic and linguistic composition of officials and that of the mission population reflected the needs of Spaniards and Indians alike. Franciscans and governors would have found it difficult to incorporate and control the Indians without assistance from native leaders who could effectively communicate with the mission's most populous groups, and powerful Indian groups might have rebelled had they been excluded from positions of authority.

Not until 1810, when twenty-six-year-old Teopisto José became regidor did a mission-born Indian serve as an official at San Carlos Borromeo. The policy of drawing the officials from the mission's different village and linguistic groups helps to explain why so few—only seven—were born in the mission. Indian officials were usually in their late twenties or early thirties when first elected. Thus Indians born in the 1770s at the mission could not have served until the mid-1790s, and yet they did not dominate the leadership positions when they reached maturity. Rather, the representation of different village groups, some of which did not come to the mission until the mid-1780s, took precedence over the selection of the individuals who, having spent their entire lives in the mission, might have been the most acculturated to Spanish ways and loyal to Franciscan wishes. Even after 1810, Indians born at the mission filled only one quarter of the leadership positions; those baptized before age ten took only slightly more than half.

To most Indians in Alta California, Spaniards brought disease, cultural dislocation, and an early grave; to some, they also provided political opportunity. The prominence of individuals like Baltazar, and the coherence of the groups they led suggest that the political system the Spaniards relied on to control the missions—and the Indians' ability to shape that system to their needs—fostered the preservation and creation of Indian authority. Indians who held legitimate authority among their people frequently served as officials, and the composition of the Indian cabildos reflected the divisions of village groups in the missions. When officials did not reflect the community, disgruntled or excluded Indians sought redress from Spanish authorities. When Indian officials contradicted or challenged Spanish authorities, they courted dismissal. Still, it was never in the interest of Spaniards to replace uncooperative officials with Indians whose legitimacy was not recognized by their own people. Nor was it in their interest to level the distinctions of rank among Indians. To have done so would have provoked opposition from the Indians who could most effectively assist in controlling the missions.

Doubtless, there were Indian officials in the missions of Alta California whose malleability rather than their kinship or lineage recommended them to the Franciscans. But for the most part the alcalde system depended on the extent to which native villages, leadership, and traditions were incorporated into the missions. The authority of Indian officials in colonial California originated from more than brute force, Franciscan missionaries, or the Spanish state. It was carried over from native villages, legitimated and re-created in annual mission elections, and ultimately strengthened by the extent to which the staff of Indian leadership remained embedded in a network of shifting family relations that defined Indian communities throughout the colonial period.

FURTHER READING

Aron, Stephen. *How the West Was Lost: The Transformation of Kentucky from Daniel Boone to Henry Clay* (1996).

————. *American Confluence: The Missouri Frontier from Borderland to Border State* (2006).

Bolton, Herbert E. "The Mission as a Frontier Institution in the Spanish American Colonies," [1917]. In *Bolton and the Spanish Borderlands*, ed. John F. Bannon, 187–211 (1964).

Brooks, James F. *Captives and Cousins: Slavery, Kinship, and Community in the Southwest Borderlands* (2002).

Calloway, Colin G. *The American Revolution in Indian Country: Crisis and Diversity in Native American Communities* (1995).

Cumfer, Cynthia. *Separate Peoples, One Land: The Minds of Cherokees, Blacks, and Whites on the Tennessee Frontier* (2007).

Edmunds, R. David. *The Shawnee Prophet* (1983).

Ethridge, Robbie. *Creek Country: The Creek Indians and Their World* (2003).

Frank, Ross. *From Settler to Citizen: New Mexican Economic Development and the Creation of Vecino Society, 1750–1820* (2000).

Giltlin, Jay. *The Bourgeois Frontier: French Towns, French Traders, and American Expansion* (2009).

Griffin, Patrick. *American Leviathan: Empire, Nation, and Revolutionary Frontier* (2007).

Gutiérrez, Ramón A., and Richard J. Orsi, ed. *Contested Eden: California before the Gold Rush* (1998).

Hackel, Steven W. *Children of Coyote, Missionaries of Saint Francis: Indian-Spanish Relations in Colonial California, 1769–1850* (2005).

Hahn, Steven C. *The Invention of the Creek Nation, 1670–1763* (2004).

Holland Braund, Kathryn E. *Deerskins and Duffels: Creek Indian Trade with Anglo-America, 1685–1815* (1993).

Hoxie, Frederick E. *Parading Through History: The Making of the Crow Nation in America* (1995).

Hoxie, Frederick E., Ronald Hoffman, and Peter J. Albert, eds. *Native Americans and the Early Republic* (1999).

Hu-DeHart, Evelyn. *Yaqui Resistance and Survival: Struggle for Land and Autonomy, 1821–1910* (1984).

Hudson, Angela Pulley. *Creek Paths and Federal Roads: Indians, Settlers, and Slaves and the Making of the American South* (2010).

Hurtado, Albert L. *Indian Survival on the California Frontier* (1988).

Jones, Oakah L. Jr. *Los Paisanos: Spanish Settlers on the Northern Frontier of New Spain* (1979).

———. "Rescue and Ransom of Spanish Captives from the *indios bárbaros* on the Northern Frontier of New Spain." *Colonial Latin American Historical Review* 4 (Spring 1995): 129–148.

Loomis, Noel M., and Abraham P. Nasatir. *Pedro Vial and the Roads to Santa Fe* (1967).

Magnaghi, Russell M. "Plains Indians in New Mexico: The Genízaro Experience." *Great Plains Quarterly* 10 (Spring 1990): 86–95.

Mapp, Paul W. *The Elusive West and the Contest for Empire, 1713–1763* (2011).

Marez, Curtis. "Signifying Spain, Becoming Comanche, Making Mexicans: Indian Captivity and the History of Chicana/o Performance." *American Quarterly* 53 (June 2001): 267–307.

Miles, Tiya. *Ties That Bind: The Story of an Afro-Cherokee Family in Slavery and Freedom* (2005).

Mooney, James. *Calendar History of the Kiowa Indians* (1898; reprint, 1979).

Moorhead, Max L. *New Mexico's Royal Road: Trade and Travel on the Chihuahua Trail* (1958).

———. *The Apache Frontier: Jacobo Ugarte and Spanish-Indian Relations in Northern New Spain, 1769–1791* (1968).

Piker, Joshua. *Okfuskee: A Creek Indian Town in Colonial America* (2004).

Poyo, Gerald E., and Gilberto M. Hinojosa, eds. *Tejano Origins in Eighteenth-Century San Antonio* (1991).

Sandos, James A. *Converting California: Indians and Franciscans in the Missions* (2004).

Santiago, Mark. *Massacre at Yuma Crossing: Spanish Relations with the Quechans, 1779–1782* (1998).

Saunt, Claudio. *A New Order of Things: Property, Power, and the Transformation of the Creek Indians, 1733–1816* (1999).

Silver, Peter. *Our Savage Neighbors: How Indian War Transformed Early America* (2007).

Smith, F. Todd. *From Dominance to Disappearance: The Indians of Texas and the Near Southwest, 1786–1859* (2005).

Taylor, Alan. *The Civil War of 1812: American Citizens, British Subjects, Irish Rebels, and Indian Allies* (2010).

———. *The Divided Ground: Indians, Settlers, and the Northern Borderland of the American Revolution* (2006).

———. *William Cooper's Town: Power and Persuasion on the Frontier of the Early American Republic* (1995).

Teja, Jesús F. de la, and Ross Frank, eds. *Choice, Persuasion, and Coercion: Social Control on Spain's North American Frontiers* (2005).

Usner, Daniel H. Jr. *Indians, Settlers, and Slaves in a Frontier Exchange Economy: The Lower Mississippi Valley before 1783* (1992).

CHAPTER 7

∿

The Mexican North

In 1821, the three-centuries-old Spanish Empire collapsed, and Mexico became an independent republic. Mexico City set out to turn its slice of the empire into a national domain, and gradually the Spanish borderlands became the Mexican borderlands. There were fundamental continuities from the Spanish into the Mexican era. The Mexican North attracted few immigrants, and the old families continued to inhabit the borderlands. Mestizaje still conditioned social life. But there were also ruptures and new beginnings. Less concerned about foreign infiltration than the Spanish Crown, the Mexican government opened borders to U.S. merchants. Where the Spanish crown had expressed growing interest in developing the far northern borderlands, the Mexican government, beleaguered by fiscal crisis and political instability, often neglected the borderlands. Ignored by Mexico City, borderlanders took matters in their own hands, fashioning practices and policies that were not necessarily in line with Mexico City's expectations.

Whereas Mexico struggled to bring its northern borderlands into the national fold, the United States, bolstered by propitious land acquisitions and a booming economy, extended its reach deep into the Southwest, where it collided with Mexico's nation-building project and still powerful native societies. The history of the Southwest is generally divided into Mexican and American periods, starting in 1821 and 1848, respectively, but such neat divides do not always match the reality on the ground. Mexican and American eras blended into one another, and both were marked by indigenous power, giving rise to a borderlands history that pulled simultaneously in several directions. That the United States would absorb the Southwest seems inevitable only in hindsight; few contemporaries expected such an outcome in 1821. The Mexican government opened Texas to U.S. immigrants in 1825 with the expectation that they would become loyal Mexican subjects, and, for a while, the newcomers seemed to be doing just that. The majority of Americans in the East considered the acquisition of northern Mexico too ambitious and risky, fearing that their fragile republic would dissolve in an enlarged form. This concern did not start to recede until the 1840s, when Manifest Destiny, a belief that the United States was preordained to spread democracy across the continent, galvanized the nation.

This chapter explores how the collision of the native peoples, Mexicans, and Anglo-Americans in the Southwest borderlands played out on several levels: sovereignty and loyalty, nation-building and cross-cultural alliances, sex and intermarriage, and capitalist expansion and identity formation. The Mexican North did not survive the collision, but the Mexican borderlands era should not be dismissed as just a transitional episode, a passage to U.S. dominance. Many developments of the turbulent era—the secularization of the California missions, the ascent of Spanish-speaking californios, the proletarianization of Texas Mexicans, the localization of politics, the Anglo-American recasting of Mexicans as racial inferiors—continued to shape the borderlands long after the Mexican flag had been lowered.

∿ DOCUMENTS

Anglo-Americans began moving to Texas immediately after Mexico's independence, and, in 1825, Coahuila and Texas—the two provinces had been joined together a year before—passed a colonization law that allowed foreigners to obtain land in the state. Yet, Mexican officials soon grew anxious over Anglo-American influence in Texas. Led by empresarios—immigration agents who recruited settlers, allocated lands, and maintained order—Anglo colonists arrived in thousands, building distinct and seemingly inassimilable colonies. In 1828, the Mexican government sent General Manuel Mier y Terán to lead a special commission to inspect conditions in East Texas, where most Anglo newcomers lived. The first document is from the journal of José María Sánchez, a member of the Terán expedition, which reveals a diminishing Mexican influence in the region. Sánchez was struck by the cultural differences between Tejanos (Mexican Texans) and Anglo Americans, and he was skeptical of the prospects of mutual accommodation. He criticized Tejanos for their failure to contain Anglo influence and deplored their character, revealing a cultural chasm between Mexico's core region and its borderlands, but he also identified historical and structural factors that made the task of curbing Anglo-American power almost impossible. The findings of the Terán expedition became the basis of the law of April 6, 1830, which was intended to close Texas to further U.S. immigration but largely remained a dead letter. The second document is the petition sent by San Antonio's prominent Tejanos to the legislature of Coahuila and Texas, which identified a series of problems in Texas and criticized the state government for inadequate support. The petition reveals how local Tejano leaders viewed Anglo-American immigration and how their views differed from those of outsiders like Sánchez. Document 3, an extract of proposals that Donaciano Vigil, one of New Mexico's leading citizens, delivered to the New Mexico Assembly in 1846, provides a critical view of the U.S. commercial expansion into the Mexican borderlands that had begun in 1821 with the opening of the Santa Fe trade. Vigil deplores how the arrival of Anglo Americans changed relations between New Mexico and Indians and regrets the central government's failure to support New Mexico.

U.S. immigrants and markets were not the only foreign challenge Mexican authorities faced in the far North. Distracted by internal political instability, Mexican authorities failed to maintain the Indian alliance network they inherited from Spain, and, by the 1830s, independent Indians were raiding across Mexico's northern borderlands from California to Texas. A new war zone emerged in

New Mexico's western borderlands, where the Navajos began intensive raiding in the mid-1830s, in part in retaliation for New Mexican slave raids and in part as a response for the cessation of gift distributions. Navajos had adopted Spanish horses, cattle, and sheep in the seventeenth century, and, by the eighteenth century, they lived by a dual economy of farming and animal herding that supported some seven thousand people in the foothills and canyonlands west of New Mexico. In Document 4, written in 1837, Albino Chacón, a member of Governor Albino Pérez's administration, describes the effects of Navajo raiding in New Mexico and reports on Pérez's ill-fated expedition into Navajo territory. Chacón also discusses the factors that made New Mexico so vulnerable to Navajo attacks.

The devastation that Navajo raiding caused in New Mexico—and Mexican authorities' failure to suppress it—formed an undercurrent of fear and discontent that erupted in a popular uprising, the Chimayó Rebellion, in 1837. In 1835, political power in Mexico City moved from liberal federalists to conservative centralists, who imposed a new national charter known as *Las Siete Leyes* ("seven laws"), or Departmental Plan. The plan aimed to reduce the autonomy of the states, introduce direct national taxation, and impose nationwide religious reforms, and it sparked an armed rebellion in Texas and then in New Mexico, which until then had been exempted from national taxes. A coalition of thousands of poor *vecinos* (citizens), mestizos, and Pueblo Indians rose against Governor Pérez, beheaded him, and placed José González, a mixed-blood bison hunter and militia captain, in his stead. The rebels, headed by a war council known as *Cantón de la Cañada*, took hold of northern New Mexico and, on August 3, the cantón issued a proclamation of five objectives, reproduced here as Document 5. A coalition of conservative New Mexicans led by Manuel Armijo, ex-governor of New Mexico, staged a counterattack that suppressed the revolt by January 1838. Document 6 is a report written by Armijo on October 11, 1837, when the rebels had agreed to a treaty in Tomé pueblo (the revolt flared up again soon after). Armijo's description suggests how the Chimayó Rebellion had taken on an aspect of class conflict, and it reveals Armijo's distrust toward the border villagers with close ties to Pueblo Indians and independent native nations. The victorious conservative coalition launched a vigorous nationalistic program in New Mexico, but the state's incorporation into the national fold remained incomplete: A few months after the collapse of the Chimayó Rebellion, the president of Mexico extended New Mexico's historical exemption from national taxes for seven more years.

In 1834, California missions were secularized by a new liberal government in Mexico, which saw missions as colonial relics out of pace with a modernizing nation. Indians were emancipated, mission lands were privatized, and missionaries were replaced with parish priests. Document 7 is a report written in 1830 by Juan Bandini, a customs official in San Diego. It offers a local view into the secularization process. In the course of the 1820s, New England companies had taken over much of California's lucrative hide and tallow trade, and Bandini envisioned a modern California of private ranchos, international trade, and foreign immigration. A border crosser himself—he was born in Lima, Peru, in 1800—Bandini imagined California as a future transnational nexus. After the secularization of missions, some California Indians obtained sizable tracts of land, but most secured only small plots or remained landless. The governors of California approved some seven hundred land petitions, granting vast holdings to wealthy *californios*, whose large private ranchos replaced missions as California's dominant economic institution.

1. José María Sánchez Criticizes Tejanos and Anglo-American Immigrants in Texas, 1828

The commerce, which is carried on by foreigners and two or three Mexicans, is very insignificant, but the monopoly of it is very evident. I could cite many instances to prove by assertion, but I do not wish to be accused of ulterior motives. Although the soil is very rich, the inhabitants do not cultivate it because of the danger incurred from Indian attacks as soon as they get any distance from the houses, as the Indians often lurk in the surrounding country, coming in the silence of the night without fear from the troops, for by the time the latter notice the damage done it is already too late. No measures can be taken for the maintenance of a continuous watch on account of the sad condition of the troops, especially since they lack all resources. For months, and even years at times, these troops have gone without salary or supplies, constantly in active service against the Indians, dependent for their subsistence on buffalo meat, deer, and other game they may be able to secure with great difficulty. The government, nevertheless, has not helped their condition in spite of repeated and frequent remonstrances. If any money arrives, it disappears instantly, for infamous hands are not lacking to take it and give the poor soldiers goods at double their normal value in exchange for what they have earned, suffering the inclemencies of the weather while these inhuman tyrants slept peacefully in their beds. I am not exaggerating; on the contrary, I keep silent about many worse things I could say. The character of the people is care-free, they are enthusiastic dancers, very fond of luxury, and the worst punishment that can be inflicted upon them is work.

The Americans from the north have taken possession of practically all the eastern part of Texas, in most cases without the permission of the authorities. They immigrate constantly, finding no one to prevent them, and take possession of the *sitio* [location] that best suits them without either asking leave or going through any formality other than that of building their homes. Thus the majority of inhabitants in the Department are North Americans, the Mexican population being reduced to only Bejar, Nacogdoches, and La Bahía del Espíritu Santo, wretched settlements that between them do not number three thousand inhabitants, and the new village of Guadalupe Victoria that has scarcely more than seventy settlers. The government of the state, with its seat at Saltillo, that should watch over the preservation of its most precious and interesting

José María Sánchez, "A Trip to Texas in 1828," trans. Carlos E. Castañeda, *Southwestern Historical Quarterly* 29 (April 1926): 258, 260, 270–271, 273–274, 283.

department, taking measures to prevent its being stolen by foreign hands, is the one that knows the least not only about actual conditions, but even about its territory.

Villa de Austin [San Felipe de Austin], April 27 [1828]—We continued along hills without trees, the ground being wet and muddy, until we arrived at a distance of four or five leagues from the settlement of San Felipe de Austin, where we were met by Mr. Samuel Williams, secretary of the empresario, Mr. Stephen Austin; and we were given lodging in a house that had been prepared for the purpose.

This village has been settled by Mr. Stephen Austin, a native of the United States of the North. It consists, at present, of forty or fifty wooden houses on the western bank of the large river known as *Rio de los Brazos de Dios*, but the houses are not arranged systematically so as to form streets; but on the contrary, lie in an irregular and desultory manner. Its population is nearly two hundred persons, of which only ten are Mexicans, for the balance are all Americans from the North with an occasional European.... They are in general, in my opinion, lazy people of vicious character. Some of them cultivate their small farms by planting corn; but this task they usually entrust to their negro slaves, whom they treat with considerable harshness. Beyond the village in an immense stretch of land formed by rolling hills are scattered the families brought by Stephen Austin, which today number more than two thousand persons. The diplomatic policy of this empresario, evident in all his actions, has, as one may say, lulled the authorities into a sense of security, while he works diligently for his own ends. In my judgment, the spark that will start the conflagration that will deprive us of Texas, will start from this colony. All because the government does not take vigorous measures to prevent it. Perhaps it does not realize the value of what it is about to lose.

May 12.—Our beasts of burden not being used to this climate suffered a great deal because of the bad forage. For this reason the general ordered that I should go to Mr. Groce, an American, to buy corn; and Mr. Chovell, wishing to accompany me, we started on our mission.... At about three in the afternoon we arrived at Groce's place and secured the corn we were to take back. We asked for some food, and it was given to us in the house, consisting, as is customary among Americans, of bacon, milk, and coffee; and when we had finished, we were taken upstairs to see Mr. Groce who was in bed and unable to move. Our visit was very short because we could not understand each other. After a short while, Mr. Groce's son came out with a doctor who appeared to be a pedant, and another young man, the son-in-law of Mr. Groce, all of them Americans, and by signs and sentences in Latin written with pencil they carried on a conversation with us, trivial in the main, but they did not deign to offer us shelter in the house, even though they saw us camping under the trees. Later, they asked us into the house for the sole purpose of showing us the wealth of Mr. Groce and to introduce us to three dogs called Ferdinand VII, Napoleon, and Bolívar. The indignation at seeing the name of the Colombian Liberator thus debased caused Mr. Chovell to utter a violent oath which the impudent fellows did not understand or did not wish to understand. We returned immediately to our camp and went to bed without supper because we could not get anything. Groce is a man of 45 or 50 years of age; he came from the United States to establish himself on the eastern bank of the Brazos River in order to avoid paying the numerous creditors that were suing him. He brought with him 116 slaves of both sexes, most of which were stolen. These wretched slaves are the ones who cultivate the corn and cotton, both of which yield copious crops to Mr. Groce. Likewise, he has a great many head of cattle, innumerable hogs, and a great number of horses; but he is a man who does not enjoy his wealth because he is extremely stingy, and he treats his slaves with great cruelty.

The population [of Nacogdoches] does not exceed seven hundred persons, including the troops of the garrison, and all live in very good houses made of lumber, well built and forming straight streets, which make the place more agreeable. The women do not number one hundred. The civil administration is entrusted to an *Alcalde*, and in his absence, to the first and second *regidores*, but up until now, they have been, unfortunately, extremely ignorant men more worthy of pity than of reproof. From this fact, the North American inhabitants (who are in the majority) have formed an ill opinion of the Mexicans, judging them, in their pride, incapable of understanding laws, arts, etc. They continually try to entangle the authorities in order to carry out the policy most suitable to their perverse designs.

Different tribes of Indians such as the Tejas, Nadacos, Yguanes, Savanos, Cherokees, Kickapoos, Delawares, Cutchates, Alabamas, Quichas, and Cados, continually enter Nacogdoches, but they are all peaceful and carry on their trade in the city with skins, corn, pumpkins, and beans. These tribes are located in the neighborhood of Nacogdoches, their *pueblos* being intermingled with the settlements of the Americans who are scattered throughout Texas, but more particularly along the frontier because the greater part of them are settled without the consent of the government of the country. The Mexicans that live here are very humble people, and perhaps their intentions are good, but because of their education and environment they are ignorant not only of the customs of our great cities, but even of the occurrences of our Revolution, excepting a few persons who have heard about them. Accustomed to the continued trade with the North Americans, they have adopted their customs and habits, and one may say truly that they are not Mexicans except by birth, for they even speak Spanish with marked incorrectness.

2. Tejano Leaders Give Their Opinion of Anglo-American Immigrants, 1832

This town of [San Antonio de] Béxar was established 140 years ago, La Bahía del Espíritu Santo and Nacogdoches 116 years ago, and the fort of San Sabá, the towns of Jaén, San Marcos, and Trinidad, were founded in the intervening years along with other military establishments on the Guadalupe, Colorado and Brazos

David J. Weber, ed., *Troubles in Texas, 1832: A Tejano Viewpoint from San Antonio*, pp. 16–17, 19–21 (Dallas: DeGolyer Library, Southern Methodist University, 1983).

rivers. These communities have disappeared entirely; in some of them the residents dying to the last man. Many early settlers and their descendants have been sacrificed to the barbarians, and not a few others have died of hunger and pestilence, which have caused havoc in this part of the republic due to the inaction and apathy of those who govern. Other frontier communities, located toward the west have, perhaps, suffered much more, and every last one of us is probably threatened with total extermination by the new Comanche uprising.

And what shall we say concerning evils caused by the general law of April 6, 1830, which absolutely prohibits immigration by North Americans? The lack of troops and other officials capable of supervising it has made it impossible to enforce this law. On the other hand, the law prevents immigration of some capitalists and of some industrious and honorable men who have refrained from coming because of it, but has left the door open to wicked adventurers and others who constitute the dregs of society. Since they have nothing to lose, they have arrived furtively in large numbers and may cause incalculable harm.

The same is true of the numerous tribes of semicivilized Indians. Expelled from the United States of North America, they have crossed the Sabine River and, unchallenged, have established themselves in our territory. It will be very difficult to uproot them and even more so if we intend to make them observe our legal system. Yet, risking all kinds of dangers and inconveniences, North Americans reclaimed a considerable part of these lands from the desert prior to the passage of the law of April 6, 1830, and toiled assiduously to further agriculture and to introduce crafts unknown in these parts since the discovery of this land by the old Spanish government. They planted cotton and sugar cane, introduced the cotton gin, and imported machinery for the cultivation of sugar and sawmills to cut wood economically. We owe these advances to the efforts of these hard-working colonists, who have earned a comfortable living within seven or eight years. Theirs is not a precarious existence, the only kind known in Mexican towns, which depend solely upon the troops' payroll that circulates so slowly among us.

Immigration is, unquestionably, the most efficient, quick, and economical means we can employ to destroy the Indians and to populate lands they now occupy—directing the immigrants to the northern interior whenever possible. This goal can only be achieved by freely admitting these enthusiastic North Americans so they may live in this desert. They already are experienced in dealing with the barbarians in their native land, where they have done similar work. Not a single European nation that might be interested in colonizing offers their people similar advantages. Because they have been very regimented, the Europeans' transportation, climate, customs, and forms of government are very different from those of the neighboring republic and are not as suitable for Mexico.

The opening of roads going directly from Texas ports to New Mexico, Paso del Norte, or even Chihuahua, would place Texas at the rank it should occupy in the Mexican federation. This achievement, too, is the result of the immigration of North American capitalists. They built these at least more economically and in less time than could be accomplished by any other nation and even by Mexico itself. The same is true of direct communication from all the far northern parts of our republic with the state of Missouri of the neighboring nation, which is maintained today despite great risk and cost of freight. The population of those lands [between Texas and Missouri, and between Texas and New Mexico] would benefit Texas and would be the best barrier against the Indians. It would thrust population 200 leagues farther north than it is today, and protect the entire line of defense for Coahuila, Nuevo León and Tamaulipas, and even that of Chihuahua.

3. Donaciano Vigil Mourns the Changing Relationships among New Mexicans, Anglo Americans, and Indians, 1846

In some ways, the lot of the heathens around New Mexico improved at the same time that ours worsened. Many Americans, persuaded by their own interests, established forts on the Platte, Arkansas, and Red rivers. Through these forts, heathens have been supplied amply with as much as they might need, in exchange for furs. Thus, little by little, all the heathens forgot us and lost their affection for us. As soon as they became familiar with firearms and considered themselves well supplied with them, they no longer feared offending us. Since then, one also notes, the livestock and buffalo, which once abounded even on the common lands of our villages, have been progressively diminishing so quickly that now we have come to feel their scarcity or their complete disappearance in many areas. Now our hunters travel over 100 leagues in search of them—a long journey of four months. For the last two years there has not been enough meat to sustain them on their return trip without coming home empty-handed. Under these circumstances [of shortage of game] the barbarians, incited by necessity, attack us in order to save themselves.

Gentlemen: Most of the inhabitants of New Mexico, and especially those who are most exposed to attacks by barbarians, are armed only with bows and arrows and these are scarce because they do not have the means to buy more—not to mention guns and ammunition. The central government of the nation, continually distracted and occupied with more general concerns, has not been able to provide us with the protection we need and that we have wanted for our security. The few troops that are in this Department are employed in this capital (which is the theater of all contests when there are any) in sustaining the authorities and in keeping order among the inhabitants. Due to their number and due to the deterioration of most of their equipment, even if the troops were free from this service [of keeping order in Santa Fe], they would not be able to defend more than the place where they live. The arrogance of our barbaric enemies requires us to defend our extensive borders with thousands of disciplined troops. These troops must be provisioned in the manner of the presidial system that was here in the era of the Spanish government—something that the National Treasury has not been able to do.

Donaciano Vigil, *Arms, Indians, and the Mismanagement of New Mexico*, ed. and trans. David J. Weber (El Paso: University of Texas at El Paso, 1986), 5–7.

In any event, to wait for such protection from the central government of the nation would be to wait in vain. This is especially true given the degree to which the Republic has been weakened by the different [political] factions that are continually forming, as well as conflicting interests and unbridled ambitions. Thus, for our personal security and our interests (at least in regard to the barbarians), I believe we should not count on any protection or resources other than those the New Mexicans themselves can provide. But, so that the New Mexicans might display some new energy, we should obtain means of defense for them—arms and munitions. It is a calamity that we have always lacked these two very important items here. Although some of the wealthy class have acquired some luxurious guns from merchants who brought them for their own use, these cannot be obtained by most people. Nor is it the rich who usually go in pursuit of the barbarians when they have carried out a raid. The introduction of arms and munitions is prohibited by our laws, and the government has no public arsenal here for either arms or ammunition. Nonetheless, they are indispensable for us if we wish to exist in this Department. We are exposed to the same or worse horrors than those that occur in departments more populous and wealthy than ours, and that do not defend themselves well, no doubt due to some of the same problems we suffer here.

Gentlemen: I have heard reports regarding the barbaric tribes: of the number of Mexican captives, and especially of young Mexican women who serve the bestial pleasures of the barbaric Indians; of the brutal treatment they receive; and of the kinds of deaths that the barbarians are accustomed to inflicting for whatever capricious reason. Those reports have made me tremble with horror, have made me grieve, and have made me ashamed as I consider the degree to which bad luck has dogged our nation. The more so when I contemplate what the fate will be of many people whom I esteem, if timely measures are not taken to guard against such degrading misfortunes.

4. Albino Chacón Describes Navajo Raiding and Mounting Discontent in New Mexico, 1837

New Mexico, abandoned from the beginning of independence, did not appear to have any other relation with the rest of the republic other than that which comes from a common origin, language, and customs. Its only resources since then had been the product of duties [taxes] that a small annual caravan of North Americans paid on the goods that they introduced, which in even the most profitable years never, by far, had been sufficient to pay for the entire necessities of the presidial company's complement of personnel which, since that time, has not been complete. The geographical situation of New Mexico, separated from the rest of the republic by great distances, surrounded by barbaric tribes, some powerful and experienced in warfare, and almost all of them ferocious to its

Jacqueline Dorgan Meketa, ed., *Legacy of Honor: The Life of Rafael Chacón, a Nineteenth Century New Mexican*, pp. 23–26 (Albuquerque: University of New Mexico Press, 1982).

inhabitants, was subject to furious attacks from its barbaric neighbors which patriotic love and national honor have made it resist, always with firmness, and
many times it succeeded in giving severe retaliation to the Indians, even to the
very center of their own territory. This [resistance], always at the expense and
fatigue of its [New Mexico's] own inhabitants, and certainly the general government [Mexico] has not given assistance, not even one time, of arms and ammunition. During a series of hardships and sacrifices of many years, it had been
represented many times to the supreme government about the critical situation
of payment which, with each passing day, had been becoming more alarming
because the number of its enemies was growing and because they were perfect-
ing themselves in the art of warfare and were much more well supplied with
arms and ammunition than the inhabitants of New Mexico, but the supreme
government did not understand and for these reasons never heeded them. These
poor inhabitants, their haciendas and the rest of their resources ruined, lost their
enthusiasm and means of fighting, and their enemies became encouraged in the
same proportion, coming to commit depredations with impunity, even on the
outskirts of settlements. Reduced, then, in spite of such hardships, to such extreme misery that in various places they did not dare to plant their fields because
of the great danger that they ran, the people began to manifest some discontent
as is only natural in such misery.... New Mexico was in this state when it was
learned that Señor Colonel Don Albino Pérez was arriving as governor, of
whom the supreme government, upon announcing him, gave distinguished recommendations as to his character. This announcement raised hopes of improving the situation as much because of his talent and experience as because of his
high military rank and important connections he had in the capital of the republic, which would enable him to obtain from the supreme government the aid
that New Mexico needed so desperately. The arrival of Pérez in Santa Fe reinforced the notion that had formed at the announcement of his coming. His personal appearance, the accounts of the great services he had rendered to his
country that were told by members of his retinue and those men who had close
access to him, the military actions in which he had distinguished himself, the
plans he had already formed to place in motion the troops of the territory and
to procure the necessities to support them and to annihilate the Navajo Indians
who, at that time, had continued to be very hostile, made most of the people
form a promising opinion of him.... But as he could not get enough [funds] to
continue the services or the troop by this means, and since he received nothing
from Mexico in spite of his repeated requests, he went to the natives of the
country whom he thought might be able to advance him what was needed individually or through the credit they had. For this reason, of course, he was observed to visit more frequently the houses of certain gentlemen who, without
acceding to his aim, were persuaded of the influence they had and wanted to
use it in protecting themselves against competitors.... Lacking the means to support the troops in arms, he had to give it up, forcing the troop to look for its
own subsistence wherever it could find it, and the employees and officials were
left reduced to their individual credit or that which the credit of the governor
could procure for them in case there was not sufficient to maintain their ranks.

This condition, together with the bad feelings of some particular people, gave rise to recriminations in which the general calamity was blamed, by different individuals, on each other.... in the end everything became confusion. The Navajo tribe, at the same time, was not idle, committing depredations of all kinds in all areas, stealing large numbers of livestock, carrying away captives, burning various persons alive in their homes, and they even sent some parties to commit murders near Santa Fe, which was the best-guarded jurisdiction in all the territory. All with impunity.

There was made, it is true, among others, a general campaign against the Navajos, to which the governor went in person, but it produced no more effect than the loss of the major part of the animals it carried, and with this finished the ruin of many unhappy farmers. The public, in the midst of many misfortunes, was trying to find the cause of their misery. Some attributed it to the corruption and bad management of the civil employees, giving substance to the accusations being spread. Others blamed the governor, saying that the number of officials who worked with him consumed all the assets of the troop which, if well directed, could defend the territory.

5. New Mexico's Chimayó Rebels Denounce Mexico City's Plan for National Reform, 1837

Long live God and the Nation and the faith of Jesus Christ, for the most important issues they stand for are following:

1. To sustain God and the nation and the faith of Jesus Christ.
2. To defend our country until the last drop of blood is shed to achieve the desired victory.
3. Not to allow the Departmental Plan.
4. Not to allow any tax.
5. Not to allow the excesses of those who try to carry this out.

God and the Nation, Santa Cruz de la Cañada, August 1, 1837, in camp.

6. Manuel Armijo Reports on the Suppression of the Chimayó Rebellion, 1837

This department has been involved in the horrors of a disastrous and barbarous revolution into which perverse men led it, setting the people against the constitutional laws and government that rule us; after they committed in their exhilaration every kind of crime, impiously assassinating persons of the highest offices,

Janet Lecompte, *A Rebellion in Río Arriba*, p. 20 (Albuquerque: University of New Mexico Press, 1985).

Janet Lecompte, *A Rebellion in Río Arriba*, pp. 136–139 (Albuquerque: University of New Mexico Press, 1985).

and when they were preparing another bloody explosion even more dangerous, having for its only object general desolation and ruin, on the eighth of September last I pronounced in Tomé for order, constitution and laws.

On the 14th of September, as soon as I arrived in this capital where the worthy permanent company, which had been disbanded, again took up arms along with the citizenry with the greatest enthusiasm for repelling the cantonment of rebels who were expected any moment, I was recognized as commander in chief of all the troops, with the rank of colonel of the liberating army. The forces at my command were a thousand-odd men, whom I trained in the management of arms, for as citizens they knew almost nothing about it, and I saw to the mounting of artillery, repair of broken arms, and reinforcement of supplies, expecting also to enter into communications with the Cantón of rebels, now approaching; before fighting them, inasmuch as their force, numbering three thousand men, was considerable, and their position on high ground very advantageous, my object being to avoid battle and the loss of Mexican blood if possible, for I knew that most of the mob had been deceived in their ignorance by false promises, and that others of them had joined out of fear of the rebel force. I took the opportunity of having the commander of the Cantón, Don Pablo Montoya, direct a letter to Governor Gonzales (elected by the same factions) who had already been arrested in Santa Fe.

It was necessary to receive these men in the manner that had been offered to them, and to use them with all the prudence necessary for success in the undertaking, without loosing the torrents of blood they were prepared to shed, and as I used the greatest persuasion in conjunction with an energetic decision to fight them, it resulted in the drafting of terms of agreement by which they were obliged to dissolve their Cantón, declare their government and laws invalid, and subject themselves to my orders, giving me the position of superior head of both political and military commands until the resolution of His Excellency the president of the republic.

In this manner concluded a revolution that presented a most horrible aspect of misfortunes so frequent and so great that they filled the inhabitants of this soil with confusion, having no other recourse but to succumb, for fear of the terrifying army they saw committing crimes with the most outrageous cruelty. In fact, the way they killed the governor, Colonel Don Albino Pérez, district judge Don Santiago Abréu, prefect Don Ramón Abréu, secretary of government Don Jesús María [sic], Lieutenant Don Joaquín Hurtado, Alférez Don Diego Sáenz, Don Miguel Sena and others, cannot be described without the consternation humanity feels in the highest degree, being better, then, to omit the circumstances of such horrendous assassinations, even more criminal than merely having deprived the victims of life. One feels surprise and fear to know that these evildoers, with the show of authority that they pleased to put on, invited the barbarous nations that surround this department to form an allegiance against the supreme government, and to help by cutting off communication with the interior of the republic, counting as well on the Pueblo Indian people whom as a weak, credulous, ignorant people very addicted to the sack and spoils of war, they easily seduced, persuading them that the departmental laws would take from them a third part of the fruits of their labor, taxing heavily the common benefits of water, wood, pastures, and even their own children and wives.

The aim of the factions was, as is evident, to remain independent of the government of the Mexican nation; to put an end to every person who has an average education; to be governed by no established law, which was their excuse for sentencing all the archives to the flames; to destroy fortunes in a general sack; and to live without subjection to any precept or authority, identifying themselves with the savage tribes and putting themselves on the same level, making the same cause with their same interests.

There is no doubt but that the Mexican nation would have lost, perhaps forever, this integral part of its territory had not some of its people taken a strong stand, seized the right opportunity, and shown great fortitude; but it is even more doubtful that this would have succeeded had not the supreme government extended its protecting hand to this unfortunate territory, providing the help required to quell the rebellion without much difficulty.

7. Juan Bandini Envisions an International Future for California, 1830

The possessions of the missions extend from one end of the territory to the other. Their borders come right up to each other. Even though they might not need all the land they appear to have for the care of the crops and the maintenance of their herds, they have insensitively appropriated all the area. They have constantly been opposed to any private person becoming involved in the affairs of the missions. With that sinister notion, they occupy the best lands and water sources. With but a small flock of sheep they rejoice at having come into possession of everything. They desire exclusive control over the productions of the country, whose bad condition stems from that deeply rooted source.

Counting all the missions, there are about twenty to twenty-one thousand indigenous listed in the mission registers. However, they are not equally distributed among the missions. Some missions have close to three thousand souls, while others can scarcely muster four hundred. The population at a mission more or less determines its prosperity.

By their nature, the Indians are careless and lazy. Even though they are able to imitate, they are not very clever. They can be educated, of course, but that would not be the most fitting way to develop their ability to reason. It is true that their inclinations are not of the type apt to create good impressions, since thievery, treachery, deceit, and lethargy are their dominant passions. From this, one can deduce that little usefulness can be drawn out of these Indians.

Generally speaking, the production of all the missions is the raising of cattle, sheep, horses, wheat, corn, beans, and other vegetables. The more southern missions are extensively engaged in vineyards and olives. However, the most lucrative

Rose Marie Beebe and Robert M. Senkewicz, eds., *Lands of Promise and Despair: Chronicles of Early California, 1535–1846*, pp. 380–385. (Berkeley: Heyday Books, 2001).

production is that of cattle, for there is an active, high demand on the part of the ships engaged in the coastal trade for their hides and crops. Indeed, these articles are the only items in demand which both the missions and private persons have in order to meet their needs. This is why all are anxious to stimulate this branch of trade as much as possible and why it receives the attention of everyone.

Foreign vessels have been allowed to collect hides here for the past eight years. Previously, it had been approved only on a case-by-case basis, but now those who export from the missions will deliver thirty thousand hides [annually] and about the same number of *arrobas* of tallow produced in the slaughters. And, in view of the method used in the these slaughters, it seems certain that within three or four years' time the quantity exported of one or more of these items will double.

Hemp, wine, olive oil, grains, and other agricultural products could be cultivated more extensively if there were some stimulus to export more, but since there is none, they only plant enough for domestic consumption.

The only thing that makes the foreigners want to trade here is the untanned cattle hides and tallow. It is well known here that nothing else will ever be able to serve as money, for scarcely any money circulates. So it is that all who come here seek to exchange their goods for other goods. The items the ships bring as imports are designed for this kind of purchase. They know that the missionaries are not interested in money, but rather items the Indians need. Some ships that have arrived here only with cash have lost their business because they have not been able to obtain goods.

Therefore, if there is only one type of export, which barely produces enough to allow the settlers to purchase the absolute necessities to survive, what would happen if restrictions were placed on trading at the moment in which the exports were beginning to increase? It seems to me that the consequences would be more than obvious, yet I find it necessary to mention them here: (1) no ship would sail along these coasts, and the nation would lose the money that its wares bring in; (2) neither the missions nor private individuals would be able to obtain those articles which they most need for the field work, not to mention what they need in order to live with respectability and culture; (3) since the raising of cattle is the only useful branch of industry, and the one on which all are pinning their hopes, if harvesting the carcasses were thwarted, the populace here would once again become submerged in the poverty of eight years ago, which they attributed to this limited commerce; (4) there are many foreigners in the territory who have become naturalized citizens, but if they thought they would not be able to survive here in the future, they would abandon a country which only promised them misery. This would have an adverse affect on the whole colonization effort.

Only a few missions can transport their goods to another port at minimal cost, and these missions are precisely the poorest ones and the ones that produce the least. The missions that are going to attract the attention of the sailors are obviously the ones that are going to suffer due to the unfeasibility of their commerce. In addition, one should not forget the *pueblo* of Los Angeles, which is worthy of consideration because it has the wealthiest population in California and a number of different foreigners also reside there. This *pueblo* is located one hundred and thirty leagues to the south of Monterey, and the course and fostering of its growth is due to the hide and tallow trade. If it becomes impossible to dispose of the hides and tallow, the city inevitably will be ruined.

As a result of this explanation, I can say with certainty that if foreigners are excluded from all ports except Monterey, I repeat, the commerce of Alta California will be completely finished.

Mission *ranchos*, and private ones as well, are found only in a narrow strip of the territory from north to south. Only a few are more than ten or twelve leagues inland, because the mountain range that also runs from north to south is a barrier. The missions have the best *ranchos* with the most abundant water and pastures. Private *ranchos* have had to face a thousand obstacles and barely have been able to obtain some small sites for a limited amount of cattle. Only around Los Angeles are there private *ranchos* of any consequence.

The climate and fertile valleys of California offer all types of vegetation a person could hope for. In addition to what has been stated previously, California produces the highest quality flax and hemp. The best vineyards are found in abundance here and there is no lack of cotton. Pear, apple, orange, and several types of peach trees abound, as well as other fruits. The olive tree is unsurpassable. It is very unusual to find a plain anywhere in the territory that is not able to produce fruitfully. In addition, all the fields and hillsides produce infinite types of wild fruit, such as strawberries and other exquisite and diverse herbs, many of which have not been botanically classified. The territory does not lack wood for the construction of ships, particularly around San Francisco, where pines and oaks are abundant everywhere around the mountains. Livestock reproduces with the most astonishing ease, especially the cattle, which become pregnant and are ready to give birth at two years of age. The wild horses are so numerous that it is necessary to round them up every year and kill a large number because of the damage they do to the fields. Also, their wildness can affect horses that already have been broken.

The sheep give the most exquisite wool and they reproduce wildly. The value of the livestock is about equal: a newly born calf is worth five *pesos*, and a horse is worth a bit more. The country also abounds in deer, rabbits, and hare. Unfortunately, there is also an abundance of bears, wolves, coyotes, squirrels, and moles, which do a good amount of damage in the fields, especially the latter three. Geese, cranes, and ducks are plentiful in season, and a unique type of quail is abundant. In sum, Alta California lacks none of the essential elements for an inexhaustible production. The only thing it does lack is people.

∾ ESSAYS

In the first essay, Andrés Reséndez, professor of history at the University of California at Davis, challenges the conventional view of the U.S. takeover of northern Mexico as a simple tale of U.S. expansionism, which saw a belief in an inexorable expansion merging with a willingness to back up that belief with military might. The U.S. incorporation of the Southwest, Reséndez argues, began not with propaganda and armies but with markets and merchants: The military conquest was preceded and propelled by a softer process of economic conquest. Far from being a passive observer of its national dismemberment, Mexico encountered U.S. economic penetration with nationalist rhetoric and rituals, turning the borderlands into a cultural battleground where the spoils were the resources and loyalty of local residents. In analyzing this history of colliding national projects and shifting cross-cultural alliances, Reséndez engages several questions that are central to the study of borderlands in general and the Southwest borderlands in particular: How do people construct identities in borderlands that are being pulled toward two competing national cores? Can identity be situational, a strategic choice, or is it something that is deeply engrained in our psyche and thus not easily moldable? What is the difference between personal identity and national identity; is it possible to say where one ends and the other begins? Why did New Mexico stay with Mexico twelve years longer than Texas?

The second essay, by Albert L. Hurtado, professor of history at the University of Oklahoma at Norman, explores the intersection of sex, gender, and power in the multicultural milieu of Mexican California. Hurtado analyzes intimate ties of incoming Anglo-American men with elite Mexican women and impoverished Indian women, focusing on how marital and sexual relationships shaped race, class, and power relations in the province. Intimate bonds and family formation, more than economic or military strength, he argues, decided who would rule California. Anglo-American immigrants may have modified but rarely abandoned their preconceived notions of Mexicans and Indians as racial inferiors and tended to assess relationships with both groups in utilitarian terms. Unions with women of high-status *californio* families—self-identified Hispanic families—opened access to social circuits and land ownerships and were eagerly pursued: Numerous Anglo men converted to Catholicism and became Mexican citizens in order to marry a *californiana*. Relationships with Indian women, by contrast, were social dead ends and therefore rarely developed beyond sexual encounters. As the essays in previous chapters suggest, multicultural unions had the potential of promoting mutual understanding, racial tolerance, and balanced power relations, but, in Mexican California, the opposite often held true: Attitudes hardened, whiteness and status conflated, and power flowed into the hands of Anglo-American patriarchs of racially mixed households. What factors made Mexican California different?

Markets, Persuasion, and Identity in the Southwest Borderlands

ANDRÉS RESÉNDEZ

Traditionally, we have told the story of how nations emerged as a triumphant tale of domination exerted by a determined center over reluctant peripheries and by persuasive officials over skeptical masses. The literature depicts state

Andrés Reséndez, "National Identity on a Shifting Border: Texas and New Mexico in the Age of Transition, 1821–1848," *Journal of American History* 86 (Sep. 1999): 668–688.

formation and nation building as originating from the core outward and from top to bottom. Sitting at the apex of all political and social organizations, the state has been granted the leading role. After all, it was the state that built the infrastructure linking the center to all corners of the nation, increasing the network of communications within a territory and thus helping integrate a national market. Under the auspices of the state, a nationalist ideology was fashioned and disseminated to all prospective citizens. Whether accounts spotlight institutions or identities, the underlying theme is centralization: The national state wins out over lesser political organizations and potential challengers, and the people divest themselves of previous ethnic or local loyalties as the nation becomes their overriding identity.

This core-periphery, top-down model has recently come under criticism. Although nations tend to be promoted from above, they nevertheless have to be analyzed and understood from below.... People's perceptions (and not nationalist propaganda) constitute the most critical yardstick against which we can measure the success of attempts at national construction. Historians and theorists have been understandably concerned with state-sponsored nationalist discourse, but they have been less adept at explaining why this discourse was adopted by local communications and non-elite groups.

An approach that pays attention to both state designs and responses from local communities is badly needed to rethink the story of how Mexico's Far North became the American Southwest. This episode has long been explained through a sweeping narrative, that of American expansionism. Undoubtedly, expansionism was a powerful 'mood' that prevailed in the United States throughout the first half of the nineteenth century. But expansionism has been used in the historiography as a catchall, explain-all concept to describe the social psychology of early Americans, to elucidate the relations between American settlers and Native Americans, and to provide a rationale for the policy pursued by the United States toward the Spanish/Mexican possessions. The dramatic territorial exchanges of this era have been presented almost as logical outcomes of that irresistible ideology; they thus require no further explanation. Worse still, by emphasizing how Anglo-Americans expanded their domain, we have left unexamined how other peoples reacted to this offensive, often confining non-Anglo-Americans to the role of passive victims as they watched their homelands being taken away.

Yet when we look closely at this process, we obtain a starkly different image. Expansionism, at least on Mexico's northern frontier, meant first and foremost *economic* penetration that afforded local Hispanic and Native American elites the opportunity to profit. This circumstance led those local elites consciously to shift their allegiances to accommodate their interests, even in the face of opposition from other members of their own ethnic groups. Economic expansion provided the medium in which cross-cultural alliances were forged along Mexico's northern frontier. Rather than idle players, local elites were active agents who made choices of far-reaching consequences.

Just as we have tended to oversimplify the United States' drive for Mexico's territory, we have assumed that the northern frontier provinces were unproblematically a part of Mexico, as if national identity had emerged full-blown right after Mexico gained independence from Spain in 1821. Municipal and state authorities resisted the intervention of the national government on several fronts, from elections of local officials to the regulation of economy or the organization of the military. In its most basic form, this tension between local and national elites acquired a clear nationalist dimension. In the fractious political environment of early-nineteenth-century Mexico, national leaders began to equate local and regional autonomy with territorial disintegration of the country and, accordingly, started to brand some power brokers in the Far North as separatists.

We need to recast the story of Mexico's northern frontier, paying attention to how the Mexican and the American national projects collided there and how conflicts played out at the local level. Did different provinces experience the change of sovereignty in the same manner? Did different social groups among Hispanics understand their loyalties and national attachments in the same way? Did Native Americans play the same role in California, New Mexico, and Texas as these provinces were being incorporated into the United States? Instead of a simple tale of domination in which a handful of resourceful Anglo-Americans managed to conquer an enormous territory, we have to unearth a far richer story of cross-cultural and cross-class alliances and counteralliances, each side struggling to define and shape whatever nation was emerging in its locality. In the following pages I attempt to trace some of the struggles over the nation, focusing on the cases of Texas and New Mexico. My contention is that communities in these two provinces were caught between two opposing forces. On the one hand, a web of local and regional economic interests increasingly tied Texas and New Mexico to the economy of the United States, thus affecting the livelihood and ultimately the loyalty of key social groups within the Hispanic, Anglo-American, and Native American communities. On the other hand, the Mexican government responded to this challenge by fashioning a defensive, antiforeign, patriotic rhetoric and by fostering rituals aimed at creating a sense of nationhood.

In the aftermath of independence, Mexico's political leadership, a clique of independence heroes and ardent nationalists, became fully aware of the difficulties of bringing the northern frontier into the national fold. They did not delude themselves about the fact that the enormous arc of provinces from Texas to Alta California was exposed to the designs of other nations and most alarmingly to those of the United States. They also knew that the northern frontier society was committed to deeply entrenched regional attachments, *las patrias chicas*. The people of the frontier gave primacy to their cherished identities as *tejanos, nuevo-mexicanos,* or *californios,* and understandably viewed with a certain skepticism newer and more abstract appellations such as *mexicano/a.* And finally, the heterogeneity of frontier society made the task of forging the nation there quite daunting. In Texas, for instance, the part of the population that was called "Mexican" was a tiny minority, amounting to some 2,000 inhabitants mostly concentrated in the San Antonio-Goliad region. In comparison, the Texas Indian population was larger, far more diverse, and dominant in a greater geographic area.

Similarly, the Anglo-American immigrants who came to Texas in waves during the 1820s and early 1830s ended up outnumbering Mexican Texans ten to one on the eve of the Texas Revolution of 1835-1836. New Mexico's demography was more favorable to the construction of the Mexican nation, but there was considerable heterogeneity. The Hispanic population amounted to close to 30,000 inhabitants. Yet Hispanics coexisted with the 10,000 Pueblo Indians living in twenty settlements who maintained significant autonomy. Moreover, Hispanics and Pueblo Indians were surrounded by nomadic groups that were generically called *barbarous, gentile,* or *errant* nations, including the powerful Comanche confederation, the Navajo, and the Apache. Although nomadic Indians were not generally considered Mexican citizens, they nevertheless, as contemporaries put it, formed part of "the extended Mexican family" whose members could one day become citizens if they were to abandon their wandering ways, pledge allegiance to the Mexican government, and convert to Catholicism.

Thus many of Mexico's early leaders at the national, provincial, and local levels attempted to impose uniformity and nationalist devotion along the northern frontier. One vehicle to create national awareness was the printed word. Newspapers, journals, gazettes, and random manifestos proliferated throughout the northern frontier during the first half of the nineteenth century. The impetus behind the majority of those—often fleeting—publications was political bickering, but regardless of their political orientation, editors and writers always cloaked themselves in the nationalist mantle. Benedict Anderson has argued that in postcolonial Latin America such printed material "created an imagined community among a specific assemblage of fellow-readers," and he thus assigns "the decisive historic role" of creating the nation in Latin America to Creole functionaries and provincial Creole journalists. Although the printed word undoubtedly helped foster a sense of nationhood in Texas and New Mexico, it is hard to contend that such publications played a decisive role, for very few people knew how to read and write. Even if we assume that the contents of the publications were spread by word of mouth beyond the actual readers, the number was nonetheless rather small. Geographic dispersion and cultural disparities added insurmountable barriers. Pueblo and nomadic Indians, for instance, simply could not participate in this virtual community of readers and writers, while Anglo-American colonists in Texas and New Mexico had their own publications where the symbology of the Mexican nation was greatly diluted, if it appeared at all, or where a different and incompatible national project was promoted.

Primary education became a more deliberate vehicle to bolster national loyalties. In Texas and New Mexico an educational crusade flourished between 1827 and 1834.... However, the educational crusade was short-lived. By 1834 most public schools in Texas and New Mexico operated very precariously or had closed down. Scarce funds were frequently diverted toward more immediate concerns such as fighting Indians or paying the troops their back wages.

For the vast majority of the frontier inhabitants, neither the print media nor the schools went very far in promoting a sense of nationhood. For them, the most pervasive and perhaps the only indications of the existence of the Mexican nation were rituals and symbols. Officials in Texas and New Mexico introduced an endless succession of *reminders* of the nation: flags, coins, elections, commemorations of the birthdays and deaths of independence heroes. The crowns that had hitherto embellished public buildings and carriages during colonial times were mercilessly erased, and the word "imperial" was systematically replaced by "national." Emblems planned to the last detail and always boasting the eagle standing on a prickly pear devouring a serpent—symbolizing the foundation of the Aztec empire—sprung up even in the smallest and most remote villages.

From Mexico City the ritualistic onslaught was projected across the entire national domain.... Both New Mexico and Texas submitted to the mysterious new rituals, even though New Mexico did so belatedly. Gov. Agustín Melgares reported that the people of Santa Fe celebrated with what he ironically described as "inexplicable joy" in a program that included, among other features, an Indian dance, an allegorical parade with children dressed as angels and a little girl as the Virgin, and a patriotic performance in which three leading citizens (an alderman, the vicar general, and the military chaplain) played the parts of the three guarantees upon which the Mexican nation had just been brokered: independence, Catholicism, and unity.

It is exceedingly difficult to ascertain how people felt about these ceremonies. Melgares somewhat sardonically remarked that it was his hope that those "exteriorities" revealed genuine support for "our holy cause." Indeed, it is likely that such newfound patriotism was at least partly a fabrication of zealous local and state officials desirous of showing their constituencies in a good light to their superiors. But regardless of private feelings, Independence Day celebrations in Texas and New Mexico quickly became elaborate and ritualized affairs organized by patriotic committees that labored for months every year to reach all segments of society. All of this required substantial outlays of money by leading citizens, who were thus able to show how solvent and patriotic they were. Repetition and anticipation became powerful conduits. From the enthusiasm displayed in San Antonio for the festivities of September 16, 1835, one would not have suspected that Texas was in the throes of a major rebellion. In addition to the usual tolling bells, pyrotechnic fires, and cannon shots, a mass with *Te Deum*, and the party and dance *de rigueur*, a gas-filled globe was released from the main plaza to commemorate Mexico's deliverance from Spain. Even more enthusiastic was the Independence Day celebration of 1844 in Santa Fe, which lasted six entire days, including three days of bullfights.

Notwithstanding these attempts at national construction, sweeping economic changes tended to foil such efforts, imposing capricious cross-national alliances and intranational cleavages and in general making the logic of the market—free trade, free movement of peoples, unencumbered exploitation of natural resources—prevail over the designs of nationalist officials. Mexico's national leaders generally supported the pursuit of capitalist development in the northern frontier, but toward the 1830s, as they became more wary of real or imagined secessionist tendencies in the North, they attempted to regulate the region's integration with the economy of the United States and put obstacles in the way of increasing Anglo-American immigration. However, in so doing national officials met with decided resistance from local and regional Hispanic and Indian elites as well as Anglo-American newcomers who had interests revolving around commerce and land and depended on laissez-faire policies for their well-being.

Initially, commerce provided the impetus for change. The Spanish colonies in America were long barred from trading with the United States and European countries other than Spain, and although the Bourbon monarchs did away with some trade regulations in the 1760s and 1770s, freedom of commerce outside the empire came only after independence from Spain. Trade liberalization had a particularly strong impact on Mexico's northern provinces as they were tantalizingly close to the United States, which was rapidly becoming one of the most dynamic trading areas in the world. In New Mexico the beginning of a new commercial era can be dated with precision. The people of Santa Fe were still digesting the news of separation from Spain in mid-November 1821 when word spread of an approaching caravan of Missouri merchants. This time New Mexico's governor allowed the Anglo merchants to trade with the locals unmolested. It was the beginning of the Santa Fe Trail, which within a few years became the most important trading route between the United States and northern Mexico.

Commerce brought a new set of social relations and interests to these provinces. In New Mexico the Santa Fe Trail was at first monopolized by an exclusive group of Anglo-American traffickers and a few Frenchmen who had preceded them. They controlled the bulk of the profits and wielded commensurate political influence. But New Mexico's traditional Hispanic elite soon made the transition from land-based and sheep-raising enterprises to commercial ventures. Manuel Armijo, three times governor of New Mexico, was the most striking example. He rapidly found a way to profit from the Santa Fe Trail, as the crafty governor began to sell foreign goods to other parts of northern Mexico where he had previously sold only sheep. He was hardly alone. Such families as the Chávez, Ortiz, Otero, and Perea became successful international merchants in their own right. By 1843, nuevomexicano merchants accounted for a full 45 percent of New Mexico's total exports and 22 percent of all shipments of foreign goods going into Mexico's interior.

Texas went through a similar transition. By 1826 Anglo-Americans dominated the trading business in San Antonio and Goliad, introducing merchandise at various times of the year. But as in New Mexico, it did not take long before entrepreneurial native sons staged a return to the commercial arena. Indeed by the early 1830s Anglo-American merchants squarely competed against a powerful tejano clique. These men had developed extensive trading networks comparable to those of their Anglo counterparts, webs stretching from New Orleans suppliers to Texas customs officers and store owners. This tejano group became a formidable power to reckon with.

Although relations between Anglo and Hispanic merchants in both Texas and New Mexico were sometimes contentious, the two groups generally got along well and often forged profitable and long-lasting partnerships. In many respects the two groups of merchants were complementary. While Anglo-Americans could make introductions and pave the way for their Hispanic counterparts with suppliers in Missouri and Louisiana, Hispanic traders could reciprocate, helping their Anglo-American colleagues deal with Mexican customs officers and other authorities. The two groups were forced to travel together and to extend credit to one another. Many Anglo-American merchants married into nuevomexicano and tejano families. Above all, the merchants, regardless of ethnicity, were keenly opposed to outside meddling that threatened to interrupt the flow of profits coming from the north.

The emergence of a trading economy in Texas and New Mexico stimulated land deals, which provided yet another network of common interests. In Coahuila and Texas, state officials contracted with private developers or *empresarios* whose task was to settle at least one hundred families and to establish self-sustaining colonies in exchange for land. The majority of both *empresarios* and colonists turned out to be Anglo-American. The *empresario* system completely changed the face of Texas. In the 1810s Texas had been an undeveloped province with enormous *baldíos* (vacant lands) visited only by occasional Indian groups, hunters, and adventurous Texans. Within a few years, most of the land was parceled out among numerous settlers who showed claims under the authority of overlapping *empresario* contracts and other land development schemes. State officials in Coahuila and Texas created a powerful patronage system on the basis of land distribution. In secretive deliberations, state legislators and the governor conferred princely land grants, approved colonization enterprises, granted exclusive rights to navigate Texas rivers, and made profitable appointments for customs and land officials. From these transactions emerged a web of economic as well as political alliances that ran from state officials to *empresarios*, land commissioners, and colonists themselves, including widely diverse groups from tejano landowners to Anglo-American developers and speculators to Indian allies such as the Cherokees, who also secured a grant.

New Mexico went through a similar ... land drive.... As in Texas, these transactions naturally bound the grantees to New Mexican officials and created a network of interests that would be critical when war between Mexico and the United States broke out and the department of New Mexico tottered between the two countries.

Commercial and land transactions hindered the consolidation of the Mexican nation in Texas and New Mexico. This occurred not so much because there were cozy partnerships between local authorities and foreign businessmen as because the prosperity of those provinces hinged on the continuation and accretion of economic ties with the United States. Prominent tejanos and nuevomexicanos, with their Anglo-American partners, staked their future on the development of those provinces along federalist lines, which meant unrestricted trade with the United States, increasing immigration of Anglo-Americans, and flexible land policies that insured property rights for foreigners and recent arrivals. Given the demographic and economic imbalance between Hispanics and Anglos, this policy would eventually result in an overwhelming preponderance of Anglo-Americans along the frontier. On the eve of the Texas Revolution, northeastern Texas was largely inhabited by Anglo colonists who had prospered in a thriving cotton and cattle economy. In the years immediately before the

Mexican-American War, northern New Mexico was falling inexorably into the hands of wealthy Anglo-American merchants and some of their nuevomexicano partners.

These developments did not go unnoticed in centralist circles, and they eventually elicited a strong nationalist reaction.

Citizens who felt displaced by outsiders repeatedly resorted to patriotic rhetoric to strengthen their claims.... In sum, patriotic rhetoric became a potent cement binding local, regional, and national political groups who often pursued different immediate objectives but were all united under the same banner: to preserve the territorial integrity of Mexico.

The Texas Revolution would set the terms of the national identity struggles in Mexico's Far North in the decades to follow. Most traditional histories either trace the revolt of 1835–1836 to cultural or ethnic incompatibility between Mexicans and Americans or adopt a sweeping Manifest Destiny explanation, casting the revolution as merely a step in the westward drive of Anglo-Americans into Spanish America. Yet a growing interest in Mexican Texans has shown that the revolution was not carried out exclusively by dissatisfied Anglo colonists but that tejanos as well were actively involved. Indeed, the initial momentum to organize state militias and resist the central government's authority, even if that entailed using force, originated in Coahuila and the San Antonio–Goliad region, not in the Anglo colonies. Indians also played a crucial part in this story.... It was an unwieldy coalition of Anglo-American colonists, tejanos, and Indian tribes fighting against the national government and its local and regional allies.

The origins of the Texas Revolution have to be traced back to the clash between regional and national elites in Mexico, especially as their struggle affected the network of interests that had flourished in Texas in the 1820s. Those who advocated autonomy for the states and defended local interests against national encroachment—a heterogeneous group that came to be known as "radical liberals" or "federalists"—began to chafe after the offensive launched by their "centralist" opponents in the early 1830s.... The national government instituted reforms that threatened to alter the fundamental economic and political relations prevalent in Coahuila and Texas.

Having said this, however, we should avoid another form of historical reductionism—following contemporary rhetoric—that described the Texas Revolution as a quest for freedom against military despotism from Mexico's heartland. First, the nationalist rhetoric employed by centralists commanded enormous popular support, especially given the truly scandalous speculation and the rapid Americanization of Texas. Even within Coahuila and Texas a vocal antifederalist faction responded enthusiastically to the patriotic harangues to regain Texas for Mexico. Second, federalists and revolutionists in Texas—whether Anglo, tejano, or Indian—may all have been fighting under the collective banner of "freedom," but "freedom" was often linked to self-interest.... Both Anglo-American and tejano merchants objected to the establishment of customs houses, and both remained generally supportive of the revolution even as secession from

Mexico became permanent. Undoubtedly, in the course of the fighting, ethnic and racial tensions surfaced, but initially Texans made a revolution to protect their freedoms, their beliefs, and their interests; in the process they took the momentous decision to create a new nation.

Ten years after the Texas Revolution, in the summer of 1846, Col. Stephen W. Kearny found himself marching along the Santa Fe Trail, commanding a small army, with instructions from the United States government to take possession of New Mexico. War had begun between Mexico and the United States. On August 18, about two thousand weary and dusty American soldiers marched unopposed into Santa Fe. Their commander formally took possession of the territory of New Mexico. The Army of the West had conquered New Mexico "without the firing of a shot or the shedding of a single drop of blood," according to a contemporary description that historians have repeated ever since. Yet five months later, an anti-American rebellion broke out in the northern and western districts of New Mexico. The uprising eventually claimed the lives of the recently appointed American governor of New Mexico, several other Anglo-American residents, and at least two nuevomexicano "collaborationists." The two episodes, the unopposed march of American troops into Santa Fe and the Taos rebellion, marked the two ends of the pendulum swing in the sovereignty struggles unfolding in New Mexico. The war created an environment in which local political grievances, economic interests, and evolving identities played themselves out throughout Mexico's Far North against the backdrop of an impending invasion and possible annexation to the United States. It is tempting to interpret the war squarely as a conflict between two clearly defined nations, and it is easy to understand the ensuing territorial exchange as solely a military outcome. And yet, from the perspective of the border society—rather than that of Mexico City or Washington, D.C.—what we find is an army of invasion negotiating with local and regional actors whose loyalties did not always conform to simple national lines.

Much in the attitudes of leading nuevomexicanos toward Kearny's Army of the West in the summer of 1846 has to be traced back to a network of interests that had developed among key nuevomexicano officials and Anglo-American merchants and residents during the 1840s. Some days before the arrival of the Army of the West, Manuel Alvarez, the Spanish-born consul of the United States in Santa Fe, tried to persuade Governor Armijo not to resist. Alvarez found Armijo "vacillating to the last" and utterly undecided. Although the consul admitted that he could not persuade the governor to turn over the Department of New Mexico to the Americans, he asserted that he had had more success with "other officers" and Armijo's "confidential advisers." Santiago (James W.) Magoffin, a seasoned merchant of the Santa Fe Trail who had been commissioned by President James K. Polk to use his connections to win the northern provinces over to the American side, reported that prior to Kearny's arrival he had met many of the "rich" and the militia officers of New Mexico and, with only one exception, had found that they would be perfectly satisfied if the area became a territory of the United States. Magoffin told nuevomexicano officers that they would be happy under the star-spangled banner because their property would be respected, their houses would rise in value, and the political system would change for the better. Robert B. McAfee, another merchant, sarcastically summed up this phenomenon for President Polk: "Touch their money and you reach their hearts. Make it their interest to have peace and we will soon have it."

The events that followed are not entirely clear. The governor began preparations to face the American army of occupation at a formidable pass called *el Cañón*, fifteen miles east of Santa Fe. Yet two days before the showdown would have occurred, Governor Armijo took the momentous decision to disband the volunteers he had summoned. With seventy soldiers the governor retreated to Chihuahua, thus clearing the path of the invading army.

McAfee may have been accurate in describing the outlook of the privileged few whose interests depended on the Santa Fe Trail, but displaced elites and commoners thought otherwise. In the aftermath of the American takeover, significant discontent surfaced throughout New Mexico. The Pueblo Indians of Taos, for instance, resented the encroachment of Anglo-American and Mexican merchants on their land. Aided by the influential parish priest of Taos, José Antonio Martínez, Pueblo Indians had denounced the Miranda-Beubien land grant, claiming that it included communal lands that belonged to the Taos Pueblo and were used for hunting buffalo. They managed to persuade nuevo-mexicano officials to suspend the grant in 1844, but only temporarily. After the American occupation, Pueblo Indians feared that land encroachment would proceed more rapidly.

New Mexico's Catholic establishment also fiercely opposed annexation to the United States. Even before the military occupation of New Mexico, Father Martínez had been the most outspoken critic of Armijo's administration for "caving in" to the Americans and had delivered a series of sermons "arousing the people to a determined resistance." He warned his congregation of impending disasters and told them of his nightmares about the national government disposing of New Mexico. As the embattled priest interpreted New Mexico's situation with some hyperbole, a mob of "heretics were ready on its confines to overrun this unfortunate land." Father Martínez's patriotic rhetoric drew on a wellspring of religious symbology and Pueblo Indian mythology.

The conflicts that rocked Mexico's northern frontier in the first half of the nineteenth century, including the Texas Revolution and the Taos rebellion, were ultimately struggles over sovereignty and identity. These events cannot be reduced to ethnic conflicts between Hispanics, Native Americans, and Anglo-Americans. The surprising decision of tejano merchants to support the Anglo-American drive to secede from Mexico in 1835–1836 or the Pueblo Indians' intention to restore Mexico's sovereignty over New Mexico in 1847 seem to defy common sense because their loyalties did not conform to previous ethnic solidarities. For this reason those events well illustrate how much national identity depended on economic arrangements as well as an imagery able to speak to the needs and longings of diverse peoples.

The Mexican government, having inherited the Spanish imperial bureaucracy and its political-religious mental world, attempted to forge a Mexican identity in the northern frontier by developing patronage lines leading from the center to the remote provinces by using the overlapping administrative structures of church, military, and civil government; by promoting civic and religious rituals derived chiefly from the independence struggle; and by fashioning—often unwittingly—a defensive, antiforeign, nationalist rhetoric that was appropriated by border communities and political groups to advance their own interests and agendas. Yet, this nationalist project went against the grain of a network of economic, social, and political cross-cultural alliances brought about by the prodigious economic development of the frontier region and its growing integration into the economy of the United States.

Adopting the perspective of the people living in these border provinces, we can recast the sovereignty struggles as a vast project to organize society. The decision to become Mexican or American or Texan was not only a question of placing or imagining oneself within one collectivity; most critically, it involved choices about the organization of the economy, the contours of the political system, and religious and moral values. And in making all of those critical choices, different social groups, classes, and ethnicities that coexisted in Mexico's Far North had different and often conflicting ideas. Tejanos, federalists, indigenous communities, nuevomexicanos, centralists, merchants, *empresarios*, Anglo-Americans, and common people attempted to shape the nation to their own wishes and their best interests. In this frontier world where interests, political ideology, and national allegiances were inextricably intertwined, the deployment of Mexicanist rhetoric—or its absence—became another weapon in their everyday life struggles. The nation did not emerge full-blown right after emancipation from Spain in 1821, nor was it purposefully constructed according to blueprint laid out by the "Mexican founding fathers," it was simply a by-product of complicated alliances and counteralliances contingent on a set of local arrangements in constant flux.

Sex, Marriage, and Power in Mexican California

ALBERT L. HURTADO

Alfred Robinson, twenty-seven-year-old native of Massachusetts, figuratively kissed the hand of his future father-in-law, Don José Antonio Julián de la Guerra y Noriega. Robinson was an agent for Bryant, Sturgis and Company, a Boston-based firm that dominated California's hide and tallow trade. Don José was a native of Spain, soldier, respected man of affairs, and the richest man in the Santa Barbara region. His principal business was in raising thousands of cattle that he slaughtered for their tallow and hides, which he sold to Bryant, Sturgis, and similar companies. Doña Anita, the object of Robinson's desire, was thirteen years old.

The betrothal of Doña Anita to Alfred Robinson was emblematic of California's changed state of affairs. In 1821 Mexico had achieved its independence

Albert L. Hurtado, *Intimate Frontiers: Sex, Gender, and Culture in Old California*, pp. 21–44 (Albuquerque: University of New Mexico Press, 1999).

from Spain and California became a part of the new American nation. Mexico re-formed the antiquated trade laws of Spain that in most cases had restricted colonies to trading only with the mother country. Consequently, enterprising Mexicans and Americans began to carry goods along the Santa Fe Trail, and California ports became open to merchants who obtained the necessary license in Monterey, the provincial capital. But what did California have to trade? There were hundreds of thousands of horned cattle grazing on the yellow coastal hills, but before the days of refrigeration it was impossible to ship fresh meat over great distances and markets for salt and jerked beef were limited. Bryant, Sturgis soon sent an agent who gained a share of the market and eventually dominated the California hide and tallow business, although they had many competitors.

Under Spain, missions had been the primary economic institution of California. Franciscan missionaries controlled most of the arable land, vast livestock herds, and a workforce of thousands of Indians who tended the herds and plowed mission fields. The Mexican government would secularize the missions—convert missions to small parish churches and convey the vast pastoral holdings of the church to private ownership. Theoretically, mission Indians would receive land grants from the missions where they had lived and worked, but this seldom happened. Because the missions were so important to the economic well-being of California, the governors at first appointed secular administrators, who administered the missions as they were being broken up. Administrators could compel the former neophytes to labor on mission lands even as they were granted status as citizens. Few Indians were willing to work for new masters at their old missions. Most of them went to work for Mexican rancheros and became peons in the process, or moved to the interior where they lived with independent Indian communities. Secular administrators liquidated the mission property and arrogated mission revenue to themselves. Ultimately, the Mexican government gave more than five hundred grants of land to applicants, who got tens of thousands of acres after paying a small filing fee and meeting nominal government requirements. Most of these grants were made from former mission lands. This transfer of property created a private latifundio system and an elite that was land-and cattle-rich, but money-poor. It also made the daughters of the de la Guerra, Carrillo, Bandini, Vallejo, and other California families exceedingly attractive marriage partners. By making favorable matches, landed californio families could consolidate holdings through marriage, and new-comers—such as Robinson—could become a part of the gentry.

The hide and tallow trade would dominate the Mexican California economy through the mid-1840s. Every year American and British traders bartered manufactured goods for thousands of hides destined to be made into harness, boots, shoes, and leather goods. Some of these finished products returned "round the horn" to California, and were bartered to Californians for more dry hides and bags of tallow—at a profit handsome enough to attract Yankee investors and competitors from the United States and England. One observer claimed that more than 100,000 hides were shipped from California each year.

Virtually no cash changed hands in the hide trade. Cow hides were known as California banknotes and were worth about $1.50, although the value varied according to the market. Sea captains and the few permanent merchants who established stores advanced credit to Californians who guaranteed their debts with hides from future slaughters. Thus the californios, seemingly so rich in land and cattle, were snared in a system of debt and credit and made dependent on an international trade in which they traded raw materials for manufactured goods. This was a relationship that historian David Weber has called "the new colonialism." Mexicans had cast off their old political masters, but in their haste to enter the capitalist marketplace they failed to recognize that as providers of raw materials in exchange for manufactured goods they were in a disadvantageous position. They were accustomed to doing business on a small scale with people whom they knew and often to whom they were related either by blood or by *compadrazgo*—a system of godparentage that linked Californians in a fictive kin network. Children received *compadres* (godparents) at birth and other important life events. These authority figures provided advice, security, and sometimes became foster parents in the event of the birth parents' death. This elaborate network of blood and fictive kin connected californio families in the Spanish and Mexican periods and beyond. These extended biological and fictive families gave Mexican Californians identity and security. Additional kinship ties with Yankee and Anglo traders seemed to assure mutuality in trade and a degree of continuity with familiar traditions. It was logical that the de la Guerra family added William Hartnell, the first hide and tallow trader in California, as a son-in-law. Many another californio family would follow the de la Guerra's example.

While the hide and tallow trade embodied a colonial relationship between frontier Mexico and the industrializing United States, marriages like Robinson's evoked another old institution—patriarchy. When Robinson begged for the hand of Don José's daughter, he was not merely observing a formality that had lost its literal meaning. Truly, Don José held the key to Robinson's happiness, "in this world," as the suitor said. The father could have prevented the marriage of Alfred and Doña Anita had he so desired, for in California the father's permission was required before a woman could marry. In theory a woman was not required to marry against her will, but law and traditions that spanned the Spanish and Mexican eras supported fathers' control over their daughters' marital future. Moreover, elite families often arranged the marriages of their children so that a good match would be assured rather than leaving this important matter to the whims of mere youthful passion. Betrothals of girls who had yet to reach menarche—which may have been the case with thirteen-year-old Doña Anita— were not unknown. In theory, Mexican Californians could have married Indian women, and some of them did. Most californios were in fact from mixed or entirely non-Spanish stock, but elite families that claimed to have pure Spanish blood were deeply concerned about maintaining the supposed racial purity of their line. In this respect Anglo Americans could be helpful. Even though they were not Spanish they were white, and on that account were eligible to marry in the best families.

Studies of the marriage record show that only a small fraction of Spanish and Mexican colonists married Indians during the Spanish period.

In colonial California, as in other frontier regions, there were far more men than women, a condition that drove male competition for eligible women and fostered early betrothal of some young girls.

Not all of the young women who were married by arrangement were complacent or content, but there was little that they could do about it. Marriage, the production of legitimate children, and the protection of family honor were the common duties of most California women. Those who resisted faced the combined wrath of brothers, husbands, and fathers both temporal and spiritual.

Lack of power, however, did not keep all women from accusing men of sexual crimes or of violating sexual mores themselves.... californianas denounced seducers, and accused rapists. The record also shows that women had their share of illicit affairs. In one case, Juan Francisco Bernal threatened to beat his mother after learning that she was having carnal relations with Marcelo Pinto, a notorious soldier. There were accusations and counteraccusations of adultery, corruption of minors, and dishonor. Priests recorded the births of illegitimate babies in the mission registers and were accused of fathering some of them. Sexual competition for females and women's desire to control their sexual lives made it impossible to uphold the absolute standards that Spanish-Mexican patriarchy demanded.

This was the society that foreigners entered in the nineteenth century. For New Englanders like Robinson, the California world was quite different from their homeland in several respects. Of course, Bostonians had their own forms of patriarchy, and Anglo-Protestant men and women were as capable of rape, fornication, and adultery as were Hispanic Catholics. The formal rules of Anglo sexual behavior and marriage were in some ways similar to those that pertained in Hispanic California. Men and women were both supposed to be virgins when they married; extramarital sex was forbidden; divorce was very difficult to obtain. In 1821 women's rights were as strictly limited in Boston as they were in Monterey. Women were legal appendages of their husbands, who usually retained custody of children in the rare event of divorce. In one respect, Anglo American women were even less free than their California counterparts because they lost control of their property when they married; californianas did not.

In the early nineteenth century Anglo American beliefs about female sexuality differed markedly from Hispanic ideas. Until the mid-1700s Anglos believed that women enjoyed sex, although ideally sex was for procreation and not merely for pleasure. In the nineteenth century medical men and moralists began to propose a new notion—that women were naturally frail, nervous creatures who lacked much interest in sex except as a means to have babies. These theories emerged as women began to challenge patriarchal authority and the United States was experiencing the upheavals and uncertainties that accompanied industrialization. In such an unsettling time many men preferred women who did not challenge authority in or out of the marriage bed. The "cult of true womanhood" was the prevailing ideology that governed women's behavior. Women were supposed to be pure, pious, and domestic. They aspired—or so it was thought—to nothing more than raising children, keeping house, and making the home an undisturbing sanctuary for the husband/father when he returned from his worldly struggle to gain a living for his wife and family.

On the other hand, Spanish-Mexican men believed that women were naturally lustful creatures who were apt to meekly submit to the sexual demands of a would-be seducer. That is why families chaperoned young couples, even when they were engaged. It was important to maintain family honor and the unquestioned virginity of daughters. If a young woman was rumored to have had sex, her value on the marriage market was diminished—at least as far as making a good match with an elite family was concerned. Here was another reason to betroth very young girls and to marry them as soon after menarche as possible. Of course, neither Anglo nor Hispanic women necessarily lived according to the sexual ideologies that prevailed in the nineteenth century. But the ideals of their respective societies conditioned expectations about sexuality of Anglo and Mexican men and women alike.

The Anglo American hide traders who went to California in the Mexican era knew that they would have to remain for an extended time, perhaps for many years. Those who wished to marry during their sojourn would almost certainly have to marry a californiana, a match that would, it was hoped, secure domestic happiness as well as property and an advantage in trade. Hide traders would have to adjust to California marriage customs to marry a daughter from one of the elite families. Among other things, they would have to become Catholics. Church and state required that Protestants convert to Catholicism before a marriage took place and foreigners had to apply to the governor for permission to marry. Naturalization was not required to marry, but for Mexican citizens there was land to be had for the asking. Religious and national qualms seldom deterred Robinson and his colleagues from marrying or acquiring land. Many a Boston man renounced his U.S. citizenship in order to gain the landed wealth that was so enticingly available.

Robinson worked hard in the hide business, sailing up and down the coast trading with the ranchers and learning the ropes. He became a Catholic, but evidently did not become a Mexican citizen. With the approval of Doña Anita's father, Robinson's citizenship proved to be no bar to marriage, although they waited until she was fifteen before marrying (perhaps delaying until she was sexually mature). The people of Santa Barbara celebrated the alliance between the Bryant, Sturgis agent and the de la Guerra family as if it were a state affair.

While Robinson's financial interests in California and the de la Guerras were obvious, it is also evident that he had more than a pecuniary association with his in-laws. He affectionately corresponded with them about family matters, even after Doña Anita died in 1853. He seemed to take great pleasure in discussing political matters with his father- and brother-in-law, and took special delight in satirizing the Democratic party. Surely, Robinson married for more than money.

The precise number of marriages between californianas and Americans is not known, but nineteenth-century historian Hubert Howe Bancroft compiled brief biographies of all of the prominent California pioneers, including marriage data. While his list is incomplete, it provides a reliable source of information on the best-known mixed marriages. He recorded eighty such unions between 1817 and 1848. Half of the men were from the United States and nearly one-third were from the northeastern states—mostly from Massachusetts. Forty percent of the grooms came from the British Isles (nearly one-quarter were English). The men who married into California's elite families truly were Anglo American.

Mixed marriages began as soon as foreigners began to arrive and continued throughout the Mexican period.... Five to six years was the median period that grooms spent in California before marrying, although part of that time may have been spent on voyages back to Massachusetts, or waiting through a long engagement. Nevertheless, it is clear that most foreigners did not jump into marriages with californianas. This may have been due to the californios' strict rules of propriety as well as circumspection on the part of the prospective husbands. Bancroft's "Pioneer Register" is a limited source of data for mixed marriage, but it suggests that grooms and prospective in-laws considered marriage a very serious undertaking that should not be rushed into. Marriage was meant to be a permanent arrangement that would benefit the family for as long as it lasted.

While maritime merchants married into Mexican families on the coast, a new group or Europeans and Americans began to filter into the great central valley of California. In 1827, Jedediah Smith led a party of trappers into the interior in search of beaver pelts. He found some, and he also found another potentially valuable export commodity—horses. Smith purchased horses from the ranchos on the coast and drove them north to Oregon, hoping that he could eventually sell them at a profit. Umpqua Indians foiled his scheme, took the horses, killed most of Smith's men, and barely missed putting an end to Smith. Nevertheless, scores of American trappers followed Smith into California by the southwestern route, and the British Hudson's Bay Company sent expeditions from Oregon as well. Some trappers emulated Smith's horse-trading venture, but not all of them relied on legal purchases to acquire stock. Instead, they teamed up with Indians who lived in the interior—Yokuts, Miwoks, and ex-mission Indians—and who raided the coastal herds. Thus engaged in horse rustling, these newcomers cared nothing about maintaining good relations with elite Mexican families. Nor did they live permanently in the interior, preferring instead to make an annual journey to California and drive their stolen stock back to the Missouri frontier. While all this was going on, Mexican rancheros and soldiers periodically raided Indian communities in the central valley.

Even though the California interior was an isolated region, between 1827 and 1839 it became an international frontier where Indians, agents from the Hudson's Bay Company, American trappers, horse thieves, Mexican soldiers, and rancheros converged. They struggled to control California's horse herds, a critical resource in an economy based on wild, long-horned cattle. Until 1839, however, Indians did not have to worry about any of these newcomers settling in the interior. Spanish and Mexican officials had deemed new mission projects too expensive and risky, so they left the venture to private parties who, they hoped, would take up land grants east of coastal settlements. Mexican rancheros were not quick to move into a region where they had been fighting with Indians for decades, so the government relied on foreigners to occupy this disputed district. In 1837, John Marsh, a former U.S. Indian agent who claimed to be a physician, made his home on a grant that he purchased on the western edge of the San Joaquin Valley. Two years later, John A. Sutter convinced Governor Juan Alvarado that he was a man of great military experience who would be useful in suppressing Indian livestock raiding. Alvarado permitted Sutter to colonize the Sacramento Valley where the American River flowed into the Sacramento.

Marsh and Sutter not only made permanent settlements for themselves, they inspired other Americans to make the overland journey and settle in the California interior. Sutter's Fort, near the confluence of the American and Sacramento rivers, was the military heart of the Swiss-American's New Helvetia agricultural business and became the destination for overland immigrants to California. Sutter employed scores of American immigrants and hundreds of Indian laborers who kept his enterprise humming. To obtain Indian labor, Sutter relied on diplomacy, trade, and blunt force. He established an Indian army that intimidated surrounding tribes and protected his herds and those of his neighbors.

While imposing his military and economic will on the Indian communities of the Sacramento and San Joaquin valleys, Sutter altered native traditions of courtship and marriage. Formerly Central California Indians forged alliances through marriage. Usually the prospective husband asked permission of the parents of his intended spouse. If they were agreeable, the young man brought meat from the hunt and other goods to the home of his in-laws. Then the couple could marry. Some powerful and rich men had two or more wives, but most had only one. As usual, marriages were meant to link families in a kinship network that assured friendship, prosperity, and allies in troubled times.

Sutter, the self-proclaimed patriarch of New Helvetia, took it upon himself to intervene in the Indians' long-established marriage customs. Years later, he reminisced that "polygamy obtained among the Indians and I determined to stop it" because "the chiefs had so many wives that the young men ... could have none." Claiming that he had the interests of young Indian men at heart, Sutter put all of the marriageable men and women in rows facing each other. "Then I told the women one after another to come forward and select the man they wanted." Sutter denied "the chiefs more than one or two wives each," but he did not mention that white men were also competing for Indian women, including the lord of New Helvetia himself. Taking Indian helpmeets—at least temporarily—was a time-honored practice among fur trappers and traders, although fur men often abandoned their Indian wives when they left Indian country or when racially suitable wives became available.

While Sutter subverted Indian marriage customs, he arrogated the authority of the Catholic Church and Mexican state in matrimonial matters as well. He evidently believed that he had civil authority to marry people because he was the New Helvetia *alcalde*. In 1844, he therefore married several American couples, including Cyrus Alexander (an American) and Rufina Lucero, who was from New Mexico. "Oh yesh," Sutter reputedly assured Alexander, "I ish der law, I cans perform der serremony, und all ish den right." Alexander accepted

Sutter's bland assurances and allowed the captain to marry him at the fort. Some time later a priest from the Mission Santa Clara informed the Alexanders and other couples whom Sutter had joined that they were not legally married, and that their wives must return to their parents until they were married in the church. Alexander was outraged because he believed that the priests were merely trying to extort money from him, and because his young son was now illegitimate. Three other couples who had married under Sutter received similar notification, but only two of them and the Alexanders dutifully—and angrily—went to Santa Clara to be married again. The disobedient man later teased the couples because the war with Mexico soon limited the priests' authority over civil marriages and asserted that by obeying the priests Alexander had admitted that his marriage under Sutter was illegal. Alexander retaliated by saying that his tormentor and his wife simply had no shoes and didn't want to get married barefoot. Such were the airs of propriety among Americans in the 1840.

The custom of taking an Indian wife may have been time honored, but it was not universally respected or admired in Anglo American society. "Squaw man" and "half-breed" were racial slurs that condemned interracial sex and the progeny that came from it. Once the frontier era had passed, male pioneers and their biographers often extolled their heroic exploits while politely forgetting to mention the Indian women who baked their bread and bore their children. Yet they often sneeringly divulged the sexual adventures of other fellows who crossed the color line. Captain Sutter was especially vulnerable to rumormongers. He had abandoned his wife and children in Switzerland to escape debtors' prison. In the Sandwich Islands Sutter picked up a Hawaiian mistress, Manaiki, who was his favorite consort at New Helvetia, but she had to share him with Indian women. Heinrich Lienhard, who was critical of everyone's behavior but his own, charged that there was a special room for young Indian women adjoining Sutter's apartment in the fort. Worse, he accused Sutter of having sexual relations with Indian girls as young as ten. Lienhard may have embellished his accusations, but Sutter's own correspondence explicitly reveals a trade in boys and girls that hints at a sexual dimension. Sutter captured these children during his attacks on Indian communities and sold or leased them to other ranchers. John Chamberlain, Sutter's blacksmith, said that "it was customary for Capt Sutter to buy and sell Indian boys & girls." Accusations that Sutter was a pedophile are not proven, but charges of child abuse are conclusive.

Just as Chamberlain exposed Sutter's transgressions, John Yates pointed to Chamberlain's sexual habits. The blacksmith was "given to gazing on the native females," Yates reported, and Chamberlain did more than look at Indian women. "I learnt that he had been married nineteen times to native women & to my own certain knowledge he was when I last saw him newly married to an American girl of thirteen." Neither was Yates altogether blameless in this regard, for Yates kept two Indian mistresses. Eventually he married a sixteen-year-old immigrant, but the marriage foundered because the Indians refused to give up their white husband. And so it went. Up and down the valleys, Americans and Europeans mated with Indian women in the 1840s, then the esteemed pioneers snickered and pointed their fingers at others a quarter-century later.

For most whites, these unions were doubtless alliances of convenience that were necessary when frontier conditions prevailed and Indians were a large majority in the region. In addition to the domestic and sexual services of their Indian wives, whites gained friends, laborers, and allies through Indian kinship ties. Once equipped with a local Indian wife, these men were no longer mere interlopers but members of an Indian community. This status, reinforced with Sutter's military presence, enabled a small group of whites to live among Indians in relative security and to benefit from Indian labor. After the discovery of gold and the ensuing rush of new people to California, the need for native workers and soldiers subsided, so white men usually abandoned their Indian wives for new mates. The Indians—wives and kin alike—who joined in these unions gained temporary access to trade goods and a modicum of security in rapidly changing times. When times changed and the connubial arrangements with whites dissolved, they had to find new ways to satisfy these needs. In the end, they were left to rely on their own resources for survival during the extravagant upheavals of the gold rush and its aftermath.

Intermarriages in the interior and on the coast occurred according to the needs of the people who lived in their respective regions. On the coast californios were clearly in political control, so Americans and others seldom violated the prevailing marriage laws and customs. Rancheros may have been in a disadvantageous position in a colonial trade network, but they were unquestioned patriarchs at home. Yankees like Alfred Robinson therefore kissed the hands of their fathers-in-law, joined the Catholic Church, and ofttimes became citizens of Mexico. More than that, Yankee husbands often displayed more than perfunctory attention to their religious and marital obligations after the change in national sovereignty in 1848. To be sure, they had material reasons for keeping up appearances. Most of them had acquired substantial landholdings and might inherit even more when their fathers-in-law passed on. They also had children of their own to provide for. In American and californio minds alike, there was no racial problem in the marriages to elite California families. Californios insisted that they were white, that they were of unmixed blood, and they often claimed to be descended from Spain's noble lines. Whatever the facts may have been, Americans happily accepted this bleached version of California family history. It was a good thing for an American to be married into a California family.

A connection to an Indian woman, whether solemnized with Sutter's supposed authority or more casually effected, had little lasting value for the white men involved. American society scorned "squaws," "squaw men," and their "half-breed" children. Indians were not part of a landed gentry, but a despised racial minority whose fate, as far as most Americans were concerned, was to be dispossessed and obliterated. Once the country was settled, an Indian family could only hinder the social advancement of pioneers. Thus, the custom of mixed marriage in Mexican California proceeded along two paths. One was seemingly a highway to material wealth and social status; the other was a dead end to be abandoned at first opportunity. Both were well-traveled roads.

FURTHER READING

Blackhawk, Ned. *Violence over the Land: Indians and Empires in the Early American West* (2006).

Brooks, James F. *Captives and Cousins: Slavery, Kinship, and Community in the Southwest Borderlands* (2002).

Brown, William E. *The Santa Fe Trail: The National Park Service 1963 Historic Sites Survey* (1988).

Casas, Maria Raquél. *Married to a Daughter of the Land* (2007).

Craver, Rebecca McDowell. *The Impact of Intimacy: Mexican-Anglo Intermarriage in New Mexico, 1821–1846* (1982).

Griffen, William B. *Utmost Good Faith: Patterns of Apache-Mexican Hostilities in Northern Chihuahua Border Warfare, 1821–1848* (1988).

Hackel, Steven W. *Children of Coyote, Missionaries of Saint Francis: Indian-Spanish Relations in Colonial California, 1769–1850* (2005).

Iverson, Peter, and Monty Roessel. *Dine: A History of the Navajos* (2002).

Jackson, Jack, ed., and John Wheat, trans. *Texas by Terán: The Diary Kept by General Manuel de Mier y Terán on His 1828 Inspection of Texas* (2000).

Kenner, Charles L. *The Comanchero Frontier: A History of New Mexican-Plains Indian Relations* (1969; rev. ed., 1994).

Langum, David J. *Law and Community on the Mexican California Frontier: Anglo-American Expatriates and the Clash of Legal Traditions, 1821–1846* (1987).

Lecompte, Janet. *A Rebellion in Río Arriba.* (1985).

Matovina, Timothy M. *Tejano Religion and Ethnicity: San Antonio, 1821–1860* (1995).

McNitt, Frank. *Navajo Wars: Military Campaigns, Slave Raids, and Reprisals* (1972).

Monroy, Douglas. *Thrown Among Strangers: The Making of Mexican Culture in Frontier California* (1990).

Moorhead, Max L. *New Mexico's Royal Road: Trade and Travel on the Chihuahua Trail* (1958).

Mulroy, Kevin. *Freedom on the Border: The Seminole Maroons in Florida, the Indian Territory, Coahuila, and Texas* (1993).

Pubols, Louise. *The Father of All: The de la Guerra Family, Power, and Patriarchy in Mexican California* (2010).

Ramos, Raúl A. *Beyond the Alamo: Forging Mexican Ethnicity in San Antonio, 1821–1861* (2008).

Reséndez, Andrés. *Changing National Identities at the Frontier: Texas and New Mexico, 1800–1850* (2005).

Tijerina, Andres. *Tejanos and Texas Under the Mexican Flag 1821–1836* (1994).

Walker, Henry Pickering. *The Wagonmasters: High Plains Freighting from the Earliest Days of the Santa Fe Trail to 1880* (1966).

Weber, David J. *Taos Trappers: The Fur Trade in the Far Southwest, 1540–1846* (1968).

———. *The Mexican Frontier, 1821–1846: The American Southwest Under Mexico* (1982).

CHAPTER 8

~

Anglo-American Takeover
of the Southwest Borderlands

Between 1836 and 1845, through two votes and two wars, the Mexican North became the American Southwest. In 1835, disillusioned by Mexico City's attempts to create a tightly centralized nation, the Anglo-American colonists in Texas, together with a nucleus of Texas Mexicans, voted to sever the province from Mexico, a move that brought about a war with Mexico, the battles of the Alamo and San Jacinto, and a tenuous independence. In 1845, after years of wavering, the U.S. Congress voted to annex the Republic of Texas, triggering a war with Mexico that delivered to the United States a territory that today comprises California, Nevada, Utah, Arizona, and parts of New Mexico and Colorado. These were epoch-shifting events that ushered in a new era—the United States was now a continental power—but they also marked the culmination of an older history. That history can be only partially understood through a national prism, through the aspirations and actions of nation-states. For a more complete picture, it is necessary to look at the borderlands and the ways in which their inhabitants embraced, emulated, exploited, detested, and, eventually, rejected one another. The U.S.-Mexico borderlands were not putty in the hands of national governments; the borderlanders played an active role in the process that brought an international border in their midst.

The previous chapter discussed how market and marital relations reconfigured identities and loosened loyalties in the Mexican North, pushing local communities to envision alternate futures for the borderlands. American commodities, merchants, immigrants, and customs became ubiquitous, and the borderlands began to turn from Mexico toward the United States. This reorientation raised the specter of U.S. takeover, preparing the borderlands for a more purposeful and aggressive conquest. This chapter explores how Americans maneuvered politically and militarily to absorb the Mexican North and how Mexicans responded to those efforts. It also discusses how the enduring indigenous power in the borderlands shaped Mexican and American policies during the years leading up to the U.S.-Mexican War and how that war revealed deep divisions within both U.S. and Mexican societies.

∿ DOCUMENTS

On March 2, 1836, while the Alamo in San Antonio was under siege by the Mexican Army, delegates from several Texas communities gathered at Washington-on-the-Brazos and declared independence. Historians have identified many causes for this Texas revolt: strict customs regulations, the prohibition of slavery in Mexico in 1829, and the 1830 ban on further immigration from the United States had alienated Anglo immigrants and members of the Tejano elite from Mexico. But the final spark came in 1835, when a new centralist regime came to power in Mexico City and set out to curtail state rights. The first document is the Texas Declaration of Independence, which echoes the U.S. Declaration of Independence almost sixty years earlier. The document contains two main sections: a statement on the nature of good government and a list of grievances. The second document is a map drawn by Stephen F. Austin, a prominent empresario and Anglo-Texas political leader, in 1835. The map captures the process of "cartographic dispossession" by which Euro-American colonists used maps to diminish and ultimately revoke native territorial claims. Most of the land marked on this map as Anglo-Texan empresario grants was actually controlled by the Comanches, who here seem to hover in the air, unattached to land and the political landscape. Austin's map anticipated the appropriation of Comanche and other Plains Indian lands by the United States in the late nineteenth century.

In the years leading up to the U.S.-Mexican War, anti-Mexican sentiments became increasingly prevalent in the United States. Rufus B. Sage, a journalist and a fur trapper, both built on and inflamed the growing anti-Mexican rhetoric in his *Scenes of the Rocky Mountains*, published in 1846 and excerpted here as Document 3. Sage blended common Anglo-American stereotypes about Mexicans into a highly negative portrayal that found a ready audience among those Americans who believed that Mexico deserved to be conquered by a more progressive and industrious United States. Document 4 offers a different kind of window into Anglo-American attitudes toward Mexicans and the Mexican Republic. In September 1841, Thomas Catesby Jones, the commander of the Pacific fleet of the United States Navy, received a message that war between the United States and Mexico was imminent. Jones sailed to Monterrey, where, on October 19, he issued a proclamation announcing the U.S. takeover of California. Jones's proclamation portrays the U.S. Navy not as an occupying force, but as a liberating one, and his list of American blessings reads as an inverse list of Mexican failures. Once Jones learned that war had not broken out, he sailed out of Monterrey.

On May 11, 1846, following a clash between Mexican and U.S. troops on the north side of the Rio Grande, President James K. Polk sent a war message to Congress, which, with overwhelming majorities in both the Senate and the House, declared war on Mexico on May 13. Document 5 is the speech Abraham Lincoln delivered to the U.S. House of Representatives in January 1848, condemning the way the United States had entered the war with Mexico and the way President Polk was leading the war effort. Lincoln, then serving his only term in the House, centered his criticism on the uncertainty of the exact location of the U.S.-Mexico border before the war, a legacy of Texas's long history as a contested borderland with fluid, undetermined boundaries.

The U.S.-Mexico War ended on February 2, 1848, with the signing of the Treaty of Guadalupe Hidalgo. The treaty consisted of twenty-three articles, three of which—VIII, IX, X—concerned the rights of the Spanish-speaking inhabitants who stayed in the transferred lands. Before ratification, however, the U.S. Senate revised Article IX and eliminated Article X altogether. Document 6 includes Articles VIII and IX as ratified by the U.S. Senate on March 19, 1848, and by the Mexican legislature on May 25, 1848. The document also includes the expunged Article X and Article XI, which concerned Indian raiding across the border. Finally, the document includes Article IX prior to the amendment. These articles—the ratified, the revised, the eliminated—invite several questions. If territorial conquest of the Mexican North created the category of "Mexican Americans," the Treaty of Guadalupe Hidalgo gave that category meaning. Was "Mexican American" an ethnocultural, legal, national, or historical designation? What possible motives did the U.S. Senate have for the revisions of the original treaty? Why would the enforcement of Article XI pose serious difficulties for the United States?

The Treaty of Guadalupe Hidalgo decreed that pre-existing land titles from the Spanish and Mexican periods would be protected in New Mexico, Arizona, and California (Texas was exempted), but in reality Mexican Americans lost their land at an accelerating pace. In 1851, three years into the California Gold Rush, Congress passed the California Land Act, which put the burden of proof of titles upon claimants. To confirm their titles, Mexican Americans had to engage in costly litigation in an unfamiliar judicial system and in a foreign language, and many of them lost their lands. Document 7 is a petition of mostly Spanish-speaking landowners to the U.S. Senate and the House of Representatives in which they argue that California's process of verifying land ownership violated their rights as defined in the Treaty of Guadalupe Hidalgo.

1. Texan Rebels Declare Independence, 1836

When a government has ceased to protect the lives, liberty and property of the people, from whom its legitimate powers are derived, and for the advancement of whose happiness it was instituted; and so far from being a guarantee for their inestimable and inalienable rights, becomes an instrument in the hands of evil rulers for their oppression. When the federal republican constitution of their country, which they have sworn to support, no longer has a substantial existence, and the whole nature of their government has been forcibly changed, without their consent, from a restricted federative republic, composed

---

H. P. N. Gammel, comp., *The Laws of Texas, 1822–1897* (Austin: Gammel Book Co., 1898), 1: 1063–1066.

of sovereign states, to a consolidated central military despotism, in which every interest is disregarded but that of the army and the priesthood, both the eternal enemies of civil liberty, the ever ready minions of power, and the usual instruments of tyrants. When, long after the spirit of the constitution has departed, moderation is at length so far lost by those in power, that even the semblance of freedom is removed, and the forms themselves of the constitution discontinued, and so far from their petitions and remonstrances being regarded, the agents who bear them are thrown into dungeons, and mercenary armies sent forth to enforce a new government upon them at the point of the bayonet.

When, in consequence of such acts of malfeasance and abduction on the part of the government, anarchy prevails, and civil society is dissolved into its original elements, in such a crisis, the first law of nature, the right of self-preservation, the inherent and inalienable right of the people to appeal to first principles, and take their political affairs into their own hands in extreme cases, enjoins it as a right towards themselves, and a sacred obligation to their posterity, to abolish such government, and create another in its stead, calculated to rescue them from impending dangers, and to secure their welfare and happiness.

Nations, as well as individuals, are amenable for their acts to the public opinion of mankind. A statement of a part of our grievances is therefore submitted to an impartial world, in justification of the hazardous but unavoidable step now taken, of severing our political connection with the Mexican people, and assuming an independent attitude among the nations of the earth.

The Mexican government, by its colonization laws, invited and induced the Anglo American population of Texas to colonize its wilderness under the pledged faith of a written constitution, that they should continue to enjoy that constitutional liberty and republican government to which they had been habituated in the land of their birth, the United States of America.

In this expectation they have been cruelly disappointed, inasmuch as the Mexican nation has acquiesced to the late changes made in the government by General Antonio Lopez de Santa Anna, who, having overturned the constitution of his country, now offers, as the cruel alternative, either to abandon our homes, acquired by so many privations, or submit to the most intolerable of all tyranny, the combined despotism of the sword and the priesthood.

It hath sacrificed our welfare to the state of Coahuila, by which our interests have been continually depressed through a jealous and partial course of legislation, carried on at a far distant seat of government, by a hostile majority, in an unknown tongue, and this too, notwithstanding we have petitioned in the humblest terms for the establishment of a separate state government, and have, in accordance with the provisions of the national constitution, presented to the general congress a republican constitution, which was, without a just cause, contemptuously rejected.

It incarcerated in a dungeon, for a long time, one of our citizens, for no other cause but a zealous endeavour to procure the acceptance of our constitution, and the establishment of a state government.

It has failed and refused to secure, on a firm basis, the right of trial by jury, that palladium of civil liberty, and only safe guarantee for the life, liberty, and property of the citizen.

It has failed to establish any public system of education, although possessed of almost boundless resources, (the public domain,) and although it is an axiom in political science, that unless a people are educated and enlightened, it is idle to expect the continuance of civil liberty, or the capacity for self government.

It has suffered the military commandants, stationed among us, to exercise arbitrary acts of oppression and tyranny, thus trampling upon the most sacred rights of the citizen, and rendering the military superior to the civil power.

It has dissolved, by force of arms, the state congress of Coahuila and Texas, and obliged our representatives to fly for their lives from the seat of government, thus depriving us of the fundamental political right of representation.

It has demanded the surrender of a number of our citizens, and ordered military detachments to seize and carry them into the interior for trial, in contempt of the civil authorities, and in defiance of the laws and the constitution.

It has made piratical attacks upon our commerce, by commissioning foreign desperadoes, and authorizing them to seize our vessels, and convey the property of our citizens to far distant parts for confiscation.

It denies us the right of worshiping the Almighty according to the dictates of our own conscience, by the support of a national religion, calculated to promote the temporal interest of its human functionaries, rather than the glory of the true and living God.

It has demanded us to deliver up our arms, which are essential to our defence—the rightful property of freeman—and formidable only to tyrannical governments.

It has invaded our country both by sea and by land, with the intent to lay waste our territory, and drive us from our homes; and has now a large mercenary army advancing, to carry on against us a war of extermination.

It has, through its emissaries, incited the merciless savage, with the tomahawk and scalping knife, to massacre the inhabitants of our defenceless frontiers.

It has been, during the whole time of our connection with it, the contemptible sport and victim of successive military revolutions, and hath continually exhibited every characteristic of a weak, corrupt, and tryannical government.

These, and other grievances, were patiently borne by the people of Texas, until they reached that point at which forbearance ceases to be a virtue. We then took up arms in defence of the national constitution. We appealed to our Mexican brethren for assistance: our appeal has been made in vain; though months have elapsed, no sympathetic response has yet been heard from the interior. We are, therefore, forced to the melancholy conclusion, that the Mexican people have acquiesced in the destruction of their liberty, and the substitution therefor of a military government; that they are unfit to be free, and incapable of self government.

The necessity of self-preservation, therefore, now decrees our eternal political separation.

2. Stephen F. Austin's Map of Empresario Land Grants in Texas, 1835

Map of Texas by Stephen F. Austin. Published by H. S. Tanner. Courtesy of Center for American History, University of Texas at Austin.

3. Rufus Sage Condemns the Inhabitants of New Mexico, 1846

The mountains are rich in minerals of various kinds. Gold is found in considerable quantities in their vicinity, and would doubtless yield a large profit to diggers, were they possessed of the requisite enterprise and capital. At present these valuable mines are almost entirely neglected,—the common people being too ignorant and poor to work them, and the rich too indolent and fond of ease.

The Mexicans possess large *ranchos* of sheep, horses, mules, and cattle among the mountains, which are kept there the entire year, by a degraded set of beings, following no business but that of herdsmen, or *rancheros*.

This class of people have no loftier aspirations than to throw the *lasso* with dexterity, and break wild mules and horses.

They have scarcely an idea of any other place than the little circle in which they move, nor dream of a more happy state of existence than their own. Half-naked and scantily fed, they are contented with the miserable pittance doled out to them by the proud lordlings they serve, while their wild songs merrily echo through the hills as they pursue their ceaseless vocations till death drops his dark curtain o'er the scene.

There are no people on the continent of America, whether civilized or uncivilized, with one or two exceptions, more miserable in condition or despicable in morals than the mongrel race inhabiting New Mexico. In saying this, I deal in generalities; but were I to particularize the observation would hold good in a large majority of cases.

Next to the squalid appearance of its inhabitants, the first thing that arrests the attention of the traveller on entering an [*sic*] Mexican settlement, is the uninviting mud walls that form the rude hovels which constitute its dwellings.

These are one story high and built of *adobies* [*adobes*], with small windows, (like the port-holes of a fortification,) generally without glass. The entrance is by an opening in the side, very low, and frequently unprotected by a door. The roof is a terrace of sod, reposing upon a layer of small logs, affording but poor protection from the weather.

The interior presents an aspect quite as forbidding;—the floors are simply the naked ground,—chairs and tables are articles rarely met with. In case of an extra room, it is partitioned off by a thin wall of mud, communicating with its neighbor through a small window-shaped aperture, and serves the double purpose of a chamber and store-house.

A few rags, tattered blankets, or old robes, furnish beds for its inmates, who, at nightfall, stow themselves away promiscuously upon the ground or in narrow bins, and snooze their rounds despite the swarms of noxious vermin that infest

LeRoy R. and Ann W. Hafen, eds., *Rufus B. Sage: His Letters and Papers, 1836–1847, With an Annotated Reprint of His "Scenes in the Rocky Mountains, and in Oregon, California, New Mexico, Texas and the Grand Prairies"* (Glendale, CA: The Arthur H. Clark Company, 1956), 2: 82–87. This document is also available in David J. Weber, ed., *Foreigners in Their Own Land: Historical Roots of the Mexican Americans* (Albuquerque: University of New Mexico Press, 1973), 73–75.

them, (companions from which they are seldom free, whether sleeping or waking,—and afford them, perhaps, in greater number and variety of species than any other known people.)

During the winter months, these filthy wretches are seen, day after day, basking at the sunny side of their huts, and bestowing upon each other certain friendly offices connected with the head, wherein the swarming populace of the pericranium are had in alternate requisition.

The entire business of the country is in the hands of the rich, upon whom the laboring classes are mainly dependent for support; and, as a natural consequence, the rich know no end to their treasures, nor the poor to their poverty.

The common laborer obtains only from four to six dollars per month, out of which he must feed and clothe himself. In case he runs in debt beyond his means, he is necessitated by law to serve for the required amount, at two dollars per month;—thus, once in debt, it is almost impossible ever to extricate himself.

Having faintly depicted the real condition of a large majority of the degenerate inhabitants of New Mexico, it will be expected of me to say something of their intelligence and morality; and here a still more revolting task awaits my effort.

Intelligence is confined almost exclusively to the higher classes, and the poor "palavro" comes in for a very diminutive share.

Education is entirely controlled by the priests, who make use of their utmost endeavors to entangle the minds of their pupils in the meshes of superstition and bigotry. The result of this may be plainly stated in a few words:

Superstition and bigotry are universal,—all, both old and young, being tied down to the disgusting formalities of a religion that manifests itself in little else than senseless parade and unmeaning ceremony,—while a large majority can neither read nor write.

These conservators of intelligence and morals are often as sadly deficient in either as those they assume to teach. Gambling, swearing, drinking, Sabbath-breaking, and sundry other vices, are the too frequent concomitants of their practice;—under such instructors, who can fail to foresee the attendant trains of evils? The abject condition of the people favors the impress of unsound instruction and deteriorating example, reducing public morals to a very low ebb.

Property and life are alike unsafe, and a large proportion of the whole community are little other than thieves and robbers. Profanity is their common language. In their honesty, integrity, and good faith, as a general thing, no reliance should be placed. They are at all times ready to betray their trust whenever a sufficient inducement is presented.

With the present of a few dollars, witnesses may be readily obtained to swear to anything; and a like bonus placed in the hands of the *Alcaldi* [alcalde] will generally secure the required judgment, however much at variance with the true merits of the cause.

Thus, justice becomes a mere mockery, and crime stalks forth at noon-day, unawed by fear of punishment, and unrebuked by public opinion and practice.

But fear, in most cases, exercises a far more controlling influence over them than either gratitude or favor. They may be ranked with the few exceptions in the family of man who cannot endure good treatment. To manage them successfully, they must needs be held in continual restraint, and kept in their place by force, if necessary,—else they will become haughty and insolent.

As servants, they are excellent, when properly trained, but are worse than useless if left to themselves.

In regard to the Mexican women, it would be unfair to include them in the preceding summary.

The ladies present a striking contrast to their countryman in general character, other than morals. They are kind and affectionate in their disposition, mild and affable in their deportment, and ever ready to administer to the necessities of others. But, on the score of virtue and common chastity, they are sadly deficient; while ignorance and superstition are equally predominant.

One of the prime causes in producing this deplorable state of things may be attributed to that government policy which confines the circulating medium of the country within too narrow limits, and thus throws the entire business of the country into the hands of the capitalist.

A policy like this must ever give to the rich the moneyed power, while it drains from the pockets of the poor man and places him at the mercy of haughty lordlings, who, taking advantage of his necessity, grant him but the scanty pittance for his services they in tender compassion see fit to bestow.

The higher classes have thus attained the supreme control, and the commoners must continue to cringe and bow to their will. In this manner the latter have, by degrees, lost all ambition and self-respect, and, in degradation, are only equalled by their effeminacy.

Possessed of little moral restraint, and interested in nothing but the demands of present want, they abandon themselves to vice, and prey upon one another and those around them.

4. Thomas Catesby Jones Announces United States Takeover of California, 1842

To the inhabitants of the two Californias:

Although I come in arms, as the representative of a powerful nation upon whom the central government of Mexico has waged war, I come not to spread desolation among California's peaceful inhabitants.

It is against the armed enemies of my country, banded and swayed under the flag of Mexico, that war and its dread consequences will be enforced.

United States National Archives. Naval Records Collection of the Office of Naval Records and Library. Record Group 45. Letters from Officers Commanding Squadrons: 1841–1846, Pacific Squadron: 1841–1846. This document is also available in Rose Marie Beebe and Robert M. Senkewicz, eds., *Lands of Promise and Despair: Chronicles of Early California, 1535–1846* (Berkeley: Heyday Books, 2001), 460–461.

Inhabitants of California! You have only to remain at your homes in pursuit of peaceful vocation to ensure security of life, persons, and property from the consequences of an unjust war into which Mexico has suddenly and rashly plunged you.

Those Stars and Stripes, infallible emblems of civil Liberty—of Liberty of speech, freedom of the press, and above all, the freedom of conscience, with constitutional rights and lawful security, to worship the Great Deity in the way most congenial to each one's sense of duty to his Creator, now float triumphantly before you and henceforth and forever will give protection and security to you, to your children, and to unborn countless thousands.

All the rights and privileges which you now enjoy, together with the privilege of choosing your own magistrates and other officers for the administration of justice among yourselves, will be secured to all who remain peaceably at their homes and offer no resistance to the forces of the United States.

Each of the inhabitants of California, whether natives or foreigners, as may not be disposed to accept the high privilege of citizenship and to live peaceably under the Free Government of the United States will be allowed time to dispose of their property and to remove out of the country without any other restriction, while they remain in it, than the observance of strict neutrality, total abstinence from taking part directly or indirectly in the war against the United States or holding any intercourse whatever with any civil or military officer, agent, or other person employed by the Mexican Government.

All provisions and supplies of every kind furnished by the inhabitants of California for the use of the United States, their ships, and their soldiers will be paid for at fair rates.

No private property will be taken for public use without just compensation.

5. Abraham Lincoln Condemns the War with Mexico, 1848

Some, if not all the gentlemen on, the other side of the House, who have addressed the committee within the last two days, have spoken rather complainingly, if I have rightly understood them, of the vote given a week or ten days ago, declaring that the war with Mexico was unnecessarily and unconstitutionally commenced by the President. I admit that such a vote should not be given, in mere party wantonness, and that the one given, is justly censurable, if it have no other, or better foundation. I am one of those who joined in that vote; and I did so under my best impression of the *truth* of the case. How I got this impression, and how it may possibly be removed, I will now try to show.... The President, in his first war message of May 1846, declares that the soil was *ours* on which hostilities were commenced by Mexico; and he repeats that declaration, almost in the same language, in each successive annual message, thus showing that he esteems that point, a highly essential one.

Roy P. Basler, ed., *Collected Works of Abraham Lincoln* (New Brunswick: Rutgers University Press, 1953), 1: 431–444. Courtesy of the Abraham Lincoln Association.

Now I propose to try to show, that the whole of this,—issue and evidence—is from beginning to end, the sheerest deception.

I now proceed to examine the Presidents evidence, as applicable to such an issue. When that evidence is analized, it is all included in the following propositions:

1. That the Rio Grande was the Western boundary of Louisiana as we purchased it of France in 1803.

2. That the Republic of Texas always *claimed* the Rio Grande, as her Western boundary.

3. That by various acts, she had claimed it *on paper*.

4. That Santa Anna, in his treaty with Texas, recognised the Rio Grande, as her boundary.

5. That Texas *before*, and the U. S. *after*, annexation had *exercised* jurisdiction *beyond* the Nueces—*between* the two rivers.

6. That our Congress, *understood* the boundary of Texas to extend beyond the Nueces.

Now for each of these in it's turn.

His first item is, that the Rio Grande was the Western boundary of Louisiana, as we purchased it of France in 1803; and seeming to expect this to be disputed, he argues over the amount of nearly a page, to prove it true; at the end of which he lets us know, that by the treaty of 1819, we sold to Spain the whole country from the Rio Grande eastward, to the Sabine. Now, admitting for the present, that the Rio Grande, was the boundary of Louisiana, what, under heaven, had that to do with the *present* boundary between us and Mexico? How, Mr. Chairman, the line, that once divided your land from mine, can *still* be the boundary between us, *after* I have sold my land to you, is, to me, beyond all comprehension. And how any man, with an honest purpose only, of proving the truth, could ever have *thought* of introducing such a fact to prove such an issue, is equally incomprehensible. His next piece of evidence is that "The Republic of Texas always *claimed* this river (Rio Grande) as her western boundary[.]" That is not true, in fact. Texas *has* claimed it, but she has not *always* claimed it. There is, at least, one distinguished exception. Her state constitution,—the republic's most solemn, and well considered act—that which may, without impropriety, be called her last will and testament revoking all others—makes no such claim. But suppose she had always claimed it. Has not Mexico always claimed the contrary? so that there is but *claim* against *claim*, leaving nothing proved, until we get back of the claims, and find which has the better *foundation*. Though not in the order in which the President presents his evidence, I now consider that class of his statements, which are, in substance, nothing more than that Texas has, by various acts of her convention and congress, claimed the Rio Grande, as her boundary, *on paper*.... I next consider the President's statement that Santa Anna in his *treaty* with Texas, recognised the Rio Grande, as the western boundary of Texas.

.... I believe I should not err, if I were to declare, that during the first ten years of the existence of that document, it was never, by any body, *called* a treaty—that it was never so called, till the President, in his extremity, attempted, by so calling it, to wring something from it in justification of himself in connection with the Mexican war. It has none of the distinguishing features of a treaty. It does not call itself a treaty. Santa Anna does not therein, assume to bind Mexico.... He did not recognise the independence of Texas; he did not assume to put an end to the war; but clearly indicated his expectation of it's continuance; he did not say one word about boundary, and, most probably, never thought of it.

Next comes the evidence of Texas before annexation, and the United States, afterwards, *exercising* jurisdiction *beyond* the Nueces, and *between* the two rivers. This actual *exercise* of jurisdiction, is the very class or quality of evidence we want. It is excellent so far as it goes; but does it go far enough? He tells us it went *beyond* the Nueces; but he does not tell us it went *to* the Rio Grande. He tells us, jurisdiction was exercised *between* the two rivers, but he does not tell us it was exercised over *all* the teritory between them.

If, as is probably true, Texas was exercising jurisdiction along the western bank of the Nueces, and Mexico was exercising it along the eastern bank of the Rio Grande, then *neither* river was the boundary; but the uninhabited country between the two, was.... As to the country now in question, we bought it of France in 1803, and sold it to Spain in 1819, according to the President's statements. After this, all Mexico, including Texas, revolutionized against Spain; and still later, Texas revolutionized against Mexico. In my view, just so far as she carried her revolution, by obtaining the *actual*, willing or unwilling, submission of the people, *so far*, the country was hers, and no farther. Now sir, for the purpose of obtaining the very best evidence, as to whether Texas had actually carried her revolution, to the place where the hostilities of the present war commenced, let the President answer the interrogatories, I proposed, as before mentioned, or some other similar ones. Let him answer, fully, fairly, and candidly. Let him answer with *facts*, and not with arguments.... How like the half insane mumbling of a fever-dream, is the whole war part of his late message! At one time telling us that Mexico has nothing whatever, that we can get, but teritory; at another, showing us how we can support the war, by levying contributions on Mexico. At one time, urging the national honor, the security of the future, the prevention of foreign interference, and even, the good of Mexico herself, as among the objects of the war; at another, telling us, that "to reject indemnity, by refusing to accept a cession of teritory, would be to abandon all our just demands, and to wage the war, bearing all it's expenses, *without a purpose or definite object*[.]" So then, the national honor, security of the future, and every thing but territorial indemnity, may be considered the *no-purposes*, and *indefinite*, objects of the war!... So again, he insists that the separate national existence of Mexico, shall be maintained; but he does not tell us *how* this can be done, after we shall have taken *all* her teritory. Lest the questions, I here suggest, be considered speculative merely, let me be indulged a moment in trying [to] show they are not. The war has gone on some twenty months; for the expenses of which, together with an inconsiderable old score, the President now claims about one half of the Mexican teritory; and that, by far the better half, so far as concerns our ability to makeany thing out of it. *It* is comparatively uninhabited; so that we could establish land offices in it, and raise some money in that way. But the other half is already inhabited, as I understand it, tolerably densely for the nature of the country; and all it's lands, or all that are valuable, already appropriated as private property. How then are we to make any thing out of these lands with this incumbrance on them? or how, remove the incumbrance? I suppose no one will say we should kill the people, or drive them out, or make slaves of them, or even confiscate their property. How then can we make much out of this part of the teritory?

6. The Treaty of Guadalupe Hidalgo, 1848

ART. VIII.—Mexicans now established in territories previously belonging to Mexico, and which remain, for the future, within the limits of the United States, as defined by the present treaty, shall be free to continue where they now reside, or to remove, at any time, to the Mexican republic, retaining the property which they possess in the said territories, or disposing thereof, and removing the proceeds wherever they please, without their being subjected, on this account, to any contribution, or tax, or charge, whatever.

Those who shall prefer to remain in said territories, may either retain the title and rights of Mexican citizens, or acquire those of citizens of the United States. But they shall be under the obligation to make their selection within one year from the date of the exchange of ratifications of this treaty; and those who shall remain in the said territories, after the expiration of that year, without having declared their intention to retain the character of Mexicans, shall be considered to have elected to become citizens of the United States.

In the said territories, property of every kind, now belonging to Mexicans not established there, shall be inviolably respected. The present owners, the heirs of these, and all Mexicans who may hereafter acquire said property by contract, shall enjoy, with respect to it, guaranties equally ample as if the same belonged to citizens of the United States.

ART. IX.—The Mexicans who, in the territories aforesaid, shall not preserve the character of citizens of the Mexican republic, conformably with what is stipulated in the preceding article, shall be incorporated into the union of the United States, and admitted as soon as possible, according to the principles of the federal constitution, to the enjoyment of all the rights of citizens of the United States. In the mean time, they shall be maintained and protected in the enjoyment of their liberty, their property, and the civil rights now vested in them according to the Mexican laws. With respect to political rights, their condition shall be on an equality with that of the inhabitants of the other territories of the United States, and at least equally good as that of the inhabitants of Louisiana and the Floridas, when these provinces, by transfer from the French republic and the crown of Spain, became territories of the United States.

N. C. Brooks, *The Complete History of the Mexican War: Its Causes, Conduct, and Consequences* (Baltimore: Hutchinson and Seebold, 1949), 546–550.

The same most ample guaranty shall be enjoyed by all ecclesiastics and religious corporations or communities, as well in the discharge of the offices of their ministry as in the enjoyment of their property of every kind, whether individual or corporate. This guaranty shall embrace all temples, houses, and edifices dedicated to the Roman Catholic worship, as well as all property destined to its support, or to that of schools, hospitals, and other foundations for charitable or beneficent purposes. No property of this nature shall be considered as having become the property of the American government, or as subject to be by it disposed of, or diverted to other uses.

Finally, the relations and communication between the Catholics living in the territories aforesaid, and their respective ecclesiastical authorities, shall be open, free, and exempt from all hindrance whatever, even although such authorities should reside within the limits of the Mexican republic, as defined by this treaty; and this freedom shall continue, so long as a new demarkation of ecclesiastical districts shall not have been made, conformably with the laws of the Roman Catholic church.

ART. X.—All grants of land made by the Mexican government, or by the competent authorities, in territories previously appertaining to Mexico, and remaining for the future within the limits of the United States, shall be respected as valid, to the same extent that the same grants would be valid if the said territories had remained within the limits of Mexico. But the grantees of lands in Texas, put in possession thereof, who, by reason of the circumstances of the country, since the beginning of the troubles between Texas and the Mexican government, may have been prevented from fulfilling all the conditions of their grants, shall be under the obligation to fulfil the said conditions within the periods limited in the same, respectively; such periods to be now counted from the date of the exchange of ratifications of this treaty; in default of which, the said grants shall not be obligatory upon the State of Texas, in virtue of the stipulations contained in this article.

The foregoing stipulation in regard to grantees of land in Texas is extented to all grantees of land in the territories aforesaid, elsewhere than in Texas, put in possession under such grants; and, in default of the fulfilment of the conditions of any such grant, within the new period, which, as is above stipulated, begins with the day of the exchange of ratifications of this treaty, the same shall be null and void.

The Mexican government declares that no grant whatever of lands in Texas has been made since the second day of March, one thousand eight hundred and thirty-six; and that no grant whatever of lands, in any of the territories aforesaid, has been made since the thirteenth day of May, one thousand eight hundred and forty-six.

[The above article was expunged by the Senate.]

ART. XI.—Considering that a great part of the territories which, by the present treaty, are to be comprehended for the future within the limits of the United States, is now occupied by savage tribes who will hereafter be under the control of the government of the United States, and whose incursions within the territory of Mexico would be prejudicial in the extreme, it is solemnly agreed that all such incursions shall be forcibly restrained by the government of the United States, whensoever this may be necessary; and that when they cannot be prevented, they shall be punished by the said government, and satisfaction for the same shall be exacted—all in the same way, and with equal diligence and energy, as if the same incursions were committed within its own territory, against its own citizens.

It shall not be lawful, under any pretext whatever, for any inhabitant of the United States to purchase or acquire any Mexican, or any foreigner residing in Mexico, who may have been captured by Indians inhabiting⁻ the territory of either of the two republics, nor to purchase or acquire horses, mules, cattle, or property of any kind, stolen within Mexican territory by such Indians: nor to provide such Indians with fire-arms or ammunition, by sale or otherwise.

And in the event of any person or persons captured within Mexican territory by Indians, being carried into the territory of the United States, the government of the latter engages and binds itself in the most solemn manner, so soon as it shall know of such captives being within its territory, and shall be able to do so, through the faithful exercise of its influence and power, to rescue them and return them to their country, or deliver them to the agent or representative of the Mexican government. The Mexican authorities will, as far as practicable, give to the government of the United States notice of such captures; and its agents shall pay the expenses incurred in the maintenance and transmission of the res-cued captives; who, in the mean time, shall be treated with the utmost hospital-ity by the American authorities at the place where they may be. But if the government of the United States, before receiving such notice from Mexico, should obtain intelligence, through any other channel, of the existence of Mexican captives within its territory, it will proceed forthwith to effect their release and delivery to the Mexican agent, as above stipulated.

For the purpose of giving to these stipulations the fullest possible efficacy, thereby affording the security and redress demanded by their true spirit and intent, the government of the United States will now and hereafter pass, without unnec-essary delay, and always vigilantly enforce, such laws as the nature of the subject may require. And finally, the sacredness of this obligation shall never be lost sight of by the said government when providing for the removal of Indians from any portion of said territories, or for its being settled by the citizens of the United States; but, on the contrary, special care then shall be taken not to place its Indian occupants under the necessity of seeking new homes, by committing those inva-sions which the United States have solemnly obliged themselves to restrain.

Article IX Prior to Amendment by the U.S. Senate

The Mexicans who, in the territories aforesaid, shall not preserve the character of citizens of the Mexican Republic, conformably with what is stipulated in the preceding Article, shall be incorporated into the Union of the United States,

David J. Weber, ed., *Foreigners in Their Own Land: Historical Roots of the Mexican Americans* (Albuquerque: University of New Mexico Press, 1973), 164–165.

and admitted as soon as possible, according to the principles of the Federal Constitution, to the enjoyment of all the rights of citizens of the United States. In the
mean time, they shall be maintained and protected in the enjoyment of their
liberty, their property, and the civil rights now vested in them according to the
Mexican laws. With respect to political rights, their condition shall be on an
equality with that of the inhabitants of the other territories of the United States;
and at least equally good as that of the inhabitants of Louisiana and the Floridas,
when these provinces, by transfer from the French Republic and the Crown of
Spain, became territories of the United States.

The same most ample guaranty shall be enjoyed by all ecclesiastics and religious corporations or communities, as well in the discharge of the offices of their
ministry, as in the enjoyment of their property of every kind, whether individual
or corporate. This guaranty shall embrace all temples, houses and edifices dedicated to the Roman Catholic worship; as well as all property destined to its support, or to that of schools, hospitals and other foundations for charitable or
beneficent purposes. No property of this nature shall be considered as having
become the property of the American Government, or as subject to be, by it,
disposed of or diverted to other uses.

7. Antonio Maria Pico and Others Criticize California's Land Policy, 1859

We, the undersigned, residents of the state of California, and some of us citizens
of the United States, previously citizens of the Republic of Mexico, respectfully
say:

That during the war between the United States and Mexico the officers of
the United States, as commandants of the land and sea forces, on several occasions offered and promised in the most solemn manner to the inhabitants of
California, protection and security of their persons and their property and the
annexation of the said state of California to the American Union, impressing
upon them the great advantages to be derived from their being citizens of the
United States, as was promised them.

When peace was established between the two nations by the Treaty of
Guadalupe Hidalgo, they joined in the general rejoicing with their new
American fellow countrymen, even though some—a very few indeed—decided
to remain in California as Mexican citizens, in conformity with the literal interpretation of that solemn instrument; they immediately assumed the position of
American citizens that was offered them, and since then have conducted themselves with zeal and faithfulness and with no less loyalty than those whose great
fortune it was to be born under the flag of the North American republic—believing, thus, that all their rights were insured in the treaty, which declares that
their property shall be inviolably protected and insured; seeing the realization of the

Robert Glass Cleland, *The Cattle on a Thousand Hills: Southern California, 1850–1880* (San
Marino, CA: Huntington Library, 1951), 238–242.

promises made to them by United States officials; trusting and hoping to participate in the prosperity and happiness of the great nation of which they now had
come to be an integral part, and in which, if it was true that they now found the
value of their possessions increased, that was also to be considered compensation
for their sufferings and privations.

The inhabitants of California, having had no choice but to dedicate themselves to the rural and pastoral life and allied occupations, ignorant even of the
laws of their own country, and without the assistance of lawyers (of whom there
were so few in California) to advise them on legal matters, elected from among
themselves their judges, who had no knowledge of the intricate technical terms
of the law and who were, of course, incompetent and ill-fitted to occupy the
delicate position of forensic judicature. Scattered as the population was over a
large territory, they could hardly hope that the titles under which their ancestors
held and preserved their lands, in many cases for over half a century, would be
able to withstand a scrupulously critical examination before a court. They heard
with dismay of the appointment, by Act of Congress, of a Commission with the
right to examine all titles and confirm or disapprove them, as their judgment
considered equitable. Though this honorable body has doubtless had the best
interests of the state at heart, still it has brought about the most disastrous effects
upon those who have the honor to subscribe their names to this petition, for,
even though all landholders possessing titles under the Spanish or Mexican governments were not forced by the letter of the law to present them before the
Commission for confirmation, nevertheless all those titles were at once considered doubtful, their origin questionable, and, as a result, worthless for confirmation by the Commission; all landholders were thus *compelled de facto* to submit
their titles to the Commission for confirmation, under the alternative that, if
they were not submitted, the lands would be considered public property.

The undersigned, ignorant, then, of the forms and proceedings of an
American court of justice, were obliged to engage the services of American lawyers to present their claims, paying them enormous fees. Not having other means
with which to meet those expenses but their lands, they were compelled to give
up part of their property, in many cases as much as a fourth of it, and in other
cases even more.

The discovery of gold attracted an immense number of immigrants to this
country, and, when they perceived that the titles of the old inhabitants were
considered doubtful and their validity questionable, they spread themselves over
the land as though it were public property, taking possession of the improve-
ments made by the inhabitants, many times seizing even their houses (where
they had lived for many years with their families), taking and killing the cattle
and destroying their crops; so that those who before had owned great numbers
of cattle that could have been counted by the thousands, now found themselves
without any, and the men who were the owners of many leagues of land now
were deprived of the peaceful possession of even one vara.

The expenses of the new state government were great, and the money to
pay for these was only to be derived from the tax on property, and there was
little property in this new state but the above-mentioned lands. Onerous taxes

were levied by new laws, and if these were not paid the property was put up for sale. Deprived as they were of the use of their lands, from which they had now no lucrative returns, the owners were compelled to mortgage them in order to assume the payment of taxes already due and constantly increasing. With such mortgages upon property greatly depreciated (because of its uncertain status), without crops or rents, the owners of those lands were not able to borrow money except at usurious rates of interest.

The petitioners, finding themselves unable to face such payments because of the rates of interest, taxes, and litigation expenses, as well as having to maintain their families, were compelled to sell, little by little, the greater part of their old possessions. Some, who at one time had been the richest landholders, today find themselves without a foot of ground, living as objects of charity—and even in sight of the many leagues of land which, with many a thousand head of cattle, they once had called their own; and those of us who, by means of strict economy and immense sacrifices, have been able to preserve a small portion of our property, have heard to our great dismay that new legal projects are being planned to keep us still longer in suspense, consuming, to the last iota, the property left us by our ancestors.

The manifest injustice of such an act must be clearly apparent to those honorable bodies when they consider that the native Californians were an agricultural people and that they have wished to continue so; but they have encountered the obstacle of the enterprising genius of the Americans, who have assumed possession of their lands, taken their cattle, and destroyed their woods, while the Californians have been thrown among those who were strangers to their language, customs, laws, and habits.

It would have been better for the state, and for those newly established in it, if all those titles to lands, the *expedientes* [documents] of which were properly registered in the Mexican archives, had been declared valid; if those holders of titles derived from former governments had been declared perpetual owners and presumptive possessors of the lands (in all civilized countries they would have been acknowledged legitimate owners of the land); and if the government, or any private person or official who might have pretensions to the contrary, should have been able to establish his claim only through a regular court of justice, in accordance with customary judicial procedure. Such a course would have increased the fame of the conquerors, won the faith and respect of the conquered, and contributed to the material prosperity of the nation at large.

～ ESSAYS

Many of the recent histories on the Anglo-American takeover of the Southwest borderlands have been histories from below: They focus on the dynamic tensions between metropolitan designs and local agency and emphasize slow changes in peoples' everyday lives over diplomatic and military interventions. Where does this historiographical shift leave such famous borderlands leaders as Stephen Fuller Austin or Sam Houston, who figured so prominently in the older scholarship?

Is there room for their lofty visions and momentous decisions in the expanded cast of historical agents, or has their historiographical stature become irreversibly diminished? Great figures are still worthy of our attention, argues Gregg Cantrell, professor of history at Texas Christian University, but their historical roles and influence must be placed in proper context. In his essay, Cantrell does just that to Stephen F. Austin, the man who has been mythologized as the "Father of Texas." Rather than trying to determine how Austin shaped history, Cantrell suggests, we might be better served by asking how history shaped him. The Austin he portrays was a southerner, a Missouri slaveholder, and a promoter of plantation agriculture who in Texas reinvented himself as a multicultural border-lander. The "Father of Texas" was a conscientious empresario who became a bilingual land speculator, a loyal Mexican citizen, a political mediator, and, only towards the end, a revolutionary separatist.

The second essay, by Brian Delay, professor of history at the University of California at Berkeley, discusses how three parallel historical tracks—Mexico's internal troubles, Native American power politics, and U.S. expansionism—converged after 1830 to change the history of the Southwest borderlands. As previous chapters have shown, Apaches, Comanches, Kiowas, Navajos, and other native groups had raided Spanish colonial outposts since the early seventeenth century; indeed, along with cross-cultural accommodation through diplomacy, commerce, intermarriage, and mixed communities, raiding is a defining strand of the Southwest borderlands history. Yet, as Delay shows, the 1830s and 1840s witnessed a dramatic increase in intercultural violence, as Indians launched devastating raids on Mexican settlements across nine states. Delay discusses the complex political, economic, and cultural impulses that fueled the violence, but his main focus is on its many and often unexpected consequences. In what ways did violence shape how Americans, Mexicans, and Indians viewed one another, and how did it alter the balance of power among them? How did the Mexico-bound raids serve native communities and why, in the end, did they backfire on them? How do the existing national narratives change if viewed from the vantage point of the borderlands?

Stephen F. Austin, Empresario and Borderlander

GREGG CANTRELL

The Anglo-American colonists who came to Mexican Texas brought with them some heavy cultural baggage. Most came from slaveholding states and subscribed to southern notions of white supremacy—notions that might easily be applied to dark-skinned Mexicans as well as to African Americans. Many undoubtedly embodied the other forms of ethnocentrism peculiar to the Jacksonian era, such as a strident prejudice against Catholics and an intense hatred of Indians. Moreover,

Gregg Cantrell, "Stephen F. Austin: Political and Cultural Mediator," in *Major Problems in Texas History*, ed. Sam W. Haynes, Cary D. Wintz, and Thomas Paterson, pp. 104–110 (Wadsworth Publishing, 2001).

few settlers would have questioned the basic tenets of the ideology that would someday be called "Manifest Destiny:" the belief that the United States would inevitably spread American-style democracy and cultural institutions westward across the continent. Given these realities, many recent scholars have viewed the Anglo settlement of Texas as little more than an American invasion, a racist land grab of Mexico's northern frontier in which Mexicans and Indians were the chief victims.

At first glance, the foremost leader of this "invasion" seems to sustain these interpretations. Stephen Fuller Austin was a Virginia native who had grown up mostly on the Missouri frontier, where he utilized slave labor on a large scale in his family's lead-mining operation. In Texas, he worked repeatedly to ensure that slavery would be protected by the government. He had also served in the Missouri militia during the War of 1812, participating in a military campaign that burned Indian villages in Illinois. His credentials as a white supremacist seemed secure.

The same might be said for his standing as a proponent of Manifest Destiny. In an Independence Day speech in 1818, he delivered an address extolling the virtues of American civilization and the Founding Fathers. Near the end of the oration, he alluded to Mexico's ongoing independence struggle:

> ... the same spirit that unsheathed the sword of Washington and sacrificed servitude and slavery in the flames of the Revolution, will also flash across the Gulph of Mexico and over the western wilderness that separates independent America from the enslaved colonies of Spain, and darting the beams of intelligence into the benighted souls of their inhabitants awake them from the stupor of slaves to the energy of freemen, from the degradation of vassals to the dignity of sovereigns.

After emigrating to Texas, he frequently defined his mission as that of "[spreading] over it North American population, enterprise, and intelligence."

In addition to his racial beliefs and his pro-American chauvinism, Austin also seemed typically American in his attitudes toward Mexican Catholicism. On his first trip through the interior of Mexico, he wrote that "the people are bigoted and superstitious to an extreem, and indolence appears to be the general order of the day." And in another, oft-quoted passage, he added, "to be candid the majority of the people of the whole nation as far as I have seen them want nothing but tails to be more brutes than the apes.... Fanaticism reigns with a power that equally astonishes and grieves a man of common sense."

Austin's words and deeds seemed to confirm his ethnocentrism when Texas began to wage war against Mexico. Not only did he publicly advocate independence several months before the actual declaration, but he justified the revolution on the grounds that "A war of extermination is raging in Texas, a war of barbarism and of despotic principles, waged by the mongrel Spanish-Indian and Negro race, against civilization and the Anglo-American race." He recounted the fifteen years in which he had labored "like a slave to *Americanize Texas*" so that the southwestern frontier of the United States would be safe. "But the Anglo-American foundation, this nucleus of republicanism, is to broken up," he declared, "and its place supplied by a population of Indians, Mexicans, and renegadoes, all mixed together, and all the natural enemies of white men and civilization." In other statements he raised the cry of anti-Catholicism, claiming that the revolution was being fought for "religious liberty" and against the "banner of the inquisition." With such actions and statements coming from the man who initiated the Anglo-American colonization of Texas, who could doubt that racism, imperialism, cultural chauvinism, and greed were the main impulses behind the American occupation of Texas all along?

Despite all of this, the case of Stephen F. Austin—when considered in its entirety—actually tells a very different story. For the better part of fifteen years, the young Missourian served as a political and cultural mediator between Anglo Texans and Mexicans. When examined objectively, Austin's career demonstrates the very real potential for political, economic, and social cooperation across racial and cultural lines. The history leading up to the Texas Revolution emerges as a far more complex story than it appears.

When Austin received permission in 1821 to introduce 300 American families into the region between the Brazos and Colorado, his timing was perfect. The newly independent government of Mexico, as well as the local Tejano leadership of Texas, recognized the need to populate the sparsely settled province with hardworking, taxpaying citizens who would contribute to the economic development of northern Mexico, help fight hostile Indians, and hopefully prevent the loss of Texas to the rapidly expanding United States. Austin's title was *empresario*, which meant that he was responsible for recruiting settlers, surveying and issuing land titles, enforcing the laws, and acting as liaison between his colonists and the Mexican government. From the start, Austin labored tirelessly and took his responsibilities as empresario seriously.

One of the first indications of that seriousness was his approach to the language barrier. Austin spoke little or no Spanish when he first arrived in Texas, but he dedicated himself to learning the language not just passably but fluently. Most of this effort took place in 1822 when he was forced to travel to Mexico City to secure confirmation of his grant from the new government of Mexico. Within a few weeks of his arrival there, Austin was conducting business in Spanish and even acting as spokesman for other Americans in their business with the government.

We get a glimpse of Austin's attitudes toward the language issue in his letters to his younger brother, Brown Austin. Stephen had left Brown, who was only nineteen, behind in Texas when he went to Mexico City. But rather than leave Brown with Anglo friends in the new colony, he placed Brown in the household of the prominent Tejano citizen Erasmo Seguín of San Antonio with instructions to spend every waking moment studying Spanish and learning Mexican ways. "Remember," Stephen lectured Brown, "that all your hopes of rising in this country depend on lear[n]ing to speak and write the language correctly. Without that, you will do nothing." Ten years later he would take a similar course with his teenage nephew, Moses Austin Bryan.

By the time Austin returned to Texas in 1823, he could speak Spanish and was personally acquainted with a host of major Mexican leaders. Arriving home, he issued a proclamation reminding the settlers of their obligation to the government. He instructed them "to remember that the Roman Catholic is the religion of this nation" and urged them to "respect the Catholic religion with all that attention due to its sacredness and to the laws of the land." Two years later, when the new national constitution was published, he summoned the colonists to San Felipe for a grand celebration of the new system of government. There, in the village he had laid out in a traditional Spanish pattern with streets named for Mexican statesmen, Austin raised the Mexican flag, read the constitution, and administered the oath of allegiance. Good order prevailed the entire day, and the people expressed "general enthusiasm in favor of the Government of our adopted Country." Austin made the phrase "fidelity to Mexico" his motto and for years preached it like gospel to the colonists, frequently reminding them that they lived under "the most liberal and munificent government on earth to emigrants."

Austin soon formed harmonious working relationships with important Tejanos as well as Mexicans from the interior. When the national congress combined Texas with Coahuila to form one state, he succeeded in forging an effective three-pronged political coalition between Anglo colonists, Tejanos, and a group of powerful Coahuilan politicians/businessmen headed by the Viesca brothers of Parras. Together, they dominated the politics of the vast frontier state for more than a decade, finding common ground on a wide range of issues.

Prominent Tejano José Antonio Navarro of San Antonio was one of Austin's key allies in this coalition. Navarro represented Texas in the 1828 state legislature, at a time when Austin, along with other Anglo colonists, feared that the state was on the verge of enforcing its prohibitions on slavery. Navarro came to the rescue, quietly securing the passage of a bill that allowed Americans to continue to bring their slaves into Texas. Modern sensibilities will condemn the purpose of Navarro's labors, but the point here is to show the close cooperation and identification of mutual interests between these two men who came from such different cultural backgrounds.

Equally telling is the *personal* relationship that apparently developed between Austin and Navarro. Stephen F. Austin was not the sort who formed intimate friendships easily, and he tended to be a very private and reserved man, rarely mentioning personal matters to business or political associates. But in 1829, he faced one of the greatest personal crises of his life when his beloved younger brother, Brown, suddenly died of yellow fever. The stress of this event triggered a severe attack of fever in Austin, who lingered near death for weeks. When he finally was able to sit up in bed and write a few letters, Navarro was one of the first people he contacted—and one of the few in whom he confided. Austin poured out his grief to his Tejano friend, poignantly writing of the "terrible blow" he had received. That Austin would share his anguish with Navarro (who would later sign the Texas Declaration of Independence) says much about the degree of trust and friendship that existed between the two men.

Similarly strong and enduring was Austin's relationship with the Seguín family. Erasmo Seguín was among a group of Tejanos who traveled to Louisiana in 1821 to escort Stephen F. Austin to the site of his grant. The men became friends, and Brown Austin apparently lived with the Seguíns for the entire year that Austin was gone. Several years later, Austin made efforts to purchase cotton ginning equipment for Erasmo in New Orleans because Erasmo had refused to accept any reimbursement for the time that Brown had boarded with him.

Like the Austin-Navarro relationship, the Austin-Seguín relationship extended into the period of the Revolution itself. In the fall of 1835, when Austin was commanding Texan troops in the field, into the camp galloped Juan Seguín—Erasmo's son—along with a company of Tejano cavalrymen, volunteering their services in the Texas cause. Austin welcomed them into the ranks, commissioning Seguín as a lieutenant colonel. Austin would later praise the Tejano troops, saying that "They uniformly acquitted themselves to their credit as patriots and soldiers."

But Austin did not simply cooperate with Mexicans when they were willing to take the side of Anglos in some conflict. There were also times when he stood by the Mexican government in conflicts with other Anglos. Perhaps the most famous case involved the Fredonian Rebellion of 1826–27. In 1825, an Anglo-American, Haden Edwards, received an empresario contract from the state government to introduce 800 settlers into the Nacogdoches area. Edwards, a reckless and undiplomatic man, soon angered both Anglo and Tejano settlers who had long predated him in the region, and finally the Mexican government canceled his contract and ordered him expelled from Texas. He responded by declaring the independence of the "Fredonian" republic, and he made an alliance with a portion of the local Cherokee Indian tribes who had failed in their attempts to gain land titles from the Mexican government. Political chief José Antonio Saucedo assembled Mexican troops from Goliad and San Antonio, marched to San Felipe where they were joined by Stephen F. Austin and his colony's militia, and together the mixed force marched to Nacogdoches and put down the rebellion with minimal difficulty.

In hindsight, the Fredonian rebellion resembles comic opera, but for those willing to read the lessons carefully, it indicates more about the real nature of the Texas frontier from 1821 to 1835 and of racial and ethnic relations than almost any other incident. The temptation is to look only at surface facts and to see the rebellion as a precursor of the 1836 revolution—a land grab by aggressive, ungrateful Anglos. But the realities are much more complex. Consider several points. Before the granting of the Edwards empresario contract, the Nacogdoches region was occupied by an incredibly diverse population of Tejanos and Anglos, with a sprinkling of other ethnic Europeans. The region was also home to a number of indigenous Texas Indian tribes, plus the semi-Europeanized Cherokees, who were themselves recent emigrants from the American southeast. Edwards's contract was granted by a state legislature in far-off Saltillo, by Mexican elites whose own financial interests depended on the economic development of Texas. Edwards antagonized both Anglos and Tejanos in Nacogdoches, and the actual fighting that took place there was by no means an Anglo vs. Mexican affair. When Austin learned of the revolt, he called the Fredonians "a party of infatuated madmen," and Austin's Anglo colonists turned out unhesitatingly to aid the Mexicans in putting down the rebellion. Furthermore, facts show that the Cherokees themselves were actually sharply divided over the affair, and a sizable portion of them repudiated their comrades who had sided with Edwards and instead aided the Tejanos and Anglos in opposing the rebels. When the revolt disintegrated, the Cherokee leaders who had joined with the Fredonians were condemned by a tribal council, hunted down, and executed by their own people. In the aftermath of the rebellion, Anastacio Bustamante, commandant general of Mexico's northern frontier states, wrote Stephen Austin a letter expressing his gratitude for Austin's colonists' support, saying he wanted personally to give Austin "*un Extrechisimo abrazo*"—a very strong embrace—for "the happy result of the Expedition to Nacogdoches."

Like so much Texas history during this period, the simple dichotomies break down. In the Fredonian episode, Austin and his Anglo colonists marched side by side with Mexican troops against other Anglo-Americans. Even the Indians were bitterly divided. At Austin's suggestion, the Mexicans later granted amnesty to all but the ringleaders of the revolt, and he remained in East Texas several weeks, traveling the region with the Mexican leaders to calm the fears of the inhabitants and restore peace and order. Brown Austin undoubtedly spoke for his brother when he wrote that the insurgents were "treated with a degree of lenity by the Mexicans they had no right to expect from the nature of their crimes—and which I vouchsafe would not have been shewn them in their native country for similar offences." The actions of Austin and his colonists, as well as the response of the Mexican authorities, suggest a degree of cooperation and identification of common interests that transcended cultural differences.

After the notorious Law of April 6, 1830 disrupted the empresario system and initiated a Mexican crackdown on Anglo Texas, Austin once again sought to act as mediator. Although he potentially had more to lose under the law than almost anyone else, he counseled calmness and continued loyalty toward Mexico, even pointing out to his colonists the beneficial aspects of the much-hated decree. Over the next four years, every time that Texans grew dissatisfied with the actions of the government in Mexico City, he tried to forge solidarity between the Tejanos and Anglos of Texas and to encourage the Tejanos to take the lead in petitioning the government for redress. Even after Austin's arrest and imprisonment in 1833, he continued to call for calm in Texas. Indeed, after four months in a dungeon, he was still asking friends in Texas to "Remember me to Ramón Músquíz [the Tejano political chief in San Antonio] particularly—I shall feel grateful to him as long as I live...."

Austin's friendship and respect for a long list of Mexican and Tejano leaders never faltered. His efforts to build a society in Mexican Texas where enterprising men of Anglo and Hispanic backgrounds might live in harmony and prosperity remained constant for fifteen years prior to the outbreak of revolution. He tried to avoid warfare against Indians, and he even accepted a few free blacks as settlers in his colony.

Given these efforts, how are the seemingly bigoted statements that he occasionally uttered to be explained? Take, for example, his famous 1823 complaint about Mexicans being as being as uncivilized apes. It is easy to take such a statement out of context, but if one continues reading that same letter, Austin predicts optimistically that the Mexican nation would soon "assume her rights in full, and bursting the chains of superstition declare that *man has a right to think for himself.*" In other words, Austin directed his criticism at the Church itself and what he perceived as its oppression of the Mexican people, not at Mexicans for any inherent defect of character. In 1833, he was even more explicit on this theme, actually defending Roman Catholicism as "a religion whose foundation is perfect harmony, a union of principles, & of action." But he condemned the *type* of Catholicism then being practiced in Mexico, saying it was "in theory divine, in practice infernal." These were not the words of a knee-jerk nativist.

But what about the harsh racial invective that he employed in 1835–1836? What are we to make of his support for independence, his 1836 outburst about the "war of barbarism" being "waged by the mongrel Spanish-Indian race, against civilization and the Anglo-American race," and his declaration that the non-Anglos of Texas were "the natural enemies of white men and civilization?" Was this the chauvinistic American finally showing his true colors? How do we reconcile such statements with his actions during the previous fifteen years?

Again, context is everything, and placing Austin's racist-sounding comments in context reveals the great tragedy of Anglo-Tejano relations in the Texas Revolutionary period. Austin wrote these words at a point in the Revolution when he was desperately trying to arouse sympathy and support from citizens of the United States. His main audience was made up of Jacksonian Democrats—and *southern* Democrats at that. His rhetorical transformation of the Texian struggle into a war against racially inferior Mexicans was carefully calculated to stir the deepest fears and emotions of southerners. One of the tragic consequences of this war—and of almost all others in which the enemy is of a different race, ethnicity, or culture—is that such wars almost inevitably generate this sort of propaganda. Portray your enemies as somehow less than human, and killing them becomes much easier. Recall how Germans were portrayed in American propaganda during World War I, or the Japanese during World War II, and the genesis of Austin's words can be understood. Was he wrong to resort to racist appeals when his actions over a fifteen-year period clearly contradicted such sentiments? Of course he was. In this one instance, Austin sacrificed his principles in a desperate attempt to reverse the tide of a war that by all appearances was about to be lost. We may wish that he had possessed the superhuman strength of character needed to resist such a sellout, but in the end he was only human.

Returning to his beloved Texas in the critical summer of 1836, Austin reverted to his tried-and-true philosophy of seeking reconciliation and national unity. He never had the opportunity to visit his old Tejano friends in San Antonio, but there is no indication that he would have treated them any differently than before. The harsh rhetoric was never repeated at home. Nothing from his short, ill-fated presidential campaign against Sam Houston that September suggests that he would have changed his longstanding policy of working to build a Texas in which Anglos and Tejanos could honorably cooperate and coexist. And his willingness to accept a cabinet appointment from his rival, Sam Houston, and to support Houston in all broad policy matters, further suggests that he, like Houston, would have resisted the movement toward persecution and recrimination against Tejanos that grew in intensity over the coming years.

However, Stephen F. Austin was a man of his times in one important respect. He believed that American-style democracy—flawed though it may have been by the stain of slavery—was the best system of government yet devised. He only gave up on Mexico when he became convinced that his adopted country had utterly failed to secure the blessings of democracy for its people, Anglo and Hispanic. Having reached that determination, he was willing to employ whatever necessary means to win the Revolution and bring Texas under a better government. That decision—and those means—could give the appearance that he was motivated by an unthinking bigotry against all things not American. But to arrive at such a conclusion, based on a selective reading of the evidence, is to overlook the fifteen-year reality of Austin as a genuine political and cultural mediator.

How Indians Shaped the Era of the U.S.-Mexican War

BRIAN DELAY

In the early 1830s, following what for most had been nearly two generations of imperfect peace, Comanches, Kiowas, Navajos, and several different tribes of Apaches dramatically increased their attacks upon northern Mexican settlements. While contexts and motivations varied widely, most of the escalating violence reflected Mexico's declining military and diplomatic capabilities, as well as burgeoning markets for stolen livestock and captives. Indian men raided Mexican ranches, haciendas, and towns, killing or capturing the people they found there, and stealing or destroying animals and other property. When able, Mexicans responded by attacking their enemies with comparable cruelty and avarice. Raids expanded, breeding reprisals and deepening enmities, until the searing violence touched all or parts of nine states.

These events had powerful but virtually forgotten consequences for the course and outcome of the U.S.-Mexican War. In pursuing their own material, strategic, and cultural goals, indigenous polities in the Mexican north remade the ground upon which Mexico and the United States would compete in the mid-1840s. Raids and counter-raids claimed thousands of lives, ruined critical sectors of northern Mexico's economy, stalled the north's demographic growth, depopulated much of its vast countryside, and fueled divisive conflicts between Mexicans at nearly every level of political integration. Exhausted, impoverished, and divided by fifteen years of war, and facing ongoing and even intensifying Indian raids, northern Mexicans were singularly unprepared to resist the U.S. Army in 1846 or to sustain a significant insurgency against occupation forces.

Indian raiders shaped how Americans and Mexicans viewed each other in advance of the war. From Texas to Washington, Anglo-American observers

Brian DeLay, "Independent Indians and the U.S.-Mexican War," *American Historical Review* 112 (Feb. 2007): 35–68. Permission granted by University of Chicago Press.

began looking at Mexico *through* the autonomous native peoples of the border-lands, as if these Indians were lenses calibrated to reveal essential information about Mexicans, their lands, and their futures in North America. Schooled in Indian removal—that supreme exhibition of state power over native peoples—Americans watched Indians driving Mexicans backward, and this observation in-spired ambitions and tactics for continental expansion. Mexicans living through the conflicts could not afford the same creative detachment, but they too came to gaze through Indians rather than at them. Mexicans saw Americans standing behind *los indios bárbaros*, employing them as proxies in a plan to seize Mexico's territory.

Thus U.S. expansion into Mexican territory should be viewed not as the culmination of one story, but rather as the collision of two. The more familiar tale about competition between a thriving and a faltering republic intersected in neglected but decisive ways with a story—or, more precisely, multiple stories—about independent Indian peoples pursuing their own interests at the margins of state power.

Recovering the significance of Indians to the U.S.-Mexican War advances the project of integrating native peoples into the international history of the Americas.

As nineteenth-century North America's defining international conflict and an event with enduring consequences for all of the continent's peoples, the U.S.-Mexican War is an ideal starting place for reconceptualizing indigenous contributions to the hemisphere's international history. By taking seriously both what Indians did and how their deeds informed discourse in the U.S. and Mex-ico, it is possible to see how native polities could "powerfully influence political relations" between rival states in North America and beyond.

In 1830, Northern Mexicans enjoyed relatively peaceful relations with most independent Indians. Despite frequent animal thefts, killings and kidnappings were relatively rare and were met more often with negotiation than with orga-nized violence. Conditions deteriorated rapidly during the next decade, until overlapping theaters of war canvassed the whole of the north. By the early 1830s, Apaches in the northwest were raiding in five states: "Western" Apaches in Sonora and Chihuahua; Chiricahuas, in Sonora, Chihuahua, and southern New Mexico; and Mescaleros in Chihuahua, Coahuila, and Durango. As the decade progressed, New Mexicans became embroiled in renewed war with Na-vajos, and during the early 1840s they provoked narrower quarrels with Utes and Arapahos as well. Lipan Apaches on the Lower Rio Grande broke a wary peace with Mexicans repeatedly in the 1830s and 1840s, raiding ranches and settle-ments throughout the northeast. Finally, Comanches and Kiowas dramatically escalated their raids on Chihuahua in the early 1830s, turned to Tamaulipas, Nuevo León, and Coahuila by mid-decade, and by 1840 were even campaigning across Durango, northern Zacatecas, and parts of San Luis Potosí.

While all of these conflicts had local and regional proximate causes, a few broad changes help explain why violence metastasized across the north when it did. Following independence in 1821, the Republic of Mexico found itself without the financial and, to a lesser extent, the diplomatic resources that had helped Bourbon New Spain foster a delicate system of alliances, regulated trade, and gift-giving with independent Indians. Presents to Indians became fewer and shabbier, provoking "humiliating" excuses from cash-poor northern Mexican officials and violent outbursts by Indian visitors. The consequences of Mexican parsimony were nowhere more calamitous than in the northwest, where Apaches resorted to widespread raiding only after the cancellation of a decades-old ration program.

For most independent Indians, the costs of conflict diminished along with the benefits of peace. The presidios (garrisons) that had anchored Spanish military force on the frontier went into steady decline beginning in the 1810s.

By making peace attractive and war dangerous, the regional system established in the late colonial era had put a brake on the contest for animals and, to a lesser extent, captives that fueled nearly all organized conflict between independent Indians and northern Mexicans. Native and nonnative economies alike depended on domestic animals for transportation of goods and people, and for hunting and war. Throughout northern Mexico, horses, mules, and (especially for Mexicans and Navajos) sheep also served as markers of wealth, as resources that bound together networks of patrons and clients, and as the gifts most commonly used for bride-price. Without access to animals, then, young men could not participate in basic aspects of economic and social life. Indian and Mexican societies likewise placed a premium on captive women and children, who could be treated as commodities, slaves, or dependent kin. Across northern Mexico, inequalities and unrealized ambitions encouraged men to improve their own fortunes by taking animals and captives from ethnic others.

Meanwhile, maturing connections to outside markets made theft all the more lucrative. American commercial activity in the Mexican north increased dramatically after 1821. Mexican officials denounced U.S. merchants whom they labeled "traders of blood" for supplying raiders with arms and ammunition in return for stolen Mexican animals. There is evidence of such activity among Apaches, and especially on the southern plains, where American and Texan merchants established several trading houses on the edges of *la comanchería* in the 1830s and 1840s.

... Economic explanations for raiding should be situated within a larger political framework. First, changes in Comanche and Kiowa raiding indicate coordination of policy rather than coincidence of ambition. Over the 1830s and 1840s, the geography and intensity of raiding expanded in sharply defined stages, each stage corresponding to geopolitical events on and around the southern plains. Second, large campaigns were the norm rather than the exception. On more than thirty occasions between 1834 and 1846, Comanches and Kiowas sent parties of one hundred men or more below the Rio Grande. More than a third of these groups included at least five hundred warriors, and on four occasions Mexican officials reported expeditions of eight hundred to a thousand men. These largest campaigns involved perhaps half of the total fighting force of the southern plains.

Third and finally, the tremendous destruction of these campaigns often worked against the very material ambitions that seem to have motivated raiders in the first place. In addition to plundering homes, taking captives, and seizing horses and mules, southern plains men exerted great energy and took great risks to kill Mexicans, slaughter thousands of pigs, cows, goats, and sheep, and set fire to dwellings, barns, and granaries. Comanches and their allies killed at least two thousand Mexicans in the twelve years before the U.S.-Mexican War—a figure that amounts to five Mexicans killed for every two the raiders tried to capture. Indeed, southern plains Indians occasionally became so engrossed with the work of killing people, slaughtering animals, and destroying property that Mexican forces had time to converge on the scene and deprive them of their spoils.

... One feature in particular of the Comanche and Kiowa political traditions helps to explain the coordination, size, and extreme violence of the campaigns into Mexico: vengeance. Like most non-state peoples, individual Comanches and Kiowas could call upon kin to help them avenge loved ones killed by outsiders.

In the abstract, the huge campaigns organized in this way were supposed to be brief, to culminate with an enemy's death, and to remain conceptually distinct from the much smaller and informal "raids" targeting animals and captives. But these distinct endeavors seem to have collapsed into one in the years before the U.S. invasion, thanks to the peculiar manner in which profits intersected with dangers in northern Mexico. While many Comanches and Kiowas made reputations and fortunes raiding Mexicans between 1834 and 1846, at least five hundred southern plains men lost their lives in the attempt.

Rather than simply promote the individualistic, economic benefits of raiding Mexican settlements, then, Comanches and Kiowas united their broader communities in the enterprise in part by submerging economics in a discourse about honor, pity, and, especially, revenge. Doing so enabled them to assemble enough men to penetrate deep into Mexican territory for weeks at a time, to take hundreds of captives and steal tens of thousands of horses and mules. But because vengeance provided the political gravity necessary to organize these armies of raiders, Comanches and Kiowas crossed the river to hurt Mexicans as well as take from them. Hence the vast destruction during the 1830s and 1840s, destruction that often undermined the economic objectives that fueled raiding in the first place.

The scale and intensity of interethnic violence increased at a sickening pace across all of northern Mexico after 1830, but subregions endured significant episodic conflict before then. Texas was one such place. Soon after Mexico's War for Independence began in 1810, Spanish authority went into sharp decline in Texas, Indian diplomacy faltered, and native peoples began raiding *tejano* settlements. Spanish officials saw Indian violence as one important factor retarding the development of Texas, and in 1820 began allowing limited Anglo-American colonization in the troubled province. Following independence in 1821, Mexican authorities expanded the pace of colonization. This decision they soon came to regret, as colonists quickly outnumbered *tejanos*, conflicts mounted, and, finally, Texans declared independence from Mexico in 1836.

The rebels dispatched their most illustrious citizen, Stephen F. Austin, to tour the United States and capitalize on sympathy for the movement. Austin delivered a stump speech in several states, laying out the Texan case.

This story, which we can call the Texas Creation Myth, was retold and refined in books, articles, and pamphlets published in cities across the U.S. Texan ambassadors to the United States chanted the Creation Myth like a mantra, and sympathetic U.S. politicians soon knew it by heart. The myth contained three basic components: First, Texas had been a wasteland before Anglo-American colonists arrived, because the Mexicans, "either through a want of personal prowess or military skill ... were unable to repel the frequent incursions of their savage neighbors." Second, officials in Mexico invited American colonists into Texas both to redeem the wilderness from the Indians and to protect northeastern Mexico from Indian attack. Third, the Americans quickly accomplished these twin tasks. As one author put it, "the untiring perseverance of the colonists triumphed over all natural obstacles, expelled the savages by whom the country was infested, reduced the forest to cultivation, and made the desert smile."

The myth introduced a set of ideas about Indians and Mexicans into American political discourse at a moment when the nation was taking notice of the whole of northern Mexico for the first time.

But while Comanches overwhelmed Mexicans, informants assured their readers, the Indians became craven wretches in the presence of armed Anglo-American men. The popular *New Orleans Picayune* explained that Comanches "care little for the Spaniards, but they dread the Americans." [American trader and historian of the Santa Fe Trail Josiah] Gregg agreed, insisting that Comanches appeared "timid and cowardly" when they encountered Americans. Another author added that Comanches "recede as fast as encroachments are made upon their territory."

In other words, the same Indians who had in American minds so efficiently dismantled northern Mexico supposedly dissolved into hapless cowards in the presence of Anglo-Americans. This idea was as essential as it was self-serving. By denigrating Comanches, critics excoriated the Mexican men who allowed themselves to be bested by such contemptible enemies. As in the Texas Creation Myth, American discourse about northern Mexico made Indians into the great signifiers of, rather than the reason for, Mexico's failures. Like Texas prior to colonization, northern Mexico was in tatters not because Indians were strong, but because Mexicans were weak.

And why were Mexicans weak? Many commentators emphasized deficiencies of courage or intelligence. American observers also tried to explain Mexico's Indian problem as a consequence of Mexican sloth, physical weakness, and stupidity. More holistic thinkers gathered all of these condemnations together under the roof of what during the Jacksonian period had become increasingly sophisticated pseudo-scientific theories about racial difference.

Stories about Indian raids from elsewhere in northern Mexico had the effect of rhetorically invalidating Mexico's claim to the land, only on a much larger scale. Waddy Thompson, who had nothing but contempt for Comanches, thought that Mexico's unending ordeal with Indian raids presented the best evidence against that nation's future in North America. "That the Indian race of Mexico must recede before us, is quite as certain as that that is the destiny of our own Indians, who in a military point of view, if in no other, are superior to them."

Mexicans also arrived at a rough consensus on why Indians had done such damage to the northern third of their nation, but it took them more than a decade to get there. Everyone acknowledged that the once-formidable Spanish defenses had declined and that Indians found it easier to raid than before. But that opportunity spoke more to how Indians accomplished their raids than to why they launched them in the first place. In reaching for ultimate causes, northern Mexicans tended initially to attribute the violence to what they saw as the base, animalistic, evil nature of *los salvajes*, whereas prominent authorities in Mexico City pointed to the Indians' disadvantaged, pitiable condition.

Undoubtedly northerners held a range of shifting views about raiders. Still, by the early 1830s, most northern policymakers and writers began framing the "war against the barbarians" as one pitting civilization, religion, and political organization against savagery, faithlessness, and chaotic individualism. *Los bárbaros* were animal, elemental, something, in the words of political geographer José Agustín Escudero, that "the ground seems to vomit forth in its pain." Editors wrote that the enemy strikes without reason or warning, "kills the poor shepherd ... wretched woodcutter ... washer women ... little children." Hence the only rational, indeed the only possible, response, according to Sonora's legislature, was "destruction and eternal war against these barbarians."

Presidents and prominent ministers in the nation's capital thought the northern rhetoric excessive, and insisted not just that Apaches, Comanches, Navajos, and other raiders were human, but that they were Mexican. This was consistent with the sweeping claim of the Constitution of 1824 that everyone born inside Mexico's territorial limits was *mexicano*, but it was also important because Mexican political elites contrasted their own enlightened, inclusive benevolence with the aggressive exclusionism of the United States, and especially with remembered Spanish cruelties.

The conceptual chasm between these two positions aggravated the security crisis. Northerners viewed their fight against *los bárbaros* as an "eminently national" war, albeit one waged against an incomprehensible enemy. National officials saw raiders as something closer to Mexican "banditti," and hence as domestic agents of local or regional crime waves—not as alien threats to national security. Without a single interpretive framework that situated Indian raiders in an unambiguously national context, frontier defense remained disorganized, ineffective, and hobbled by bitter competition for inadequate resources.

After a decade of disagreement, Mexicans finally began to construct a unified discourse about Indian raiders. As was the case in the United States, the nationalization of Mexico's conversation started with Texas, and emerged from a combination of deliberate political calculation, ideological reasoning, and honest observation. In the early 1840s, as the Republic of Texas adopted more belligerent rhetoric toward Mexico, northern officials observed that the word "Texan" commanded Mexico City's attention in a way that "Apache" or "Comanche" never had. Editors of northern newspapers began discerning heretofore underappreciated links between Texans and *los salvajes*. Northern governors started doing the same, informing their constituents and superiors that the Indian invasions were "directed by the Texans," and successfully linking the two threats in appeals for resources.

Mexico City felt comfortable with such notions. Observers in the capital had long believed that Texans and Americans provided Indians with their firearms, and pronouncements and policies from the early 1840s suggest that national officials were coming to see connections more sinister still. In 1841, for example, when Texan officials started boasting of plans to make the Sierra Madre their southern boundary, the editors of Mexico's official newspaper insisted that Texans were inciting Indian raiders to prepare the way for a planned invasion.

Once the purported Texan-Indian connection started coming into focus at the frontier and in the capital, two things happened to turn this rhetorical convergence into something resembling a national consensus. First, U.S. president John Tyler presented Congress with a plan for the annexation of Texas in the spring of 1844. Tyler's scheme failed, but Mexico's leaders took it to mean that annexation was only a matter of time. While officials in Mexico considered the implications of this, the second change took place: Indians dramatically escalated their raiding activities across the whole of northern Mexico.

... After a relatively uneventful 1843, Comanches and Kiowas launched several destructive campaigns into Tamaulipas, Coahuila, Chihuahua, Durango, and Zacatecas in 1844 and 1845. This surge in raiding coincided with the consummation of a formal peace between the Republic of Texas and the Hois, the southernmost Comanche tribe. The treaty indirectly encouraged raiding by establishing vigorous new trade relationships and by improving security for the families and fortunes that Indian men would have to leave behind while campaigning in Mexico. But the timing of the attacks convinced Mexicans of a direct relationship between raiders and *norteamericanos*.

As international tension increased, more and more Mexicans started seeing in the security crisis evidence of Indian-*norteamericano* collusion. James Polk won the U.S. presidential election in November 1844 thanks to his strong support for annexing Texas, and the U.S. Congress responded by approving annexation days before his inauguration. Soon after Polk took office, Mexico's minister of war, Pedro García Conde, confidently explained to Mexico's house and senate that the "hordes of barbarians" were "sent out every time by the usurpers of our territory, in order to desolate the terrain they desire to occupy without risk and with perfidy." García Conde described an agreement whereby the U.S. provided Indians not only with arms and ammunition, but also with a political education, with "the necessary instruction they need to understand the power they can wield when united in great masses."

The emerging national consensus on why Indians did what they did—because unscrupulous *norteamericanos* and possibly even agents of the U.S. government encouraged and instructed them to—was as much a fiction as the Texas Creation Myth. Apaches and Comanches doubtlessly obtained some arms and ammunition from Americans, and there is evidence that a few merchants tried to increase business by fomenting raids. But *norteamericano* traders had little or no influence over native policy—Indians in Mexico's far north were much more likely to trade with and seek council from other Indians. And as for the

U.S. government, it had little contact with Comanches and Kiowas in the 1830s and early 1840s, and none with Apaches and Navajos.

Nonetheless, the consensus had its uses. It provided a conceptual framework that finally seemed to promise unanimity of national purpose in coping with Indian raiders. By putting an American stamp on the long lists of dead and the numbingly familiar news stories of empty corrals, burned-out ranches, and childless parents, the new consensus also fueled anti-Americanism in advance of an increasingly likely war.

But consensus came too late. The U.S. Army invaded northern Mexico in the spring of 1846, and Americans won striking victories over Mexican troops due in large part to advantages in light artillery. As Polk's army moved through the north, it found a land already scoured by war. From New Mexico to Tamaulipas, the invaders saw abandoned homes, overgrown fields, and hastily finished graves. Sometimes northern Mexicans confided in the *norteamericanos*, telling tales of perpetual insecurity, lamenting dead or stolen kin, and promising cooperation in return for protection from Indians.

Polk and his war planners had counted on this. While the war would eventually end when U.S. troops took Mexico City and the "Halls of the Montezumas," initially the president intended to wage the war entirely in the north, in those same regions that had been devastated by Indian raids. Polk and his advisors were anxious to obtain the friendship, or at least neutrality, of the northern Mexicans who would fall under U.S. occupation. American generals had to worry about tens of thousands of civilians swelling the ranks of the Mexican army, about coordinated efforts to deny Americans necessary supplies, and, perhaps most importantly, about the possibility of a broad-based guerrilla insurgency against the occupation. Anxiety over such scenarios prompted Polk and his subordinates to craft detailed instructions for commanders on the ground, ordering them to exploit Mexicans' fears and dissatisfaction with their government. Indians would be central to this task. "It is our wish to see you liberated from despots," General Zachary Taylor was to announce at each town conquered or surrendered, "to drive back the savage Cumanches, to prevent the renewal of their assaults, and to compel them to restore to you from captivity your long lost wives and children." General Stephen W. Kearny delivered a New Mexican variant. "From the Mexican government you have never received protection," he proclaimed. "The Apaches and the Navajoes come down from the mountains and carry off your sheep, and even your women, whenever they please. My government will correct all this."

Given Mexican assumptions about the causes of Indian raiding, we can imagine people in the crowds shaking their heads and exchanging knowing looks. But help from hypocrites surely seemed better than no help at all, because conflicts with Indians would only intensify during the U.S.-Mexican War.

Northern Mexicans suffered grievously. "And to think that we owe all this," raged the editors of the *Registro Oficial*, "to those infamous North American enemies who push the bloody hordes of savages upon us and direct their operations with unparalleled astuteness and ferocity! Such are the methods through which a nation that styles itself enlightened and just wages war."

Therefore, when northern Mexicans spoke of the "enemy" in 1846 and 1847, they as often meant *indios* as *norteamericanos*. The ruinous legacy of fifteen years of raiding and the ongoing threat of Indian violence left large segments of northern Mexico's population unable and probably unwilling to resist the U.S. Army. In the northeast, for example, state officials were ordered to muster all males between the ages of sixteen and fifty against the Americans. While the orders exempted those places most exposed to raids, many local authorities still demurred, insisting that their communities needed the men to patrol against Indians. Occasionally this scenario unfolded on a grand scale. In late 1846, Santa Anna labored to amass a huge army and defeat Taylor near Monterrey. Mexico City called upon the states to raise men, but, recognizing the troubles that the north faced from both Indians and Americans, insisted on contributions from only three northern states: Chihuahua, Durango, and Zacatecas. Suspicious of Santa Anna and, more importantly, facing acute threats from Apaches and Comanches, none of the three sent any men. In February 1847, the Mexican army lost the battle of Buena Vista by the narrowest of margins. Had Chihuahua, Durango, and Zacatecas met their quotas, Santa Anna's force would have been increased by one-fifth, perhaps enough to win the battle and shift the entire dynamic of the war.

In defeat, certain Mexican leaders denounced what they saw as northern indifference, even complicity with the invader. Durango's editors assailed those who accused the state's population of treason. "Why? Because we have not fielded armies that have been impossible to raise, because they need be composed of men paid in cash, and our brothers have been assassinated by the barbarians, or else fled far away from their fury?" Chihuahua's representatives likewise tried to defend their honor. They reminded their compatriots that Chihuahua had been "afflicted and desolated for fifteen years by the savages, drowned in the blood of the men and in the lamentations of the widows and the orphans, an ideal theatre in which to showcase the power of the United States."

Subtract the irony, and expansionists in Washington would have agreed. To their way of thinking, Chihuahua and the rest of northern Mexico was not only an ideal showcase for U.S. power, but a land in desperate need of it. By the time senators began openly debating how much territory to demand from Mexico, expansionists could draw on more than a decade of observations to describe a Mexican north empty of meaningful Mexican history, and, by all appearances, increasingly empty of Mexicans themselves.

U.S. leaders turned to tales of Indians attacking Mexicans for more than just rhetorical cover. Congressmen, editors, and administration officials pointed to Mexico's ruinous war with frontier Indians as compelling and, to their minds, honest evidence that Mexicans were incapable of developing their northern lands. This is not to say that everyone subscribing to this view also wanted to acquire Mexican territory. Politicians ambivalent about or even opposed to the war also talked about raiding, but they incorporated Indians into arguments against a cession—for example, invoking the "well-known fact" that raiders had "encroached upon and broken up many of the settlements of the Spaniards" in the north, leaving behind mainly indigenous Mexicans unfit for American political life. In other words, rhetoric about Mexico's Indian war was not so much part of a calculated expansionist argument as it was indicative of assumptions that by 1846 had become common across the political spectrum.

Northern Mexico's security crisis had therefore become foundational to how U.S. politicians thought about the proposed cession, irrespective of their position on the war. But that was only half of the story. The other half, fully realized in the Texas Creation Myth but as yet only potential in the ongoing conflict with Mexico, concerned the Anglo-American capacity and even destiny to do what Mexico could not: defeat the Indians and provide security to the long-suffering residents of northern Mexico.

Polk had instructed his generals to promise precisely this to Mexicans in the field, and he took pains to assure Congress that this was his intention when he finally made explicit his territorial ambitions in late 1847. The Mexican government should desire to place New Mexico "under the protection" of the U.S., the president explained, because Mexico was too feeble to stop bands of "warlike savages" from committing depredations not only above the Rio Grande, but also upon more populous states below. Thus the cession would improve life for Mexicans north of the line, but more importantly "it would be a blessing to all the northern states to have their citizens protected against [the Indians] by the power of the United States. At this moment many Mexicans, principally females and children, are in captivity among them," Polk continued. "If New Mexico were held and governed by the United States, we could effectually prevent these tribes from committing such outrages, and compel them to release these captives, and restore them to their families and friends."

Confident talk, but did anyone believe it? Every senator had to decide for himself, because Article Eleven of the proposed Treaty of Guadalupe Hidalgo bound U.S. authorities both to restrain Indians residing north of the new border from raiding into Mexico, and to rescue Mexican captives held by Indians. The article echoed Polk's self-assured rhetoric, but more importantly it called such confidence to task. All the talk about incompetent and cowardly Mexicans, contemptible Comanches, Anglo-Americans easily defeating the Indians and turning deserts into gardens—was this bravado or conviction?

It is telling that the opposition to Article Eleven was led by those who understood Mexico's security problem best. Unlike nearly everyone else in Washington, representatives of the new state of Texas had an appreciation for how difficult it would be to prevent Indian raids into Mexico.

The majority of senators, men better versed in the rhetoric than the reality of Mexico's conflicts with Indians, voted to ratify a treaty that enshrined U.S. obligations for preventing Indian raids into Mexico. They apparently did so because they had persuaded themselves that the United States would indeed save northern Mexico, simply by letting Anglo-Americans and their superior energies flow into the new territories. They would quickly defeat the wandering savages, redeem the helpless Mexican captives, and rescue the vast, derelict garden of western North America from Mexican neglect.

That representatives from both nations felt confident about and pleased with Article Eleven testifies to an essential congruity between American and Mexican conceptions of Indian raiders. Americans believed that Apaches, Navajos, Kiowas, Comanches, and the like were undisciplined, craven opportunists. Above all, Americans considered these Indians reactive. Mexican weakness, racial impurity, cowardice, and stupidity induced, even compelled, Indians to raid. Most U.S. politicians believed that American strength would quickly reverse the trend. For their part, Mexico's negotiators assumed that *los salvajes* drew much of their strength, most of their weapons, and perhaps even their tactics and political coherence from *norteamericanos*. So it was that Mexican representatives championed Article Eleven as the "only advantage" that could compensate Mexico for all it had sacrificed in the war.

These were vain hopes, born out of a shared nineteenth-century worldview that held only nation-states and empires to be entities of hemispheric significance. Despite an abundance of evidence, national leaders in both Mexico and the United States had been incapable of seeing non-state Indian peoples as consequential political communities pursuing their own collective goals—goals that, however indirectly, might alter the course of nation-states. So it was confusing and infuriating for leaders in both capitals to see raiding surge in the aftermath of the war, and grow progressively worse through the early 1850s. There was evidently more behind raiding campaigns than Mexican incompetence or American provocation. Mexicans responded with outrage and threatened lawsuits into the tens of millions of dollars, based on the violation of Article Eleven. U.S. administrators grumbled about Mexican passivity and asked for patience. Cross-border raids by native peoples would continue in diminished form through the 1880s, but Washington was not prepared to wait nearly that long. Despairing of its ability to honor Article Eleven, the United States bought its way out of it in 1854, with the Gadsden Purchase.

It is unsurprising that nineteenth-century Americans weathered this embarrassment without reevaluating assumptions that had helped them appropriate half of Mexico's national territory. What *is* surprising is that historians on both sides of the modern border retain many of the same assumptions about the capacity of America's indigenous peoples to influence geopolitics in the postcolonial era. But the evidence above suggests that the transformations we associate with the U.S.-Mexican War emerged from a nexus of American, Mexican, and *Indian* politics. U.S. expansion into Mexican territory appears considerably more contingent in its outcome once Indian actors are included in the story. This can only be for the good, given that a perception of inevitability has contributed to collective disinterest in the U.S.-Mexican War, despite its immense and enduring continental consequences.

More broadly, we need to rethink the significance of autonomous native peoples to the interlocked histories of American states. By the early 1820s, more than a dozen generations after Columbus, indigenous polities still controlled between half and three-quarters of the continental landmass claimed by the hemisphere's remaining colonies and newly independent states. The fact that the scope of Indian power is rarely cast this way, in hemispheric terms, speaks to the grip that national teleologies have upon our historical imaginations.

FURTHER READING

Cantrell, Gregg. *Stephen F. Austin, Empresario of Texas* (1999).

Castillo, Richard Griswold del. *The Treaty of Guadalupe Hidalgo: A Legacy of Conflict* (1990).

Crisp, James E. *Sleuthing the Alamo: Davy Crockett's Last Stance and Other Mysteries of the Texas Revolution* (2004).

Delay, Brian. *War of a Thousand Deserts: Indian Raids and the U.S.-Mexican War* (2008).

De Leon, Arnoldo. *They Called Them Greasers: Anglo Attitudes Toward Mexicans in Texas, 1821–1900* (1983).

Francaviglia, Richard, and Douglas W. Richmond, eds. *Dueling Eagles: Reinterpreting the U.S.-Mexican War, 1846–1848* (2000).

González, Deena J. *Refusing the Favor: The Spanish-Mexican Women of Santa Fe* (1999).

Haas, Lisbeth. *Conquests and Historical Identities in California, 1769–1936* (1995).

Heizer, Robert F., ed. *The Destruction of California Indians* (1993).

Hurtado, Albert L. *Indian Survival on the California Frontier* (1988).

———. *John Sutter: A Life on the North American Frontier* (2006).

Johnson, Susan Lee. *Roaring Camp: The Social World of the California Gold Rush* (2000).

Lindheim, Milton. *The Republic of the Rio Grande: Texans in Mexico, 1839–40* (1964).

Miller, Edward L. *New Orleans and the Texas Revolution* (2004).

Montejano, David. *Anglos and Mexicans in the Making of Texas, 1836–1986* (1987).

Nance, Joseph Milton. *After San Jacinto: The Texas-Mexican Frontier, 1836–1841* (1963).

Pitt, Leonard. *The Decline of the Californios: A Social History of Spanish-Speaking Californians, 1846–1890* (1966).

Pubols, Louise. *The Father off All: The de la Guerra Family, Power, and Patriarchy in Mexican California* (2010).

Teja, Jesús F. de la, ed. *A Revolution Remembered: The Memoirs and Selected Correspondence of Juan N. Sequin* (1991).

———, ed. *Tejano Leadership in Mexican and Revolutionary Texas* (2010).

Tijerina, Andrés. *Tejanos and Texas under the Mexican Flag, 1821–1836* (1994).

Valerio-Jiménez, Omar. "Neglected Citizens and Willing Traders: The Villas del Norte (Tamaulipas) in Mexico's Northern Borderlands, 1749–1846." *Mexican Studies/Estudios Mexicanos* 18 (2002): 251–291.

———. "Avenues for Domestic Dispute and Divorce Lawsuits along the U.S.-Mexico Border, 1832–1893." *Journal of Women's History* 21 (Spring 2009): 10–33.

Vázquez, Josefina Zoraida, ed. *México al tiempo de su guerra con Estados Unidos (1846–1848)* (1997).

Velasco Avila, Cuauhtémoc José, ed. *En manos de los bárbaros* (1996).

Velasco-Márquez, Jesús. *La Guerra del '47 y la opinión publica (1845–1848)* (1975).

Vizcaya Canales, Isidro, ed. *La invasión de los indios bárbaros al noreste de México en los años de 1840 y 1841* (1968).

Weber, David J. *The Mexican Frontier, 1821–1846: The American Southwest Under Mexico* (1988).

———. *Myth and the History of the Hispanic Southwest* (1988).

CHAPTER 9

Negotiating National Borders

In the early nineteenth century, after two centuries of European colonization, most of North America was still a world of porous borderlands rather than sharp borders. European mapmakers drew Spanish claims with assertive lines, and the 1819 Adams-Otis Treaty defined a Spanish-U.S. boundary—soon to become the U.S.-Mexico boundary—that stretched from the Mississippi Valley to the Pacific Coast. The Southwest had transitioned, in the terminology of Jeremy Adelman and Stephen Aron from their essay in Chapter 1, from borderlands to bordered lands.

But these were paper boundaries; on the ground, people visited, traded, raided, hunted, and married across imperial and national demarcations virtually at will. A more formidable border came to the Southwest in 1848, when the United States and Mexico agreed on a new boundary in the Treaty of Guadalupe Hidalgo. Yet, as earlier, the old borderland ways persisted. People, goods, and ideas crossed the international border, frustrating metropolitan dreams of discrete sovereign spaces. Indeed, various groups—Indians, slaves, smugglers, outlaws, laborers, migrants—found the new border useful for their own, sometimes subversive purposes.

By crossing the border, their members could win access to things—plunder, markets, freedom, salaried work, land—that were not readily available on the other side. Moreover, they could also evade official control, because often the agents of law and enforcement lacked their transnational mobility. These border crossings exploited the paradoxical nature of the U.S.-Mexico boundary, which often curbed the actions of nation-states more than it did those of their malcontents. Like the borderlands that it was meant to stamp out, the border sustained quiet accommodations, informal economies, and places of refuge that existed outside the effective reach of institutional power. The U.S.-Mexico border region remained a fugitive landscape that the distant centers of national power could neither fully understand nor fully pin down.

The U.S.-Mexico border was not the only international boundary to emerge from the early nineteenth-century nation-building projects in the West. In 1818, the United States and Great Britain set the middle section of their North American border along the 49th parallel. In 1846, after a heated dispute over the Oregon Country, the boundary was extended from the Rocky Mountains to the Pacific, again along the 49th parallel. At first glance, the U.S.-Mexico and U.S.-Canada borders have little in common. The former was forged in a major war that lingers in historical memory; the latter was a product of diplomacy *that averted an international war. The former evokes images of illegal immigrants, drug traffic, border patrols, migrant deaths, and waste trade, all underwritten by a yawning wealth gap; the latter, the world's longest non-militarized border, is associated with light security measures, bustling commerce, and Niagara Falls. Yet there are also similarities, which were especially pronounced in the nineteenth century when the borders were still new and highly permeable. Much like the U.S.-Mexico border, the U.S.-Canada border arbitrarily divided long-existing communities, and like its southern counterpart, it has held different meanings for different peoples. For government agents, it was a boundary separating two sovereign political entities. For native peoples and the Métis—descendants of marriages between native women and French-Canadian fur traders—it signified opportunity and sanctuary, a line that allowed them to evade national policies that aimed to keep them in place. Like the U.S.-Mexico border, the U.S.-Canada border failed to create inviolable national spaces. Rather, it spawned a transnational space that stretched across the border, defying the exclusionary territorial logic of nation building.*

This chapter explores the ways in which diverse communities dealt with these new borders in the decades after their creation. Some borderlands groups refused to accept the legitimacy of the borders as they were drawn, fighting for their own continued autonomy, their own visions of peoplehood, and their own territory. Armed rebellions erupted in both the Mexico-U.S. and Canada-U.S. border regions from the 1840s to 1870s, requiring the intervention of the federal military forces of all three nations. Independent Indian peoples, including the Comanches and the Apaches, whose raids deeply influenced the U.S.-Mexico War, succeeded in defying conquest for decades. Equally important, a wide range of people found uses for international borders that governments had never anticipated. American slaves knew full well that crossing borders into Canada and Mexico could bring them a freedom unimaginable in the South or even in the free states of the United States. Mexican laborers bound by debt found similar opportunity in the United States, and similarly aggravated their masters when they fled. Even some of the native peoples most victimized by national expansion could use borders to their own benefit. The sharp and unambiguous appearance of the young borders on maps masked a reality that was much more complicated— and more interesting.

∿ DOCUMENTS

The willingness of different groups to uproot themselves and move across international boundaries invested borders with meanings that generals, diplomats, and treaties did not anticipate. The first three documents explore the ways that visions of freedom prompted American slaves and Mexican laborers to cross borders. In Document 1, William Wells Brown, an escaped slave, abolitionist, and author, describes the appeal that Canada, then still a part of the British Empire, held for American slaves. In Document 2, Frederick Law Olmsted recounts the glimpse into the world of escaped slaves in Mexico that he had while visiting the Mexican border town of Piedras Negras, Coahuila, in 1853. In his widely read travel book, Olmsted, a passionate opponent of slavery, recorded slaves' experiences in Texas, their motives for escape, and their prospects for a new life south of the border. What did border crossing mean for people enslaved in the United

States? Do you think that conditions in Canada and Mexico were as good for those who fled as Brown and Olmsted assume?

If some felt that they had to leave the United States to find freedom, then others chose to cross borders into that country. In the early 1870s, the Mexican government established a commission to investigate problems on its northern frontier, especially extensive livestock theft and raids mounted from U.S. soil by both Indians and Anglo-Americans. The commission received extensive complaints from large landowners in the North about the flight of their servants to Texas, where wages were higher and where debts that kept many in conditions of peonage in Mexico could not be collected. Document 3, an excerpt from the commission's report, summarizes the impact of this flight on the Mexican North. How do the authors characterize fugitive laborers, and is this characterization believable? To what extent do these complaints echo the earlier complaints of Texas slaveholders that Sean Kelley describes in the essay to follow?

National authorities also found that independent Indian peoples still traveled and made war across the new borders. In the 1848 Treaty of Guadalupe Hidalgo, which ended the U.S.-Mexico War, American authorities committed themselves to suppressing "incursions into the territory of Mexico" by Comanches, Apaches, and others. Three years later, as Document 4 shows, they had abandoned this effort, unable to subdue independent Indians. This letter from U.S. Secretary of State Daniel Webster to the U.S. ambassador in Mexico reveals just how little control either country had over most of their shared border. Why was the border region so hard to subdue? Were these Indians meaningfully "United States Indians," as Webster calls them?

Native peoples would use borders to their advantage even as they were being dispossessed and forced onto reservations, as Documents 5 and 6 illustrate in the case of Lakota leader Sitting Bull and Apache leader Geronimo. In 1876, the Seventh Cavalry of the United States Army under George Armstrong Custer attacked a Lakota, Cheyenne, and Arapaho Indian village near the Little Big Horn River on the northern Great Plains. Outnumbered, the Seventh Cavalry was destroyed in a battle that sent shock waves across the United States. The government sent thousands of soldiers to the area, forcing most of the Indians to surrender. Sitting Bull, a Hunkpapa Lakota leader and holy man, refused to submit and instead led his band across the border into Canada, where the U.S. Army could not pursue them. He and his followers crisscrossed the border to hunt bison and avoid government authorities on both sides of the border until 1881, when starvation forced their surrender to U.S. authorities and confinement on a reservation in the United States. In October 1877, General Alfred Howard Terry of the U.S. Army visited Sitting Bull in Saskatchewan and offered a pardon in exchange for moving into a reservation in the Dakota Territory. Document 5 presents some of this exchange. What knowledge did Sitting Bull and other Lakotas demonstrate of the border? Why might they have been so warm toward the British officers present? Document 6 is an 1884 interview with General George Crook, who a year earlier had been sent to Arizona to rein in Geronimo and his Chiricahua Apache followers, who had left their Arizona reservations and returned to raiding on both sides of the border. The U.S. military finally secured the surrender of

Geronimo and a few dozen followers in 1886, after nearly a quarter of the nation's standing army was deployed to the Arizona-Sonora borderlands in pursuit of Geronimo. What made Apaches so difficult to conquer, and what role did the U.S.-Mexico border play in this? Why did Crook rely so much on Apache scouts in his efforts?

Indians were not the only ones who defied the control of national authorities. Document 7 presents extracts from two proclamations that Juan Nepomuceno Cortina, a rancher and political leader, delivered in 1859 in south Texas near the Mexican border, calling Tejanos to resist their abuse, dispossession, and economic marginalization by Anglo-American newcomers. In the early 1850s, when the Texas-Mexico border remained little more than a line on a map, Cortina had done business and engaged in politics on both sides of the boundary; virtually un-regulated, the border was a site where both Anglos and Tejanos could pillage, trade, campaign, and seek retribution with little official supervision. But Cortina's border-straddling existence became increasingly difficult with the consolidation of Anglo-American hegemony in south Texas in the 1850s. In 1859–61, amidst rising tensions in the region, Cortina led a paramilitary Tejano force against local militias, Texas Rangers, and Mexican and U.S. troops in two conflicts. What is his attitude toward the United States and Anglo Americans? Is he entirely critical? Is it clear whether he considers himself a Mexican or an American?

In 1869, two years after the establishment of the Canadian Confederation, the Canadian government appointed William McDougall as the governor of North-west Territories, provoking resistance from the Métis inhabitants along the Red River of the North. Led by Louis Riel, the French-speaking Métis prevented the English-speaking McDougall from entering the territory, created a provisional government, and opened direct negotiations with Ottawa over the establishment of a separate province. Although this bold gambit resulted in the formation of Manitoba, with provisions for bilingual society and for the preservation of Métis landholding, Anglo-Canadian dominance of the new province led most Métis to migrate west in search of continued freedom. Many would again rebel against the Canadian government in 1885 under the leadership of Louis Riel. (Some, as the Gerhard Ens essay in this chapter describes, found refuge in the United States.) In Document 8, issued in both English and French, Riel explains the basis of Métis actions in 1869. What is his basis for resisting Canadian authority? What is his attitude toward Canada? In what ways is he similar to Cortina?

1. Escaped Slave Describes Appeal of Canada, 1847

… I was hired to Capt. Otis Reynolds, as a waiter on board the steamboat Enterprize, owned by Messrs. John and Edward Walsh, commission merchants at St. Louis. This boat was then running on the upper Mississippi. My employment on board was to wait on gentlemen, and the captain being a good man, the situation was a pleasant one to me;—but in passing from place to place, and seeing

William Wells Brown, *Narrative of William W. Brown, a Fugitive Slave, Written by Himself.* (Boston: The Anti-slavery office, 1847), 31, 84, 104–105, 109–110.

new faces every day, and knowing that they could go where they pleased, I soon became unhappy, and several times thought of leaving the boat at some landing place, and trying to make my escape to Canada, which I had heard much about as a place where the slave might live, be free, and be protected.

... The anxiety to be a freeman would not let me rest day or night. I would think of the northern cities that I had heard so much about;—of Canada, where so man of my acquaintances had found refuge. I would dream at night that I was in Canada, a freeman, and on waking in the morning, weep to find myself so sadly mistaken.

> "I would think of Victoria's domain,
> And in a moment I seemed to be there!
> But the fear of being taken again,
> Soon hurried me back to despair."

... [During his flight North] I found that I was about fifty or sixty miles from Dayton, in the State of Ohio, and between one and two hundred miles from Cleaveland, on lake Erie, a place I was desirous of reaching on my way to Canada. This I know will sound strangely to the ears of people in foreign lands, but it is nevertheless true. An American citizen was fleeing from a Democratic, Republican, Christian government, to receive protection under the monarchy of Great Britain. While the people of the United States boast of their freedom, they at the same time keep three millions of their own citizens in chains; and while I am seated here in sight of Bunker Hill Monument, writing this narrative, I am a slave, and no law, not even in Massachusetts, can protect me from the hands of the slaveholder!

... [After escaping to the North] It was my great desire, being out of slavery myself, to do what I could for the emancipation of my brethren yet in chains, and while on Lake Erie, I found many opportunities of "helping their cause along."

It is well known, that a great number of fugitives make their escape to Canada, by way of Cleaveland; and while on the lake, I always made arrangement to carry them on the boat to Buffalo or Detroit, and thus effect their escape to the "promised land." The friends of the slave, knowing that I would transport them without charge, never failed to have a delegation when the boat arrived at Cleaveland. I have sometimes had four or five on board, at one time.

In the year 1842, I conveyed, from the first of May to the first of December, sixty-nine fugitives over Lake Erie to Canada. In 1843, I visited Malden, in Upper Canada, and counted seventeen, in that small village, who owed their escape to my humble efforts.

2. Frederick Law Olmsted on Slaves Escaping to Mexico, 1857

We told him, that being about to make a short trip into Mexico, we had called on him to pay our respects, and at the same time offered him an informal passport, we had obtained of the Mexican consul at New York. He called the young

Frederick Law Olmsted, *Journey Through Texas; Or, a Saddle-Trip on the Southwestern Frontier* (New York: Dix, Edwards, and Company, 1857), 322–325.

man who had received us at the door, and asked him to read the passport, and then told us he was glad we had taken this precaution, for such was the state of the country, he should otherwise have been under the painful necessity to deny us permission to travel in it. He then inquired by what route we had come from New York; and on our mentioning Natchitoches, in Louisiana, he asked, with interest, how that town now appeared, and what was its present population. Thirty years ago, he informed us, he was a lieutenant in the Spanish garrison there.

After half an hour's conversation, Woodland being our interpreter, he conducted us into the adjoining room. It was less than half the size of the first, and had a projecting window, not glazed, but strongly barred. Six beds, with patchwork coverlids, more or less highly ornamented, were set around the sides of the room, which also contained several packing-boxes, doing duty as wardrobes, and a table with writing materials.

Following his example, we reclined upon the beds, while his clerk made a lengthened examination of us, and recorded our age, birth-place, residence, occupation or profession, state (married or single), religion, our purpose in visiting Mexico, the route we proposed to follow, our proposed destination, the time we expected to spend in the country, a minute description of our persons, etc., to a copy of which we were requested to append our signatures. The original was then given to us, on payment of the very moderate fee of twelve-and-a-half cents; and we were told that one copy of it would be retained in the capitan's official bureau (which appeared to be a small box, distinctly labeled, "COLGATE'S PEARL STARCH—NEW YORK"), and that the other would be sent to the city of Mexico. Woodland told us, that a few weeks before, he had called with a gentleman who had been obliged to pay three dollars apiece for the passport of every man in his company.

RUNAWAY SLAVES IN MEXICO

As we turned a corner near the bank, we came suddenly upon two negroes, as they were crossing the street. One of them was startled, and looking ashamed and confounded, turned hesitatingly back and walked away from us; whereat some Mexican children laughed, and the other negro, looking at us, grinned impudently—expressing plainly enough—"I am not afraid of you." He touched his hat, however, when I nodded to him, and then, putting his hands in his pockets, as if he hadn't meant to, stepped up on one of the sand-bank caverns, whistling. Thither, wishing to have some conversation with him, I followed. He very civilly informed me, in answer to inquiries, that he was born in Virginia, and had been brought South by a trader and sold to a gentleman who had brought him to Texas, from whom he had run away four or five years ago. He would like right well to see old Virginia again, that he would—*if he could be free.* He was a mechanic, and could earn a dollar very easily, by his trade, every day. He could speak Spanish fluently, and had traveled extensively in Mexico, sometimes on his own business, and sometimes as a servant or muleteer. Once he had been beyond Durango, or nearly to the Pacific; and, northward, to Chihuahua, and he professed to be competent, as a guide, to any part of Northern Mexico. He had joined the Catholic True Church, he said, and he was very well satisfied with the country.

Runaways were *constantly* arriving here; two had got over, as I had previously been informed, the night before. He could not guess how many came in a year, but he could count forty, that he had known of, in the last three months. At other points, further down the river, a great many more came than here. He supposed a good many got lost and starved to death, or were killed on the way, between the settlements and the river. After they had learned the language, which did not generally take them long, if they chose to be industrious, they could live very comfortably. Wages were low, but they had all they earned for their own, and a man's living did not cost him much here. The Mexican Government was very just to them, they could always have their rights as fully protected as if they were Mexicans born. He mentioned to me several negroes whom he had seen, in different parts of the country, who had acquired wealth, and positions of honor. Some of them had connected themselves, by marriage, with rich old Spanish families, who thought as much of themselves as the best white people in Virginia. In fact, a colored man, if he could behave himself decently, had rather an advantage over a white American, he thought. The people generally liked them better. These Texas folks were too rough to suit them.

I believe these statements to have been pretty nearly true; he had no object, that I could discover, to exaggerate the facts either way. They were confirmed, also, in all essential particulars, by every foreigner I saw, who had lived or traveled in this part of Mexico, as well as by Mexicans themselves, with whom I was able to converse on the subject. It is repeated as a standing joke—I suppose I have heard it fifty times in the Texas taverns, and always to the great amusement of the company—that a nigger in Mexico is just as good as a white man, and if you don't treat him civilly he will have you hauled up and fined by an alcalde. The poor yellow-faced, priest-ridden heathen, actually hold, in earnest, the ideas on this subject put forth in that good old joke of our fathers—the Declaration of American Independence.

3. Mexican Government Complains of Laborers' Fight to the United States, 1873

The *ranchos* of Texas swarming with fugitive servants from Mexico, whose habits and inclinations are not of the best, have always fostered a element of demoralization which, added to that already existing in Texas, has caused evils on either bank of the river. The Mexican shore has suffered a triple loss: in the absence of men, considered as an instrument of labor; in the capital, which at the time of his flight the servant owes his master (a positive loss of capital), for in order to secure

Reports of the Committee of Investigation Sent in 1873 by the Mexican Government to the Frontier of Texas (New York: Baker and Godwin, 1875), 401–404.

the services of these men it is necessary to advance their salaries; and lastly, through the depredations committed by these men, who after their flight dedicate themselves to the theft of horses from the grazing lands with which they are well acquainted, in order to dispose of the animals to speculators, who purchase the stolen goods without scruple, and even hire these men to commit the crime.

The immense losses suffered by the Mexican frontier, through the flight of servants, may be computed at over one million [pesos] a year ...

From less than one half of the municipalities of the two states [Nuevo León and Coahuila] referred to, which have furnished data upon this matter, there appears to have fled into Texas, since 1848 to the present, two thousand eight hundred and twelve servants, who have transported thither their families numbering two thousand five hundred and seventy two persons. The liabilities of two thousand and twenty eight of these fugitives from proprietors of Nuevo Leon, amount to a sum of ... $255,996.80 [pesos] and that of the others, who are from Coahuila, amount to ... $123,120.80 [pesos].

Nearly half a million of [pesos] of actual loss; but it is not so much the loss of money that attracts the attention of the Commission, as that of labor to places where the population is sparse, the lack of men being a loss of capital to the country, considered as they are instruments of labor.

Dr. Engel, a famous German statistician, calculates that it requires the sume of one thousand one hundred and twenty-five dollars to place a person of either sex in a condition to become a producer. If under this rule, an estimate is made of the amount lost by the Mexican frontier, including the debts of the fugitives, we have a sum of ... $15,429,623, an amount which does not include any elements except those which ought to be considered and which refers to the double character of producers and consumers borne by the five thousand two hundred and eighty-four person emigrating from Mexico, to escape the labor to which they were in duty bound.

The United States, whose prosperity is in a great measure accountable to this personal capital or labor furnished by other countries to augment its wealth, cannot have benefitted much by that acquired from Mexico, for, unfortunately, they bring with them a vicious element which, added to that of the floating population congregated there from all parts of the world, and composing a considerable mass of the inhabitants, imperils the preservation of good habits of order and peace, as is demonstrated by the existing demoralization in the State of Texas.

The fugitive servants referred to are for the most part criminals, for they always steal before fleeing or have already been prosecuted for other crimes, and it is only reasonable to suppose that in the United States, where they take refuge, they do not maintain any better conduct. These criminals and others of another class, especially the cattle thieves who have managed to escape, all reside in Texas ...

Freedom of labor having been established as a constitutional principle, the institution of *servants*, once a specialty and considered necessary on a frontier, cannot today be sustained, nor would it be advisable, either morally or economically considered. But the annoyances endured, and the evils involved are of the most paramount interest to both frontiers, as regards the peace and harmony of each. The matter deserves consideration, and a stop should be put to the abuses, by laws, which properly enforced, would close the door to the system of roaming, which is indulged in by the people of the states of Nuevo Leon, Coahuila, and Tamaulipas, towards the frontier of Texas.

The institution of field labor having undergone a radical change, by action of law and a better knowledge of true economy, the old system is fast disappearing. Whilst this change is taking place, the energies of the authorities should be employed in causing, directly or indirectly, the return of servants, by means of extradition, when they have committed robberies or other crimes, and by the collection of debts in Texas. This last might be effected through the public agents charged with facilitating extradition, agreeably to the principle proposed by the Commission.

When it will be known to the fugitives that Texas is no longer a place of refuge where they can flee with impunity, after swindling their creditors, the tide of emigration will be diminished on the part of men who, by their habits of idleness, are no less pernicious to the state of Texas than to the frontier of Mexico, and beneficial effects will be enjoyed by all parties through the advantageous measures which may be adopted, to produce this result.

4. U.S. Government Seeks Release from Treaty Obligation to Control Indian Raids into Mexico, 1851

Daniel Webster, Secretary of State of the United States, to Robert P. Letcher, United States Minister to Mexico, August 19, 1851.

Sir: The President deems it of the utmost importance that we should be released from the stipulation in regard to Indians contained in the 11th article of the Treaty of Guadalupe Hidalgo ... [They] are unlimited in duration and impose upon this government the obligation to prevent and punish the depredations of United States Indians in Mexico ...

There can be no doubt that the inhabitants of the northern States of Mexico have suffered severely from Indian depredations since the Treaty of Guadalupe Hidalgo went into operation, and the Mexican government has complained of them both in representations to our Legation at Mexico and to this Department. It is understood that they suffering parties intend to ask amends from this government for the losses and injuries which they have sustained ... The hostile acts of the Indians whose homes are in the territory ceded to the United States by the Treaty of Guadalupe Hidalgo, have not been confined to Mexican citizens only, but have probably been as frequent, as destructive and as barbarous on citizens of the United

Daniel Webster, Secretary of State of the United States, to Robert P. Letcher, United States Minister to Mexico, Washington, Aug. 19, 1851, in *Diplomatic Correspondence of the United States: Inter-American Affairs, 1831–1860, vol. IX, Mexico, 1848 (mid-year)–1860,* William R. Manning, pp. 89–92 (Washington: Carnegie Endowment for International Peace, 1937).

States, especially of North Western Texas, New Mexico, and California … It is obvious that along a frontier of such an extent, most of it a rugged wilderness, without roads of any kind and impassable, not only by wheeled vehicles but perhaps even by horses, no means which could have been employed since the Treaty of Guadalupe Hidalgo went into operation, would have sufficed to prevent incursions of United States Indians into Mexican territory. The subsistence, forage, and ammunition of the troops must necessarily have been conveyed from one or the other extremity of the line of boundary, and without roads, this would have been impracticable. It is also notorious that that part of the boundary which extends from the Rio Grande to the Gila [roughly modern-day El Paso to central Arizona], and which is not a natural line, such as those rivers afford, has not yet even been marked. This would in any event have rendered it uncertain where a road for the conveyance of our military stores ought to have been constructed or where our troops should have been posted. The probability, also, that savages dwell on both side of at least this part of the line, would render it uncertain, in the absence of land marks, whether depredations from that quarter have been committed by United States of Mexican Indians.

The objects which Mexico sought to encompass by the 11th Article of the Treaty of Guadalupe Hidalgo, will in all probability be accomplished with as much certainty and as soon, by means of the ordinary Indian policy of the United States as if that Article were to remain in operation. That policy has generally been successful. As the territories of the nomadic tribes have been narrowed by the advancing tide of civilization, the savages have been restrained by the military force which has preceded or accompanied the settlers, or by means of treaties stipulating peace, which the Indians have found it for their interest to observe. The same course will be pursued in respect to the Indians mentioned in our treaties with Mexico. The vastness of the regions over which they roam, may be an obstacle to its comparative success there, but if the white population shall spread over them with anything like the rapidity with which it has occupied the Indian territory in other quarters of the Union, its ultimate triumph within a reasonable time will be sure.

5. Sitting Bull Crosses into Canada to Elude U.S. Authorities, 1877

Department of the Interior, Washington City, September 6, 1877

GENTLEMEN: The President desires you to proceed at your earliest convenience to Fort Benton, and thence to a point on our northern frontier, from which the present encampment of the Sioux chief, Sitting Bull on British

Report of the commission appointed by direction of the President of the United States: under instructions of the Honorables the Secretary of War and the Secretary of the Interior, to meet the Sioux Indian chief, Sitting Bull, with a view to avert hostile incursions into the territory of the United States from the Dominion of Canada (Washington, D.C.: Government Printing Office, 1877), vol. 2, pp. 6–8.

territory, is most easily accessible At the frontier you will be met by a detachment of mounted Canadian police, detailed by the Government of the Dominion of Canada for your protection.

It is the object of your mission, undertaken at the suggestion of the Government of the Dominion, to ascertain what danger there may be of hostile incursions on the part of Sitting Bull and the bands under his command upon the
territory of the United States, and, if possible, to effect such arrangements, not
unacceptable to the Government of the Dominion, as may be best calculated to
avert that danger ...

In the month of February last, Sitting Bull and his bands engaged in armed
hostilities against the United States, and pursued by our military forces, crossed
the boundary line of the British possessions, for the purpose of escaping from that
pursuit. At that time the fugitive Indians appeared to be well armed, but their
ammunition was so nearly exhausted that they were no longer able to continue
the struggle. Under such circumstances they took refuge on British soil, where
the troops of the United states could not follow them without violating the territory of a friendly power. It is reported, and there is good reason for believing,
that these hostile Indians have availed themselves of the protection and security
thus enjoyed to replenish their stock of ammunition, and thus to enable themselves to resume their hostilities against the United States as soon as they may
find it convenient to do so.

Fort Walsh, October 17, 1877

The commission assembled at 3 o'clock p.m. in Major Walsh's quarters ... The
Indian Chiefs were then brought in ... General Terry then read to them the
propositions ...

The President has instructed us to say to you that he desires to make a lasting
peace with you and your people ... and he has instructed us to say that if you
will return to your country, and hereafter refrain from acts of hostility against its
government and people, a full pardon will be given to you for all acts committed
in the past ... Of all of the bands which were at war with the United States a
year ago, this band of yours, which has sought refuge in the British possessions, is
the only one which has not surrendered; every other one has come into some of
the agencies established for the Sioux nation ...

We ask you to take these propositions into consideration; to take time, consult together, and to weigh them carefully. When you have done so, we shall be
glad to meet you and receive your answer.

Sitting Bull then said: For 64 years, you have kept me and my people and
treated us bad; what have we done that you should want us to stop? It is all the
people on your side that have started us to do all these depredations. We could
not go anywhere else, and so we took refuge in this country. It was on this side
of the country we learned to shoot, and that is the reason why I came back to it
again ... I was raised in this country with the Red-River Half-Breeds [Métis],
and I intend to stop with them. I was raised hand in hand with the Red River

Half-Breeds, and we are going over to that part of the country, and that is the reason why I have come over here. (Shaking hands with the British officers) ... You have got ears, and you have got eyes to see with them, and you see how I live with these people? You see me? Here I am! If you think I am a fool you are a bigger fool than I am. This house is a medicine-house. You come here to tell us lies, but we don't want to hear them ... Don't you say two more words. Go back home where you came from. This country is mine, and I intend to stay here, and to raise this country full of grown people. See these people here. We were raised with them. (Again shaking hands with the British officers.) That is enough; so no more. You see me shaking hands with these people.

"Nine," a Yankton Indian, who joined the Santee band that left Minnesota some years ago during the [1864] massacre, said, after shaking hands all around: I have shaken hands with everybody in the house. You come over here to tell lies on one another. I want to tell you a few, but you have got more lies than I can say ... There are seven different tribes of us. They live all over the country. You kept part of us over there, and part of us you kept on this side. You did not treat us right over there, so we came back over there. The people sitting around here, you promised to take good care of them when you had them over there, but you did not fulfill your promises ...

A squaw named "The-one-that-speaks-once," wife of "The-man-that-scatters-the-Bear," said, I was over to your country; I wanted to raise my children over there, but you did not give me any time. I cam over to this country to raise my children and have a little peace. (Shaking hands with the English officers.) That is all I have to say to you. I want you to go back where you came from. These are the people that I am going to stay with, and raise my children with.

6. General Crook Describes Difficulty of Capturing Geronimo, 1883

Q: What is the direct cause of your late campaign against the Apaches into Mexico?

A: In the month of March [1883] those Apaches, who we now hold as prisoners made raids through Arizona, killing citizens, depredating, and committing all kinds of outrages to such an extent that the entire country was aroused, and the people so incensed that it was absolutely necessary that something should be done.

After they had spread terror through the country and had moved further south, I had information that they were coming back to renew their raids, and of course there was only one way to stop that, and that was to go down and meet them in their strongholds, because it is impossible to catch a raiding party of Indians while they are on the rampage. I was satisfied that they could not be brought into the reservation unless we punished them, and I felt that if we could not locate them from this side, it would be necessary to extend the expedition into Mexico.

When I found that they had gone so far into Mexico, I went to Sonora for the purpose of having an understanding with the Mexican authorities, and did it upon my own responsibility. We found the people kindly disposed, and they assured us that they would do everything in their power to assist us.

To supply my expedition I got all the pack mules I could raise in that country—about 350. I obtained two months' rations to guard against any possible contingency, for I did not want to stop at a critical moment for want of food ...

Q: How was your force divided with respect to Indian scouts and soldiers?

A: I had forty-two soldiers, 193 Indians, and fifty packers, but the latter I did not include in my fighting force.

Q: What is the distance from the border to the rendezvous of the Apaches in the Sierra Madre Mountains?

A: About two hundred miles, and one hundred miles from the railroad to border.

Q: And it required how much time to march to the place where you discovered the Apaches?

A: We started from the border on May 1 and arrived on the fifteenth of the month.

Q: What method of strategy did you adopt in pursuing the savages?

A: Of course, my plan in fighting Indians is first to locate them. When located we make forced marches and attack them. You cannot surprise them with a large command, particularly in a mountainous region, where they occupy positions overlooking many miles of territory. When we got to within twenty or thirty miles of where they were located, I sent Captain Crawford in with the Indian scouts, who carried with them three days' rations and blankets, which were strapped to their backs, in order that they might more readily climb precipices and canyons, the mules and soldiers remaining in the rear. It was a case of playing Indian on Mr. Indian.

Q: By what means did you locate the hostiles?

A: Our Apache scouts told us where they were. Peaches, our leading scout, said they were in there somewhere.

They hid on these peaks until nearly starved and then started forth on their raids. The raid they made in March was divided, one band being sent to Sonora to steal stock and another to Arizona to get ammunition, but they got so little from the people whom they killed that they carried out no more than they brought in. Geronimo led the party through Sonora, and Chatto headed that which went through Arizona.

Another evidence of their success in predatory warfare is the fact that about 120 bucks have paralyzed all business interests for hundreds of miles around their rendezvous and have totally depopulated that country ...

7. Juan Cortina Condemns Anglo Americans for Land Theft, 1859

An event of grave importance, in which it has fallen to my lot to figure as the principal actor since the morning of the 28th instant; doubtless keeps you in suspense with regard to the progress of its consequences. There is no need of fear. Orderly people and honest citizens are inviolable to us in their persons and interests. Our object, as you have seen, has been to chastise the villainy of our enemies, which heretofore has gone unpunished. These have connived with each other, and form, so to speak, a perfidious inquisitorial lodge to persecute and rob us, without any cause, and for no other crime on our part than that of being of Mexican origin, considering us, doubtless, destitute of those gifts which they themselves do not possess.

To defend ourselves, and making use of the sacred right of self-preservation, we have assembled in a popular meeting with a view of discussing a means by which to put an end to our misfortunes....

Innocent persons shall not suffer—no. But, if necessary, we will lead a wandering life, awaiting our opportunity to purge society of men so base that they degrade it with their opprobrium. Our families have returned as strangers to their old country to beg for an asylum. Our lands, if they are to be sacrificed to the avaricious covetousness of our enemies, will be rather so on account of our own vicissitudes. As to land, Nature will always grant us sufficient to support our frames, and we accept the consequences that may arise. Further, our personal enemies shall not possess our lands until they have fattened it with their own gore.

It remains for me to say that, separated as we are, by accident alone, from the other citizens of the city, and not having renounced our rights as North American citizens, we disapprove and energetically protest against the act of having caused a force of the national guards from Mexico to cross unto this side to ingraft themselves in a question so foreign to their country that there is no excusing such weakness on the part of those who implored their aid....

There are, doubtless, persons so overcome by strange prejudices, men without confidence or courage to face danger in an undertaking in sisterhood with the love of liberty, who, examining the merit of acts by a false light, and preferring that of the same opinion contrary to their own, prepare no other reward than that pronounced for the "bandit," for him who, with complete abnegation of self, dedicates himself to constant labor for the happiness of those who suffering under the weight of misfortunes, eat their bread, mingled with tears, on the earth which they rated.

If, my dear compatriots, I am honored with that name, I am ready for the combat.

The Mexicans who inhabit this wide region, some because they were born therein, others because since the treaty Guadalupe Hidalgo, they have been attracted to its soil by the soft influence of wise laws and the advantages of a free

---

U.S. Congress, House, *Difficulties on the Southwestern Frontier*, 36th Congress; 1st Session, 1860, H. Exec. Doc. 52, pp. 70–82.

government, paying little attention to the reasoning of politics, are honorably and exclusively dedicated to the exercise of industry, guided by that instinct which leads the good man to comprehend, as uncontradictory truth, that only in the reign of peace can he enjoy, without inquietude, the fruit of his labor. These, under an unjust imputation of selfishness and churlishness, which do not exist, are not devoid of those sincere and expressive evidences of such friendliness and tenderness as should gain for them that confidence with which they have inspired those who have met them in social intercourse. This genial affability seems as the foundation of that proverbial prudence which, as an oracle, is consulted in all their actions and undertakings. Their humility, simplicity, and docility, directed with dignity, it may be that with excess of goodness, can, if it be desired, lead them beyond the common class of men, but causes them to excel in an irresistible inclination towards ideas of equality, a proof of their simple manners, so well adapted to that which is styled the classic land of liberty. A man, a family, and a people, possessed of qualities so eminent, with their heart in their hand and purity on their lips, encounter every day renewed reasons to know that they are surrounded by malicious and crafty monsters, who rob them in the tranquil interior of home, or with open hatred and pursuit; it necessarily follows, however great may be their pain, if not abased by humiliation and ignominy, their groans suffocated and hushed by a pain which renders them insensible, they become resigned to suffering before an abyss of misfortunes.

Mexicans! When the State of Texas began to receive the new organization which its sovereignty required as an integrate part of the Union, flocks of vampires, in the guise of men came and scattered themselves in the settlements, without any capital except the corrupt heart and the most perverse intentions. Some, brimful of laws, pledged to us their protection against the attacks of the rest; others assembled in shadowy councils, attempted and excited the robbery and burning of the houses of our relatives on the other side of the river Bravo; while others, to the abusing of our unlimited confidence, when we intrusted them with our titles, which secured the future of our families, refused to return them under false and frivolous pretexts; all, in short, with a smile on their faces, giving the lie to that which their black entrails were meditating. Many of you have been robbed of your property, incarcerated, chased, murdered, and hunted like wild beasts, because your labor was fruitful, and because your industry excited the vile avarice which led them. A voice infernal said, from the bottom of their soul, "kill them; the greater will be our gain!" Ah! This does not finish the sketch of your situation. It would appear that justice had fled from this world, leaving you to the caprice of your oppressors, who become each day more furious towards you; that, through witnesses and false charges, although the grounds may be insufficient, you may be interred in the penitentiaries, if you are not previously deprived of life by some keeper who covers himself from responsibility by the pretense of your flight. There are to be found criminals covered with frightful crimes, but they appear to have impunity until opportunity furnish them a victim; to these monsters indulgence is shown, because they are not of our race, which is unworthy, as they say, to belong to the human species. But this race, which the Anglo-American, so ostentatious of its own qualities, tries so much to blacken, depreciate, and load with insults, in a spirit of blindness, which goes to the full extent of such things so common on this frontier, does not fear, placed even in the midst of its very faults, those subtle inquisitions which are so frequently made as to its manners, habits, and sentiments; nor that its deeds should be put to the test of examination in the land of reason, of justice, and of honor. This race has never humbled itself before the conqueror, though the reverse has happened, and can be established; for his is not humbled who uses among his fellow-men those courtesies which humanity prescribes; charity being the root whence springs the rule of his actions. But this race, which you see filled with gentleness and inward sweetness, gives now the cry of alarm throughout the entire extent of the land which it occupies, against all the artifice interposed by those who have become chargeable with their division and discord. This race, adorned with the most lovely disposition towards all that is good and useful in the line of progress, omits no act of diligence which might correct its many imperfections, and lift its grand edifice among the ruins of the past, respecting the ancient traditions and the maxims bequeathed by their ancestors, without being dazzled by brilliant and false appearances, nor crawling to that exaggeration of institution which, like a sublime statue, is offered for their worship and adoration.

Mexicans! Is there no remedy for you? Inviolable laws, yet useless, serve, it is true, certain judges and hypocritical authorities, cemented in evil and injustice, to do whatever suits them, and to satisfy their vile avarice at the cot of your patience and suffering; rising in their frenzy, even to the taking of life, through the treacherous hands of their bailiffs. The wicket way in which many of you have been often-times involved in persecution, accompanied by circumstances making it the more bitter, is now well known; these crimes being hid from society under the shadow of a horrid night, those implacable people, with the haughty spirit which suggests impunity for a life of criminality, have pronounced, doubt ye not, your sentence, which is, with accustomed insensibility, as you have seen, on the point of execution.

Mexicans! My part is taken; the voice of revelation whispers to me that to me is entrusted the work of breaking the chains of your slavery, and that the Lord will enable me, with powerful arm, to fight against our enemies, in compliance with the requirements of that Sovereign Majesty, who, from this day forward, will hold us under His protection. On my part, I am ready to offer myself as a sacrifice for your happiness; and counting upon the means necessary for the discharge of my ministry, you may count upon my cooperation, should no cowardly attempt put an end to my days. This undertaking will be sustained on the following bases:

First. A society is organized in the State of Texas, which devotes itself sleeplessly until the work is crowned with success, to the improvement of the unhappy condition of those Mexicans resident therein; extermination their tyrants, to which end those which compose it are ready to shed their blood and suffer the death of martyrs.

Second. As this society contains within itself the elements necessary to accomplish the great end of its labors, the veil of impenetrable secrecy covers

"The Great Book" in which the articles of its constitution are written; while so delicate are the difficulties which must be overcome that no honorable man can have cause for alarm, if imperious exigencies require them to act without reserve.

Third. The Mexicans of Texas repose their lot under the good sentiments of the governor elect of the State, General Houston, and trust that upon his elevation to power he will begin with care to give us legal protection within the limits of his powers.

Mexicans! Peace be with you! Good inhabitants of the State of Texas, look on them as brothers, and keep in mind that which the Holy Spirit saith: "Thou shalt not be the friend of the passionate man; nor join thyself to the madman, lest thou learn his mode of work and scandalize thy soul."

8. Métis Defy Canadian Rule, 1869

Whereas it is admitted by all men, as a fundamental principle, that the public authority commands the obedience and respect of its subjects. It is also admitted that a people, when it has no government, is free to adopt one form of government in preference to another, to give or refuse allegiance to that which is proposed...

Now, therefore—

1st. We, the representatives of the people in council, assembled at Upper Fort Garry, on the 24th November, 1869, after having invoked the God of Nations, relying on these fundamental moral principles, solemnly declare, in the name of our constituents, and in our own names, before God and man, that from the day on which the Government we had always respected abandoned us, by transferring to a strange power the sacred authority confided to it, the people of Rupert's land and Northwest became free and exempt from all allegiance to the said Government.

2nd. That we refuse to recognize the authority of Canada, which pretends to have a right to coerce us, and impose upon us a despotic form of government, still more contrary to our rights and interests as British subjects than was that Government to which we had subjected ourselves through necessity up to a certain date.

3rd. That by sending an expedition ... charged to drive back Mr. William McDougall and his companions, coming in the name of Canada to rule us with the rod of despotism, without a previous notification to that effect, we have acted conformably to that sacred right which commands every citizen to offer energetic opposition to prevent his country being enslaved.

4th. That we continue, and shall continue, to oppose, with all our strength, the establishing of the Canadian authority in our country under the announced form. And in case of persistence on the part of the Canadian government, we

---

Alexander Begg, "Declaration of the People of Rupert's Land and the Northwest," in *History of the North-West*, vol. 2, pp. 416–417 (Toronto: Hunter, Rose, and Company, 1894–95).

protest beforehand against such an unjust and unlawful course: and we declare the said Canadian Government responsible bfore God and men for the innumerable evils which may be caused by so unwarrantable a course. Be it known, therefore, to the world in general, and to the Canadian government in particular, that as we have always heretofore successfully defended our country in frequent wars with the neighboring tribes of Indians who are now on friendly relations with us, we are firmly resolved in future, not less than in the past, to repel all invasions from whatsoever quarters they may come.

And, furthermore, we do declare and proclaim, in the name of the people of Rupert's Land and the North-West, that we have, on the said 24th of November, 1869 … established a provisional government, and hold it to be the only and lawful authority now in existence in Rupert's Land and the North-West which claims the obedience and respect of the people.

That meanwhile we hold ourselves in readiness to enter into such negotiations with the Canadian Government as may be favorable for the good government and prosperity of this people.

~ ESSAYS

Borderlands had long compromised slavery in North America by offering places of refuge from bondage. In the antebellum United States, slaves fled the southern plantations to the North; earlier, in colonial North America, they mostly pushed to the South. For over a century, Spanish Florida represented a refuge for runaway slaves—both African and Native American—from Carolina, Georgia, and other English colonies. In the Southwest, the border between Mexico and Texas played a similar emancipatory role. Although most Americans thought of Mexico as a weak and backward nation, slaves had reason to see it in a different light: Mexico had abolished slavery in 1829, within a decade of gaining its independence, while slaveholders still dominated the highest offices in the United States. Human beings who were property North of the Rio Grande belonged to nobody but themselves on the South side. In the first essay, Hartwick College Professor Sean Kelley analyzes the flight of slaves from Texas to Mexico. Texas slaves, he shows, paid close attention to Mexican politics and understood well that they might gain their freedom by crossing the border. They did so by the thousands, angering and frightening their masters. Even decades after the abolition of slavery, African Americans in Texas and Oklahoma remembered this exodus and understood the border as a marker of freedom and racial equality.

In the second essay, Gerhard Ens, professor of history and classics at the University of Alberta, discusses how the Métis people of the northern Great Plains negotiated the U.S.-Canada border that cut across their territory and how they eventually had to choose between the two nation-states. It is a story that overturns usual assumptions. One revelation is how meaningless the border was to the people living near it, and for how long. For half a century, the boundary, unmarked and widely ignored, had little effect on the Métis, who continued to live and hunt on both sides of it, providing food and hides for the fur trade industry they helped expand to the West. Unexpected, too, was the choice the Métis made when forced to give up their transnational existence. The United States Indian policy is often contrasted with the supposedly more benevolent and humane First Nations policy of Canada. Why did the boundary initially matter so little for the Métis, and why, in the end, did it come to mean so much? Why did the Plains Métis abandon Canada, the place of their origin and home for numerous Métis communities, for life in the United States, a country whose government did not grant them status as a distinct people?

In the third selection, Samuel Truett, professor of history at the University of New Mexico, examines the Arizona-Sonora borderlands in the late nineteenth century, when the region emerged as the world's leading copper producer. Truett describes the wide range of people who found opportunity in these borderlands, from Anglo-American mining executives and their families, Mexican miners, and Yaqui Indians, to polygamist Mormons fleeing the U.S. government. The Mexican and U.S. governments and some of their nations' most powerful corporations tried to control and transform this region. The wide-ranging Apaches had been confined on reservations, railroads had arrived, corporate finance and management were in place, and deep craters dotted the landscape around Bisbee, Nacozari, Cananea, and other mining towns. But Truett underscores just how incomplete and messy these efforts were, even by the early twentieth century. Fluid borderlands refused to become a domesticated transnational landscape of extraction. Borderlanders continued to live, move, work, and consume in ways that confounded state and corporate designs. Their resilience kept human life in much of the region local, mobile, informal, and beyond the grasp of would-be modernizers, anticipating the labor strikes, racial violence, and worker mobility that would destabilize the copper borderlands in the new century. Decades before aggressive mining exhausted ore reserves and the Great Depression collapsed copper prices, the transnational industrial ties that once knit the southern Arizona and northern Sonora together were already fraying.

Slavery and the Texas–Mexico Border, 1810–1860

SEAN KELLEY

In September 1851, six years after Texas was annexed by the United States and fifteen years after independence from Mexico, Guy M. Bryan, politician and slaveholder of Brazoria County, wrote his brother-in-law in response to a proposal to swap a tract of land for a slave. Bryan seems to have liked the idea and planned to inspect his brother-in-law's slave that evening, but a disturbing rumor prompted him to reconsider. "The negroe he has got Mexico in his head," he wrote, referring to the prospect of seeing the slave escape to the south, adding, "on this account I may not buy." The record is silent on whether Bryan went ahead with the deal, but his dilemma reveals something of the nature of slavery

Sean Kelley, "'Mexico in His Head': Slavery and the Texas–Mexico Border, 1810–1860," *Journal of Social History* 37 (Spring 2004): 709–723. Reprinted by permission.

in the U.S.-Mexico borderlands: enslaved residents of Texas invested the border with a set of meanings that formed the core of an oppositional culture, shaping numerous acts of resistance.

Historians of Texas slavery have long recognized that Mexico attracted and harbored refugees from the state's plantations. But in chronicling the efforts of enslaved Texans to reach freedom in Mexico, scholars have overlooked two important issues. First, they have generally treated the border itself as an unproblematic given, ignoring not only the conflicts that resulted in the frequent redrawing of the boundary between the U.S., the Texas Republic, and Mexico/New Spain, but also the changing significance of the border that accompanied each shift. The issue warrants serious consideration. National boundaries delineated the scope of state power, which, through military support and the passage of slave codes, was vital to the maintenance of slavery. A second, and closely related issue is the ability of enslaved Texans to project a definition of the border. They did not simply react to the various redrawings of the border; in the crucible of their own interpretive communities they invested the border with liberationist significance, helping to set off a chain of events that resulted in Texas independence and the establishment of a slaveholding republic. Ironically though, the drawing of a clear border between slavery and non-slavery only inspired more flight toward the Rio Grande.

If historians of Texas slavery have largely ignored the issue of borders and boundaries, historians of Mexico and the U.S. West certainly have not. The concept of a borderland has evolved considerably since Herbert Bolton first envisioned it in the early 20th century as the meeting place of rival European empires in western North America. Cultural and literary critics, such as Gloria Anzaldúa, have seen the borderlands as a "third country in-between" Anglo-American and Mexican cultures, characterized by a high degree of hybridity and resistance. Although most historians have embraced Anzaldúa's concept of a cultural borderland, her tendency to treat it as continuous and timeless has generated calls for greater historical specificity. In response, Jeremy Adelman and Stephen Aron have proposed a three-part typology consisting of "frontiers," "borderlands," and "bordered lands," with each ideal type defined by the degree and nature of state control over the area in question. Frontiers, according to Adelman and Aron, are simply meeting places of peoples; borderlands are the meeting places of empires; bordered lands are the formally recognized meeting places of sovereign states. The succession of one form by the other, they argue, had important consequences for those "in between," presenting them with different sets of problems and opportunities.

In Texas slaves created different meanings for the border as it moved. We may divide the process by which the Mexican border became associated with nonslavery into four periods. In the first, which lasted until approximately 1820, the geographic boundary between the United States and New Spain (soon to be Mexico) was undetermined. Because slavery was legal in both areas, slaves did not attach any particular significance to the border, although some fled to Texas recognizing that it would be difficult for masters to pursue runaways into Spanish territory. The second period, approximately 1820 to 1829, saw the beginnings of plantation slavery, but as yet only a faint connection between Mexico and the idea of freedom. The third period, 1829 to 1845, saw tensions escalate between Anglo Texans and the Mexican government over a number of issues, including slavery, resulting in the establishment of an independent slave-holding republic and culminating in the annexation of Texas as a slave state, so-lidifying once and for all the linkage of Mexico with freedom. Thousands of slaves acted on this vision and fled across the Rio Grande. Finally, in the years after emancipation, the image of Mexico symbolized not only a collective history of resistance to slavery, but also served as a reminder that the racial hierarchies of the postwar South were by no means natural, inevitable, or just.

The Mexican War for Independence, which began in 1810, altered the region's relationship with slavery in two ways. First, by bringing into existence a Mexican state, the war focused attention on the U.S.-Mexico boundary. Napoleon's sale of Louisiana in 1803 set off a round of claims and counter-claims between the United States and Spain. An 1819 treaty between Spain and the United States settled the matter two years before Mexican independence, and the newly created stare accepted the boundary, which ran from the Gulf up the Sabine River, westward along the Red River, then through the Rocky Mountains to the Pacific Coast. Despite grousing from some Anglo-Americans who felt their claims had been ignored (and who mounted occasional filibustering expeditions), the border held. Coahuila-Texas had passed from "borderland" to "bordered land," to borrow Adelman and Aran's term.

The creation of a Mexican state raised a second issue, which, combined with the newly drawn boundary, lent a special texture to slavery in the region. Though ultimately rather conservative, the Mexican state was forged in a revolutionary atmosphere hostile to slavery. Father Hidalgo's 1810 *Grito de Dolores*, traditionally seen as the catalyst of the independence movement, contained an explicit call for the institution's abolition. That same year, José Maria Morelos, Hidalgo's eventual successor, called for an end to slavery, along with the distinctions of indio, mestizo, and mulatto. As the Hidalgo movement lost momentum in the 1810s, the reluctance of some liberals to interfere with masters' property rights prevented decisive action against slavery But with no Mexican slavehold-ing interest to register objection, antislavery rhetoric persisted into the 1820s, if for nothing more than symbolic reasons.

New Spain had been a haven for fugitive U.S. slaves for some time before the establishment of a formal boundary with the United States. Even before the formalization of a U.S. New Spain border in 1819, U.S. diplomats complained to Spanish officials that Mississippi Valley slaves, were escaping to the region west of the Sabine River.

With the formalization of the border in 1819, followed two years later by Mexican statehood and Anglo/African-American colonization, the geographic logic of slave flight changed. Coahuila-Texas was now a slave-owning society. For runaways and those contemplating flight, the Sabine no longer constituted the practical limit of the slaveholders' reach. Two options emerged for fugitives. Some, it appears, sought freedom even further south in Coahuila or Tamaulipas, drawn perhaps by the lingering antislavery rhetoric of the Hidalgo movement and the war for independence. In the actions of these fugitives we can detect the early linkages between the image of Mexico and ideas of freedom, although not yet as strong as they would be in the 1830s. One Anglo resident recalled Jim, a slave on John McNeel's plantation in the 1820s, who "openly announced his determination to leave, and, acting on impulse, threw down his hoe and started away." McNeel's son, Pleasant, aimed his rifle at Jim and threatened to shoot him if he did not return to work. Jim continued on his way, and Pleasant McNeel promptly shot him dead, which undoubtedly strengthened whatever connection his slaves may have made between Mexico and antislavery. It can hardly be coincidental that when the Mexican Army approached the Brazos in 1836, the McNeel family lost "a great many of there Negroes."

Although they left no direct evidence of their thoughts or reactions, Texas slaves undoubtedly took note of the ongoing conflict between the Mexican government and Anglo settlers on these issues, especially slavery. Ironically, the Mexican government's commitment to antislavery was inconsistent, and its antislavery measures frequently fell victim to the desire to populate Texas and make it profitable. Time and again, officials undercut their own antislavery policies by permitting exceptions and reinterpretations. What mattered, however, was not the government's stance on slavery per se, but how the slaves themselves interpreted the government's equivocations.

And equivocations they were. The declarations of Hidalgo and Morelos, the strongest expressions of Mexican antislavery, were null and void after the collapse of their movement in the 1810s. The political struggles of the 1820s muddied the waters even further, as both state and federal governments steered an erratic and often-conflicting course on the issue of slavery. Disputes between federalists and centralists over the scope of the Mexican state made it difficult to know which jurisdiction took priority. Between 1823 and 1829, national authorities decreed the following: a prohibition of the foreign slave trade (1823); the emancipation of slave children under fourteen (1823); an extra, grant of land to settlers who brought in large numbers of enslaved laborers (1823); a reconfirmation of the proslavery article in the national colonization law (1824); the abolition of the internal slave trade (1824); the abolition of slavery in Mexico (1829); and the subsequent exemption of Texas from the abolition decree (1829). The state government at Saltillo was equally erratic. Among its decrees were: a six-month period during which slaves could be brought into the state (1824); a six-month sunset period for slave importations (1827); a post-nati emancipation law (1827); a law providing for the emancipation of ten percent of the slaves on any estate undergoing sale or transfer (1827); and a contract labor law that allowed Anglo slaveowners to sign their bondsmen to ninety-nine year indentures, essentially undercutting all previous antislavery legislation (1827).

Anglo slaveowners took advantage of the confusion to bring more slaves into Texas, but through its equivocations, the Mexican government had actually weakened slavery in a variety of ways. Most of the slave societies of the Western Hemisphere sought legitimization of the institution from the state in the form of a slave code. Nineteenth-century Anglo Southerners in particular were accustomed to a rather extensive body of statutory and case law that shaped all aspects of the master-slave relationship. If bondage were to be replicated in Texas, the obligations of the master-slave relationship would require legal definition. In addition, since slavery required community acquiescence, the relationships between the free members of society to each other's slaves needed to be spelled out. How, for example, would society treat interference by one free person with another's slaves when the law did not sanction the right of the first to hold slave property? An unambiguous body of slave law was economically essential since slaves represented not only labor, but capital as well. Could they be mortgaged in order to raise money? Were slaves real or personal property? How would the succession of titles proceed? Were there any limits on the domestic or international sale of slaves? Could slaves be seized and sold for debt? Did slave families have legal standing? Could slave children be separated from their mothers? Mexican law, while failing to abolish the institution outright, gave little support to the master-slave relationship.

Mexican equivocation on slavery would have been inconsequential if the interpretive community of slaves had not endowed Mexico with special significance, one that helped inspire overt acts of resistance. Throughout the New World, slaves appropriated whatever language they encountered and turned it to their own ends. This tendency of slaves to reinterpret the pronouncements and political rhetoric issuing from distant sources that made Mexican rule intolerable to slaveowners. In the hands of slaves, the idea of Mexico was transformed into a symbol of non-slavery, much as Christianity and revolutionary France had been reinterpreted by enslaved Africans a generation before.

There can be little doubt that the various pronouncements on slavery issuing from Saltillo and Mexico City led Texas slaveowners to view the Mexican state as a potential threat. Although the presence of the Mexican state was minimal in the Anglo regions of Texas, masters did all they could to shield their bondsmen from its influence. Such was the experience of a state expedition that traveled to Texas in 1828 amid fears of Anglo secessionism. That May, a small detachment led by General Manuel Miet y Terán happened past Bernardo Plantation, where, despite the sweltering May heat, its members received a frosty reception from Texas' first and wealthiest planter, the normally hospitable Jared Groce. After grudgingly giving the soldiers some corn for fodder, Groce refused the party food or shelter, leaving it to camp underneath some trees. Taking the hint, the interlopers left the following day.

If masters increasingly viewed the Mexican state as a threat to their interests, slaves soon demonstrated that they saw it as an ally. In 1835—1836, the simmering tensions between Anglo settlers and the Mexican government boiled over. A number of issues, not the least of which was slavery, lay behind the rift. As the Mexican army approached the Austin Colony in 1836 to put down what had become an open rebellion, thousands of Anglos fled toward the U.S.-Mexico border at the Sabine River with their slaves, an event memorialized in Texas history (usually without any sense of irony) as the "Runaway Scrape." An unknown, but certainly sizable number of slaves ran the opposite direction. Ann Thomas, wife of slaveholder John Thomas, began her flight with nine slaves. Three were immediately seized by other Anglo settlers for her husband's debts, leaving her with six.

Within a week, four of the men fled to the Mexican army, "being promised their freedom on doing so," as Ann Thomas surmised. The only slaves who remained were two women, who may have deemed the risks of camp life, including possible harassment and abuse, not worth taking.

Slaves who reached Mexican lines did not always see their dreams of freedom realized. Some of the fugitives were freed and sent further south, as was the case with the fourteen families encountered by General José Urrea's forces in April 1836, whom he "sent free" to Victoria. Other commanders were not as liberal. According to Urrea, General Vicente Filisoia returned several runaways, including a man who had served as his own coachman, to Anglo slaveholders as he retreated from Texas. Moreover, Filisola also seems to have permitted slaveholders to enter Mexican camps to recover stolen property, including slaves. As with Mexican legal support for slavery, actual military policy did not consistently grant freedom to the enslaved. Yet, as with the issue of legality, what mattered was not the actual policy, but the significance slaves attached to Mexican equivocation. To them, the Mexican Army was an army of liberation.

The most dramatic expression of the linkage between the ideas of Mexico and freedom came in the form of a slave revolt in October 1835. As the army approached the fast-developing plantation district on the lower Brazos River, the enslaved population rebelled. Virtually all that is known about the incident is contained in a letter dated Octoher 17 from B. J. White to Stephen F. Austin, which read in its entirety:

> I now have some unpleasant news to communicate, the [sic] negroes on Brazos [sic] made an attempt to rise. Majr Sutherland came on here for a few men to take back, he told me—John Davis returned from Brazoria bringing the news that near 100 had been taken up and many whipd nearly to death some hung etc. R.H. Williams has nearly Kild one of his.—The carancawa Indians is in the Navidad country killing (stealing) etc.
>
> [signed] B.J. White
>
> PS—The negroes above alluded to had devided [sic] all the cotton farms, and [sic] they intended to ship the cotton to New Orleans and make the white men serve them in turn [sic]

The militia, it seems, managed to quell the disturbance without too much difficulty. But the incident again shows the potential power of the slaves' vision of Mexico.

With the Brazos slave rebellion crushed and the Mexican army expelled, Anglo Texans established an independent, slave-holding republic. Delegates to a constitutional convention approved several proslavery clauses, guaranteeing the right to hold slave property, the right to import slaves from the United States, and forbidding free blacks to enter or reside in Texas without the special authorization of the legislature. Earlier legal ambiguities on the succession of slave property, the status of slave families, and other points of law soon vanished as the legislature and courts elaborated on the slave code. The border between the Texas Republic and Mexico, now drawn along the Rio Grande, finally became the unequivocal boundary between slavery and freedom that black Texans had imagined years earlier. In 1845 the United States Congress voted to annex Texas, then fought and won a war to put permanent rest to Mexican claims to the area between the Nueces the Rio Grande, Enslaved Texans would hardly have celebrated the consolidation of the new slave regime, but its very existence stemmed partly from Anglo fears that the institution could not exist under Mexican sovereignty. If slave flight during the U.S. Civil War presented U.S. authorities with the fait accompli of self-liberation, propelling Lincoln and Congress toward the revolutionary policy of emancipation, the flight of Texas slaves helped provoke the opposite sort of revolution in Texas—a proslavery one.

Although the border between slavery and freedom was redrawn, it was not erased; Texas and Mexico were still "bordered lands." The boundary persisted on maps, in practice, and in the minds and memories of enslaved Texans. The most telling evidence is the stream of runaways chat continued beyond independence and annexation and persisted through the antebellum period, aided at times by both Mexicans and Anglos. In 1844 a reputed horse thief named Jesse Blades and an accomplice named Robert Redding, alias Lascum, confessed plotting to "seduce" ten slaves from six different Brazoria County estates into paying $100 each for safe transport to Mexico. The effort failed "owing to the want of means to defray necessary expenses, and to the repentence and failure of some negroes." Nine of the ten were soon captured by authorities, and a tenth, a man named Dennis, was seized after hiding out for a week.

The number of slaves who managed to survive the long and hazardous journey to the Rio Grande is almost certainly in the thousands. On an 1854 visit to Piedras Negras, a small town on the Mexican side of the river, Frederick Law Olmsted reported seeing several former Texas slaves. One, a native of Virginia who had come to Texas with his master, spoke Spanish fluently, was a member of the Catholic Church, and had traveled throughout northern Mexico. The fugitive estimated that forty slaves had come through the town in the preceding three months. Some of the former slaves scattered and married into local families, but Olmsted also reported hearing of a community of runaways settling a few days outside Piedras Negras and comprising a virtual maroon colony. "The Mexican Government was very just to them," Olmsted quoted his informant, adding, "They could always have their rights as fully protected as if they were Mexicans born."

Texas and U.S. officials understood that ignoring the southward hemorrhage of slaves deprived the state of valuable labor and destabilized its plantation system. Both the state and private individuals launched expeditions to recover fugitives but found that Mexican opposition limited their effectiveness. Among the failures was the expedition of James H. Callahan, who led Texas Rangers into Piedras Negras in 1855 in pursuit of a group of Lipan Apaches, with a second goal being the recapture of runaways. A Mexican force soon expelled Callahan, and his rangers burned the town of Piedras Negras as they left. State officials also pressed the United States government to negotiate an extradition treaty, but that effort failed as well.

Flight was not the only form of border-oriented resistance to persist after annexation. In 1856, officials in Colorado County, in Central Texas, uncovered what they believed was a plot by 200 local, slaves to kill all the white men and "make wives" of the women. A search reportedly turned up a stockpile of pistols, long guns, ammunition, and bowie knives. A vigilance committee hanged the three men accused of being the ringleaders, while the lives of the rest were spared. As with so many other incidents, the border figured prominently. According to county officials, the rebels had resolved to "fight their way to a 'free state' (Mexico)." In addition, officials claimed that every Mexican in the county, "without exception," was involved in the plot. One man in particular, known only as Frank, was reputed to be one of the leaders, prompting officials to conclude "that the lower class of the Mexican population are incendiaries in any country where slaves are held, and should be dealt with accordingly." This sentiment translated into the expulsion of all Mexicans from Colorado and several nearby countries. Although it is difficult to say for certain how much of the plot was real and how much was a figment of Anglo imaginations, it demonstrates the continuing linkage of Mexico and antislavery in master-slave discourse.

The consequences of this linkage were felt in a variety of ways. In a simple economic sense, the loss of several thousand bondspeople was felt on the ledgers of the state's slaveowners. If we accept one contemporary estimate of 4,000 successful runaways by 1855, the aggregate loss works out to approximately 3.3% of the slave population. If the true number of successful escapees were only half that, it would still represent a noticeable proportion of the labor force. Even recaptured fugitives temporarily deprived their owners of labor, further cutting into productivity and profits. One Bastrop County master paid slave catchers $200 to track two fugitives 750 miles to the Rio Grande, only to hear that the slaves had "escaped & not [been] found." It is easy to understand why planters like Guy M. Bryan, quoted at the beginning of this essay, thought twice before purchasing laborers who had "Mexico in their heads." Other planters undoubtedly shared Bryan's apprehensions and factored the possibility of flight into their economic calculations.

The effects of flight to Mexico were not confined to the realm of economics, nor were they limited to the fugitives. For those who remained behind, Mexico appeared, rightly or not, as a republic built on a more inclusive model of citizenship. The image persisted in countless retellings of the slave experience, although with the end of slavery the meaning of the border shifted from one of freedom to one of racial equality. Almost seventy years after emancipation, Felix Haywood of San Antonio told a WPA interviewer, "In Mexico you could be free. They didn't care what color you was, black, white, yellow, or blue. Hundreds of slaves did get to Mexico and got on all right. We would, hear about 'em and how they was goin' to be Mexicans." Coming front a man who had experienced not only slavery, but the stifling racism of the Jim Crow South, Haywood's Mexico was a perfect inversion of the world north of the border, a poignant critique of a nation that liked to see itself as more progressive and enlightened than its southern neighbor.

The end of slavery in 1865 may have slowed, but it did not halt the flow of black Texans across the border, as the case of former slave Sallie Wroe's father demonstrates. During the Civil War, Wroe's father escaped by paddling a bale of cotton across the Rio Grande. He returned after the war, but finding his chances poor in post-emancipation Texas, he returned to Mexico, earned some money, and used it to buy clothing for his family on his return. Although the border no longer marked the spatial division between freedom and slavery, it could still be put to good use by those who understood how to manipulate it.

Texas slaves were not unique in attaching liberationist significance to the world beyond the boundaries of their own. The tendency was especially pro-nounced during the late eighteenth and early nineteenth centuries, as interpretive com-munities of slaves received, translated, and appropriated the language of liberty and freedom in settings ranging from Virginia, to Saint Domingue, to Bahia. None of this is to suggest that slave communities were incapable of generating subversive ideas internally; the history of New World slave resistance demon-strates clearly that they were. In fact, the very notion of interpretive community suggests that members drew on an internal and pre-existing collective experience in their encounters with metropolitan ideas and texts. Among these texts were political boundaries, not only the Mexican border, but the Haitian coast, the Mason–Dixon Line, the Ohio River, and eventually the picket lines of the Union Army. Slaves were among the world's most persistent border crossers.

The Border, the Buffalo, and the Métis of Montana

GERHARD J. ENS

In the late 1860s and early 1870s, large numbers of Plains Métis began to move into Montana to exploit the last large herds of buffalo in North America. The Métis are those descendants of native women and European men who forged a new identity in the fur trade that was neither Indian nor white. These Métis communities arose in various geographic locations such as the Great Lakes, Up-per Missouri, Red River, and the Canadian Northwest. The Plains Métis who could be found almost anywhere on the northern plains were a buffalo-hunting variant of this "New People." Most of these Métis had their origins further east, and many were Canadian or British by birth. The temporary *hivernants* or win-tering communities that the Méis established in Montana during this period be-came the basis of more permanent Métis communities in the 1880s when the United States/Canadian border became even more impermeable and the buffalo disappeared. They stayed in Montana even though the American government gave no recognition or rights to the Métis as a separate people. The questions this chapter addresses are why many of these Plains Métis, largely of Canadian or British origin, chose to stay on the American side of the border after the

Gerhard J. Ens, "The Border, the Buffalo, and the Metis of Montana," in *The Borderlands of the Canadian and American Wests: Essays on Regional History of the Forty-ninth Parallel*, ed. Evans, pp. 139–154 (Lincoln: University of Nebraska Press, 2006). Reprinted by permission of the Uni-versity of Nebraska Press. Copyright 2006 by the Board of Regents of the University of Nebraska.

buffalo disappeared, and what role the border and national consciousness played in the choice of whether the Métis would become American or Canadian.

The Plains Métis had been borderland people for more than fifty years in the Canadian and American Wests before the 1870s, and to the extent that they recognized the border as a meaningful entity, it was a "white" or "English" construct to be manipulated. The Métis lived, worked, and hunted on both sides of the line, and they recognized its existence only when it was to their benefit. After 1870, however, the border began to play an ever-increasing role in their identity.

Before the 1870s the American/British border on the northern plains was of little consequence to the Métis who exploited the buffalo herds in this region. The Plains Métis who first came to prominence in the Red River/Pembina region began to spread westward in the 1840s and 1850s as the buffalo withdrew from the more easterly parts of the northwestern plains and as the number of the Red River Métis rapidly increased from 3,646 in 1835 to 12,000 in 1870. By the 1850s and 1860s their wintering villages could be found anywhere in the ecological zone where the buffalo wintered, irrespective of the international boundary.

The Convention of 1818, which had established the forty-ninth parallel as the boundary between the United States and the British possession, went largely unrecognized by the native peoples of the northern plains. For the Métis, the main repercussion was that the Hudson's Bay Company (HBC), realizing that their post along the border was now in American territory, moved the Pembina post to the Red River Settlement and put pressure on the Roman Catholic Church to relocate the Pembina mission to Red River, bringing the Métis with them. The HBC feared that if left at Pembina the Métis would take advantage of their new citizenship to flout the company's monopoly and go into the trade themselves. Even though the majority of the Pembina Métis did relocate to Red River in the British Territory, they lived and hunted where they wished and where it was safe to do so. Given that the Plains Métis' way of life was almost wholly dependent on the buffalo—they acted as provisioners for the fur trade and later became heavily involved in the buffalo robe trade—the Métis traveled as far as necessary to find the herds they needed. In the 1830s, 1840s, and 1850s they hunted in Sioux territory as far south as Devils Lake and as far west as the Grand Coteau. They had permanent villages in the Red River Settlement, Pembina, and St. Joseph. By the 1850s and 1860s they were hunting as far west as Wood Mountain, Milk River, and the Cypress Hills, and the distance from their former villages necessitated the establishment of temporary wintering villages near the buffalo and where there was enough shelter and wood to allow them to survive a winter on the plains. From the 1850s onward these wintering villages stretched from the Souris (Mouse) River in the east to the Cypress Hills in the west and from Devils Lake in the south to the North Saskatchewan River in the north. They survived in these locations because of their kinship connections to surrounding Indian bands (Sioux, Ojibway, Cree, and Assiniboine) and their military prowess.

From the time the Métis began expanding southwestward in the 1840s there were almost yearly conflicts with Sioux. By 1858, however, the Chippewa

(Ojibwa), Métis, and Dakota met in a Grand Council north of the Sheyenne River and west of Devils Lake to set tribal boundaries and establish peace among the three groups. The Métis were recognized as a legitimate band in the region and were represented by Jean-Baptiste Wilkie of St. Joseph (aka Norbexxa) and allowed to hunt in Sioux territories. The other factor that reduced Sioux/Métis conflicts was the "Minnesota Massacre" of 1862, which put the Sioux at war with the U.S. Army. The Sioux needed allies among the British Métis, who were their main trade source for guns and ammunition, and in 1863 the Sioux traveled to St. Joseph to reaffirm the peace treaty. Although these treaties signifi-cantly reduced the hostilities between the Sioux and Métis and allowed the Métis access to buffalo hunting grounds north and south of the border, the expansionary nature of both the Métis and Sioux in these years led to sporadic conflicts into the 1870s.

Before the 1870s the border was no impediment to the Métis, who manip-ulated it for their own purposes. The history of the Métis' use of the interna-tional boundary is a study in itself, and so I will provide only one example. When the Red River Métis heard that the U.S. government was planning to negotiate a treaty with the Pembina and Red Lake Chippewa, many decided to relocate to the American side of the boundary to take advantage of the ben-efits of this treaty. During the negotiations, the Métis claimed that "it was they who possessed the country really, and who had long defended and maintained it against the encroachments of enemies." The treaty that was signed between the United States and the Pembina Chippewa on September 20, 1851, however, did not include the Métis as signatories, as the government believed it should not deal with people whom it regarded "as our *quasi* citizens." The government negotiator did stipulate that he would not object "to any just or reasonable arrangement or treaty stipulation the Indians might choose to make for their benefit." As a result the Chippewa inserted a clause into the treaty that $30,000 be given to their Métis relatives. The treaty, however, was not ratified by Con-gress, and many of those who had claimed U.S. residence returned to the Red River Settlement in British Territory. The Métis' cavalier attitude toward the border was expressed more explicitly to Gen. Isaac-Stevens, who was exploring a route for a railway from the Dakota plains in the summer of 1853. The first group he encountered was from Pembina, but the second group, led by a hunt chief named De L'orme (Delorme), had come from the Red River Settlement in British Territory. De L'orme told Stevens that they had a right to hunt in American territory, being residents of the territory on both sides of the boundary line. Stevens reported that "they claim the protection of both governments, and the doubt as to the position of the boundary makes them uncertain as to the government upon which they have the most claim. During the hunting season they carry with them their families and their property. Many children are born during these expeditions, and they consider that children born upon our soils during the transit possess the heritage of American citizens."

By the 1860s, however, the boundary was becoming of increasing impor-tance in Indian/white relations. Advancing American settlement, Sioux hostilities in Minnesota, and the Canadian government's interest in acquiring the British

Northwest made the border a major factor in determining the responsibilities of the various governments in recognizing and protecting the rights of the various Indian groups in the region. As both the Métis and Indians were increasingly using the border to shield themselves from reprisals by the 1870s, it is not surprising that both governments would want better control of the border region. Within a few years the western boundary between the United States and Canada had been surveyed, and both the U.S. Army and the Canadian North-West Mounted Police were patrolling the border, significantly limiting cross-border traffic. These factors, combined with the southwestward retreat of the buffalo, would increasingly force the Plains Métis to choose a U.S. residence.

These developments brought the Plains Métis into Montana for the first time. Wintering villages had begun to appear in the 1840s at places like Turtle Mountain, Souris Basin, Riding Mountain, Wood Mountain, and along the Assiniboine, Qu'Appelle, and Saskatchewan rivers. They were a response to the westward retreat of the buffalo herds and the changing nature of the fur trade on the Upper Missouri River. Before 1840 the Plains Métis of Red River had secured most of the pemmican, dried meat, buffalo robes, and leather they required from the summer and fall buffalo hunts out of Red River and Pembina. Beginning in the 1840s, however, the buffalo retreated further and further west, and the Métis hunters had to travel hundreds of miles before even spotting a herd. Buffalo robes became increasingly important in the fur trade of the Missouri at this time. Beaver stocks had been depleted, and buffalo robes found lucrative markets in New York, Montreal, St. Paul, and St. Louis. These robes consisted of the skin of the buffalo with the hair left on and the hide tanned. Prime robes, those taken from November to February and in excellent shape, fetched good prices of ten to twelve dollars per robe by the 1870s. The Métis responded to this new market by smuggling their furs and robes across the border to American traders.

Beginning in the late 1840s and accelerating in the 1850s and 1860s, observers began to notice an increase in Métis' wintering communities west of Red River and Pembina in response to these new economic opportunities. While it was still possible to winter in St. Joseph in the 1850s and be close enough to the winter range of the buffalo to get winter robes, it was certainly no longer possible to do so wintering in the Red River Settlement or Pembina. As a result, more and more Plains Métis began spending their winters in small temporary communities west of Red River, where they could hunt the buffalo in winter. By the late 1860s and early 1870s, even the Métis of the settlement of St. Joseph were leaving en masse to winter on the plains. As time went on, these wintering villages moved in a southwesterly direction following the retreat of the northern herd, and by the 1870s, the orientation of most Plains Métis was south of the border. In 1878 prairie fires swept a wide area of grassland in the boundary region between Montana and what today is Alberta. The buffalo moved south, and what was left of the northern herd remained south of the border between the Milk River and the Judith Bain. The large herds never returned to Canada. Not only were the last remnants of the northern herd concentrating in northern Montana, but increasing military vigilance along the international boundary by both the U.S. Army and the NWMP forced the Métis to choose an American residence. While the U.S. Army and the NWMP were primarily interested in stopping the arms and whiskey trade that was stirring up Indian hostilities, this increased border vigilance also ended the Métis' practice of taking their buffalo robes across the border to traders at Fort Benton. Given these factors, it became much more convenient for the Métis to claim American residency.

The Métis had began wintering in Montana in the 1860s, locating their communities on the Milk River where the Riviere Blanche branches off into Canada. By the early 1870s, Métis settlements were springing up all over the Milk River country. Father Lestanc, who had built a mission at Wood Mountain for the Plains Métis, was forced to relocate to Montana because most of his group had left Wood Mountain. In 1871 he reported that there were sixty families wintering at Riviere Blanche, and by 1873 his camp alone had ninety families. He noted that no one knew precisely where the border was or if they were living in American or Canadian territory. George M. Dawson, traveling with the British Boundary Commission in 1874, met numerous Métis groups between Wood Mountain and Montana, and noted that Wood Mountain had "seen its palmy days. Buffalo & Indians already too far west. Most of the families speak of wintering next at Cypress Hills." On July 19, 1874, he visited a Métis camp on the Milk River that numbered two hundred lodges and two thousand horses. This group of Plains Métis was wintering on Riviere Blanche well within the United States, and he noted they traded their goods via the Missouri River posts.

The presence of these Canadian Métis in Montana worried the U.S. Army and Indian agents. Convinced that the Métis from Canada were trading whiskey and guns to the Sioux and using the border to shield themselves, the U.S. Army resolved to eliminate this traffic. According to A. J. Simmons, the Indian agent of the Milk River Agency in Montana, the Métis had "urged Sitting Bull to resist the construction of the North Pacific Rail Road. So long as Sitting Bull's people remain hostile they have the exclusive trade and barter with them from which they derive large profits and so long as these Indians can procure ammunition from this source, it will be found a serious obstacle in the way of their effecting peace with the Government."

On October 19, 1871, the Seventh Infantry stationed at Fort Shaw was ordered to proceed to the Milk River where this large group of "British" Métis had established their wintering villages. The Seventh Infantry was ordered to destroy all trade goods and drive the Métis out of the country. The army arrived at the Riviere Blanche on November 1, finding a camp of several hundred Métis. The settlement, consisting of houses and lodges scattered along four or five miles of the creek, was captured without any resistance. The houses of the two traders, consisting of nine buildings, as well as the whiskey and trade goods valued at $10,000 were all burned, and John Kerley was arrested. The Métis were told that they were in violation of American law by selling liquor and ammunition to Indians, and they were thereby helping the Indians to make war on the United States. They were ordered to leave the country and not return. The Métis, for their part, argued that the whiskey and ammunition were the property of white traders who had only recently joined them, and they had lived on the plains (including the United States) all their lives. Besides, they argued, they could not move north because the plains were burnt. They begged to be allowed to remain, promising they would allow no traders among them. In consideration of their good conduct on this occasion, and because the destruction of the entire camp would have inflicted great hardship and suffering, the Métis were allowed to remain in their settlement if they obeyed American laws.

This and other encounters with the U.S. Army convinced many Plains Métis that American residence and citizenship were crucial not only to hunting the buffalo but also to being able to trade buffalo robes to American posts along the Missouri. When 140 Métis were stopped by the U.S. Army in Montana in 1879 and asked what nationality they were, all but 10 replied they were American. The 10 who declared they were British were escorted across the border, and the others were advised to go to the Judith Basin.

By 1882 the buffalo herds had disappeared, even in Montana. This represented a real crisis for the Plains Métis, and they were faced with hard decisions as to what to do next. Those who had close kinship connections to tribal groups in Montana, such as the Blackfoot and Flathead, went into treaty. Some Métis who had come to Montana from Manitoba and North Dakota went back and reinvented themselves as the Turtle Mountain Chippewa and took treaty in 1892. Others moved north to Canada and took scrip (a negotiable certificate entitling the holder to receive an allotment of public land) after 1885, but a large number, despite their British Canadian roots, remained in Montana and refused to leave.

Those Plains Métis who remained in Montana after 1882 did so not only because there were employment opportunities but also because a significant number had come to see the United States as a homeland—something the Canadian Northwest no longer was. By the late 1870s and early 1880s, the border had become more than a line on a map; it had become something of a state of mind with its own mythology. This new way of looking at the border and the Canadian Northwest had begun shortly after the Riel Resistance in Red River and the transfer of the British Northwest to Canada in 1870, and it crystallized with the military suppression of the Riel Rebellion in the Northwest in 1885.

With the arrival of troops in Red River in the summer of 1870, the increasing pace of Canadian immigration to Manitoba, and the delays in fulfilling the land grants to the Métis promised in the Manitoba Act, many of the Plains Métis came to believe that they had been treated unjustly by the Canadian government. This feeling only increased as the government was slow to acknowledge Métis rights in the Northwest. By 1873 numerous reports were coming back to Alexander Morris, the lieutenant governor of Manitoba and the Northwest Territories, that the Indians and Métis of the Canadian Northwest were full of anxiety regarding the intentions of the Canadians toward them. Robert Bell, who wrote a report for Morris on the state of the West, noted that the notion that "the English have ceased to be their friends appears to be fostered ... if not promoted by the half breeds." The Métis, he wrote, wanted nothing to do with surveys, treaties, railways, or settlement, and they considered the Canadians cowards. When Pascal Breland was appointed by the Canadian government to investigate the presence of Sioux at Wood Mountain, he met with numerous Plains Métis who eventually would settle in Montana. He was informed that the state of affairs on the plains was critical and dangerous. In regard to the Métis, Edward McKay told him that the Métis, who lived and hunted on both sides of the border, had little respect for the Canadian government and were close to taking the law into their own hands. They were spreading rumors that the Canadian government wanted to exterminate the Indians and rob them of their country. The Métis, he said, "have so little public spirit that it is utter nonsense to depend on them for assistance." The talk of them being loyal, he said, "is outrageous as the majority don't know what it means and most of them scorn the idea.... Louis Riel is still their idol and should he or any smart fellow come out to lead them there will be a grand row.... They are becoming bolder every day under the inactive policy of the government and if the call be given a rebellion worse in every respect than the last will spread like a fire on the plains." Many of the most troublesome Métis, he noted, were those who had left the British Territory several years earlier to live on, the American side. They had recently returned to Wood Mountain to excite the Métis and Indians against the Canadian government and British rule. They promised assistance from the United States if the Métis and Indians could not prevent the Dominion from disposing of their lands.

This discontent was evident as far north as St. Albert on the North Saskatchewan River. A large group of St. Albert Métis wintering at Buffalo Lake told Bishop Grandin in 1875 that "we know too well that we have nothing to hope from the Canadian Government except ill will and contempt. Rather than be ill treated (browbeaten) like our parents, we have decided to locate ourselves on the territories of the United States." Grandin refused this request, but noted the Métis were still planning to head south and cross the boundary when the time was right.

These simmering hostilities continued throughout the 1870s, and when Louis Riel returned to the West in 1878, he quickly saw the potential for a new offensive against the Canadian state. From his base in Carroll, Montana (a settlement in the heart of the badlands or "breaks" of the Upper Missouri near the Judith Basin), Riel planned an invasion of Canada by the Métis allied to various Indian bands. This invasion would be the prelude to the establishment of a Confederacy of Métis and Indians in the Canadian Northwest. Riel sent for Ambroise Lepine, his former adjutant-general from Red River days, who agreed to meet Riel at Fort Assiniboine in late 1879 or early 1880. Archbishop Taché, aware that Lepine had gone west to meet Riel and aware of the potential trouble the two could create, contacted Lepine and warned him not to meet with Riel. Not wanting to offend the Catholic Church, and aware of the risk to his own safety if he got involved with Riel again, Lepine returned to Manitoba without meeting Riel. As he wrote Taché, it would not take a very large spark to light a fire in the West, as the Métis were very unhappy with how they were being treated by the Canadian government. To Riel he wrote that he was not prepared to sacrifice more for the Métis, as he had already seen the noose at close hand and was not prepared to risk all again.

Riel was just as unsuccessful in persuading the Montana Métis and Indians to support his plan, and after a year or two he moved on to other projects. Riel's plan to attack Canada and establish a Métis and Indian Confederacy, farfetched as it may have been, does indicate the Métis' discontent with the Canadian government and provides some explanation for why the Métis of Montana had no interest in returning to Canada after the buffalo disappeared.

These Montana Métis, the remnant of the buffalo-hunting Plains Métis, settled in railway towns along the line of the Great Northern Railway (Fort Buford, Poplar, Oswego, Wolf Point, Havre, Chinook, Harlem, Malta, Glasgow, Kipp, Box Elder). Given that the Great Northern ran parallel to the Milk River, some of these towns such as Malta, Havre, and Glasgow were, in fact, very close to old Métis wintering sites. As railway towns they offered the Métis jobs as construction workers, dirt movers, wood choppers, and buffalo bones collectors. Others settled away from railway centers where it was still possible to hunt small game and farm (Dupuyer, Teton River, Sweetgrass, Choteau). Still others settled at Lewis town, Fort Benton, St. Peters, St. Ignatius, Augusta Hill, and Fort McGinnis, either homesteading, working as laborers on ranches and farms, or freighting. Some indication of the distribution and concentration of former Canadian Métis living in Montana comes from scrip applications by the Canadian government between 1900 and 1904 from Métis living in the United States.

One of the larger Métis settlements in Montana was located in the Judith Basin at Spring Creek (now known as Lewistown). It was settled by Plains Métis buffalo hunters led by Pierre Berger. These families originated in the Red River/ St. Joseph region of Manitoba and North Dakota. As the buffalo had retreated westward, this Métis band had relocated first to Wood Mountain and then to Milk River. By 1879 they were wintering on the Milk River between Harlem and Chinook, but with the herds growing smaller every year Pierre Berger began looking for a better location to winter and a location where his people might settle permanently. The larger wintering camps on the Milk were breaking up, and so Berger and twenty-five families decided to move to the Judith Basin where the last big herds were located and where there were other small game and lots of timber. Here they hunted the last buffalo. When these disappeared, they took up homesteads. Within a few years they were joined by other Plains Métis hunters from the Milk River, increasing the settlement to more than 150 families. This latter group had been told by the U.S. Army to leave the country or settle somewhere permanently. These Métis raised stock or worked on area ranches after more settlers moved in.

The 1885 North-West Rebellion was the crystallizing event that changed a transborder people into the Montana Métis who regarded the border as protection from the Canadian government. After the Canadian military crushed Riel's forces at Batoche in the spring of 1885, hundreds of Indians and Métis fled south to escape persecution. These Métis, settling among the Métis who had been in Montana for at least a decade and a half, reinforced the mythology of the evils of the Canadian government. Approximately sixty Métis refugee families settled on Dupuyer. Creek south of Blackfoot Reservation, arid another group chose the south fork of the Teton River near Choteau. Hiding in the canyons for fear of being sent back to Canada, these Métis lived off the land, hunting small game, "woodhawking," selling buffalo bones, and working on area ranches and farms. Their anti-Canadianism and fear of deportation stayed with the Montana Métis for good reason. In 1896 the American government decided to solve the social problems created by these "indigent" Canadian-born Crees and Métis by forcibly shipping them back to Canada. In all, 537 persons were shipped by rail to Canada, but almost all returned, slipping back across the border over the next few weeks.

Those Plains Métis who settled permanently in Montana had, over the course of a decade and a half, been transformed from a borderland people into American Métis. They willingly and deliberately chose an American residence and citizenship, at least in part, because of their belief that they had suffered an injustice at the hands of the Canadian government and that their rights and livelihood were better protected in the United States. They believed this despite the fact that the American government did not recognize the Métis as a separate group and accorded them no special political or economic rights. By 1885 the border had assumed almost mythical status as protection from persecutions by the Canadian state. This history of the Plains Métis should give pause to those historians who still hold the belief that the Canadian West was settled peaceably and that the Canadian government treated its native peoples more generously than the United States. For the Montana Métis, the demons of the "Western Civil War of Incorporation" were the Canadian state and military. They chose incorporation in the American body politic.

Passages into the Sonora–Arizona Borderlands

SAMUEL TRUETT

Shadows are worlds in motion; to appreciate them, we must trace their passages. When the U.S. mining engineer Morris B. Parker came from Chihuahua to Sonora in 1900, he took a passage familiar to many miners in the colonial era, from the old trade center of Casas Grandes through the Púlpito Pass to the highlands of northeastern Sonora. Squeezing through this "rough, rocky bottle-neck" in a rickety buckboard, he paused at Colonia Oaxaca, a new Mormon colony on the Bavispe, before pushing on to his destination, the mining region below Nacozari. Four years later, a traveler like Parker would have taken a train north to El Paso, east to Douglas, and south into Sonora on the Phelps Dodge rail network. In May 1900, however, Douglas was still Whitewater Draw, a rural landmark beyond the industrial frontier. Púlpito Pass, open to mule and wagon, was the shortest way to Sonora. Except for the nearby Carretas Pass, the next road across the sierras lay a thousand miles to the south.

Parker's journey was far from unusual. He was one of many mining engineers who shuttled back and forth between New Mexico, Chihuahua, Arizona,

Samuel Truett, *Fugitive Landscapes: The Forgotten History of the U.S.-Mexico Borderlands* (New Haven: Yale University Press, 2006), 104–130.

and Sonora at the turn of the century to sell his expertise to miners. He began his borderland odyssey as a teenager in the 1880s, when he moved with his family to White Oaks, a gold mining town in southern New Mexico. By the 1890s, he and his neighbors had begun to look to Mexico. "I was lured into that cornucopia in 1895," Parker later recalled, "and from then until 1932 a goodly portion of my time was spent below the border." In 1898, as William Cornell Greene was peddling mines on Wall Street, Parker became superintendent of the San Pedro mine, 125 miles southwest of El Paso near the Sierra Madres of Chihuahua. It was here that he was called west in 1900 to assess the wealth of Sonora.

Parker's journey offers a snapshot of Sonora on the brink of a new industrial age. Two things that stand out in his diary are times and distances. From Colonia Morelos, he and his partner headed for Fronteras, twenty miles west as the crow flies, but seventy miles for mule and buckboard, which had to swing north to avoid one of Sonora's many mountain ranges. Driving "by ruts and gullies" through pastures, mescal ranches, and customs outposts, they finally hit Ochoa's wagon road between Naco and Nacozari. Suddenly the world spun into motion. At meal stations spaced to match the speed of freighters, they dined with captains of industry. Louis D. Ricketts breezed by en route to Nacozari, as did John P. Ramsey, manager of the Rio Grande, Sierra Madire, and Pacific Railroad. Like Parker, Ramsey was "looking over country" but with a bolder eye: he envisioned himself driving rails west across the sierras from Chihuahua and thus knitting together northern Mexico into a larger, industrial whole.

With Phelps Dodge's machine dreams still "bogged axle deep in the black adobe soil" of Sonora, such talk must have seemed like idle chatter. This was still a profoundly local world, bound together by modest desires. North of Nacozari, "where we expected to get B'fast and didn't," Parker found Americans struggling to make ends meet with "a small rattle trap stamp mill." In Cumpas, south of Nacozari, he dined with a doctor who had found his way into Mexican society by marrying a local woman. In Moctezuma, he was the guest of the oldtimer George F. Woodward and his Mexican wife, who was "very kind and feeds us *fine!*" His journey revealed a different sort of human landscape than that oriented around the industrial pace of Ochoa's wagon road. These rural pathways, structured by economic isolation, family ties, and local custom, had changed little since the 1820s, when Moctezuma and Cumpas residents guided Robert Hardy and Simon Bourne through the haunted remains of former empires.

The road one took made all the difference, but so did the starting point. Another pilgrim in Sonora at the time was Maud Kenyon-Kingdon, the young wife of George Kingdon, a mining engineer of Parker's cohort. Kingdon had served his apprenticeship in Arizona and Mexico, prospecting and supervising mines, at times traveling, like Parker, to inspect properties. Maud met him in the Arizona copper town of Globe and joined him on a new path. "We unfurled our sails upon life's matrimonial sea and anchored across the Mexican border in one of the remotest, uncivilized little towns," she wrote of a move around 1903 to Pilares, where George found work as a superintendent. It was a "barren, desolate place," she wrote. Douglas was booming, and Phelps Dodge was laying tracks south, but not yet to Pilares. "Roads were forced to surrender to the rough and winding footpaths" winding up "precipitous slopes," she recalled of her new home, a "wild spot" she could hardly regard "without some trepidation."

Above all, this was a world of men. "I was about the first American woman that had ever come to this place," she wrote. She pressed George to make her feel at home. Mexicans were "put to work with spades, pickaxes and dynamite" to excavate a garden, and "in the matureness of time we had a garden blooming in wondrous profusion," she wrote. Embellished with a new rosebush, a Madeira vine around the veranda, and rows of "thrifty cottonwoods" nearby, it made for "a most attractive setting—a veritable garden spot ... and this was home." Yet Maud felt hemmed in. "Violent gales," she noted, "howled around our premises in weird, uncanny sounds, portending, as it were, some dark omen, some hidden tragedy awaiting this unsuspecting land." A ravine opened behind their house, and here miners played cards at night. They "were a law-breaking gang of thieves," she feared, addicted to "a vile and poisonous beverage of their own distillation, and which would likely result in some terrible feud.

Yet in time the copper borderlands became more fixed and less confined for the likes of Kenyon-Kingdon. In 1913, after a hiatus in the States, George took a job in Cananea. "It was a violent shock" to think of returning to Mexico, Maud wrote, but Cananea was not what she expected. The streets were "wide and very well laid out," and "the homes for American people were attractively built." Their house had a manicured lawn, Chinese servants, and French doors opening onto "verandas, walks and sweet-scented flower gardens." Cananea was a larger town than Pilares, but in a decade the borderlands also had changed. Her "haven of refuge" in a land controlled by others had now become a cosmopolitan cross-roads, managed—or so it seemed—with her own dreams in mind. "It was so very civilized," she happily admitted. "An unruffled world, it seemed, stretched its length before us."

Cananea's metropolitan intensity also attracted others. Coming to Cananea was like "entering another world," wrote Jesús Corral, who moved there as a child from the small mining town of La Dura in southern Sonora. Compared to La Dura, it seemed like a lost city of gold. "American and Mexican money flowed freely," Corral recalled. "The smell of luscious fruits and the din of silver dollars on the counter, as miners were being paid at the end of a week's work, made this place far different from the sleepy towns where [my] family had been before." Like Maud and George, Jesús saw the shift from hinterland to core as a migration from danger to safety, for southern Sonora in the early 1910s was be-ginning to spiral into a renewed cycle of ethnic violence among Yaqui Indians and Mexicans. "Fear of Yaqui raids was far from everybody's mind" in Cananea, he wrote. In terms of its economic promise for working families and its isolation from ethnic warfare, it was "a mecca for those desiring a better life."

If Jesús Corral, Maud Kenyon-Kingdon, and Morris B. Parker took different roads into the borderlands, they had at least this in common: their worlds were in constant motion. Places like Nacozari and Cananea were stopping places on larger, transnational circuits that knit together local spaces: gardens and dance halls, meal stations and rural hosts, the refuge and quaking earth of Billy Goat Hill. The itinerary of the Corral family linked the contested countryside to a working-class mecca and eventually pointed farther north. After toiling under Chivatera Ridge, Jesús's brother, Emilio, frequented the male refuges of Cananea's pool halls. "It was there, where men gathered, that he heard that farmers in the United States were recruiting large families to help harvest cotton crops in Arizona and California," Corral wrote. "That announcement presented an alternative to the Corral family. We now had a choice." If Parker chased nature's bounty over hill and dale, and Kenyon-Kingdon settled for French doors in a wild land, the Corrals ultimately chose the "open fields" of Arizona as the final stop on their journey of toil.

These roads were as diverse as those who took them, and they suggest a human side to the borderlands that we miss by perusing contracts, annual reports, and booster tracts. They also suggest the *range* of transnational tales: U.S. mining engineers stringing together disparate landscapes on a tenuous scientific thread; Yaqui and Mexican villagers working and fighting for traditional homelands; Chinese servants working to sustain a new life abroad; mining directors and railroad builders seeking to wring dividends from a rebellious land; *rancheros* and *mescaleros* chasing more modest dreams at the edges of the copper borderlands; immigrants passing through to the other side; worlds of women and men, their work, play, fantasies, and fears.

Such relationships approximated the modern electrical grid that Thomas Edison manufactured from copper in the late nineteenth century. Circuits of human energy led in all directions, yet each strand had its own logic and bundle of connections. Each was linked to discrete places, the human equivalent of transformers, insulators, pole lines, switchboards, and generators. It was a network that made connections and also created distinctions. Yet the analogy of electrical networks only goes so far, for unlike systems conceived by the Edison Electric Company and Westinghouse, these were anything but static fixtures. Spatial coordinates shifted over time as Mexicans, Americans, Yaquis, Chinese, and others migrated between spaces that corporate and state elites could see— smelters and mines, company towns, corporate reports, censuses—and "subterranean" spaces of ethnicity, culture, and family: regions of refuge from the official gaze. These unseen worlds burrowed beneath the more visible arteries of capital and state power to provide the essential human bedrock of the borderlands.

At a basic level, the rise of industrial mining mapped a modern world on frontier foundations. From a Mexican perspective, copper mining promised to help reorganize a landscape that was already generations old. As Mexican entrepreneurs entered the new corporate realms of Cananea and Nacozari, they sought to regenerate and improve upon older pathways with the help of outsiders. And yet there was more to the story than new immigrant pathways being mapped onto older Mexican foundations, for part of the story is also about Mexican migrations. If copper corporations required massive inputs of energy in the form of hoisting machinery, concentrators, mills, smelting furnaces, and railroads to carve up places like Pilares Mountain and the Cananeas and get their pieces to market, they also needed more human labor than the local countryside could provide. To transform the U.S.–Mexico borderlands, Phelps Dodge and the CCCC needed to remake the region's Mexican population.

This process began as early as 1902, when the El Paso and Southwestern Railroad began to ship carloads of Mexicans south into Sonora to build the Nacozari road and work in the mines and smelters of Pilares and Nacozari. Local accounts about the workers' origins are vague, but they probably came via El Paso from Chihuahua, Durango, and other states on the far side of the Sierra Madres. Unlike the Sonora Railway, which was not extended south of Sonora until 1907, the Mexican Central Railroad below El Paso tapped the entire central plateau of Mexico and its vast pool of labor. In 1903, additional workers came from Chihuahua to complete the Nacozari Railroad. The road's labor contractor, Enrique Rodriguez, also supplied crews around Naco, and many of his men, whom he assembled at El Paso, were newcomers even to Chihuahua. Many had traveled hundreds of miles from villages in southern Mexico to take advantage of new industrial wages at the Arizona–Sonora border.

Cananea managers also had to reassemble "native" labor from afar. In 1903, CCCC officials noted that even though workers were arriving daily from all over Sonora, the company had also imported labor from Baja California. Like Phelps Dodge and its contractors, the CCCC manufactured mobility to pin their mining landscapes down. If this seemed paradoxical, it was a contradiction that workers willingly took advantage of. The Mexicans bound for the Lucky Tiger, a gold mine near Nacozari, benefited from the railroad journey but to the company's dismay kept moving. "No amount of herding would keep the gang intact," a reporter later noted. Some "skipped out" before the train reached the station. It was hard to keep these workers tied down, Greene acknowledged, "as they are never satisfied." In a climate of high demand for labor, they "work for a few days in one place and then go to another camp and so on," pursuing tales—and there were many—of higher wages elsewhere.

If corporate elites grumbled about Mexican mobility and opportunism— they also found that putting workers in place once they got to camp was anything but straightforward. For labor may have seemed to move as freely (and, indeed, as abstractly) as capital, but spatial and cultural distinctions mattered. In 1905, the CCCC imported miners from Aguascalientes and San Luis Potosí, Mexico, to the Cananea mining camp of Buenavista, only to find that local Sonorenses ridiculed their appearance, dress, and habits. The mining manager, Arthur S. Dwight, finally asked Cananea's chief of police, Pablo Rubio, to post a policeman near their new homes "until they have acclimated to their new surroundings and made the locals understand they're here to stay."

Ethnicity, class, and nationality also inflected urban divides in Sonora. Entering Cananea by train, one passed through the town on the mesa, upwind from the smelter. Here Kenyon-Kingdon and her cohort had their French doors, Chinese servants, and lawns. "Life in a Mexican mining town for an American group is rather like an Army outpost in that they adhere as far as possible to their own customs, and life is not so different from that of the United States," recalled Mildred Young Wallace, the daughter of CCCC Secretary George Young "There were breakfasts, luncheons, numerous afternoon and evening … parties, tennis, dances at the American Club, horseback rides and moonlight picnics." Mexico entered this world, but in a selective fashion. The center of town was the plaza, where Wallace remembered "listening to the band concert and watching the slowly-moving throng" and admiring "the gaily dressed *señoritas*, with their *dueñas* or chaperones." Here Americans encountered Mexico, but not the Mexico that most Mexicans saw when they came to Cananea.

To get to this Mexico, one had to continue to the edge of the mesa and wander down into working-class Ronquillo or climb to mountain barrios such as Chivartera. Like Chihuahua Hill and Tintown, these were regions of refuge. This was especially true for the camp of Buenavista, a nerve center of Cananea's labor movement. Like Chihuahua Hill, mining camps and smelter-side homes were perilous places, as Jesús Corral's mother knew well. Pneumonia killed in Chivatera, "where the accommodations for the miners are of a primitive character" but also near the smelter. "When anyone living in the vicinity of the smelter is afflicted with the disease," a resident wrote, "it is almost certain that death will follow" since "fumes of sulphur prevent the curing of the lungs." This was far from the Mexico where Mildred Young lived. "My wife and daughters go about the streets at will unattended," George Young bragged. For his family and others, Mexican Cananea lay beyond the pale: a mere shadow of the familiar and domesticated landscapes of Anglo-American Mexico.

These borders were especially clear in Pilares, where an artificial terrace halfway up the mountain divided the camp in two halves. "The Mexican town swarmed up to it and covered it," wrote the mining engineer Ralph Ingersoll in the 1920s, "but above, the odd hundred feet before the topography came to a sharp point at the top, was reserved for the American quarter." Here were "attractive" houses on a "fashionable thoroughfare," each with a garden, "where the almost-green grass and peach- and fig-trees were neatly fenced off from the roving burro." Each had "a Mexican girl to help out, and every modern convenience included in a realtor's paean of praise—electric lights, hot and cold water, and two minutes' run (down-hill) to work. In the morning the vegetable man, a withered old Chinaman, came along with a string of burros loaded with fresh vegetables, and the wife stood at her gate and selected what she wished, and argued with the huckster, in the six or eight Spanish phrases she had picked up."

Ingersoll likened Pilares to white settler enclaves of the British Empire. "I have read of Englishmen who go into the wilderness and, living there, dress for dinner, play cards in the evening, and build golf-courses on Sunday," he wrote, but Anglos at Pilares played another game. Most "came from Main Street towns," where "they had not amounted to much socially," he wrote, "but when they journeyed into a foreign land ... there was not the, slightest doubt that they were all used to much better things, much more exclusive friends, and in general an entirely different (and higher) rung of the social ladder." Here in the American colony, transnational dreams became imperial fantasies.

It is hard not to see Anglo houses—prefabricated abroad, designed for a life on the interior—as a metaphor for the U.S. transnational experience. This was a world of refuge, patrolled by the paternalism of corporate capital. Phelps Dodge even prepared a guide to help new U.S. employees navigate Pilares.

It introduced newcomers to special American rentals, hotels offering board, a market selling beef from the company's ranch, the company store, the Chinese peddlers selling produce door to door, how to get home deliveries of wood and milk. One could remain completely inside, like Maud Kenyon-Kingdon and the U.S. wives in Ingersoll's portrait. Phelps Dodge also managed mobility with special railroad passes, available at its local office. The Nacozari Country Club and Nacozari Boole Club offered other refuges bounded by class, culture, and language. The paternalism of company towns was familiar to mining engineers, but in Mexico it had an additional purpose: to keep them from getting lost in a foreign land.

Mexican spaces were less contained and less managed, Held together by culture and family ties, they were also supported by pathways that wandered off the corporate map. Like Anglo enclaves, Mexican barrios served as refuges: not because corporations sheltered them, but because they pushed them to the margins. Mexicans moved in and out of focus, tracing shadow circuits that met in Zacatecas Canyon, Tintown, Buenavista, and Chivatera Ridge. These pathways ran through the male spaces of the mines, smelters, and pool halls and the domestic spaces of the company homes, where extended families came together for work, fiestas, or casual visits. For those from Chihuahua and beyond, these circuits were often far-reaching and attenuated. In Sonora, they formed sinews of a regional community that ran south along the Yaqui, Sonora, and San Miguel valleys, a community that had changed little in its geographical contours since Mexican and Opata grandparents had cycled in and out of Tubac.

One saw these regional lifelines in Huépac, an Opata-Mexican outpost one hundred miles south of Cananea and Nacozari. Huépac's fields, pastures, and orchards fed a few local mining ventures, but workers and products also took a longer road to the copper mines. Unsettled conditions often triggered migrations: floods in 1914 and 1926, for instance, washed away much of Huépac's land, pushing farmers to become miners. Conversely, the periodic reduction of workforces in Cananea and Nacozari could push miners south toward rural safety nets. The roads between city and country were in constant motion, and mobility just as often reflected good times. When conditions were flush in Cananea and Nacozari, the roads teemed with livestock, cheese, meat, and agricultural surpluses heading north from Huépac and nearby villages to feed miners. The children of farmers thereby consumed the fruits of their families' lands as industrial workers, while sending wages south to help keep the other half of the regional community alive.

If copper mines anchored regional communities in place, so did their mercantile adjuncts. Howard Carroll Groton, a sales representative of the Phelps Dodge Mercantile in Nacozari, learned about these commercial ties in the 1920s. He saw them from the tail end of the Nacozari railroad, where trains unloaded carloads of corn, flour, coffee, and lard from the United States, fine thread from Glasgow, and every ten months or so a full carload of cigarette papers from Italy. The Phelps Dodge wholesale trade in Sonora was enormous. At any given time, "thirty or forty pack animals" were in line behind the warehouse from villages to the south, Groton recalled. Freighters "always had a certain amount of trading to do as soon as they hit camp." They peddled *panocha* (brown sugar cakes), *carne seca* (dried meat), cheese, oranges, squash, tobacco, molasses, and chickens, most of it ending up at the company store for resale. They then loaded up green coffee, sugar, lard, flour, rice, cigarette papers, candles, plows, dynamite, fuse and caps, roofing iron, kerosene, lace, thread, and cloth before returning south.

Yaqui Indians also wove the mines and smelters of Cananea and Nacozari into broader transnational circuits, migrating from lowland villages in the Yaqui River delta of southern Sonora to copper towns along both sides of the border to supplement the annual harvests. Their migration from lowland to *sierra*, from farm to mine, built on a colonial strategy of moving between their Jesuit mission towns on the Yaqui River delta and mines in the Opata and Pima highlands.

Yaquis moved between village and mine well into the nineteenth century, but their relationship to Mexico became increasingly volatile. They resisted efforts to open up their homeland to development, and by the twentieth century, battles for the Yaqui homeland raged as *broncos*, or "hostile" Yaquis, launched raids from the mountains to defend their lands while *pacíficos*, "peaceful" Yaquis, worked in mines and haciendas. They drifted not only between village and wage work, but also between imposed categories of *bronco* and *pacífico*.

Yaqui mobility and resistance led to pathways that resembled the roads taken by Mexicans and Opatas but that were harder for outsiders to pin down. In every respect, this was fugitive terrain: it was based on relations of mobility, it was invisible to most Americans and Mexicans, it drew on shifty categories, and it often harbored fugitives from the law. As a land of shadows, it also provided refuge and power. Morris B. Parker snatched glimpses of this autonomous realm at Pilares, whose Yaqui workers "were quick to learn and, after a short period of training made excellent miners, the best in Mexico." Mine managers paid a premium for this labor, for twice a year, during the planting and harvesting seasons, Yaquis. "simply stopped work and went home." All managers could do was anticipate the exodus and cope. Before they left, the company had Yaquis break up as much ore as possible, so that in their absence others could carry out the less skilled work of shoveling the broken ore and bringing it to the surface.

These migrations made it hard not only to manage time, but also to police space, for unless managers were careful, fragments of the mining landscape also flowed south. One year Parker found some of the canvas hose that ran air into the shafts was missing. When Yaqui workers returned from the harvest, they were wearing canvas pants, "stiff, uniform in circumference, baggy, and wearing quality to last a lifetime." When accused of pilfering, "the only reply was a mischievous grin—*'Muy buenos pantalones, señor'*—the Yaquis considered their trousers a big joke." During these migrations, drill steel also ran low. Yaquis allegedly used the steel for planting sticks, but that was not all: "Yaqui blacksmiths forged this steel into weapons of war, knives, machetes, spear and arrow points," Parker wrote, "many of which were among the weapons used by the Yaquis in their revolt against the state and federal troops." Technologies of development from one borderland were thereby used to resist capital and state power in another.

Yaquis also converted their industrial wages into weapons of resistance, "Every one of them who comes to Arizona and works, goes back to Sonora with either a rifle or ammunition," claimed one mining entrepreneur. Yaquis working in Douglas bought guns from U.S. merchants, and most probably came from the Copper Queen Mercantile. This commerce, proposed President Díaz in 1906, contributed greatly to the prolongation of Yaqui campaigns, causing the unnecessary deaths of both Mexicans and Americans. Yet when the Díaz regime began to deport Yaquis to the Yucatán peninsula later that same year, many U.S. entrepreneurs pointed the finger at Mexico. Hunger forced the Yaquis "to the trails and roads to plunder," insisted one: "they cannot work in the mines or on the ranches; they cannot cultivate their lands or raise cattle." Consigned to the shadows, "they must either rob or die of starvation."

As Yaquis were driven underground by Mexican efforts to make them outlaws in their own land, many crossed the border into Arizona. Refugee pathways to the north, which built on previous networks between U.S. mines and fields and Yaqui villages in the Yaqui River delta, eventually gave rise to new communities north of the border, such as Pascua Village and Barrio Libre in Tucson and Guadalupe in Phoenix. From these "expatriate" communities, Yaqui migrants sustained cultural, religious, and family ties to villages in Sonora. Like many of their Mexican and Anglo-American neighbors, they were relatively free to cross the border well into the twentieth century, and many would continue to do so to their advantage.

In this world, even the dominant dialect trailed off into the shadows. Americans remade their lives with power and privilege in Cananea and Nacozari, but in the copper hinterlands, beyond the pull of copper and steel, gravity weakened. Here one found an exile community of immigrants who crossed borders—like the Chinese—as refugees from worlds of exclusion. In 1882, weeks before voting to exclude Chinese, the U.S. Congress passed the Edmunds Act, outlawing polygamy. In 1884, federal marshals began making arrests in Utah, Idaho, and Arizona, where Mormons practiced plural marriage as one of the cardinal Mormon doctrines. As marshals swept through Mormon country to impose new domestic laws at home, many Mormons, like their Chinese neighbors, began to take their families and households abroad.

William Carroll McClellan was among these refugees. A resident of the Mormon enclave of Pleasanton, New Mexico, he was in constant fear of Indians, since "Geronimo and his renegades were on the rampage." But U.S. marshals were also "invading remote frontiers, bent on arresting every man having more than one wife." Ironically, McClellan soon took a path familiar to Geronimo, leading south into the Sierra Madres. Here, church officials hoped, polygamists might find "a place of refuge under a foreign government." Starting at the Mormon town of St. David—along the San Pedro near Tombstone—a party left for Chihuahua in 1885, camping near Casas Grandes. After gaining permission from the Díaz regime, church officials bought land on the Casas Grandes and Piedras Verdes rivers and in the nearby highlands, where they created six new colonies: Colonias Díaz, Juárez, Pacheco, Dublán, García, and Chuhuichupa.

In 1892, Mormons expanded into Sonora after colonists bought two hundred square miles of land on the Bavispe River from the customs officers and landowners Juan Fenochio and Emilio Kosterlitzky. They founded Colonia Oaxaca at the mouth of Púlpito Pass in 1893, followed by Colonia Morelos, established just to the north in 1900. Both places appealed to the exiles precisely because they were so isolated.

One could measure its isolation by Parker's grueling trip from Colonia Oaxaca to Nacozari or the equally long journey to the nearest railhead, across the Púlpito Pass into Chihuahua. This was "a pioneer road," wrote one Mormon: "It was solid rock for miles and in places it was like a staircase." One point, called The Squeeze, was nightmarish for wagons. "I could only take one wagon at a time, taking it to the top of the mountain, leaving it, and going back after the next," explained another resident. "High mountains tapped with snow, dark canyons where wild beasts made their lair," and "wild" Indians encircled this distant realm, embellished another writer.

Yet, for exiles who wanted "a place where they wouldn't be mixed up with [the] outside," these newcomers were remarkably well connected to the world around them. Connections started at home: the trademark brick buildings of Colonia Morelos, whose facades were made of local clay fired in local kilns, were supported by frames harvested in the pine forests of Chihuahua. Their doors, window frames, porch pillars, and lathed ornamental dowels came from workshops in Colonia Juárez, across Púlpito Pass, roofs were topped with pine shingles from the towering Sierra Madres, and plaster was made from gypsum from mountains in southwestern New Mexico. Compared to the Anglo-American homes of Pilares, prefabricated in California, these were local spaces—but not nearly as local as Mexican adobes farther south along the Bavispe, in the Opata-Mexican villages of Bavispe, Bacerac, and Huachinera.

In the end, these nomadic pathways were not much different from those taken by Chinese, Yaqui, Mexican, and Opatas. As difficult as it could be, this was also a world of possibilities. Mormons such as the Haymores gravitated to rural work, moving from the Turkey Track Ranch of Sonora to the Empire Ranch of Arizona to the Ojitos Ranch in Chihuahua. William Claude Huish, Isaac Alldredge, and David Alvin McClellan cycled through mines and smelters in Sonora, and in Chihuahua they hauled goods, cut trees, and laid track for Greene's mining and timber empire. It was an uneven world, one in which, like freighters crossing Nacozari Creek, one had to keep moving. Men like David Alma Stevens could hardly stop to breathe. He started out as a freighter in Chihuahua, shifted to railroad construction, and then hit the Cananea-Nacozari freighting boom. After that, he returned to Chihuahua, where he farmed, freighted, and raised cattle, barely making ends meet. In 1905, he hauled supplies for the Kansas City, Mexico, and Orient Railroad in Chihuahua and then crossed the Sierra Madres to do the same work for the Southern Pacific. The intense heat finally drove him back across the *sierras*, where he finally came to rest on a farm near Casas Grandes.

As he drifted, Stevens covered terrain that would have been familiar to Morris B. Parker, Maud Kenyon-Kingdon, Jesús Corral, Hop Sing, the Yaqui

Indians of Pilares, and countless others who came to call the borderlands home at the turn of the century. Yet even though they had landmarks in common, each of these travelers charted different journeys, set off from the others by culture, class, ethnicity, nationality, and any number of individual idiosyncrasies. What they had in common was the nature of their traffic: these were all people in motion, turning border space to their own ends and stirring up endless clouds of human sediment that both nurtured and obscured transnational space. It nurtured this space through dreams, labor, and cultural exchanges that motivated and underwrote economic development, but it obscured this space because at the end of the journey, the local worlds made more human sense than the expanding networks of rails, mines, capital, and contracts that connected nations to each other.

Many things set these worlds apart. Borders often emerged from the uneven and unequal relationships of development: some people moved to the centers of power, and others were pushed to the margins; some anchored their lives in smelters and cities, and others toiled at the rural frontiers. Yet even the ragged edges of the copper borderlands had ways of empowering people by creating regions of refuge, autonomy, and mobility that allowed people to inhabit the region on their own terms. Mormons followed their own path by moving between mines, roads, and utopian villages on the Bavispe; Yaquis took similar journeys to preserve autonomy and power vis-à-vis the Mexican state; rural and urban Chinese entrepreneurs found ways to maintain both legal and illegal webs of commerce and migration; and Mexicans, Opatas, Yaquis, and even Mormons frequently left the industrial borderlands during planting and harvesting seasons to sustain safety nets for an unstable modern world in which jobs and wages came and went. Indeed, as it had for generations, mobility offered the best means for living in a world at the margins of state, entrepreneurial, and corporate power.

Ultimately, these separate seen and unseen worlds underscored the gap that still persisted between corporate and state dreams of pinning the borderlands down, and the complicated, messy, and ever-shifting worlds that people called home. The more power corporate and state elites tried to exert over the region— the more space their rails, mines, and smelters consumed—the more it slipped from their grasp. The lustrous dream of the modern world cast a series of long shadows, and these shadows, some feared, seemed to be taking on fugitive lives of their own.

FURTHER READING

Bartlett, John Russell. *Personal Narrative of Exploration and Incidents in Texas, New Mexico, California, Sonora, and Chihuahua, Connected with the United States and Mexican Boundary Commission, during the Years 1850, '51, '52, and '53.* 2 Vols. (1965).

Carrigan, William. *The Making of a Lynching Culture: Violence and Vigilantism in Central Texas, 1846–1916* (2004).

Cazneau, Mrs. William (Cora Montgomery). *Eagle Pass; or, Life on the Border.* Edited, with an introduction by Robert Crawford Cotner (1852; reprint, 1966).

Cerutti, Mario. *Economía de Guerra y poder regional en el siglo XIX: Gastos militares, aduanas, y comerciantes en los años de Vidaurri (1855–1864)* (1983).

Cerutti, Mario, and Miguel González-Quiroga, eds. *Frontera e historia ecónomica: Texas y el norte de México, 1850–1865* (1993).

Cozzens, Peter, ed. *Eyewitnesses to the Indian Wars, 1865–1890. Volume I: Apacheria* (2001).

———. *Eyewitnesses to the Indian Wars, 1865–1890. Volume IV: The Long War for the Northern Plains* (2001).

Flanagan, Thomas. *Louis "David" Riel: Prophet of the New World* (1978).

García-Martínez, Bernardo. "El espacio del (des)encuentro." In *Encuentro en la frontera: mexicanos y norteamericanos en un espacio común*, ed. Manuel Ceballos-Ramirez, pp. 19–54 (2001).

González Quiroga, Miguel A. "Los inicios de la migratión laboral mexicana a Texas (1850–1880)." In *Encuentro en la frontera: mexicanos norteamericanos en un espacio común*, ed. Manuel Ceballos-Ramírez, pp. 345–372 (2001).

Hall, Dawn, ed. *Drawing the Borderline: Artist-Explorers of the U.S.-Mexico Boundary Survey* (1996).

Herrera Pérez, Octavio. *El norte de Tamaulipas y la conformación de la frontera México-Estados Unidos, 1835–1855* (2003).

Hogue, Michel. "Between Race and Nation: The Creation of a Métis Borderland on the Northern Plains, 1850–1900." In *Bridging National Borders in North America: Transnational and Comparative Histories*, ed. Benjamin H. Johnson and Andrew R. Graybill, pp. 59–89 (2010).

Howard, Joseph Kinsey. *Strange Empire, a Narrative of the Northwest* (1952).

Hudson, Linda S. *Mistress of Manifest Destiny: A Biography of Jane McManus Storm Cazneau, 1807–1878* (2001).

Jacoby, Karl. *Shadows at Dawn: An Apache Massacre and the Violence of History* (2008).

LaDow, Beth. *The Medicine Line: Life and Death on a North American Borderland* (2001).

McGrady, David. *Living with Strangers: The Nineteenth-Century Sioux and the Canadian-American Borderlands* (2006).

McManus, Sheila. *The Line Which Separates: Race, Gender, and the Making of the Alberta-Montana Borderlands* (2005).

Miller, Susan A. *Coacoochee's Bones: A Seminole Saga* (2003).

Mora, Anthony. *Border Dilemmas: Racial and National Uncertainties in New Mexico 1848–1912* (2011).

Mora Torres, Juan. *The Making of the Mexican Border: The State, Capitalism, and Society in Nuevo León, 1848–1910* (2001).

Morganthaler, Jefferson. *The River Has Never Divided Us: A Border History of La Junta de los Ríos* (2004).

Nugent, Daniel. *Spent Cartridges of Revolution: An Anthropological History of Namiquipa, Chihuahua* (1993).

Rebert, Paula. *La Gran Línea: Mapping the United-States Mexico Boundary, 1849–1857* (2001).

Seltz, Jennifer. "Epidemics, Indians, and Border-Making in the Nineteenth-Century Pacific Northwest." In *Bridging National Borders in North America: Transnational and Comparative Histories*, ed. Benjamin H. Johnson and Andrew R. Graybill, pp. 91–115 (2010).

Sharp, Paul F. *Whoop-Up Country: The Canadian-American West, 1865–1885* (1955; reprint, 1973).

Stanley, George F., ed. *Mapping the Frontier: Charles Wilson's Diary of the Survey of the 49th Parallel, 1858–1862* (1970).

Thompson, Jerry. *Cortina: Defending the Mexican Name in Texas* (2007).

CHAPTER 10

$\sim$

Pacific Ties

In addition to dealing with the challenges of land borders, the three North American nation-states—the United States, Canada, and Mexico—also met the Pacific World on their west coasts. The Pacific was at once an attraction and a challenge to these nations and their majority populations. From Columbus on, it lured European explorers of North America with the prospect of a lucrative trade route from western Europe to Asia, especially India and China. The Spanish Empire linked Mexico with East Asia, by way of the Spanish Philippines. By the 1600s, Latin American silver and corn penetrated deep into the Chinese interior, with Chinese luxury items to be found in wealthy households in Spanish America. People from China lived in Mexico as early as the 1630s.

The prospects for continental dominion from sea to sea helped fan the flames of U.S. expansionism, and the struggle for attractive ports pitted Americans and their government against British, Spanish, and Mexican authorities. The cultural and economic impulses that drove U.S. expansionism in North America lead to military interventions and ultimately to the conquest and acquisition of territory in East Asia and the Pacific. A U.S. fleet entered Tokyo Bay to force Japan to open to American trade in 1853, just five years after the end of the U.S.-Mexico War. By 1900, the United States had begun active trade and missionizing in China, acquired the Philippines upon defeating Spain in the 1898 Spanish-American war, and overthrown Hawaii's monarchy and annexed the archipelago.

East Asia and North America, then, had become tightly linked. Among those who were most aware of this were the residents of southern Chinese provinces, who had long had mercantile and shipping ties with Southeast Asia and much of the Pacific basin. From the 1840s to the end of the century, several million residents of southern China moved to Hawaii, Australia, New Zealand, Thailand, Africa, the Philippines, and the Americas in search of work and trading opportunities. Several hundred thousand came to Canada and the United States, where they played critical roles in railroad construction and agricultural labor. The overwhelming preponderance of the migrants were men, and most hoped to earn enough money to return home with greater economic independence. Although they were a small proportion of the North American population, they were highly concentrated in the West, at one point constituting around 10 percent of the population of California and 30 percent of Idaho. Japanese and Filipino migrants would come to the west coasts of

Canada and the United States (and, to a lesser extent, Mexico) later in the century and in smaller numbers.

Majority populations treated Asians in North America with great hostility and brutality. They demeaned them as drudges and opium fiends, subjected them to mob violence and job discrimination, and banned them from marrying people of other backgrounds. White racial self-conception in much of the western United States and Canada centered on profound contrasts with Asians. By the early twentieth century, a large set of laws restricted the ability of Asian migrants to live in certain places, own property, or become citizens. Similar resentments toward Asians rose to the fore in Northwestern Mexico in the early twentieth century, resulting in parallel laws and practices.

This chapter explores the ways that regulating Asian migration shaped the international borders in the late nineteenth and early twentieth centuries. Although conflict and controversies over migration since the 1950s have centered on Latin Americans entering the United States, Asian migration was foundational in prompting the development of laws, bureaucracies, and practices aimed at border enforcement. And although contemporary immigration debates would seem to highlight the economic and racial differences between Americans and Canadians on the one hand, and Mexicans on the other, from the vantage of Asian migration, North America's three nations seemed more alike than different. Prompted by white laborers in the West, the U.S. and Canadian governments implemented restrictions against migration from China and Japan, the first measures aimed explicitly at banning the entry of specific racial groups. Those migrants who subverted the regulations became, from the perspective of the U.S. government, the first "illegal aliens." And the lives of all Asians and Asian Americans were deeply marked by this illegality, just as all Latinos have been impacted by immigration enforcement more recently. The term wetback, which later in the twentieth century would come to be used as a derogatory term for Mexican migrants in the United States, was first applied to people from China after the 1882 Chinese Exclusion Act severely curtailed their entry into the United States. Americans living in the Northeast sometimes called French Canadian immigrants the "Chinese of the eastern states." Chinese migrants were the first targets of U.S. immigration enforcement, decades before the 1924 founding of the United States Border Patrol. Just as the United States expelled many Mexicans (and Mexican Americans) during the 1930s, so, too, did the Mexican state of Sonora expel most of its Chinese-descent population in the same years, as Mexican nationalists condemned Chinese in terms very similar to those Canadians and Americans had used decades before.

In short, we cannot understand the modern borders of North America and their enforcement without understanding the historical ties between North America and Asia.

∿ DOCUMENTS

The 1882 passage of the Chinese Exclusion Act marked the first specific exclusion of a national group in U.S. history. The law, whose text we present as Document 1, banned the entry of Chinese laborers into the United States. Its detailed provisions for identity certificates would later be expanded into the modern system of passports and green cards, and its provisions for the careful inspection and identification of immigrants would come to be standard practice with all border crossers.

Mexico and Canada saw similar anti-Chinese movements, whose adherents believed that the Chinese could never become part of their nations. In Document 2, the Sonora Legislature bans marriages between Mexican women and Chinese men, even if the men became Mexican citizens (as many did). In Document 3, a British Columbian labor leader condemns Asian laborers in ways that similarly permanently place them outside the boundaries of the nation and the working class on whose behalf he spoke. And he downplays the significance of the Canada-U.S. boundary, asserting that the white workers of both countries share the same interests and are representatives of the same civilization.

Chinese migration and efforts to halt it were a leading public issue in the late nineteenth century. In Document 4, Julian Ralph, a journalist writing for a popular news magazine, describes the illicit entry of Chinese into the United States from British Columbia. The ambivalence of the Canadian government about Chinese exclusion, the ability of would-be immigrants to forge documents and assume false identities, and the landscape of the border all worked together to allow for extensive Chinese entry into the United States in the early years of exclusion.

Document 5 is an excerpt from the memoirs of Clifford Perkins, who worked for the U.S. federal government as a "Chinese Inspector" in Arizona starting in 1910. Writing decades later, Perkins recalled both the challenges of identifying and capturing Chinese migrants banned from entry and his relationships with Chinese who were allowed to live in the country. He presents himself as at once sympathetic to the migrants and intent upon doing his job of enforcing Chinese exclusion. Intentionally or not, his writings offer a glimpse of the Chinese community in the United States that endured despite social hostility and legal harassment.

The final two documents are cartoons from mass circulation magazines in the late nineteenth century. Famed artist Frederick Remington, best known for his depiction of nineteenth-century cowboys and Indians, drew the image reproduced in Document 6. It captures the dangers of border crossing. Is it sympathetic toward its subject or more stereotypical in its portrayal? How does it compare to images in circulation today about the suffering of migrants? Document 7, entitled "And Still They Come!" depicts Chinese migrants entering the United States by way of British Columbia and Mexico behind the back of a guileless American eagle.

1. The United States Government Passes Chinese Exclusion, 1882

An Act to execute certain treaty stipulations relating to Chinese.

Whereas in the opinion of the Government of the United States the coming of Chinese laborers to this country endangers the good order of certain localities

An act to execute certain treaty stipulations relating to the Chinese, May 6, 1882;
Enrolled Acts and Resolutions of Congress, 1789–1996; General Records of the United
States Government; Record Group 11; National Archives.

within the territory thereof: Therefore, *Be it enacted by the Senate and House of Representatives of the United States of America in Congress assembled*, That from and after the expiration of ninety days next after the passage of this act, and until the expiration of ten years next after the passage of this act, the coming of Chinese laborers to the United States be, and the same is hereby, suspended; and during such suspension it shall not be lawful for any Chinese laborer to come, or having so come after the expiration of said ninety days to remain within the United States.

SEC. 2. That the master of any vessel who shall knowingly bring within the United States on such vessel, and land or permit to be landed, any Chinese laborer, from any foreign port or place, shall be deemed guilty of a misdemeanor, and on conviction thereof shall be punished by a fine of not more than five hundred dollars for each and every such Chinese laborer so brought, and maybe also imprisoned for a term not exceeding one year.

SEC. 3. That the two foregoing sections shall not apply to Chinese laborers who were in the United States on the seventeenth day of November, eighteen hundred and eighty, or who shall have come into the same before the expiration of ninety days next after the passage of this act, and who shall produce to such master before going on board such vessel, and shall produce to the collector of the port in the United States at which such vessel shall arrive, the evidence hereinafter in this act required of his being one of the laborers in this section mentioned; nor shall the two foregoing sections apply to the case of any master whose vessel, being bound to a port not within the United States, shall come within the jurisdiction of the United States by reason of being in distress or in stress of weather, or touching at any port of the United States on its voyage to any foreign port or place: Provided, That all Chinese laborers brought on such vessel shall depart with the vessel on leaving port.

SEC. 4. That for the purpose of properly identifying Chinese laborers who were in the United States on the seventeenth day of November eighteen hundred and eighty, or who shall have come into the same before the expiration of ninety days next after the passage of this act, and in order to furnish them with the proper evidence of their right to go from and come to the United States of their free will and accord, as provided by the treaty between the United States and China dated November seventeenth, eighteen hundred and eighty, the collector of customs of the district from which any such Chinese laborer shall depart from the United States shall, in person or by deputy, go on board each vessel having on board any such Chinese laborers and cleared or about to sail from his district for a foreign port, and on such vessel make a list of all such Chinese laborers, which shall be entered in registry-books to be kept for that purpose, in which shall be stated the name, age, occupation, last place of residence, physical marks of peculiarities, and all facts necessary for the identification of each of such Chinese laborers, which books shall be safely kept in the custom-house.; and every such Chinese laborer so departing from the United States shall be entitled to, and shall receive, free of any charge or cost upon application therefor, from the collector or his deputy, at the time such list is taken, a certificate, signed by the collector or his deputy and attested by his seal of office, in such form as the Secretary of the

Treasury shall prescribe, which certificate shall contain a statement of the name, age, occupation, last place of residence, persona description, and facts of identification of the Chinese laborer to whom the certificate is issued, corresponding with the said list and registry in all particulars. In case any Chinese laborer after having received such certificate shall leave such vessel before her departure he shall deliver his certificate to the master of the vessel, and if such Chinese laborer shall fail to return to such vessel before her departure from port the certificate shall be delivered by the master to the collector of customs for cancellation. The certificate herein provided for shall entitle the Chinese laborer to whom the same is issued to return to and re-enter the United States upon producing and delivering the same to the collector of customs of the district at which such Chinese laborer shall seek to re-enter; and upon delivery of such certificate by such Chinese laborer to the collector of customs at the time of re-entry in the United States said collector shall cause the same to be filed in the custom-house anti duly canceled.

SEC. 5. That any Chinese laborer mentioned in section four of this act being in the United States, and desiring to depart from the United States by land, shall have the right to demand and receive, free of charge or cost, a certificate of identification similar to that provided for in section four of this act to be issued to such Chinese laborers as may desire to leave the United States by water; and it is hereby made the duty of the collector of customs of the district next adjoining the foreign country to which said Chinese laborer desires to go to issue such certificate, free of charge or cost, upon application by such Chinese laborer, and to enter the same upon registry-books to be kept by him for the purpose, as provided for in section four of this act.

SEC. 6 That in order to the faithful execution of articles one and two of the treaty in this act before mentioned, every Chinese person other than a laborer who may be entitled by said treaty and this act to come within the United States, and who shall be about to come to the United States, shall be identified as so entitled by the Chinese Government in each case, such identity to be evidenced by a certificate issued under the authority of said government, which certificate shall be in the English language or (if not in the English language) accompanied by a translation into English, stating such right to come, and which certificate shall state the name, title or official rank, if any, the age, height, and all physical peculiarities, former and present occupation or profession, and place of residence in China of the person to whom the certificate is issued and that such person is entitled, conformably to the treaty in this act mentioned to come within the United States. Such certificate shall be prima-facie evidence of the fact set forth therein, and shall be produced to the collector of customs, or his deputy, of the port in the district in the United States at which the person named therein shall arrive.

SEC. 7. That any person who shall knowingly and falsely alter or substitute any name for the name written in such certificate or forge any such certificate, or knowingly utter any forged or fraudulent certificate, or falsely personate any person named in any such certificate, shall be deemed guilty of a misdemeanor; and upon conviction thereof shall be fined in a sum not exceeding one thousand dollars, and imprisoned in a penitentiary for a term of not more than five years.

SEC. 8. That the master of any vessel arriving in the United States from any foreign port or place shall, at the same time he delivers a manifest of the cargo, and if there be no cargo, then at the time of making a report of the entry of the vessel pursuant to law, in addition to the other matter required to be reported, and before landing, or permitting to land, any Chinese passengers, deliver and report to the collector of customs of the district in which such vessels shall have arrived a separate list of all Chinese passengers taken on board his vessel at any foreign port or place, and all such passengers on board the vessel at that time. Such list shall show the names of such passengers (and if accredited officers of the Chinese Government traveling on the business of that government, or their servants, with a note of such facts), and the names and other particulars, as shown by their respective certificates; and such list shall be sworn to by the master in the manner required by law in relation to the manifest of the cargo. Any willful refusal or neglect of any such master to comply with the provisions of this section shall incur the same penalties and forfeiture as are provided for a refusal or neglect to report and deliver a manifest of the cargo.

SEC. 9. That before any Chinese passengers are landed from any such line vessel, the collector, or his deputy, shall proceed to examine such passenger, comparing the certificate with the list and with the passengers; and no passenger shall be allowed to land in the United States from such vessel in violation of law.

SEC. 10. That every vessel whose master shall knowingly violate any of the provisions of this act shall be deemed forfeited to the United States, and shall be liable to seizure and condemnation in any district of the United States into which such vessel may enter or in which she may be found.

SEC. 11. That any person who shall knowingly bring into or cause to be brought into the United States by land, or who shall knowingly aid or abet the same, or aid or abet the landing in the United States from any vessel of any Chinese person not lawfully entitled to enter the United States, shall be deemed guilty of a misdemeanor, and shall, on conviction thereof, be fined in a sum not exceeding one thousand dollars, and imprisoned for a term not exceeding one year.

SEC. 12. That no Chinese person shall be permitted to enter the United States by land without producing to the proper officer of customs the certificate in this act required of Chinese persons seeking to land from a vessel. And any Chinese person found unlawfully within the United States shall be caused to be removed therefrom to the country from whence he came, by direction of the President of the United States, and at the cost of the United States, after being brought before some justice, judge, or commissioner of a court of the United States and found to be one not lawfully entitled to be or remain in the United States.

SEC. 13. That this act shall not apply to diplomatic and other officers of the Chinese Government traveling upon the business of that government, whose credentials shall be taken as equivalent to the certificate in this act mentioned, and shall exempt them and their body and house-hold servants from the provisions of this act as to other Chinese persons.

SEC. 14. That hereafter no State court or court of the United States shall admit Chinese to citizenship; and all laws in conflict with this act are hereby repealed.

SEC. 15. That the words "Chinese laborers," wherever used in this act shall be construed to mean both skilled and unskilled laborers and Chinese employed in mining.

Approved, May 6, 1882.

2. Sonora Legislative Bans Mexican Chinese Marriage, 1923

ALEJO BAY, Constitutional Governor of the Free and Sovereign State of Sonora, to its inhabitants makes known:

That the Honorable State Congress, has passed the following Law 31 PROHIBITING MARRIAGE AMONG MEXICAN WOMEN AND CHINESE INDIVIDUALS.

ARTICLE 1—Marriages between Mexican women and individuals of the Chinese race are prohibited, even if said individuals obtain a Mexican naturalization certificate.

ARTICLE 2—Marriages or illicit unions between Chinese men and Mexican women shall be punished by a fine of $100.00 to $500.00, depending upon the case, and shall be applied by local authorities in the place in which the infraction in committed.

—State Congress, Hermosillo, Sonora. December 13, 1923.

3. British Columbia Labor Leader Warns of Dangers of Asian Migration, 1907

Fraternal Delegate M.A. Beach, representing the Vancouver, British Columbia, Trades and Labor Council, read his report at this time, which was received with great pleasure by the Convention, and was ordered made a part of the proceedings, as follows:

Mr. Chairman and Delegates to the State Federation of Labor:

I assure you it is a very great pleasure for me to be able to meet with you on this most important occasion. While I am sent here from a foreign country, I feel quite at home here, in your beautiful city, as I have had the pleasure of being here and surrounding country on various occasions, in fact have spent a number of years on this side of the imaginary boundary line. I say, Mr. President, imaginary line, because I suppose from a national standpoint or a political standpoint we are divided, but from a wage-earners' standpoint we are not divided, we must not be divided. We are working for a common cause, the bettering of conditions for the wage-earner; what is good for you is good for me, and what is god for me is good for

José Ángel Espinoza, *El Ejemplo de Sonora* (Mexico City: n.p., 1932), 35. Translation by Julia María Schiavone Camacho.

Proceedings of the Washington State Federation of Labor Held at Bellingham, Washington, January 2-3-4-5, 1907 (Seattle: Washington State Federation of Labor, 1907), 27–28.

you; and, Mr. President and Brother Delegates, while I bring you greeting from a foreign land, I do so as a brother, as one of you, and not as a stranger ...

We in British Columbia have existing conditions which are very dangerous to the welfare of the white wage-earner of this country, namely the influx of cheap coolie labor, the Japanese, Chinese, Hindoo and Dukhoboores. We have succeeded in a measure in getting the ears of a capitalistic government to listen to our cries when we got the head tax on the Chinese increased from $50 to $500, which has made a very noticeable difference in the influx of Chinese, but we shall not rest until we get total prohibition of the yellow evil.

4. Journalist Julian Ralph Describes Human Smuggling in the Pacific Northwest, 1891

Our Exclusion Act bears date October, 1888.... Bearing the date of this act in mind, and understanding that there is only one steamship line to Canada from Asia, the extent of the smuggling (of new-comers) must be apparent in the number of Mongolians which that line of ships has brought from their country. The whole number is 4008, with and without certificates, in the period between 1887 (a year before our Exclusion Act) and the month of July, 1890. Of this 4000, some were returning on certificates and some were new immigrants. It is generally understood that 99 in 100 of these latter go to British Columbia in tending to smuggle themselves over our border. In all, since '87, these number 1910. The steamers of the Canadian Pacific Line arrive at intervals of about three weeks, and bring from 100 to 150 Chinamen at a time. One came while I was in Victoria. It carried 125 Mongols, 74 with certificates and 51 without. Several of those who carried certificates had obtained them improperly—nearly a dozen, as I remember the case—and were detained on the ship. Three weeks before that another steamer arrived with 140 Chinamen, 94 without certificates and 46 with those documents. Out of the 46 were 18 accused of having obtained their papers fraudulently, and 15 confessed their guilt. The other three were stubborn and stolid, and were released.

Every Chinaman who leaves Canada takes a certificate which shall serve as his passport when he returns. He may take out a certificate when he does not mean to leave the country. He may take one when he is merely going to smuggle himself over our border, and never means to go back to the Dominion. Or he may take a certificate when he has made all the money he needs, and is on his way to China to end his days there, after years of that luxurious idleness which the average laborer counts upon obtaining in China from the judicious investment of $2000—the coolie's plum. Of course it is fair to presume that in many cases the certificates are demanded by men who mean to return. At all events, these certificates, which are passports to Canada, and indirectly to the United States, have a money value. They are sold in China. They can be purchased openly to-day in the streets of Hong-Kong, like ducks or chopsticks. There

Julian Ralph, "The Chinese Leak," *Harper's* 82 (March 1891): 517–521.

they possess a fluctuating value, and have been known to fetch as high as $65. Sometimes they are let go at a less price than the $50 they are expected to save in the avoidance of the poll-tax, the fluctuations being governed by the demand at the time of the departure of a vessel, because only so many uncertified Chinese laborers may take passage on the steamers under the Canadian law— one to every fifty tons of the ship's burthen. Of those who carry certificates and of those not of the laboring class as many as choose may come.

It is to guard against trickery with the certificates that the customs officials at Victoria and Vancouver have all that they can manage. "When a Chinaman enters the office of the collector to apply for a certificate, several men are called in—the interpreter and a clerk or two. The Chinaman gives his name, age, place of birth, and other particulars of value in identifying him. He is asked to step upon the platform of a measuring machine, such as is in use in our army and elsewhere— an upright pole marked off into feet and inches, and fitted with a sliding rod that gives the man's height when it rests upon his head. All this the Chinaman per- fectly comprehends; but what he does not know is the description of himself that the men around him are going to write down in the big government book after he has gone, a description which takes in his general appearance, the pecu- liarities of his features and limbs and shape, with notes of every scar or pit or mark upon his hands, neck, face, and head.

And yet, in spite of these precautions, Chinamen who go away from Canada looking at least forty years of age, return appearing to be only twenty-four; and others who measure five feet and nine inches when they depart, come back in a few months several inches shorter or taller than when they sailed for China. They are new-comers, with the certificates of other men, of course. The silent scanning of the features of applicants for certificates does not pass unnoticed by these shrewd and intelligent people. The manner in which they endeavor to make themselves appear like the persons whose certificates they carry shows this. They frequently go as far as to disfigure themselves for life in order to save the $50, and to bear out what they judge must be written in the customs book against the numerals that mark each of the certificates—which, by-the-way, con- tain no word of the descriptions of the men who take them out. While I was in Victoria one of these tricksters arrived with a great scar burned in his forehead, a cut disfiguring one cheek, and a deep pit burned in his neck. When questioned, and proven to be a fraudulent fellow, he confessed that he had never been to Canada before.

The men who sell the certificates accompany' the sales with descriptions of themselves, and with a great amount of the information they acquired of the local- ities they were familiar with. As to the general facts about Caucasian life, there are plenty of men in China and on the ships to post the immigrants fully.

Yet, petty as the smuggling is, it is worth while to have measured it, and it will be equally well to understand why it is possible, and how it is carried on. Whoever would understand it must know that the entire northern boundary of our nation, from the Lake of the Woods to the Pacific coast, is a gigantic wilder- ness. The prairie, the plains of the western provinces, and the thick-clustered mountains of British Columbia are repeated in our Minnesota, North Dakota,

Montana, Idaho, and Washington. Geologically and naturally there is no difference between the countries; the boundary line is an arbitrary mark. At intervals
of a mile apart this otherwise intangible division is established by means of surveyors' "monuments," that are imbedded in the earth, and stand slightly above
it, each marked "B. A." on one side and "U.S.A." on the other. There are few
settlements on the line—almost none—and the whole region is practically
known to men only as they cross it by the watercourses in canoes, or the far-
apart trails of the great grass plateaus, and of the valleys between the mountains.
There is no part of it over which a Chinaman may not pass into our country
without fear of hinderance; there are scarcely any parts of it where he may not
walk boldly across it at high noon. Indeed, the same is measurably the case all
along our northern boundary—even upon the St. Lawrence north of our State,
where smuggling has always been a means of livelihood whenever varying tariffs
made it remunerative.

The lawless practice does go on from one end of the border to the other.
Chinamen at work in the forests beside the Columbia steal in by the Kootenay
trail; others cross the St. Lawrence, others the plains and prairie, others the Great
Lakes. But, all combined, this defiance of our laws is so inconsiderable as to be
unworthy of serious attention. What it might become if the Chinese really
"swarmed" in Canada, and the waters of Washington State were closed against
the invaders is quite another matter.

For it is in those waters that nearly all the smuggling goes on at present. Let
those who are unfamiliar with that region glance at the map. They will see that
the northwest corner of the State of Washington is torn off, and the space that is
left is filled with water dotted with an archipelago. The island of Vancouver fits
partially into the gaping corner as if it had been torn out by some gigantic con-
vulsion. The tatters and débris of the rent form the archipelago. Our national
interest centred in that corner long ago when that portion of the boundary was
in dispute, and the tension of a war feeling was only relieved when a foreign
arbitrator settled the boundary, and gave us the island of San Juan, the most important in the group. The city of Victoria confines nearly all the population on
that corner of Vancouver Island; the city of Vancouver is the main settlement on
the British Columbia shore; and on our borders are such little places as What-
com, New Dungeness, and Port Angeles, in the State of Washington. Port
Townsend, on Puget Sound, is the principal American town near by, and the
headquarters of the scanty force of customs officials who are supposed to guard
against the smuggling, and who are entitled to the presumption that they are
doing their best in this direction. Victoria has only 20,000 population, Vancouver fewer still, and the islands only here and there a house. Deer abound upon
these islands, which are heavily timbered, and the waterways between them feel
the keels of but few vessels—of none at all, except the smallest craft, outside the
main channels. It would be hard to imagine a more difficult region to police, or
a fairer field for smugglers. Old London itself has scarcely a greater tangle of
crooked and confusing thoroughfares than this archipelago possesses, and these
waterways are so narrow and sheltered that mere oarsmen can safely and easily
travel many of them. It is a smugglers' paradise.

5. Clifford Perkins Describes Work as "Chinese Inspector" in Arizona, 1978

Tucson's commercial and professional establishments were operated primarily by Anglos, as were the firms catering to the expanding winter tourist trade and to the growing list of sanitariums built for health seekers. The restaurants and laundries, on the other hand, were operated almost entirely by Chinese brought into the country originally as laborers. Forbidden by law to own property or engage in commerce, their search for work had carried them away from the west coast. They were industrious and maintained gardens well past any area close enough to town to be considered by most citizens as desirable, and they provided most of the local residents with their fresh vegetables, chickens and eggs. Horse drawn, flat roofed wagons, with scales and brass scoops dangling from the tops, carried fresh produce, poultry and eggs to housewives every day.

These "Orientals" and their colony became a major focus of my activities a few days after my arrival [in 1910].

Chinese inspectors and Immigrant inspectors, working with Customs line riders, made it increasingly difficult for Chinese to get into the country via busy ports and populated areas, and as a result smuggling activities shifted to the sparsely inhabited sections of southern New Mexico, Arizona and California. By the time I joined the Service, few Chinese were coming in east of El Paso. Some continued to enter through gulf and west coast ports, but by far the greatest numbers were entering in the vicinity of towns on or near the Mexican border and, for a while, through Canada. This border phase of law enforcement, carried on by a comparatively small number of inspectors working twelve to fifteen hours a day, seven days a week, continued until about 1917, when the Service was faced with new problems arising from the passage of the Literacy Act.

After 1893 every Chinese alien was required to carry identification, including a photograph. Such procedures invariably led to forgeries and duplications. Photography in 1893 was rather rudimentary, and many pictures on certificates of residence faded with time. Also, most of the Chinese who were required to register were adults, since the immigrants up to that point had consisted almost entirely of males over twenty-one years of age. Eighteen to twenty years later, it was almost impossible to be sure the photograph on a certificate of residence was of the person presenting it. Copies of the originals, with photographs, were supposed to have been filed in the office of the U.S. collector of internal revenue of the district where the application was made, but records were sketchy. Additionally, the forms varied from one locality to another, so the fact that one document did not look exactly like another meant very little.

It was important to prove that a suspect picked up coming into the United States after a trip to China had actually been out of the country and was here illegally. Of course when he was apprehended at Tucson, Phoenix, or some other point near the border and was suspected of having just reentered the

Clifford Alan Perkins, *Border Patrol: With the U.S. Immigration Service on the Mexican Boundary, 1910–1954* (El Paso: Texas Western Press, 1978), 6, 9–11, 16–17, 19–21, 23–24.

country from Mexico, he was thoroughly searched and his clothing was examined. In some cases identifying marks were found, but the Chinese soon learned to remove all such markings. Strangely enough, it was sometimes possible to trap them by making a casual comment to them in Spanish. This they might answer unthinkingly, though they would not respond to questions put to them in English. This was not prima facie evidence, but it often served as a lever to cause a suspect to confess where he had been.

For a time the Service hired Mexicans in Nogales, Sonora, to photograph Chinese on their arrival by train from the south and, if possible, to take pictures of new arrivals living in Nogales. Such pictures were supplied to the Tucson and other border Immigration offices, where they were filed by approximate age, shape of face, and body type. This reference material was often useful in establishing the fact that apprehended Chinese had been in Mexico as recently as a few weeks or months previously.

We also arranged to have pictures taken in Tucson of persons suspected of illegal entry from Mexico and sent to ports and agents on the border for referral to residents and officials in or near Mexico. In a number of instances we were able to secure witnesses who could swear in court that the alien had been in Mexico on a certain date. Bringing witnesses in from Mexico to testify in court had to be discontinued after a couple of years, however; they got to making a good thing of it since they received money to cover their expenses up and back. Their credibility suffered when one witness identified our Chinese interpreter, maintained in the office full-time by the Service, as a man he had seen getting off a train in Mexico.

With only ten inspectors to cover Tucson and the surrounding countryside for forty or fifty miles, we were on duty twelve to fifteen hours a shift, seven days a week, alternating from days to nights and back every two weeks. My room was close enough to the depot so when a passenger train was due I could clean up a little before putting on my uniform without wasting too much time, but there was many a day when one more change of clothing would have finished me with the Service. Sometimes, in addition to inspecting two or three passenger trains, we opened as many as three hundred freight cars on a shift, regular loaded freights usually having from fifty to sixty cars and empties as many as seventy.

Chinese attempting to reach inland cities undetected hid in every conceivable place on trains: in box cars loaded with freight, under the tenders of the locomotives, in the space above the entryway in the old passenger cars, in staterooms rented for them by accomplices, and even in the four-foot-wide ice vents across each end of the insulated Pacific Fruit Express refrigerated cars, iced or not. We also had to check the passenger cars in the depot for travelling Chinese, making a record of their names, where they had boarded, their destinations, and any documents they carried. The information was then verified with the conductors to be sure it was correct insofar as they knew it. They were familiar with our work and told us right away whenever they had seen a Chinese board the train at a small station, especially if it had been on the side of the car away from the platform or under other circumstances that might indicate he was being put aboard by smugglers.

Entering the United States by wagon or on foot through that country was a hazardous, lonely proposition, and must have been a bewildering experience to the majority of Chinese who made the attempt. They had made a long and no doubt miserable ocean voyage; they had to learn a new language, become proficient at unaccustomed work in a foreign land, adapt to different customs, clothing and surroundings. About the time things became familiar, the aliens would be put aboard a mechanical conveyance they probably had never seen before. It would carry them north through uninhabited, barren and sometimes mountainous country and leave them in a sun-baked town of drab adobe buildings.

Nobody wanted them; few people made any attempt to understand them; and detection would make futile all of the effort and money expended. Mexican railroad section hands seldom would help them because they did not want anyone around who might get them in trouble; the native Indians seemed to resent their passage through the harsh land; and uniformed officials who knew the country were sent out on horseback with guns to catch them. It was little wonder so few of the Chinese we apprehended gave us trouble and so many appeared to be almost glad they were going to be sent back to China. Often it was hard not to feel sorry for some of them, even though enforcing immigration laws was our job. They had come so far, and their wants were so few in a land of so much opportunity. I did not know it then, but there would be many times when I would be caught between the natural inclination to help another human being and my responsibilities as an officer, and guided by the conviction that it is far easier not to take the first wrong step than the second.

6. Frederick Remington Depicts Suffering of Chinese Migrant, 1891

Frederick Remington, "Dying of Thirst in the Desert," *Harper's* 82 (March 1891): 522.

7. Cartoonist Points to Chinese Use of Canadian and Mexican Borders to Enter the United States, 1880

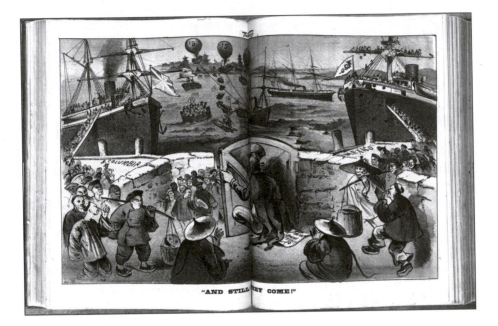

"AND STILL THEY COME!"

〰 ESSAYS

Chinese exclusion led to the first patrolling of North American borders to halt the entry of an entire category of people. In the first essay, Patrick Ettinger of California State University–Sacramento shows just what a difficult task this was. Chinese and other migrants were able to draw on a number of advantages, including the physical and social geographies of both border regions, to elude understaffed federal agencies and to enter the United States illicitly. Professional smuggling rings, a detailed knowledge of the loopholes in American law, and heavy local cross-border traffic expedited their crossings. Ettinger concludes that early border enforcement efforts enjoyed limited success at best. These were landscapes beyond the control of governments.

"And Still They Come," *Wasp*, Dec. 4, 1880.

Chinese exclusion, however, did have an enormous impact on Chinese living in the United States. In the second essay, University of Minnesota History Professor Erika Lee takes her readers into the daily lives of these people, arguing that they led a "shadowed existence" because of immigration law and its enforcement. Chinese immigrants were virtually the only residents of the country to face deportation, and they—along with American-born citizens of Chinese descent—were subjected to harassment, extortion, raids that disrupted normal business and social life, and outright physical violence. The federal government may not have been powerful enough to effectively patrol American borders, but its efforts haunted the lives of all Chinese-descent people in the country.

The Limits of Early U.S. Border Enforcement

PATRICK ETTINGER

In January 1929, William Whalen and G. C. Wilmoth, United States Immigration Service supervisors employed on the U.S.-Mexico border, traveled north to Washington, D.C., to a conference addressing the problems of the Immigration Service. Drawing on his experience supervising south Texas ports of entry on the border, Whalen contributed an hour-long address, "Mexican Border Problems." He spoke in an exasperated but bemused manner of the resourcefulness of migrants attempting to circumvent U.S. immigration laws along the U.S.-Mexico border in south Texas. Wilmoth gave a similar talk about border crossings in West Texas, New Mexico, and Arizona. Together, their speeches detailed the host of ruses, disguises, deceptions, and tricks that northward immigrants, predominantly Mexican, used to make their way past U.S. immigration inspectors on the border. Migrants and smugglers, Whalen confessed with a mix of admiration and chagrin, had demonstrated such ingenuity that "[w]e sometimes wonder what they will spring on us next."

Their 1929 conference reports no doubt reflected well the experiences of the dozens of immigration inspectors working along the southern U.S. border—and perhaps too the sentiments of many of the newly commissioned Border Patrol agents who worked in the vast expanses between formal ports of entry. For historians, they provide a glimpse of the everyday shuffle of life on the international boundary line joining the United States and Mexico in the 1920s. But they also offer insight into the complex history of undocumented immigration, in particular the persistent difficulty of effectively enforcing immigration laws on land boundaries. For Whalen, Wilmoth, and their Immigration Service colleagues on the Canadian and Mexican border were not *initiating* a system of

Patrick Ettinger, "'We sometimes wonder what they will spring on us next': Immigrants and Border Enforcement in the American West, 1882–1930," *Western Historical Quarterly* 37 (Summer 2006): 159–181.

border inspections in the late 1920s. Rather, their 1929 status reports came on the heels of a forty-five year, multi-million dollar effort on the part of the federal government to establish and enforce immigration regulations on the nation's international borders. In detailing the difficulties attendant to the enforcement of the national boundary and highlighting the continued permeability of the border, their reports nicely conveyed the state of the American border control regime. They also relate the enigmatic nature of the "official" border as it stood in the late 1920s. Border inspection stations were both highly visible, commanding features of the borderlands and, for many a determined migrant, almost insignificant.

This article looks closely at evolving patterns of illicit border crossing on the Canadian and Mexican borders at the turn of the twentieth century, providing a snapshot of the concomitant rise of unsanctioned immigration and border-crossing controls. In terms of border enforcement, remarkable transformations occurred along the American sides of both borders in this era. But amidst dramatic change came stubborn continuities as well. Border-crossing patterns changed, but practices of illicit entry survived, practices that had profound implications for the history of the twentieth-century American West.

Whether focusing on borders through either the prism of the Chinese or Mexican experience, much scholarship emphasizes the successful imposition of state power at the international boundaries. That is, the authors accentuate the power of the state to put in place bureaucratic fortifications to govern border crossings. Without a doubt, that is part of the story, for both the Canadian and Mexican borders did change dramatically between 1882 and 1929 in terms of the rigor of immigration controls. They went from being virtually unguarded in the 1880s to heavily controlled by 1924. By the end of the 1920s, highly visible immigration inspection and patrol forces had been put in place on the nation's borders, and they enjoyed some considerable successes in enforcing immigration laws.

From another perspective, however, continuity, rather than change, seems the more important story. Borders are part of the visible apparatus by which states attempt to effect state power, but the extent to which state borders can "impose their jurisdiction on 'the people'" is contested. One common feature in the construction of modern borders, wrote Michiel Baud and William Van Schendel, authors of a comparative study of international borderlands, has been "the efforts of people to use, manipulate, or avoid the resulting border restrictions." In late-nineteenth-century American West, migrants and smugglers took on this role. Faced with new restrictions on border crossings, they created methods of illicit entry that kept these borders open—and border officials such as William Whalen at their wit's end. In effect, the period saw the simultaneous "drawing" and "erasing" of the official border, its gradual articulation and elaboration in the midst of consistently successful efforts to undermine it.

Efforts to "draw" or fortify American land borders in the 1880s and beyond began in the political imagination. In fact, they were the incidental consequence of complex and competing political efforts, begun in earnest in the 1870s, to have the federal government define and filter out those deemed to be the wrong sort of immigrant aliens. Proponents of placing restrictions on immigration achieved two initial successes in 1882, with the passage that year of two seminal pieces of restrictive legislation. Responding to anti-Chinese agitation in the West, Congress passed the Chinese Exclusion Act in the spring of 1882, which instituted a ten-year suspension on the immigration of Chinese laborers. Months later, faced with warnings about the dangers of pauper and convict immigration from Europe, Congress approved a general Immigration Act that prohibited the landing of "any convict, lunatic, idiot, or any person unable to take care of himself or herself without becoming a public charge" and provided for the onboard inspection of all arriving immigrants. Both pieces of legislation ultimately would introduce changes to the Canadian and Mexican borderlands, but the ban on Chinese immigration had an immediate effect.

The surreptitious passage of Chinese immigrants into the U.S. across the western reaches of the Canadian border in the 1880s marked the beginning of unsanctioned immigration into the United States. That an illicit cross-border traffic in Chinese laborers would first develop on the Washington Territory-British Columbia frontier is not surprising. Chinese had lived and worked in British Columbia in substantial numbers since at least 1858, when Chinese from California and China joined the thousands of miners entering the region during the Fraser River gold rush. The Chinese population in British Columbia swelled in the early 1880s when recruitment of Chinese labor for construction of the Canadian Pacific Railway brought an additional 15,000 Chinese from the United States and China. After the Chinese Exclusion Act closed the door to the U.S., those who desired entry to the U.S. began to do so surreptitiously. In so doing, they availed themselves of natural advantages found in the physical and cultural geography of the Canadian-American borderlands.

According to contemporary accounts, border crossings followed close on the heels of exclusion. An October 1883 newspaper report from San Francisco warned that it was "a fact well known to the residents of British Columbia that at the present time Chinamen are crossing the [United States] border in batches of 20 or 30" by means of Puget Sound. Although newspaper accounts of the volume of smuggling ought to be treated skeptically, a fair amount of smuggling was, without a doubt, going on. One border official testifying to a congressional committee in 1890 placed the figure at 2,500 annually, although an investigative article published on the subject the following year suggested that only 1,500 Chinese entered by way of Canada each year. Opium smuggling syndicates based on Vancouver Island, British Columbia, apparently organized much of this human trafficking across Puget Sound. Labor contractors with ties to Chinese merchants across the West Coast used the extant opium smuggling network to orchestrate the entry of Chinese workers after 1882.

The remote, sometimes rugged terrain of the northwestern border enhanced smuggling efforts. The physical geography of Puget Sound, with hundreds of sparsely populated small islands situated amid narrow channels, made it a smugglers' paradise. "It would be hard to imagine a more difficult region to police, or a fairer field for smugglers," wrote journalist Julian Ralph. "Old London itself has scarcely a greater tangle of crooked and confusing thoroughfares than this archipelago possesses, and these waterways are so narrow and sheltered that mere oarsmen can safely and easily travel many of them." Smugglers adopted myriad routes across the Sound, sometimes sailing directly south across the Straits of Juan de Fuca to Port Angeles on the Olympic Peninsula, at other times crossing the twelve miles of bay to San Juan Island, or carrying the Chinese past the customs headquarters at Port Townsend and directly into the Seattle area. Perhaps two-thirds of the Chinese entry in Washington territory occurred on Puget Sound.

Chinese also slipped across the border on the eastern side of the Cascade mountains. The wooded, remote region of north central Washington territory provided an equally ideal crossing point. Sparsely populated, the area had only a few American customs officers patrolling it in the 1880s, and they principally focused on monitoring cattle crossings in the river valleys. Such open expanses invited defiance of the border. Chinese came down the Columbia River into the United States "in boats and on horseback and on foot," but since that waterway provided a natural point for customs officers to conduct inspections, many stopped at a point just north of the American border. From there, they headed westward to the wagon roads and trails that crossed the border near the Kettle River and Rock Creek. On the one hundred miles of international border between Kettle River and the Cascade Mountains, one customs inspector noted in 1890, "there is no difficulty for them in getting across. It is not necessary for them to take a trail to get across.... It is open country to the Cascade Mountains, and Chinese coming across avoid[ed] the trail as much as they [could]" because they knew inspectors patrolled it. Thanks to the enormous length of the border, another American observer wrote, "there is no part of it over which a Chinaman may not pass into our country without fear of hindrance; there are scarcely any parts of it where he may not walk boldly across it at high noon."

The cultural geography of the region facilitated illicit entry as well. Numerous Chinese enclaves lay scattered inside U.S. territory. Fresh across the border, Chinese workers typically gravitated toward the nearest ethnic Chinese community, whether in Seattle or in a rural mining camp. There, they could intermingle with local residents and become virtually invisible to customs authorities. Once "they get into the Chinese camp and mix with the balance of the Chinese," one inspector reported, "it is very difficult to tell who the recently arrived Chinese are." As a result, frustrated inspectors along the northern border could only watch as the small Chinese communities in Seattle and regional mining camps slowly swelled with new arrivals from across the border.

A substantial Chinese presence in British Columbia had made smuggling through Washington in the 1880s an unsurprising development, but the emergence of Chinese smuggling routes through Mexico was more unexpected. The Chinese population in Mexico did not reach significant proportions until after 1900. But entry of Chinese started to attract notice in press and in Congress by the mid-1880s. California and Arizona, by virtue of their proximity to the Pacific Ocean, were favored routes. Initially, Chinese smuggling rings based in Hong Kong and San Francisco devised a plan to land U.S.-bound Chinese workers at the small Mexican fishing village of Ensenada, located sixty miles south of San Diego. Chinese immigrants would sail from Hong Kong to San Francisco and, without landing in the U.S., transfer to Mexican steamers heading for Mexican Pacific coast cities. When the Mexican steamer first touched Mexican soil, the Chinese would disembark and make their way north, either by boat or wagon, into the U.S. by way of Southern California.

When a shipload of eighty Chinese on the steamboat *New Berne* disembarked in Ensenada on 3 April 1890, the U.S. consul in Ensenada took notice and immediately telegraphed customs authorities in San Diego. Within a matter of days, customs authorities in San Diego intercepted thirteen Chinese crossing the border near Tijuana and another ten trying to enter San Diego harbor aboard a small vessel captained by a Portuguese fisherman.

Foiled by the American officials, smugglers modified their plans, opting for the more circuitous route of sending Chinese workers to the mainland Mexican port of Guaymas and thence to the Arizona border by rail. When the *New Berne* sailed again from San Francisco on the 25th of April, laden now with fifty Chinese, the San Francisco customs collectors sent along two undercover officials. When fifteen Chinese disembarked at Ensenada on the 28th of April, the customs officials wired San Diego to warn authorities. They then continued on board as the steamer headed toward Mazatlan and Guaymas with the balance of the Chinese passengers. The Chinese disembarked at Guaymas and "every one of them took passage by railway to points within 35 or 40 or 50 miles from the border of the United States." The undercover inspectors stayed in Mexico another six weeks, tracking the movements of the Chinese and eventually coordinating with customs authorities in Arizona to intercept various small groups as they tried to enter the U.S. near Tombstone and Nogales.

The roundabout, dangerous, and expensive routes that they took spoke volumes about Chinese migrants' desire to enter the United States as well as their smugglers' tenacity in pursing that objective. They also reveal the ways in which the terrain and cultural geography of the southwestern border conspired against American efforts to prevent illicit entries. In testimony before congressional hearings on Chinese smuggling in 1891, customs authorities familiar with the Mexican border time and again emphasized the difficulties attendant upon watching the border. The solitary officer assigned to the customs house at Tombstone, Arizona, found "the border [there] is so large and so long and so rough that he [could not] do his work." In the mountainous and isolated terrain just east of San Diego, Chinese might safely cross any of the more than 150 remote trails and passes. The tranquility of the San Diego coast also offered opportunities for small boats to land Chinese migrants in area inlets and bays. Rural, remote, and mostly uninhabited, the southwest border invited subversion of the national border. In the course of a typical year, "more Chinamen came across and were never captured and never seen" than were captured.

Chinese migrants coming across the Mexican border in the 1880s and 1890s enjoyed the same advantage that crossers through Canada exploited: the presence of ethnic Chinese communities situated on both sides of the border. The Treasury Department's 1890 reports to Congress on smuggling routes through Ensenada and Guaymas included a "Map of Chinese Underground Railway." The crude map detailed the Baja California villages—Real de Castillo, Burro Valley,

Yalecites, and Carisco—through which Chinese immigrants passed as they moved north from Ensenada. Ethnic Chinese who lived and worked in these and other Baja towns, American officials believed, conspired in efforts to pass them across the American border. Chinese immigrants who made it to the American side of the border found substantial Chinese communities there as well. In the borderland cities of El Paso, Tucson, and San Diego, Chinese communities stood ready to receive and support, at least temporarily, smuggled immigrants. Tucson had a Chinese population approaching seven hundred in 1890, while nearly one thousand Chinese worked in San Diego county during the same period. Members of the San Diego Chinese community worked principally as house servants, orchard hands, and fishermen, but, according to one Chinese resident at the time, earning a little extra money by assisting smugglers could be lucrative as well.

The fact that only a skeletal force of customs officers existed to patrol these vast spaces presented one seminal problem. Not surprisingly, border officials called to testify before Congress on Chinese smuggling in the West quickly introduced what would become a familiar refrain of American border authorities: provide funding for more manpower.

Alongside their appeals for greater numbers of inspectors, customs authorities also suggested that certain technological innovations might improve their ability to perform their work. One inspector suggested that Congress adopt the Mexican practice of equipping its customs inspectors with horses so that they could better patrol the line. The San Diego collector of customs testified that only with the addition of a steamship would his force have adequate means to guard the San Diego coastline.

In their efforts to craft a more effective border, officials also spent a fair amount of time arguing for changes in the Chinese exclusion laws. Under the terms of the current law, Chinese detected entering the country illegally had to be deported to the "country from whence they came." Most federal courts had interpreted this provision strictly, insisting that Chinese apprehended on either the Canadian or Mexican borders could only lawfully be deported back across those borders. But Treasury Department officials wished to send illegal entrants directly back to China instead. Deportation to the contiguous countries was, of course, largely ineffectual; deported Chinese simply continued to attempt entry until they succeeded.

This phenomenon highlighted a centrally important third advantage that the contiguous borders afforded Chinese immigrants seeking entry into the U.S.: the convenience of a nearby staging area that offered opportunities for multiple efforts at illegal entry. At a maritime port such as San Francisco, customs officials returned rejected migrants to the ship on which they sailed, presumably for the long voyage back to China. In contrast, the land border importantly circumscribed the power of American officials over the Chinese. Chinese workers detained along the Canadian or Mexican border were set back only a matter of yards.

By 1890, many officials imagined the best solution to the Chinese smuggling problem would be to export U.S. immigration policy to its neighbors.

They pressed political leaders to support efforts to encourage the neighboring Republic of Mexico and Dominion of Canada to adopt bans on Chinese immigration. In May 1890, the U.S. House and Senate had, by concurrent resolution, asked President Grover Cleveland to negotiate treaties with Great Britain and Mexico to prevent the illegal entry of Chinese across American borders. Many border officials hoped that the two nations might be persuaded to ban Chinese labor immigration outright.

But officials crafting visions of a more effective border control regime did so at the precise moment that trans-border flows of U.S.-bound migrants became increasingly complex. An unprecedented infusion of federal personnel on the international borders coincided with confusing new migration patterns that increased the volume of surreptitious entry.

In the first place, in a dynamic that would become an axiomatic feature of immigration border enforcement in the twentieth century, a "solution" somewhere on the border simply created a "problem" elsewhere. As Chinese traffic waned on the northern border, it waxed on the southern. "Having been practically defeated at every turn along the Canadian frontier," the Bureau reported in 1906, "the Chinamen who desire to enter this country are now turning their attention more than ever to the opportunity afforded by the natural conditions existing along our southern frontier."

Looking at the remarkable successes of immigrants and smugglers in crossing the border in the opening decade of the twentieth century reveals a great deal about the inherent difficulties of border enforcement. Most authorities attributed the Chinese smuggling successes of the 1880s and 1890s to the existence of vast, virtually unpatrolled borders north and south. But the continued success of the Chinese and other foreign nationals in crossing the Mexican border even after the establishment of a port-of-entry inspection system and border patrols suggested that undocumented immigration might be a far more subtle, intractable problem. Coupled with the natural advantages the borderlands offered, the creative energy of individual migrants—and of the smugglers who marketed services to them—had the potential to keep the border functionally permeable.

For migrants, the Mexican border offered two attractions—an opportunity for both legal entry and, for those who failed, illicit entry. Most of the non-Mexican immigrants pressing at the southern border probably either knew or believed that they were excludable under American immigration law; they were therefore attracted by the notion that they might encounter less rigorous inspection on the remote Mexican border, where the routines of inspections had only recently been introduced. If efforts at legal entry failed, Mexican soil provided a safe staging area for illegal entry "a few miles to the right or to the left, of the particular Immigrant Station" from which they had been rejected. Migrants made use of both methods of entry during this time, but it is most startling to examine their efforts to enter the U. S. at official ports of entry. For while one can hardly be surprised at the ease with which they managed to cross the lightly patrolled border at points far away from official ports, it is a bit more surprising to discover how often they simply slipped under the noses of port-of-entry inspectors. But from the debut of border inspections through the 1920s, thousands of excludable immigrants of various nationalities successfully passed into the United States, often uninspected, by deceiving American immigration authorities at Mexican ports of entry.

Often they did so under the tutelage of professional smugglers. The small towns on the Mexican side of the border became the natural marketplace for those peddling smuggling services to the northward-bound Italians, Greeks, Lebanese, Japanese, and Chinese. As they made their way north from the Mexican port cities of Vera Cruz and Guaymas, migrants got advice from fellow countrymen and Mexican railroad conductors about whom to contact for smuggling services on the border. Arriving at Nogales, Ciudad Juárez or Nuevo Laredo, migrants at once sought out the lodging houses, restaurants, or saloons recommended to them.

American authorities regarded the hotels and other enterprises, many run by ethnic Lebanese and Japanese, as little more than "schools for coaching immigrants as to what they should say during inspection at the border."

Whether on their own or under the guidance of smugglers, migrants undermined the new border controls by relying heavily on the art of deception, on appearing or posing, on the practice of making themselves invisible, inconspicuous, or misunderstood. The possibilities for "passing" as someone other than who one was were especially rich at land-border (as opposed to maritime) ports of entry. Immigrants traveling in steerage represented the preponderance of steamship passengers arriving at maritime ports of entry, and inspectors could expect to question almost everyone coming ashore. On the border, however, immigration inspectors in the 1900s discovered that most border-crossing individuals were non-immigrant locals. In an ordinary day's business at Laredo or El Paso or Nogales in the 1900s, individuals subject to inspection as immigrants might be the exception rather than the rule.

From the very first, then, immigration inspectors at these ports of entry did not ask every single individual crossing to demonstrate his or her right to pass. Instead, inspectors did then what they do now: they made preliminary judgments about the admissibility of border crossers largely on the basis of their physical appearance. And the criteria used to visually sort through the crowds were individual, highly subjective, and unevenly applied. Border crossers understood that determinations of their "legality" ultimately could be quite superficial and frequently hinged on perceptions of race. As a result, those with something to hide tried to meet inspectors' expectations about the proper appearance of an innocent crosser.

Ironically, given later developments in immigration control, appearing to be Mexican generally ensured an easy, unchallenged border crossing prior to 1917. An undercover immigration service inspector investigating Asian smuggling from Mexico in 1906 similarly reported the practice of Chinese disguising themselves as Mexicans. "[The Chinese] cut off their queues, exchange their blue jeans and felt slippers for Mexican apparel, and begin training in the Mexican language, at least to the extent of being able to say 'Yo Soy Mexican'"—words that could get them past the border.

Migrants and smugglers understood the ways in which federal immigration officials accommodated local, everyday patterns of border commerce, and they used that knowledge to their advantage. On any given day from Brownsville to San Diego, most of the border crossings might be local residents crossing for work, shopping, or to visit kin. It was a pattern to which immigration inspectors and customs inspectors had both become accustomed and which could, over time, lull them into a state of lower vigilance. Since border crossers were overwhelmingly local, inspectors discovered that their "real work" of conducting inspections of head-tax-paying aliens was episodic at best. Lax monitoring ensued.

Pretending to be a local Mexican—and thereby avoiding inspection—was but one of many strategies that "excludable aliens" used to gain entry at immigration ports of entry on the border during the 1900s. At least some of the Lebanese, European, and Japanese immigrants who feared exclusion nonetheless attempted to enter the United States legitimately. Rather than trying the dodge of appearing Mexican, they dutifully appeared for inspection at a designated port of entry. Yet manipulating appearances remained important in this instance as well.

Migrants routinely used other fraudulent documents to cross the border. The contiguous border created unique opportunities for trafficking in "head tax receipts," the official documents given to aliens after they had been inspected, paid their head tax, and been admitted into the United States as immigrants. After the closing of the border to Japanese migrants in 1907, an illicit trade in head tax receipts flourished. Those in the United States in possession of receipts reportedly "rented" them to aspiring Japanese immigrants on the Mexican side, who, assuming the identity of the people named on the receipt, presented themselves at the port of entry with the receipt as proof they had already been admitted into the United States. At the same time entrepreneurs in Ciudad Juárez had commissioned an El Paso printing company to produce documents that could be used in the production of forged Japanese passports.

Yet, for all the successes of immigrants in outwitting immigration inspectors manning American ports of entry, Bureau of Immigration inspectors clearly held their own at the ports of entry. After 1900, border immigration authorities annually barred thousands of immigrants from entering the U.S. from Mexico. As American officials became more familiar with the border setting and practices, their efficiency and effectiveness increased. The undercover investigations of 1906 and 1907 revealed the central port-of-entry strategies of borderland smugglers and resulted in a new insistence that immigration inspectors carefully scrutinize all border crossers, Mexicans included. At the same time, objections to an increase in Mexican labor migration were putting Mexican migrants under increased scrutiny as well. By 1910, the ports of entry themselves had acquired some meaning as a barrier to open immigration.

But even this "progress" in enforcing the border was chimerical. Already in the 1900s the largest portion of migrants entering from Mexico at this time avoided ports of entry entirely. Immigrants near El Paso in 1908 came "across the river practically at their pleasure without risk of being caught" because only two inspectors watched the entire river front. In southern Arizona in the 1900s, it was still "a relatively simple matter for aliens to cross the line away from inhabited areas, shepherded by smugglers along river washes and through brush-covered areas." Near Laredo, Texas, a Mexican smuggler guided Greek and Lebanese clients south a few miles to where the Rio Grande was easily forded. Across the river waited the smuggler's brother, a hack driver from Laredo, who placed the migrants in a closed express wagon and took them into town. The newly fortified border could only be as strong as its weakest point, and it still largely consisted of weak points.

By the mid-1920s, officials had resigned themselves to creating a border that might serve as a deterrent, rather than barrier, to undocumented immigrants. "If we had the Army on the Canadian border and on the Mexican border, we couldn't stop them; if we had the Navy on the water-front we couldn't stop them," Secretary of Labor James Davis explained in 1927. "Not even a Chinese wall, nine thousand miles in length and built over rivers and deserts and mountains and along the seashores, would seem to permit a permanent solution." But the vision of the border as, at best, a deterrent to illicit entry (rather than a guarantee against it) seemed a bitter pill for many ardent restrictionists to handle in 1920, and dreams of somehow sealing the border against unwanted immigrants helped drive the creation of the Border Patrol in 1924. Still, by the late 1920s, border officials like William Whalen understood that promises of something beyond deterrence were impossible to keep and foolish to make. The goal of border enforcement, in the words of another federal official, was to "at least make attempts to cross the border dangerous and to hold illegal entry down to small proportions."

The development of an American border control and screening regime at the turn of the twentieth century involved both change and continuity to the northern and southern borders of the West. In general, the Immigration Service made steady progress in its efforts to understand and counter the deceptive practices of excludable aliens trying to cross the borders. But for every smuggling scheme detected and stymied another two seemed to succeed; for every undocumented migrant apprehended, countless others escaped detection. In large part, continuities prevailed. We discover not simply the same cast of characters in 1882 and 1929—determined, economically driven migrants, organized smuggling rings, professional border guides or *coyotes*, and technology-obsessed federal enforcement officials—but also familiar themes and strategies: ingenuity, courage, subterfuge, pretense, and blending. Far from achieving any long-term diminution in illicit border crossings during this period, enforcement officials had in fact witnessed tremendous growth in smuggling and undocumented entry. Although perseverant and at times optimistic, immigration authorities rarely deceived themselves about the overall inadequacy of their activities. Efforts to fashion an effective system of control over cross-border migration along the boundaries of the United States were ultimately undermined by migrants too determined, a labor market too attractive, and a border too long.

The first three decades of American immigration restriction efforts on the Mexican border portended poorly for visions of tight border control. The relative ease with which the Chinese used the lightly patrolled borders in the 1880s West to subvert the Chinese Exclusion Act—and the subsequent success of European, Japanese, and other barred immigrants in doing the same across an increasingly patrolled Mexican border in the 1890s and 1900s—demonstrated the degree to which enforcing these latest borders in the West would prove difficult, resource intensive, and intensely frustrating.

The Impact of Exclusion on the Chinese in America

ERIKA LEE

While detained in the barracks of the immigration station on Angel Island, Chinese immigrants dreamed of the day when they might finally be admitted into the United States. Passing through America's gates, however, did not mean freedom from the exclusion laws. The government's failure to prevent or deter illegal immigration resulted in an expansion of the exclusion laws into the nation's interiors and a vigorous policy of surveillance, arrest, and, finally, deportation. As part of the 1882 Chinese Exclusion Act, deportation became a primary means of controlling and disciplining the Chinese community in America. This shadow of exclusion extended not only to legal and illegal Chinese immigrants but also to native-born Chinese American citizens, whose plight was inextricably connected to that of their immigrant brethren. Consequently, members of the Chinese community in America began to reevaluate both their place in the United States and their status as Americans. Deportation was the government's last chance to protect its citizens from allegedly dangerous aliens. Viewed as an essential feature of exclusion enforcement, American deportation policy further racialized Chinese immigration as a serious threat to national peace and security. As Commissioner-General of Immigration Frank Sargent remarked in 1903, "Any reasonable amount of success in the continuance of the exclusion policy [depends upon] the success of the expulsion [policies] as well." In other words, if one failed, the other might succeed.

The Chinese Exclusion Act provided the legal means for deporting Chinese. The act gave local and state police officers (listed as "peace officers") and U.S. marshals the authority to arrest any Chinese person suspected of being in the country unlawfully. After being brought before a justice, judge, or commissioner of a federal court in a deportation hearing, the person was either released if found innocent, or, if found guilty, returned to the "country from whence he came," at the expense of the U.S. government. The establishment of the deportation clause in the Chinese Exclusion Act was immensely significant. Just as they were the first to be excluded on the basis of their race and class, Chinese immigrants also became the first group to be classified as deportable. By the time the Chinese exclusion laws were repealed in 1943, Chinese were no longer an anomaly, and the U.S. government had added many other classes of immigrants to the deportable list.

Amendments to the exclusion laws passed after 1882 refined the deportation policies relating to Chinese immigrants and established the system by which deportation would be accomplished. In 1888, the Scott Act reaffirmed the nation's legal right to deport Chinese found to be in the country unlawfully, but it did allow them to appeal the decision. The 1892 Geary Act expanded and centralized the system by which the government could identify and track Chinese immigrants. All laborers found without the certificate of residence that the Geary Act required were arrested and taken before a deportation hearing. Although exempt-class Chinese did not have to register, they were subject to harassment by immigration officials just the same. Moreover, since the Bureau of Immigration required them to leave their exempt-class (Section 6) certificates with the agency, Chinese merchants, students, teachers, and diplomats were often left without proof of lawful residence and, in the event of a raid, were vulnerable to arrest.

The Chinese community challenged both the registration and the deportation provisions of the 1892 Geary Act through the courts, and one case made it all the way to the U.S. Supreme Court in *Fong Yue Ting v. United States*. Some justices argued that the power to expel should not apply to lawful and long-term resident aliens. They contended that the Tenth Amendment to the Constitution offered constitutional protection to citizens and aliens alike. Thus, any expulsion of lawful residents would be in violation of constitutional guarantees of liberty and due process of the law. However, the majority of justices ruled that the power to exclude aliens and the power to expel them were within the rights of a sovereign government. After the 1893 Supreme Court ruling, the power of Congress to enact legislation expelling aliens, even long-term residents, from the United States remained unchallenged, and the government began to exercise this new power of the state vigorously and forcefully.

The initial intent of the country's deportation activities had been to catch, arrest, and deport those who failed to produce the necessary documentation proving their status as legal residents in the United States. By the 1900s, however, the deportation system expanded to include additional classes of Chinese not originally covered in the 1882 act, such as border crossers. Beginning in 1908, the immigration service also began to deport Chinese under the general immigration laws whenever possible, thereby bypassing the judicial hearings required under the exclusion laws. Chinese who failed to maintain the professional or exempt status under which they were admitted also became targets for deportation. Prior to the 1924 Immigration Act, the courts uniformly held that treaties between the United States and China exempted from deportation those Chinese whose status changed from exempt to laborer (that is, former merchants who had suffered business losses and were now laborers) unless their original entries were fraudulent. In practice, immigration officials ignored these judicial decisions and increased their efforts to find and deport Chinese who had lost their exempt status. In 1905, for example, the Bureau of Immigration authorized its agents to arrest a number of students who were found to be working in Chinese laundries and restaurants. Moreover, beginning in 1909, all persons of Chinese descent, including U.S. citizens, were required to carry a certificate that identified them as having been legally admitted to the country. Chinese American citizens could work as laborers, but if exempt-class Chinese were caught performing manual labor, their certificates of identity were confiscated and they were liable for arrest and deportation.

By the early 1900s, deportation became an essential tool of control and security in the nation's interiors. In 1902, the number of Chinese arrested (1,128) was more than double the number in 1900 (539), and in 1904, a record 1,793 Chinese were arrested based on their suspected illegal residence. Court cases also supported the government's deportation policies. In *Li Sing v. U.S.* (1901), for example, the court ruled that aliens were not protected against unreasonable search or seizures, nor could they claim the right of trial by jury. Moreover, only white witnesses could testify on behalf of potential deportees.

In 1915, however, Bureau of Immigration guidelines expanded the parameters of what constituted an "illegal immigrant" as part of the government's efforts to crack down on Chinese who entered the country illegally from Mexico or Canada. Agency regulations of that year gave inspectors the right to examine "all Chinese persons in the United States not personally known to them" to determine if they were legally entitled to be and remain in the country. In essence, that meant that any Chinese immigrant whom an officer did not personally know could be suspected of having entered the country illegally. The regulations also allowed for the deportation of any wives and children of exempt-class Chinese who were found to be in the country illegally, even if this meant disrupting families.

The strictest deportation provisions were established in the 1924 Immigration Act, which further codified the requirement that Chinese immigrants maintain their exempt-class status in order to remain in the country. Although the number of arrests and deportations remained far lower after 1924 than during the government's intense crackdown in the early 1900s, the harsh new provisions served to punish not only Chinese who had entered illegally but also long-term residents and those who were ignorant of the changes in the law or innocently overstayed their visas. In 1940, sociologist Wen-hsien Chen pointed to the explicitly racist component of the country's deportation policies. Such expulsions, she charged, were "peculiar only to the Chinese.... Some with an established good reputation were held deportable, not because of undesirability but because they were Chinese and ineligible for citizenship."

As were all other aliens residing in the United States, Chinese were entitled to the safeguards of the Constitution and to the protection of the laws regarding their rights of person and property. But the deportation policies established by the exclusion laws, affirmed by the Supreme Court, and expedited by the Bureau of Immigration made the Chinese in America more vulnerable to infringements on their rights than other immigrant groups. Moreover, because the Chinese community had little political power, American politicians did little to ameliorate abuses against them, and there was little public outcry on their behalf.

Chinese immigrants and residents thus often lived a shadowed existence, constantly anxious about their immigration status, about harassment by immigration officials and others, and about their personal safety in general. All Chinese were required to produce on demand the documentation verifying their right to remain in the United States. If the officers were not satisfied with the proof or if the individual under question could not immediately produce the documentation, he or she could be arrested.

One of the most effective tools of the immigration service was the immigration raid. Instituted in the early twentieth century under Commissioner-General Frank Sargent, raids proved to be particularly useful means of catching and arresting a large number of suspected illegal immigrants at one time. No neighborhood, place of business, school, or church was beyond the government's reach. As the Chinese Chamber of Commerce complained, vegetable gardens, stores and other places of business, as well as private residences and homes, were "raided repeatedly, sometimes as often as once a month, even though the Immigration Inspectors generally fail[ed] to find contraband Chinese employed or concealed there." Moreover, the Chinese-American League of Justice in Los Angeles charged that immigration officials routinely acted with "the grossest insolence and most brutal conduct." Inspectors forcibly broke locks and crashed through doors, unlawfully searched through trunks and baggage, and physically abused and insulted the Chinese under their control.

Immigration officials were required to get the commissioner-general's approval before they conducted an immigration raid on suspected illegal Chinese, but apparently they did not need to provide much evidence to support their suspicions. For example, in 1903, the immigrant inspector in charge at New Orleans sought and received permission from Sargent to conduct a raid on the Chinese community in that city based on his belief that it was "not unreasonable to suppose that some Chinamen may have affected an unlawful entrance ... and are now hiding here."

One of the best-known raids occurred in Boston on October 11, 1903. Prior to the raid, local police officers had informed the U.S. district attorney that they suspected that many Chinese residing in Boston were illegal immigrants. It was also rumored that members of a Chinese secret society were blackmailing Chinese residents into paying large sums of money in exchange for not reporting their illegal status to immigration authorities. Together with the police department and the district attorney, the Bureau of Immigration consented to rectify the "evil conditions" in Boston not by going after the blackmailers, but by deporting all Chinese who were in the country in violation of the law. Accordingly, on the evening of Sunday, October 11, 1903, a number of immigration agents from Boston, New York, and other cities, assisted by the local police, made a sudden and unexpected descent upon the Chinese quarter of Boston. As one witness reported, the police and immigration officials "fell upon their victims without giving a word of warning" and surrounded all of the area's private homes and clubs, as well as restaurants and other public places. No warrants for arrest were produced, and all Chinese residents who failed to show their identification papers were detained. The raid resulted in the arrest of 234 Chinese. After they spent twelve hours in jail, 122 of them were found to be legal residents. In the end, only 45 Chinese were deported back to China.

The raid in Boston was not an isolated event. Smaller, less-publicized raids occurred on a regular basis over the next several years, causing sociologist Mary Coolidge to write that "all Chinese are treated as suspects, if not as criminals." The *Nation* reported that in the early 1900s, police and immigration officials swept into the Chinatowns of Cleveland, Chicago, Boston, Philadelphia, New York, and other cities, smashing down doors and arresting "thousands of peaceful Chinese waiters, laundrymen, merchants, and laborers." They jailed the offenders without warrant and left the broken homes and businesses unguarded and vulnerable to looting.

By the 1910s, vocal Chinese complaints made the rounds in Washington, D.C. In 1918, the Chinese Six Companies grew so infuriated by the mistreatment of Chinese residents that they sent a telegram to President Woodrow Wilson. "No matter how long their residence or how firm their right to remain, Chinese are being arrested, hunted, and terrorized," they charged. As a result, they continued, the Chinese population of the Pacific Coast was "fast decreasing." Despite such complaints, the government raids and harassment continued. In 1923, San Francisco's Chinese community complained that the Bureau of Immigration had instituted nothing less than a "veritable Reign of Terror" against them.

Immigration raids on Chinese communities became the public face of the government's efforts to control Chinese immigration within the nation's interiors. They also served to sanction the harassment of Chinese throughout the country by other law-enforcement officials and the general populace as well. Thus, Chinese residents found themselves constantly at risk of being questioned, detained, or physically or verbally assaulted. Aggressive government deportation policies had effectively brought Chinese exclusion into every corner of the country, making every place potentially dangerous for Chinese. Longtime Chicago resident and merchant Hong Sling experienced this harassment first hand in 1901. While on a train en route to Decatur, Illinois, Hong was pounced upon by a U.S. marshal. After the marshal declared that it was his intention to "arrest every Chinaman in this district," he demanded that Hong show proof of his right to be in the country. Hong complied, giving his name, place of residence, and a description of his business. He also provided other evidence of his status as a merchant, including a letter signed by Secretary of the Treasury Lyman Gage, who certified that he personally knew Hong to be a merchant. The marshal was not satisfied and searched Hong's baggage. Upon finding Hong's registration certificate, the officer let him go, but only after kicking and hitting Hong in front of a large crowd gathered around him.

Such abuses were apparently widespread. In 1905, Reverend Leighton Parks of New York City complained to the Department of Commerce and Labor that the Chinese residents of that city lived in "continual dread" of the Chinese inspectors, because they were blackmailed and subjected to other unjust treatment by them. By 1914, the Chinese Consulate felt it necessary to file a formal protest with the immigration service in Los Angeles against its unnecessary force in apprehending Chinese. The immigration officials, the consul-general complained, "make a big show of force where absolutely none is necessary, and that in many cases, exceptionally high bonds have been asked in cases where the ordinary amount would have answered all purposes. In other words, they are making the matter one of *persecution* as well as prosecution." Those who were most vulnerable to persecution were, of course, Chinese who had entered the country under fraudulent purposes, lost their legal immigration status, or possessed no documentation whatsoever. San Francisco immigration agents, for instance, chased down Wong Bew in 1908 after learning that although he had been granted admission into the country as a Chinese merchant, he was actually working as a cook in a local hospital. When inspectors unexpectedly showed up at the hospital, Wong immediately fled the kitchen through a back alley but was eventually caught and brought in for questioning.

Similarly, a merchant, Wu Wah, and his wife, Ngoon Shee, found themselves hunted by immigration officials for five years beginning in 1932, because Wu had been forced to sell his Oakland, California, business in the wake of the economic depression. Although they had six children, all born in the United States as citizens, immigration officials issued a warrant for the arrest of both parents in 1932, charging the couple with violating the Immigration Act of 1924 and failing to maintain their exempt-class status. The two were apparently aware of the government's intentions and hurriedly left their home in Oakland just a few days before immigrant inspector E. C. Benson arrived with the arrest warrant. Benson attempted to track them down through the U.S. postal system and the California Department of Motor Vehicles. Meanwhile, Ngoon Shee and Wu Wah were forced into a life of hiding and secrecy, moving from place to place, but never staying in one location for very long. When immigrant inspectors finally caught the family in 1937, the couple hired attorney W. H. Wilkinson, a former law officer in the Bureau of Immigration, who argued that both legal precedent and the service's own regulations nullified the government's charges against the couple. Immigration officials in San Francisco had no choice but to cancel the arrest warrants for Ngoon Shee and Wu Wah. In October of 1937, their deportation cases were finally closed, five years after they had first been filed.

For illegal and undocumented immigrants, exploitation and extortion came from many quarters. Oppressive employers, corrupt government bureaucrats, other Chinese, suspicious Americans, and lawyers and con artists all preyed upon Chinese whose vulnerable legal status made them unable or unwilling to press charges. In 1895, Chinese immigrants in San Francisco complained through their attorney, Thomas D. Riordan, that two men, representing themselves as customs inspectors, were extorting money from Chinese immigrants. The two suspects continually entered Chinese stores without warrants and searched the premises for illegal immigrants and opium for the purpose of blackmailing the residents. The following year, other Chinese also complained of harassment by another officer who visited homes in Chinatown and charged the Chinese with being in the country illegally. If the family paid him enough money, he would leave them alone. If not, he threatened to take the case to the immigration service....

In the 1930s, sociologist Paul Siu found that Chinese immigrants and Chinese American citizens suffered from a deep-rooted sense of insecurity, a "psychology of fear" brought on by the fact that the Chinese "did not feel at home under the conditions of exclusion and race prejudice." This fear reinforced the process of social, political, and economic segregation of Chinese communities, resulting in a high rate of return migration and perpetuating the sojourning pattern. Unwelcome in the United States, plagued by a tenuous legal status, and prevented from becoming full-fledged citizens, many Chinese immigrants continued to view the United States as a sojourner would: a place in which to make money and then leave. As one Chicago laundryman interviewed by Paul Siu explained: "I have no other hope but to get my money and get back to China. What is the use of staying here; you can't be an American here. We Chinese are not even allowed to become citizens. If we were allowed, that might be a different story. In that case, I think many of us Chinese would not think so much of going back to China. Many would get a woman and settle down here."

Many immigrants shared these views about the United States and their intentions to return to China. Indeed, in 1928, sociologist R. D. McKenzie identified return migration as the most significant effect of exclusion upon the Chinese immigrant community. He observed that "exclusion tends to expel the resident population of the race in question in addition to preventing newcomers from entering." While other immigrant groups came in large numbers at the end of the nineteenth and beginning of the early twentieth centuries, more Chinese left the United States than came. From 1908 to 1923, 36,693 Chinese came to the United States, but 47,607 departed, or, for every 100 hundred Chinese who came in during that period, 130 departed. During the same period, the ratio of immigration to emigration was 100:5 for Jewish immigrants, 100:11 for Irish immigrants, and 100:33 for Japanese immigrants. The high rate of departures over arrivals suggests many Chinese chose to give up their immigrant status in the United States and return to China instead of staying and being subjected to harassment and discrimination. In addition, the number of new immigrants remained small during the same period. As a result, the census reports also indicate a rapid decrease in the Chinese resident population. While the exclusion laws may not have succeeded in closing all of the gates to Chinese immigration, the atmosphere they created drastically reduced the size of the Chinese community in America.

Another significant consequence of Chinese exclusion was its impact on native-born Chinese American citizens who were also the targets of discriminatory legislation and policies affecting their rights of travel and citizenship. They found that their status offered little protection from government harassment. Although the 1898 Supreme Court case *Wong Kim Ark* protected their birthright citizenship, this status was constantly attacked well into the twentieth century. In 1913 and 1923, politicians introduced bills in Congress designed to disfranchise citizens of Chinese ancestry. In addition, the 1922 Cable Act revoked the citizenship of women who married "aliens ineligible for citizenship," a code phrase that applied to Asians only. The main victims of this law were Asian American women who married Asian male immigrants. Once a woman lost her citizenship, her rights to own property, vote, and travel freely were also revoked. When Lon Thom, one of the first American-born Chinese in New York City's Chinatown, met and married Chinese student Wing Ark Chin in 1922, she was stripped of her citizenship. She remained in the country of her birth as a noncitizen for eighteen years. Only in 1940, when Congress amended some of the provisions of the Cable Act, did Lon Thom regain her American citizenship. Though American-born, she had to face a naturalization hearing and swear her allegiance to the United States just like an immigrant alien. The Immigration Act of 1924 also explicitly excluded "aliens ineligible to citizenship," which barred alien wives of citizens.

The impact of these immigration laws on Chinese American citizens was great. They were subjected to inconvenience and even harassment every time they reentered the country, tried to sponsor a relative, or even happened to be in Chinatown during an immigration raid.

Chinese American citizens were unable to escape the shadow of exclusion. Citizens interviewed in 1931 expressed a marked loss of admiration for the United States, as well as a frustrated sense of alienation. One explained, "I speak fluent English, and have the American mind. I feel that I am more American than Chinese. I am an American citizen by birth, having the title for all rights, but they treat me as if I were a foreigner. They have so many restrictions against us." Another observed, "I thought I was American, but America would not have me. In many respects she would not recognize me as American. Moreover, I find racial prejudice against us everywhere. We are American citizens in name but not in fact." Like these two individuals, many other Chinese Americans believed they were citizens in name only, with few of the benefits accorded to citizens of other ethnic and racial backgrounds.

FURTHER READING

Camacho, Julía María Schiavone. "Crossing Boundaries, Claiming a Homeland: The Mexican Chinese Transpacific Journey to Becoming Mexican, 1930s–1960s." *Pacific Historical Review* 78 (Nov. 2009): 545–577.

Chan, Sucheng. *This Bittersweet Soil: The Chinese in California Agriculture, 1860–1910* (1986).

———. *Asian Americans: An Interpretive History* (1991).

Chang, Kornel. "Circulating Race and Empire: Transnational Labor Activism and Politics of Anti-Asian Agitation in the Anglo-American Pacific World, 1880-1910." *Journal of American History* 96 (Dec. 2009): 678–700.

Cumings, Bruce. *Dominion from Sea to Sea: Pacific Ascendancy and American Power* (2009).

Delgado, Grace. "At Exclusion's Southern Gate: Changing Categories of Race and Class among Chinese *Fronterizos*, 1882–1904." In *Continental Crossroads: Remapping U.S.-Mexico Borderlands History*, ed. Samuel Truett and Elliott Young, pp. 183–207 (2004).

Ettinger, Patrick. *Imaginary Lines: Border Enforcement and the Origins of Undocumented Immigration, 1882–1930* (2009).

Geiger, Andrea. "Caught in the Gap: The Transit Privilege and North America's Ambiguous Borders." In *Bridging National Borders in North America: Transnational and Comparative Histories*, ed. Benjamin H. Johnson and Andrew Graybill, pp. 199–222 (2010).

Gómez-Izquierdo, José Jorge. *El movimiento antichino en México, 1871–1934* (1991).

González Navarro, Moisés. "Xenofobia y xenofilia en le Revolución Mexicana" [Xenophobia and xenophilia in the Mexican Revolution]. *Historia Mexicana* 38 (April-June 1969): 569–614.

Hsu, Madeline Yuan-yin. *Dreaming of Gold, Dreaming of Home: Transnationalism and Migration Between the United States and South Chine, 1882–1943* (2000).

Igler, David. "Diseased Goods: Global Exchanges in the Eastern Pacific Basin, 1770–1850." *American Historical Review* 109 (June 2004): 693–719.

Lee, Erika. *At America's Gates: Chinese Immigration During the Exclusion Era, 1882–1943* (2003).

———. "Orientalisms in the Americas: A Hemispheric Approach to Asian American History." *Journal of Asian American Studies* 8 (Oct. 2005): 235–256.

Lowe, Lisa. *Immigrant Acts: On Asian American Cultural Politics* (1996).

McKeown, Adam. *Melancholy Order: Asian Migration and the Globalization of Borders* (2008).

Okihiro, Gary Y. *Margins and Mainstreams: Asians in American History and Culture* (1994).

Ota, María Elena Mishima, ed. *Destino México: un estudio de las migraciones asiáticás a México, siglos XIX y XX* (1997).

Rénrique, Gerardo. "Race, Region, and Nation: Sonora's Anti-Chinese Racism and Mexico's Postrevolutionary Nationalism, 1920s–1930s." In *Race and Nation in Modern Latin America*, ed. Nancy P. Applebaum et al., pp. 219–226. (2003).

Romero, Robert Chao. "Transnational Chinese Immigrant Smuggling to the United States via Mexico and Cuba, 1882-1916." *Amerasia Journal (UCLA Journal of Asian American Studies)* 30 (2004/2005): 1–163.

———. *The Chinese in Mexico, 1882–1940* (2010).

Yu, Henry. *Thinking Orientals: Migration, Contact, and Exoticism in Modern America* (2001).

Zhu, Liping. *A Chinaman's Chance: The Chinese on the Rocky Mountain Mining Frontier* (1997).

CHAPTER 11

∿

The Mexican Revolution

In 1876, Mexico entered a long period of political stability with the advent of the regime of Porfirio Díaz. Díaz, a former general, ruled the country until he stepped down in 1911 in the face of a massive revolt. He presided over an economic transformation that saw the influx of foreign capital, especially in the form of railroads (which expanded from less than four hundred miles of track to fifteen thousand) and mining enterprises. Textile manufacturing and export crops such as sugar and cotton boomed. Politically, Díaz centralized power, effectively ending partisan warfare and the frequent regime change that had plagued Mexico since its independence. On the other hand, dispossession and rising inequality were a fundamental part of Porfirian Mexico. Violence, fraud, and debt stripped millions of peasants of their land; by 1910, nearly two-thirds of the population were landless peasant families. Wages remained flat as the prices of staple foods spiraled upward. And the regime provided no real outlet for discontent over such conditions: It banned opposition political parties and used force to crush strikes and other protests.

In 1908, the wealthy Coahuilan Francisco Madero began a daring presidential campaign against Porfirio Díaz, who was planning his eighth reelection. Madero, the scion of one of northern Mexico's wealthiest and most influential families, called for free elections, an independent judiciary, and an uncensored press. Hampered by fraud and violence, his forces failed to win a single congressional seat in the 1910 elections, and Madero fled to San Antonio, Texas, where he declared himself provisional president of Mexico and called for the armed overthrow of Díaz. A series of revolts—mostly unplanned by Madero—erupted by the spring of 1911. Madero's supporters captured Ciudad Juárez, opposite El Paso, Texas, in March. Díaz resigned in May. Another presidential election was held, and Madero won decisively.

Building a new order that could rule Mexico and meet the enormous and conflicting expectations of its people proved much more difficult than toppling the Díaz regime. Madero devoted most of his energies to formal legal and political reform, generally rejecting calls for land redistribution. The key constituents of the old regime—regional political bosses, wealthy hacienda owners and industrialists, and the federal army—never accepted his rule, believing him perilously weak and unable to prevent the lower orders from tearing society apart. On the other hand, those like Morelos peasant leader Emiliano Zapata, hoping for a sweeping reform of landholding, were angered by Madero's unwillingness to heed their calls. In 1913, the commander of the federal army assassinated Madero and dismissed the congress. His forces desperately fought to undo the revolution. Venustiano Carranza, a Coahuilan, sought to restore Madero's liberal and moderate rule, whereas others, like Pancho Villa in the North and Emiliano Zapata in the South, fought for a more radical vision of land reform. A plethora of local rebellions and alliances, many unconnected to larger factions or ideologies, also emerged by the end of 1913. Civil war—at first between the revolutionaries and the federal army, and then among the different revolutionary factions—would wrack Mexico for the rest of the decade. By the early 1920s, a central government under the leadership of one of Carranza's former generals had asserted control over most of the nation. The post-revolutionary regime enjoyed much broader support than Porfirio Díaz had, and, in the next few decades, it would launch programs of mass education, infrastructure construction, economic development, and land redistribution that would substantially improve the lives of most Mexican citizens.

This chapter explores the enormous impacts of the Revolution on Mexican Americans, U.S. border policy, and diplomatic relations between Mexico and the United States. Nearly one in ten Mexican citizens fled to the United States over the course of the decade, dramatically transforming the culture and demography of the borderlands. The Mexican-descent population of the United States tripled between 1910 and 1920, most visibly in places like Los Angeles that had until that time become overwhelmingly Anglo-American. At the same time, relations between the Mexican and U.S. governments were badly frayed. United States military forces occupied Mexican territory twice, nearly bringing the two nations to outright warfare for the first time since 1848. Revolutionary violence and radicalism transformed the ways that much of the American population and its government perceived their border with Mexico and provided a rationale for the increasingly brutal treatment of Mexican-descent people in the United States. The Mexican Revolution was a turning point for Mexico, the United States, and their shared border.

∿ DOCUMENTS

The tumult of the revolution, as well as the rapid economic development of the U.S. Southwest and Mexican North in the decades beforehand, led to a dramatic increase in Mexican migration to the United States. Indeed, this migration continues to the present, pausing only in the 1930s because of the Great Depression, and forced expulsion campaigns directed at ethnic Mexicans. In Document 1, journalist Samuel Bryan describes Mexican migration in the early 1910s. He captures the way that Mexicans were treated by their employers and the social tensions that their expanded settlements provoked. How would you characterize Bryan's attitude toward his subjects? Can his depiction of them as passive and content to live in squalor be reconciled with their willingness to migrate and to work in low-paying and arduous jobs?

Many of the Mexicans who came to the United States in the 1910s were deeply involved with different factions of the Mexican Revolution. Such was the case with Flores de Andrade, whose memories of political activism in Chihuahua and El Paso are excerpted in Document 2. Born into a life of privilege, Andrade turned against the Díaz dictatorship, at great risk to herself. Like many of the regime's opponents, she found refuge in the United States and used the American side of the border as a base from which to struggle against the regime.

Many more left Mexico for economic reasons. In Document 3, Anastacio Torres, a native of Guanajuato, recounts his varied experiences in the United States. He entered the United States through El Paso, whose railroad connections made it the largest point of entry for Mexicans, and eventually settled in California, the major destination for Mexicans, after working in a number of states. His ambivalent feelings toward the Mexican government, Americans, and Mexican-Americans were widely shared by Mexican migrants.

Mexicans in the United States, along with Mexican Americans, were treated as racial outcasts and exploitable laborers. Even as their numbers grew with the flight from the Revolution, the harshness of their treatment in the United States increased. In certain areas—southern California, northern New Mexico, and much of the Texas border region—Mexican-descent people had maintained substantial political and economic power for decades after the U.S. conquest of the Southwest in 1848. In these enclaves, they maintained themselves as independent landowners, voters, and elected officials. By 1910, however, segregation, disfranchisement, and economic dislocation had come to even these places. In south Texas, in 1915, dispossessed Tejanos launched a revolt against Anglo-American dominance, one that was associated with the Plan of San Diego, a manifesto supposedly drafted in San Diego, Texas, that is reproduced in Document 4. (These events are described at greater length in the second essay in this chapter.) The manifesto captures the grievances of ethnic Mexicans in Texas and reflects the belief—inspired by the Mexican Revolution—that redress could be found through armed struggle.

The Plan of San Diego uprising was not the only organized violence associated with the Mexican Revolution that took place on U.S. territory. On March 9, 1916, General Francisco "Pancho" Villa led a force of some five hundred in an attack on Columbus, New Mexico, engaging U.S. cavalry units in pitched battle. This attack, intended to punish the United States government for what Villa believed to be its support for his rival Venustiano Carranza and its interference in Mexican affairs, prompted U.S. President Woodrow Wilson to dispatch ten thousand soldiers to track down and capture Villa. Document 5 is his announcement of this punitive expedition. It is most notable for its understatement: Wilson is careful to describe the goals of the military intervention in limited terms, as applying only to Villa and not representing an invasion, as in 1846. Nevertheless, nationalist sentiment in Mexico forced Carranza to demand the withdrawal of American military forces, and the two nations reached the brink of war later that year. Wilson withdrew the expedition in early 1917, having failed entirely to capture Villa or defeat his faction of the revolution.

The Plan of San Diego and Villa's raid shaped other events in the borderlands, as was the case in Bisbee, Arizona, in 1917. As many as 90 percent of the copper-mining workers in the town had joined a strike aimed at increasing pay, improving safety, and ending the blacklisting of union members. This action, by a polyglot workforce comprised of Anglo-Americans, European immigrants, and Mexicans and Mexican-Americans, also threatened a long-standing dual-wage system that confined ethnic Mexicans to the most dangerous and low-paying jobs. Working closely with the mining companies, local law enforcement authorities assembled an enormous posse of some two thousand (nearly all Anglo-American), which then forcibly placed the strikers (90 percent of whom were born outside the United States) in boxcars, in which they were taken to the New Mexico desert, some 180 miles away, and dumped. This action, known as the "Bisbee Deportation," was condemned by labor leaders, many newspaper editorialists, and the federal government. Nevertheless, it broke the strike, crippled organized labor in Arizona for a generation, and hardened the lines between Whites and Mexicans. Document 6 is the testimony of county sheriff Harry Wheeler, one of the chief architects of the deportation, to a U.S. Senate committee. Wheeler's explanation for his actions reveals the extent to which the Mexican Revolution prompted the fear—and perhaps a pretext—for such extreme measures. Many Americans had come to see Mexican migration and the still easily crossed border as a threat.

Concerns about border security and opposition to immigration (largely from southern and eastern Europe) by native-born Americans prompted Congress to enact systematic immigration legislation in 1917. Document 7 is an excerpt of the text of the Immigration Act of 1917. This measure was the most restrictive immigration legislation in American history. It continued the practice of excluding almost all Asians, made literacy a requirement for entry, and created a long list of reasons for barring entry into the United States. These reasons gave immigration inspectors enormous latitude in their decisions of who to admit and who to exclude, as they included factors difficult to evaluate, such as insanity, alcoholism, anarchism, and the likelihood that people would not be able to support themselves.

The 1917 Immigration Act was directed primarily at European migrants entering the United States by ship. The land borders were still lightly patrolled by today's standards, with official crossing and inspection stations isolated and avoidable. In some places, however, local authorities took more aggressive measures of inspection of border crossers. In El Paso, Texas, customs officials were particularly wary of Mexican border-crossers. By 1917 they had implemented a policy of making some migrants take baths in gasoline if they wanted to cross the border. Carmelita Torres, who crossed daily into El Paso from its sister city of Juárez to clean houses, refused to submit to this procedure, finding it humiliating and unsafe. As reported in the newspaper account of the Bath Riots reproduced in Document 8, her refusal prompted hundreds of protesting women to block traffic into El Paso and to clash with American and Mexican authorities trying to disperse them. Despite the mocking tone of the newspaper's coverage, the protestors' actions resonated with the increasing numbers of people subjected to what they considered humiliating treatment. Why might this scene have prompted an onlooker to yell "Viva Villa"?

1. Samuel Bryan Analyzes Increases in Mexican Immigration, 1912

Previous to 1900 the influx of Mexicans was comparatively unimportant. It was confined almost exclusively to those portions of Texas, New Mexico, Arizona and California which are near the boundary line between Mexico and the United States. Since these states were formerly Mexican territory and have always possessed a considerable Mexican population, a limited migration back and forth across the border was a perfectly natural result of the existing blood relationship. During the period from 1880 to 1900 the Mexican-born population of these border states increased from 66,312 to 99,969—a gain of 33,657 in twenty years. This increase was not sufficient to keep pace with the growth of the total population of the states. Since 1900, however, there has been a rapid increase in the volume of Mexican immigration, and also some change in its geographical distribution.

In 1908, it was estimated that from 60,000 to 100,000 Mexicans entered the United States each year. This estimate, however, should be modified by the well-known fact that each year a considerable number of Mexicans return to Mexico. Approximately 50 percent of those Mexicans who find employment as section hands upon the railroads claim the free transportation back to El Paso which is furnished by the railroad companies to those who have been in their employ six months or a year. Making allowance for this fact, it would be conservative to place the yearly accretion of population by Mexican immigration at from 35,000 to 70,000. It is probable, therefore, that the Mexican-born population of the United States has trebled since the census of 1900 was taken.

This rapid increase within the last decade has resulted from the expansion of industry both in Mexico and in the United States. In this country the industrial development of the Southwest has opened up wider fields of employment for unskilled laborers in transportation, agriculture, mining, and smelting. A similar expansion in northern Mexico has drawn many Mexican laborers from the farms of other sections of the country farther removed from the border, and it is an easy matter to go from the mines and section gangs of northern Mexico to the more remunerative employment to be had in similar industries of the southwestern United States. Thus the movement from the more remote districts of Mexico to the newly developed industries of the North has become largely a stage in a more general movement to the United States. Entrance into this country is not difficult, for employment agencies in normal times have stood ready to advance board, lodging, and transportation to a place where work was to be had, and the immigration officials have usually deemed no Mexican likely to become a public charge so long as this was the case. This was especially true before 1908...

Most of the Mexican immigrants have at one time been employed as railroad laborers. At present they are used chiefly as section hands and as members of construction gangs, but a number are also to be found working as common laborers about the shops and powerhouses. Although a considerable number are

Samuel Bryan, "Mexican Immigrants in the United States," *Survey* 20 (Sep. 1912): 726, 730. As excerpted in *Major Problems in Mexican-American History*, 212–214.

employed as helpers, few have risen above unskilled labor in any branch of the railroad service. As section hands on the two more important systems they were paid a uniform wage of $1.00 per day from their first employment in 1902 until 1909, except for a period of about one year previous to the financial stringency of 1907, when they were paid $1.25 per day. In 1909 the wages of all Mexican section hands employed upon the Santa Fe lines were again raised to $1.25 per day. The significant feature is, however, that as a general rule they have earned less than the members of any other race similarly employed. For example, 2,455 Mexican section hands from whom data were secured by the Immigration Commission in 1908 and 1909, 2,111, or 85.9 percent, were earning less than $1.25 per day, while the majority of the Greeks, Italians, and Japanese earned more than $1.25 and a considerable number more than $1.50 per day.

In the arid regions of the border states where they have always been employed and where the majority of them still live, the Mexicans come into little direct competition with other races, and no problems of importance result from their presence. But within the last decade their area of employment has expanded greatly. They are now used as section hands as far east as Chicago and as far north as Wyoming. Moreover, they are now employed to a considerable extent in the coal mines of Colorado and New Mexico, in the ore mines of Colorado and Arizona, in the smelters of Arizona, in the cement factories of Colorado and California, in the beet sugar industry of the last mentioned states, and in fruit growing and canning in California. In these localities they have at many points come into direct competition with other races, and their low standards have acted as a check upon the progress of the more assertive of these.

Where they are employed in other industries, the same wage discrimination against them as was noted in the case of railroad employees is generally apparent where the work is done on an hour basis, but no discrimination exists in the matter of rates for piecework. As pieceworkers in the fruit canneries and in the sugar beet industry the proverbial sluggishness of the Mexicans prevents them from earning as much as the members of other races. In the citrus fruit industry their treatment varies with the locality. In some instances they are paid the same as the "whites"—in others the same as the Japanese, according to the class with which they share the field of employment. The data gathered by the Immigration Commission show that although the earnings of Mexicans employed in the other industries are some-what higher than those of the Mexican section hands, they are with few exceptions noticeably lower than the earnings of Japanese, Italians, and members of the various Slavic races who are similarly employed. This is true in the case of smelting, ore mining, coal mining, and sugar refining. Specific instances of the use of Mexicans to curb the demands of other races are found in the sugar beet industry of central California, where they were introduced for the purpose of showing the Japanese laborers that they were not indispensable, and in the same industry in Colorado, where they were used in a similar way against the German-Russians. Moreover, Mexicans have been employed as strikebreakers in the coal mines of Colorado and New Mexico, and in one instance in the shops of one important railroad system.

Socially and politically the presence of large numbers of Mexicans in this country gives rise to serious problems. The reports of the Immigration Commissions show that they lack ambition, are to a very large extent illiterate in their native language, are slow to learn English, and most cases show no political interest. In some instances, however, they have been organized to serve the purposes of political bosses, as for example in Phoenix, Arizona. Although more of them are married and have their families with them than is the case among the south European immigrants, they are unsettled as a class, move readily from place to place, and do not acquire or lease land to any extent. But their most unfavorable characteristic is their inclination to form colonies and live in a clannish manner. Wherever a considerable group of Mexicans are employed, they live together, if possible, and associate very little with members of other races. In the mining towns and other small industrial communities they live ordinarily in rude adobe huts outside of the town limits. As section hands they of course live as the members of the other races have done, in freight cars fitted with windows and bunks, or in rough shacks along the line of the railroad. In the cities their colonization has become a menace.

In Los Angeles the housing problem centers largely in the cleaning up or demolition of the Mexican "house courts," which have become the breeding ground of disease and crime, and which have now attracted a considerable population of immigrants of other races. It is estimated that approximately 2,000 Mexicans are living in these "house courts." Some 15,000 persons of this race are residents of Los Angeles and vicinity. Conditions of life among the immigrants of the city, which are molded to a certain extent by Mexican standards, have been materially improved by the work of the Los Angeles Housing Commission. However, the Mexican quarter continues to offer a serious social problem to the community.

In conclusion it should be recognized that although the Mexicans have proved to be efficient laborers in certain industries, and have afforded a cheap and elastic labor supply for the southwestern United States, the evils to the community at large which their presence in large numbers almost invariably brings may more than overbalance their desirable qualities. Their low standards of living and of morals, their illiteracy, their utter lack of proper political interest, the retarding effect of their employment upon the wage scale of the more progressive races, and finally their tendency to colonize in urban centers, with evil results, combine to stamp them as a rather undesirable class of residents.

2. Flores de Andrade Recalls Her Revolutionary Activity as an Immigrant in El Paso, Texas, 1931

I was born in Chihuahua, [Mexico,] and spent my infancy and youth on an estate in Coahuila which belonged to my grandparents. As I was healthy and happy I would run over the estate. I rode on a horse bareback and wasn't afraid of anything. I was thirteen years of age when my grandparents died, leaving me a good inheritance.

Manuel Gamio, *The Mexican Immigrant: His Life-Story* (Chicago: University of Chicago Press, 1931), 29–35. As excerpted in *Major Problems in Mexican-American History*, 209–211. © University of Chicago Press. Reprinted by permission.

The first thing that I did, in spite of the fact that my sister and my aunt advised me against it, was to give absolute liberty on my lands to all the peons. I declared free of debts all of those who worked on the lands which my grand-parents had willed me and what there was on that fifth part, such as grain, agri-cultural implements and animals, I divided in equal parts among the peons. I also told them that they could go on living on those lands in absolute liberty without paying me anything....

Because I divided my property, my aunt and even my sister began to annoy me.

They annoyed me so much that I decided to marry, marrying a man of German origin. I lived very happily with my husband until he died, leaving me a widow with six children. Twelve years had gone by in the mean time. I then decided to go to Chihuahua, to the capital of the state, and there ... I began to fight for liberal ideals, organizing a women's club which was called the "Daugh-ters of Cuauhtemoc," a semi-secret organization which worked with the Liberal Party ... in fighting the dictatorship of Don Porfirio Dìaz.

My political activities caused greater anger among the members of my family.... Under these conditions I grew poorer and poorer until I reached extreme poverty. I passed four bitter years in Chihuahua suffering economic want on the one hand and fighting in defense of the ideals on the other. My relatives would tell me not to give myself in fighting for the people, because I wouldn't get anything from it.... I didn't care anything about that.... I would have gone on fighting for the cause which I considered to be just.

My economic situation in Chihuahua became serious, so that I had to accept donations of money which were given to me as charity by wealthy people ... who knew me and my relatives....

Finally after four years' stay in Chihuahua, I decided to come to El Paso, Texas. I came in the first place to see if I could better my economic condition and secondly to continue fighting in that region in favor of the Liberal ideals ... to plot against the dictatorship of Don Porfirio. I came to El Paso ... together with my children and comrade Pedro Mendoza....

With comrade Mendoza we soon began the campaign of Liberal propa-ganda. We lived in the same house ... and as we went about together all day working in the Liberal campaign the American authorities forced us to marry. I am now trying to divorce myself from my husband for he hasn't treated me right....

... A group of comrades founded in El Paso a Liberal women's club. They made me president of that group, and soon afterwards I began to carry on the propaganda work in El Paso and in Ciudad Juarez.... I took charge of collecting money, clothes, medicines and even ammunition and arms to begin to prepare for the revolutionary movement, for the uprisings were already starting in some places.

The American police and the Department of Justice began to suspect our activities and soon began to watch out for me, but they were never able to find either in my house or in the offices of the club documents or arms or anything....

In 1910, when all those who were relatives of those who had taken up arms were arrested by order of the Mexican federal authorities, I had to come to Ciudad Juarez.... I was then put into prison, but soon was let out and I went back to El Paso to continue the fight....

... Sr. Madero ... came to El Paso, pursued by the Mexican and American authorities. He came to my house with some others. I couldn't hide them in my house, but got a little house ... and put them there.

... One day Don Francisco Madero entrusted my husband to go to a Mexican farm on the shore of the Bravo river so as to bring two men who were coming to reach an agreement concerning the movement. My husband ... didn't go. Then I offered my services to Sr. Madero and I went for the two men who were on this side of the border, ... in Texan territory.... Two Texan rangers who had followed me asked me where I was going, and I told them to a festival and they asked me to invite them. I took them to the festival and there managed to get them drunk; then I took away the two men and brought them to Don Francisco. Then I went back to the farm and brought the Rangers to El Paso where I took them drunk to the City Hall and left them there.

Later when everything was ready for the revolutionary movement against the dictatorship, Don Francisco and all those who accompanied him decided to pass over to Mexican territory. I prepared an afternoon party so as to disguise the movement. They all dressed in masked costumes as if for a festival and then we went towards the border. The river was very high and it was necessary to cross over without hesitating for the American authorities were already following us... Finally, mounting a horse barebacked, I took charge of taking those who were accompanying Don Francisco over two by two. They crossed over to a farm and there they remounted for the mountains.

A woman companion and I came back to the American side, for I received instructions to go on with the campaign. This happened the 18 of May, 1911. We slept there in the house of the owner of the ranch and on the next day when we were getting ready to leave, the Colonel came with a picket of soldiers. I told the owner of the ranch to tell him that he didn't know me...When the authorities camp up..., the owner of the ranch said that he didn't know me and I said that I didn't know him. They then asked me for my name and I gave it to them. They asked me what I was doing there and I said that I had been hunting and showed them two rabbits that I had shot. They then took away my ... rifle and my pistol and told me that they had orders to shoot me because I had been conspiring against Don Porfirio. I told them that was true and that they should shoot me right away because otherwise I was going to lose courage. The Colonel, however, sent for instructions from his general.... He sent orders that I should be shot at once.

This occurred almost on the shores of the Rio Grande and my family already had received a notice of what was happening to me and went to make pleas to the American authorities.... They were already making up the squad to shoot me when the American Consul arrived and asked me if I could show that I was an American citizen so that they couldn't shoot, but I didn't want to do that I told I them that I was a Mexican....

The Colonel told me to make my will for they were going to execute me. I told him that I didn't have anything more than my six children whom I will to the Mexican people....

The Colonel was trying to stave off my execution so that he could save me, he said. An officer then came and said that the General was approaching. The Colonel said that it would be well to wait until the chief came so that he could decide concerning my life, but a corporal told him that they should shoot me at once for if the general came and they had not executed me then they would be blamed.... The corporal who was interested in having me shot was going to fire when I took the Colonel's rifle away from him and menaced him; he then ordered the soldiers to throw their rifles at the feet of the Mexican woman..., for the troops of the General were already coming. I gathered up the rifles and crossed the river in my little buggy. There the American authorities arrested me and took me to Fort Bliss.... On the next day the authorities at Fort Bliss received a telegram from President Taft in which he ordered me to be put at liberty, and they sent me home, a negro military band accompanying me through the streets.

At the triumph of the cause of Sr. Madero we had some great festivities in Ciudad Juarez....

Afterwards Sr. Madero sent for me and asked me what I wanted. I told him that I wanted the education of my six children and that all the promises which had been made to the Mexican people should be carried out.

During the Huerta revolution I kept out of the struggle, ... and little by little I have been separating myself from political affairs.

3. Mexican Migrant Describes Working Life in the United States, 1927

ANASTACIO TORRES

I was about seventeen years old, in 1911, when I came to the United States with my brother-in-law. I had worked until then as a clerk in a small store in my home town and also knew something about farm work. My brother-in-law managed to get me across the border without much trouble. We crossed the border at Ciudad Juarez and when we got to El Paso, Texas, we signed ourselves up for work in Kansas. We first went to work on the railroad and they paid us there $1.35 for nine hours of work a day. As that work was very hard I got a job in a packing house where I began by earning $1.25 a day for eight hours work but I got to earning as much as $2.00 when the foreman saw that I was intelligent and that I was very

Manuel Gamio, *The Mexican Immigrant: His Life-Story* (Chicago: University of Chicago Press, 1931), 55–58. © University of Chicago Press. Reprinted by permission.

careful about my work. They almost always paid me a cent or two more an hour than my companions and as I was intelligent they didn't give me the hardest jobs.

I was educated in a Catholic school and if it hadn't been that my mother was poor, I might perhaps have been a doctor or a lawyer, for I was one of the most advanced in the school. I even learned how to help to say mass although that has hardly helped me in any way in this country. I keep on being Catholic although I don't go to church very often. I was married to a girl from La Piedad, Michoacan, in Kansas City. She died there after we had been married about a year, leaving our little son. While working in the packing plant I broke my leg and then I wanted to collect damages but I wasn't able to. I was thinking of going to ask the Mexican Consul there to help me but some countrymen told me not to go to that Consul because he didn't help anybody. At about that time the time of the Great War came and they gave me a war registry questionnaire. They wanted me to go to the war with the American army but I told them that I wasn't an American. They then asked me why I lived in this country and they kept on trying to persuade me. I told them that I had a son and finally, so that they wouldn't keep on bothering me, I went to California where a brother of mine was. I worked for a long time in California and then I did register for the draft, but at the same time declaring that I was a Mexican citizen and that I wasn't willing to change my citizenship. I was in the Imperial Valley, in Calipatria. I worked there first as a laborer with some Japanese. As they are very good and intelligent they showed me how to run all the agricultural implements, a thing which I learned easily with my intelligence. About the end of 1918 I went to Ciudad Juarez for my sister and her children. My father also came with her. Then we went to Calipatria and the whole family of us engaged in cotton picking. They paid very well at that time. They paid us $2.00 or $1.75 for every 100 pounds of cotton which we picked and as all of the family picked we managed to make a good amount every day. When the cotton crop of 1919 was finished we went to Los Angeles and then I got a job as a laborer with a paper manufacturing company. They paid me $3.40 a day for eight hours work. I was at that work for some time and then returned to the Imperial Valley for lemon picking. They paid me $3.00 a day for eight hours work. I became acquainted with a young lady in Valley from San Francisco del Rincon, Guanajuato, and was married to her. This was my second marriage. In 1921 a Japanese friend for whom I was working as a laborer told me to keep the farm, for he was going to go soon. The owner of the land who was an American furnished the land, the water and the seeds, and we went on halves on the other expenses. Half of the crop was his and half mine. The first planting that I made was of 13 acres of lettuce. I also planted squash and tomatoes. We did very well on those for the crops turned out first class. I don't have anything to say against the Japanese for they have been very good people to me. They showed me how to use a plow, the cultivator, the disc and the planting machines and they have been my best bosses. Neither can I complain of the Americans, for in Kansas City when I was working in the packing plant, as well as in Los Angeles and wherever I have been and have worked with them they have treated me.

Afterwards, encouraged by the first good crop that I got, I rented forty acres of land at $30 a year for each acre. I had to furnish the water and the seed and this time things went bad time for me. The crop wasn't any good, the seed was lost and I had to go and look for work elsewhere. I went from one place to another working in different ways. At times I earned $2.00 a day and at others as much as $4.00. Recently I had a job as a gardener in Beverly Hills. I was very well there, for they paid me $4.00 a day for taking care of the garden. I also had a piece of land on which I could plant vegetables, which also bought in something. But one day they told me that as I wasn't American citizen they were going to take away my job and put an American in my place. Then I went back to cultivating some land with an American. I planted forty acres again on halves. The crops turned out well, but the American took the products to a packing house which went bankrupt, so my partner and I were left without anything.

"I believe in God, but I have my doubts, for I was convinced in the Catholic school that all those beliefs are useless. They exploit the poor man anyway and steal his work."

He has had four children by his second wife, so that he has five children in all. He has baptized all of them according to what he says. He says that his wife is and isn't a Catholic, for she doesn't go to church very often nor does she have any saints in the house. Referring to his first days in school he says:

"I might perhaps have been a lawyer or a doctor if my parents had even sent me to a government school. But the school where I was was Catholic and they had us praying all day. As I was the most advanced in the class, for I had learned to read in less than a year, the parish priest taught me how to say Mass. I was getting big then and saw that they didn't do anything but pray in the school so I once asked the teacher to show me something about numbers so that I could keep accounts I was then given some multiplication, which was foolish, for I couldn't even add. I then told the teacher that perhaps he himself couldn't do that multiplication and for that reason I stopped going to school.

"I don't have anything against the *pochos,* but the truth is that although they are Mexicans, for they are of our own blood because their parents were Mexicans, they pretend that they are Americans. They only want to talk in English and they speak Spanish very poorly. That is why I don't like them.

4. South Texas Rebels Issue Manifesto, "The Plan of San Diego," 1915

"We will rise in arms against ... the United States."

—Plan of San Diego
(January 6, 1915)

1. On the 20th day of February, 1915, at 2 o'clock in the morning, we will rise in arms against the Government and country of the United States and North

---

Translated copy of Plan of San Diego, *Records of the Department of State Relating to the Internal Affairs of Mexico, 1910–1929,* 812.00/1583.

America, one as all and all as one, proclaiming the liberty of the individuals of the black race and its independence of Yankee tyranny, which has held us in iniquitous slavery since remote times; and at the same time and in the same manner we will proclaim the independence and segregation of the States bordering on the Mexican nation, which are: Texas, New Mexico, Arizona, Colorado, and Upper California, of which States the Republic of Mexico was robbed in a most perfidious manner by North American imperialism.

2. In order to render the foregoing clause effective, the necessary army corps will be formed under the immediate command of military leaders named by the supreme revolutionary congress of San Diego, Texas, which shall have full power to designate a supreme chief who shall be at the head of said army. The banner which shall guide us in this enterprise shall be red, with a white diagonal fringe, and bearing; the following inscription: "Equality and Independence"; and none of the subordinate leaders or subalterns shall use any other flag (except only the white for signals). The aforesaid army shall be known by the name of "Liberating Army for Races and Peoples."

3. Each one of the chiefs will do his utmost by whatever means possible, to get possession of the arms and funds of the cities which he has beforehand been designated to capture in order that our cause may be provided with resources to continue the fight with better success, the said leaders each being required to render an account of everything; to his superiors, in order that the latter may dispose of it in the proper manner.

4. The leader who may take a city must immediately name and appoint municipal authorities, in order that they may preserve order and assist in every way possible the revolutionary movement. In case the capital of any State which we are endeavoring to liberate be captured; there will be named in the same manner superior municipal authorities: for the same purpose.

5. It is strictly forbidden to hold prisoners, either special prisoners (civilians) or soldiers; and the only time that should be spent in dealing with them is that which is absolutely necessary to demand funds (loans) of them; and whether these demands be successful or not, they shall shot immediately, without any pretext.

6. Every stranger who shall be found armed and who can not prove his right to carry arms, shall be summarily executed, regardless of race or nationality.

7. Every North American over 16 years of age shall be put to death, and only the aged men, the women and children shall be respected. And on no account shall the traitors to our race be respected or spared.

8. The Apaches of Arizona, as well as the Indians (red skins) of the territory shall be given every guarantee, and their lands which have been taken from them shall be returned to them, to the end that they may assist us in the cause which we defend.

9. All appointments and grades in our army which are exercised by subordinate officers (subalterns) shall be examined (recognized) by the superior officers. There shall likewise be recognized the grades of leaders of other complots which may not be connected with this, and who may wish to co-operate with us; also those who may affiliate with us later.

10. The movement having gathered force, and once having possessed our-selves of the States above alluded to, we shall proclaim them an independent republic, later requesting, if it be thought expedient, annexation to Mexico without concerning ourselves at that time about the of government which may control the destinies of the common other country.

11. When we shall have obtained independence for the negroes we shall grant them a banner which they themselves shall be permitted to select, and we shall aid them in obtaining six States of the American Union, which States border upon those already mentioned, and they may from these six States form a republic and they may therefore be independent.

12. None of the leaders shall have power to make terms with the enemy without first communicating with the superior officers of the enemy, bearing in mind that this is a war without quarter, nor shall any leader enroll in his ranks any stranger unless said stranger belongs to Latin, the negro or the Japanese race.

13. It is understood that none of the members of this complot (or any one who may come in later) shall upon the definite triumph of the cause which we defend, fail to recognize their superiors, nor shall they aid others who with bastard designs may endeavor to destroy what has been accomplished with such great work.

14. As soon as possible each local society (junta) shall nominate delegates, who shall meet at a time and place beforehand designated; for the purpose of nominating a permanent directorate of the revolutionary movement. At this meet-ing shall be determined and worked out in detail: the powers and duties of the permanent directorate and this revolutionary plan may be revised or amended.

15. It is understood among those who may follow this movement that we will carry as a singing voice the independence of the negroes, placing obligations upon both races, and that on no account shall we accept aid, either moral or pecuniary, from the government of Mexico, and it need not consider itself under any obligations in this, our movement.

EQUALITY AND INDEPENDENCE.

5. President Woodrow Wilson Sends U.S. Army into Mexico, 1916

The Secretary of State to All American Consular Offices in Mexico

Washington, March 10, 1916.

The following statement has just been given to the press by the President:

An adequate force will be sent at once in pursuit of Villa with the single object of capturing him and putting a stop to his forays. This can and will be done in entirely friendly aid of the constituted authorities in Mexico and with scrupulous respect for the sovereignty of that Republic.

Papers Relating to the Foreign Relations of the United States, 1916 (Washington: Government Printing Office, 1925), 484.

6. Sheriff Justifies Deporting Striking Miners
from Arizona Town, 1917

SENATOR FALL. Did you regard the position at that time (1917) in the town of Bisbee, and in that vicinity, as warranting you in calling upon the Federal Government for assistance in the preservation of peace?

CAPT. WHEELER. I did.

SENATOR FALL. In connection with your activities and the performance of your duties as peace officer, were your actions thereafter investigated by any commission or department of the Government of the United States?

CAPT. WHEELER. Yes, sir.

SENATOR FALL. By whom were your acts investigated aside from any subsequent court proceedings?

CAPT. WHEELER. Secretary of Labor Wilson and a man by the name of Frankfurter—Felix Frankfurter, I believe—Marsh, and I forget the other name.

SENATOR FALL. They constituted what was known as the mediation committee appointed by the President of the United States, were they not?

CAPT. WHEELER. Yes, sir.

SENATOR FALL. In connection with this occurrence at Bisbee to which we have just been referring, did you come in contact with any citizens of Old Mexico?

CAPT. WHEELER. Yes, sir.

SENATOR FALL. Were such Mexicans involved in these occurrences at Bisbee?

CAPT. WHEELER. A great many.

SENATOR FALL. What did you learn from these Mexicans, if anything in reference to their action, and proposed action as to the causes leading them to pursue the course which they were pursuing?

CAPT. WHEELER. You understand, Senator, that a sheriff will frequently have stories related to him, both correct and incorrect, many of which he is unable personally to run down, but I was frequently told that the Mexicans of the Villa army had cached arms and ammunition in the mountains of Sonora, upon their retreat from Sonora; that many of these Mexicans were former Villa soldiers, and knew

U.S. Congress, Senate, Committee on Foreign Relations, *Investigation of Mexican affairs: preliminary report and hearings of the Committee on Foreign Relations, United States Senate, pursuant to S. res. 106, directing the Committee on Foreign Relations to investigate the matter of outrages on citizens of the United States in Mexico* (Washington: Government Printing Office, 1920): vol. 2, pp. 1882–1886.

where these caches were and intended to secure them at the proper time. I personally heard one Mexican—if you will remember a few weeks before that, or a month or two, the Mexicans ran the Americans out of Cananea, Sonora.

SENATOR FALL. Drove them out?

CAPT. WHEELER. Drove them out.

SENATOR FALL. The Americans took refuge on the American side.

CAPT. WHEELER. Most of them at Bisbee. After six weeks or two months, when peace was restored in Cananea, a great many of the Mexicans came into Bisbee. I heard one Mexican distinctly, heard him remark to an American workman going up the hill with his lunch pail: "We run you out of Cananea a short while ago; we will run you. out of here." That is one of the remarks I heard.

SENATOR FALL. Did you hear what character of arms and ammunition had been cached by the Villistas in the mountains?

CAPT. WHEELER. I heard that, he had left most of his artillery in the mountains, but the arms spoken of at that time were their rifles. Most of his men were armed with Mausers.

SENATOR FALL. From information which you obtained through your deputies, and which you regarded as a reliable source, was the purpose disclosed of using those arms in connection with trouble at Bisbee?

CAPT. WHEELER. When the proper moment arose.

SENATOR FALL. Did you ever hear of the plan of San Diego, Captain?

CAPT. WHEELER. Yes, sir.

SENATOR FALL. Where did you first hear of it, do you know?

CAPT. WHEELER. I heard of it in various places. The time I remember best of all was in Tombstone. I heard a Mexican speak of it and say that the time would soon arrive when this country would be restored to Mexico, and the Mexicans would take their proper station; they would receive what was due them.

SENATOR FALL. That was the first time you heard of the plan of San Diego?

CAPT. WHEELER. I don't know that it was the first time; it was the time most distinct in my memory; I remember the Mexican and his looks; he was a stranger in town

SENATOR FALL. By this country being restored to Mexico he meant Arizona?

CAPT. WHEELER. Arizona and these border States.

SENATOR FALL. The border States which had formerly been a part of Mexico; and at Bisbee you heard at least one Mexican say that in a short time—they had run these American miners out of Cananea—in a short time they would run them out of Bisbee?

CAPT. WHEELER. "We ran you out of Cananea; we will run you out of here."

SENATOR FALL. How many—about how many Mexican miners were there is Bisbee during these disturbances?

CAPT. WHEELER. Oh, that would be hard to say; I have seen about—extending probably four or five hundred yards in length, column of twos, each day marching up to the I. W. W. headquarters to receive their rations. The I. W. W. was feeding them, all of them on strike.

SENATOR FALL. These were Mexicans?

CAPT. WHEELER. Mexicans; and, of course, a great many Mexicans did not cease work, and there were many Mexicans in camp not interested one way or another.

SENATOR FALL. Now, who were these Mexicans who were being fed by the I. W. W., as near as you could ascertain; where were they from?

CAPT. WHEELER. I believed, and still believe, the majority of them were former Villistas.

SENATOR FALL. Soldiers in Villa's army?

CAPT. WHEELER. Ex-soldiers.

SENATOR FALL. And you had reasons to believe that more than one of them knew of the arms which had been left by Villa?

CAPT. WHEELER. Absolutely.

SENATOR FALL. Did you have any reason to fear that some arms might be used by these Mexicans in connection with threatened disturbances at Bisbee?

CAPT. WHEELER. Yes, sir; I did.

SENATOR FALL. Was this one of the reasons that guided you in pursuing the course which you did with reference to the lawless element at Bisbee?

CAPT. WHEELER. It was.

SENATOR FALL. Then there were several hundred Mexicans, who, as near as you could ascertain—the largest proportion of whom, as near as you could ascertain, had been with Villa, who were in Bisbee being fed by the I. W. W.?

CAPT. WHEELER, Yes, sir.

SENATOR FALL. And who were causing the disturbance there?

CAPT. WHEELER. Yes, sir.

SENATOR FALL. Now, do you know of any statement being made by the I. W. W. who were there to the Mexicans with reference to their purpose—how it would affect the Mexicans themselves?

CAPT. WHEELER. Yes, sir.

SENATOR FALL. What statement do you know of?

CAPT. WHEELER. I had arrested A. E. Embree, I believe under indictment now in the Federal court, one of the leaders of the I. W. W. He was brought to Tucson and tried in this court and acquitted by a jury; I believe eight of the jury were Mexicans, but during that trial the statement was sworn to by a Mexican whose name was Peralta—Antonio Peralta—saying that the Mexicans were induced to quit work. This was subsequent, all having been told by these head men in Bisbee, that it was to their interest that Germany should win the war; it was to the interest of the Mexicans and to Mexico that Germany should win the war. That was the inducement to them to cease work by the head men. That testimony can be corroborated because it is in the court records here in Tucson.

SENATOR FALL. Do you know whether the Mexican citizens passed backward and forward with comparative freedom across the line between Cananea and Bisbee about this time? You spoke of some.

CAPT. WHEELER. It is much more difficult now than it was in those days. In those days anyone could go a mile east or west of these ports and cross.

SENATOR FALL. The country is not very thickly settled?

CAPT. WHEELER. No, sir.

SENATOR FALL. And there is no canal or river such as exists below El Paso on the international boundary?

CAPT. WHEELER. No, sir.

SENATOR FALL. The boundary line between Arizona and Old Mexico generally, particularly that portion within your jurisdiction, simply is an imaginary line, marked by monuments, and in some places by wire fences?

MR. WHEELER. By wire fences; yes, sir.

SENATOR FALL. Now, Captain, to refer back a moment to what was known as the Bisbee trouble, resulting later in what was known as the Bisbee deportation cases, you took action upon your own initiative finally after appealing to both the State and the National Government, which was investigated by this committee of which you have spoken?

CAPT. WHEELER. Yes, sir.

SENATOR FALL. That action resulted in the driving out, or escorting out of Bisbee of quite a large number of people whom you regarded as threatening to disturb the peace of other law-abiding citizens of Bisbee?

CAPT. WHEELER. Yes, sir; and in the interest of the country, which at that time was in war.

SENATOR FALL. And threatening to cut off the production of copper, which was necessary to this country in carrying on the war?

CAPT. WHEELER. Yes, sir.

SENATOR FALL. You took the action which you did under those conditions and under that belief.'

CAPT. WHEELER. Yes, sir. I will state had it been in time of peace that action would not have been taken.

SENATOR FALL. Was the gravity of the situation there, in your judgment, increased by the fact that there were a large number of Mexicans over there from the other side, and the fact that it was claimed that they knew where there were at least a thousand rifles cached which they could avail themselves of at the proper time when that time might arise. Did those facts increase the gravity of the situation as you understood it?

CAPT. WHEELER. Yes, sir; as I said before it was a factor in summing up the situation.

SENATOR FALL. Did you know of arms which could be supplied from any other particular source?

CAPT. WHEELER. Senator, these men, the majority of them, were strangers. We did not know where they came from. We did not know what they had. While I did not see arms on them exactly they would not work around in their shirt sleeves with arms, though they may have had arms in their domicile, or out in the hills in caches.

SENATOR FALL. Did you have information leading you to believe there were any large caches of arms available outside of these which you have mentioned, as available to the Mexicans who were among those strikers?

CAPT. WHEELER. No, sir.

SENATOR FALL. Did you, from what you have learned, and your observation, did you believe—is it your opinion that any number of Mexicans around through the State, Bisbee or elsewhere, Tombstone or elsewhere in Arizona, actually believed that the proper moment would arrive when, through the activities of Mexicans, assisted by others, that a successful attempt might be made to restore Arizona to Mexico?

CAPT. WHEELER. We did not think it would be successful.

SENATOR FALL. No; but did you learn—entertain the idea—that the Mexicans themselves believed it?

CAPT. WHEELER. Oh, yes, sir.

SENATOR FALL. That they were confident that such an opportunity would arise.

CAPT. WHEELER. They even went to the extent of organizing; a working nucleus of organization was called into existence.

SENATOR FALL. In accordance with the general plan of San Diego?

CAPT. WHEELER. And we had rifle clubs in this country formed. At one time we feared they were going to take things into their own hands but that was prevented by this deportation.

7. U.S. Congress Imposes Restrictions on Migration, 1917

CHAP. 29.—An Act To regulate the immigration of aliens to, and the residence of aliens in, the United States.

Be it enacted by the Senate and House of Representatives of the United States of America in Congress assembled.

Sec. 2. That there shall be levied, collected, and paid a tax of $8 for every alien, including alien seamen regularly admitted as provided in this Act, entering the United States: That the said tax shall not be levied on account of aliens who enter the United States after an uninterrupted residence of at least one year immediately preceding such entrance in the Dominion of Canada, Newfoundland, the Republic of Cuba, or the Republic of Mexico, for a temporary stay.

SEC. 3. That the following classes of aliens shall be excluded from admission into the United States: All idiots, imbeciles, feeble-minded persons, epileptics, insane persons; persons who have had one or more attacks of insanity at any time previously; persons of constitutional psychopathic inferiority; persons with chronic alcoholism; paupers; professional beggars; vagrants; persons afflicted with tuberculosis in any form or with a loathsome or dangerous contagious disease; persons not comprehended within any of the foregoing excluded classes who are found to be and are certified by the examining surgeon as being mentally or physically defective, such physical defect being of a nature which may affect the ability of such alien to earn a living; persons who have been convicted of or admit having committed a felony or other crime or misdemeanor involving moral turpitude; polygamists, or persons who practice polygamy or believe in or advocate the practice of polygamy; anarchists, or persons who believe in or advocate the overthrow by force or violence of the Government of the United States, or of all forms of law, or who disbelieve in or are opposed to organized government, or who advocate the assassination of public officials, or who advocate or teach the unlawful destruction of property; persons who are members of or affiliated with any organization entertaining and teaching disbelief in or opposition to organized government, or who advocate or teach the duty, necessity, or propriety of the unlawful assaulting or killing of any officer or officers, either of specific individuals or of officers generally, of the Government of the United States or of any other organized government, because of his or their official character, or who advocate or teach the unlawful destruction of property; prostitutes,

An Act to Regulate the Immigration of Aliens to, and the Residence of Aliens in, the United States.
H.R. 10384; Pub.L. 301; 39 Stat. 874. 64th Congress; Feb. 5, 1917.

or persons coming into the United States for the purpose of prostitution or for any other immoral purpose; persons who directly or indirectly procure or attempt to procure or import prostitutes or persons for the purpose of prostitution or for any other immoral purpose; persons who are supported by or receive in whole or in part the proceeds of prostitution; persons hereinafter called contract laborers, who have been induced, assisted, encouraged, or solicited to migrate to this country by offers or promises of employment, whether such offers or promises are true or false, or in consequence of agreements, oral, written or printed, express or implied, to perform labor in this country of any kind, skilled or unskilled; persons who have come in consequence of advertisements for laborers printed, published, or distributed in a foreign country; persons likely to become a public charge.

8. Mexican Migrants Protest Gasoline Baths, 1917

Order to Bathe Starts Near Riot Among Juarez Women.

Auburn-Haired Amazon at Santa Fe Street Bridge Leads Feminine Outbreak.

Rumor Among Servant Girls That Quarantine Officers Photograph Bathers in the Altogether Responsible for Wild Scenes.

Luckless Laborer Mistakes Character of Demonstrations, Shouts "Viva Villa," and His Career Is Promptly Ended by Bullets from Carranza Cavalry.

Street Carts Seized and Detained for Hours and Conductors and Motormen, One with a Black Eye, Are Escorted Back to El Paso.

Juarez women, incensed at the American quarantine regulations, led a riot yesterday morning at the Santa Fe Bridge. From the time the street cars began to run until the middle of the afternoon thousands of Mexicans thronged the Juarez side of the river and pushed out to the tollgate on the bridge. Women ringleaders of the mob hurled stones at American civilians, both on the bridge and on the streets of Juarez. Four street cars which crossed into Juarez early in the morning were seized, and the eight members of the crew sent afoot back to El Paso, one of the bringing a black eye and bruised face as a memento. A Villa sympathizer who started a diversion during the excitement by shouting "Death to Carranza! Viva Villa!" was promptly shot by a Carranza soldier. Four bullets took effect, killing him instantly.

    Mounted Men Disperse Crowd.

    Toward the middle of the afternoon, when the excitement had died down somewhat, mounted men disperse the crowd on the Juarez side of the bridge. American soldiers also forced back the Mexicans on the bridge to the international line at the middle of the river, the Mexicans having previously pushed as far as the tollgate, where they hung over the railing to jeer their compatriots who entered the bathhouse to comply with the requirements.

El Paso Times, Jan. 29, 1917, p. 1.

Street Car Traffic Interrupted.

The street cars which had been stopped in Juarez were brought back about 2 o'clock, undamaged. A Mexican official brought the first one to the middle of the bridge and volunteers were obtained by the street car company to go after the others. Car service to Juarez was resumed about 3 o'clock, but after one car made the trip it was discontinued for the rest of the day.

False Reports Responsible for the Trouble.

When women were ordered to get off the street cars and submit to being bathed and disinfected before passing to the American side the rioting started. Reports were circulated that the women were being insulted in the bathhouse and photographed while nude. The greater part of them refused to go to the bath and became indignant when they were ordered off the street cars after having paid their fares, and could not have their nickels refunded.

Carmelita Torres Leads Demonstration

When refused permission to enter El Paso without complying with the regulations the women collected in an angry crowd at the corner of the bridge. By 8 o'clock the throng, consisting in large part of servant girls employed in El Paso, had grown until it packed the bridge half way across. Led by Carmelita Torres, an auburn-haired young woman of 17, they kept up a continuous volley of language aimed at the immigration and health officers, civilians, sentries, and other visible Americans. Small stones were thrown, but the missiles were little more dangerous than the language. Some few automobiles which braved the fury and pushed through to the other side were showered with mud and stones.

Motormen's Grotesque Revenge

One of the streetcar motormen, finally making his way back to the American side, emerged from the mob with half a dozen women clinging to him endeavoring to drag him down. The controllers of the street cars were carried away by the women and used for weapons or thrown into the river.

Carranza cavalrymen were unable during the morning to make any headway against the crowd, although they drew their sabers threateningly. Women laughingly caught their bridles and turned the horses aside, holding the soldiers sabers and whips.

American sentries had to be placed under the bridge to prevent Mexicans from jumping off upon the sand and reaching the American side in that manner. Those sentries were exposed to the marksmanship of a gang of small Mexican boys, who threw sticks and mud.

Carranza Cavalry Arrive

One of the significant incidents of the disturbances across the river yesterday morning was the actions of the Mexican military authorities in parading their forces on Juarez avenue. Not only was the civil population of Juarez permitted to make a disgusting exhibition, but the Mexican soldiers were turned out as though to encourage the civilians in their anti-cleanup demonstration.

A surprisingly large number of soldiers were revealed when the Mexican commander marshaled his forces on the avenue. With the famous skull and crossbones flag of the Murgia division flying and a band playing the forces of General Murgia made a picturesque showing. Just why they were placed on parade could not be fathomed by the few Americans who happened to see them.

At the American end of the bridge quiet efficiency prevailed. The handful of American soldiers who patrolled the grounds around the customs house continued to walk their beats just as though a seething Latin mob scene was not being enacted a few feet away.

Girls Attack Automobiles

Those who witnessed the actions of the Mexican mob at the end of the bridge will never forget it … the mob remained bent on destroying anything that came from the American side. As soon as an automobile would cross the line the girls would absolutely cover it. The hands of the feminine mob would claw and tear at the tops of the cars. The glass windows of the autos were torn out, the tops torn to pieces and parts of the fitting such as lamps and horns were torn away. All of this happened in view of the Mexican military, who had a sufficient force at hand to stop any kind of difficulty. But the commanders and the soldiers seemed in sympathy with the mob. The impulse was to injure and insult Americans as much as possible without actually committing murder.

Jose Maria Sanchez Stops Bullets

Later in the morning, when the crowd had grown to several thousand, including a large percentage of men, the Villa sympathizer above mentioned made his unfortunate outbreak and received the four bullets. His name was given as Jose Maria Sanchez, a laborer.

Consul General Garcia Appeals to Crowd

About 10 o'clock, Andres Garcia, Mexican consul general, drove out upon the bridge in his automobile and succeeded, to some extent, in quieting the mob. When he started back to the American side the crowd seized the wheels of his car, endeavoring to keep him on the Mexican side. An automobile carrying mail was turned back when it tried to cross in to Juarez, the crowd refusing to give way and ordering the driver's return to El Paso.

Mexicans Survive Bath

Early in the afternoon, as Mexicans continued to come out of the bathhouse without appreciable injury, the crowd began to break up. Mounted Mexican soldiers drove them away from the river bank and cleared the end of the bridge, allowing none to pass the custom house except those who wished to enter El Paso. Similar restrictions had been put into effect on the American side. Crowds of spectators had gathered near the El Paso end of the bridge to watch the excitement, and groups were strung for some distance along the banks.

Bad Day for Americans

There were few Americans visiting in Juarez yesterday, as the early developments caused immigration officials to warn all who attempted to cross. Dozens turned back every hour on being informed that it was a "bad day for Americans." Some Americans who went to the race track made their return without being interfered with. Others had to run the gauntlet of rocks and abuse, and there were rumors of several Americans resenting insults and being jailed, but these reports were not confirmed. Consul General Garcia, after a trip through Juarez in the afternoon, said there had been no disturbance of consequence except at the bridge. He said no American had been arrested, and declared that the report of the Villista killed was untrue. He said four shots were fired to frighten rioters.

Amusement Resorts Closed

The race track, gambling houses and amusement places of Juarez were closed all day.

In spite of protests made by so many, there were enough Mexicans who submitted to the orders of the immigration officers to keep the bathhouse and disinfection equipment busy. Each individual who crossed the bridge was questioned and inspected, and the greater part of them ordered to the cleaning house. They came out with clothes wrinkled from the steam sterilizer, hair wet and faces shining, generally laughing and in good humor. The immigration men predict that as soon as the Mexicans become familiar with the bathing process they will not only submit to it but welcome it.

At east one "professional bather" has already been developed by the quarantine. A man of about 60 years was found to be taking his fifth cleansing of the day, with the object of selling the certificates to his countrymen.

Certificates Required of Travelers

The certificates read "United States Public Health Service, Mexican Border Quarantine. The bearer, ...has been this day deloused, bathed, vaccinated, clothing and baggage disinfected."

No railroad tickets will be issued out of the city to Mexicans unless such certificates are presented. Many Mexicans were refused transportation yesterday for this reason.

The owner of a bathhouse in Juarez was among the instigators of the riot and was seen inciting the women throughout the morning.

Many laughable incidents were reported by the health officers, quoting their conversations with Mexicans ordered to the baths. One argued eloquently that he had bathed well in July. Another put up a logical debate with the officers, alleging there was more typhus in El Paso than Juarez, proving American methods wrong.

∿ ESSAYS

The U.S.-Mexico border played a key role in the Mexican Revolution, and in turn the Revolution transformed the border. In the first essay, Friedrich Katz, formerly a history professor at the University of Chicago, describes how the policies of the Porfirian regime in northern Mexico helped cause the Mexican Revolution. In need of self-sustaining settlements that could form a military bulwark against the formidable Apaches, national leaders had granted many northern settlements more political rights and economic independence than was typical of Mexico's peasantry. These communities governed themselves and enjoyed a comparatively egalitarian distribution of land and livestock. But in the 1880s, the conquest of Apaches and other Indian peoples (described in Chapter 9 of this volume) removed the need for such treatment. Economic development, especially railroads, made northern lands attractive targets for appropriation by regional elites and leading figures in Díaz's circles. Increasingly alienated by the Díaz regime, northern communities became the mainstay of the Revolution. And they had a critical resource that other regions of Mexico lacked: the border with the United States, which gave them access to arms and sanctuary.

The Revolution had enormous impacts north of the border as well. In the second essay, University of Wisconsin-Milwaukee historian Benjamin H. Johnson examines the failed uprising in south Texas associated with the Plan of San Diego (Document 4). The attempted rebellion prompted a massive and violent backlash, one which accelerated the dispossession of Mexican Americans and heightened racial tension with Anglos. On the other hand, Johnson argues, it prompted a key group of Tejanos to seek their rights as American citizens, thus helping to launch a Mexican-American civil rights movement. The Mexican Revolution continued to reverberate in the borderlands and beyond, if in unpredictable ways.

Mexico's Northern Border and the Coming of the Revolution

FRIEDRICH KATZ

Prior to Díaz's assumption of power, the states of Sonora, Chihuahua, and Coahuila enjoyed a fair measure of autonomous existence. Remote and isolated, not just from the rest of Mexico but from the rest of the world as well, and well-nigh independent politically and self-sufficient economically, they formed the mainstay of Mexico's northern "frontier." In the last quarter of the nineteenth century, however, with the advent of Díaz and the influx of unprecedented amounts of foreign, especially American, capital into Mexico, the country's northern frontier underwent a radical change when Díaz and the United States, respectively, imposed their political and economic controls on the region. Railway construction, begun in the 1880s, offered the most dramatic piece of evidence of the degree to which the former enclave was to be integrated into the rest of Mexico and the American sphere of influence. The railways illustrated in the most palpable way possible that what had once been a frontier was being transformed into "the border" and that what had once been largely beyond the reach of any country was now within the reach of two countries at once.

The political transformation was launched when Díaz set out to demolish systematically the almost independent principalities that regional caudillos such as Ignacio Pesqueira in Sonora and Luis Terrazas in Chihuahua had established.

The economic transformation was mainly the work of American investments that began pouring into all of Mexico at unprecedented rates during the 1880s. Northern Mexico had always had a large share of this investment. By 1902, for instance, more than 22 percent of all U.S. investment in Mexico had gone into these three northern states, 6.3 percent went to Chihuahua, 7.3 percent to Sonora, and 9.5 percent to Coahuila, primarily in mining, farming, and transportation.

Friedrich Katz, *The Secret War in Mexico* (Chicago: University of Chicago Press, 1981), 7–21.

The repercussions of this dual transformation of the frontier, the political and the economic one, caught up most quickly and unkindly with the very people who had done the most to make the frontier habitable in the first place and who were its unique product: the military colonists. In the mid-eighteenth century, the Spanish crown had established military colonies along the northern frontier to fend off roaming bands of Apaches and other nomads. The method employed was always the same: land along this frontier was granted to anyone willing to take possession of it and defend it with his life. In the nineteenth century, Benito Juarez followed this example and established more such colonies.

The inhabitants of the colonies were privileged in many respects compared to the free villagers of central and southern Mexico. Unlike the villagers, they were not wards of the crown during the colonial period but enjoyed rights generally reserved for Spaniards and their descendants, the criollos. They owned their land individually and were allowed to sell it, or buy additional land. They usually owned more land and more cattle than the free peasants of Mexico's other areas. Their communities were entitled to greater internal autonomy, and the military colonists had not only the right but the duty to bear arms.

By 1885 great changes took place in the Mexican frontier region. The Apaches were finally defeated, and the frontier became appreciably quieter. Neither the hacendados nor the government any longer needed the military support of the peasants, but what they felt they did need was the land the peasants had so assiduously reclaimed, and they felt no qualms about turning against their former allies.

After the first railways linked northern Mexico to the central parts of the country and to the United States in 1885, the increasing value of the peasants' land ushered in a wave of expropriation. First hit were the most recently established settlements, but even the oldest and most prestigious ones were not spared. Resentment was acute. "We are deeply concerned that lands we consider our own, since we have received them from our fathers and worked them with our own hands, are now passing into other hands," the inhabitants of the village of Namiquipa wrote to President Díaz in 1908 (without much success).

The northern military communities lost not only their lands but also their cherished political rights, the most precious among them their municipal autonomy. The right of a village to elect its own municipal authorities had been conferred on many settlements in the eighteenth century by the Spanish crown. The right was reconfirmed after independence and extended to newly founded settlements as well. The greatest guarantor of that autonomy, however, was not the official charter of any short-lived government but the atomized and isolated pattern of settlements that prevailed along the frontier until about the mid-nineteenth century. Because it was no longer a factor after Díaz came to power, state authorities were able to disregard with impunity those hallowed rights and traditions and to usurp for themselves the privilege of appointing such officials as the *jefes políticos* (district administrators) and *presidentes municipales* (mayors) at their own discretion.

The loss of municipal autonomy aroused almost as much passion as the loss of land. On 16 November 1910, when the populace of the old frontier village of Cuchillo Parado shouldered their rifles and enlisted in the revolutionary forces, the removal of the mayor who had been imposed on them was the most burning issue. And it was the removal of a popularly elected mayor by the state authorities and his replacement by a village usurer that drove the inhabitants of the mountain town of Bachíniva in Chihuahua to join the revolution in 1910.

While peasant unrest did not assume revolutionary proportions until 1910, the expropriation of land and the suppression of traditional rights did precipitate sporadic uprisings long before the revolution began. In Chihuahua, for instance, the government lost more than five hundred men in a two-year struggle with about sixty insurgent peasants of the village of Tomochic, who, in 1892, declared themselves bound only by the law of God and revolted against the encroachments of the government.

Repercussions of the frontier transformation affected another group of peasants, the Indian tribes that had managed to retain their lands and a measure of autonomy throughout the Spanish colonial period as well as during the first half-century of independence. Unlike the military colonists who were mainly concentrated in Chihuahua, the most militant Indian tribe came from the neighboring state of Sonora. They were the Yaqui Indians, who inhabited one of the most fertile regions of Sonora, the Yaqui Valley. Several abortive attempts to seize their lands had been made before, but it was not until Díaz came to power that a concentrated offensive was mounted to expel them from their lands. The offensive met with fierce resistance. Long and bloody battles took a heavy toll on both sides, and, although the federal troops finally succeeded in defeating the most formidable force among the Yaquis and in capturing its leader Cajeme, they never managed to root out all guerrilla resistance.

Both of these traditional peasant groups—the frontiersmen and the Indians—thus found themselves helpless in the face of blatant assaults on their property and independence until the turn of the century. The only allies they found before 1900 were former caudillos, landowners who had been ousted from positions of political power.

The peasants, however, did not receive the support of any nonrural classes in these states before 1900. The simple reason was that the transformation of the frontier had beneficial effects for the middle classes and the industrial working class who therefore had little reason to support the fighting peasants. Foreign investment in such projects as railroad construction greatly multiplied the economic opportunities of these classes and, until 1900, brought about a significant rise in real wages. Moreover, Díaz's overthrow of the old political oligarchies had created vacancies that the middle class was able to fill and from which it was able to exercise, for a time at least, some real power, until once more displaced by another emerging oligarchy.

Not until 1900–1910 was the favorable disposition of these groups toward the regime reversed, for, in those ten years, foreign investment began to show its ugly underside. It was accelerating at a breathtaking rate: between 1900 and 1910 investments in Mexico leaped to three times the amount invested between 1876 and 1900. One of the results of this increase was a soaring inflation rate that cut deep into the real wages of the middle and industrial working classes and sharply curtailed the investment opportunities of middle class entrepreneurs by tightening available credit. The government added to the burden on these two groups when it sought to raise their taxes to make up for the reduced value of taxes paid by foreign investors and the local oligarchy. Another result of increased foreign investment was a heightened vulnerability to the business cycle of the United States, which manifested itself most painfully during the economic crisis of 1907. Again the burden on the middle and working classes was increased by an external factor—the return of thousands of Mexican workers discharged from American mines and factories during each recession.

For the middle classes, falling income and rising taxes constituted only two elements of a rapidly deteriorating social and economic situation. Between 1900 and 1910 their opportunities for upward mobility were dramatically reduced through new political structures implemented by Díaz in northern Mexico. In the last years of his regime Díaz gave up his attempts to divide political from economic power and to limit the political power of the regional oligarchies in their native states. As a result political positions and patronage jobs, which in Mexico had always been crucial to the survival of the middle classes, came under the exclusive control of the state's oligarchies. At the same time these powerful groups exercised an increasing degree of control over regional and local authorities, frequently a traditional fiefdom of the middle classes. Among the latter a profound resentment against the state's oligarchies began to emerge.

Discontent within the industrial working class and the middle classes manifested itself in an upsurge of nationalist sentiment and growing resentment toward foreign investors, who were largely held responsible for their plight, and toward the Díaz regime, which refused to curtail their advance. In the final account, then, despite an auspicious beginning, the transformation of the frontier eroded support for the Díaz regime among the nonrural population.

In this period manifestations of discontent also emerged among a rural group that until then had remained passive and docile to both the large landowners and the state and national governments. These were the traditional hacienda peons, a sector of the agrarian population that, since the colonial period, was proportionately much more prominently represented in the North than anywhere else in the country.

On northern haciendas, an important role was played by yet another group, present in the South only to a limited extent—the vaqueros, or cowboys. Cattle raising, naturally enough, became the chief industry in those regions of northern Mexico where the lack of an adequate water supply had severely checked the spread of agriculture. The vaqueros were well armed and often owned their own horses; they were indeed a privileged class. They were better off than the peasants, many owned their own cattle, which grazed on the hacienda lands, and their opportunities for social mobility were greater than were those of the peasants. For every seven or eight vaqueros, there was a foreman who received twice the salary of a regular cowboy. Anyone who remained on the hacienda long enough had a good chance of rising to this position. On the whole, then, the situation of resident workers on northern haciendas was better than that of their counterparts elsewhere in Mexico, and yet their relations with the hacendados often were more antagonistic.

This antagonism may be explained by the breakdown of the patriarchal relationship between the traditional peon (whose ancestors in most cases had lived on the hacienda for centuries) and the hacendado, a relationship that had characterized both northern and central Mexico for the greater part of the nineteenth century. It continued to characterize central Mexico even during the revolutionary period, for here many peons had become a kind of privileged retainer on haciendas where the bulk of the laborers consisted of expropriated peasants. Such was not the case, however, in the North, for on the eve of the revolution, Luis Terrazas complained bitterly, "Since the beginning of the unrest, I have been trying to arm the peons of my haciendas, but, I must tell you honestly these workers are infected with ideas of revolution and only a few of them are loyal to me. Arming disloyal people, as you shall see, would be counterproductive because they will go over to the enemy with their weapons and equipments." This breakdown of patriarchal bonds on northern estates was not due to a lack of effort on the part of the hacendados to maintain them. Luis Terrazas made it a point to visit each of his haciendas at least once a year. On those occasions a holiday was declared, and the peons lined up to receive him and the gifts he brought. He went to great pains to remember the name and history of each peon.

But the transformation of the frontier tended to vitiate those efforts. First, the traditional patriarchal relationship was strained intolerably by the enormous growth of the estate holdings of Terrazas and other barons of the North, which made it more and more difficult for the landowners to establish personal relationships with their peons. Second, it was drained of much of its meaning with the defeat of the Apaches in 1884. Until then the hacendado, like the medieval lord of Europe, had been able to offer protection from attacks by furnishing his peons with a safe refuge in his thickly fortified *casco* (the central residence hall of the hacienda which in northern Mexico had been built as both a refuge and a fortress) and by sending out retainers to fight the wandering Indian bands. When the attacks ceased, that protection was no longer needed. Characteristically, the one region in northern Mexico where relations between peons and hacendados remained the closest—many hacendados even armed their peons and led them into the revolution—was southern Sonora, where the danger of attacks by rebellious Yaquis persisted. Third, the patriarchal relationship was undermined by the peons' growing awareness of higher wages and better living conditions on ranches in the neighboring United States. Thousands of them, especially vaqueros, left to find work on the ranches of the American Southwest. Those who returned to Mexico did so with fresh doubts about the patriarchal goodness of the Mexican hacendados, who paid them a fraction of what they had earned in the United States.

One additional element of discontent seems to have been limited mainly to the peons on the huge Terrazas haciendas of Chihuahua. Here, in contrast to the great majority of all haciendas in the North, restrictions on the freedom of movement of many peons, such as debt peonage, had not disappeared. The old caudillo's unwillingness to break with traditional forms of servitude was combined with a unique capacity to avoid doing so. Because of his enormous economic and political power, Terrazas had the means, which few other northern hacendados possessed, to enforce an increasingly unpopular system of debt peonage among his largely recalcitrant laborers.

In contrast to the "traditional" peons found mainly in Chihuahua, and to a lesser degree in Sonora, a new kind of "modern" estate laborer emerged, especially in the third state that was to provide an important segment of the northern revolutionary movement—Coahuila.

The term "modern peon" is perhaps the most appropriate one to designate the thousands of migrants from central Mexico, many of them expropriated peasants, who streamed into the newly developed regions of northern Mexico. The majority settled in a small area where perhaps the most rapid economic growth of the Porfirian period took place, the Laguna area of Coahuila and Durango. In its cotton fields they earned the highest agricultural wages paid anywhere in Mexico. In addition, all forms of forced labor, such as debt servitude, had practically disappeared in that region. Even the *tienda de raya,* the ubiquitous company store, was different in the Laguna from that on most haciendas in Mexico. Workers were paid in cash rather than scrip and thus were not obliged to limit their purchases to the company store. The hacendados, who frequently charged lower prices in their shops than neighboring merchants, used the *tienda de raya* as a supplementary incentive to attract scarce laborers rather than as a means to increase their profits or to force workers to remain on their estates.

In spite of these advantages the region where these immigrants had settled, especially the Laguna, became an inexhaustible reservoir of revolutionary troops in the years 1910–20. The basic reason for this was not primarily opposition to the region's landowners. By comparing their situation with conditions in central and northern Mexico, from whence they had come, many migrants saw it in a favorable light. Only twenty years and one generation later would the Laguna's peasants (now born and bred in the North) turn against the region's estate owners.

In the 1910–20 revolution in fact many of the permanent resident peons on the haciendas revolted not against but together with their hacendados. Like medieval lords in Europe, some of the landowners of Sonora and the Laguna even led their well-paid and well-treated peons into battle.

By 1910 only one Mexican group finally benefited from the transformation of the frontier, the new caudillo class in Chihuahua and Sonora, which had begun to rise from the ashes of the old one in the last quarter of the nineteenth century.

The new class was an amalgam of "blue-blooded" and upstart caudillo dynasties. Some of the older ones who had been removed from power in the course of Díaz's transformation were able to make a comeback. Most prominent among them was the Terrazas clan, which made its peace with Díaz in 1903: Luis Terrazas was reappointed to the governorship of Chihuahua, to which he was succeeded by his son-in-law Enrique Creel and somewhat later by his son Alberto Terrazas. Other members of the new caudillo class were recruited by Diaz from the lower end of the old ruling stratum in the course of his political revamping of the region. Most prominent of these were Luis and Lorenzo Torres, military men who headed Díaz's faction in Sonora during Díaz's successful revolt of 1876; they ousted Ignacio Pesqueira, who had dominated the state for many years.

The caudillos of Coahuila were an exception to all this. Unlike Sonora and Chihuahua, Coahuila saw no lasting alliance formed between the new oligarchy and the Díaz government. In fact, by the time the new century dawned, the two were in open conflict.

In 1885, Porfirio Díaz had sent a close confidant, General Bernardo Reyes, to the northeastern states of Nuevo León and Coahuila as military commander with the directive to break the hold of the local caudillos so that their power could be assumed by the central government. Reyes was successful at first, but after he was appointed governor of Nuevo León in 1887 he allied himself closely with the old oligarchic circles and became one of the most powerful caudillos in Mexico. He was able to increase his already considerable support in the armed forces when he was given the post of minister of defense in 1900. He became the only new caudillo to call into question the power of Mexico's financial and political oligarchy, popularly called the Científicos because they espoused Auguste Comte's positivism and Herbert Spencer's social Darwinism. The ambitions of Reyes and the northeastern groups tied to him soon aroused the mistrust of Díaz, who sent Reyes back to Nuevo León in 1903 and put an end to his role as minister of defense.

The mounting enthusiasm that part of the northeast's upper classes (and to a lesser degree some Sonoran hacendados) manifested toward Reyes led to an increasing hostility toward them on the part of the Díaz administration. Unlike the elites of Chihuahua and Sonora, some of whose representatives Díaz had accepted into his administration, the wealthy and powerful merchants and landowners of the Laguna were excluded from representation in the federal government.

Díaz's opposition to this group of the northeastern elite as well as the latter's mounting bitterness may have been compounded by their increasing conflicts with foreign interests. The best-known, but by no means unique, conflict of this kind concerned the Laguna's (and probably all of Coahuila's) wealthiest family, the Maderos. (This family had never supported Reyes but one of its most prominent members, Francisco Madero, had for some years attempted to set up political opposition to the Díaz administration.) In contrast to the Torres and Terrazas families, the Madero clan, which was the wealthiest and most powerful family in Mexico's northeastern region, had never cooperated harmoniously with the U.S. companies and had become notorious among those companies for its ill-concealed confrontation tactics. At the turn of the twentieth century, Francisco Madero had formed and led a coalition of hacendados in the Laguna region to oppose attempts by the Anglo-American Tlahualilo Company to monopolize the water rights of that irrigation-dependent area. When the Maderos cultivated the rubber substitute guayule, they had clashed with the Continental Rubber Company. Another conflict developed because prior to 1910 the Maderos owned the only smelting oven in northern Mexico that was independent of the American Smelting and Refining Company.

The Maderos were not alone in their fight. Many other members of the northeastern upper class were interested in water rights in the Laguna, in the cultivation of guayule, and in the operation of independent smelting ovens in northern Mexico.

Most of the Laguna had been unpopulated wasteland before the hacendados reclaimed it. They did not have to confront a mass of peasants whom they had expropriated. The fact that the peons on their estates received the highest wages and enjoyed the greatest freedom found anywhere in the Mexican countryside had created a new kind of paternalistic relation between these landowners and their peons. The hacendados attempted to strengthen this relationship by providing schools and medical care to their workers. Some enlightened landowners, such as Francisco Madero, even extended many of these services to nonresident peons, thus earning their loyalty.

In the long run the hacendados' confidence in the passivity and loyalty of their peons proved to be completely unfounded. In the 1930s the second and third generation of Laguna peons set up the most militant peasant movement in Mexico. As a result the most radical agrarian reform that took place in Mexico in the thirties occurred in the Laguna. For the period 1910–20, however, with some significant exceptions, the hacendado's optimism was not unrealistic. Rather than rebel against the landowners, most of the peons of the Laguna preferred to join them in their fight against the federal government. Thus the northeast's hacendados, in addition to strong motivation to revolt, had a unique kind of mass support that allowed them to do so.

These uneven developments raise two obvious questions: Why did the North become the mainstay of the Mexican Revolution from which both its victorious leaders and armies emerged? And why, among the many frontier regions that developed on the American continent, was northern Mexico practically the only one where a large scale and successful revolutionary movement took place?

The answer to the first question is obviously linked to the rapid, largely foreign-induced, economic change in the North which led to large-scale economic and social dislocation. Northern Mexico, however, was not the only region so affected. Rapid growth linked to dislocations occurred elsewhere in Mexico, for example, in Morelos, Veracruz, and Yucatán. Radical social movements did emerge in all those regions, though not simultaneously; the Zapata revolt broke out in Morelos in 1910, but in Veracruz and Yucatán radical protest movements developed in the 1920s.

What distinguished the revolution in northern Mexico from these other movements was the diversity of social classes and strata that joined the revolution, on the one hand, and the access of the northern revolutionaries to arms, on the other.

What was unique to the North was that substantial portions from all classes of society participated in the revolution. It was the only part of Mexico, for example, with a relatively large stratum of revolutionary hacendados, whose support for anti-Díaz political movements threw them into alliance with middle classes and even the lower classes of society.

A dissatisfied middle class which resented the fact that it was excluded from political power, that it seemed to garner only the crumbs of Mexico's economic boom, and that foreigners were playing an increasingly important role in the country's economic and social structure existed in most parts of Mexico.

Nowhere, however, had it grown as rapidly as in the North, and nowhere had it suffered such losses in so short a span of time. Not only was the northern middle class profoundly affected by the cyclical crises of 1907 that hit the North far more than any other part of Mexico, but it also suffered greater political losses. In the nineteenth century because of the isolation of the frontier states it had enjoyed a degree of municipal and regional autonomy which was equaled in no other part of the country. The absorption of the North by the central government cost this class most of these traditional rights.

Nevertheless these losses were at first compensated for by two advantages the Díaz regime brought them: one was rapid economic growth and the building of railroads from which many of them benefited. The other was what could be called the introduction of the two-party system into some of the northern states. In Chihuahua for instance, after he became president, Dìaz removed the traditional oligarchy from power and imposed his own men on the state. The Mexican president was not strong enough, however, to prevent the old ruling group from forming its own political party and challenging the new rulers of the state. In the resulting conflict both sides sought the support of the state's middle classes which thus gained a certain degree of political and economic leverage.

When Díaz, in a profound political reversal at the turn of the century, gave political control of their states to the oligarchy, he put an end to the two-party system and completely excluded large segments of the middle classes from political power. At the same time their economic situation grew drastically worse. They were first hit by inflation and rising taxes and many of them were ruined by the crisis of 1907–10.

The same crisis affected the North's industrial working classes to a degree unprecedented in their experience and unparalleled in the rest of Mexico. With the possible exception of the city of Mexico it was in the North of the country that the greatest number of unemployed workers could be found on the eve of the revolution.

Also the agricultural population of northern Mexico exhibited a number of traits that distinguished them from their counterparts in the rest of the country.

Because of the Apache wars, they had a far greater fighting tradition and more arms than peasants in any other part of the country. Because so many of them were engaged in industry and mining, many more peasants in the North had links to the nonagricultural population than in any other part of Mexico. The migrants and the vaqueros who formed a large part of the population of the northern countryside had no deep-rooted traditional attachment to a specific community.

These three factors were obviously conducive to their joining revolutionary armies.

To all of these characteristics that distinguished most social classes in the North from their counterparts in the rest of Mexico must be added a tradition of cooperation among all classes of society which first emerged in the Apache wars and which reemerged in the course of the revolution. While uprisings of peasants, industrial workers, and members of the middle classes occurred in different parts of Mexico, only in the North were all of them able to unite among themselves and to join forces with a group of revolutionary hacendados.

The proximity to the United States was the last element that helped to transform the dissatisfaction of nearly all segments and classes of frontier society into revolutionary activity. The transformation of the frontier into the border did more than change many frontiersmen into revolutionaries. It also gave them the means for carrying out a revolution. Proximity to the United States provided them with an easy solution to the perennial problem facing all revolutionaries—access to arms. In spite of its neutrality laws, the United States was used as a sanctuary by revolutionaries preparing to launch a movement in Mexico. The ideological consequences of the economic symbiosis between Mexico's frontier and the American Southwest were as strange as the practical ones. A pronounced anti-American nationalism was combined with the desire of the Mexican middle and working classes to obtain the rights and freedoms enjoyed by their counterparts in the United States.

All these elements provide an explanation of why the Mexican North played a role so different from the rest of the country during the revolution. It also helps to explain why the Mexican North was the only frontier region in Latin America which became a center of large-scale revolutionary activity.

The Mexican Revolution and the Birth of the Mexican-American Civil Rights Movement

BENJAMIN JOHNSON

One of the most prolonged episodes of racial violence in United States history occurred at the southern tip of Texas from 1915 to 1919. It began in the summer of 1915 as a series of raids on ranches, irrigation works, and railroads by ethnic Mexicans and quickly developed into a full-blown rebellion. Groups of armed men—some from across the Rio Grande, others seemingly from out of nowhere—stole livestock, burned railroad bridges, tore up tracks, killed farmers, attacked post offices, robbed stores, and repeatedly battled local posses, Texas Rangers, and the thousands of federal soldiers dispatched to quell the violence. The groups ranged from two or three assailants who quickly vanished into the brush to scores of well-organized and disciplined mounted men.

The rebels, who came to be called "Sediciosos" or "Seditionists," killed dozens of Anglo farmers. Many Anglo residents fled the region. Hundreds, perhaps several thousand, clustered in urban areas.

The raids appeared to be the fulfillment of a manifesto entitled the "Plan de San Diego." This document came to light early in 1915 but remained largely ignored until the outbreak of violence. It called for a "liberating army for races

Benjamin H. Johnson, "The Plan De San Diego Uprising and the Making of Modern of Texas-Mexican Borderlands," in *Continental Crossroads: Remapping U.S.-Mexico Borderlands History*, ed. Samuel Truett and Elliot Young, pp. 273–298 (Durham: Duke University Press, 2004). Copyright, 2004, Duke University Press. All rights reserved. Reprinted by permission of the publisher.

and peoples" composed of Mexicans, blacks, and Indians to kill all white males over the age of sixteen and overthrow United States rule in Texas, Colorado, New Mexico, Arizona, and California. The freed territory would form an independent nation, perhaps to rejoin Mexico at a future date. Modeled after other proclamations of the ongoing Mexican Revolution, the Plan seemed to promise—or threaten, depending on where one stood—that a revolution would erupt north of the Rio Grande.

The reprisals that followed the insurrectionary violence were even worse. Texas Rangers and local vigilantes led a brutal counterinsurgency that included indiscriminate harassment of ethnic Mexicans, forcible relocation of rural Tejanos, and mass executions. A San Antonio reporter observed that "finding of dead bodies of Mexicans, suspected for various reasons of being connected with the troubles, has reached a point where it creates little or no interest. It is only when a raid is reported or an American is killed that the ire of the people is aroused." On a single day in late 1915, for example, "near Edinburg ... the bodies of two more Mexicans were found. They had been slain during the night. During the morning the decapitated body of another Mexican roped to a large log floated down the Rio Grande." Respectable citizens openly made statements of near-genocidal racism: "The recent happenings in Brownsville country indicate that there is a serious surplus population there that needs eliminating," argued the editor of the *Laredo Times*.

At first glance these events seem sadly characteristic of the Southwest in the decades after its conquest by the United States. Ostensibly endowed with the full rights of citizenship by the 1848 Treaty of Guadalupe Hidalgo, many ethnic Mexicans remained north of the border. Those who stayed, and their descendents, saw the victorious Anglos seize political and economic power. Even many formerly proud landowners ended up doing field work on land that had once belonged to them. In some places—most notably, South Texas and northern New Mexico, but for several decades also southern California—ethnic Mexicans remained a majority. In these enclaves, Anglos generally inserted themselves into the preexisting social hierarchy, often marrying into elite Mexican families and relying on their paternalist social relations to wield power without constantly resorting to force.

In South Texas, although a political "machine" run by Anglos and their elite ethnic Mexican compatriots ruled for nearly seventy years, popular resentment of marginalization and racism led to instances of open and even concerted rebellion. The region witnessed repeated clashes between defiant Tejanos and Rangers and other security forces. Two major uprisings, one led by Juan Cortina in 1859 and the other by Catarino Garza in 1891, were only defeated after intervention by the U.S. Army.

Such defiance was often articulated in the lingo of Mexican nationalism. Where their Anglo oppressors denigrated Mexican culture, rebels proclaimed their pride. Where Anglos celebrated the "manifest destiny" epitomized by their defeat of the Mexican nation, rebels often linked the protection of Mexicans in the United States to the redemption of the Mexican state.

A closer look at the tumult of the Plan de San Diego undermines this dualistic notion. The uprising not only became the occasion for massive and horrific racial violence but also precipitated protracted conflict among Tejanos. Its crushing defeat weakened the appeal of irredentist and Mexican nationalist politics, strengthening the position of those willing to use U.S. institutions and citizenship rights to advance the interests of ethnic Mexicans. Even as the Plan's failure solidified Anglo dominance and racial segregation in South Texas, it also helped push some Tejanos to embrace identities as Mexican Americans. Instead of continuing the contest of which nation would rule what territory, they aimed to change what United States rule would mean for those not of Anglo descent.

This essay examines the conflict between different Tejano factions during the Plan de San Diego uprising. In the decade before the uprising, ethnic Mexicans responded in divergent ways to an agricultural boom and consequent influx of Anglos. As their socioeconomic and political position became ever more tenuous, some continued to cooperate with the region's Anglo–dominated political machine. Others, inspired by the Mexican Revolution, advocated a violent redistribution of land. A third group, the "Tejano Progressives," embraced many of the region's economic changes even as it called for a revitalized Tejano community to combat discrimination and oppression. The revolt and backlash pit these groups against one another. The Texas-Mexico borderlands would continue to be influenced by the governments, capital, culture, and citizens of both Mexico and the United States. But the Plan de San Diego uprising transformed the pattern of future resistance to Anglo domination.

Cattle ranching, dominant since colonization by the Spanish empire in the mid-eighteenth century, lay at the heart of South Texas's social structure, politics, and identity. Though the U.S. conquest in 1848 did change the region, in many ways the Anglo newcomers assimilated themselves to Tejano social mores and institutions. Cattle ranching became more tightly linked to the U.S. market but remained the region's dominant economic institution. Anglos married into elite ranching families. Ethnic Mexicans were thus subordinated but not entirely dispossessed. They retained a measure of land, independence, and political power into the early twentieth century.

For the daily lives of Tejanos, 1904 was more of a turning point than 1848. On July 4, 1904, the first passenger train from the rest of the nation's railroad system arrived in Brownsville. The connection that it represented fatally undermined the social and political accommodation that Anglos and Tejanos had maintained for the previous six decades. By providing rapid and easy connection to major market centers, the railroad unleashed an agricultural boom. Real estate developers aggressively marketed the Lower Rio Grande Valley to farmers in Midwestern states, who soon flooded the area, founding dozens of new towns and nearly doubling the Valley's population in the years 1905–1910.

The agricultural boom subjected the ranching economy to a new set of pressures. Before the railroad, unimproved pastureland sold from fifty cents to two dollars per acre. By 1912, undeveloped land cost between one hundred and three hundred dollars an acre, and property that was easily irrigated or had particularly rich soil was sold for five hundred dollars or more per acre. These rapid increases strained the operations of *rancheros* who were not interested in or sufficiently capitalized to do well in this new market. Inability to pay property taxes led to a dramatic increase in the number of sheriff's sales of tax-delinqnent lands in Hidalgo County, sales that almost always transferred land from Tejanos to Anglos. The rise in land values also intensified conflict over land ownership. Land became too valuable to remain unoccupied or lightly used.

The combination of economic pressure, title challenges, and outright violent appropriation led to significant Tejano land loss shortly after the railroad's construction. From 1900 to 1910 Hispanic-surnamed individuals lost a total of more than 187,000 acres in Cameron and Hidalgo counties. In Hidalgo County during this decade, the percentage of rural land in Tejano hands declined from 28.6 percent to 16.8 percent. The corresponding drop in Cameron County was from 20 percent to 16.4 percent.

If the new agricultural economy strained the position of Tejanos, changing political dynamics in South Texas were even more hostile. Whereas Tejanos played an indispensable part in South Texas's political machine, the farmers' politics threatened to leave them with no political power at all. The newcomer farmers were fiercely antimachine, wanting little to do with what they perceived as a hopelessly corrupt political system that made the terrible mistake of enfranchising their racial inferiors. The solution to this problem, from their perspective, was simple: eliminate Tejano political power by disenfranchising those of Mexican descent. The tools for this strategy were readily at hand, for by 1910, Texas, like most of the South, had created the system of poll taxes, white primaries, and vigilante violence that all but stripped African Americans of the vote.

The new agricultural order affected Tejanos in different ways. Many became semimigrant laborers, working in towns like Brownsville or McAllen for part of the year, serving on land-grubbing crews, or picking crops from South Texas all the way to Oklahoma or Arkansas. A few prospered as merchants and land developers, carving out niches for themselves in sectors dominated by Anglo newcomers. And yet others continued as ranchers, whether as large market-driven businesses or small, subsistence-oriented family operations.

Tejano politics was similarly diverse. Some families continued to play an indispensable role in the machine as vote-deliverers and candidates for low to midlevel offices. In contrast, two more ideological factions of Tejano politics arose in the early twentieth century in response to the agricultural boom and influx of Anglos. Radicals, inspired by the Mexican Revolution, believed that violence was required to restore ethnic Mexican power in South Texas, a project which would in turn depend on the overall revitalization of Mexico vis-à-vis the United States. Others, whom I have termed "Tejano Progressives," saw hope in many of the political and ethnic developments of the Progressive Era United States. They encouraged ethnic Mexicans to combat their marginalization through economic success, education, and political power. They pointed to useful traditions and examples from both Mexico and the United States. These two currents fed both the Plan de San Diego and Mexican American politics.

Merchants and small businessmen of cities like Brownsville and Laredo, joined by elements of landed wealth, dominated Tejano progressivism. Progressives adapted many of the tenets of Mexican liberalism to the circumstances of life in the United States. The ideal liberal society was one dominated by autonomous individuals equal before the law, unrestrained by such corporate entities as an established church or Indian communities. A central government with powers authorized by a written constitution and private property rights were the foundational institutions for such a society. Liberal elites and intellectuals were vehemently anticlerical and opposed to village commons and other collective lands. As the industrial revolution lifted western Europe and the United States to new heights of economic wealth and global power, Mexican liberals struggled to modernize their own country by preparing and even forcing its citizens to compete in a market economy. Steeped in this liberal tradition, the Progressives argued that Tejanos needed education and economic success to overcome the racism and political corruption confronting them. They aimed inward, seeking to remold Tejanos as a modern people, and outward, to secure their rights in an increasingly racist society.

South Texas's agricultural boom stimulated Progressives with the hope that economic development would both make Tejanos more industrious and give them a much-needed base of economic security. Laredo's Idar family, writers and publishers of the influential newspaper *La Crónica,* were so impressed with the Valley's transformation that they called for ethnic Mexican landholders farther upstream to construct their own rail system. The Idars' compatriot in Brownsville, lawyer and politician José Tomás Canales, described the arrival of the railroad as "the beginning of a new era in the Valley: the Era of Progress."

An awareness of Tejano land loss and the rise of segregationist politics tempered this enthusiasm. The ascendant farmers were not content with just economic dominance but also failed to respect the established social and political position of ethnic Mexicans in South Texas. "The rapid industrial and agricultural development of the lower Rio Grande daily brings to our land … numerous elements unfamiliar with our prior rights as old inhabitants of the border," *La Crónica* noted in an article on Brownsville politics. Given "our lack of political foresight," the paper warned that "the newcomers," with their "new ideas, resources and lofty ambitions, will not hesitate to fleece us … of the representation that we have collectively exercised for many years in banking, commerce, society, and politics."

The rising tide of racial segregation elsewhere in Texas particularly alarmed Progressives. Tejanos who witnessed Jim Crow in the rest of Texas or other parts of the South often feared that they saw their own future in whites-only train cars, restaurants, and waiting rooms. If this was what deepening the border's ties with the rest of the country meant, then they wanted none of it.

Fears like García's haunted Progressives, who watched as Jim Crow subsumed more and more areas where Mexicans previously enjoyed a measure of political power and social respectability: "In San Antonio, Corpus Christi, Seguin, Goliad and other currently important cities, founded by Mexicans," lamented the Idars, "there is no public place for Mexicans except for the inferior and poorly-paid jobs allowed them."

Avoiding this fate, according to the Progressives, required Texas Mexicans to increase their power through individual education, ethnic unity, and economic success. Although the Progressive position obviously demanded changes from Anglos—an end to lynchings, an undoing of segregation, respect for Mexican culture and traditions—it also insisted that Tejanos transform themselves, collectivity and individually.

The Progressives held ambivalent and sometimes contradictory notions about their own national identity. They kept one foot planted in the soil of Mexican liberalism, frequently condemning Catholicism and other "superstitious" beliefs, while lauding such Mexican heroes as Benito Juárez. At the same time, they looked beyond Mexico to other ethnic and racial groups as examples of the successful implementation of their strategy. Clemente Idar called for "la Raza Mexicana" in Texas to follow the model of numerous ethnic groups within the United States. He hoped that Texas Mexicans would wield the same sort of political power that European ethnics exercised in the areas where they were numerically superior. Citing the Swedes in Minnesota as the preeminent example of such a group, Idar argued that "in this country, from its founding, even when all lived loyally under the national flag and as American citizens, its inhabitants have always divided themselves into peaceful factions along lines of racial origin."

Despite an important sense of kinship, Tejanos were for the Progressives different from Mexico-born Mexicans. "They have their own ways of living in their own country," Emeterio Flores said of Mexican nationals, "and it is absolutely different from ours. We people who were born in this country feel for them because they are our own race, although we were born and educated here in this country; we feel for those poor unfortunates, and we would not like to see them come here any more unless "conditions changed a great deal."

Tejano Progressives harbored a similarly ambivalent attitude about the United States. Like the Latin American liberalism in which much of their own politics was steeped, they had deep admiration for some U.S. political traditions. In opposing the poll tax, for example, La Crónica referred to the "glorious and sublime principles of individual liberty and civil rights embodied by the Declaration of Independence and the Federal Constitution of the American Republic." The Idars encouraged Mexicans and Texas Mexicans to invoke such freedoms to protect themselves from discrimination and violence. They demanded protection for Texas Mexicans from lynchings and believed that such protection was more likely to come from federal power than from either Texas or the Mexican government. Given their harsh criticism of segregation and racial violence, their praise for the openness of U.S. life was high indeed.

The Idars even demonstrated at least a strategic interest in adopting some aspects of U.S. culture. They admired the business sense of Americans—even that of the farmers whose racism so offended them. As part of their education campaign, they wanted Texas Mexicans to learn "the language of the country in which they live."

Despite the Progressives' attachment to aspects of United States politics and culture, the currents of Mexican nationalism tugged at them. While some American traditions were admirable, Tejanos risked losing their Mexicanness. Houston resident J. J. Mercado, for example, argued that Anglicisms corrupted the Spanish spoken by Texas Mexicans. For Mercado the use of terms like "bordeando" for the English "boarding" demonstrated that the isolated social life of Mexicans in Texas stunted their culture and even their mental faculties. Whatever their resentment of Mexican politics—or even of many of the Mexicans in Texas—and whatever the attraction of aspects of U.S. politics and culture, many Progressives hoped for the redemption of the Mexican national project.

The 1911 toppling of Porfirio Díaz and subsequent election of liberal Francisco Madero to the presidency of Mexico bolstered this hope. The Idars speculated that Mexicans might be able to leave the increasingly inhospitable Texas and return to "the sacred native ground of our ancestors." Indeed, the increasing likelihood of such a return was all the more reason "that before our relocation, we should study some lessons in democracy." Later that year, on Mexico's Independence Day, Tejano Progressives from Laredo and beyond hosted the "Primer Congreso Mexicanista," which drew delegates from dozens of Texas and Tamaulipas towns in an effort to defend the beleaguered rights of Mexicans in Texas. The largest ethnic Mexican civil rights meeting ever held up to that point, the conference hewed to the Progressive position on many ideological and pragmatic issues. At the same time, Mexican nationalism clearly dominated the attendees' political consciousness. Where the Idars and other Progressives were conflicted in their national consciousness, speaker after speaker at the conference emphasized that Texas Mexicans' future lay within the institutions and culture of Mexico.

If the advent of the Mexican Revolution seemed to turn Tejano Progressives away from their experimentation with U.S. citizenship rights, then in another sense it also energized Texas-Mexican politics. The plethora of Mexican politicians, military leaders, and intellectuals who found refuge in Texas brought with them a wide spectrum of political philosophies and visions of the future of Mexico.

Ricardo and Enrique Flores Magón were some of the earliest and most influential exiles. First fleeing to Texas, then St. Louis, and ultimately to Los Angeles, they achieved remarkable success in spreading their newspaper, *Regeneración,* across the Mexican community in the United States and into Mexico itself. By 1906 nearly 20,000 people in both nations paid for subscriptions and avidly read the brothers' calls for formal political reforms such as a four-year presidential term with no reelection, classical liberal proposals such as taxing church property, and social reforms such as an eight-hour workday and an end to child labor. Their manifesto circulated across Mexico, gaining the support of many local liberal organizations, including groups involved in major industrial strikes, and helped to spark numerous small and unsuccessful uprisings in Mexico's North over the next several years.

Enrique and Ricardo, relocated in Los Angeles, became both more explicitly radical and less influential by the time that Francisco Madero became president in October 1911. Whereas liberals like Madero thought that private property allowed individuals to function as autonomous members of society, the Flores Magón brothers came to embrace the anarchist idea that property needed to be redistributed so that the direct and decentralized control of the means of production could create an egalitarian and just society. They denounced Madero as a "traitor to the cause of liberty" and called for an armed struggle to redistribute land and wealth and destroy the power of the church, foreigners, and the rich. This stance cost them the support of Tejano Progressives, many of whom enthusiastically supported Madero.

In south Texas, Aniceto Pizaña, a rancher who lived near Brownsville, appears to have been the single most active Partido Liberal Mexicano (PLM) partisan. Pizaña not only faithfully contributed his own money to the legal defense of jailed PLM partisans; he also raised money and sold PLM literature in the Brownsville area. The *ranchero* was introduced to *Regeneratión* by a friend in 1908 and soon distributed, as he put it, "the propaganda of Land and Liberty for all." Pizaña founded a South Texas PLM *grupo* named "Perpetual Solidarity." The anarchist condemnation of wage labor as a form of servitude would have had enormous resonance with rancheros like Pizaña, who found such labor (which was almost always in agriculture) exploitive and humiliating.

Soon enough Texas itself became the site of a rebellion. In 1915, *rancheros'* anger at their displacement boiled over into a sustained uprising. Aniceto Pizaña, attacked at his own ranch by Anglo vigilantes, joined the rebellion along with several of his PLM compatriots. Receiving some aid from a revolutionary commander based in Matamoros, the Sediciosos mounted an impressive series of raids in the fall of 1915 They attacked irrigation pump houses, derailed a passenger railroad car leaving Brownsville, terrorized and killed Anglo farmers against whom they bore grudges, and attacked a branch of the enormous King Ranch. Vigilantes, in response, began killing ethnic Mexicans—in some cases engaging in mass executions—and driving many rancheros off their lands. In the midst of this clearly racial violence, Tejanos were also set against one another. The three pre-uprising political factions—machine lieutenants, PLM-inspired radicals, and the Progressives—found themselves at odds and sometimes even at arms.

The first apparent killing of a Tejano by the rebels occurred on July 12, about a week after the first sustained flurry of raids on Anglo farmers. Ignacio and Adelair Cantú shot and killed Brownsville deputy constable Pablo Falcón while he was on duty at a dance. The Cantús, according to witnesses, called out to Falcón and Cameron County deputy marshal Encarnación Cuellar and then shot both men from behind.

But Harbert Davenport, a Brownsville lawyer and sometimes legal partner of J.T. Canales, later described Falcón as "the raiders' first victim" and expressed his confidence that if he had the chance, Falcón "would have undoubtedly, warned me of the trouble brought about by the 'Plan of San Diego.'" Another Cameron County deputy sheriff, Carlos Esparza, who "allegedly had a reputation of mistreating local residents," was killed some two weeks before Falcón. Esparza's family had a long-standing dispute with the nearby Escamillas, some of whom soon joined the uprising. Two weeks after Falcón's shooting, one of the bands active in Cameron County killed a local Tejano, José María Benavides, during a raid on the Los Indios Ranch.

Low-level office holders such as Falcón were not the only Tejanos affiliated with the machine to be targeted by the Sediciosos. Pizaña and his comrades resented the complicity of many machine figures in the agricultural boom. The political establishment's willingness to resort to violence to crush the uprising only exacerbated this resentment. Indeed, the estate of a key Hidalgo County *jefe político* became the rebels' favorite target. The small town of Progreso, right along the river in the portion of eastern Hidalgo County known as Ojo de Agua, was a virtual private kingdom for Don Florencio Saenz. Saenz's prosperous store, his integrated farming and ranching operation (more than 40,000 acres, complete with its own private irrigation system), and the post office set up to cater to his community's needs reflected his success in navigating the currents of the Valley's new commercial order. Like most ranchers who benefited from the agricultural boom, Saenz relied on a nexus of economic and political power. He served as Hidalgo County commissioner from 1852 to 1905, delivering the numerous votes of his tenants, retainers, and kin to the Hidalgo County machine. According to one neighbor, "he practically controlled the votes of the eastern part of Hidalgo County for years and years."

Saenz's store had been robbed in May of 1914, more than a year before the wider-scale uprising began. Saenz named two local Tejano residents as participants in the robbery. They became some of the earliest lynching victims in 1915. The Sediciosos struck back hard, attacking Progreso four times in August and September of 1915. Soldiers and raiders exchanged gunfire on August 17 and 25, a four day-battle raged in the area from September 2 to 5, and another sustained and bloody fight took place on September 24.

If the rebels wanted to punish Saenz, they certainly succeeded. The September attacks forced him to shut down his store and transfer his goods to Mercedes. Although he hired a private security force to defend his vast estate, the frequent raids forced most of his tenants and nearby population out of the area for the better part of three years.

The reprisals and vigilantism launched by the newly unified Anglo newcomers exacerbated the divisions among Tejanos. Rancheros opposed to the uprising found themselves in a very difficult position, fearing both vigilante posses, often led by Texas Rangers, and attacks by the Sediciosos. As the raids and vigilantism continued into the fall of 1915, the Sediciosos seemed to prompt something of a backlash. Some Tejanos began cooperating with the army and local law enforcement officers to put an end to the raids. L. H. Bates wrote to the Texas adjutant general, the commander of the Texas Rangers, that "most all Mexican ranchmen in this section [near Brownsville] are ready to cooperate and do all they can to aid militia with aid of scouts and Mexican-Texas ranchmen who know the country."

Key Tejano Progressives joined the backlash. The Progressives found themselves in an awkward and in-between position. On the one hand, they wanted little to do with any violent upheaval or radical overthrow of established economic power. The Sediciosos' attacks on the railroad and the farmers affronted the Progressive support of economic development in general, and of South Texas' agricultural boom in particular. On the other hand, the Progressives abhorred the growing vigilantism. The events of 1915 and 1916 must have confirmed their fear that a loss of Tejano economic power subjected them to marginalization and social violence. The machine's inability or unwillingness to limit such violence reflected the Progressive judgment that it held little promise for the betterment of Tejano lives.

Because no early raids occurred near Laredo, the Idars did not have to confront these tensions directly in the fall of 1915. J. T. Canales, on the other hand, was caught in the middle of them. His family's land (which included five different ranches at the time) and his own enthusiasm for agricultural development made Canales a staunch opponent of the uprising. He proved to be an active opponent as well. Although not part of a large meeting held in late October to coordinate a response to the raids, Canales chose his own method of action, organizing a regular patrol of like-minded Tejanos who assisted the army's efforts to turn back all raids at the river. Canales's efforts bore fruit. Soon, cavalry officers were reporting that the scouts he recruited had allowed them to detect and halt raids that otherwise would have slipped past their own patrols.

At the same time, Canales also made efforts to stop the vigilantism. Convinced that Aniceto Pizaña had been the victim of a neighbor who coveted his land, Canales did what he could to help the ranchero's family. When Aniceto's brother Ramón was charged with attempted murder for defending his ranch, Canales served as his legal counsel, ultimately winning his acquittal on the grounds of self-defense in an appeals court. On at least one occasion Canales secured the release of Tejanos detained for suspicion of involvement with the uprising. When the vigilantism grew more extreme in the fall of 1915, he spoke out publicly against the Texas Rangers' brutality. In 1919, again a member of the state legislature, Canales launched an investigation into the conduct of the Rangers that would document their worst crimes.

If Canales was in a difficult position, a split between the army and the Texas officials and citizens responsible for the vigilantism made it more tenable than it otherwise would have been. While local Anglos set aside their differences to face a shared threat, federal and state authorities found themselves increasingly at odds. Federal officers and the U.S. Army took a dim view of vigilantism. Because it generated support for the uprising among both the local Tejano population and some of the revolutionary forces across the river, such violence made the government's goal of restoring order more difficult. Consequently, army officers did not engage in arbitrary executions, killings, or removals. Some even made some efforts to prevent Rangers and civilians from doing so. Tejanos showed themselves to be very aware of the differences between state and local officers, sometimes asking for army units to be assigned for their protection. The deployment of federal soldiers could offer protection from Sedicioso reprisals and Ranger vigilantism alike.

The experiences of Laredo's Tejano Progressives indicate how the suppression of the South Texas uprising also silenced a wide range of political dissent. Although the Idars, living in Laredo, were removed from the majority of the raids and reprisals in 1915, the shock waves of the Plan de San Diego soon reached them. Like J.T. Canales, they showed little sympathy for the Plan or its adherents. In the early stages of the Mexican Revolution, the Idars sided with Francisco Madero, even as the Flores Magón brothers denounced him as a sell-out, and would have had little sympathy for calls for a violent revolution on the north side of the Rio Grande. Clemente Idar actively opposed the Plan when the opportunity presented itself. After the June 1916 clashes in the Laredo area, local and federal authorities needed a reliable Spanish-speaking witness and translator to deal with the captured raiders. Court documents name a "C. N. Idar" as a witness to the statements of three men captured after the Webb Station raid on June 12. Idar copied and translated the letter from one of the prisoners to Mexican general Alvaro Obregón. Moreover, when it looked as though the Sediciosos would extend their campaign to the Laredo area in May and June of 1916, Clemente also served as an agent of the U.S. Department of Justice, passing along information about a raid nearby.

By 1919, when the end of World War I finally led to the withdrawal of the armed forces sent to quell the uprising, South Texas was in important respects a different place than it had been before. The defeat of the Plan de San Diego in 1916, high commodity prices, and vigorous marketing prompted a resumption of the region's agricultural boom. The balance of political and economic power shifted decisively to newcomer farmers. The machine and its Tejano lieutenants lost much of their power. Soon the Jim Crow–style segregation and disfranchisement that the Progressives had feared became a reality for all too many Tejanos. The land that produced Juan Cortina, Catarino Garza, and the Plan de San Diego would never again witness another sustained uprising. Seventy years after the Treaty of Guadalupe Hidalgo, the South Texas borderlands were politically and economically integrated into the United States, with dire results for ethnic Mexicans. Conquest, it seemed, was finally complete.

But it was not so simple, as subsequent events would demonstrate. Tejanos did not stop struggling for political rights and economic security in the modern borderlands. What distinguished their protests from those of their ancestors was their use of the language of U.S. nationalism to articulate their grievances. The 1920s saw the emergence of a Mexican American civil rights movement, with the embrace of American citizenship and the struggle for political and social freedoms under its rubric. Tejano Progressives, pitted against Mexican revolutionaries and Anglo segregationists during the uprising, shed their previous ambivalence about United States citizenship and played a key role in shaping the political platform and institutions of the first generation of Mexican Americans. At the founding convention of the League of United Latin American Citizens (LULAC), the principal organization of this new political impulse, J. T. Canales and Clemente wrote much of the constitution and sponsored the controversial motion limiting membership to United States citizens.

Most of LULAC's platform and techniques had been anticipated by the Tejano Progressives in the decade before the Plan de San Diego. The Progressives were as intent on the modernization of their own people, the fitting of them with the skills and attitudes necessary to compete in twentieth-century United States, as they were on confronting Anglo racism. So was LULAC. Earlier in the century,

Canales, the Idars, and J. Luz Saenz pinned many of their highest hopes on the transformative potential of education, thereby singling out educational inequality and segregation as particularly offensive. So did LULAC. The Progressive current included politically engaged women and men who welcomed such activity. So did LULAC. The Progressives hoped that Mexican Americans would seek and gain political power on their own terms, rather than the machine's. So did LULAC. "One generation visualizes that which another brings into practice," wrote Clemente Idar shortly after the new organization's founding. "In the history of all peoples, that is exactly what human progress has brought about."

There was one critical difference, however, between LULAC and the Tejano Progressives. Where the Progressives had been able to pick and choose between U.S. and Mexican nationalism, LULACers were now enthusiastic American citizens. This was not because they had turned their backs on Mexican culture or customs, but rather because what they had endured during the Plan de San Diego convinced them of the dangers of statelessness: that they risked becoming a people belonging to no nation at all. Mexican Americans had fallen through the crack between the two nations. "We are becoming a new people on the margin of two great and powerful nations," editorialized *El Paladin* in its announcement of the founding of LULAC, "and continue being Americans to religiously fulfill all of our obligations, and Mexicans when it comes to sharing rights, especially in the South of Texas." "Mexican-Americans," emphasized Castulo Gutiérrez, "as long as we do not elevate ourselves to the level of citizens, will be nothing more than the conquered."

LULAC and its ideology of U.S. citizenship still competed with the machine and the nationalist politics of exile for Tejano loyalties. The remnants of South Texas's once mighty machine, which still ruled portions of the region's ranching areas, condemned the new organization. At times they even called in the Texas Rangers to harass and arrest LULAC organizers. Although vehemently opposed to the radicalism of the Flores Magón brothers and Aniceto Pizaña, the Mexican government created by the revolution called upon the loyalties of those of Mexican descent, insisting that their true home was south of the river. Angered by LULAC's American citizenship politics, Mexico's consul general in San Antonio warned those of Mexican descent "that they should always remember that they live in a foreign nation, that they came by their own choice to the United States and that they have no right to disturb the existing social conditions here." If "luck is bad in one place," he concluded, "they should seek their fortune in another or return to their country."

Such appeals fell on deaf ears. The Plan de San Diego uprising, intended to cast off United States rule, had instead helped to create the category of Mexican American. A critical mass of Tejanos had come to believe that the borderlands could be the site not merely of clashing sovereignties but also of multiracial democracy.

FURTHER READING

Benton-Cohen, Katherine. *Borderline Americans: Racial Division and Labor War in the Arizona Borderlands* (2009).

Gilly, Adolfo. *La revolución interrumpida; México, 1910–1920: una guerra campesina por la tierra y el poder* (1971; reprint, 1998).

Hall, Linda B., and Don M. Coerver. *Revolution on the Border: The United States and Mexico, 1910–1920* (1988).

Hart, John Mason. *Revolutionary Mexico: The Coming and Process of the Mexican Revolution* (1987).

————. *Empire and Revolution: The Americans in Mexico since the Civil War* (2002).

Horne, Gerald. *Black and Brown: African Americans and the Mexican Revolution, 1910–1920* (2005).

Johnson, Benjamin Heber. *Revolution in Texas: How a Forgotten Rebellion and Its Bloody Suppression Turned Mexicans Into Americans* (2003).

Katz, Friedrich. *The Secret War in Mexico: Europe, the United States, and the Mexican Revolution* (1981).

————. *Life and Times of Pancho Villa* (1998).

Knight, Alan. *The Mexican Revolution*. 2 Vols (1986).

Martinez, Oscar. *Fragments of the Mexican Revolution: Personal Accounts from the Border* (1983).

Romo, David Dorado. *Ringside Seat to a Revolution: An Underground Cultural History of El Paso and Juárez, 1893–1923* (2005).

Sánchez, George. *Becoming Mexican American: Ethnicity, Culture, and Identity in Chicano Los Angeles, 1900–1945* (1993).

Sandos, James. *Rebellion in the Borderlands: Anarchism and the Plan of San Diego, 1904–1923* (1992).

Tinker-Salas, Miguel. *In the Shadow of the Eagles: Sonora and the Transformation of the Border During the Porfiriato* (1997).

Vanderwood, Paul J. *The Power of God Against the Guns of Government: Religious Upheaval in Mexico at the Turn of the Nineteenth Century* (1998).

Womack, John. *Zapata and the Mexican Revolution* (1969).

Zamora, Emilio. *World of the Mexican Worker in Texas* (1993).

CHAPTER 12

~

Vice

The Mexican Revolution and immigration restrictions implemented in the 1910s made North America's international borders much more tightly policed and monitored than before. But that did not mean that central states were able to control who and what crossed their borders. By the 1920s, distinctive vice industries centered on liquor, prostitution, gambling, and illegal drugs had visible presences on both the Mexico-U.S. and Canada-U.S. lines. These industries were hardly new to the decade, but they increased dramatically because of burgeoning consumer demand from the comparatively populous and wealthy United States and the simultaneous banning of many products. Key here was Prohibition, the outlawing of alcoholic beverages in the United States, in effect nationally from 1920 to 1933. Mexican border towns had attracted tourists before this measure, but the American ban on alcohol did more than any other factor to create a dynamic entertainment and lodging industry in both Mexican and Canadian border towns. The ban, along with measures outlawing various drugs, also created powerful new incentives to smuggle across international borders.

This chapter explores the ways that the so-called vice industries shaped border life and the popular images of borders that circulated across the continent. On the one hand, these industries accentuated the extent to which national borders marked the edges of supposedly different societies. This was particularly true of the U.S.-Mexico border. Despite the revolutionary violence of the previous decade, by the 1920s, when most Americans thought of the border, they thought above all about liquor and sex. This border offered for easy money what they could only get at home with much greater expense and trouble. Countless trips into Mexico brought the border into American consciousness in another way: By the 1920s, pornographic cartoon books in the United States were popularly known as "Tijuana Bibles." The border's risqué reputation was further secured by a series of powerful radio stations, located just south of the river to avoid more restrictive American signal limits. Holding station names that began with the letter 'X', these were among the first to play the once-controversial hillbilly, country and western, Mexican ranchera, and rock and roll music. The stations were so powerful that, like the other cultural echoes of the border, they could be heard across most of the United States. Americans did not generally thought of their border with Canada with the same mix of fear and fascination that their southern border held, but nonetheless many of the same industries drove the economies of towns on the Canadian border.

If border vice industries traded in national difference, then at the same time they also revealed some of the divisions within nations. Whereas some Canadian and Mexican entrepreneurs took great advantage of the American tourist dollar, other citizens resented the incursions of what they often encountered as rowdy, boorish, and even dangerous drunks. And who would benefit from this commerce was often in dispute; in the early 1920s, for example, the overwhelming majority of Tijuana bartenders, waitresses, and hotel staff were American citizens, but protests from Mexican unions led the state governor to mandate that hotels, bars, and clubs fill at least half of their positions with Mexican nationals. The extensive smuggling of consumer goods into Mexico, a pattern begun in the nineteenth century that continued throughout the twentieth, often pitted citizens of the Mexican North in search of bargains against the national government down in Mexico City and against many of their own industries. Americans were just as conflicted: Whereas Prohibitionists and anti-prostitution reformers attempted to extend their regulations into Mexican border towns, their fellow citizens were equally determined to escape such restrictions. The divisions within nations could be as pronounced as the differences between them.

〰 DOCUMENTS

In Document 1, former El Paso reporter Chester Chope recalls the El Paso-Juárez area in the 1920s, when both towns were marked by the open sale of alcohol, drugs, sex, and guns. Although El Paso reformers succeeded in getting the U.S. government to close its border crossings early in the evening, Chope's account suggests that they were unable to combat the deep allure that Juárez nightlife held for Americans of all walks of life. The Mexican Revolution and Mexican migration made Americans look on their southern border with fear and suspicion, and, indeed, Chope also remembers that violence accompanied smuggling, whether of arms into Mexico or liquor into the United States.

But this border had developed an allure as well. By the 1920s, Mexican border towns drew tourists from across the United States, who believed that they could have wild times there that they could not enjoy at home. In Document 2, writer Duncan Aikman satirizes American tourists in Juárez. Border towns, he implies, were not nearly as wild as their exaggerated reputations implied. Despite his mocking tone, Aikman's piece captures the enormous reach of the Mexican border's reputation in American life. In Document 3, C. D. Smith, a columnist for a British Columbian newspaper, described American tourists drawn to Canada for similar reasons. Smith pokes gentle fun at his neighbors to the south.

If the border vice industries provoked fascination, resentment, and ridicule, then for some they also prompted outright admiration. Document 4 is a *corrido*, or border ballad, lauding the exploits of Mexicans who smuggled tequila into the United States during Prohibition. One of a number of songs about the exploits of smugglers composed and sung in the lower Rio Grande Borderlands in the early twentieth century, "Los Tequileros" portrays American law enforcement agents as brutal murderers and the smugglers as honest men trying to make a living. For its singers and listeners, the song thus placed smuggling alcohol in the context of the long history of Anglo-Mexican conflict in the borderlands. In subsequent decades, drug smugglers became the subjects of similar ballads, which came to be called *narcocorridos*. Like earlier corridos of border outlaws and heroes—or, for that matter, like Anglo-American ballads about notorious criminals or the American gangster rap of recent decades—narcocorridos generally expressed admiration and fascination with the lives of drug smugglers. Such is the case in "Contrabando y traición" ("Contraband and Betrayal"), a version of an older song made wildly popular by the then teen-aged group "Los Tigres del Norte" ("The Tigers of the North") in 1972, which is reproduced in Document 5. Widely purchased and played on radio stations across Mexico and the western United States, the song made Los Tigres enormously successful and marked the advent of what one writer has called "the narcocorrido boom."

Americans and their elected officials often view their country as the victim of the smuggling of goods banned in order to protect the public interest. In many ways, Mexicans and their government think of themselves in the same way. Mexican law, for example, is much more restrictive of private gun ownership than American law, and so, in recent years, most guns used in killings in Mexico related to the drug industry involve arms purchased north of the border and brought into the country illegally. Document 6, an account of the smuggling of electronics and other consumer goods from Laredo, Texas, into Mexico, reveals a similar dynamic at work. In the 1930s, after the consolidation of the Mexican political order created in the Mexican Revolution, the national government imposed high tariffs on many manufactured goods in the hope that they would foster domestic industry and keep the nation's employment rates and wages high. As writer Tom Miller describes, this created enormous incentives to smuggle such goods into Mexico, since their legal price was so much higher there than in the United States. Borderlanders from both countries thus undermined national policy.

In Document 7, Don Henry Ford Jr., a former drug smuggler, describes the circumstances that first drew Oscar Cebello, a prominent resident of Piedritas, Coahuila, into the drug trade. Marijuana farming seemed like one of the few options for residents of this remote and impoverished town, and, at first, growing the crop and smuggling it into the nearby United States seemed like a good strategy. But the violence and corruption that soon overtook Cebello made the high price of this plan clear. The appeal of the vice industries that were so critical to North American borders brought with them much danger and destruction.

1. El Paso Reporter Recalls Lure of Juárez in 1920s, 1968

Mr. Chester Chope
Interviewed by Wilma Claveland
July 27, 1968

CC: I came to El Paso to work in 1917. I went to work for the *El Paso Times* the day I got here. At that, El Paso was a city of about 75,000 people. In addition to that, there were numerous troops that had been brought

Chester Chope, interview by William Cleveland, July 27, 1968, interview 27, transcript,
Institute of Oral History, University of Texas at El Paso, pp. 1–2, 13–20.

here to the border following the Columbus Raid in which Villa attacked Columbus.

In those days, El Paso was a wide open town. The prisoners were primarily dope addicts, drunks, etc. Marijuana was common in those days and narcotics addicts came to El Paso because it was easy to get drugs. The drugs were manufactured across the border. There were frequent fights and killings; every Saturday night we espected to have a shooting before the first edition.

In the Roaring Twenties, Juárez was a Mecca for thousands of thirsty Americans. Bars and cafés—they were called cabarets in those days—stood wall to wall on the 16th of September Street. Owners imported bands and orchestras from the United States for the cabarets. People came here, especially on weekends, to make 'whoopee'. Part of the time the bridge closed at 10:00 or at 12:00, depending on the conditions at that time. At one time I was the only newspaper reporter who had a pass to return across the border after 12:00. It was issued by the Assistant Customs Collector, Mr. Warren Carpenter. Customs inspector, Louie Holzman, was in charge of the bridge at night. It was his duty to open the gate for me when I yelled for admission into the United States. On some occassions he was too busy to come down and open the gate, so I had to climb over. I recall that one time I tore the seat of my pants and became very angry. I reported the incident to Mr. Carpenter and then he issued strict orders that thereafter the gate was to be opened for me.

On many occasions, people were trapped in Juárez when the early closing hours were inaugurated. One time when the bridge was to stay open until 12:00 but orders came to close it at 9:00, El Pasoans didn't believe that the bridge would be closed at that hour and remained in Juárez. When they came to the bridge it was closed and they couldn't get over. I usually telephoned my office before returning from the Río Bravo, which was the best hotel in Juárez at that time, On this occassion, the lobby was filled with young women, most of them members of prominent families of El Paso, most of them wailing that they wouldn't get home at the time they had promised their families. They were using the phone and when they saw me using the phone they tried to get me to use my influence to get them through the gate, which I could not do, of course. On such occasions, some El Pasoans slept on tables, especially in the Big Kid Cáfe.

One of the most interesting people in Juárez in the twenties during the period when I was working there, was U.S. Consul John W. Dye. Mr. Dye was the tweed type. He was slender, quiet, and retiring. He was very courageous. He was the source of several interesting stories that I covered. One occasion he received a note that was brought to him by messenger from a young woman who said she was being held prisoner by a Chinese in an abandoned dance hall on the Street of the Devil, which was the zone of tolerance in Juárez. He asked me to investigate for him. I went to the place and found the woman lying on a mattress filled with straw in the back room of this building that was partially dilapidated. At one time it had been a huge house of prostitution and dance hall. I conferred with Mr. Dye and decided we had better get help. I contacted Mother Mary Warren of the Salvation Army. She had never been to Juárez prior to that time. She accompanied me to that place, and by candlelight as the vesper bells were ringing in the old church in Juárez, she knelt on the ground beside the bed and took this dirty disheveled woman in her arms and prayed. She immediately arranged to take this woman to El Paso.

During Prohibition days, battles between the gangsters and the border guards were frequent. One time, it was not liquor that was the cause of the fight, but ammunition that was being smuggled to Juárez. Two smugglers attempted to carry two cases of ammunition across the river which was very low, immediately west of the Santa Fe Street bridge. U.S. soldiers, who were on guard at the bridge, saw them and shouted for them to stop. When the soldiers attempted to apprehend the men, they were fired upon by the men from the Juárez side of the river. The smugglers dropped the cases of ammunition and fled to the Juárez side of the river under cover of gunfire from men on the Juárez side of the river. The U.S. soldiers took refuge behind a pile of adobe brick on the river side. Customs agents and immigration men telephoned for police. Captain Bill Simpson of the police force and two other men including Charlie Wood, a patrolman, hurried to the Santa Fe Street bridge. Captain Simpson spoke Spanish fluently; he shouted across the river that he was going out into the river to recover the ammunition. At that time, no one knew what was in the cases. Later it was presumed that the ammunition was destined for the Juárez garrison. When he was fired upon, Captain Simpson retreated hurriedly behind the pile of adobe brick. The soldiers returned the fire and the gunfire across the river lasted several minutes.

2. American Journalist Satirizes American Tourists in Juárez, 1925

There are three kinds of legends about the fringe of frowzy hamlets and small towns that have been placed by Providence, working through the Treaty of Guadalupe Hidalgo, just across the southern border of the Federal Union. They are said (mainly by railroad folders and the local guide-books of the American metropolises opposite them) to posses a 'piquant foreign atmosphere' and to wield a 'quaint Old World spell.' They are said to be unsafe for Americans visiting them who do not wear their oldest clothes, raise three-day bears and leave their jewelry behind. And they are said to offer Bacchanalian revels on such a lavish scale that only a millionaire's pocket-book can take care of the check.

Throughout the United States vast numbers of people believe in these droll sayings. In El Paso, where I am expiating the evil done in my youth, some stranger from the Corn Belt or the high Sierras drops into my office almost weekly to ask my advice as to whether he (or she) should risk a visit to Ciudad Juarez at all. Even in the border cities themselves there are hordes of Angles and Saxons no better informed. They are the men and women who, for fear of being seen in more than one half of one percent alcoholic surroundings by customers, clients, patients, pastors or rivals in local social-climbing, never cross the Rio Grande. Thus the life of the Mexican towns becomes as romantically remote to

Duncan Aikman, "Hell Along the Border," *American Mercury* 5 (May 1925): 17–23.
Reprinted by permission.

them as the life of the Falkland Islands. And thus they take on faith the declaration of the Rev. Dr. Bob Jones, a favorite evangelist of the Southern backwoods, that "I would rather shoot my son and throw his body in the river than have him spend an hour in the raging inferno of Juarez," or the equally gorgeous fantasies of visiting inebriates who, having lost $7 in a Mexican gambling den, raise it to a robbery of $7,000 on complaining to the police on the American side.

The Mexican border towns, it is true, offer a certain show of moth-eaten adobe architecture, and have dark brown inhabitants who speak Spanish, and an occasional visitor from the interior flourishing a serape or the high-peaked sombrero by which Mexicans may be recognized in the movies. Mexicali, in addition, provides a few turbaned Hindus and black-pajamaed Chinese. Tia Juana sometimes—and not always veraciously—supplies a Hollywood star indulging publicly in his or her bacchanals. But the only "quaint old-world spell" really worth noticing is exactly the same spell which was cast by the row of two- and three-story "store construction" buildings on the west side of Court House Square in any bibulous middle western county seat on a Saturday afternoon 20 years ago. It is the spell of a noisy and confused babble mixed vaguely with drums and fiddles, and the whirr of swinging doors plied busily, and a rich alcoholic smell. The charm, the prosperity, the usefulness of the border resorts are all rooted in the fact that they are the only relatively accessible, reasonably inexpensive, all-year-round, snow-free life-saving stations for the arid population of the inland United States: in short, cheap Bahamas to which minor Babbits can come from Kansas by Ford.

Their charm for the conveniently located sociologist is that the minor Babbitts keep on coming. In Winter, the endless string of motor and train traffic seeking the snow-free routes to California strikes the border at El Paso and clings to it all the way to Tia Juana's near neighbor, San Diego. In general, this Winter visitation is mid-western in origin. The bar-room clamor at the Big Kid's Palace of Jimmie O'Brien's in Juarez, the feminine chatter from the immaculate tables at the Central or from behind the naughtily curtained booths at the Office or the Lobby, is shrill with the harsh, flat *a*'s and the insistent *r*'s of the Corn Belt. In Summer, when terror of the desert drives this migration over the northern routes, the same places are pleasant with the musical accents of the lower Old South, mixed with the whiny drawls of East Texas and Arkansas.

Either season the procession is made up, as to class, of much the same elements: small-town bankers and grocers seeking retirement and mild dementia praecox in the suburbs of Los Angeles; dissatisfied young clerks and mechanics seeking "new openings" somewhere "on the coast," and their pert young flapper wives seeking new ideas in bungalows and bathing suits in Long Beach and La Jolla; occasional sportsmen on their way to chase big game in Mexico; fairly well-to-do tourists, embracing all classes from church deacons to racing touts, seeing the country on long vacations; traveling salesmen and other special agents, often accompanied by their wives, and eager to enliven business with serious intervals of pleasure; floaters looking for jobs, locality of no consequence, that will not seriously inhibit their floating; semi-nomads in battered Fords bound from Nowhere to the same place. Either season, too, the outward-bound procession encounters another flood—the thinner but constant ebb of the disillusioned from California back to where they came from.

In any case, they are bound from and for localities infinitely more arid than thirst-begetting desert. They have either sorrows to drown or pleasures to accelerate in a way that is relatively difficulty and expensive, and sometime socially inexpedient at home. Juarez, the first border resort encountered by probably seventy-five percent of them, is the place where more convinced Prohibitionists, including those from States where their cause triumphed a generation ago, gloriously escape from the régime they have made, than are to be found anywhere else. Even the trans-Atlantic liners, speeding north-eastward twelve miles of Sandy Hook, carry smaller passenger lists. Even on the Quebec border there is no spot where so many trails converge for rich and poor alike.

So it goes. The more one frequents the Mexican border resorts, the more one is brought to realize that the great American gift in depravity is for playing devilish rather than being it. Even in the wildly denounced gambling halls of Juarez, which are open or shut for months at a time according to the fluctuations of obscure arrangements with the Mexican officials, the frantic playing of nickels and dimes on mechanical devices is what takes one's breath away. Tia Juana draws on the wealth of southern California and is sometimes more thrilling, but more often not so. For, due to the regions and populations from which they border resorts mainly draw their customers, the very business of being devilish is mainly on the small-town, high-school alumnus scale.

The truth seems to be that the tourist from the American inland, whether he comes by Ford or Cadillac, by day coach or Pullman, is looking for thrills at a low price. So the establishments which are content to do most of their business in those bar-room simples, beer, gin, and whiskey, and which cut down about fifty per cent on the normal chile allowance in their Mexican viands, are the only ones that can pay the exorbitant Mexican license rates and still prosper. The real thrill, obviously and always sought in a border debauch, is to carry the memory of from two to nine drinks back to some town like Coon Rapids of Memphis, and to be able to say at the next gathering of cronies or lodge brothers: "Lemme tell you, li'l old Juarez is some town to raise hell (feminine equivalent: raise the roof) in. And, boy, we sure raised it!"

3. Columnist C. D. Smith Lampoons American Tourists in Search of Drink in Canada, 1925

Refugees from Albania have enlisted sympathy for generations. Refugees from Poland have aroused tender pity in the breasts of thousands. Refugees from Belgium were objects of extreme commiseration during the war. The exodus of the Israelites from the land of Egypt will never be forgotten. But none of

---

C. D. Smith, "Refugees From Volstead," *Daily Colonist* (Victoria, British Columbia), Aug. 30, 1925, p. 1.

these events exceed in sympathetic interest the refugees from Volstead, driven forth by the Eighteenth Amendment for a recompensing "life-saver." Their case is indeed a sad one.

Here in the wonderfully attractive Capital of British Columbia, in which place so many of the sufferers from the South of us fly for shelter, protection and safety from the rigors and aridity of their own country, their arrival has now become a commonplace. For two reasons its ceases to attract any particular attention; one, because we are used to it and the other from the fact that, living in the land of plenty—however we make look upon the Prohibition question— we take it as a matter of course. Every weekday sees the coming in of large numbers of these distressed exiles who, so to speak, turn themselves loose on the moistened ranges of the Canadian Pacific Coast to assuage the pangs caused by lack of the stimulating liquids of which they are deprived in their homeland.

The news has gone forth to the uttermost parts of the United States that throughout the haven of this Province there are located seventy-one hospices where the respective monks in charge dispense all brands of succor to the weary, travel-stained refugees. And also that there are two hundred and twenty-nine additional places, known euphemistically as beer parlors, where fermented liquors, made from malted grain with hops and other bitter flavoring matters, are dispensed at ten cents per glass, froth included. The result was a foregone conclusion.

This city [Victoria] possesses two of these fully-fledged refuge camps, or hospices, one close to the wharf at which tourists arrive by steamer, and the other in the centre of the shopping district. Residents, of course, are fully aware of this fact. It is pathetic indeed to see how quickly the parched arrivals from the weary treks over the intervening desert to this oasis discover the first-mentioned hospice and, bearing on their faces a look exceeding great gladness, make for its helping arms. It would, indeed, be difficult for them to miss their road, for waving in the breeze at the corner of the street the Stars and Stripes indicates the happy way.

This flag, which hangs from the first floor of the building in which is situated the offices of the United States Immigration Department, indicates a curious paradox. Under the shelter of the United States flag—"Old Glory"—is one of the legalized places where alcoholic drinks of all and every description can be procured. Yes, Old Glory is to many glory indeed.

Mostly, the refugees are men. It is naturally distressing in the extreme when women, children and helpless babes are the victims of cruel circumstance which cause them, through political crisis, to leave their native land. But when the sufferers are strong men it is heart-rending.

The pains of the strong who have battled long and manfully should, perhaps, make a greater sympathetic appeal than the afflictions of the weak who habitually endure submerged conditions of life, and never kick. These latter have capitulated without a struggle, whereas the others have fought, and some—resisting decrees they held to be aimed at their sacred liberty—have taken to moonshine and died.

Many of these refugees, however, have succeeded in bringing their womenkind safely with them through the arid deserts to the promised land. They reach this country flowing, not with milk and honey, but with more potent liquids, full details of which can be inspected in the tabulated lists prepared by the monks of the hospices according to the rates at which the Providential Fathers of the Order are prepared to supply alcoholic goods without loss to Provincial revenues.

It is not found that the refugees arrive in trucks, trains, and moving lorries in regular refugee style. They are not huddled together, nor do they sleep on straw sacks. Their appearance does not all suggest privation in the sense of their being starved, hollow-eyed, with haggard faces, torn feet and bleeding hands, caused by the dangers and privations of the journey. Neither are they attired in conventional garb of harassed wanderers, subsisting on what they can beg from kind-hearted peasants in route. All that is not a bit like it. They are mostly clothed in plus-fours and their one look is of assured triumph and anticipation. Nothing else matters.

4. Ballad Praises Liquor Smugglers, 1920s

The Tequila Runners

On the second day of February, what a memorable day!
The *rinches* from the other side of the river killed three tequila runners.

They reached the Rio Grande and then they stopped and thought,
"We had better go see Leandro, because there are only two of us."

They asked Leandro to go with them, and Leandro said he could not:
"I am sorry, but I'm sick. I don't want to go this way."

They kept asking him to go, until Leandro went with them;
in the hills of Almiramba, he was the first one to die.

The contraband they were taking was tequila *anisado;*
the direction they were taking was toward famed San Diego.

They left from Guerrero in an easterly direction;
two cars with many men were waiting for them there.

When they crossed the river, they traveled along a canyon;
then they stopped and built a fire without any regard for danger.

The captain of the *rinches* was saying, speaking in measured tones,
"It is wise to stack the odds because these men are from Guerrero."

They fired a volley at them in the middle of the road;
Gerónimo fell dead, and Silvano fell badly wounded.

They shot Leandro off his horse, wounding him in the arm.
He could no longer fire back at them; he had several bullet wounds.

The captain of the *rinches* came up close to Silvano;
and in a few seconds, Silvano García was dead.

Américo Paredes, *A Texas-Mexican Cancionero: Folksongs of the Lower Border*
(Austin: University of Texas Press, 1976), 101–102.

The *rinches* are very brave, there is no doubt of that;
the only way they can kill us is by hunting us like deer.

If the *rinches* were really brave and met us face to face,
then things would be quite different for us tequila runners.

So all three of them died, and these stanzas are at an end;
the *rinches* were able to accomplish the killings they wanted.

He who composed these stanzas was not present when it happened;
these verses have been composed from what people were saying.

Now here is my farewell, in the midst of three flower vases;
this is the end of the ballad, the stanzas of the tequila runners.

5. "Contrabando y tracíon" Marks Popularity of Narcocorrido, 1972

"Contrabando y traición" 1972, Los Tigres del Norte

They left San Isidro, coming
from Tijuana,
They had their car tires full of
"bad grass," (marijuana)
They were Emilio Varela and
Camelia the Texan.

Passing through San Clemente,
they were stopped by
Immigration.
He asked for their documents,
he said, "Where are you from?"
She was from San Antonio,
a woman with a lot of heart.

A woman so loves a man that
she can give her life for him.
But watch out if that woman
feels wounded,
Betrayal and smuggling do not
mix.

They arrived in Los Angeles,
they went to Hollywood.
In a dark alley they changed
the tires.

"Contrabando y traición," Los Tigres Del Norte. http://www.arlindocorreia.com/
080604.html, accessed May 10, 2010.

There they delivered the grass,
and there also they were paid.

Emilio says to Camelia, "Today
is your farewell,
With your share you can make a
new life.
I am going to San Francisco
with the mistress of my life."

Seven shots rang out, Camelia
killed Emilio.
All the police found was the
discarded pistol.
Of Camelia and the money
nothing more was ever known.

6. Writer Tom Miller Describes Smuggling Electronics into Mexico to Avoid Duties, 1981

"I work in a small retail store. Someone comes in and buys twenty television sets. He pays cash, he gets a sales receipt, everything is clean. But he wants the TVs smuggled into Mexico, so he brings them to a man in town who seals them in a boxcar headed for Mexico City. I know the man smuggles because I deliver the goods to him. That's what I do for a living—I help Mexican shoppers get their purchases into Mexico."

The short man with the skin problem was explaining the facts of life, Laredo style. He had lived there since birth, seen generations of stagnant poverty among the townfolk, seen the wealth grow among the nouveau merchant class. Like so many others in this town of ninety-two thousand, he recognizes that shipping consumer goods into Mexico, in violation of that country's laws, can be a lucrative enterprise, condoned and even encouraged by pillars of the community. Mexicans spend so much money in Laredo that the city, whose residents earn among the lowest wages in the United States, ranks among the very highest in per capita retail sales. Mexican shoppers generally prefer U.S. products—televisions, clothing, stereos, appliances, blenders, furniture, cameras—to homemade ones. Superior American technology usually means a longer product life span. Many consumer goods are simply not manufactured in Mexico at all. Additionally, Mexican consumers often attach status to American products even if a similar item is available in-country. As the American town most accessible to the greatest number of Mexicans, Laredo, Texas, has become Mexico's shopping center.

Smuggling goods into Mexico is commonplace because of the prohibitively high import duties imposed by that country's government. The complex and

Tom Miller, *On the Border: Portraits of America's Southwestern Frontier* (New York: Harper and Row, 1981), 48–51. Reprinted by permission.

well-established pipeline of Mexican smugglers imports items not only by freight train but over major highways as well. *Aduana*—customs—officials throughout the Republic receive systematic payoffs in the process. For Laredo merchants to sell goods to Mexican customers is perfectly legal. The merchandise becomes contraband only when it enters Mexico untaxed. Smuggled goods are called *fayuca*.

J. C. Penney, 80 percent of whose business is from Mexico, is located in River Drive Mall, a downtown shopping center virtually on the banks of the Rio Grande. *Chiveras,* or smugglers (literally, goatherds), come to town with shopping lists for a dozen or so families and fill the Penney's parking lot in the afternoons. They take their purchases out of the store wrappings and rip out any tags indicating they are new. Often clothes are worn immediately, two and sometimes three layers at a time. More clothes are crammed into suitcases—also just purchased for the return trip. The rest is concealed from the *aduana* in door panels, under seat covers, beneath trunk liners, and elsewhere. At La Posada, the city's best hotel, high-volume *chiveras* convert their rooms to warehouses, storing clothes for the return trip to the interior. Paper bags from shops all over town litter the hotel's hallways.

When the bridge is "tight"—that is, when high customs officials from Mexico are in town to monitor their underlings—Laredo department stores such as Montgomery Ward will keep purchased appliances destined for the interior until the situation returns to normal. Sales clerks and *chiveras* throughout the city maintain a cozy relationship, each profiting from the other. In Laredo, clandestine activity is business as usual. The town has become an American Andorra.

To spot the *chiveras,* simply cross the International Bridge to Nuevo Laredo and watch Mexicans pass their own customs. Shoppers on foot carrying paper bags of new purchases often leave a ten- or twenty-peso note on top as *mordida,* which is considered nothing more than a gift to speed things along. The *aduana* pocket the money, nod slightly, and move on to the next person.

Enrico, a friend from Monterrey, 150 miles south of Laredo, explained how the game is played when driving home. "You have to pull around to the rear of the port building where the *aduana* go through your luggage pretending they're looking for *fayuca*. Actually they are looking for their money. It's best to leave the *mordida* on top so they don't mess up your suitcase. For a little two hundred dollar television set, the *aduana* may get fifty dollars, but the total expense is still cheaper than buying a similar set in Mexico. Another *aduana* checkpoint is at twenty-six kilometers out, and another one as you drive into Monterrey. If Mexico City is the destination, there may be ten or twelve *aduana* payoffs along the way. The government is very lenient about this. These customs men retire very well."

Enrico's observations had historical precedent. John Russell Bartlett, the U.S. survey commissioner who traveled the border in the mid-nineteenth century, noted that "the duty ... imposed by Mexico on many items of merchandise amounts to a prohibition. Yet owing to the laxity of customhouse officials, the law has been evaded, and goods regularly admitted at a nominal rate. Each collector knows that if he exacts the legal duty, either the merchandise will be smuggled in or some brother-collector, less conscientious and anxious to pocket the fees, will be ready to compound for a smaller sum. It accordingly became the practice ... to admit merchandise for the interior of Mexico by paying five hundred dollars on each wagon load."

In one major appliance store a twenty-four-inch color console television was tagged at $1,125. The store manager said he could deliver the set to Monterrey for another $315. "The bridge is still tight," he lamented. "When it loosens up, here's how we'll do it: You pay for the set here and we give you the receipt. When our *chivera* gets ready to deliver in Monterrey, he'll call you and you pay him the delivery cost. If the television is confiscated, we'll send out another one. We guarantee delivery."

In an office supply shop the story was similar. A new office-model electric typewriter cost $825. "Oh, you want it sent to Mexico? That will be an extra one hundred fifty dollars. Delivery guaranteed."

The pattern repeated itself in store after store. Each had its own *chivera,* each guaranteed delivery, and each undercut the legal Mexican price. At one store a salesman apologized that he had to delay smuggling because a new customs man was being broken in at the *aduana* station and the *chivera* had to negotiate his contract.

7. Former Smuggler Don Henry Ford Jr. Describes Why Border Community Drawn to Smuggling Marijuana, 2005

People around Piedritas dug fluorite out of the mountains by hand, earning in the vicinity of five bucks a day for a brutal day's effort. More than one man remains buried in a deep mineshaft which collapsed and crushed him. Others poisoned themselves digging cinnabar and extracting mercury destined for the United States, a practice which also yielded little money. Children suffered from curable diseases like a virulent form of conjunctivitis which leads to blindness, where a dollar's worth of antibiotic ointment would have saved their eyes. They suffered and died from dysentery caused by drinking out of contaminated water sources. There were no sewer systems. And nobody on either side of the river cared.

This is the world Oscar was raised in. Maybe because his dad did a better job of feeding him as a child, Oscar was more intelligent than his peers or even than his own father. Not only was he more intelligent, but he was bigger, stronger and more compassionate. Because of this, he inherited the burden of taking care of the needs of his community at an early age. He was elected their representative in the state legislative body that ruled the area, but that did little to bring aid to the community. Piedritas had nothing those in power wanted, and consequently they had nothing to offer Pledritas.

A few aborted attempts to help did take place. A water tower was built but the water system that should have accompanied it was not. So the tower stood rusting off in the distance, like some huge monument to the good will of the

Don Henry Ford, Jr., *Contrabando: Confessions of a Drug-Smuggling Texas Cowboy* (El Paso: Cinco Puntos Press, 2005), 58–60.

Mexican government, while women and kids pulled water to the surface from a well in the center of town, using ropes and buckets. A large dam and gravity flow system was built to collect rainwater for irrigation purposes and a lake-full of water accumulated. For a few years crops flourished, but the government screwed the farmers out of what they should have received. The people had no machinery to work the soil or harvest their crops. The Mexican government provided these things. Then, when the crops were harvested, they paid the people with a few sacks of flour and kept the money. The *ejiditarios* became disillusioned and quit.

Oscar made contact with the rich world of the United States at some point in his young life and discovered there was something Mexico had that the people of this country wanted and would gladly pay for: marijuana. Not only would they pay for it, they would pay a lot for it. Oscar didn't have any interest in getting high, but he did need money—desperately—more than he could earn working legally in the United States. He found the sources, and then American buyers found him.

Celerino [Oscar's father] had reservations about entering the marijuana business. He had heard all the propaganda but remained undecided about whether it would be a bad thing. Oscar entered the business nonetheless and gained his father's favor by investing profits into legitimate businesses for the community: cattle, horses, pickup trucks and a limited amount of farm equipment. In time, nearly the entire village worked for the Cabello family—farming, ranching and smuggling marijuana. Those who didn't starved, trying to make a living collecting candelilla or digging fluorite. Celerino fed the old, retarded and incapacitated of the town and paid a traveling doctor to come by on occasion.

Oscar began to move larger and larger loads through the region, and he made more and more money. Then came setbacks. One man, who had always been reliable, simply drove off with a ton of marijuana—bought on credit—and disappeared, never to be seen again. Oscar had to make good on the debt to those higher in the food chain who were supplying him with his product. If he didn't, the results could be tragic.

Then came the ill-fated shootout at the San Vicente crossing. An American narc set up a deal to buy a load of marijuana. The van to be used to haul the load concealed American drug agents. The agents jumped out after the Mexican vehicle containing the load arrived on the U.S. side. Shots were exchanged during the attempt to arrest the man. The Mexicans fled, leaving the marijuana behind. While this may be attributed to [cartel leader Pablo] Acosta, it happened on Oscar's turf, and he suffered much of the financial loss since most of the marijuana was his. But Oscar had nothing to do with any shooting that day. Perhaps Acosta's people did. In any event, Acosta was inclined to take credit for what happened, and smarter men were more than glad to let him.

It was about this time that Oscar began to look for new buyers. He needed someone he could trust in the United States. And I needed someone I could trust in Mexico. I had no money to speak of, but Oscar was willing to front me the dope. And a man with dope will soon find those willing to pay for it in this country. Matter of fact, they'll find him.

I did not want to sell to West Texas locals. To me it seemed like shitting in my own bed. Besides, no one out there had much money. Instead I approached Arnold Kersh and his crew in Plainview, who could supply the Lubbock area. Later I also contacted my cousin Phil who lived in the Dallas-Fort Worth metroplex. So Oscar bought from his connections in Mexico, he sold the marijuana to me, and I carted it across the river and sold it to Arnold, Phil and others. Their job was to collect everybody's paychecks. Oscar—and the rest of us too—started to make lots of money.

All of this wealth eventually took its toll on Oscar. While he did continue to turn over healthy amounts to his dad for distribution into the poor community of Piedritas, he also developed a liking for cocaine and whores. It seems to go with the business. Oscar moved his family to Fort Stockton, Texas, and bought a small conservative home. His children learned English and enjoyed the privileges of most Americans. Oscar began to spend more and more time gone from home in the company of people like [cartel leader] Amado Carrillo and high-ups in the Mexican government—drinking brandy, snorting lines and screwing. No matter how much money a man makes, there's never enough for that lifestyle. Maybe there're days when, to him, the cash seems unlimited, but mark my words—the day comes when he'll look up and it's gone.

∿ ESSAYS

In the first essay, Stephen T. Moore, a history professor at Central Washington University, analyzes the impact of the U.S. ban on alcoholic beverages on the border between Canada and the United States. Because Canada did not institute such a sweeping ban, in the 1920s Americans crossed the border in unprecedented numbers in search of alcoholic refreshment. Canadian entrepreneurs took advantage of this with a spate of hotel and other hospitality development. Moreover, the high prices for alcohol Prohibition created provided an irresistible lure for Canadian liquor smugglers. By the end of the 1920s, the alcohol-oriented American tourist trade was one of Canada's leading industries. American tourists and their often boisterous behavior strengthened the widespread Canadian belief in the border as a bulwark against their cruder, more philistine southern neighbors. At the same time, the violence and political corruption associated with liquor traffic led many Canadians to view the border as a threat, a "zone of peril" in Moore's words, perhaps similar to the way in which many Americans saw their border with Mexico after the Mexican Revolution. Moore concludes by arguing that the experience of Prohibition led Canadians to see the Canada-U.S. border as "a metaphor for everything that was significantly different about Canadians and Americans."

In the second essay, historian Gabriela Recio, a staff member at Mexico's National Archives, examines similar dynamics on the U.S.-Mexico border during the same period. In the late 1800s, the use of drugs such as cocaine and marijuana was legal and open in the United States. Recio describes the increasing regulation and outright banning of many of these substances, arguing that racial fears played a prominent role. These measures, and the banning of alcohol, created strong economic incentives for the production and shipping of drugs and alcohol in Mexico, where anti–drug and -alcohol campaigns had enjoyed much less success. American Prohibition was, in practice, an enormous subsidy for the Mexican brewing industry, which rapidly expanded in the 1920s. The governors of Mexican border states were able to strengthen their hold on power and independence from Mexico City by skimming some of the profits of drug production and transportation. By the end of the 1920s, Recio concludes, the Mexican Northwest had become a key supplier and transportation hub for the enormous U.S. appetite for drugs. The American government viewed its long border with Mexico as an obstacle for its drug policies, but its inability to limit demand for these substances by its own citizens meant that its enforcement efforts met with little success—a pattern that continues in the twenty-first century.

Canadians, Americans, and the Multiple Meanings of Border during Prohibition

STEPHEN T. MOORE

Canada is a border nation. With over 75 percent or its population living within a hundred miles of the boundary, the border is a reality of virtually every Canadian's daily life. Not only does it define citizenship, it contributes to how Canadians think, what they believe, and how they work. It should come as no surprise then that the border is tied very closely to Canada's national identity. Even Canadian nationalists, quick to point out that being Canadian means much more than simply being "not American" (and it does), concur that the border plays an important role in shaping their identity. One of the English-Canadian writers with the greatest national and international reputation in the 1920s was the humorist Stephen Leacock who, not coincidentally, found much of his material in the border and Canada's relationship with the United States. He once observed, "By an odd chance the forty-ninth parallel, an astronomical line, turned out to *mean* something." But what? This question is not unimportant, even beyond the ways in which it informs the Canadian national identity, for it also helps to explain the relationship between Canadians and Americans more generally. To that relationship the border is central.

Never was this more true than during America's "noble experiment." Between 1920 and 1933, no issue in Canadian-American relations proved more contentious or more intractable than the liquor problem. When the Eighteenth Amendment took effect in January 1920, no longer could Americans make, sell, transport, or import any "intoxicating beverage" that contained more than 0.5 percent alcohol. They could, however, legally drink it, and thus it was left to the Amendment's enforcement mechanism, the Volstead Act, to insure that they didn't have access to it. Predictably, from the Pacific to the Atlantic,

Stephen T. Moore, "Defining the 'Undefended': Canadians, Americans, and the Multiple Meanings of Border during Prohibition," *American Review of Canadian Studies* 34 (Spring 2004): 3–32.

American dollars promptly headed north, and (usually) pure, unadulterated Canadian whisky, south. Canadian distillers, brewers, export houses, rumrunners, and bootleggers were more than happy to assuage the parched throats of their American brethren. However, what was a boon to the Canadian economy was bane to American diplomats and enforcement officials who sought help from their Canadian counterparts in stemming this illegal torrent of booze. Part of the focus of this essay is to explore this problem and the reasons for its intractability.

The "undefended" border had always been a porous one. Yet during the 1920s there was an extraordinary increase in the pace and scope of what Marcus Lee Hansen referred to as the "mingling of the Canadian and American peoples." Its chief cause was the automobile and the ease with which travelers were able to cross the border. By the end of the decade, four million American cars and twenty million Americans crossed the border each year. The effect, according to one historian, was a "turning point" in the cultural history of Canada, as Americans—in pursuit of liquor, scenery, and other things "Canadian"—brought with them other (sometimes less desirable) aspects of American culture.

In ever-increasing numbers, it follows that they spent a greater amount of time thinking about that border and what it meant. One way of exploring the "fabric" of the prohibition-era relationship then is to explore how the shifting meanings of an increasingly permeable border factored into what would have otherwise remained merely a diplomatic problem. Did the border's various meanings magnify distinct sovereign loyalties or did they magnify shared cross-border loyalties? Ultimately, which mattered most?

Even beyond the prohibition question, a study of this sort has much to say about Canadians, Americans, and their respective values and institutions. While the casual (especially American) observer may see or cross the border without recognizing its significance, many academics too often see it as a definitive line and, in so doing, fail to make the valuable comparative discoveries the border offers. Both countries originated from European expansion and evolved from a common, largely English, heritage. Both adopted federal, constitutional democratic systems, place an emphasis on liberal values, and share many social, economic, and historical experiences. It is because Canada and the United States have so much in common that they help us understand not only the other, but ourselves as well. It places into question the notion of American "exceptionalism," or at least forces us to reframe it in a "North American" context.

During prohibition, the border assumed a variety of meanings. As scholars have shown in other contexts, these meanings are not exclusive to the prohibition era. Nonetheless, in examining these sometimes overlapping, sometimes conflicting meanings, we discover answers to why the prohibition problem remained so intractable for Canadian and American diplomats. In the meanings of border, we also discover a microcosm of the larger Canadian-American relationship and a window into the ever-elusive Canadian identity.

In North America, the quest for a temperate society lasted roughly a century, from the 1830s to the Great Depression. The movement's first upsurge coincided with the religious revival known as the Second Great Awakening, and urged voluntary individual temperance for spiritual and social purposes. Temperance borrowed religion's proselytizing methods and emotionalism to convince followers that society's ills could be cured in a world without drink. It was World War I that propelled prohibition to the national stage in both Canada and the United States. With the war, prohibition became synonymous were patriotism. The results were the Eighteenth Amendment, approved by Congress in December 1917, and the War Measures Act, approved by Parliament in 1918.

National prohibition continued in force in the United States until 1932, but in Canada prohibition took a decidedly different turn. When the War Measures Act expired in December 1919, most provinces retained prohibition at the provincial level. Quebec and British Columbia, however, became the vanguard of a new experiment when they adopted a system of government monopoly of liquor sales.

While springing from the same movement and propelled by the same people, it is not accidental that Canada and the United States took different approaches in the temperance cause. Instead it reflects, at a deeper level, very different institutions and value systems.

For prohibition, this had significant consequences, not least of which was a tendency for Canadians to view the provincial or local level as the appropriate arena for social reform legislation, while prohibition advocates in the United States counted on the enforcement machinery of a powerful federal government. By statutorily regulating liquor at the provincial level, Canada enjoyed a degree of flexibility not found in the American constitutional experiment. It certainly confirmed to many Canadians that the Canadian political system was "far more responsive to the ebb and flow of public thought than the plan handed down by the fathers of the Republic." Neither was this irony lost on Americans, especially as the difficulties of enforcing prohibition on a national level became increasingly apparent. The *Boston Globe* commented enviously, "It seems so easy for Canadians to change their minds. We might be trying similar experiments if Prohibition were not a part of the Federal Constitution."

Canada's divergent approach also stemmed from a set of social values that were less likely to use the power of government to regulate social morality. As the Canadian Richard de Brisay commented during prohibition, "The Americans, as a nation, believe their souls can be saved by prohibitory laws. With Canadians it is not so.... We do not believe that there can be salvation by legislation for anyone, anywhere, anytime."

If it did nothing else, national prohibition in the United States convinced Canadians that they were somehow more thoughtful or more temperate in matters of reform. Sociological surveys of this period indicate that many Canadians tended to believe that Americans "resort hastily to extreme measures and yield to social forces which a tougher minded, or at any rate firmer-minded people might resist." Having rejected national prohibition themselves, they became rather cynical of the moral experiment in the United States, especially as a steady stream of American tourists looking for liquor in Canada clearly indicated that a large portion of the American population was not in accord with their own constitutional law.

As an interface, the border tied Canadian and American reformers together even while it reflected fundamentally different approaches toward a common goal. They were different approaches that reflected different values and institutions, but nonetheless influenced each other. On another meaning of the border, however, Canadians and Americans could agree wholeheartedly. The border meant opportunity. It always had. Throughout the border's shared history, smuggling had always been a integral part of the relations between inhabitants, north and south.

But with national prohibition in the United States, the potential of border smuggling took on an almost surreal quality. Once the Volstead Act took effect, the border provided even the lowest of rumrunners with lucrative employment. A case of liquor wholesaling for sixteen dollars in Canada could easily fetch as much as eighty dollars in the States. Canadian or American, rumrunners found that liquor sent across the border in boats, automobiles, aircraft, hip flasks, tin corsets, hog carcasses, shipments of lumber, or farm screenings more than paid for the method of conveyance. The risks were few, but the profit almost without limit.

At the heart of the diplomatic intransigence American diplomats faced in their Canadian counterparts was the boost the liquor trade gave to the Canadian economy. It is impossible to calculate accurately the value of the liquor traffic. Smugglers were no more eager to report their exports to Canadian authorities than American, since Canada heavily taxed liquor exports destined specifically for the United States. Still, from official export figures, one can at least determine the lower limit of Canadian liquor shipped to United States. In 1920, Canada exported only $707,099 worth of alcoholic beverages to the United States. Within only three years, official liquor exports increased to $3,178,908 and, by 1925, to $11,610,169. These figures continued to increase until, for the last three years of the decade, they routinely exceed $30,000,000 annually. For Canada's distilling industry, this was no small change. Having a thirsty, captive audience to the South was a monopoly worth keeping, and distillers made certain that the politicians who represented them were well aware of it.

Entrepreneurs were especially quick to take advantage of the opportunity the border provided to attract American tourists. As with the earlier gold rushes, they recognized that the real profits lay not necessarily in liquor sales, but in providing comfortable places for Americans to drink. Hotels, roadhouses, and personal residences, many of them owned by Americans or financed by American dollars, sprang up all along the international border.

Like liquor exports, American tourism favorably affected Canada's balance of trade. As an "invisible export," if Americans spent $150 million in Canada, it was like Canada sending to the United States goods of an equal value. At its high point in 1929, Commerce Department statistics suggest that American tourists spent $300 million in Canada, and Canadian Department of Trade and Commerce figures place that value at an even higher $309 million. By the late 1920s, the American tourist trade was so important that it ranked among the top three industries in the Dominion.

Whether for smugglers of the distant past, or the rumrunners, distillers, and hospitality industry of the roaring twenties, the border indeed represented unbridled opportunity. For American tourists the border also meant opportunity. But for these travelers it held an overlapping meaning, one that Canadians believed the border to represent as well—refuge or sanctuary. Throughout American history, the border has served as a refuge for those seeking to escape some threat or oppression: for deserters in the War of 1812, for African Americans on the underground railroad, for Sitting Bull and Chief Joseph and their bands of followers, or for opponents of the Vietnam War. For each, the border is a place across which one may escape when internal pressures become too great. This version of the border as refuge most often manifests itself in a south to north direction; that is, it is held more often by Americans fleeing north than it is for Canadians fleeing south. As we will later see, Canadians also saw the border as a refuge, but in a different way.

Even before the Eighteenth Amendment, the concept of Canadian-American "relations" invariably brought to the American mind the vague reminder that Canada was sort of a northern extension of the United States. It was the one country into which American tourists could drive their own motor cars and, save for a brief examination at a customs station, barely know that a border had been crossed. The American tourist could continue to drive on the same side of the road, speak in English, use American money, buy American magazines, and drink "drinks that were his own once but are so no longer."

Ardent drinkers who lived near the Canadian border knew exactly why they were crossing the border, and it wasn't for the scenery. They followed the advice of a popular refrain,

> Forty miles from whiskey
> And sixty miles from gin
> I'm leaving this damn country.
> For to live a life of sin.

No sooner had prohibition taken effect in the United States than the *Seattle Post-Intelligencer* began to joke about the northward migration: "One thing about prohibition, you don't need surveyors to find the boundary line of Canada." The trail left by migrating tourists clearly marked the way. Soon, even those who did not live near the border, and who may never have visited Canada before, found the trek irresistible. Americans sought Canada because of the refuge it afforded them, not only to drink, but to drink without worrying about spies or "stool pigeons." The border offered sanctuary from American temperance run amok and, as the *Chicago Tribune* noted, "freedom in the Provinces which [the tourist] is denied at home."

As Russell Brown notes, the view of Canada as a sanctuary or refuge is one of the "few places where an American version of Canada and the Canadian one correspond, but this apparent similarity actually arises from an important cultural difference." While for Americans the border is a line across which one may escape internal pressures, "In Canada, the border is seen as protecting the country, making it a place of safe refuge from the outside world." In this context, "outside world" most often refers to the United States and all of its excesses. Northrop Frye has noted that Canada's national identity is informed by a "garrison state" mentality. One of the most enduring images of Canada, one that continues to inform the Canadian identity, portrays the Dominion as a tranquil kingdom. Its corollary is the belief that the border juxtaposes "Peace, Order, and Good Government" with "Life, Liberty, and the Pursuit of Happiness." Sociological studies conducted in the 1930s found Canadians believing Americans to be "lawless," "more corrupt," "less moral," and "less cultured." Other popular catchphrases created a picture of a country well on its way to hell: "companionate marriage," "easy divorce," "gangsters," "kidnapping," and "racketeering." On the other hand, words used to describe Canadians included "honourable," "law-abiding," "quieter, slower in tempo, and saner in quality."

In many ways, prohibition in the United States and the adoption of government control in most of the provinces reinforced in the Canadian mind the belief that Canada had found a superior route toward the temperance objective both nations otherwise shared. With reports of prohibition-related violence in the United States an almost-daily occurrence, Canadians tended to look upon their own untroubled waters with an air of smugness. One reader of the *Victoria Daily Colonist* commented that Chicago alone had more criminals in its penitentiary than in all the penitentiaries of Canada. "If this is the record of dry Chicago," he continued, "let us thank God we live in wet British Columbia, where we do not, like the U.S.A., have to build armored cars to transfer a little money or merchandise from one place to another."

American tourists who saw Canada as a wet refuge were, in turn, viewed by Canadians with a certain ambivalence, because American tourism occasionally threatened the Canadian version of border as refuge. While enamored by the profits, many were also wary about the negative effect tourists had on the Canadian social and cultural fabric. Not all Americans who came north in search of drink were congenial to Canadians of the steadier sort. When American tourists brought their philistine culture, they challenged the "peace, order, good government" mantra Canadians held so dear. They also kept the border from being the refuge Canadians needed it to be.

Clearly central to Canada's thinking was the belief that there was little incentive, but great expense, for helping the United States enforce the Eighteenth Amendment. By 1930, however, when the Mackenzie King administration finally found a consensus for cooperation, that illusion had been shattered. The border had taken on yet another, darker meaning. Borders, while they may be crossed, are nonetheless risky places either in a physical sense or, more subtly, for one's identity. Crossing the border means, at least for a moment, to make oneself vulnerable and to be dangerously between. One early traveler commented, "We were across the yet undefined survey line, the 49th parallel. Somewhere here it must run, and for a few miles we were in doubt as to where we were at."

It was when Canadians began to view the border as a zone of peril, that calls began to come from throughout the Dominion to rethink Canada's diplomatic position. Facilitating rumrunners, while profitable, began to seem inimical to Canada's best interests. The border had become a dangerous place for the nation's physical well-being, for its way of life, and for its identity and reputation. A Vancouver daily alluded to this newly discovered reality:

> It is all very well to argue that the enforcement of the prohibition law in the United States has nothing to do with Canada and there is no reason why this country should make any special efforts to assist her neighbor. Up to a point this is technically correct; but the situation which has developed along the international border involves Canada's own vital interest and compels her to consider the question from a broad standpoint.

What the paper was referring to, at least in part, was a new understanding of just how dangerous the rumrunning traffic could be, as well as the corrupting nature of the liquor industry in the Canadian polity.

In the fall of 1924, an abandoned, blood-strewn rumrunning vessel by the name of the *Beryl* G was discovered drifting aimlessly in the Puget Sound, just south and east of the border. The investigation that followed, the most sensational in British Columbia's history, indicated the Canadian vessel had been hijacked and its disemboweled Canadian crew attached to the anchor and thrown overboard. The murderers, though American, had committed this heinous crime in Canadian waters. They had then fled across the border, were eventually arrested in the United States, extradited to Canada, and, after a lengthy trial, executed by hanging. For many years afterward, the hijacking of the *Beryl* G remained the defining incident of the rumrunning era in the Pacific Northwest. While inhabitants of the region recalled the specifics of the *Beryl* G with varying degrees of accuracy, common to all recollections was that the hijackers were Americans.

As the *Beryl* G incident made abundantly clear, the border was more an abyss than the impenetrable and protective barrier many thought. It could not protect Canada from the disorder that emanated from the American side. Not only was the violence associated with the liquor traffic contagious but, by participating in the traffic, Canada undermined her international reputation as well.

Many meanings of the border serve to define the ways in which Canadians and Americans differ. When one thinks of border, it is the idea of division that most quickly comes to mind. Borders divide states, peoples, and identities. But borders also serve as margins. As a border nation, Canadians have often felt as though they were *on* the margin of something else—merely a delightful northern playground for their more numerous neighbors to the south. At other times, to be Canadian means to actually *be* the margin—merely a second-tier power serving as interlocutor, interpreter, or linchpin between two greater powers. Used in these contexts, being on the margin means to be marginal or marginalized. By occasionally defining themselves as "not American," Canadians have had to deal with these mostly negative connotations of margin. More positively, however, margin implies a zone of transition, where interests on one side blend ever gradually with those on the other. The border as margin implies that Canadians and Americans share something positive in common, perhaps a "special," or at least a unique relationship and that the border need not be considered entirely perilous.

As we have seen, that is not to say that Canadians do not defend against American economic, political, or cultural intrusion. However, while myriad "pinpricks" occasionally disrupt the sense of neighborliness, the reality of the border is that it is physically undefended, more a porous fence than a brick wall.

As one American daily pointed out in 1922, "Our border is as open as the prairie just as it should be, for we like the Canadians and some of them have learned to put up with us." Many Canadians agreed but were concerned that prohibition threatened to undermine "three thousand miles of undefended boundary over which not a shot has been fired for a hundred years." This concern took on increasing importance in January 1930 when President Herbert Hoover proposed stationing ten thousand agents along the northern border. The proposal was a mixed blessing for Canadians. Many were glad to see the United States finally taking responsibility for its problems, or at least paying attention to the border for other than expansionist reasons. Others were more concerned. The *Chronicle Telegraph* of Quebec worried, "Experience has shown that the type of man employed as a prohibition agent is not conspicuous for his judgment or responsibility and even with the greatest care in selection, there are bound to be a number ... who are not fit to be trusted with firearms."

The more important concern over the border patrol was the damage a standing patrol would do to that most enduring symbol of the Canadian American relationship. A border patrol, noted the Vancouver *Daily Province,*

> Cannot fail to emphasize everything which divides Canada and the United States. It will give to our border an aspect which it has never had in a hundred years and more—the aspect of an armed frontier, where soldiers patrol the highways of international communication, where guns guard the line which, gunless and peaceful, has been the honorable boast of our friendship.

Even the sovereignty issues seemed to become less important as the border began to lose its characteristic meaning. The *Daily Province* noted, "We are jealous of our sovereignty. We insist that what we do within our borders is the business of nobody but ourselves, and we should resist any attempt on the part of an outside nation to interfere with our decisions."

Others soon began touting the importance of Canada being a good neighbor. Prohibition organizations and dry newspapers throughout Canada petitioned Ottawa to cooperate with the United States with a vigor equal to that expended on the earlier campaign for prohibition. Many in Ottawa at first discounted these petitions, for prohibitionists were not the majority in Canada. Yet with prohibitionists came a large segment of the population who agreed that, wet or dry, it was neither decent nor neighborly for Canada to undermine American public policy. Soon, these groups had attracted the support of Conservatives who saw in agitating for cooperation with the United States a moral high ground from which they could attack the slow-moving Liberals. Coming shortly before a Dominion general election, it would prove a compelling argument. In the end, the idea of the border as a neighborly margin won out.

U.S. Prohibition and the Drug Trade in Mexico

GABRIELA RECIO

In recent years the international community has been increasingly concerned with the rise in volume of illegal drug trafficking. The wide attention and media coverage that the issue has received might indicate that it is a relatively recent problem. However, the drug trade has been the subject of international concern and debate for almost a century. In 1909 the first international conference on opium traffic and control was held in Shanghai—under a joint British and US government initiative. This meeting, attended by delegates from thirteen different countries, marked the beginning of a series of multilateral conferences convened in order to eliminate the manufacture, consumption and trade of opium, initially, and in later years of morphine, cocaine and marihuana.

Although Mexico has been an important participant in the history of the drug trade, little is known regarding how and when the country began to specialise in such illegal endeavours. This article explores the nature of Mexico's involvement in the drug trade at the onset of the twentieth century, arguing that the role Mexico has played as 'bootlegger', the routes that have been developed and the states within the country that have been heavily involved in this traffic have roots that can be traced to 1910 at least.

Such an analysis would not be complete if it did not discuss regulations introduced by the United States regarding drug and alcohol consumption, marketing and production early in the twentieth century. The article will examine the transformation of the drug market between 1900 and 1930, by which time drug production and distribution were totally prohibited in the USA. By examining drug regulation changes that occurred within the United States between 1912 and 1928 and their effects on Mexico, we can begin to understand how drug distribution networks geared to supplying the US market with illegal substances developed in the latter.

How Drug Consumption and Distribution Became Illegal: Changes in U.S. Policies and Regulations

In 1900 opium and its derivatives (morphine and heroin), cocaine and marihuana were legal substances that could be purchased, sold and used without any difficulty in the United States. These drugs could be bought or ordered by mail through different stores. Additionally, their use was not restricted to reducing pain or countering insomnia. For example, until 1903 cocaine was an active ingredient of the Coca–Cola formula, and Parke Davis (the multinational pharmaceutical company, now part of Pfizer, inc.) sold cigarettes, liquor, tablets and an injectable liquid based on coca leaves. Similarly, Sears Roebuck's 1897 catalogue offered 'hypodermic cases' that included a syringe, two needles, two morphine bottles and a case for only $1.50.

Gabriela Recio, "Drugs and Alcohol: US Prohibition and the Origins of the Drug Trade in Mexico, 1910–1930," *Journal of Latin American Studies* 34 (Feb. 2002): 21–42.

Nevertheless, by this date several groups were already indicating that the use of certain medications, such as morphine, could cause addiction.

By 1895, around three percent of the population of the United States was addicted to morphine. The majority were high-income women—known as habitués. These women were not considered outcasts nor socially ostracised. On the contrary, they were believed to have a physiological problem, which could be solved with certain medications. Nonetheless, other groups of addicts were feared by the majority: mostly poor minorities such as the Chinese and Mexicans (who lived mainly in the West) and the Blacks (mostly in the South).

In the South, public perception regarding cocaine was linked to racist prejudices against blacks. It was believed that cocaine consumption by the black community could make them disregard the barriers that society had established between different races. It was thought that 'cocaine transformed hitherto inoffensive, law-abiding negroes into a constant menace to the community … sexual desires are increased and perverted, peaceful negroes become quarrelsome, and timid negroes develop a degree of "Dutch courage" that is sometimes almost incredible. Similarly, the West began an anti-Chinese and anti-opium campaign; in 1875, opium could not be smoked in the city of San Francisco and between the years 1877 and 1900, eleven western states proclaimed anti-opium laws. Correspondingly, the American Federation of Labour (AFL) warned in its brochures against the Chinese, who were portrayed as assiduous opium smokers.

By the 1900s 'racist anti-vice' groups joined forces with other groups that were fighting prostitution and alcohol consumption and began to lobby for drug and liquor control, inculcating a different view towards drug and alcohol consumption and commercialisation in United States public opinion. By the beginning of the twentieth century a new perception was emerging that drug consumption could not be morally accepted and therefore its use should be seriously restricted.… Both pharmacists and the medical profession wanted to regulate the use of drugs but were opposed to total prohibition. These conflicting views led to the formulation of the Pure Food and Drug Act in 1906. This law established that all patented medication containing narcotics in its formula should indicate this information on the label.

Nonetheless, the anti-vice groups were not satisfied with the new regulations and sought stricter laws, lobbying for total drug and alcohol control on a national scale.

The Harrison Narcotics Tax Act and the Volstead Act: Prohibition Begins

In 1914 the United States Congress approved the Harrison Act, which established three mandates for those who distributed or manufactured drugs:

1. All transactions should be registered with the Federal Government.

2. A sales tax was to be imposed on the sale of such substances.

3. A medical prescription was required to buy any drug.

By 1922 a range of different court rulings had transformed the Harrison Act into a totally prohibitionist law. However, drugs were not alone in the 'forbidden substance' category, since the 1919 Volstead Act had already prohibited alcohol production and consumption. During those years addicts began to be considered as criminals and traffickers replaced physicians. Narcotics' markets had few restrictions at the end of the nineteenth century, but by the early twentieth century became illegal endeavours, producing millions of dollars in profits for those involved.

By the early 1920s an important interest group opposed to drug consumption had developed within the Treasury Department, with some sympathisers inside the State Department. This group not only started to fight consumption inside the United States but also believed that the problem could be solved by reducing production in the countries responsible for supplying different narcotics. It was hypothesised that if producer countries totally prohibited drug production, then prices would become exorbitant hence leaving US consumers unable to purchase drugs. Therefore, Mexico—which was a producer as well as distributor of different drugs and liquors—came under systematic Treasury—as well as State Department—surveillance during this prohibitionist phase.

The Effects of Prohibition in Mexico

The new regulations imposed by the US government on alcohol consumption and production as well as on drug consumption, import and manufacturing had profound consequences in Mexico. Total prohibition created black markets worth millions of dollars, and the long border shared with the United States encouraged the expansion of liquor and narcotic markets on the Mexican side.

Even though alcohol prohibition was repealed in the United States in 1933, it is important to analyse the effects of such prohibition on Mexico. Apparently, the Mexican states that were involved in smuggling this product were not necessarily the same as were engaged in drug production and distribution. In fact, there was a 'country' as well as 'state' specialisation in product manufacture and commercialisation. As a result, Canada began by exporting liquors to the United States while Mexico mostly specialised in opium and marihuana distribution. Within Mexico the states that engaged in drug production and distribution were those in the Northwest (Baja California, Sonora, Chihuahua, Sinaloa and Nayarit). The border states, however, were mostly involved with alcohol trafficking, illegally distributing beers and attempting—without much success—to distil some beverages.

By 1915, the states of California and Arizona had prohibited the establishment of alcohol vending saloons. Even though California had not been declared a 'dry state', the Women's Christian Temperance Union of Imperial Valley, California, was lobbying in favour of alcohol prohibition and hoped that regulations would be imposed and enforced promptly. The group's main concern was that the water that the Valley received originated closely to the town of Mexicali in the Baja California territory on the Mexican border. Mexicali as the women pointed out, was filled with numerous saloons that sold alcohol and could therefore pollute the water that they drank. They therefore demanded that if the state of California went 'dry', it should also include the city of Mexicali. The secretary of state consequently instructed the person in charge of Mexican Interests at Mexico City to discuss the matter with the Mexican government.

At the time, not only were people in the USA worried about alcohol consumption. Some Mexican groups, including Venustiano Carranza (president 1917–1920), were worried about alcoholism in Mexico.

Even though Mexico and the USA were concerned about the consumption and production of alcohol in their territories, important differences also existed. Both countries wanted to solve the 'addictive' nature of the problem, but the groups that proposed more stringent regulations differed substantially in both nations. In the USA it was public opinion, in the form of different pressure groups—such as the Women's Christian Temperance Unions—that lobbied for more rigorous regulations. In contrast, in Mexico rules were imposed from top to bottom: the president and the governors issued regulations with apparent lack of public support. During the Mexican Revolution (1910–1920) several states prohibited liquor production and consumption. For example, the state of Durango prohibited the sale and manufacture of alcohol and in Mexico City all *pulquerias* were forced to close down by decree. Sanctions for violating alcohol prohibition differed in kind, the most extreme being death in Chihuahua and Sinaloa.

Although the state governments issued laws prohibiting the production and sale of different liquors, these were often disregarded by officials due to their negative impact on fiscal revenues. The US consul at Durango explained that anti-alcohol laws had not been enforced because no other source had been found to compensate for the loss of fiscal income generated by alcohol sales. Although some members of Mexico's ruling elites favoured anti-alcohol laws, they were reluctant to apply them due to their inability to find alternative sources of fiscal revenue in the midst of the Revolution.

Fiscal earnings were not the only reason why some governors were unwilling to enforce these laws. On the other side of the border, Prohibition had created lucrative black markets, which could provide vast amounts of money to those willing to participate in them.

The passing in 1919 of the Volstead Act in the United States had different consequences in Mexico. As mentioned above, California and Arizona had prohibited saloons and casinos in their states prior to 1919, stimulating the opening of these businesses on the Mexican side of the border. After 1919, the saloon enterprises in Mexico were booming and alcohol trafficking into the United States had become even more profitable.

By the 1920s much of the brewing and distilling factories in the USA were closing down. Some, however, decided to move their entire factories to Mexico, as was the case of a new whisky plant inaugurated in the city of Piedras Negras, Coahuila, in 1920. The factory owners were Mexican and US citizens who planned to sell their product in Mexico and other Latin American countries.

In the years of 1922 and 1923 there were several projects by US brewery owners from the state of California—to establish a brewery in the border city of Nogales in Sonora. Prohibition had seriously affected these businessmen and they were trying to sell their factories or to relocate them entirely to Mexico so that they could resume production.

Prohibition in the United States had other important consequences. It tremendously encouraged the expansion of the Mexican beer industry during a dire economic period. By 1923 Consul Bowman in Mexico City reported that this industry was second in importance within the manufacturing sector. The consul observed that this expansion was due to an increase in beer demand, but most importantly to the absence of US beer within the Mexican market. Prohibition left Mexican brewers with no competition from imported US beers for more than a decade. Thus, a direct correlation existed between the industry's expansion and the imposition of the Volstead Act.

Liquor smuggling increased considerably during the 1920s. Most of this illegal traffic was handled by land, but maritime routes on the Pacific as well as the Gulf Coast were also important. The consul in Progreso, Yucatán, indicated that Pérez Island served as a storage place for liquors in transit that were finally transported by vessels from Florida to the United States. On the Pacific coast the port of Ensenada served as an important base for all the liquor in transit to the Western United States. The consul in that city reported in 1924 that US demand was quite considerable since most of the liquor that arrived in the city was rapidly shipped to US markets.

The Harrison Act and Its Impact on Mexico

The drug trade in Mexico has long been the focus of investigation of Mexican as well as United States government agents. Collaboration between the two countries to attempt to regulate the traffic can be traced to the beginning of the twentieth century. By 1912—two years before the Harrison Act was passed—the Consul at Chihuahua was already working together with special agents of the Treasury Department in El Paso, Texas, and with the Governor of Chihuahua to capture opium shipments that had originated in the port of Manzanillo, Colima.

By 1916 the Treasury Department had begun exerting pressure on Mexico through the State Department to prohibit smoking opium imports. Mexico had signed the International Opium Convention, which had agreed to ban imports of such substances (Chapter 2, Article 7). Nevertheless, Treasury Department reports indicated that Mexico continued to import the drug through the port of Ensenada in Baja California. The Treasury Department was concerned since it had evidence that Mexico imported crude opium, converting it into the smoking version and later exporting it to the United States.

Governor Cantú: The Rent-Seeker

Governor Cantú not only obtained a considerable income from alcohol smuggling, but his earnings were also vastly increased by opium trafficking. It seems that Cantú's involvement in drug smuggling was associated with his authority as governor to issue different types of licenses and concessions. Clearly, Cantú had fruitful drug dealings; as Governor he single-handedly prohibited opium consumption and trade, thus legally allowing him to seize such substances. According to Treasury Department agents, confiscated drugs were sold by the governor or resold to the original owners at a much higher price.

The State Department correspondence suggests that in the period 1916–1920 all opium related traffic was circumscribed to Baja California and in some way or another involved the Cantú family. In terms of describing the opium market that developed in those years in the Baja California territory, it can be reasonably established that opium was imported through the Ensenada Port and later consumed locally as well as exported to the United States. Opium was not commercially planted in Mexico and was therefore imported from Liverpool, Geneva and Germany. The cargo ships travelled from Europe through the Panama Canal and had stopovers at Corinto in Nicaragua; Salina Cruz, Oaxaca; Manzanillo, Colima; Mazatlán, Sinaloa; and finally arrived in Ensenada, Baja California. Once the opium arrived in Baja California, Cantú sold the merchandise to the Chinese in the city of Los Angeles.

Some studies have evaluated Cantú's term in office as a by-product of the autonomy from central government in Mexico City that he enjoyed. These indicate that the distance separating the Baja California territory from central Mexico, as well as the lack of transportation such as railways explain the territory's lack of involvement during the Revolution. It is also mentioned that Cantú was able to obtain resources (which proceeded from cotton as well as canteens) within the territory and thus was relatively free to make decisions compared to other Governors at the time. The correspondence analysed so far suggests that the origin of Cantú's income derived mainly from vice-related operations and that this, in conjunction with the territory's isolation, probably allowed him greater freedom during his term in office. The Governor even affirmed that his government would gladly prohibit the opium trade once he could obtain alternative resources that would compensate the loss incurred from such a lucrative business.

Lastly, it should be mentioned that Cantú—and Mexicans in general—were not alone in the drug trafficking business of the time. It also involved US citizens, Chinese, Rumanians, Palestinians, Spaniards, French, Greeks and Japanese. The involvement of so many nationalities as well as the distribution routes in the opium traffic indicate that narcotic illegal markets have for a long time been international in character. It also points to the fact that Mexico and the United States—as supplier and consumer respectively—were already playing an important part in such a lucrative international market from the beginning of the twentieth century.

The 1920s: The Beginnings of Drug Production in Mexico and the Professionalisation of Trafficking

The 1920s saw the emergence of more stringent laws regarding drug consumption and commercialisation in the United States. Rigorous laws were imposed on a national and state level in Mexico and it was in this decade that traffickers became planters in several states. Smugglers took the offensive and began planting opium in the states of Sonora, Sinaloa, Nayarit, Chihuahua and Durango. Along with planting, the northwestern territory consolidated itself as the most important drug distribution network in the country whose principal market was the United States.

During the decade the Mexican government established that special permits should be obtained in order to import marihuana and opium into the country. It was also ruled that drug stores should record all transactions that involved these substances in special books. In addition, in 1920 the government published the Provisions regarding the trade of products that can be used to encourage vices which degenerate mankind (or race) and on the planting and harvesting of plants that can be used for that purpose.

Provision five prohibited cultivating and marketing marihuana but the sixth established that 'opium poppies as well as extraction of its byproducts could only be handled with a Health Department permit.' At the state level, similar laws were imposed.

Not only the states were addressing the drug-smuggling issue, in 1921 the Mexico City newspaper *Excélsior* launched an intense campaign, informing its readers about drug trafficking operations that were taking place in different border states. The article indicated that several customs employees in Nuevo Laredo, Tamaulipas and Ciudad Juárez, Chihuahua, were involved in drug smuggling. It also mentioned that a man had been captured because he had introduced a kilogram of heroin from the United States for his personal use. The newspaper disapproved of the way that the authorities had handled the case, since after spending only five days in jail and paying a small fine, the man had been set free. This article is interesting in that it illustrates how some groups in Mexico were already concerned about the drug problem, while others saw no harm in consuming heroin.

Some authors have claimed that the current United States government war on drugs has for some years been focused mainly on attacking the supply side, while the demand side problem has been seriously ignored. The correspondence analysed thus far indicates that, as early as the 1920s, the Treasury and State Departments considered that the 'drug problem' could be solved if the drug producer countries could be controlled. Moreover, this view received backing from different pressure groups, since they had been lobbying the Secretary of State to impose severe restrictions on those countries illegally exporting drugs to the United States. These groups viewed consumers as innocent and helpless victims that were being poisoned and killed by those countries that allowed the production of different drugs. According to this view, if the producer country did nothing to prevent drug production then the United States should impose severe sanctions in order to protect its citizens.

It is interesting to note that not only the United States government focused on solving the 'supply side' of the drug problem; Mexico, had adopted a similar strategy at both federal and state level. Nevertheless, it seems that the US strategy was somewhat incomplete since drug consumption was climbing among its own citizens.

Early measures should have been taken to fight both sides of the problem in such a way that coordinated policies by both countries could have been made more effective in curtailing drug trafficking and consumption. Nevertheless, the United States decided to deal with the problem by implementing the Harrison Act. This new prohibitionist atmosphere, as well as the lucrative black markets that resulted from these, induced traffickers to take more aggressive measures. Thus in the 1920s opium began to be planted in the states of Sonora, Sinaloa, Nayarit, Chihuahua and Durango and by the end of the decade the northwestern region had consolidated itself as the most important distribution drug network whose final market was the United States.

In 1923 the consul in Ciudad Juárez reported that marihuana seized during a police raid had been planted in the property of a rich local merchant. In 1924 the Federal Narcotics Control Board reported that opium poppies were being planted in the Sonoran towns of Caborca, Oquitoa and Pitiquito as well as in the city of Mazatlán in Sinaloa. Apparently most of these fields were in the experimental stage and research was been carried out to see if the land was suitable for opium production. Only four years later opium was planted regularly in these towns and the fields were spreading to the fertile Yaqui and Mayo Valleys in southern Sonora.

Another region that became appropriate for opium planting was the area extending from the city of Culiacán, Sinaloa, to the city of Tamazula in Durango (just a few kilometres east from Culiacán). In this territory the planting and manufacture was handled by a group of Chinese who were later arrested and sent to Mexico City for trial. Not only the Chinese were involved in this illegal market; some state public employees in northern Sinaloa played an important role in such a lucrative business.

This suggests that the opium illegal business was expanding and that poppy crops were spreading along several northwestern states. For example, there is evidence that in the 1920s the state of Nayarit was also producing opium and sending it to the United States, and in the city of Mulegé in southern Baja California, the drug started to be planted in 1927. Even though Mexico already had experience in planting and sending such drugs to the United States, the country was not self-sufficient in production; to judge from the reports on opium seizures, the drug entered Mexico illegally quite frequently.

There is evidence to suggest that the role that certain cities played in the drug smuggling markets was constantly changing, a fact that brings to mind contemporary trends in the drug business in Mexico and elsewhere. Whether or not a city or town was more permissive towards drug planting and smuggling depended mainly on the governor's and mayor's tolerance, as well as on the different state and federal controls imposed at various times.

Traffickers changed their *modus operandi* whenever certain routes became more restricted for their operations. This ability to quickly rearrange distribution routes suggests that different means of transportation were crucial in smooth day-to-day operations. As already mentioned, much of the drugs came from Europe through the Panama Canal, with different stopovers along the Mexican Pacific Coast. Once the merchandise reached Mexico it was transported to the United States by sea and land. There is also evidence that the Southern-Pacific Railway was unlawfully used to transport drugs through the states of Nayarit, Sinaloa and Sonora. Finally, it should be said that drug trafficking into the United States was becoming such a profitable business that technological innovations in transport, such as aviation, were also employed by various smugglers as early as the

1920s in order to transport drugs to the northern market. This technological innovation seriously hindered the security measures that the United States had been able to establish along the Mexican border in order to curb drug smuggling.

Conclusion

Whether a country decides to ban (or for that matter permit) narcotic and liquor distribution and production, the consequences are hard felt not only by its citizens but also by those living in adjacent countries. However, little is known about how regulatory changes imposed in the 1920s in the United States affected Mexico once prohibition was put into practice.

This article has explored Mexico's participation in the drug and alcohol trade once its northern neighbour implemented the Volstead and the Harrison Acts. It suggests that the country entered these illegal markets early in the twentieth century, mostly as a result of the new anti-vice regulations that the United States implemented during the 1920s. These stricter regulations—which Mexico also carried through—resulted in the creation of very profitable black markets.

Illicit operations enticed drug traffickers in Mexico to explore the possibilities of opium planting in the country's northwestern territory and also encouraged them to rearrange distribution channels on the Mexican side in a more efficient manner. Although, alcohol prohibition was only in effect between 1919 and 1933, it is interesting to observe how in this period Mexico also began manufacturing whisky to be exported to the United States and Mexican beer factories had an important boost in their activities.

Finally, and more importantly, what emerges as striking is the longevity of Mexican drug distribution channels. The Mexican states that now play an important role in drug trafficking began their activities in this trade around 1916. The northwestern states of Mexico have approximately ninety years' experience of developing and improving channels to distribute drugs into the United States.

FURTHER READING

Campbell, Howard. *Drug War Zone: Frontline Dispatches from the Streets of El Paso and Juarez* (2009).

Cocks, Catherine. "The Welcoming Voice of the Southland: American Tourism across the U.S.-Mexico Border, 1880–1940." In *Bridging National Borders in North America: Transnational and Comparative Histories*, ed. Benjamin H. Johnson and Andrew Graybill, pp. 225–248 (2010).

Díaz, George Thaddeus. *Contrabandista Communities: A History of Smugglers and Smuggling on the Lower Rio Grande Border* (forthcoming).

Cohen, Andrew Wender. "Smuggling, Globalization, and America's Outward State, 1870–1909." *Journal of American History* 97: 2 (Sep. 2010): 371–398.

Ford, Don Henry Jr. *Contrabando: Confessions of a Drug-Smuggling Texas Cowboy* (2005).

Fowler, Gene and Bill Crawford. *Border Radio: Quacks, Yodelers, Pitchmen, Psychics, and Other Amazing Broadcasters of the American Airwaves* (2002).

Gecelovsky, Paul. "Canadian Cannabis: Marijuana as an Irritant/Problem in Canada–U.S. Relations." *American Review of Canadian Studies* 38 (Summer 2008): 207–212.

Gootenberg, Paul, ed. *Cocaine: Global Histories* (1999).

Maleck, Dan. "An Innovation from across the Line: The American Drinker and Liquor Regulation in Two Ontario Border Communities, 1927–1944." *Journal of Canadian Studies* 41 (Winter 2007): 151–171.

Marak, Andrae and Elaine Carey, eds. *Smugglers, Brothels, and Twine: Historical Perspectives on Contraband and Vice in North America's Borderlands* (2011).

McCrossen, Alexis, ed. *Land of Necessity: Consumer Culture in the United States–Mexico Borderlands* (2009).

Medrano, Marlene. "Regulating sexuality on the Mexican border: Ciudad Juarez, 1900–1960." Ph.D. dissertation, Indiana University, 2009.

Miller, Tom. *On the Border: Portraits of America's Southwestern Frontier* (1981).

Mottier, Nicole. "Drug Gangs and Politics in Ciudad Juárez: 1928–1936." *Mexican Studies/Estudios Mexicanos* 25 (Winter 2009): 19–46.

Musto, David. *Drugs in America: A Documentary History* (2002).

Nadelmann, Ethan A. *Cops Across Borders: The Internationalization of U.S. Criminal Law Enforcement* (1993).

Sandos, James. "Northern Separatism During the Mexican Revolution: An Inquiry into the Role of Drug Trafficking, 1919–1920." *Americas* 41 (Oct. 1984): 191–214.

Schantz, Eric. "From the Mexicali Rose to the Tijuana Brass: Vice Tours of the U.S.-Mexico Border, 1909–1965." Ph.D. dissertation, University of California, Los Angeles, 2002.

Tagliacozzo, Eric. *Secret Trades, Porous Borders: Smuggling and States Along a Southeast Asian Frontier, 1865–1915* (2009).

Vanderwood, Paul. *Juan Soldado: Rapist, Murderer, Martyr, Saint* (2004).

———. *Satan's Playground: Mobsters and Movie Stars at America's Greatest Gaming Resort* (2010).

Wald, Elijah. *Narcocorrido: A Journey into the Music of Drugs, Guns, and Guerrillas* (2002).

∿

CHAPTER 13

Migration, Race, and Border Enforcement

If illicit commerce in such goods as alcohol and drugs did much to structure national borders and their perception in the early twentieth century, then the movement of people would become more salient in subsequent decades. Which people would governments allow to freely enter their territory? Which would they restrict, and which ban outright? The nations of North America began to address these questions in the nineteenth century, when they looked with wariness on the movements of indigenous peoples and fugitive laborers (see Chapter 9) and turned against Asian migration (see Chapter 10). In the twentieth century, national governments became much more involved in regulating movement across their borders. The United States became particularly preoccupied with this question because its robust economy continued to attract migrants, even as these migrants provoked animosity and calls for exclusion. Mexican migrants took central stage in these debates because the porous border expedited their entry, and they provoked intense and often violent racial animosity from many white Americans. Although French-Canadians in the Northeastern United States faced some discrimination and ostracism, migration from Canada attracted comparatively little controversy. The Canadian border thus became nearly invisible for most Americans.

This chapter examines the subject of the regulation of Mexican migration to the United States from the 1920s to the early 1990s. The changing patterns of border enforcement had enormous impacts on the lives of Mexican migrants, Mexican Americans, and others living in the borderlands, and raised fundamental social and economic questions. By the twenty-first century, Latinos (of which Mexican-descent people were by far the largest component) had become the largest minority group in the United States and were predicted to be a quarter of the national population by 2050. The border that joined the United States to Latin America, once a lightly populated region far from national centers of power and population, had become a central feature of U.S. and Mexican life.

〰 DOCUMENTS

In the early twentieth century, much of the U.S. population responded to ethnic Mexicans (people of Mexican descent, regardless of their nationality) with great hostility and fear. Document 1 contains portions of a speech by Texas congressman John Box calling for sharp limits on Mexican migration. Box treats Mexicans as a fundamentally different and inferior race and warns of what he sees as the dangers of attempting to incorporate them into American society. At the time, federal law did not ban or limit the entry of Mexican nationals per se. Nevertheless, as discussed in Chapter 11, immigration agents could use literacy and public health provisions to exclude particular Mexicans from the United States, and thus the racial animosity so clear in this document often led to intrusive and hostile inspections of Mexicans crossing into the United States. Although Box's views may have been widely shared by Anglo Americans, they did not carry the day. Instead, farmers' associations, railroad companies, and other employers of Mexican labor succeeded in keeping Mexico and the rest of Latin America out of the immigration quota system established in 1924. As it is now, American society was deeply divided on the question of immigration policy and border enforcement.

The U.S. Border Patrol, established in 1924, was charged with enforcing American immigrant laws. In Document 2, longtime agent Clifford Perkins captures some of the challenges that the new bureaucracy faced in doing so. Anglo landowners had little use for the organization, whose early agents were, according to Perkins, prone to wanton violence. In the rich agricultural area of south Texas, hostile farmers dependent on Mexican labor and the overwhelming number of migrants presented the Border Patrol with what seemed like an impossible task.

The advent of the Great Depression in 1929 greatly strengthened anti-Mexican sentiment. Viewing Mexicans (and Mexican Americans) as competitors for scarce jobs, Anglo Americans pressed government agencies to exclude them from the unemployment benefits, relief programs, and employment measures designed to ameliorate the Depression. Employers began to actively discriminate against Mexicans, firing them first, and hiring them last, if at all. In many places in the U.S. Southwest, local governments organized active campaigns of repatriation, or return to Mexico, with some support from the Mexican government. These campaigns pressured many who were unwilling to go, including numerous U.S. citizens of Mexican descent, into Mexico. As a result of these measures and the Depression itself, the 1930s became the only decade since the outbreak of the Mexican Revolution to see a net migration of Mexicans (about 1.6 million) from the United States into Mexico. Document 3 captures some of worker and trade unionist Jesús Pilares's memories of this time. The 1930s deportations, Pilares makes clear from his own experiences, were also tools of labor control that aided employers' efforts to prevent unionization.

In the subsequent decade, the economic recovery caused by the entry of the United States into World War II quickly reversed this pattern. Concerned that labor shortages could hamper the war effort, the U.S. government actively sought Mexican labor. In 1942, the governments of Mexico and the United States struck an agreement, which lasted in different forms until 1964, to bring Mexican workers into the United States under contracts intended to protect their rights to workplace safety and fair compensation. These agreements, collectively called the "Bracero Program," provoked controversy in both nations. American labor organizations and farm workers, including Mexican Americans, feared that the influx of temporary, non-citizen labor would be used to break strikes and reduce wages for agricultural labor. Some Mexicans saw their government's role in the program as less a defender of Mexican labor and more an enabler of its exploitation. The Bracero Program proved similarly divisive for Mexican Americans. The most prominent Mexican-American civil rights group of the time, the League of United Latin American Citizens (LULAC), formally opposed it. Document 4 is an excerpt from a 1951 report, "The Wetback in the Lower Rio Grande Valley," that key LULAC figures funded and advised. Conducted by two University of Texas sociologists, the report examined the living and working conditions of illegal migrants and their impact on Anglos and Mexican Americans in south Texas. The authors concluded that migrants were exploited precisely because their illegal status limited their contact with the rest of society (including Mexican Americans) and rendered them vulnerable to deportation. Furthermore, the report concluded, their presence weakened the economic position and social status of Mexican Americans. Other Mexican-American civil rights advocates, however, were appalled by the report and furious at LULAC's support for it. They charged that the authors uncritically accepted the worse of anti-Mexican stereotypes and damaged their own cause by repeating them, along with such derogatory terms as "wetback" and "peon." In short, Mexican Americans could not agree on how to deal with continued migration from Mexico. The border that linked the United States and Mexico thus deeply divided American society.

Mexican migrants also had mixed experiences with the Bracero Program, as Document 5, an interview with migrant laborer and former bracero Manuel Padilla suggests. A native of Jalisco, Padilla moved around Mexico in search of work starting in the 1930s. The harsh conditions of the Chihuahua silver mine in which he worked drew him to the Bracero Program, which at first allowed him to find work in the United States relatively easily. In subsequent years, however, the chaos caused by bureaucratic requirements and the sheer numbers of people in search of work led Padilla to cross the border on his own. Regularly returning to his home and family in Juárez, Padilla worked in numerous jobs in the United States for decades, always at risk of imprisonment and deportation. The migration from Mexico, driven by economic forces, proved difficult for either government to regulate or control.

The laws governing Mexican migration changed substantially in 1965, when Congress repealed the 1924 Immigration Act (see Chapter 11). Whereas the old system had aimed at maximizing immigration from western Europe, limiting it from eastern and southern Europe, and banning Asians almost entirely, the new law allowed for migration from across the globe, with preferences for family re-unification and those with particular skills and expertise. The 1965 Act changed the patterns of immigration to the U.S. in important ways, particularly in allowing for the dramatic growth of the Asian-American population. Document 6 excerpts President Lyndon B. Johnson's signing statement, which he delivered at the feet of the Statue of Liberty. Johnson celebrates the Act as a reflection of the diverse and egalitarian character of American society.

The 1965 Immigration Act may have marked a new era in immigration to the United States, but it lead to few changes on the U.S.-Mexico border. The strong pull of the U.S. economy continued to attract hundreds of thousands of Mexican workers every year, far more than could be admitted legally under the provisions of the 1965 Act. Some Americans resented them for their illegal entry, the lowering effect that they could have on wages and working conditions, and, in many cases, for their race. On the other hand, these migrants were welcomed by their employers, by friends and relatives already in the United States, and by other citizens and residents who saw their struggles in much the same terms as Lyndon Johnson had cast immigration. This border thus remained, paradoxically, both permeable and increasingly policed. Nevertheless, the steady expansion of the Border Patrol and increase in deportations and immigration raids heightened the impact of immigration enforcement on the residents of the U.S. Southwest. In Document 7, novelist Leslie Marmon Silko describes being stopped by the border patrol. Her charges that the force ignored whites and deliberately harassed dark-skinned people, including American citizens, were often voiced by borderlands residents, even after the Border Patrol began to recruit large numbers of Hispanic agents. Silko's particular criticism of immigration enforcement emerges from her understanding of native American history, which views national borders as continuations of the conquest of Indian peoples. Even for those who may not be convinced by her argument, her essay underscores the extent to which the enforcement of American immigration law cast a long shadow over race relations in the American southwest.

1. U.S. Congressman John Box Warns of Dangers of Mexican Migration, 1928

... During the present session of Congress immigration discussion and legislation will probably center around four important questions:

1. Shall our deportation laws be strengthened, extended, and better enforced?

2. Shall the endless chain of relationship existing between immigrants and their kindred abroad be permitted to start dragging out of Europe tens of thousands of those whom the laws now exclude?

3. Shall we retain in the law the national-origins provision, written into the acts of 1924, making it more accurately and adequately serve the Nation's purpose to keep itself American, or shall they be suspended or repealed at the dictates of certain hyphenated minorities of our population?

4. Shall the quota provisions of the immigration law be made applicable to Mexico, South America, and adjacent islands?

U.S. Congress, House, Committee on Immigration and Naturalization, *Immigration from Countries of the Western Hemisphere: Hearings: 1930.* 71st Congress, 2d Session, p. 221.

To this last question I shall devote my brief remarks.

The people of the United States have so definitely determined that immigration shall be rigidly held in check that many who would oppose this settled policy dare not openly attack it. The opposition declares itself in sympathy with the policy and then seeks to break down essential parts of the law and opposes any consistent completion of it making it serve the nation's purpose to maintain its distinguishing character and institutions. Declaring that they do not believe that paupers and serfs and peons, the ignorant, the diseased, and the criminal of the world should pour by the tens and hundreds of thousands into the United States as the decades pass, they nevertheless oppose the stopping of that very class from coming out of Mexico and the West Indies into the country at the rate of 75,000, more or less, per year.

Every reason which calls for the exclusion of the most wretched, ignorant, dirty, diseased and degraded people of Europe or Asia demands that the illiterates, unclean, peonized masses moving this way from Mexico be stopped at the border. Few will seriously propose the repeal of the immigration laws during the present Congress, but the efforts of those who understand and support the spirit and purpose of these laws is to complete them and make them more effective by the application of their quota provisions to Mexico and the West Indies, will be assiduously and strenuously opposed.

The admission of a large and increasing number of Mexican peons to engage in all kinds of work is at variance with the American purpose to protect the wages of the working people and maintain their standard of living.

Another purpose of the immigration laws is the protection of American racial stock from further degradation or change through mongrelization. The Mexican peon is a mixture of Mediterranean-blooded Spanish peasant with low-grade Indians who did not fight to extinction but submitted and multiplied as serfs. Into that was fused much negro slave blood. This blend of low-grade Spaniard, peonized Indian, and negro slave mixes with negroes, mulatoes, and other mongrels, and some sorry whites, already here. The prevention of such mongrelization and the degradation it causes is one of the purposes of our laws which the admission of these people will tend to defeat.

2. Border Patrol Agent Clifford Perkins Recalls Early Challenges of the Organization, 1978

Within two years the Border Patrol in the El Paso District was a healthy, coordinated outfit that was beginning to inspire a considerable amount of public confidence. The officers were well trained and disciplined; they could be counted on in any tight spot they encountered; generally, they reflected the efforts expended to set up a model for the nationwide, responsible division of the Immigration Service we hoped the Patrol would become. Walter E. Carr, the District Director in

Clifford Perkins, *Border Patrol: With the U.S. Immigration Service on the Mexican Boundary, 1910–1954* (El Paso: Texas Western Press, 1978), 100–103, 106–107.

California, had taken almost as active a part in the establishment of the Border Patrol as George Harris, the man probably most responsible for providing the initial impetus necessary to put the new organization into successful operation. As a result, the Patrol in California progressed almost as rapidly as it did in El Paso, and proved to be every bit as deserving of public support. The story in the San Antonio District during the same period, however, was quite different. There, due to politics in and out of the Service, the Patrol's primary accomplishment was to gain a bad reputation practically the entire length of the Rio Grande.

Influence peddling and the spoils system have been more a way of life in Texas than perhaps any other state in the Union, the result, I suspect, of the thousands of miles of onetime practically uninhabited country brought under a semblance of control only by tough, determined ranchers who had little or no help to start with from local or federal law officers. To survive, as well as to protect their property against rustlers, renegades, and raiders from below the border, the successful early settlers had to shoot first and ask questions later. To continue to hold onto what they had acquired with such difficulty, they and their descendants, with the assistance of equally tough hired hands, enlarged and consolidated their islands of rugged individualism into self-sufficient empires, giving, little more than lip service to outside authority.

The first effective law enforcement officers along the Rio Grande were counterparts of these early ranchers: the determined Texas Rangers, who had to be tough to tame the country and its inhabitants. Not surprisingly, growing numbers of federal law enforcement officers who served the expanding population received little help from either local officials or the Rangers; the federals found their efforts often triggered confrontations with landowners long accustomed to being laws unto themselves. Right or wrong, many felt they had the right to keep what they had by whatever means they could. Resorting to less deadly but equally devastating methods of preserving their positions, they turned to circumvention of the laws through pressure, favoritism, and eventually through political corruption. In such a climate, the life of any law officer or organization was apt to be both difficult and short. It was therefore understandable that the district director of the Immigration Service in the San Antonio District was a political appointee instead of an officer who had come up through the ranks, as was the case elsewhere. Also, it followed that he allowed personnel under him to carry on in any way they saw fit, so long as their actions did not interfere with his prerogatives, and that beyond recruiting enough men to bring the Border Patrol up to its authorized strength after funds were appropriated, he did nothing to build an organization. As a consequence, operations were slipshod; the men were disrespectful to their superiors as well as to each other, inefficient in what work they did and careless in their appearance, showing up for duty out of uniform or wearing only parts of it, which was worse.

To clean up the situation in this district, I was transferred to the San Antonio headquarters as Chief Patrol Inspector in June of 1926 and was promoted to Assistant Superintendent of the Border Patrol on my arrival. This was both a substantial advancement and a tremendous challenge, for the San Antonio District extended north to the Texas-Oklahoma state line.

Many early Patrolmen were acquainted with the Texas Rangers and their activities and started to emulate them despite the fact that the Patrol was dealing with the general public, not criminals. It makes a lot of difference whether an officer is in a shoot-out with a bunch of rustlers or winnowing out a small percentage of aliens engaged in unlawful activities. It took considerable indoctrinating to convince some of the inspectors they were not chasing outlaws, and we never did get it out of the heads of all of them, for we had to discharge several for being too rough. A good percentage had not been well trained, so that once in a while conditions arose that became serious before either the sector or district offices were aware of what was going on. Not all of the problems were obvious, and a few would have proved very injurious to the Patrol had there been any publicity. One involved a Mexican arrested as a smuggler, whose case was referred back to our office by the judge when it came to trial because was no evidence against the man's beyond his confession. During the ensuing investigation it developed that the main confession was all the evidence in the case. Two officers had apprehended him near the river in what happened to be rather suspicious circumstances, had tied his feet together, and had dragged him into the water to conduct an interrogation. Every time they asked and he denied that he was a smuggler, they jerked his feet out from under him. After enough dunkings, they obtained what they considered a satisfactory admission of guilt and took the fellow in.

Opposition to the Border Patrol in the Brownsville Sector was considerable and stemmed from ranchers and farmers in the lower Rio Grande Valley who had benefitted greatly before the Patrol entered the picture by using Mexican wetbacks to plant and harvest their crops. The laborers were paid practically nothing, and such exorbitant prices were charged for food, clothing and other essentials at ranch commisaries that they were usually in debt to their employers by the end of their stay. Inspectors picking up illegal entrants literally by the thousands and sending them back across the line aroused the resentment of the growers, and they were not reluctant to register complaints that would make trouble for the Patrol. To make matters worse, the head of the Republican Party in Texas resided in the Brownsville Sector and made himself accessible to anyone with a real of imaginary complaint to make about Patrol activities.

The Brownsville Sector was by far the best organized in the district when I became assistant superintendent, though that was not saying much. Considering the others, however, it was a good deal, and all the credit went to Chief Patrol Inspector Portus Gay, a longtime resident of Brownsville and former Texas Ranger. In an effort to cope with the wetbacks pouring into the country during the growing season, he kept very few men in the sector office, scattering the better part of his force along the river as far up as Rio Grande City. Their efficiency and reputation were slightly better than elsewhere, but so much feeling existed against them at the time of my first inspection trip, that their morale was shaky or nonexistent, and it showed in their sloppy appearance. The lack of cooperation from residents and the overwhelming numbers of illegal entrants contributed greatly to the men's discouragement. Officers at one station reconciled themselves to their difficult situation by setting a daily quota of wetbacks to be picked up. Once that number had been reached, they quit looking, knowing inspectors at the ports of entry would be unable to process more out of the country, a procedure involving not much more than putting the aliens back across the river after identifying data were taken.

3. Philip Stevenson Describes the Deportation of Jesús Pallares, 1936

On June 29, [1936,] Jesús was deported as an undesirable alien. Jesús Pallares is a skilled miner. He has spent twenty-three of his thirty-nine years in the United States. Born in the state of Chihuahua, Mexico, Jesus joined the Madero revolution at the age of fifteen, fought four years, and mustered out in 1915 with part of his lower jaw missing. He entered the United States legally and obtained work as a miner. As miners' standards went, Jesús did well. He was an exceptional worker. There never was a time when he could not get a job. On the whole he got along with his bosses.

The onset of the depression, 1930, found him working for the Gallup-American Coal Company, a subsidiary of the Guggenheim giant, Kennecott Copper. In 1930 Gallup was unorganized. So when Jesús found himself being paid ... irregularly ... , he kicked—as an individual—and like individual protestors in all depressed coal fields, was promptly fired.

Jobs were scarce now... But after several months of unemployment he obtained work at Madrid, New Mexico. The town is company-owned.

Jesús was elected local union organizer. Jesús and his aides decided to ask the aid of the federal government in enforcing Section 7-a.[*] When the company prohibited all union meetings in Madrid, the unionists walked four miles to Cerrillos for meetings, passed resolutions, drew up petitions, framed protests, and sent them to the coal board, ... to the state Labor Commissioner. From the coal board came a promise of a hearing—if the miners would withhold their strike and wait. And wait they did. Not until... February, 1934 did T. S. Hogan, chairman of the Denver District Coal Board, arrive in Madrid for an "impartial" hearing.

... Grievances went unredressed. Union meetings continued to be prohibited. A new coal code went into effect, only to be violated even more flagrantly by the company. They struck. The strike failed. Jesús was marked for riddance.

Under the NRA [National Recovery Administration] he could not be fired for union activity.[†] He finished work ... in the mine and was assigned a new location. He could make at best sixty-seven cents a day here—and the mine

---

Philip Stevenson, "Deporting Jesus," *Nation*, July 18, 1936. As excerpted in *Major Problems in Mexican-American History*, 279–282. Reprinted with permission. For subscription information, call 1-800-333-8536. Portions of each week's Nation magazine can be accessed at http://www.thenation.com

[*]Section 7-A of the 1933 National Industrial Recovery Act (NIRA) guaranteed workers the right to organize and bargain collectively through representatives of their own choosing interference by employers. *Ed.*

[†]The NRA was one of the two major recovery programs of the Roosevelt administration. Through the NRA, major public works projects were established to increase employment. *Ed.*

was then working only one day a week—while his rent alone amounted to $3 per week. Yet the boss refused him any better location. Then a fellow worker offered to share his place with Jesús. Jesús asked the superintendent's permission to accept this offer.

"No. Take the place assigned you, or none." ...

... Jesús refused. His fifth child was expected shortly. His savings went for food. Arrears on his rent to the company piled up. He was told to vacate his house or be evicted. He stayed put. The child arrived.

... Jesús was charged with "forcible entry" of his house. The "court" was the company office, the justice of the peace a company employee. Evicted, blacklisted as a miner, Jesús moved to Santa Fe and for the first time in his life went on relief. The family of seven lived in one room, on two cents per meal per person.

... In the fall of 1934 Jesús began organizing for the Liga Obrera de Habla Española (Spanish-speaking Workers League) which concerned itself ... with the problems of the Spanish-American rank and file. In November there had been a few hundred members. By February, 1935, the Liga had grown to some 8,000. Jesús was elected organizer for the whole district, serving without pay and hitchhiking to organize the most remote hamlets on his days off from FERA work.*

... Jesús ... won the enmity ... of the organized rulers of New Mexico. On April 23, 1935, he was arrested while at work on his FERA job and jailed on deportation charges. After three weeks' confinement, a secret hearing was held in an attempt to prove Jesús active in "communistic" organizations.

... Jesús was held for deportation under $1,000 bond pending a review of the case. The bond was promptly furnished.

He continued his task of organizing the Liga Obrera.

As a leader in the Liga Obrera, Jesus often accompanied delegations to the local relief office presenting cases of discrimination. Recently, a worker in that office has disclosed ... the methods employed against Jesús "in an effort to create reasons for his deportation"...

> Attempts were made by my office to intimidate Pallares by withholding relief and by inventing reasons by which he could be removed from relief jobs which were the only types of employment open to him. He was repeatedly called into my office where threats were made to starve his family in order to involve him in an argument which the relief agency hoped would give rise to violence on his part, which in turn would give sufficient reason for a complaint to the Labor Department. Such violence never took place. Nevertheless a complaint was made to Washington ... that Pallares was a "troublemaker."...

At the hearing on his case before the Labor Department's Board of Review last spring Jesús was represented by an attorney for the American Committee for

---

*The Federal Emergency Relief Administration (FERA), set up in 1933, provided funds for the unemployed in the form of jobs. *Ed.*

the Protection of Foreign Born. Among the papers on file ... two remarkable documents came to light, the existence of which had hitherto been kept secret.

The first was a letter to Secretary of Labor Perkins from Governor Clyde Tingley of New Mexico, urging that Jesús's deportation be "expedited" on the ... grounds that the Liga Obrera was "the New Mexico branch of the Communist organization."...

The second document was a telegram to the Immigration Bureau in Washington ... :

> Having trouble with Jesús Pallares on strike in this county. I understand he is under bond on account of the strike at Gallup, New Mexico. He is an alien from Old Mexico. We must act at once to save trouble and maybe lives in this county.
> Francisco P. Delgado, Sheriff [of San Miguel County].

In four sentences the telegram managed to utter five deliberate falsehoods. 1. The sheriff's trouble was not with Jesús but with the strikers at the American Metals Company's mine at Terrero, New Mexico. 2. Jesús was not on strike—did not even live in the sheriff's county. 3. Jesús was under bond for deportation, not for strike activity in Gallup or elsewhere. 4. At the time of the death of Gallup's sheriff, Jesús was living 230 miles away in Santa Fe. 5. The deportation of Jesús could not possibly save "trouble and maybe lives" so long as the sheriff insisted on breaking the strike by armed force and violence.

Curiously enough, two truths did creep into the sheriff's wire: first, that Jesús was indubitably "an alien from Old Mexico"; second that ... New Mexico officials and the Bureau of Immigration ... were acting in concert to railroad Jesús out of the country. And they have had their way. Jesús is deported.

4. Report Examines Migrant Labor in South Texas, 1951

Characteristics of the Wetback. Although the wetbacks are by no means a homogeneous group in every respect, there are certain attributes that tend to characterize them as a body. Preliminary analysis of our data shows that the wetback is likely to be male and from 18 to 30 years of age. The chances are about even that he is married and has one or more children. Only a few come from those Mexican states bordering on Texas; many came from the central and southern parts of Mexico, especially from the states of Guanajuato, Jalisco, San Luis Potosí, and Michoacán. They are almost invariably, farm laborers in Mexico although many own or rent small parcels of land which is cultivated in their absence by other family members. They come for relatively short periods ranging from three to six months. The peak of the migration is in the Valley cotton picking season which begins about July 1 and usually ends not later than September 1.

Lyle Saunders and Olen Leonard, *The Wetback in the Lower Rio Grande Valley of Texas,* University of Texas, Inter-American Education Occasional Papers, VII, July 1951, 84–90.

Almost all the wetbacks who enter the United States are employed in unskilled jobs. Relatively few achieve positions involving skills unless, of course, they are able to remain unmolested for a period long enough to enable them to learn a skilled occupation through apprenticeship and to master the fundamentals of English. Predominantly their jobs involve arduous, stoop, manual work such as picking cotton and cultivating and harvesting vegetable and citrus crops. Probably their nearest approach to performing skilled work is in irrigation work, which most of them learn in Mexico. Such work is considered unskilled or at most semiskilled in the Valley, however, and is paid for accordingly.

The use of wetback labor on Valley farms has become thoroughly rationalized in the thinking of the Valley farmers. Ample moral and ethical, as well as economic, justification is found for the low wages paid the wetback. Economic justification hinges upon "the many cash expenditures" involved in Valley agriculture including cost of irrigation water, mechanical equipment, and excessive shipping costs. Moral and ethical justification is found in the fact that "he still receives higher wages than in Mexico" and "here he can learn how to do scientific agriculture."

Impact of the Wetback on the Valley. This, obviously, is a complex category involving innumerable factors. Here, attention is devoted only to the more important and tangible factors that affect the two major social groupings of the Valley, the Anglo and the Spanish-speaking.

Relations of the Anglo with the wetback are limited to those of an economic nature. The two groups are in contact only in fields or in business; never or almost never do they meet socially except in the case of the few wetback children who attend the public schools. Thus, for the Anglo producer, the wetback is merely a cog in the production machine—serving as a source of cheap labor and returning to Mexico when the need for his labor ceases. The picture is somewhat different for the Anglo businessman who, to be sure, shares in the benefits to be derived from cheap, wetback labor, but, at the same time, loses to the extent that much of the money earned by wetback labor is returned Mexico and not spent locally. This is a factor frequently ignored; or overlooked by the businessman who defends the use of wetback labor.

The entrance of wetback labor into the United States affects the bulk of the Spanish-speaking people in the Valley in various ways. First they must compete with the wetback for jobs. This obviously, applies mainly to the relatively unskilled, semi-skilled and clerical jobs. Most of all, however, it applies to jobs of an agricultural nature, including the harvesting and packing of both fruit and vegetables, their canning and processing, and the picking of cotton. Since the fruit and vegetable seasons reach a peak during the winter months when other agricultural labor is not available elsewhere, many of the local Spanish-speaking people remain in the Valley to compete with the wetbacks. During the cotton picking season, however, there is agricultural work to be had elsewhere and native workers leave the Valley in large numbers. The seasonal migration of native labor from the Valley is generally considered to begin in April, however, with the migrants going first to north Texas and then into the beet fields of

Michigan and other areas. Near the end of July, 1950, a sample census through a number of Valley towns indicated that more than half the local, Spanish-speaking people were temporarily away from the Valley. Local Spanish-speaking residents consider this estimate too low. A labor union in Mission claimed that only about 30 of its winter membership of more than 600 have remained in the Valley through the summer. Although no check was made on the statement, one might well expect that a greater percentage of such a group would migrate than would be true of the general or total population. At any rate almost none of the Valley cotton picking was in 1950 being done by citizen labor. Another random check in the Valley, completed on July 20, showed that practically all workers in the Valley cotton fields were wetbacks, and that the few citizens who were working were women, children, and old people who could not migrate.

Another area in which the influence of the wetback has been enormous is in the retarding effect it has exerted on intergroup relationship, especially those between the Spanish- and English-speaking groups. This is obviously a difficult factor to measure, but its significance is evident on every hand. It is most visible in what might be called the power structure or hierarchy in the Valley, i.e., the subordinate economic and political position of the Spanish-speaking population as compared with that of the non-Spanish-speaking or Anglo. These positions have been buttressed in the past by differences in educational and employment opportunities between the two groups. Justifications or rationalizations for these differences that are current in the Valley include much-worn ideas regarding the difference in the standards of the group, e.g., "the Mexican doesn't want a good house, a variety of foods, and education for his children" and the notion that to pay a Spanish-speaking person more money is merely to increase his indulgence in leisure-time activities and idleness.

It is clear to anyone who makes an objective observation in the Valley that the local Spanish-speaking people have done much during recent years to undermine the above rationalizations. Some of the more tangible evidence for this is found in the increased enrollment of Spanish-speaking children in the higher grades and in a slow but fairly steady response to their demand for a wider range of employment eligibility and a decrease in the historical wage differential that has existed in the Valley.

The importance of the wetback migration on this situation is obvious. The wetback, first of all, is a real caricature of the Valley "Mexican" stereotype. He is illiterate, unable to speak English, and visibly poor. His historical status as a peon on the landed estates of Mexico has done little to establish in him values and attitudes in keeping with those generally believed to characterize a society of individual initiative and free enterprise. And, regardless of whether he is in the Valley a few weeks or a few years, he is able to raise himself but little from this unenviable level. This, of course, reflects back upon the native Spanish-speaking group, since society at large tends to label the entire Spanish-speaking population in terms of those characteristics possessed by a few. Hence the native

Spanish-speaking people in the Valley, with the exception of the few who are accepted in the Anglo society, are classified as "Mexicans" with no differentiation being made between them and the *bona fide* nationals of Mexico.

Attitudes in the Valley Toward the Wetback. The attitudes of the Valley people toward the wetback migration vary strikingly from one group to another. Farmers and growers, be they English-, Spanish-, or German-speaking, maintain consistently that wetback labor "has made the Valley" and that Valley agriculture could not long exist should it be prohibited. As indicated in an earlier paragraph, the use of wetback labor has its ethical and moral justifications also. These, in general, revolve around such judgments as "the native people won't work," or "the native people are becoming urbanized—are leaving the farms for the cities," or "the native laborer is not satisfied to remain in one place but wants to travel about and visit other parts of the country."

Attitudes of the local Spanish-speaking people, and especially the laboring class, toward the entrance of wetback labor is in definite contrast to that of the Anglo. The difference, of course, is rooted in the economic competition provided by the wetback and in the social and political problems already mentioned. Citizen labor will not, except where special circumstances force them to do so, work for the same pay and under the same conditions of housing, sanitation, etc., as the wetback. The acceptance of such conditions by the wetback is thus resented by the local Spanish-speaking people, a resentment that is increased by a failure on the part of many elements of the community to differentiate one group from the other. Even so, the attitudes of the local Spanish-speaking people toward the wetback are frequently ambivalent, and especially so among those who have recent and strong ties with Mexico. Then too, the cultural similarity that characterizes the two groups results in a mutual understanding and sympathy.

The total set of Valley conditions which foster identity between the wetback and legal Spanish-speaking residents of the Valley tends to bring the two groups together at various levels as well as to separate them at others. Wetbacks who drift into the towns looking for work always settle or locate in the Spanish-speaking sections of the town where they are able to rent rooms or small houses that frequently have been constructed for this purpose. This physical proximity in living has resulted in the attendance of children of the two groups in the same schools, and in the development of visiting and fraternizing relationships that frequently lead to intermarriage. Thus the attitudes of the native toward the wetback are dual and frequently conflicting, the antagonistic ones deeply rooted in economic competition, and the sympathetic ones in the sharing of many elements of a common culture, and a common set of values and standards. Conflicts imbedded in these attitudes come quickly to the surface if and when the local people are questioned about "why, if you are opposed to the entrance of wetback labor, do you rent them houses and rooms?" Obviously the easiest and most direct response to this question is, "It's business; we make a little money out of it," but some frankly admit that "they are our people and we feel sorry for them when they come to us without a place to sleep and with nothing to eat." The importance of this mixed situation is generally overlooked by those working towards solutions of attendant problems. Its recognition and effective utilization must come before any satisfactory and permanent solution of the problem can be realized.

5. Bracero and Migrant Manuel Padilla Remembers Working Life in Borderlands, 1974

The silver mine where I worked was about 900 meters deep. It had fourteen or fifteen levels. It was very hot down there, and we would work half naked, carrying sacks all day long. At times there was no air. The water would run through the ditches, and it was so hot that it would vaporize. It was dangerous work. My father ruined his life working in the copper mines of Arizona. At the time he was working, the machines that crushed the ores did not have water to settle the dust. He breathed that dust, and after some time his respiratory system was plugged up. He would wake up in the middle of the night choking and yelling. It was terrible. He suffered for seven or eight years and finally committed suicide in 1933.

In 1940 I met a schoolteacher in Los Azules. I invited her to have some ice-cream, and she accepted. At first we were friends, but later we went to a 5 de mayo [national holiday] dance. Within three months we got married and went to Torreón for our honeymoon.

I worked in Los Azules and then in San Francisco del Oro until 1944, when I decided to leave the mine and become a bracero. I went to Juárez, waited for nineteen days, but I could not get a contract. The politicians had decided that the workers should go to Mexico City to get the documentation, so I went to Mexico City with a leave of absence from the mine. In one day I was able to get my contract; there weren't too many people. That year I worked in San Bernardino, California. The following year I had to go to Mexico City once again to get my documents, but this time there were many thousands of people who wanted to go to the United States. Lines would form during the night, because the workers wanted to be ready for the following morning. They would sleep sitting down, covering themselves with their blankets. The people had great need; they were hungry. Many had been waiting around for two months without being able to get into the office. When the doors opened in the morning, there were some who would disrupt the line to create confusion so they themselves could go to the front. I saw someone throw some burning oakum, and that sure made the bunch scatter. Then the mob would form the line again.

Once there was so much confusion that one of the guards started shooting his gun into the crowd. He hit some workers who were blameless. Others soon went after the man with the gun. Then the officials sent for firemen, who came with hoses and shot water at the people to disperse them. It was a real mess,

Manuel Padilla Interview, Dec. 21, 1974, Institute for Oral History, University of Texas at El Paso. As published in Oscar J. Martínez, *Border People: Life and Society in the U.S.-Mexico Borderlands* (Tucson: University of Arizona Press, 1994), 151–155. © 1994 The Arizona Board of Regents. Reprinted by permission of the University of Arizona Press.

something terrible. There were some who got killed in the disorder, who were trampled as those in front ran back. Later they brought in some troops, who kept order with their rifles and bayonets.

For three weeks those of us from Chihuahua tried to get in, but we couldn't. We were afraid to be in line because of the tremendous crowding. About thirty or forty of us decided to go to Chihuahua City to see if the governor there could help us with a letter that we could then use to get in. We managed to get the letter, and the group took it to Mexico City, but I stayed behind in Chihuahua for a few days. When I returned to Mexico City, everyone on the list in the governor's letter had left. They had all been called over the loudspeaker and had gotten in. My brother Panchito was among them. I found a friend who gave me a note Panchito had left for me. He wrote that I and others on that list who had not been there when the names were called should contact a certain person to get our cards. The only problem was to get into the office. It was difficult because there were still so many people waiting in line. At noon I decided to go to the back entrance, and I told the guard that my name was on that list, and he let me in. I saw the official, and he signed my card right away, and that year I went to Idaho. In 1946 I got my contract in Aguascalientes, and later on I signed up about three times in Mexicali.

When I worked in the fields as a bracero, at times there were some foremen who were abusive, who would punish or fire you if you defended your rights. Once when I was loading lemons on trucks, the foreman left me to do the job of two people when he took away the other man who was helping me. I got angry and thought to myself, "Does he think I am going to do this alone all day long. He can go to hell! As soon as I have a chance I'm going to the rest room." That's what I did, but he came over and asked, "Why did you leave?" I told him I couldn't work all day long without going to the toilet, but he reported me to the "big foreman." The "big foreman" forgave me, but later I had the same trouble again and I got fired. I said, "The hell with it!"

They sent me someplace else to pick oranges, but there I got into a fight with another bracero who was one of the foreman's favorites. I was with him when he was driving a truck, and I opened the door because it was very hot. We were still in the fields; we had not entered the highway. He told me to shut the door because it would get damaged. I said, "The truck isn't yours. If the door is damaged, let the company buy another one. They have lots of money." He said, "Yes, but I am in command in this truck." I replied, "Well, you may be in command of the truck, but not of the door. I won't close it until we get to the highway." He stopped the truck, and we got into a fistfight. The "field boss" caught us fighting, and since I was new there, the following day they told me to get my things together, and I was sent to another camp nearby where it was very hot and where I didn't like the food. Also, I didn't like the scissors they gave me to do the picking.

I said, "Give me another pair. These are no good. I don't want them."

"Well, we don't have any more. You'll have to wait until the 'field boss' comes."

When he got there, he didn't have anything, so I threw the scissors at him, saying, "This thing is no good. I'm just going to pick with my bare hands." He got angry and told me to get in the truck, that he was taking me back to the camp.

At the camp I decided to desert my contract. I left without telling anyone. I went to Palo Alto, where I had an aunt. I worked there for about a month and a half, and then I went to Fresno, where I worked until the end of the year. The *migra* caught me and I was sent to Juárez, where my family was now living. I had written my wife and had told her to move to the border, that possibly things were better there. I told her it would be better for her and the kids to be at the border so I wouldn't have to go all the way to San Francisco del Oro to see them. I spent about three months in Juárez, and then I returned to the United States, hiding from the migra. I went to the state of Washington to pick apples. I knew I could earn good money there. After that, that is the way I did it for about ten years. I would return to Juárez at Christmastime, stay until April or May, and then go back to the United States.

I didn't like Juárez because of the climate; it got too hot there. Secondly, you couldn't work [on the American side] without papers because the migra patrolled the border all the time. Many from Juárez would work in El Paso with their local crossing cards, but when they were caught, they would lose them. I would head into the interior of the United States, where I had more opportunity to evade the migra. There the migra was not on top of you all the time. You could work for some time before they would come around. And if you could "escape" when they arrived, then you could stay longer. Also, the jobs around El Paso didn't pay much. If you wanted a factory job, you would have to wait for your turn to come up. If you worked in the fields, you could make about $2.50 a day maximum at that time. In California you could get a job right away, without having to apply or anything. If you picked fruit, you could work by piece-rate and earn as much as twenty-five or thirty dollars a day. I wasn't about to stay at the border.

Once I did try working in Las Cruces, New Mexico, which is near El Paso. I didn't like it. I worked weeding cotton for three dollars a day. I said to myself, I can earn more than that in one hour picking cherries in California." I lasted two weeks on the job and then went to California. In two months I would earn more than a thousand dollars picking cherries, but I had to work from sunrise until dusk. In some orchards they would let you work as much as you wanted. I would take food and spend the whole day there. There were many good pickers who would earn more than forty-five dollars a day. Since the season was only two months long, we would try hard to earn as much as we could. After cherry picking was over, I would go pick apricots, then peaches, and then pears. I preferred to work in the fields because there it was easier to avoid the migra. I felt bad leaving the family at the border all the time. But what could I do? I had to earn money so we could all eat.

In 1946 when I was in the state of Washington, I didn't like it and went on to Idaho, where I thought the migra would not bother me. I worked loading potatoes on trucks for two or three weeks, and I earned pretty good money. When I least expected it, two plainclothes officials arrived. I never thought they were immigration inspectors.

"Padilla," one of them said, "come over here!"

I thought, "Who can that be?"

He said, "Do you have papers?"

I answered, "No, I don't have papers. What papers are you talking about?

He said, "Your papers that allow you to be here. I am an immigration inspector. You'll have to come with us."

I said, "Well, all right."

Soon the farmer came over and paid me with a check. They locked me up for about a week in a nearby town and then took me to Spokane to a big jail, where they kept me for forty-six days. We ate twice a day. It was regular food; it filled us up. I would spend a lot of time playing cards, waiting for my turn to leave. Finally one day they took my group at two in the morning, and we left by plane to El Paso. I was lucky. Imagine, if they had taken us to another part of the border as punishment! When they let me go, I went to my home in Juárez.

Another time I was caught working in *el traque* [on the railroad] in Kansas. I was locked up in Kansas City also about forty-seven days, and from there they took us to San Antonio by train. We were on our way to Laredo, but I was taken off the train with a few others who had lied about their names. I had made mistake when I told them my last name. It was back to jail again, this time is San Antonio for two or three weeks. Then they took us to Laredo. When he crossed the border, the Mexican immigration official gave me a bus ticket saying "Here, take this. We don't want you here. Leave right away." Thief! From there I made my way back to Juárez through Monterrey and Torreón.

I spent two or three weeks in Juárez and re-crossed the border. I worked in Kansas for about a month, and then I was caught again. Back in Juárez I decided Kansas was too cold, so the next time I went to California. This was in 1948 or 1949. I spent about a year in Stockton and then returned to Juárez. I continued doing that for years, working for part of the year and then returning to Mexico in time for Christmas.

6. President Lyndon Johnson Signs New Immigration Law, 1965

October 3, 1965

Mr. Vice President, Mr. Speaker, Mr. Ambassador Goldberg, distinguished Members of the leadership of the Congress, distinguished Governors and mayors, my fellow countrymen:

This bill that we will sign today is not a revolutionary bill. It does not affect the lives of millions. It will not reshape the structure of our daily lives, or really add importantly to either our wealth or our power.

Public Papers of the Presidents of the United States: Lyndon B. Johnson, 1965 (Washington, D.C.: Government Printing Office, 1966), vol. 2, entry 546, pp. 1037–1040.

Yet it is still one of the most important acts of this Congress and of this administration.

For it does repair a very deep and painful flaw in the fabric of American justice. It corrects a cruel and enduring wrong in the conduct of the American Nation. And this measure that we will sign today will really make us truer to ourselves both as a country and as a people. It will strengthen us in a hundred unseen ways.

...

This bill says simply that from this day forth those wishing to immigrate to America shall be admitted on the basis of their skills and their close relationship to those already here.

This is a simple test, and it is a fair test. Those who can contribute most to this country—to its growth, to its strength, to its spirit—will be the first that are admitted to this land.

The fairness of this standard is so self-evident that we may well wonder that it has not always been applied. Yet the fact is that for over four decades the immigration policy of the United States has been twisted and has been distorted by the harsh injustice of the national origins quota system.

Under that system the ability of new immigrants to come to America depended upon the country of their birth. Only 3 countries were allowed to supply 70 percent of all the immigrants.

Families were kept apart because a husband or a wife or a child had been born in the wrong place.

Men of needed skill and talent were denied entrance because they came from southern or eastern Europe or from one of the developing continents.

This system violated the basic principle of American democracy—the principle that values and rewards each man on the basis of his merit as a man.

It has been un-American in the highest sense, because it has been untrue to the faith that brought thousands to these shores even before we were a country.

Today, with my signature, this system is abolished.

We can now believe that it will never again shadow the gate to the American Nation with the twin barriers of prejudice and privilege.

Our beautiful America was built by a nation of strangers. From a hundred different places or more they have poured forth into an empty land, joining and blending in one mighty and irresistible tide.

The land flourished because it was fed from so many sources—because it was nourished by so many cultures and traditions and peoples.

And from this experience, almost unique in the history of nations, has come America's attitude toward the rest of the world. We, because of what we are, feel safer and stronger in a world as varied as the people who make it up—a world where no country rules another and all countries can deal with the basic problems of human dignity and deal with those problems in their own way.

Now, under the monument which has welcomed so many to our shores [the Statue of Liberty], the American Nation returns to the finest of its traditions today.

The days of unlimited immigration are past.

But those who do come will come because of what they are, and not because of the land from which they sprung.

When the earliest settlers poured into a wild continent there was no one to ask them where they came from. The only question was: Were they sturdy enough to make the journey, were they strong enough to clear the land, were they enduring enough to make a home for freedom, and were they brave enough to die for liberty if it became necessary to do so?

And so it has been through all the great and testing moments of American history. Our history this year we see in Viet-Nam. Men there are dying—men named Fernandez and Zajac and Zelinko and Mariano and McCormick.

Neither the enemy who killed them nor the people whose independence they have fought to save ever asked them where they or their parents came from. They were all Americans. It was for free men and for America that they gave their all, they gave their lives and selves.

By eliminating that same question as a test for immigration the Congress proves ourselves worthy of those men and worthy of our own traditions as a Nation.

7. Leslie Marmon Silko Condemns Border Enforcement from a Native American Perspective, 1994

I used to travel the highways of New Mexico and Arizona with a wonderful sensation of absolute freedom as I cruised down the open road and across the vast desert plateaus. On the Laguna Pueblo reservation, where I was raised, the people were patriotic despite the way the U.S. government had treated Native Americans. As proud citizens, we grew up believing the freedom to travel was our inalienable right, a right that some Native Americans had been denied in the early twentieth century. Our cousin old Bill Pratt used to ride his horse three hundred miles overland from Laguna, New Mexico, to Prescott, Arizona, every summer to work as a fire lookout.

In school in the 1950s, we were taught that our right to travel from state to state without special papers or threat of detainment was a right-that citizens under Communist and totalitarian governments did not possess. That wide open highway told us we were U.S. citizens; we were free.

Not so long ago, my companion Gus and I were driving south from Albuquerque, returning to Tucson after a book promotion for the paperback edition of my novel *Almanac of the Dead.* I had settled back and gone to sleep while Gus drove, but I was awakened when I felt the car slowing to a stop. It was nearly midnight on New Mexico State Road 26, a dark, lonely stretch of two-lane highway between Hatch and Deming. When I sat up, I saw the headlights and emergency flashers of six vehicles—Border Patrol cars and a van were blocking both lanes of the highway. Gus stopped the car and rolled down the window to ask what was wrong. But the closest Border Patrolman and his companion did not reply; instead, the first agent ordered us to "step out of the car." Gus asked why, but his question seemed to set them off. Two more Border Patrol agents immediately approached our car, and one of them snapped, "Are you looking for trouble?" as if he would relish it.

I will never forget that night beside the highway. There was an awful feeling of menace and violence straining to break loose. It was clear that the uniformed men would be only too happy to drag us out of the car if we did not speedily comply with their request (asking a question is tantamount to resistance, it seems). So we stepped out of the car and they motioned for us to stand on the shoulder of the road. The night was very dark, and no other traffic had come down the road since we had been stopped. All I could think about was a book I had read—*Nunca Más*—the official report of a human rights commission that investigated and certified more than twelve thousand "disappearances" during Argentina's "dirty war" in the late 1970s.

The weird anger of these Border Patrolmen made me think about descriptions in the report of Argentine police and military officers who became addicted to interrogation, torture, and the murder that followed. When the military and police ran out of political suspects to torture and kill, they resorted to the random abduction of citizens off the streets. I thought how easy it would be for the Border Patrol to shoot us and leave our bodies and car beside the highway, like so many bodies found in these parts arid ascribed to drug runners.

Two other Border Patrolmen stood by the white van. The one who had asked if we were looking for trouble ordered his partner to "get the dog," and from the back of the van another patrolman brought a small female German shepherd on a leash. The dog apparently did not heel well enough to suit him, and the handler jerked the leash. They opened the doors of our car and pulled the dog's head into it, but I saw immediately from the expression in her eyes that the dog hated them and that she would not serve them. When she showed no interest in the inside of our car, they brought her around back to the trunk, near where we were standing. They half-dragged her up into the trunk, but still she did not indicate any stowed-away human beings or illegal drugs.

Their mood got uglier; the officers seemed outraged that the dog could not find any contraband, and they dragged her over to us and commanded her to sniff our legs and feet. To my relief, the strange violence the Border Patrol agents had focused on us now seemed shifted to the dog. I no longer felt so strongly that we would be murdered. We exchanged looks—the dog and I. She was afraid of what they might do, just as I was. The dog's handler jerked the leash sharply as she sniffed us, as if to make her perform better, but the dog refused to accuse us; she had an innate dignity that did not permit her to serve the murderous impulses of those men. I can't forget the expression in the dog's eyes; it was as if she were embarrassed to be associated with them. I had a small amount of medicinal marijuana in my purse that night, but she refused to expose me. I am not partial to dogs, but I will always remember the small German shepherd that night.

Unfortunately, what happened to me is an everyday occurrence here now. Since the 1980s, on top of greatly expanding border checkpoints, the Immigration and Naturalization Service and the Border Patrol have implemented policies that interfere with the rights of U.S. citizens to travel freely within our borders. INS agents now patrol all interstate highways and roads that lead to or from the U.S.-Mexico border in Texas, New Mexico, Arizona, and California. Now, when you drive east from Tucson on Interstate 10 toward El Paso, you encounter an INS check station outside Las Cruces, New Mexico. When you drive north from Las Cruces up Interstate 25, two miles north of the town of Truth or Consequences, the highway is blocked with orange emergency barriers, and all traffic is diverted into a two-lane Border Patrol checkpoint—ninety-five miles north of the U.S.-Mexico border.

I was detained once at Truth or Consequences, despite my and my companion's Arizona driver's licenses. Two men, both Chicanos, were detained at the same time, despite the fact that they too presented ID and spoke English without the thick Texas accents of the Border Patrol agents. While we were stopped, we watched as other vehicles—whose occupants were white—were waved through the checkpoint. White people traveling with brown people, however, can expect to be stopped on suspicion they work with the sanctuary movement, which shelters refugees. White people who appear to be clergy, those who wear ethnic clothing or jewelry, and women with very long hair or very short hair (they could be nuns) are also frequently detained; white men with beards or men with long hair are likely to be detained, too, because Border Patrol agents have profiles of "those sorts" of white people who may help political refugees. (Most of the political refugees from Guatemala and El Salvador are Native American or mestizo because the indigenous people of the Americas have continued to resist efforts by invaders to displace them from their ancestral lands.) Alleged increases in illegal immigration by people of Asian ancestry mean that the Border Patrol now routinely detains anyone who appears to be Asian or part Asian, as well.

Once your car is diverted from the interstate highway into the checkpoint area, you are under the control of the Border Patrol, which in practical terms exercises a power that no highway patrol or city patrolman possesses: they are willing to detain anyone, for no apparent reason. Other law-enforcement officers need a shred of probable cause in order to detain someone. On the books, so does the Border Patrol; but on the road, it's another matter. They'll order you to stop your car and step out; then they'll ask you to open the trunk. If you ask why or request a search warrant, you'll be told that they'll have to have a dog sniff the car before they can request a search warrant, and the dog might not get there for two or three hours. The search warrant might require an hour or two past that. They make it clear that if you force them to obtain a search warrant for the car, they will make you submit to a strip search as well.

Traveling in the open, though, the sense of violation can be even worse. Never mind high-profile cases like that of former Border Patrol agent Michael Elmer, acquitted of murder by claiming self-defense, despite admitting that as an officer he shot an illegal immigrant in the back and then hid the body, which remained undiscovered until another Border Patrolman reported the event. (Last month, Elmer was convicted of reckless endangerment in a separate incident, for shooting at least ten rounds from his M-16 too close to a group of immigrants as they were crossing illegally into No-gales in March 1992.) Never mind that in El Paso, a high school football coach driving a vanload of his players in full uniform was pulled over on the freeway and a Border Patrol agent put a cocked revolver to his head. (The football coach was Mexican-American, as were most of the players in his van; the incident eventually caused a federal judge to issue a restraining order against the Border Patrol.) We've a mountain of personal experiences like that that never make the newspapers. A history professor at UCLA told me she had been traveling by train from Los Angeles to Albuquerque twice a month doing research. On each of her trips, she had noticed that the Border Patrol agents were at the station in Albuquerque scrutinizing the passengers. Since she is six feet tall and of Irish and German ancestry, she was not particularly concerned. Then one day when she stepped off the train in Albuquerque, two Border Patrolmen accosted her, wanting to know what she was doing, and why she was traveling between Los Angeles and Albuquerque twice a month. She presented identification and an explanation deemed suitable by the agents and was allowed to go about her business.

Just the other day, I mentioned to a friend that I was writing this article and he told me about his seventy-three-year-old father, who is half Chinese and had set out alone by car from Tucson to Albuquerque the week before. His father had become confused by road construction and missed a turnoff from Interstate 10 to Interstate 25; when he turned around and circled back, he missed the turnoff a second time. But when he looped back for yet another try, Border Patrol agents stopped him and forced him to open his trunk. After they satisfied themselves that he was not smuggling Chinese immigrants, they sent him on his way. He was so rattled by the event that he had to be driven home by his daughter.

This is the police state that has developed in the south-western United States since the 1980s. No person, no citizen, is free to travel without the scrutiny of the Border Patrol. In the city of South Tucson, where 80 percent of the respondents were Chicano or Mexicano, a joint research project by the University of Wisconsin and the University of Arizona recently concluded that one out of every five people there had been detained, mistreated verbally or nonverbally, or questioned by INS agents in the past two years.

Manifest Destiny may lack its old grandeur of theft and blood—"lock the door" is what it means now, with racism a trump card to be played again and again, shamelessly, by both major political parties. "Immigration," like "street crime" and "welfare fraud," is a political euphemism that refers to people of color. Politicians and media people talk about "illegal aliens" to dehumanize and demonize undocumented immigrants, who are for the most part people of color. Even in the days of Spanish and Mexican rule, no attempts were made to interfere with the flow of people and goods from south to north and north to south. It is the U.S. government that has continually attempted to sever contact between the tribal people north of the border and those to the south.

Now that the "Iron Curtain" is gone, it is ironic that the U.S. government and its Border Patrol are constructing a steel wall ten feet high to span sections of the border with Mexico. While politicians and multinational corporations extol the virtues of NAFTA and free trade (in goods, not flesh), the ominous curtain is already up in a six-mile section at the border crossing at Mexicali; two miles are being erected but are not yet finished at Naco; and at Nogales, sixty miles south of Tucson, the steel wall has been all rubber-stamped and awaits construction, likely to begin in March. Like the pathetic multimillion-dollar antidrug border surveillance balloons that were continually deflated by high winds and made only a couple of meager interceptions before they blew away, the fence along the border is a theatrical prop, a bit of pork for contractors. Border entrepreneurs have already used blowtorches to cut passageways through the fence to collect "tolls" and are doing a brisk business. Back in Washington, the INS announces a $300 million computer contract to modernize its record keeping and Congress passes a crime bill that shunts $255 million to the INS for 1995, $181 million earmarked for border control, which is to include seven hundred new partners for the men who stopped Gus and me in our travels, and the history professor, and my friend's father, and as many as they could from South Tucson.

It is no use; borders haven't worked, and they won't work, not now, as the indigenous people of the Americas reassert their kinship and solidarity with one another. A mass migration is already under way; its roots are not simply economic. The Uto-Aztecan languages are spoken as far north as Taos Pueblo near the Colorado border, all the way south to Mexico City. Before the arrival of the Europeans, the indigenous communities throughout this region not only conducted commerce; the people shared cosmologies, and oral narratives about the Maize Mother, the Twin Brothers, and their grandmother, Spider Woman, as well as Quetzalcoatl, the benevolent snake. The great human migration within the Americas cannot be stopped; human beings are natural forces of the earth, just as rivers and winds are natural forces.

Deep down the issue is simple: the so-called Indian Wars from the days of Sitting Bull and Red Cloud have never really ended in the Americas. The Indian people of southern Mexico, of Guatemala, and those left in El Salvador, too, are still fighting for their lives and for their land against the cavalry patrols sent out by the governments of those lands. The Americas are Indian country, and the "Indian problem" is not about to go away.

One evening at sundown, we were stopped in traffic at a railroad crossing in downtown Tucson while a freight train passed us, slowly gaining speed as it headed north to Phoenix. In the twilight I saw the most amazing sight: dozens of human beings, mostly young men, were riding the train; everywhere, on flat-cars, inside open boxcars, perched on top of boxcars, hanging off ladders on tank cars and between boxcars. I couldn't count fast enough, but I saw fifty or sixty people headed north. They were dark young men, Indian and mestizo; they were smiling and a few of them waved at us in our cars. I was reminded of the ancient story of Aztlán, told by the Aztecs but known in other Uto-Aztecan communities as well. Aztlán is the beautiful land to the north, the origin place of the Aztec people. I don't remember how or why the people left Aztlán to journey farther south, but the old story says that one day, they will return.

~ ESSAYS

In recent decades, the issue of illegal immigration has dominated the ways that the U.S. media and public perceive the U.S.-Mexico border. In the first essay, Columbia University history professor Mae Ngai explores the origins of the category "illegal alien." Extensive illegal immigration, she argues, dates to the 1920s, when the U.S. government created a comprehensive system of immigration restrictions that made many migrants "illegal aliens" even as they continued to be a part of American society through their jobs, marriages, and other social relations with American citizens. This system, Ngai shows, had far-reaching consequences for American society and its borders. It required the federal government to police its borders as never before; but despite the creation of the Border Patrol in 1924, distinguishing people who were in the country illegally from citizens and legal migrants could be an impossible job. Many Americans objected to the intrusive policing and summary deportations required to enforce immigration law, and just who was and was not an illegal alien could change with time and how the law was interpreted. Over the 1920s and '30s, Nagi argues, the application of immigration law became much more lenient with Canadians and Europeans—who were more and more often granted legal status—and much more harsh with Mexicans. By the 1930s, she concludes, Mexicans had become the "prototypical illegal aliens," a perception that underscored their highly racial exclusion from American society.

The second essay, by Kelly Lytle-Hernández, a history professor at the University of California-Los Angeles, examines migration regulations in the 1940s and 1950s. Lytle-Hernández shows that the Mexican state was also very interested in regulating the migration of its citizens to the United States. Mexican officials wanted to ensure that powerful agricultural employers in Mexico had access to cheap and abundant labor, and that Mexican nationals in the United States were afforded some kind of legal protection. So Mexico cooperated with measures to restrain migration outside of the legally sanctioned channels of the Bracero Program, aiding in deporting Mexican nationals from the U.S. into the interior of Mexico, where re-entering the United States was more difficult than if they simply been removed to a border town. This cooperation with American authorities provoked deep anger by many migrants. The binational enforcement of immigration restrictions substantially increased the danger of crossing the border, but, despite the public relations claims of Border Patrol authorities, had little impact on the number of Mexicans entering the United States in search of work. The U.S.-Mexico border grew more and more heavily policed, and more and more charged with controversy, but it remained as much of a bridge as a barrier.

Deportation Policy and the Making and Unmaking of Illegal Aliens

MAE NGAI

In January 1930, officials of the Bureau of Immigration testified about the Border Patrol before a closed session of the House immigration committee. Henry Hull, the commissioner general of immigration, explained that the Border Patrol did

Mae Ngai, *Impossible Subjects: Illegal Aliens and the Making of Modern America* (Princeton: Princeton University Press, 2004), 56–89. Copyright 2004 by Princeton University Press.

not operate "on the border line" but as far as one hundred miles "back of the line." The Border Patrol, he said, was "a scouting organization and a pursuit organization." Officers operate on roads "without warrants and wherever they find an alien they stop him. If he is illegally in the country, they take him to unit headquarters."

Members of the House committee expressed concern that the Border Patrol, which was not a criminal law enforcement agency and had no statutory authority to execute search warrants, had defined its jurisdiction not just at the border but far into the nation's interior—easily one or two hundred miles but, theoretically, the entire interior. How did the officers know the difference between an alien and a citizen? Indeed, what did it mean that Border Patrol officers could stop, interrogate, and search without a warrant anyone, anywhere, in the United States?

Yet if Congress was uneasy about the Border Patrol's reach, it had nearly assured such an outcome when it passed the Immigration Acts of 1921 and 1924, which for the first time imposed numerical restrictions on immigration. Because illegal entry is a concomitant of restrictive immigration policy, the quota laws stimulated the production of illegal aliens and introduced that problem into the internal spaces of the nation. Although unlawful entry had always resulted from exclusion, in the 1920s illegal immigration achieved mass proportions and deportation assumed a central place in immigration policy. The nature and demands of restriction raised a range of problems for the modern state, which were at once administrative (how should restriction be enforced?), juridical (how is sovereignty defined?), and constitutional (do illegal aliens have rights?).

This [essay] examines the advent of mass illegal immigration and deportation policy under the Immigration Act of 1924. It argues that numerical restriction created a new class of persons within the national body—illegal aliens—whose inclusion in the nation was at once a social reality and a legal impossibility. This contradiction challenged received notions of sovereignty and democracy in several ways. First, the increase in the number of illegal entries created a new emphasis on control of the nation's contiguous land borders, which emphasis had not existed before. This new articulation of state territoriality reconstructed national borders and national space in ways that were both highly visible and problematic. At the same time, as suggested above, the notion of border control obscured the policy's unavoidable slippage into the interior.

Second, the application of the deportation laws gave rise to an oppositional political and legal discourse, which imagined deserving and undeserving illegal immigrants and, concomitantly, just and unjust deportations. These categories were constructed out of modern ideas about social desirability, in particular with regard to crime and sexual morality, and values that esteemed family preservation. Critics argued that deportation was unjust in cases where it separated families or exacted other hardships that were out of proportion to the offense committed. As a result, during the 1930s deportation policy became the object of legal reform to allow for administrative discretion in deportation cases. Just as restriction and deportation "made" illegal aliens, administrative discretion "unmade" illegal aliens.

Rather, the processes of territorial redefinition and administrative enforcement informed divergent paths of immigrant racialization. Europeans and

Canadians tended to be disassociated from the real and imagined category of illegal alien, which facilitated their national and racial assimilation as white American citizens. In contrast, Mexicans emerged as iconic illegal aliens. Illegal status became constitutive of a racialized Mexican identity and of Mexicans' exclusion from the national community and polity.

The illegal immigrant cannot be constituted without deportation—the possibility or threat of deportation, if not the fact. The possibility derives from the actual existence of state machinery to apprehend and deport illegal aliens. The threat remains in the temporal and spatial "lag" that exists between the act of unlawful entry and apprehension or deportation (if, in fact, the illegal alien is ever caught). The many effects of the lag include the psychological and cultural problems associated with "passing" or "living a lie," community vulnerability and isolation, and the use of undocumented workers as a highly exploited or reserve labor force.

Deportation was not invented in the 1920s, but it was then that it came of age. The nation's borders were "soft" and, for the most part, unguarded. Inspection at arrival sought to identify excludable persons and to deny them admission, but little could be done if they evaded detection and entered the country. Subsequent discovery was commonly the result of being hospitalized or imprisoned, yet no federal law existed mandating the removal of alien public charges from the country.

Few people were actually excluded or deported before the 1920s. Between 1892 and 1907 the Immigration Service deported only a few hundred aliens a year and between 1908 and 1920 an average of two or three thousand a year—mostly aliens removed from asylums, hospitals, and jails. Deportation appears even less significant when one considers that some one million people a year entered the country in the decade preceding World War I. Mere entry without inspection was insufficient grounds for deportation. The statute of limitations on deportation was consistent with the general philosophy of the melting pot: it seemed unconscionable to expel immigrants after they had settled in the country and had begun to assimilate.

The passage of the quota laws marked a turn in both the volume and nature of unlawful entry and in the philosophy and practice of deportation. In general, of course, legislators write laws to include sanctions against their violation. But Congress evinced a wholly different approach toward deportation in the act of 1924 than it had taken previously. The new law eliminated the statute of limitations on deportation for nearly all forms of unlawful entry and provided for the deportation at any time of any person entering after July 1, 1924, without a valid visa or without inspection.

The criminalization of unauthorized entry marked a radical departure from previous immigration policy, which deemed deportation to be a civil, or administrative, procedure.

The Immigration Act of 1924 and its attendant enforcement mechanisms spurred a dramatic increase in the number of deportations. A contemporary observed that the "extensive use of the power to expel" began in 1925 and that deportation quickly became "one of the chief activities of the Immigration

Service in some … districts." By 1928 the bureau was exhausting its funds for deportations long before the fiscal year ended.

A shift in the principal categories of deportation engendered new ways of thinking about illegal immigration. Legal and illegal status became, in effect, abstract constructions, having less to do with experience than with numbers and paper. One's legal status now rested on being in the right place in the queue—if a country has a quota of N, immigrant N is illegal but immigrant $N + 1$ is legal and having the proper documentation, the prized "proper visa."

The illegal alien that is abstractly defined is something of a specter, a body stripped of individual personage. The mere idea that persons without formal legal status resided in the nation engendered images of great danger. In 1925 the Immigration Service reported with some alarm that 1.4 million immigrants—20 percent of those who had entered the country before 1921—might already be living illegally in the United States. The service conceded that these immigrants had lawfully entered the country, but because it had no record of their admission, it considered them illegal.

Positive law thus constituted undocumented immigrants as criminals, both fulfilling and fueling nativist discourse. Once nativism succeeded in legislating restriction, anti-alien animus shifted its focus to the interior of the nation and the goal of expelling immigrants living illegally in the country. The *Los Angeles Evening Express* alleged there were "several million foreigners" in the country who had "no right to be here." Nativists like Madison Grant, recognizing that deportation was "of great importance," also advocated alien registration "as a necessary prelude to deport on a large scale."

Prohibition supplied an important cache of criminal tropes, the language of smuggling directly yoking illegal immigration to liquor-running. The California Joint Immigration Committee described illegal aliens as "vicious and criminal," comprising "bootleggers, gangsters, and racketeers of large cities." Similarly, Edwin Reeves, a Border Patrol officer in El Paso during the 1920s, recalled, "Every fellow you caught with a load of liquor on his back … was a wetback." The *National Republic* claimed that two million aliens intent upon illegally entering the United States were massed in Canada, Mexico, and Cuba, on the "waiting lists" of smugglers.

In this story, aliens were not only subjects—that is, the smugglers—they were also the objects, the human goods illegally trafficked across the border. This view that the undocumented immigrant was the least desirable alien of all denotes a new imagining of the nation, which situated the principle of national sovereignty in the foreground. It made state territoriality—not labor needs, not family unification, not freedom from persecution, not assimilation—the engine of immigration policy.

Territoriality was highly unstable, however, precisely because restriction had created illegal immigrants *within* the national body. This was not an entirely new phenomenon—it had existed since Chinese exclusion—but important consequences resulted from the different nature and scale of illegal immigration in the late 1920s. Illegal immigrants now comprised all nationalities and ethnic groups. They were numerous, perhaps even innumerable, and were diffused throughout the nation, particularly in large cities. An illegal immigrant might now be anyone's neighbor or coworker, possibly one's spouse or parent. Her illegal status might not be known to her social acquaintances and personal intimates. She might not even be aware of her own illegal status, particularly if it resulted from a technical violation of the law. She might, in fact, be a responsible member of society (employed, taxpaying, and notwithstanding her illegal status, law-abiding). Even if she were indigent or uneducated, she might have a family, social ties in a community, and interact with others in ways that arguably established her as a member of society.

The problem of differentiating illegal immigrants from citizens and legal immigrants signaled the danger that restrictionists had imagined—in their view, illegal aliens were an invisible enemy in America's midst. Yet their proposed solutions, such as compulsory alien registration and mass deportations, were problematic exactly because undocumented immigrants *were* so like other Americans. During the interwar period a majority of political opinion opposed alien registration on grounds that it threatened Americans' perceived rights of free movement, association, and privacy. The Immigration Service had through the late 1920s remained reluctant to conduct mass raids, particularly in the North.

Yet, if illegal aliens were so like other Americans, the racial and ethnic diversity of the American population further complicated the problem of differentiation. Writing about the Border Patrol in the Southwest, one author described apprehending aliens "at some distance back from the International line" a "man-sized job." She explained, "To capture an alien who is in the act of crawling through a hole in the fence between Arizona and Mexico is easy compared with apprehending and deporting him after he is hidden in the interior, among others of his own race who are legally in this country. The Border Patrol's capacious definition of its jurisdiction illustrates the nation's borders (the point of exclusion) collapsing into and becoming indistinguishable from the interior (the space of inclusion). But this is not to say that the border was eliminated. Policies of restriction and deportation reconstructed and raised the borders, even as they destabilized them. History and policy also constructed the U.S.-Mexican and U.S.-Canadian borders differently. The processes of defining and policing the border both encoded and generated racial ideas and practices which, in turn, produced different racialized spaces internal to the nation.

Before the 1920s the Immigration Service paid little attention to the nation's land borders because the overwhelming majority of immigrants entering the United States landed at Ellis Island and other seaports. The flow of immigrants into the country had been not only welcome but had been focused at fixed points that rendered land borders invisible. One immigration director described the situation as "equivalent to a circle with locked doors with no connecting wall between them." A small force of the Customs Service and the Chinese Division of the Immigration Service jointly patrolled the Mexican and Canadian borders against illegal entry by Chinese. The Chinese patrol inspector, assigned to horseback detail or inspecting freight cars, occupied the loneliest and bottommost position in the hierarchy of the service.

Immigration inspectors ignored Mexicans coming into the southwestern United States during the 1900s and 1910s to work in railroad construction, mining, and agriculture. It was not until 1919 that Mexicans entering the United States were required to apply for admission at lawfully designated ports of entry.

Before World War I the U.S.-Canada border was also soft. Throughout the nineteenth century, Canadians circulated freely into the United States: Canadian farmers participated in the settlement of the American West, which movement preceded expansion to the Canadian West; and industry and manufacturing in Michigan and New England drew labor from Canada as well as from Europe.

If both the Mexican and Canadian borders were soft until World War I, the passage of the quota laws in 1921 and 1924 threw the nation's contiguous land borders into sharp relief for immigration authorities.

Indeed, illegal European immigrants entered the United States across both borders. Belgian, Dutch, Swiss, Russian, Bulgarian, Italian, and Polish immigrants enlisted in agricultural labor programs in the Canadian west, only to arrive in Canada and immediately attempt entry into the United States, at points from Ontario to Manitoba. The most heavily traveled route for illegal European immigration was through Mexico.

By the late 1920s surreptitious entry into the United States by Europeans declined. The threat of apprehension and deportation was a deterrent but alternate legal methods also existed for circumventing the quota laws. Europeans could go to Canada and be admitted to United States legally after they had resided in Canada for five years. And, as European immigrants in the United States became naturalized citizens, they could bring relatives over legally as nonquota immigrants. In 1927 over 60 percent of the nonquota immigrants admitted to the United States were from Italy, with the next largest groups coming from Poland, Czechoslovakia, and Greece.

This is not to say that illegal immigration of Europeans and Canadians stopped. In general, the Immigration Service was more concerned with the bureaucratic burden of processing the high volume of legal traffic crossing the U.S.-Canada border in both directions.

The service's work on the Canadian border contrasted to what the commissioner general described as the "high pitch" of its work along the U.S.-Mexico border. During the late twenties the number of illegal Mexican immigrants deported across the southern border skyrocketed—from 1,751 expulsions to 1925 to over 15,000 in 1929. Deportations for entry without a proper visa accounted for most of the increase. Although Mexicans did not face quota restrictions, they nevertheless faced myriad entry requirements, such as the head tax and visa fee, which impelled many to avoid formal admission and inspection.

Mexicans coming to the United States encountered a new kind of border. Notwithstanding the lax immigration procedures before World War I, the United States-Mexico border had had a long history of contestation. After a decade of instability wrought by the Mexican Revolution and World War I, the border as a political marker became basically settled.

During the 1920s, immigration policy rearticulated the U.S.-Mexico border as a cultural and racial boundary, as a creator of illegal immigration. Federal officials self-consciously understood their task as creating a barrier where, in a practical sense, none had existed before. The service instituted new policies—new inspection procedures and the formation of the Border Patrol—that accentuated the difference between the two countries.

Inspection at the Mexican border involved a degrading procedure of bathing, delousing, medical-line inspection, and interrogation. The baths were new and unique to Mexican immigrants, requiring them to be inspected while naked, have their hair shorn, and have their clothing and baggage fumigated. Line inspection, modeled after the practice formerly used at Ellis Island, required immigrants to walk in single file past a medical officer. These procedures were particularly humiliating, even gratuitous, in light of the fact that the Immigration Act of 1924 required prospective immigrants to present a medical certificate to the U.S. consul when applying for a visa, that is, before travel to the United States. Line inspection at Ellis Island was eliminated after 1924, and at El Paso the service exempted all Europeans and Mexicans arriving by first class rail from line inspection, the baths, and the literacy test. Racial presumptions about Mexican laborers, not law, dictated the procedures at the Mexican border.

More than anything else, the formation of the Border Patrol raised the border. The Immigration Service hired former cowboys, skilled workers, and small ranchers as its first patrol officers. Almost all were young, many had military experience, and not a few were associated with the Ku Klux Klan.

The Border Patrol's work assumed the character of criminal pursuit and apprehension, although officially it was charged with enforcing civil, not criminal, laws and was not trained as a criminal enforcement agency. As discussed above, the service interpreted its authorization to apprehend illegal aliens without warrant to apply to anywhere within the interior of the nation. It also seized goods it believed were "obviously contraband or smuggled," a practice that the commissioner general acknowledged had dubious legal sanction. During the Border Patrol's first five years of service, fifteen officers were killed in the line of duty, twelve in the Mexican border districts.

As Border Patrol officers zealously pursued illegal aliens, smugglers, and criminals, the Immigration Service received complaints from white Americans who were interrogated by discourteous patrolmen or arrested without warrant. One citizen protested that the Border Patrol "enacted the role of Jesús James" on public highways. In 1929, in response to such adverse criticism, the service discontinued the "promiscuous halting of traffic" in the border area, acknowledging that it was "dangerous and probably illegal."

Thus patrolmen were trained to act with civility, courtesy, and formality when dealing with Anglo citizens, ranch owners, immigrants arriving from Europe, and "high class people com[ing] in as tourists" from Canada. But the quasi- and extra-legal practices associated with rancher vigilantism and the Texas Rangers suited the needs of the Border Patrol in the Southwest, particularly when it involved patrolling large expanses of uninhabited territory far removed from Washington's bureaucratic oversight. The Border Patrol functioned within an environment of increased racial hostility against Mexicans; indeed, its activities helped constitute that environment by aggressively apprehending and deporting increasing numbers of Mexicans. The Border Patrol interrogated Mexican laborers on roads and in towns, and it was not uncommon for "sweeps" to apprehend several hundred immigrant at a time. By the early 1930s the Immigration Service was apprehending nearly five times as many suspected illegal aliens in the Mexican border area as it did in the Canadian border area.

Moreover, many Mexicans entered the United States through a variety of means that were not illegal but comprised irregular, unstable categories of lawful admission, making it more difficult to distinguish between those who were lawfully in the country and those who were not. Mexicans living in Mexican border towns who commuted into the United States to work on daily or weekly basis constituted one category of irregular entry. The service counted these commuters as immigrants and collected a one-time head tax from them. It also required them to report to the immigration station once a week for bathing, a hated requirement that gave rise to a local black market in bathing certificates.

Many other Mexicans entered legally as "temporary visitors" to work for an agricultural season and then returned to Mexico.

It was ironic that Mexicans became so associated with illegal immigration because, unlike Europeans, they were not subject to numerical quotas and, unlike Asiatics, they were not excluded as racially ineligible to citizenship. But as numerical restriction assumed primacy in immigration policy, its enforcement aspects—inspection procedures, deportation, the Border Patrol, criminal prosecution, and irregular categories of immigration—created many thousands of illegal Mexican immigrants. The undocumented Mexican laborer who crossed the border to work in the burgeoning industry of commercial agriculture emerged as the prototypical illegal alien.

Mexican immigration abated during the 1930s, owing to the policies of deportation and administrative exclusion, as well as a lack of employment in the United States caused by the Depression. As economic insecurities among Euro-Americans inflamed racial hostility toward Mexicans, efforts to deport and repatriate the latter to Mexico grew. The movement did not distinguish between legal immigrants, illegal immigrants, and American citizens. Mexican Americans and immigrants alike reaped the consequences of racialized foreignness that had been constructed throughout the 1920s.

In addition to the deportation of illegal aliens by the INS, local and state authorities acted in myriad ways during the Depression to restrict the movement of Mexicans and Mexican Americans and to expel them from the country. California towns passed settlement laws that restricted relief to residents in order to deny welfare to unemployed migrant workers. Many towns, including the city of Los Angeles, deployed police at so-called "bum blockades" to keep indigent migrants from entering. In 1936 the governor of Colorado proclaimed martial law in the state's southern counties, giving officers of the Southern Colorado Military District instructions to turn back Mexican workers attempting to enter the state on alleged labor contracts. In El Paso, Anglos demanded that the International Bridge be closed from 6:00 A.M to 10:00 A.M. in order to keep local commuters from Juárez from going to work in El Paso. Local relief agencies, wanting "something done" about Mexicans on their rolls, reported lists of Mexicans to immigration authorities or deportation, including citizens and legal residents.

Led by the Los Angeles county relief agencies, local authorities throughout the Southwest and Midwest repatriated over 400,000 Mexicans during the early 1930s. An estimated 60 percent were children or American citizens by native birth; a contemporary observed that the "vast majority" spoke English and that many had been in the United States for at least ten years.

The repatriation movement, then, comprised voluntary departures, formal deportations by the INS, and organized repatriations by local welfare bureaus.

Despite the evident distress experienced by the repatriates and the questionable legality of "repatriating" Mexican Americans with United States citizenship, few objected to the project. In the late 1920s the fledgling Mexican American civil rights movement had supported the Box Bill, on grounds that unchecked Mexican immigration depressed wages and living standards in the Southwest and invited racial antipathy from the Anglo-American population.

Nearly 20 percent of the Mexican population in the United States returned to Mexico during the early years of the Depression. The repatriation of Mexicans was a racial expulsion program exceeded in scale only by the Native American Indian removals of the nineteenth century. But with a population of over 1.4 million, Mexicans were too numerous to be completely removed; moreover, their labor was still needed for farming, mining, and railway maintenance work throughout the Southwest.

In the same time that Mexicans and Mexican Americans were being deported and repatriated during the late 1920s and early 1930s, the volume of deportations of European immigrants also increased. These illegal aliens comprised unauthorized border-crossers, visa violators, and those who engaged lawfully but committed a deportable offense subsequent to entry. Many had already settled in the country and acquired jobs, property, and families. Unlike Mexicans, these Europeans were accepted as members of society. But their inclusion in the nation was a social reality, it was also a legal impossibility. Resolving that contradiction by means of deportation caused hardship and suffering to these immigrants and their families. It struck many as simply unjust.

Testifying before Congress in 1934, Nicholas Grisanti of the Federation of *Italian* Societies in Buffalo, New York, cited a typical case of an unjust deportation. An Italian immigrant lived most of his life in Buffalo. He was married with three small children and was gainfully employed. But, Grisanti explained, "at some previous year he had taken as a boy a half bag of coal from the railroad tracks to help keep his family warm," for which crime he was convicted and given a suspended sentence. Years later, he went to Canada for a summer vacation. The Immigration Service considered his return a "new entry" and ordered him deported, on grounds that he had been convicted of a crime involving moral turpitude before "time of entry." His deportation was thwarted after a public outcry led acting New York Governor Herbert Lehman to pardon the "little offense."

In a sense, the protest against unjust deportations stemmed from the fact that European and Canadian immigrants had come face-to-face with a system that had historically evolved to justify arbitrary and summary treatment of Chinese and other Asian immigrants.

Thus during the late 1920s and early 1930s a critique of deportation policy emerged among social welfare advocates and legal reformers. These reformers did not directly challenge deportation as a prerogative of the nation's sovereign power. But they did search for ways to reconcile conflicting imperatives of national sovereignty and individual rights.

First, they believed deportation policy was applied in arbitrary and unnecessary harsh ways, resulting in great personal hardship to individuals and in the separation of families, with no social benefit. Second, in terms of procedure, they concluded that deportation policy frequently operated in the breach of established traditions of Anglo-American jurisprudence, especially those concerning judicial review and due process. During the late nineteenth and early twentieth century the federal courts generally upheld the summary character of immigration proceedings. By the 1920s aliens had won only a few procedural rights, among them the right to an administrative hearing and the right to counsel. But critics found even these gravely lacking or undermined by the lack of other procedural safeguards, and cited a broad, range of abuses.

Specifically, critics charged, aliens were often "forcibly detained." The Boards of Special Inquiry, which conducted formal deportation hearings, were often one-man tribunals, with the immigration inspector often appearing simultaneously as arresting officer, prosecutor, and judge. The boards operated without rules of evidence, readily admitting hearsay, opinion, anonymous letters, and "confidential information."

Finally, immigrants under warrants of deportation had few avenues of appeal. The Labor Department's Board of Review, which made recommendations to the secretary of labor, had no statutory authority. Judicial review was extremely rare. During the late 1920s and 1930s the courts heard fewer than three hundred writs of habeas corpus in deportation cases and found nearly 70 percent of them in favor of the Immigration Service.

The trend may be discerned from a reading of William Van Vleck's treatise *Administrative Control of Aliens*. The treatise followed several lines of criticism that challenged traditional ideas about female dependency and sexual morality. Van Vleck cited several cases in which the Immigration Service had ordered women deported as LPC because they were without male support, even though the women were employed and self-supporting. In one case, the service deported a woman whose husband became ill with tuberculosis fourteen months after they arrived in the United States on the grounds that she was dependent on her husband—even though she was employed. Van Vleck cited other cases of single mothers supporting their children or living with other relatives, recognizing that the family was a diverse institution that included female-headed households and extended families.

The idea of the family's privacy was connected to its sanctity. One of the most tragic consequences of deportation, Van Vleck argued, was the separation of families. He pointed out, "If [the deported alien] is a poor man his wife and children have not the money to follow him. Even if they have the money and do follow him, this may mean the expatriation of American citizens."

Van Vleck's views were not isolated but articulated a trend among legal scholars and in the federal courts as well. By the early 1930s the Immigration Service tempered its use of LPC. The trend benefited Europeans and Canadians, who had comprised the vast majority of LPC deportation cases. The deportation of Europeans and Canadians as LPC dropped from a high of nearly two thousand in 1924 to fewer than five hundred in 1932.

The appeal to prevent family separation was particularly effective in areas where European immigrants were numerous and had some political influence. In New York many convicted felons received executive pardons after they served their prison terms in order to prevent their deportation, including the Italian man in Buffalo who stole a half sack of coal when he was a boy. Governor Herbert Lehman granted 110 such pardons during his tenure.

The discourse on unjust deportation referred mostly to European immigrants and only occasionally to Mexicans. Ethnic Mexicans in the United States voiced the same concerns as did Europeans; for example, the Los Angeles Spanish-language newspaper *La Opinión* criticized the deportation of Mexicans who had ten years of residence in the United States, businesses, and families. But Mexicans remained marginalized from the mainstream of immigration discourse. Among Euro-American reformers, references to immigrants of good moral character were usually not racially explicit, but by definition such immigrants were unlikely to be Mexican because "Mexican" had been constructed as a negative racial category. More important, reformers did not call for leniency in cases of unlawful entry, because this was a core component of the system based on numerical restriction, *which none of them directly opposed*. Thus while European immigrants with criminal records could be constructed as "deserving," Mexicans who were apprehended without proper documents had little chance of escaping either the stigma of criminalization or the fate of deportation.

Legislative and administrative reforms operated in ways that fueled racial disparity in deportation practices. In 1929 Congress passed the Registry Act, which legalized the status of "honest law-abiding alien[s] who may be in the, country under some merely technical irregularity." The law allowed immigrants to register as permanent residents for a fee of $20 if they could show they resided in the country continuously since 1921 and were of good moral character. The law did not formally favor Europeans over Mexicans. But of the 115,000 immigrants who registered their prior entries into the country between 1930 and 1940, 80 percent were European or Canadian. According to Berkeley economist Paul S. Taylor, many Mexicans qualified for an adjustment of status under the Registry Act but few knew about it, understood it, or could afford the fee.

During the 1930s and 1940s the Labor Department instituted a series of reforms that addressed, albeit in limited ways, questions of due process in deportation proceedings and established administrative mechanisms whereby certain illegal aliens—mostly Europeans—could legalize their status.

In 1934, the INS discontinued the practice of arresting suspected aliens without warrant at places removed from the actual time and place of entry. It also mandated that the same officer could not conduct the preliminary examination and the final hearing.

A third type of reform concerned the use of administrative discretion to grant relief from deportation for aliens for whom deportation would cause hardship.

The secretary granted waivers by invoking an obscure clause of the Immigration Act of 1917, the Seventh Proviso to Section 3, which stipulated that "aliens returning after a temporary absence to an unrelinquished United States domicile of seven consecutive years may be admitted in the discretion of the Attorney General and under such conditions as he may prescribe." Congress intended the Seventh Proviso as a hardship measure for aliens "who have lived here for a long time" who were temporarily out of the country when the Immigration Act of 1917 was passed and who, for reasons often technical in nature, were excludable upon their return. Perkins's innovation was to use the concept "returning after a temporary absence" to apply to aliens who had not yet departed and to include in its scope illegal aliens. By invoking the Seventh Proviso to waive deportations Perkins reverted to the central principle of pre-1924 immigration policy inherent in the statute of limitations on deportation, the idea that immigrants who have settled in the country should not be expelled.

The process of readjustment of status was known as the "pre-examination" procedure. Since 1933 the INS had granted letters to legal aliens going to Canada for short visits assuring them of reentry, provided that they were first examined and found admissible by immigration inspectors. It began as gesture of courtesy that allowed legal aliens departing temporarily to avoid the necessity of applying for a formal reentry permit. The Canadian authorities also required written assurance that the visitors would not remain in Canada. The practice became known in INS parlance as "pre-examination"—that is, inspection for readmission before departure.

In 1935 pre-examination was extended to illegal immigrants to facilitate their legalization. A formal agreement between the U.S. Department of State and Immigration Service and their Canadian counterparts detailed procedures whereby an immigrant in the United States without a visa could be "pre-examined" for legal admission, leave the country as a "voluntary departure," proceed to the nearest American consul in Canada, obtain a visa for permanent residence, and reenter the United States formally as a legal admission.

The INS thus suspended state territoriality in order to unmake the illegal status of certain immigrants. Although the whole procedure was a bureaucratic arrangement, the INS and State Department would not simply issue new documents granting an alien's legal status. The alien had to cooperate by physically leaving and reentering the country, to enact a voluntary departure and a legal admission. Some aliens failed to understand the necessity of the performance (or could not afford to make the trip to Canada) and wondered why, if it was willing to adjust their status, the INS would not simply leave them alone.

By the early 1940s suspension of deportation and pre-examination were available to aliens with a legally resident alien relative, those with long-term residence in the United States, and "exceptionally meritorious" cases, the latter constituting a general loophole. The expanding grounds for eligibility suggest a policy grounded in the idea that what mattered most was not the immigrant's formal status but his or her presence and ties in the community. This was a remarkable acknowledgement that undercut the premises of restriction and territoriality.

Significantly, however, the privilege of pre-examination became restricted to European immigrants. Asiatics did not qualify, because they were categorically excluded from immigration on grounds of racial ineligibility Mexicans were not initially excluded. After MacCormack formalized the pre-examination procedure, INS El Paso district director Grover Wilmoth implemented the procedure for Mexican hardship cases, but in 1938 he became stonewalled by the American consul in Juárez, William Blocker, who argued that those applying for visas at Juárez "were of the laboring class, some of them actually on relief." They should, he said, "unquestionably" be denied visas. In fact the INS Board of Special Inquiry had ruled in Canadian pre-examination cases that receipt of relief during the Depression, when no work was available, was not evidence of LPC. Blocker deliberately slowed the work of processing visas for Mexican pre-examination cases to only a handful a month in order to frustrate Wilmoth's efforts to grant relief to Mexican cases.

I found no evidence that Wilmoth's higher-ups in the INS argued with the State Department for a fair application of the policy; rather, the INS seems to have quickly scuttled the program for Mexicans.

The racism of the policy was profound, for it denied, a priori, that deportation could cause hardship for the families of non-Europeans. In stressing family values, moreover, the policy recognized only one kind of family, the intact nuclear family residing in the United States, and ignored transnational families. It failed to recognize that many undocumented male migrants who came to the United States alone in fact maintained family households in their home country and that migration-remittance was another kind of strategy for family subsistence.

For Europeans, however, the policy was clearly a boon. In fact, pre-examination became an official and routine procedure for adjusting the status of Europeans who were not legally present in the United States. By the early 1940s pre-examination was used to help adjust the status of refugees from European fascism who had entered the United States in the 1930s by way of tourist or visitor visas.

Numerical restriction legislated in the 1920s displaced qualitative reasons for inclusion and exclusion with criteria that were at once more abstract and arbitrary—the quota slot and the proper visa. Previously, territoriality had been exercised to exclude people not deemed fit to be part of the nation. In the 1920s qualitative norms of desirability remained in the law as grounds for inclusion and expulsion, but, as we have seen, they were employed in deportation cases less often than was the rule of documentation and, moreover, they were applied irregularly and with considerable discretion. As qualitative norms receded in importance, territoriality—defining and policing the national space—became both the means and the ends of immigration policy.

However, Americans increasingly believed that deportation, initially imagined for the despised and dangerous classes, was undemocratic and unjust when applied to ordinary immigrants with homes and families in the United Sates. Hence during the 1930s and early 1940s statutory and administrative reforms attempted to ease the tension between sovereignty and democracy that immigration policy had created. Family values and environmentalist views of delinquency and morality paved the way for reform, while race directed its reach.

Thus it became possible to unmake the illegality of Italian, Polish, and other European illegal immigrants through the power of administrative discretion. Of course, not all illegal European immigrants were legalized, but a rough estimation suggests that between 1925 and 1965 some 200,000 illegal European immigrants who were construed as deserving successfully legalized their status under the Registry Act, through pre-examination, or by suspension of deportation. The formal recognition of their inclusion in the nation created the requisite minimum foundation for acquiring citizenship and contributed to a broader reformation of racial identity taking place, a process that reconstructed the "lower races of Europe" into white ethnic Americans.

By contrast, walking (or wading) across the border emerged as the quintessential act of illegal immigration, the outermost point in a relativist ordering of illegal immigration. The method of Mexicans' illegal entry could thus be perceived as "criminal" and Mexican immigrants as undeserving of relief. Combined with the construction of Mexicans as migratory agricultural laborers (both legal and illegal) in the 1940s and 1950s, that perception gave powerful sway to the notion that Mexicans had no rightful presence on United States territory, no rightful claim of belonging.

The Crimes and Consequences of Illegal Immigration: A Cross-Border Examination of Operation Wetback, 1943–1954

KELLY LYTLE HERNÁNDEZ

In May of 1954, U.S. Attorney General Herbert Brownell issued an announcement. In the coming months, the U.S. Border Patrol would implement what he called Operation Wetback. As he explained it, Operation Wetback would be an intensive and innovative law enforcement campaign designed to confront the rapidly increasing number of illegal border crossings by Mexican nationals. As promised, during the summer of 1954, eight hundred Border Patrol officers swept through the southwestern United States performing a series of raids, road

Kelly Lytle Hernández, "The Crimes and Consequences of Illegal Immigration: A Cross-Border Examination of Operation Wetback, 1943–1954," *Western Historical Quarterly* 37 (Winter 2006): 421–444.

blocks, and mass deportations. By the end of the year, Brownell was able to announce that the summer campaign had been a success by contributing to the apprehension and deportation of over one million persons, mostly Mexican nationals, during 1954.

Five decades later, Brownell's public chronicling of Operation Wetback 1954 continues to draw the basic framework for understanding the campaign as an intensive, U.S. law enforcement campaign targeting undocumented Mexican nationals during the summer of 1954. Yet, Brownell's account of Operation Wetback was a decade late and a nation short. It was ten years earlier when the U.S. Border Patrol had begun its aggressive campaign against undocumented Mexican immigration. Raids, mass deportations, and an uncompromising focus on undocumented Mexican immigration had increasingly characterized U.S. Border Patrol work since the early 1940s. Further, Border Patrol efforts and in-novations to prevent undocumented Mexican immigration into the United States developed in close collaboration with Mexican officials and law enforce-ment officers seeking to limit and control unsanctioned migration out of Mexico. Therefore, when it is defined as an innovative, aggressive, and targeted campaign against undocumented Mexican immigration, Operation Wetback is only partially understood if framed as occurring just during the summer of 1954 and only north of the U.S.-Mexico border.

Rooted in archival research conducted in the United States and Mexico, this [essay] digs deep into the history of Operation Wetback to tell a binational story of migration control that began long before 1954 and extended far beyond the U.S.-Mexico border. This binational history of Operation Wetback challenges the generally accepted view of Operation Wetback as a national initiative of U.S. immigration law enforcement. While it is certainly true that the U.S. Border Patrol was the primary police force involved in migration control along the U.S.-Mexico border, the cross-border history of Operation Wetback reveals how Mexican officials actively participated in the imagination and implementa-tion of policing unsanctioned migration along the U.S.-Mexico border. Without denying the dominance of U.S. interests in U.S.-Mexican relations, Mexican of-ficials participated in migration control along its northern border according to Mexico's domestic interests in regulating the international mobility of Mexican laborers. This [essay] therefore, focuses upon Mexican collaboration with the United States Border Patrol to establish a set of law enforcement priorities and practices designed to police the crimes of Mexican laborers who exited Mexico without authorization and entered the United States without sanction.

As a focused police project dedicated to curbing undocumented Mexican immigration, Operation Wetback began as the lesser-known companion of the Bracero Program. The Bracero Program (1942–1964) was a series of agreements between the U.S. and Mexican governments that facilitated the migration of short-term Mexican contract laborers into (and out of) the United States. Known as *braceros*, these laborers generally worked on southwestern farms, and U.S. and Mexican officials closely managed their migration between the United States and Mexico. Yet, beneath the agreement to import *braceros* were commit-ments to prevent Mexican laborers from surreptitiously crossing into the United

States and to aggressively detect and deport those who had successfully affected illegal entry. At a time when detecting, detaining, and deporting enemy aliens could have emerged as a priority of migration control within the United States, the bilateral promises of the Bracero Program directed the U.S. Border Patrol's attention to policing the southern border and deporting undocumented Mexican nationals. There, along the southern border, the U.S. Border Patrol found the Mexican government to be a critical partner in the design and implementation of migration control strategies.

By the early 1940s, Mexico had several decades of experience in trying to limit and control Mexican emigration to the United States. President Porfirio Díaz (1876-1910) had routinely implored poor Mexicans to not go north and remain in Mexico as laborers of Mexico's modernizing economy. Díaz's ouster in 1910 brought years of revolution and political chaos, but the general political commitment to discourage Mexican emigration continued. The new Mexican Constitution of 1917 allowed its nationals the right to freely enter and exit the national territory, but Section 26 of Article 123 of the Constitution of 1917 required each Mexican to have a labor contract signed by municipal authorities and the consulate of the country where they intended to work. This administrative restriction rendered legal labor migration of Mexican workers to the United States virtually impossible, because U.S. law prohibited offering contracts to foreign laborers before they entered the United States. For poor Mexicans, therefore, labor migration to the United States was often a crime south of the border just as their inability to pay U.S. immigration fees and/or pass literacy exams often forced them to surreptitiously cross the border in violation of U.S. immigration law.

Still, throughout the 1920s, hundreds of thousands of Mexican laborers crossed both legally and illegally into the United States. Mexican newspapers, politicians, and activists all tried to convince them to stay in Mexico. Most often, they warned potential migrants of the humiliations of racial discrimination that awaited them in the United States and reminded them of their duty to participate in the economic development of Mexico by working south of the border. At times, Mexican officials attempted to directly interrupt illegal labor migration to the United States. But, keeping Mexicans in Mexico was a nearly impossible task when confronting poverty in Mexico and agribusiness expansion in the United States.

It was only the onset of the Great Depression that turned Mexican migrants around. In this unique moment of diminished employment opportunities in the United States, more Mexicans returned to Mexico than entered the United States. Mobilization for World War II in the United States and a campaign of rapid industrialization within Mexico, however, once again jumpstarted Mexican immigration to the United States during the early 1940s. In particular, as many U.S. citizens joined the armed services or moved into higher paying industrial jobs, agribusiness-men in the southwestern United States actively recruited laborers from Mexico to work north of the border. At the same time, the Mexican government pursued a program of industrializing its agricultural sector. Land privatization, mechanization, and the export orientation of agricultural production combined with food shortages and a dramatic rise in the Mexican population to force many Mexican *campesinos* (rural laborers) to seek economic survival through migration. They moved within Mexico and across the U.S.-Mexico border in search of work.

The Mexican government hoped to limit the loss of its citizens and laborers to its northern neighbor. Not only was massive emigration to the United States a shameful exposure of the failure of the Mexican Revolution to provide economic well-being for many of Mexico's citizens, but it also drained the country of one of its greatest natural resources, a cheap and flexible labor supply. The loss of laborers and inability to regulate labor mobility worried many social, political, and economic leaders at a time when Mexico was deeply engaged in a project of modernizing the countryside. Mexican political leaders imagined the Bracero Program as a program of managed migration that offered the Mexican government the opportunity to control the international mobility of poor Mexican *campesinos*. Control, however, was elusive as undocumented migration increased alongside the Bracero Program.

Within weeks of negotiating the Bracero agreement, tens of thousands of unemployed and underemployed Mexicans learned of the opportunity to work in the United States and headed to the recruitment center that had been established in Mexico City. When they arrived, however, many learned that they were not eligible to sign up for the program. Only healthy young men with agricultural experience, but without land, who had secured a written recommendation from local authorities verifying that their labor was not locally needed, were eligible for *bracero* contracts. Many poor Mexicans, who were too young or too old, too sick, or female, were turned away by Mexican authorities. Disappointed by the limits of the Bracero Program, many poor Mexicans headed to the U.S.-Mexico border, where they crossed without the authorization of the Mexican government or the sanction of the U.S. government. Therefore, even though the Bracero Program delivered two million legal temporary Mexican workers to U.S. farms and ranches between 1942 and 1964, an increasingly large number of Mexicans were working illegally outside of Mexico and within the United States during the same years.

Once illegal immigration to the United States grew alongside the Bracero Program, various Mexican interest groups pressured their government representatives to end unsanctioned Mexican migration across the U.S.-Mexico border. Agribusinessmen along Mexico's northern border were particularly vocal in their protests that cotton was rotting in the fields because Mexican laborers chose to cross the border for higher wages rather than work within Mexico. Agribusinessmen in these regions demanded placement of the Mexican military along the border to prevent unsanctioned border crossings into the United States by Mexican cotton pickers. Their protests were joined by the voices of *braceros* working within the United States who resented undocumented emigration because they believed undocumented Mexican workers lowered wages and worsened working conditions while many Mexicans in general resented the loss of citizens and workers to the "colossus" of the north. The Mexican government responded to these demands by improving the enforcement of its own emigration laws and used the Bracero Program as an opportunity to negotiate the deportation of illegal Mexican labor out of the United States.

Soon after the Bracero Program began, Mexican officials demanded that in exchange for participating in the facilitation of legal immigration through the Bracero Program, the United States needed to improve border control and return to Mexico those who surreptitiously crossed into the United States. These demands for improved control over unsanctioned entry into the United States linked the U.S. Border Patrol directly to the Bracero Program.

To address the mounting problem of illegal immigration alongside the Bracero Program, the U.S. Border Patrol "committed itself to strengthen the Patrol force along the Mexican Border by the means of filling all existing vacancies and detailing approximately 150 Patrol Inspectors from other areas to the Mexican border. The shift of additional Border Patrol officers to the southern border transformed the national organization of the U.S. Border Patrol. Prior to 1943, more U.S. Border Patrol officers worked along the northern border than along the southern. However, the majority of new officers hired after 1943 were assigned to stations along the U. S.-Mexico border. Growth of the Border Patrol budget in 1940 and the shift of personnel in late 1943 almost doubled the number of Border Patrol Inspectors working in the U.S.-Mexico borderlands. After 1943, the Mexican border became the center of operations for the U.S. Border Patrol, but when more officers did not automatically result in higher numbers of deportations, Mexican officials continued to press the United States for results.

On 11 December 1943, the Mexican Embassy in Washington, D. C. wrote to the U.S. Secretary of State requesting that the U.S. government "adopt the measures which may be appropriate to prevent the illegal entry" of Mexican workers not in possession of *bracero* contracts. Mexico requested such assistance because of the law enforcement challenges presented by border policing and because "the economy of Mexico is suffering serious losses through the surreptitious departure of workers."

Within six months of the Mexican Embassy's threat to revise the Bracero Program, the chief supervisor of the U.S. Border Patrol, W. F. Kelly, launched an "intensive drive on Mexican aliens" by deploying "Special Mexican Deportation Parties" throughout the country. The Special Mexican Deportation Parties were small teams of U.S. Border Patrol officers specifically directed to target, apprehend, and deport undocumented Mexican nationals. For example, on 14 June 1944, Kelly ordered the Border Patrol stations in Minnesota and North Dakota to detail officers to Chicago and to perform special raids against Mexican nationals. The next day, Border Patrol officers in McAllen, Texas, completed a drive upon Mexican nationals that resulted in over 6,900 apprehensions.

The 1943 shift in personnel to the southern border and the Special Mexican Deportation Parties of 1944 marked the beginning of the U.S. Border Patrol's intense focus upon Mexican nationals. The new focus and strategies had multiple effects. First, the number of apprehensions of deportable aliens made by U.S. Border Patrol officers in the Mexican border region increased from 11,775 in

1943 to 28,173 in 1944. Operation Wetback, a campaign of aggressively target-ing Mexican nationals for interrogation, apprehension, and deportation, had begun.

The U.S. Border Patrol's shift to the Mexican border in 1943 and focus upon Mexican nationals in 1944 created quick results by dramatically increasing the number of Mexican nationals apprehended and deported. But, the problem of increasing the number of deportations without altering the method of depor-tation was quickly apparent. When the U.S. Border Patrol released deportees at the border, deportees simply and easily re-entered the United States. Therefore, soon after the Special Mexican Deportations began, U.S. and Mexican officials initiated a conversation about how to prevent deportees from easily slipping out of Mexico and into the United States. On 11 January 1945 they reached an agreement whereby the United States Border Patrol would deport Mexican nationals who were residents of Sonora, Sinaloa, and Jalisco through Nogales, Arizona, and residents of eastern and southern Mexican states through El Paso, Texas. For their part, Mexican officials agreed to "accept delivery of the aliens in question through its immigration officials at the ports opposite El Paso and Nogales and to divert them to localities in the Interior." Therefore, rather than just releasing deportees at the border, U.S. Border Patrol officers began to deliver Mexican deportees into the custody of Mexican immigration officials who would forcibly relocate the deportees to points south of the border. After several months of preparation, this practice began in April of 1945.

Whether using trains or planes, the procedure for coordinating deportation into the interior of Mexico was similar. Typically, U.S. Border Patrol officers apprehended undocumented Mexican nationals within the United States and took them to an INS detention center along the California or Texas border. At the detention center, officers determined the method of removal that would be offered to each immigrant. If migrants were residents of an adjacent border area, they would be allowed to simply cross back into Mexico and remain in the bor-der area without further penalty or surveillance. If they were from the interior, however, Border Patrol officers tagged them for a train-lift or air-lift. Residents of northern Mexican states would generally be designated for deportation by train to Monterrey, Torreón, or Chihuahua, while residents of "the balance of Mexico" would be designated to return by plane to central Mexico.

Once all of the necessary information was gathered, the Border Patrol trans-ported deportees by plane, train, or bus to the U.S. border port from where they would be deported. While the Border Patrol released residents of the border areas from U.S. custody at the border, residents of the interior were released into the custody of Mexican officers. At this point, the deportees and the finan-cial responsibility for their detention, supervision, transportation, and care were officially transferred from the United States to Mexico.

The migrants waited until a train was ready to take them south. As they waited, perhaps they would be lectured by a Mexican official that "it was useless for them (returnees) to return to the United States as no demand existed for labor. If they complained about being forcibly removed to the interior of Mexico, an officer of the Mexican Department of Migration may have explained that they had broken Mexican law by emigrating without the proper documents and were, therefore, in no position to dispute their removal to the interior. When the trains were ready, the guards placed the migrants on board and escorted them to their final destination somewhere farther south of the U.S.-Mexico border.

Cross-border collaboration expanded the possibilities of migration control along the U.S.-Mexico border. Although police practice is defined as a site of state violence, that is limited by the boundaries of the nation-state, the cross-border policing of migrants linked the distinct territories of U.S. and Mexican police authority. At all times, U.S. and Mexican officers respected the limits represented by the border. They disembarked from the buses and exchanged custody of deportees at the line between the two countries. With cross-border collaboration, however, U.S. and Mexican officers were able to transform the line that marked the limits of their jurisdictions into a bridge that linked rather then divided the two distinct systems of migration control. Upon that bridge the consequences for unsanctioned border crossing were merged. No longer were the detentions and dislocations that accompanied migration control isolated within one nation or territory. In the United States, those identified as illegal immigrants were subject to surveillance, detention, and deportation. In Mexico, they would face the disruptions and anxieties of forced dislocation to unfamiliar places. In each location, however, the consequences of having committed the symbiotic crimes of unsanctioned emigration and undocumented immigration were bound together through the collaborative practices of U.S.-Mexican migration control.

Reports regarding the conditions of the lifts and treatment of returnees vary significantly. While Mexican officials participating in the program tended to report that the lifts were conducted "without incident" and that they were "pleased with the arrangement," journalists, migrants, and activists tended to comment less favorably. For example, Frank Ferree was a U.S. veteran and self-declared champion of the Mexican worker who was disturbed by the poor living and working conditions of undocumented Mexican laborers in South Texas. Ferree often accompanied the deportees on the train-lifts to distribute food and medicine and reported that the train-lifts were "indescribable scenes of human misery and tragedy" as poor, and often sick, deportees were forced onto guarded trains and taken to unfamiliar places. Sometimes, he reported, deportees would jump from the moving trains and be half-heartedly shot at by Mexican officers guarding the train-lift.

With a similarly negative story to tell, deportee Juan Silos spoke with a journalist from *El Heraldo de Chihuahua* as he awaited a train-lift in Reynosa, México. Silos complained that Mexican officers had beaten him over the head with an iron rod until his head bled. For years the Mexican press and politicians had warned migrants against going to the United States, where they would be subject to racial discrimination and violence. But, according to Silos, the violence experienced by him and the other deportees within Mexico made him wonder, "why they talk about discrimination towards workers abroad, when here brothers of our own race almost kill us."

While U.S.-Mexico collaboration expanded during the 1940s, the Mexican government continued to fund its own independent campaigns dedicated to preventing the unsanctioned emigration of Mexican laborers into the United States. In particular, when breakdowns in negotiations for the Bracero Program severed the cross-border negotiations for migration control, Mexico strengthened its own border enforcement.

The captain of the Mexican Border Patrol, Alberto Moreno, worked with what one Mexican newspaper described as a "hand of steel" dedicated to arresting migrant smugglers and undocumented immigrants when they illegally crossed back into Mexico. Chief Patrol Inspector Fletcher Rawls of the U.S. Border Patrol in El Paso, Texas, valued Captain Moreno's work on the southern side of the border. He "is tearing up boats by the bunches (I think shooting up a few) and is cooperating with us very good," explained Rawls to his district director within the Immigration Naturalization Serviced. "If we can keep this man over there and he continues to receive the backing from Mexico City, he is going to be a big help to us," continued Rawls, who appreciated the expanded possibilities of policing and punishing unsanctioned migration when U.S. and Mexican officers cooperated along the border.

Migrants routinely frustrated U.S. and Mexican officers by using the border as a barrier against U.S. and Mexican immigration law enforcement. The residents of Tampico, a large migrant camp just north of the South Texas border, for example, lived outside the grasp of Mexican authorities, but rushed south to flee the jurisdiction of U.S. officers when the U.S. Border Patrol raided the camp. The establishment of the Mexican Border Patrol, however, limited their ability to exploit the limits that the border placed upon the distinct jurisdictions of U.S. and Mexican law enforcement.

One of the most nagging problems for U.S. Border Patrol officers were cases of "chronic offenders" who were able to escape forced relocation to the interior by claiming residency in a border city. "You'd take them across the river and sometimes they beat you back across," explained Bob Salinger, patrol inspector in charge of the Mission, Texas, station in the early 1950s. Salinger "got fed up" with the "chronic offenders" who "you'd see … day after day" and "promoted a pair of clippers" to be carried in each Border Patrol car and instructed the officers to shave the heads of "chronic offenders. After they had put migrants through what Salinger described as "a little barbershop for the chronic offenders," he instructed his officers: "You're going to have to take them straight over the river and kick them across after you clip their heads. We can't run them through the camp. Salinger was aware that the "little barbershop" was unsanctioned and unofficial, and consciously pushed the practice underground. But soon his officers became lax in their efforts to conceal the Border Patrol barber shop. When eight chronic offenders broke free of an officer one day and began "thumbing their nose" at him, he re-apprehended them and "decided they needed their heads clipped, so he peeled all of them." He had "made an Apache out of some of them, cut crosses on their heads, just the long-haired ones. One ole boy had a big bushy mustache, he'd shaved off half of it." Salinger believed the officer had done "a good job of it," but when the head-shaven immigrants were processed through the detention center, Chief Patrol Inspector Fletcher Rawls ordered the Mission, Texas, station to stop "peeling" Mexican heads, while he investigated whether or not head shaving violated the civil rights of detainees. When

Mexican newspapers began to expose and condemn the practice, which had also independently emerged in California, Rawls was forced to put distance between the Border Patrol and head peeling. The needed political distance was available just a few feet away. Rawls contacted the head of the Mexican Border Patrol who agreed to pick up the practice of head shaving south of the border until the civil rights issues it presented within the United States could be worked out. Mexican officers conducted head shaving until several years later, when the practice was officially performed at U.S. Border Patrol detention centers for sanitary purposes."

At the same time that U.S. and Mexican officers were working to negotiate the limits that the border placed upon policing and state violence, they fortified the physical divide between the two nations to deepen the dangers that the borderlands presented to unsanctioned migrants. With fences and coordinated surveillance, U.S. and Mexican officers pushed those who dared to cross the border without sanction into the backlands and waters of the border landscape. There, in the backlands and border waters, their deaths were the product of strategies pursued by U.S. and Mexican officials and were a reminder of the most extreme consequence of being policed.

In 1945, U.S. Border Patrol authorities began to recognize a shift in illegal border crossings away from the El Paso, Texas, area to the California border. To confront the rise in illegal crossings across the California border, the Immigration and Naturalization Service delivered "4,500 lineal feet of chain link fencing (10 feet high, woven of No. 6 wire) to the International Boundary and Water Commission at Calexico, California." Although the INS was not erecting a continuous line of fence along the borderline, they hoped that strategic placement of the fence would "compel persons seeking to enter the United States illegally to attempt to go around the ends of the fence." What lay at the end of the fences and canals were desertlands and mountains extremely dangerous to cross without guidance or sufficient water. Therefore, the fences discouraged illegal immigration by exposing undocumented border crossers to the dangers of daytime dehydration and nighttime hypothermia.

The construction of the fence sparked immediate resistance in Mexican border communities. To protect the fence, the governor of Baja California detailed Mexican soldiers to patrol and protect the fence "during its erection." Therefore, although the Mexican government consistently demanded protection for Mexican *braceros* from discrimination and abuse by U.S. employers, Mexican border officials helped the U.S. Border Patrol to erect fences designed to reduce illegal immigration by making border crossings more dangerous for undocumented workers.

When the Calexico fence was completed, many migrants found ways to cut through, over and under the border fence. Others, however, became frustrated by the barricades and risked the march around its edges. For example, after being apprehended by the U.S. Border Patrol while trying to get across the border fence, a Mexican deportee reported to the *Los Angeles Times:* "[N]ext time I will cross over in the desert country. When, with companions, I will take a road through the desert sand where there are no people." He recognized that beyond the fences "it is hard, and, many die on such a road," but he hoped: "[M]aybe my water bottle will last and I will come to some place like San Bernardino, or to Los Angeles, and become lost there, from la migra." Many who shared his dream, however, perished along the way. On 4 February 1952, for example, an irrigation district employee discovered five dead Mexican males near Superstition Mountain in the Imperial Valley of California. The bodies were found "near small shrubs with a flax straw water bag, two cans of sardines and two loaves of bread." Apparently the men had readied themselves for a long trek through the desert, but had underestimated the ravages of the backlands along the U.S.-Mexico border.

Many of those who did not test the dangers of the deserts chose to cross the border's waterways, such as crossing the All-American Canal in Southern California. As with the Rio Grande in Texas, which was claiming the life of at least one undocumented border crosser each day, the United States Border Patrol and Mexican officers left the All-American relatively unguarded because of the inherent threat it presented to undocumented crossers. On 26 May, 1952, twenty-five-year-old Mario Ramírez stepped into the canal six miles west of Calexico and drowned. Several days later, canal authorities discovered the battered corpse of another young Mexican male that had been entangled in the head gate of the All-American canal for at least one month. He could have been heading north or south, because Mexican policy denied undocumented immigrants who self-deported the right to use the ports of entry forcing deportees to surreptitiously re-enter Mexico as they had entered the United States.

In February of 1950, U.S. Border Patrol Inspector Albert Quillin of South Texas launched a new strategy that would soon form the core of U.S. Border Patrol activities. "At 5 am, Tuesday, February 11" 1950, Quillin convened a detail of twelve border patrolmen with "two buses, one plane, one truck, a carryall and … nine automobiles" at a "point four miles east of Rio Hondo, Texas." There, the officers set up a miniature immigration station and split into two teams. Each team was given maps of the area and instructions to apprehend as many undocumented immigrants as possible, quickly process them through the temporary immigration station, and then place them on one of the waiting buses that would take deportees directly to the border. That day, about 100 undocumented Mexicans were deported from the Rio Hondo area. The next day, this same detail moved on to Crossroads Gin near Los Fresnos, Texas, and raided farms. By the end of the second day, an additional 561 undocumented Mexicans had been deported. On the third and fourth days, this detail moved into San Benito, Texas, from where they deported 398 Mexicans. Altogether, Quillin's detail apprehended over 1,000 undocumented laborers in four days of work. Word quickly spread regarding Quillin's accomplishments and within two weeks his model was being applied throughout South Texas. Soon, Quillin's model was given a name, "Operation Wetback," coordinated with the lifts that deported Mexicans into the interior of Mexico, and introduced to Border Patrol operations throughout California and Texas.

Along with increased personnel concentrated in the U.S.-Mexico border region and improved equipment ranging from buses to planes, the "Operation Wetback" model allowed the Border Patrol to boost the number of annual apprehensions. Between 1950 and 1953, U.S. Border Patrol apprehensions almost doubled from 459,289 to 827,440. Although the introduction of the "Operation Wetback" model and the rising number of repeat crossers made the jump in apprehension statistics a poor gauge for the overall volume of undocumented Mexican immigration, the raw increase in the number of apprehensions of undocumented Mexicans caused many in Mexico and the United States to believe that a crisis existed.

For many, the continuing spike in apprehensions along the southern border directly reflected a deepening crisis of unsanctioned border crossings by Mexican nationals and was unrelated to innovations in U.S. and Mexican immigration law enforcement. Another breakdown in Bracero Program negotiations stalled cross-border collaboration in January of 1954, but by spring, U.S. and Mexican officials resumed negotiations to aggressively combat the crisis in undocumented Mexican immigration. In the United States, President Eisenhower appointed retired Army General Swing as the commissioner of the INS. General Swing's appointment was intended to improve the efficiency of immigration law enforcement through militarization of the INS. In Mexico, preparations were made to increase the number of removals to the interior while the Mexican press warned potential migrants of the impending campaign. Officials of the two countries rushed memos and agreements back and forth regarding how they could independently and collaboratively control the flow of undocumented Mexican immigration. In May 1954, officials of each country publicly announced that the U.S. Border Patrol would soon launch Operation Wetback of 1954 as an innovative law enforcement response to the crisis of undocumented Mexican immigration. One month later, U.S. Border Patrol officers erected roadblocks on roads that led to the interior of the United States to prevent undocumented immigrants from escaping apprehension by fleeing inward. On the 17th the officers were organized into dozens of "command units" of twelve men with buses, airplanes, and mobile immigration stations that would allow them to quickly process undocumented Mexican nationals for deportation. Everywhere they went, the officers were chased and photographed by journalists who had come to witness what Brownell had promised would be a spectacular show of U.S. law enforcement, headed by the newly appointed General Swing. The journalists and U.S. Border Patrol officers, however, halted at the border while Mexican deportees were delivered into the custody of Mexican officers, who forcibly relocated them to "areas in the country [Mexico] where work was plentiful. For migrants, the process of deportation continued within Mexico as they were placed on the *S.S. Emancipación* or on one of the trains or planes that had been relocating them to far away places for almost a decade.

While General Joseph Swing is generally credited with designing and launching Operation Wetback as an innovative campaign of U.S. immigration law enforcement, the set of practices employed during the summer of 1954 had begun one decade before Swing's arrival. The focus upon Mexican nationals, mass deportations, removal to the interior of Mexico, and command units were all well-worn tactics within the recent history of migration control along the U.S.-Mexico border.

The publicity campaign of 1954 made an impact far beyond the numbers of apprehensions actually accomplished. After 1954, the long and complicated history of Operation Wetback remained camouflaged behind the public statements and press accounts of that summer. Those statements and accounts tended to limit the story of Operation Wetback to the summer of 1954 and to north of the U.S.-Mexico borderline. This article, however, utilizes U.S. and Mexican sources to retrace the longer history of Operation Wetback and highlight cross-border border dynamics of migration control that the activities and pronouncements of 1954 obscured. What emerges from a critical analysis of the development of Operation Wetback is not the story that Attorney General Brownell hoped to project about the innovation and success of U.S. law enforcement during the summer of 1954. Rather, cross-border research transforms the typically nation-bound and time-bound narrative of Operation Wetback into an unexpected story of evolving binational efforts at migration control. Those binational efforts, such as the collaborative deportations, coordinated raids, and shared surveillance, linked the crimes of unsanctioned exit from Mexico and illicit entry into the United States and extended their consequences across the U.S.-Mexico border. Although much of the cross-border history of Operation Wetback remains lost in what was never written south of the border, expanding and extending the lens applied to the campaign deepens our understanding of the penalties that migrants paid for their crimes of illegal migration when the boundaries of state violence were stitched together by collaborative police practice.

FURTHER READING

Andreas, Peter. *Border Games: Policing the U.S.-Mexico Divide* (2009).

Balderrama, Francisco, and Raymond Rodríguez. *Decade of Betrayal: Mexican Repatriation in the 1930s* (1995).

Blanton, Carlos Kevin. "The Citizenship Sacrifice: Mexican Americans, the Saunders Leonard Report, and the Politics of Immigration, 1951–1952." *Western Historical Quarterly* 40 (Autumn 2009): 299–320.

Bracero History Archive http://braceroarchive.org/

Calavita, Kitty. *Inside the State: The Bracero Program, Immigration, and the I.N.S.* (1992).

Castañeda, Antonia, Patricia Hart, Karen Weathermon, and Susan H. Armitage, eds. *Gender on the Borderlands: The Frontiers Reader* (2007).

Cohen, Deborah. *Braceros: Migrant Citizens and Transnational Subjects in the Postwar United States and Mexico* (2011).

De Genova, Nicholas and Nathalie Peutz, eds. *The Deportation Regime: Sovereignty, Space, and the Freedom of Movement* (2010).

Ettinger, Patrick. *Imaginary Lines: Border Enforcement and the Origins of Undocumented Immigration, 1882–1930* (2009).

Gutiérrez, David G. *Walls and Mirrors: Mexican Americans, Mexican Immigrants, and the Politics of Ethnicity* (1995).

———. ed. *Between Two Worlds: Mexican Immigrants in the United States* (1996).

———. "Migration, Emergent Ethnicity, and the 'Third Space': The Shifting Politics of Nationalism in Greater Mexico." *Journal of American History* 86 (Sep. 1999): 481–517.

Hoerder, Dirk, and Nora Faires, eds. *Migrants and Migration in Modern North America* (2011).

Kang, Deborah S. *The Legal Construction of the Borderlands: The INS, Immigration Law, and Immigrant Rights on the U.S.-Mexico Border* (2012).

Lytle-Hernández, Kelly. *Migra! A History of the U.S. Border Patrol* (2010).

Ngai, Mae. *Impossible Subjects: Illegal Aliens and the Making of Modern America* (2004).

CHAPTER 14

~

Economic Integration and
Mass Migration, 1994–Present

With international trade, immigration debates, and drug violence routinely making head-lines in the twenty-first century, there can be no doubt that the history of North America's borders and borderlands is still being made.

This final chapter addresses major issues concerning the continent's borders in the re-cent past and present. With the end of the Cold War in 1989, a new era of cooperation and mutuality for North America seemed in the offing. The most visible sign of this coop-eration was the negotiations for the North American Free Trade Agreement, or NAFTA. The purpose of NAFTA was to unite Canada, the United States, and Mexico into a free trade block with minimal tariffs and restrictions on one another's products. The most ambi-tious of NAFTA proponents saw it as a way of transcending past divisions, particularly between the United States and Mexico, and perhaps even as a first step toward political cooperation and coordination, as with the European Union. In this view, the borders that divided the three nations would matter less and less as they all worked toward an era of shared economic prosperity brought about by trade liberalization.

Not everybody was so optimistic. NAFTA was controversial within Mexico, Canada, and the United States. Mexican and Canadian critics charged that it would lead to economic domination by American companies and thus to an erosion of their national culture and sov-ereignty. Mexican opponents denounced the ruling party's pursuit of this agreement as proof that it had abandoned the principles of the Mexican revolution for the seductive embrace of the free-market ideology so dominant north of the border. Labor advocates from all three nations feared that it would lead to a race to the bottom for wages and working conditions. Canadian and American environmentalists similarly argued that it would gut environmental standards by encouraging companies to relocate to Mexico to avoid environmental regulation and en-forcement, and also possibly by striking down environmental laws as restraints of trade.

Nevertheless, NAFTA was approved by the governments of Canada, Mexico, and the United States. After it went into force on January 1, 1994, most tariffs and restrictions on commerce between the three nations were phased out. The increased mobility of capital, goods, and financial services allowed by the agreement, however, did not apply to labor.

509

The American economy attracted far more Mexican workers than American law allowed to enter the country. Moreover, highly capitalized and subsidized American agriculture made the operation of hundreds of thousands of small farms in Mexico economically unviable, prompting many of these farmers to move in search of work, first to Mexican cities and then often to the United States. So illegal immigration continued to grow, provoking controversy on both sides of the U.S.-Mexico border. Mexican society and officials had long looked askance at those who left for America, seeing them as embarrassing reminders of economic backwardness at best, and downright traitors to the nation at worst. But, by the 1990s, it was increasingly difficult to deny that emigration also greatly benefitted Mexico, particularly in the form of remittances, money sent home by those working aboard, which by most calculations had come to rival petroleum exports as Mexico's largest source of foreign capital. Particularly after the 2000 election of Vicente Fox, the first president from an opposition party since the Mexican Revolution, the Mexican state began to accept the permanent presence of millions of its nationals in the United States as a fact of life. The Mexican government extended itself on their behalf by providing them with identification cards, heightened consular protection, and voting rights even when abroad.

Within the United States, debates over Mexican immigration grew more heated. The September 11, 2001, terrorist attacks on New York City and Washington, D.C., shifted American priorities away from economic integration and toward national security concerns. Although none of the hijackers had entered the United States by crossing either of its land borders, there were many calls for more vigorous border policing. The Immigration and Naturalization Service, which administers U.S. immigration law, was placed under Homeland Security, an agency charged with defense against terrorism. The American and Mexican governments had begun work on comprehensive immigration reform—some new system of immigration law that would address what most viewed as the problem of more than ten million Mexicans living in the United States without legal permission. But with the American government focused on 9-11 and the subsequent wars in Iraq and Afghanistan, no further progress was made on this issue. NAFTA's trade regime remained in place, but the momentum toward greater North American integration had been reversed.

The United States began experiencing an intense anti-immigrant backlash. Nativism—opposition to the foreign-born—had not been this strong in American society since the 1920s. Anti-immigration organizations called for mass deportations and for a reconsideration of the constitutional provision that all those born on U.S. soil were automatically U.S. citizens. In response to such sentiments, the federal government increased raids on workplaces employing illegal immigrants, and residents of several states passed ballot initiatives to deny public services such as education and medical treatment to those who could not prove their legal status. A handful of municipalities in Pennsylvania and Texas sought to enforce immigration law by banning the renting of apartments to illegal aliens, although federal courts held that immigration law is a federal matter and thus found these laws unconstitutional. A 2010 law in Arizona went further than any previous measure in its requirements that immigrants carry authorization papers at all times and that police routinely check the immigration status of people they have reason to believe are in the country illegally. Hispanic civil rights organizations filed suit to block implementation of the law and charged that it would lead to rampant racial profiling and harassment of all Latinos.

Because these disputes concerned on Latin American immigration, they focused on the U.S.-Mexico border. But many of the new restrictions and border policing applied to the

U.S.-Canada border as well, to the consternation of many Canadians. The politics of border enforcement had become some of the leading and most divisive questions across the United States and between Americans, Mexicans, and Canadians. In that sense, the borderlands were everywhere.

∿ DOCUMENTS

The first document excerpts a speech given by U.S. President Bill Clinton on the signing of NAFTA. Clinton praises the creation of a continental free trade zone as a step towards prosperity and peace not only for the United States, but also as a model for a new global era of openness and free trade. When goods and services can easily and quickly cross national borders, Clinton argued, economic competition and prosperity would be the end results. In Document 2, Gene Karpinski, the head of the Public Interest Research Group, and J. Michael McCloskey, the chair of the Sierra Club, urge the U.S. Congress to vote against NAFTA. Their arguments that open borders would lead to the gutting of environmental standards were characteristic of Canadian and American opponents of the trade agreement.

The migration of workers north from Mexico was one reflection of continued North American economic integration, if not one that was provided for in the terms of NAFTA. Migrants faced numerous obstacles, including robbery, corrupt officials, and physical violence. Document 3 is a newspaper article describing some of Mexican President Vicente Fox's efforts to address these challenges. His public embrace of migrants as "heroes" symbolized the Mexican government's widely publicized reversal of silence or hostility toward migrants.

If migration to the United States was becoming more accepted in Mexico, then the opposite was the case in the United States Document 4 is Congressional testimony from the founder of an organization called the Minute Man Civil Defense Corps, originally formed in 2004 to patrol the Mexican border against unlawful migrants. Named to invoke the Americans who fought for independence in the Revolutionary War, the organization portrayed those entering the country illegally as invaders and threats to national security. These concerns had great resonance in a country still shaken by 9-11, even for many who did not endorse the organization's advocacy of vigilantism.

If the minutemen and others saw immigration policy through the lens of national security, then others believed that racism and xenophobia were more central to these debates. In Document 5, *New York Times* economics reporter David Leonhardt accuses Lou Dobbs, then a popular news anchor at the Cable News Network (CNN), and perhaps the most prominent opponent of immigration, of deception and giving a platform to white supremacists, linking him to a long strain of American nativists dating back to anti-Irish and anti-Chinese agitation in the nineteenth century. A year and a half later, Dobbs left CNN, whose management had grown concerned that his strong stances on immigration and other issues were compromising its journalistic integrity.

One of the most important political victories gained by those who perceived illegal immigration to be a threat to U.S. national security was a 2006 measure providing for the construction of a wall along the border with Mexico. Document 6 is a newspaper article about the response of the Tohon O'odham (Pima) government to this measure. O'odham leaders had long asserted the right of their people to cross the U.S.-Mexico border, which divided their traditional homeland and split the tribe into American and Mexican divisions. Critics of the wall widely echoed the O'odham spokesperson's condemnation of the waiver of environmental and labor laws in its construction.

Heightened immigration enforcement did not reduce the number of Mexicans coming into the United States. This number began to lag only with the severe recession of 2008, following the same pattern of labor demand that Mexican migration had established since the Mexican Revolution. But the process of entering the United States had become much more dangerous than in previous decades. The vast desert expanses of the Arizona-Sonora portion of the border became the primary conduit for migrants. By the early twenty-first century, on average, at least one person trying to reach the United States died each day. Document 7 is an excerpt of writer Luis Alberto Urrea's book *The Devil's Highway*, the story of a group of men from Veracruz who crossed into southern Arizona in May 2001. Fourteen of the party of twenty-six perished in the attempt. Based on extensive interviews with the survivors and the Border Patrol agents who found them, Urrea reconstructs their ordeal, hoping that his searing account will remind all who read it of the need to reckon with the human toll of migration policies.

Other factors also brought violence and suffering to the U.S.-Mexico border. In Document 8 writer Sam Quinones describes the mysterious and terrifying murders of hundreds of women in the Mexican border city Ciudad Juárez. Quinones links debates over these murders to the city's rapid industrialization and the consequent influx of young, single women workers. In the years since the article's publication, both the murders and local anger at the inability or unwillingness of the authorities to solve them have continued. In Document 9, the *New York Times* describes the increasing violence of the drug trade. Although drug traffic in Mexico exists mostly to serve the American market for illegal drugs, most of the violence associated with the cartels occurs in Mexico. This violence has sharply increased since 2006, provoking controversy and anger in both Mexico and the United States. The scale and scope of this violence suggests that neither of the countries—nor both of them acting together—can control their shared border.

1. U.S. President Bill Clinton Praises Free Trade Agreement, 1993

This whole issue turned out to be a defining moment for our Nation. I spoke with one of the folks who was in the reception just a few moments ago who told me that he was in China watching the vote on international television when it was taken. And be said you would have had to be there to understand how important this was to the rest of the world, not because of the terms of NAFTA, which basically is a trade agreement between the United States, Mexico, and

http://millercenter.Org/scripps/archive/speeches/detail/3927 (Accessed 16-04-2010).

Canada, but because it became a symbolic struggle for the spirit of our country and for how we would approach this very difficult and rapidly changing world dealing with our own considerable challenges here at home.

I believe we have made a decision now that will permit us to create an economic order in the world that will promote more growth, more equality, better preservation of the environment, and a greater possibility of world peace. We are on the verge of a global economic expansion that is sparked by the fact that the United States lit this critical moment decided that we would compete, not retreat.

In a few moments, I will sign the North American free trade act into law. NAFTA will tear down trade barriers between our three nations. It will create the world's largest trade zone and create 200,000 jobs in this country by 1995 alone. The environmental and labor side agreements negotiated by our administration will make this agreement a force for social progress as well as economic growth. Already the confidence we've displayed by ratifying NAFTA has begun to bear fruit. We are now making real progress toward a worldwide trade agreement so significant that it could make the material gains of NAFTA for our country look small by comparison.

Today we have the chance to do what our parents did before us. We have the opportunity to remake the world. For this new era, our national security we now know will be determined as much by our ability to pull down foreign trade barriers as by our ability to breach distant ramparts. Once again, we are leading. And in so doing, we are rediscovering a fundamental truth about ourselves: When we lead, we build security, we build prosperity for our own people.

We've learned this lesson the hard way. Twice before in this century, we have been forced to define our role in the world. After World War I we turned inward, building walls of protectionism around our Nation. The result was a Great Depression and ultimately another horrible World War. After the Second World War, we took a different course: We reached outward. Gifted leaders of both political parties built a new order based on collective security and expanded trade. They created a foundation of stability and created in the process the conditions which led to the explosion of the great American middle class, one of the true economic miracles in the whole history of civilization. Their statecraft stands to this day: the IMF and the World Bank, GATT, and NATO.

In this very auditorium in 1949, President Harry Truman signed one of the charter documents of this golden era of American leadership, the North Atlantic Treaty that created NATO. "In this pact we hope to create a shield against aggression and the fear of aggression," told his audience, "a bulwark which will permit us to get on with the real business of Government and society, the business of achieving a fuller and happier life for our citizens."

Now, the institutions built by Truman and Acheson, by Marshall and Vandenberg, have accomplished their task. The cold war is over. The grim certitude of the contest with communism has been replaced by the exuberant uncertainty of international economic competition. And the great question of this day is how to ensure security for our people at a time when change is the only constant.

Make no mistake, the global economy with all of its promise and perils is now the central fact of life for hard-working Americans. It has enriched the lives of millions of Americans. But for too many those same winds of change have worn away at file basis of their security. For two decades, most people have worked harder for less. Seemingly secure jobs have been lost. And while America once again is the most productive nation on Earth, this productivity itself holds the seeds of further insecurity. After all, productivity means the same people can produce more or, very often, that fewer people can produce more. This is the world we face.

We cannot stop global change. We cannot repeal the international economic competition that is everywhere. We can only harness the energy to our benefit. Now we must recognize that the only way for a wealthy nation to grow richer is to export, to simply find new customers for the products and services it makes. That, my fellow Americans, is the decision the Congress made when they voted to ratify NAFTA.

I am gratified with the work that Congress has done this year, bringing the deficit down and keeping interest rates down, getting housing starts and new jobs going upward. But we know that over the long rim, our ability to have our internal economic policies work for the benefit of our people requires us to have external economic policies that permit productivity to find expression not simply in higher incomes for our businesses but in more jobs and higher incomes for our people. That means more customers. There is no other way, not for the United States or for Europe or for Japan or for any other wealthy nation in the world.

That is why I am gratified that we had such a good meeting after the NAFTA vote in the House with the Asian–Pacific leaders in Washington. I am gratified that, as Vice President Gore and Chief of Staff Mack McLarty announced 2 weeks ago when they met with President Salinas, next year the nations of this hemisphere will gather in an economic summit that will plan how to extend the benefits of trade to the emerging market democracies of all the Americas.

And now I am pleased that we have the opportunity to secure the biggest breakthrough of all. Negotiators from 112 nations are seeking to conclude negotiations on a new round of the General Agreement on Tariffs and Trade; a historic world trade pact, one that would spur a global economic boon, is now within our grasp. Let me be clear. We cannot, nor should we, settle for a bad GATT agreement. But we will not flag in our efforts to secure a good one in these closing days. We are prepared to make our contributions to the success of this negotiation, but we insist that other nations do their part as well. We must not squander this opportunity. I call on all the nations of the world to seize this moment and close the deal on a strong GATT agreement within the next week.

I say to everyone, even to our negotiators: Don't rest. Don't sleep. Close the deal. I told Mickey Kantor the other day that we rewarded his laborious effort on NAFTA with a vacation at the GATT talks. [Laughter]

My fellow Americans, bit by bit all these things are creating the conditions of a sustained global expansion. As significant as they are, our goals must be more ambitious. The United States must seek nothing less than a new trading system that benefits all nations through robust commerce but that protects our middle class and gives other nations a chance to grow one, that lifts workers and the environment up without dragging people down, that seeks to ensure that our policies reflect our values.

Our agenda must, therefore, be far reaching. We are determining that dynamic trade cannot lead to environmental despoliation. We will seek new institutional arrangements to ensure that trade leaves the world cleaner than before. We will press for workers in all countries to secure rights that we now take for granted, to organize and earn a decent living. We will insist that expanded trade be fair to our businesses and to our regions. No country should use cartels, subsidies, or rules of entry to keep our products off its shelves. And we must see to it that our citizens have the personal security to confidently participate in this new era. Every worker must receive the education and training he or she needs to reap the rewards of international competition rather than to bear its burdens.

Next year, our administration will propose comprehensive legislation to transform our unemployment system into a reemployment and job retraining system for the 21st century. And above all, I say to you we must seek to reconstruct the broad-based political coalition for expanded trade. For decades, working men and women and their representatives supported policies that brought us prosperity and security. That was because we recognized that expanded trade benefited all of us but that we have an obligation to protect those workers who do bear the brunt of competition by giving them a chance to be retrained and to go on to a new and different and, ultimately, more secure and more rewarding way of work. In recent years, this social contract has been sundered.

It cannot continue.

When I affix my signature to the NAFTA legislation a few moments from now, I do so with this pledge: To the men and women of our country who were afraid of these changes and found in their opposition to NAFTA an expression of that fear—what I thought was a wrong expression and what I know was a wrong expression but nonetheless represented legitimate fears—the gains from this agreement will be your gains, too.

I ask those who opposed NAFTA to work with us to guarantee that the labor and side agreements are enforced, and I call on all of us who believe in NAFTA to join with me to urge the Congress to create the world's best worker training and retraining system. We owe it to the business community as well as to the working men and women of this country. It means greater productivity, lower unemployment, greater worker efficiency, and higher wages and greater security for our people. We have to do that.

We seek a new and more open global trading system not for its own sake but for our own sake. Good jobs, rewarding careers, broadened horizons for the middle class Americans can only be secured by expanding exports and global growth. For too long our step has been unsteady as the ground has shifted beneath our feet. Today, as I sign the North American Free Trade Agreement into law and call for further progress on GATT, I believe we have found our footing. And I ask all of you to be steady, to recognize that there is no turning back from the world of today and tomorrow. We must face the challenges, embrace them with confidence, deal with the problems honestly and openly, and make this world work for all of us. America is where it should be, in the lead, setting the pace, showing the confidence that all of us need to face tomorrow. We are ready to compete, and we can win.

2. Environmental Groups Warn of Damage from NAFTA, 1993

For decades, the environmental community has fought for a clean and safe environment. Laws to promote recycling, prevent pollution, protect endangered species and ensure safe food are just a few of the cornerstones of environmental successes. But the North American Free Trade Agreement could significantly weaken or wholly reverse these actions.

Many environmental laws operate by ensuring that imported goods are safe for our consumption. A case in point is the Delaney clause, which says that certain foods must be 100% free of cancer-causing pesticides. Many pesticide residues that are prohibited in the United States are allowed on Mexican produce.

Under NAFTA, the Mexican government could challenge our law as a barrier to free trade. The safety of our food supply could be determined by a panel of bureaucrats behind closed doors without public input. That's undemocratic and unacceptable.

NAFTA could encourage companies to relocate to areas where both standards and enforcement are lax. To keep those corporations in their communities, local and state regulators within the USA will be pressured to give in to industry demands on environmental regulation.

These fundamental problems have not been fixed by the environmental side agreement. In fact, it is so tortuous and riddled with loopholes it's doubtful enforcement fines ever will be applied.

A broad-based coalition of environmental, consumer and conservation groups opposes NAFTA because it will assault the laws that protect our forests, wildlife, air and water, and that keep our food safe to eat. NAFTA may mean "free trade" to multinational corporations, but it means environmental headaches for the rest of us.

3. Mexican President Defends Migrants

Mexican President Vicente Fox flew to the U.S. border yesterday to welcome home Mexicans and Mexican Americans for the Christmas holidays, and assure them that an ugly tradition would end. Many emigrants arrive in Mexico bearing gifts, and they often fall prey to extortion by Mexican customs agents, immigration officials and police. The extortion is going to stop, Fox assured returnees and about 400 government workers at a roadside customs checkpoint about 12 miles south of the Arizona border.

"There are certainly antecedents that don't speak well of public servants," Fox said.

"We want to get changes in behavior where it's necessary, and we want to come to salute these heroes who left their homes with tears in their eyes to look

Gene Karpinksi and J. Michael McCloskey, "Reject NAFTA Pollution," *USA Today*, Sep. 21, 1993, p. A 12. Reprinted with permission.

Morris Thompson, "Mexico's Leader Courts Emigrants at Border Towns," *Philadelphia Inquirer*, Dec. 13, 2000, p. A 38.

for a job, to look for an opportunity they didn't find in their own country. We respect them. We love them," said Fox, whose election ousted the party that had ruled Mexico for more than seven decades.

Fox's courtship of the millions of Mexicans who live and work in the United States, legally and illegally, is not just for their benefit. The money they wire home is Mexico's third-largest source of income after oil and tourism. Fox has urged them to invest money in their hometowns to bolster the nation's economy.

Historically, many returning Mexicans have been extorted not just at the border but also at checkpoints, like the one Fox visited, set up to control the flow of weapons, drugs and other contraband. Mariano Chavez Bernal, 30, a U.S. citizen since 1996, said at the checkpoint visited by Fox that he had been a victim in past years. "This time, [border authorities] were very nice to us, maybe because the president is here," Chavez said.

Two years ago, he was forced to pay, he said. "It was terrible, right here," said Chavez, who earns $7.50 an hour working six days a week as a farmworker in Royal City, Wash. "They took a lot of money—$20, $30—four times."

For low-paid Mexican border officials, such money is a major source of income.

An estimated 1.5 million Mexicans will cross into Mexico over the two-month period that began Nov. 20, including up to 400,000 who have entered the United States illegally.

Juan Hernandez, chief of a new presidential Office for Mexicans Abroad, said Fox was sincere in his efforts to protect returnees.

"Vicente Fox has said that he's here to supervise and check out that things are done the right way, but also to set the example," Hernandez said. "Police in Guanajuato [state] don't accept bribes anymore. It took a year and a half to filter down, but now they don't." Fox served as governor of Guanajuato before pursuing the presidency.

Hernandez said surveys indicated that returnees were being treated better so far this Christmas season. Fox visited two checkpoints yesterday south of Nogales, which is across the border from a smaller Arizona town of the same name. He will take his message today to Ciudad Juarez, across from El Paso, Texas; and to Nuevo Laredo, across from Laredo, Texas.

4. Minuteman Defense Corps Calls for Vigilante Border Enforcement, 2005

Almost four years after the terrible terrorist attacks upon our country on September 11, 2001, citizens of the United States remain concerned about our national security, specifically our outrageously porous international border with Mexico. Those who live along the border-state region with Mexico have great

From http://www.gpo.gov:80/fdsys/pkg/CHRG-109hhrg21365/pdf/CHRG-109hhrg21365
.pdf, pp. 84–88.

concern for their personal safety as well as concern over the lack of border security.

Despite repeated warning from citizens, local law enforcement and various public officials, our border remains intolerably porous and presents not only a threat to public safety but also a clear and present danger to the security of our nation. Millions of dollars have been thrown at the problem and new technology has been promised—some delivered, some conspicuously absent. Citizens who live with daily incursions of illegal aliens through our property and into the sparsely populated back country along the border realize one thing: the Department of Homeland security cannot effectively stop migrant workers, mothers carrying small children, vicious drug smugglers, known criminals and human smugglers from breaching our security—we do not feel confident that our government is able to stop terrorist elements from entering our country with the intent of inflicting harm upon our citizens.

After years of writing letters, sending faxes, sending e-mails and making countless phone calls to elected officials pleading, begging and demanding redress of our grievances, frustration led us to but one conclusion—we must act and address the problem with a citizen movement.

In November of 2002, I, Chris Simcox, began assembling a group of citizens to undertake the responsibility in assisting what we realized was a Border Patrol woefully undermanned and, as it stood, unable to provide for the safety of the citizens of our local community, Cochise County, Arizona.

We now consider the movement to be a revival of the Civil Defense movement of the World War II era. While out troops are fighting on foreign soil, while our Department of Homeland Security applies its resources and efforts to provide for our national security in other areas, we the people will take up the slack by developing civil defense volunteers to support the U.S. Border Patrol.

We consider this a no-compromise situation. Until the time that congress appropriates sufficient funding and develops personnel levels to the numbers needed to effectively secure our borders, we the people will roll up our sleeves in the time-honored tradition and creed of a "cando" society, and we will assist until honorably relieved from duty by the government of the United States.

Only one scenario is possible in convincing citizens to return to our normal everyday lives: deployment of U.S. military reserves and or assigning National Guard personnel, to augment a woefully understaffed Border patrol; only this will convince ordinary citizens to retire from this endeavor.

5. Reporter Questions Television Anchor's Anti-Immigration Crusade, 2007

The whole controversy involving Lou Dobbs and leprosy started with a "60 Minutes" segment a few weeks ago.

The segment was a profile of Mr. Dobbs, and while doing background research for it, a "60 Minutes" producer came across a 2005 news report from Mr. Dobbs's CNN program on contagious diseases. In the report, one of Mr. Dobbs's correspondents said there had been 7,000 cases of leprosy in this country over the previous three years, far more than in the past.

When Lesley Stahl of "60 Minutes" sat down to interview Mr. Dobbs on camera, she mentioned the report and told him that there didn't seem to be much evidence for it.

"Well, I can tell you this," he replied. "If we reported it, it's a fact."

With that Orwellian chestnut, Mr. Dobbs escalated the leprosy dispute into a full-scale media brouhaha. The next night, back on his own program, the same CNN correspondent who had done the earlier report, Christine Romans, repeated the 7,000 number, and Mr. Dobbs added that, if anything, it was probably an underestimate. A week later, the Southern Poverty Law Center—the civil rights group that has long been critical of Mr. Dobbs—took out advertisements in The New York Times and USA Today demanding that CNN run a correction.

Finally, Mr. Dobbs played host to two top officials from the law center on his program, "Lou Dobbs Tonight," where he called their accusations outrageous and they called him wrong, unfair and "one of the most popular people on the white supremacist Web sites."

We'll get to the merits of the charges and countercharges shortly, but first it's worth considering why, beyond entertainment value, all this matters. Over the last few years, Lou Dobbs has transformed himself into arguably this country's foremost populist. It's an odd role, given that he spent the 1980s and '90s buttering up chief executives on CNN, but he's now playing it very successfully. He has become a voice for the real economic anxiety felt by many Americans.

The audience for his program has grown 72 percent since 2003, and CBS—yes, the same network that broadcasts "60 Minutes"—just hired him as a commentator on "The Early Show." Many elites, as Mr. Dobbs likes to call them, despise him, but others see him as a hero. His latest book, "War on the Middle Class," was a best seller and received a sympathetic review in this newspaper. Mario Cuomo has said Mr. Dobbs is "addicted to economic truth."

Mr. Dobbs argues that the middle class has many enemies: corporate lobbyists, greedy executives, wimpy journalists, corrupt politicians. But none play a bigger role than illegal immigrants. As he sees it, they are stealing our jobs, depressing our wages and even endangering our lives.

That's where leprosy comes in.

"The invasion of illegal aliens is threatening the health of many Americans," Mr. Dobbs said on his April 14, 2005, program. From there, he introduced his original report that mentioned leprosy, the flesh-destroying disease—technically known as Hansen's disease—that has inspired fear for centuries.

According to a woman CNN identified as a medical lawyer named Dr. Madeleine Cosman, leprosy was on the march. As Ms. Romans, the CNN correspondent, relayed: "There were about 900 cases of leprosy for 40 years. There have been 7,000 in the past three years."

"Incredible," Mr. Dobbs replied.

Mr. Dobbs and Ms. Romans engaged in a nearly identical conversation a few weeks ago, when he was defending himself the night after the "60 Minutes" segment. "Suddenly, in the past three years, America has more than 7,000 cases of leprosy," she said, again attributing the number to Ms. Cosman.

To sort through all this, I called James L. Krahenbuhl, the director of the National Hansen's Disease Program, an arm of the federal government. Leprosy in the United States is indeed largely a disease of immigrants who have come from Asia and Latin America. And the official leprosy statistics do show about 7,000 diagnosed cases—but that's over the last 30 years, not the last three.

The peak year was 1983, when there were 456 cases. After that, reported cases dropped steadily, falling to just 76 in 2000. Last year, there were 137.

"It is not a public health problem—that's the bottom line," Mr. Krahenbuhl told me. "You've got a country of 300 million people. This is not something for the public to get alarmed about." Much about the disease remains unknown, but researchers think people get it through prolonged close contact with someone who already has it.

What about the increase over the last six years, to 137 cases from 76? Is that significant?

"No," Mr. Krahenbuhl said. It could be a statistical fluctuation, or it could be a result of better data collection in recent years. In any event, the 137 reported cases last year were fewer than in any year from 1975 to 1996.

So Mr. Dobbs was flat-out wrong. And when I spoke to him yesterday, he admitted as much, sort of. I read him Ms. Romans's comment—the one with the word "suddenly" in it—and he replied, "I think that is wrong." He then went on to say that as far as he was concerned, he had corrected the mistake by later broadcasting another report, on the same night as his on–air confrontation with the Southern Poverty Law Center officials. This report mentioned that leprosy had peaked in 1983.

Of course, he has never acknowledged on the air that his program presented false information twice. Instead, he lambasted the officials from the law center for saying he had. Even yesterday, he spent much of our conversation emphasizing that there really were 7,000 cases in the leprosy registry, the government's 30-year database. Mr. Dobbs is trying to have it both ways.

I have been somewhat taken aback about how shameless he has been during the whole dispute, so I spent some time reading transcripts from old episodes of "Lou Dobbs Tonight." The way he handled leprosy, it turns out, is not all that unusual.

For one thing, Mr. Dobbs has a somewhat flexible relationship with reality. He has said, for example, that one-third of the inmates in the federal prison system are illegal immigrants. That's wrong, too. According to the Justice Department, 6 percent of prisoners in this country are noncitizens (compared with 7 percent of the population). For a variety of reasons, the crime rate is actually lower among immigrants than natives.

Second, Mr. Dobbs really does give airtime to white supremacy sympathizers. Ms. Cosman, who is now deceased, was a lawyer and Renaissance studies scholar, never a medical doctor or a leprosy expert. She gave speeches in which she said that Mexican immigrants had a habit of molesting children. Back in their home villages, she would explain, rape was not as serious a crime as cow stealing. The Southern Poverty Law Center keeps a list of other such guests from "Lou Dobbs Tonight."

Finally, Mr. Dobbs is fond of darkly hinting that this country is under attack. He suggested last week that the new immigration bill in Congress could be the first step toward a new nation—a "North American union"—that combines the United States, Canada and Mexico. On other occasions, his program has described a supposed Mexican plot to reclaim the Southwest. In one such report, one of his correspondents referred to a Utah visit by Vicente Fox, then Mexico's president, as a "Mexican military incursion."

When I asked Mr. Dobbs about this yesterday, he said, "You've raised this to a level that frankly I find offensive."

The most common complaint about him, at least from other journalists, is that his program combines factual reporting with editorializing. But I think this misses the point. Americans, as a rule, are smart enough to handle a program that mixes opinion and facts. The problem with Mr. Dobbs is that he mixes opinion and untruths. He is the heir to the nativist tradition that has long used fiction and conspiracy theories as a weapon against the Irish, the Italians, the Chinese, the Jews and, now, the Mexicans.

There is no denying that this country's immigration system is broken. But it defies belief—and a whole lot of economic research—to suggest that the problems of the middle class stem from illegal immigrants. Those immigrants, remember, are largely non–English speakers without a high school diploma. They have probably hurt the wages of native-born high school dropouts and made everyone else better off.

More to the point, if Mr. Dobbs's arguments were really so good, don't you think he would be able to stick to the facts? And if CNN were serious about being "the most trusted name in news," as it claims to be, don't you think it would be big enough to issue an actual correction?

6. Tribal Government Condemns Border Wall, 2008

The Tohono O'odham Nation, the second largest Indian reservation recognized by the U.S. with territory and members on both sides of the U.S.-Mexico border, is calling for a halt in the construction of a fence along the Southwest border.

"As original people of the territory, the Tohono O'odham have lived on and cared for that land long before such a boundary even existed; before there was a U.S. or a Mexico," Ofelia Rivas, a representative of the Indian tribe, said Thursday in Washington.

Jerry Seper, "Southwest tribe calls for end of border fence construction," *Washington Times*, July 11, 2008, p. A 4. Copyright 2008 *The Washington Times* LLC.

"Now, however, the construction of the border wall along the entire U.S.-Mexican border is splitting border communities and indigenous nations alike, including the Tohono O'odham," Ms. Rivas said during a press conference.

The Tohono O'odham Reservation, whose 24,000 members live on 2.8 million acres on both sides of the Arizona border south of Tucson, is comparable in size to the state of Connecticut. It said the proposed border fence would "destroy the Tohono O'odham way of life, its traditions and religious practices," along with the "many rights sworn to the O'odham people that are being violated."

"This wall and the construction of this wall has destroyed our communities, our burial sites and ancient O'odham routes throughout our lands," Ms. Rivas said. "The entire international border has divided and displaced our people.

"The wall also is severely affecting the animals. We now see mountain lions going into areas where people live because of the wall," she said.

Homeland Security Secretary Michael Chertoff has said his goal is to have actual fencing along 370 miles of the U.S.-Mexico border and barriers that would allow foot traffic but prevent vehicles on another 300 miles before the end of President Bush's term, which ends in January. Mr. Chertoff has waived dozens of federal laws and regulations to build the fence.

But Tohono O'odham elders and traditionalists maintain their legacy through oral history, conducting natural ceremonies that include offerings to the land and sea. They also use many of the region's plants and environmental resources as a source of food and medicine. Many of these sacred ceremonies take place in Mexico.

Ms. Rivas said the right of the Tohono O'odham people to travel freely and safely over traditional routes in their territory had been guaranteed under U.S., Mexican and International Law. She said the American Indian Religious Freedom Act of 1978 acknowledges the rights of the O'odham people that the fence violates.

"By restricting the mobility of the O'odham people, the wall prevents the free practice of their religion and their cultural traditions. Further, rights granted by the United Nations Universal Declaration of Human Rights, the Declaration of Human Rights for Indigenous Peoples, and the American Declaration of the Rights and Duties of Man are also being ignored due to a waiver issued by the Department of Homeland Security," she said.

"Under this document, the president claims the power to waive any and all environmental and federal Indian laws in order to build the wall in the name of national security," she said.

Ms. Rivas also said the construction has increased the military presence within the O'odham territory, further affecting their lives and communities.

"This wall has militarized our entire lands," she said. "We, as original people, are now required to answer to United States armed forces as to our nationality on our own lands."

Ms. Rivas said that once she was asked at gunpoint to produce identification to establish her right to be on the lands where she was born and where her ancestors lived since before Columbus arrived.

Ms. Rivas is in Washington with members of many different indigenous nations and allies who walked from San Francisco to Washington in what was billed as "The People's Walk" to protest the fence.

7. Author Describes Death of Migrants in Arizona Desert, 2004

TUESDAY, MAY 22.

It was the high spike of the heat wave. The temperatures burned up through the nineties with the sunrise. By midmorning, it was 100 degrees. By noon, 105. By two o'clock, it was 108 degrees.

They walked.

Nahum Landa Ortiz: "I didn't watch the first ones die. Two died apart from us. They were behind us and I didn't see them die."

He says the guides took five men with them when they left. But they didn't. The group was fracturing, and small cells were moving into the landscape on their own. Francisco Morales says, "We started throwing things away. We were going to die. We threw away the things in our pockets in despair."

Edgar Martinez, who didn't have a phone at home, who had to be reached if anyone called through the phone booth in Cuautepec, a village with the name "Hill of the Eagle," middle name Adrian, nephew of José Isidro Colorado, in love with Claudia Reyes, son of Eugenio, stumbled. He righted himself and put out a hand and fell into a bush. He got to his knees, grimaced as if smiling. Perhaps he was ashamed to be falling. He was sixteen years old.

He reached a point registered on GPS coordinates as N. 32.21.85/W. 113.18.93.

He fell again. He closed his eyes. He didn't rise. He lay there for the length of the next day, lost in a delirium no one can even imagine, burning and burning.

Not a mile from Edgar, Abraham Morales tripped and hit the ground. He crawled, rolled on his side, kicked. His eyes were red. He was at N. 32.21.85/W. 113.18.94.

Nobody seemed to know him, for when they finally came and collected his body, he would lie neither claimed nor identified for a month, alone on his icy drawer.

Francisco Morales: "I do not know who was dying or how many because I too was dying."

José de Jesús Rodriguez: "That day, at three in the afternoon, I was dead. What time is it right now—it is four o'clock. Yes, I died. I was dead from three o'clock to four o'clock. I revived and came back from the dead at eleven o'clock at night."

Morales adds: "We were walking like robots."

They could not bury their dead. There is some evidence they didn't know who was dead, since they were all falling and fainting, and those who were awake didn't always know what they were seeing.

They walked three, perhaps four miles farther. Men collapsed. It looked like more deaths were inevitable. Five of them decided to go ahead and see what they could find. Perhaps they'd find Mendez. Or the way. Anything.

"Wait for us," they said, but some of the men were already un-conscious, and nobody really said anything to them.

Wait Hell, they'd already waited.

"When we got sick," José Bautista says, "there was no shade. So I crawled up to hide in the rocks. One of the boys went crazy and started jumping up and down. He started screaming, 'Mama! Mama! I don't want to die!' He ran up to a big cactus and started smashing his face against it. I don't know what his name was."

Nahum and his companions were hiding in the trees.

A voice carried on the still air, crying, "Mother, save me!"

Mario González Manzano and his brother Isidro, far ahead on their attempt to find rescue, watched their brother walk away, in search of escape.

"Somebody said the freeway was right there, right over the hills," he said. "They lied."

Isidro and Mario were in luck: they found some prickly pears—*tuna* in Spanish. "We ate the tunas to stay alive," Mario says.

The liquid in the cactus fruits spared him. He would only see dead bodies when he got to a Border Patrol truck and saw them stacked inside.

The sign of the dead could be ghastly and haunting. One of the, men tore off his shirt and tried to bury himself. The hither thither he left all around him showed violent kicking and arm flailing, as if he were swimming. He managed to get the top half of his torso buried in the ground, where he either smothered or passed out. The relentless heat baked him, literally cooking him in the ground. His face bloated and came loose from the bones tender as barbecued pork.

Reymundo Jr. collapsed in his father's arms. Reymundo held him as he died. Shook him, cried over him. He called for help, but the only thing that might have helped his son was water.

When Reymundo died and slid from his father's arms, his farther lurched away into the desert, away from the trees, crying out in despair. Some of the men said he took the American money he had saved for their trip and tore it into small bits.

Julian Ambros Malaga was also said to have torn up his money. His brother-in-law, Rafael Temich, after being prodded by Julian to walk and save himself, was helpless to save him. "That's when he took out his money and started tearing it apart. And he took off alone and I also was demented. I was demented. I couldn't help him. I couldn't carry him. Then he threw himself into the sunlight, and that's where he stayed."

Old Reymundo also threw himself into the sunlight. He was shouting and crying and throwing money into the air, and he walked until he fell, trying to swim in the dirt as if he'd fallen into a cool stream.

Nobody knows the name of the man who took off all his clothes. It was madness, surely. He removed his slacks, folded them, and put them on the ground. Then he took off his underwear, laid it neatly on the pants. He removed his shirt and undershirt and squared them away with the pants. As if he didn't want to leave a mess. His shoes had the socks tucked in them. They were placed on the clothes to keep them from blowing away.

He lay on his back and stared into the sun until he died.

Later, Kenny Smith, from Wellton Station, said, "This poor guy just crossed his ankles and went to sleep."

8. Journalist Reports on Killing of Women Maquiladora Workers in Juárez, 1997

Seven men were already in jail in Ciudad Juárez, charged in the serial murder of seventeen young women—the case apparently solved—when Sandra Juárez's body turned up on the banks of the Rio Grande.

One Saturday in July 1996 Sandra, seventeen, walked into Ciudad Juárez from Lagunillas, a village of forty adobe houses, thirty miles from the nearest telephone, in a parched region of the state of Zacatecas. She was no match for the city. On Monday she went looking for work in the *maquiladoras*—the assembly plants—that dominate the Judárez economy. A few days later they found her blouse on the Mexican side of the river. She lay strangled to death on the U.S. side. Her case has not been solved. No one knows where she went, or with whom, that Monday.

For the people of Ciudad Judárez, Sandra's case, and others that turned up that summer, played havoc with some accepted beliefs. Until then, for example, they had believed that the city's first serial-murder case, which had attracted news media from across Mexico and the United States, had been put behind them. They believed that a foreigner and a group of U.S.-style gang bangers were responsible. Given the town's border location, Juarenses are used to blaming things on people from somewhere else; 80 percent of the town's prison population is from somewhere else, is an oft-quoted statistic.

But about the time Sandra Juárez died, people in town finally had to start listening to Esther Chávez. Chávez is a thin, almost frail retired accountant who lives in a middle-class neighborhood of Juárez and wouldn't seem the type to get involved in a serial murder case. Nor did Chávez have much history of feminist involvement when she organized a women's group known as Grupo 8 de Marzo. But from newspaper clippings, Chávez had been keeping an informal list of cases involving dead young women ever since she noted the rape and murder of thirteen-year-old Esperanza Leyva on November 15, 1993. By that time the list was already thirteen cases long. "We had gone to talk to the mayor," Chávez says. "He promised to get higher authorities involved. He was my very good friend, but he never did anything for us. What we were trying to get people to see was a general climate of violence against women."

Sam Quinones, *True Tales from Another Mexico* (University of New Mexico Press, 2001), 137–141.

The cases were notable in that the identifiable victims were usually young and working-class. A good number had worked in the *maquiladoras*. These were not murders of passion, taking place in a bar or bedroom. Some of the women had been raped, many had been mutilated, and a good many more had been dumped like the worn-out parts to some machine in isolated spots in the deserts surrounding the city. Their killer or killers didn't even take the trouble to cover them with dirt, believing, with good reason, that the sun and the desert's scavengers would quickly wipe their corpses from the face of the earth. By the summer of 1996 Chávez had counted eighty-six of these cases, dating back to Esperanza Leyva in 1993.

Ciudad Juárez spreads low, bleak, and treeless across the valley floor south of El Paso and the Rio Grande. The smell of fetid sewers is a constant companion through town, a nagging reminder that the desert is no place for a major industrial center.

Years ago Juárez thrived because it understood that beneath America's puritan rhetoric, a buck was always waiting to be made. During Prohibition Juárez produced whiskey and beer and ran it across the border. Bars emerged along Avenida Juárez, the main drag leading to the bridge into El Paso, and have never left. "Divorce planes" brought American couples in to quickly end their marriages. To women looking for work, Juárez offered prostitution. Until the mid-1960s Juárez was a bustling city of sin.

Then the *maquiladoras* arrived. Over the next three decades the assembly plants turned dusty border outposts into major stops in the global economy, assembling televisions, telephones, appliances, clothes, calculators, car parts—all for export to the world's wealthiest market across the border. In Juárez several *maquiladoras* even count America's coupons.

Mexico began allowing *maquiladoras* on the border in 1964. The idea was to sop up migrant workers returning after the United States ended the so-called *bracero* treaty, a twenty-two-year-old agreement that allowed Mexicans to work seasonally and legally in America's fields. The *maquilas* began as an after-thought. But beginning in the late 1970s, the country lurched through recession after recession, and the peso steadily lost value. Many U.S. and foreign firms saw a payroll paid in a currency that always lost value as a nifty proposition. As Mexico staggered, the *maquiladora* sector along the border became an increasingly important job provider. Today [1997] some 970,000 people—mostly unskilled and low paid—work in more than 3,800 *maquiladoras*, completing in twenty-five years one of the most remarkable industrial transformations anywhere in the latter half of the twentieth century. Virtually all the plants are owned by foreign companies: General Motors, Ford, Hughes, Phillips, RCA, Sony, Toshiba, Daewoo, and on down to minor candy and clothing manufacturers.

Juárez saw the twenty-first century in the *maquiladora*. The city always had more *maquila* jobs than any other city—178,000 [by 1997]. As the *maquila* grew, so grew Juárez. The city went from 407,000 inhabitants in 1970 to about 1.5 million people [in 1997], with several thousand more wandering through in any given month.

But since in Mexico, border towns barely qualify as Mexican, Juárez is always last on the list when the central government in far-off Mexico City doled out the resources. The city couldn't provide basic municipal services for everyone the *maquiladoras* pulled from the interior. Urban planning was an impossibility. And on a *maquiladora* salary, no worker could afford much rent. So shantytowns leaped into the desert. They were without drinking water, sewers, parks, lighting, or paved streets. An apocalyptic folk craft—shack building—developed, using plastic tarp and barrels, wood pallets, card-board, wire cord—anything that was *maquiladora* detritus. Bottle caps were used for bolts.

As Juárez grew, an anonymity that characterizes many large U.S. cities settled on it. Police make a lot of the fact that so many of the dead women—more than half on Chávez's list—are unidentified. Nor do they have missing person reports matching their descriptions. No one claims these bodies. Their families in some isolated part of Mexico may believe they somewhere in the United States or simply don't care where they are. This, police say, is what they're up against.

But Juárez offered jobs, and that makes it like America in the most important way. Like the United States, Juárez attracted Mexicans from the interior who were restless and willing to risk a lot to change their lives. People from rural states of Durango, Zacatecas, and Coahuila continue to trudge into Juárez in huge numbers, figuring anything is better than the brutish life of the bankrupt Mexican *campo*. But unlike the United States, which attracts mainly men, Juárez became a magnet for women, especially young women. The *maquila* did and not, as Mexican planners hoped, employ many men returning from the United States. Instead the plants pulled young women to the border from deep in Mexico's countryside. In Juárez for many years, more than 80 percent of all *maquila* workers were women. Even today, with *maquila* work heavier, thirds of the *maquila* workforce is female. These were women with few of the skills that the industrial economy would reward. They were interchangeable and they moved frequently between jobs, which were generally similar in their monotony. Juárez thirsted for them, and the *maquilas* put up help-wanted banners that fly almost all year round.

One of the women that Juárez attracted was Elizabeth Castro, a seventeen-year-old who had come from the state of Zacatecas. On August 10, 1995, Castro's decomposing body appeared along a highway. At the time no one that much of it. For a few days she even remained unidentified. Then, the August and September, the bodies of more young women began show—several of them in Lote Bravo, a magnificent sprawl of cara-mel-colored south of the airport. The doctors autopsying the bodies said some showed of being raped. Several of them were too decomposed to identify. Presounted and head-lines grew shrill. Juárez had seen a lot, but never this, renses were comforted, however temporarily, by the arrest in early October of Abdel Latif Sharif, an Egyptian chemist. Police accused him of killing women, including Castro. (Witnesses were later found who said they'd and Elizabeth Castro in a club together.) The case finally had something Juárez was used to—Sharifez was used to—a foreigner with a history. Sharif had lived in Florida for a number of years and there had been convicted of a variety of sex crimes against girls and spent time in prison. "When the United States deported him, he didn't return to Egypt. He came to Juárez.

Police claimed the forty–nine–year–old Sharif had been prowling the down-town clubs that *maquiladora* workers frequented, seducing young women, then killing them. But Sharif said he was innocent, a scapegoat for police under public pressure. He predicted the bodies would continue to appear. He was right.

Lomas de Poleo is a stretch of desert west of town littered with the wind–blown trash of clandestine garbage dumpings. Within a few months of Sharif's arrest, the decomposing bodies of young women began appearing amid the debris. A goat herder found three of them.

It takes a lot to shock Juárez, but the continuing discovery of bodies did the trick. Civil patrols were now organized to protect children getting out of school and young women as they returned home from their *maquila* jobs. The shanty-towns of Anapra and Lomas de Poleo formed squads to comb the desert areas for more corpses. The newspapers were filled with the latest news, clues, and conjecture about the case. Police competence was routinely questioned.

Then one night in April 1996 the police raided clubs along Avenida Juárez, the bar-studded drag leading from El Paso, where officers had been working undercover. They arrested a gang called Los Rebeldes (The Rebels). The police theorized that Sharif paid Los Rebeldes to kill women while he was in jail to make it seem that the real killer was still at large. And there stood the police case.

But then came the summer of 1996. More dumped bodies showed up. They continue to be found. So while evidence points to a serial murderer in some of the cases, what now seemed clear was that Juárez had something much larger on its hands.

Indeed, since the arrests of Los Rebeldes in early 1996, the bodies of almost fifty women have turned up. Rocío Miranda, a bar owner, was raped by seventeen young men, then dumped in a vat of acid. The only parts of Miranda that remained when she was found were her hands, feet, and the silicon implants that police used to identify her. Silvia Rivera, twenty–one, was stabbed to death by her husband and buried out near the prison; she was first identified and buried as one Elizabeth Ontiveros, who'd been reported missing, until Ontiveros showed up, having run off with her boyfriend. Soledad Beltrán, a stripper known as Yesenia, turned up in a drainage ditch, stabbed to death, her killers unknown. Sonia Yvette Ramírez, thirteen, was raped and killed and left a block from police headquarters. Her father spent two months tracking down her boyfriend, who had fled south to Chihuahua City. There he cornered him in an auto-repair shop, thrashed him, and turned him over to police, who charged him with Sonia's murder. Brenda Nájera, fifteen, and Susana Flores, thirteen, were both raped, tortured, and shot in the head. An autopsy showed Susana had had four heart attacks before dying. And there were more women who turned up whose identity still is unknown, leaving behind only the grimy detritus of a dime-store novel: a tattoo on the wrist, black jeans, fingernails painted dark red, green socks, white panties, a black bra, and often the signs of rape. One woman was found with two brassieres lying by her side. Two others were found on a motorcycle racetrack in the desert, wearing slippers and bathrobes.

There was no one thing—or one person or group—to pin the bodies on anymore. If a serial murderer was at large, there was a lot of horrible other stuff going on as well. It came to seem as if Juárez was awash in dead women merely because it was Juárez.

9. Newspaper Describes Increasing Violence of Drug Trade, 2010

Although Mexico has been a producer and transit route for illegal drugs for generations, the country now finds itself in a pitched battle with powerful and well-financed drug cartels. Top police commanders have been assassinated and grenades thrown, in one case into the crowd at an Independence Day celebration.

The authorities say most of the deaths have resulted from drug cartels fighting rivals. But soldiers and police have also been killed, as well as innocents.

The upsurge in violence is traced to the end of 2006 when President Felipe Calderon launched a frontal assault on the cartels by deploying tens of thousands of soldiers and federal police to take them on. Mr. Calderon has successfully pushed the United States to acknowledge its own responsibility for the violence in Mexico since it is American drug consumers who fuel demand and American guns smuggled into Mexico that are used by the drug gangs.

With the prospect of a quick victory increasingly elusive, a rising chorus of voices on both sides of the border is questioning the cost and the fallout of the assault on the cartels.

To many Mexicans, the rising count of gruesome drug-related murders is evidence that the government's strategy is not working. In September 2009, newspapers estimated the number of killings at more than 13,600 since Mr. Calderón took office.

The struggle began to effect relations with the United States as well. On March 13, 2010, gunmen believed to be linked to drug traffickers shot a pregnant American consulate worker and her husband to death in the violence-racked border town of Ciudad Juárez. The gunmen also killed the husband of another consular employee and wounded his two young children.

The shootings took place minutes apart and appeared to be the first deadly attacks on American officials and their families by Mexico's powerful drug organizations, provoking an angry reaction from the White House. They came during a particularly bloody weekend when nearly 50 people were killed nationwide in drug-gang violence, including attacks in Acapulco as American college students began arriving for spring break.

The killings followed threats against American diplomats along the Mexican border and complaints from consulate workers that drug-related violence was growing untenable, American officials said. Even before the shootings, the State Department had quietly made the decision to allow consulate workers to evacuate their families across the border to the United States.

In response to critics, Mr. Calderón has said his government was the first one to take on the drug trafficking organizations.

The strategy "has not only reversed the rising trend of crime and drug trafficking, but it has also weakened the conditions that allowed them to reproduce and to expand," Mr. Calderón said.

But Mexicans wonder if they are paying too high a price and some have begun openly speaking of decriminalizing drugs to reduce the sizeable profits the gangs receive.

Americans, from border state governors to military analysts in Washington, have begun to question whether the spillover violence presents a threat to their own national security and, to the outrage of many Mexicans, whether the state itself will crumble under the strain of the war.

While Mr. Calderon dismisses suggestions that Mexico is a failed state, he and his aides have spoken frankly of the cartels' attempts to set up a state within a state, levying taxes, throwing up roadblocks and enforcing their own perverse codes of behavior. The Mexican government has identified 233 "zones of impunity" across the country, where crime is largely uncontrolled, a figure that is down from 2,204 zones a year ago.

The authorities have made a string of high-profile arrests of drug chieftains and have had success seizing large amounts of illegal drugs, guns and money. But the violence remains high and authorities acknowledge that they will never wipe out this multi-billion-dollar-a-year industry. The goal now is to turn what is a national security problem into one that can be handled by law enforcement.

Responding to a growing sense that Mexico's military-led fight against drug traffickers is not gaining ground, the United States and Mexico set their counter-narcotics strategy on a new course in March 2010 by refocusing their efforts on strengthening civilian law enforcement institutions and rebuilding communities crippled by poverty and crime.

The $331 million plan was at the center of a visit to Mexico in March by several senior Obama administration officials, including Secretary of State Hillary Rodham Clinton; Defense Secretary Robert M. Gates and Homeland Security Secretary Janet Napolitano.

The revised strategy has many elements meant to expand on and improve programs already under way as part of the so-called Mérida Initiative that was started by the Bush administration including cooperation among American and Mexican intelligence agencies and American support for training Mexican police officers, judges, prosecutors and public defenders.

Under the new strategy, officials said, American and Mexican agencies would work together to refocus border enforcement efforts away from building a better wall to creating systems that would allow goods and people to be screened before they reach the crossing points. The plan would also provide support for Mexican programs intended to strengthen communities where socioeconomic hardships force many young people into crime.

The most striking difference between the old strategy and the new one is the shift away from military assistance. More than half of the $1.3 billion spent under Merida was used to buy aircraft, inspection equipment and information technology for the Mexican military and police. Next year's foreign aid budget provides for civilian police training, not equipment.

Military-to-military cooperation was expected to continue, officials said, despite reports by human rights groups of an increase in human rights violations by Mexican soldiers.

This revised strategy, officials said, would first go into effect in Tijuana and Ciudad Juárez, the largest cities on Mexico's border with the United States. Ciudad Juárez, a city of 1.7 million, has become a symbol of the Mexican government's failed attempts to rein in the drug gangs.

The public outcry generated by the violence in Ciudad Juárez forced Mr. Calderón to acknowledge that the drug war would not be won with troops alone.

ESSAYS

In the first essay, York University political scientist Daniel Drache addresses the ways in which the terrorist attacks on New York and Washington, D.C., on September 11, 2001, changed border enforcement and diplomatic relations between Canada, Mexico, and the United States. In the decades before 2001, economic needs, particularly the desire for open trade and access to markets, had led the United States to keep its borders relatively porous. But in the aftermath of 9-11, national security concerns led the American government to engage in much more restrictionist measures. For the first time, Canadian citizens were required to have passports to enter the United States. The Immigration and Naturalization Service was located in the new Department of Homeland Security, the U.S. government announced plans to build a wall along most of its border with Mexico and watchtowers along much of the Canadian border, and American vigilante groups such as the Minutemen began portraying illegal migration from Mexico as a leading national security threat. The 9-11 attacks, in short, were a watershed for North American borders. Drache concludes by criticizing the leaders of Canada and Mexico for not standing up to what he sees as the short-sighted goals of U.S. policy, and encourages them to cooperate with one another and appeal to Canadian and Mexican public opinion, which is much more cognizant of border policy than before.

In the second essay, University of California–San Diego sociologist David Fitzgerald explores the mixed views that Mexicans who remain in their country have of those who have migrated to the United States. Focusing on the town of Arandas in the state of Jalisco, Fitzgerald asks how Mexican culture and institutions attempt to maintain themselves as a large proportion of the population emigrates and returns. Although most Mexicans—migrants and non–migrants alike—believe that emigration has a positive economic impact, heavy majorities also believe that the supposedly more violent and materialistic American culture to which migrants are exposed is a threat to Mexican life. Accordingly, local authorities such as the police and church closely monitor returned migrants and are likely to blame them (even in the absence of hard evidence) for social problems such as drug use and HIV/AIDS infections. Although the Mexican government has recognized dual nationality since 1998, the Mexican public continues to disapprove of Mexicans who become American citizens. Despite some predictions about the decline or disappearance of the nation-state in a new global age, Fitzgerald finds abundant evidence that nationalism is alive and well. Liberalized trade and mass migration have made border-crossing a factor of great importance all across North America, far from the international borders themselves. But North America remains a deeply divided ground in the twenty-first century.

Canada–U.S. Relations and the Impermeable Border Post 9/11: The Co-Management of North America

DANIEL DRACHE

Until September 11, 2001, Canadians had not thought very much or very hard about the long border they share with the United States. Nor had public authorities shown significant concern. There was no compelling imperative to contemplate it, particularly in this global age. Ideas passed through it, money poured over it and millions of people crossed it each year. Post-September 11, the border has changed beyond recognition. It is everywhere and everything. Issues now include enhanced security, protection of privacy rights, who Canadians want as citizens, how cross-border traffic can be expedited, and how open the border should be to political refugees.

In fact, the world's longest undefended border was never unimportant. It has always been at centre stage in North America in the exercise of power and international cooperation. For Americans it embodies the indivisibility of their national sovereignty and paramountcy of homeland security. It is symbolically as important as the constitution and the presidency. For Mexicans their frontier with the United States is the most iconic of institutions, inescapable and insurmountable linking together two radically different societies, economies and cultures in a thousand different ways. It embodies all their ambitions, pride, fears and insecurities; a remarkable contrast with the Canadian belief that its border is largely invisible and unchangeable.

Arguably, Mexicans, Canadians and Americans have come to understand each other less and less, and there are profound differences in how they think about the Great Border. The North American Free Trade Agreement (NAFTA) downsized the importance of national boundaries and minimized their importance as regulatory gates and commercial walls. Now Canada and Mexico find themselves in a new tense relationship with the United States. The security wall is forbidding and its goals and aims controversial. Many of the old notions about a porous border no longer apply. The security needs of the United States now reach into their domestic space and the effects are pronounced.

Daniel Drache, "Canada-U.S. Relations and the Impermeable Border Post 9/11: The Co-Management of North America," *CONfines* 4 (Jan.-May 2008): 69–83. Also chapter in Drache, *Borders Matter: Homeland Security and the Search for North America*, with new introduction and material (Mexico City: Siglo XXI, 2007). Originally published in *Borders Matter Homeland Security and the Search for North America* (Halifax N.S.: Fernwood Publishing, 2004). Professor Daniel Drache is a full Professor and Acting Director of the Robarts Centre for Canadian Studies, York University Toronto Canada and for more material North American integration go to www.yorku.ca/drache <http://www.yorku.ca/drache>.

Post-September 11, the border is expected to operate like a Kevlar vest, stopping everything in its path, without hindering the free movement of goods and services. What an abrupt turnaround from an age of free trade when openness was everything and security only a secondary consideration. Of course, it cannot be both, a security-tight border and a border geared for commerce with minimum restrictions at the same time. Eventually one must dominate the other Ottawa has yet to absorb the fact that the commerce-first border that every business leader worked so hard to achieve is yesterday's story. North America's elites believed that they had settled the management of the two borders for at least a generation and that the NAFTA consensus could not unravel. The commercial border was to be out of public sight and out of mind and they could get on with the business of business. A decade later how short-sighted they were. North America is not evolving towards a European style of arrangements. Relations between Canada and the United States and Mexico and Washington are cooler than ever. The United States is pursuing a traditional policy of regional bilateralism striking deals with Canada and pressuring Mexico on immigration, the investment and border security.

The dilemma is that Americans also don't want a super-tight border economically. They don't want to be body-searched and, most emphatically, corporate Unites States does not want its Canadian production facilities to face delays when shipping goods back and forth across the border. It is in their interest to trade; and the United States will do business wherever it can for oil, manufactured goods and services of every description.

Many things look different for Canada in this security-obsessed age of strategy, might, and law. The Homeland Security Act of 2002, the Public Health and Bio-terrorism Preparedness Response Act of 2002, and the Patriot Act of 2001 have placed management of the Canada-U.S. border directly under congressional and executive authority in ways that are unprecedented. All have had their authority renewed by the U.S. Congress by 2005 and this revolution in security policy will outlast the Bush presidency. These other along side measures authorize police and intelligence authorities to expand electronic surveillance and detain and remove aliens suspected of engaging in "terrorist activity."

These landmark bills grant sweeping powers to law enforcement agencies and increase the extralegal powers of the executive arm of government by means of executive and other administrative orders that do not require public hearings or obligate the president to ask Congress for additional authority. They rely on secret warrants or compulsory disclosures that expand the capability of the Justice Department to obtain warrants and conduct searches without publicly disclosing them immediately. Among other things, the new laws allow Internet monitoring, give police access to business records that include library and bookstore files, and authorize emergency searches and electronic surveillance. In the year after 9/11 the Department of Justice obtained 113 secret emergency search authorizations, compared to 47 in the twenty-three years prior to the attack. More than eight million FBI files were provided to the State Department and 85,000 records of suspected persons were turned over to the

Immigration and Naturalization Service. These expanded powers of the central security state would seem to violate the Fourth Amendment's protection against "unreasonable searches and seizures." U.S. courts have been acquiescent in defending civil rights in an era of security.

September 11 redefined not only the border but also North America as a geopolitical region. So far Ottawa and Mexico remain uncertain as to how they should define themselves on the U.S. perimeter. They can play a symbolic "filler" role in the war against terrorism. When intervention requires a military presence as in Afghanistan, experts reckon that Canada can send up to 2,500 soldiers, although even that modest contribution stretches Canada's military to the limit. From a military point of view, Canada has little to offer the U.S. war machine. Mexico is even more skeptical of formalized joint military co-operation with its neighbour. It never participated in any kind of North American Aerospace Defense Command arrangement (NORAD) with the United States. It was not part of the North Atlantic Treaty Organization. Given its size and policy of neutrality Mexico does not have a tradition of sending its military forces into joint operations. Mexico has had very limited participation in United Nations peace-keeping. Instead its security focus has been primarily domestically-oriented. No Mexican president is going to commit Mexican troops to a U.S.-sponsored initiative post 9/11.

With the Canada-Mexico-United States relationship no longer open-ended, Canada and Mexico must acquire a strategic culture for the twenty-first century. U.S. diplomacy is under intense scrutiny as never before. The transformed border is dramatically more complex with all its four dimensions in play as a security moat, regulatory fence, identity line in the sand for citizenship and a commercial opportunity. The challenge is to make all the ducks line up.

Canada has to become assertive about its side of the border. As a first priority it must conduct a full-scale audit of the U.S. Homeland Security and Patriot Acts to determine their impact on Canadian public policy and their cross-border. The Canadian government is handicapped because it has not consulted across government or with provinces about U.S. homeland security and its extraterritorial consequences for immigration, refugee policy, intelligence, commerce, and public regulation. The scope and speed of U.S. legislative and legal change is dramatic and unprecedented in recent times, and the Canadian public has not been kept fully informed.

By 2008, it is expected that U.S. border practices will have changed beyond recognition from what they were in 2003. The most telling is that Canadians will be required to have a passport to enter the U.S. and rather than the old standbys of a health card or driver's license. The era of 'flash and dash' are over. The idea of automatic access, minimum bureaucracy, and an easy going custom's officer is now a thing of the past. Every name on airline passenger lists will be checked and any that are questionable will be barred by U.S. authorities. Naturalized Canadians, those born elsewhere but have taken out Canadian citizenship, will face intense scrutiny if they emigrated from so-called high risk regions of the Middle East or South Asia. Political refugees also face new hurdles; no longer can Ecuadorians and Colombians be able to come through the United States and apply for refugee status in Canada. They now are required to apply in the United States and if they are turned back, they cannot seek asylum in Canada.

In September 2006 Homeland Security announced that the U.S. plans to set up 800 watchtowers along the northern border to block illicit migration and effectively intrude into Canadian sovereign space. This unilateral decision underlines once again that Washington does not trust Canada to screen people entering the country. Despite all the rhetoric from the Harper government about rebuilding the Canada-U.S. relationship it is obvious that Washington does not have much confidence in all the effort and money Canada has spent on its security agenda. Harper's appeasement of the Bush administration is destined to fail.

Mexico does not want to mix security with trade, but now the line between these daunting policy areas is blurred and uncertain. Eight hundred surveillance towers are to be built on the southern border with the first installations to be constructed on the Arizona frontier with Mexico. Having a green card no longer means quick and automatic entry to the U.S. Migration policy is cross–cutting– virtually touching on every aspect of Mexico-U.S. relations. Immigration has become irreversibly linked to U.S. Homeland Security. Mexico's southern border is more than ever seen as a danger zone by U.S. security authorities. Gangs, narcotics and weapons move north through Mexico into the U.S. border patrols, border police, customs' officers and U.S. vigilante organizations guard the Mexico-U.S. border up and down the line.

Many of these changes do not simply focus on the U.S. border but on the processes behind and beyond the border. The globalization of U.S. domestic policy is driven by a singular aim: to secure the future of "our nation," "American democracy" and "border security" anywhere Washington believes it is threatened. It will decide what the "security danger" is and how it should be "neutralized." The choices for Canada and Mexico are stark–to be a tactical sceptic or a trusting loyalist. Either way the answer to this fundamental quandary has to be found in Canada and Mexico, not Washington. Ottawa has not thought through its strategic response to maximize its foreign policy assets. Belatedly it still needs to.

In other areas of U.S. public policy the role and importance of the border as a marker of exclusive national sovereignty has also been broadened, contrary to the theory and practice of economic integration. Free trade was to dismantle non-tariff barriers but U.S. practice is to make the U.S. security perimeter intrusive and invasive. A primary target is Mexico and its porous border. NAFTA was not meant to dismantle the border for immigration purposes. In 2002 the INS denied immigrant status to over 170,000 immigrants, most at the U.S. southwest border. Under the old rules more than 10,000 immigrants had been removed from the United States each year since 1995. Between September 2000 and November 2001 over 300,000 illegal migrants were apprehended on the southwest border. These numbers are expected to increase in the future. By 2005 removals had topped the one million mark.

Shortly after NAFTA came into effect, the Clinton administration passed the Illegal Immigration Reform and Immigrant Responsibility Act of 1996 in order to closely monitor and control the cross-border movement of all non-U.S. citizens, or "aliens" as they are termed under U.S. law. The Act required the INS "to collect and record the departure of every alien from the United States and match the records of departure with the record of the alien's arrival in the United States." It was aimed at Canadians and Mexicans who entered the United States illegally or remained beyond the permissible time period. The INS estimated that Canada was the fourth largest source of illegal immigrants, with about 120,000 Canadian aliens residing in the United States as of 1996. The INS studies also found that about 40 percent of all illegal immigrants enter the United States legally but stay without a visa.

Despite the protest from both Canadian and Mexican governments that this new legislation would impede entries and exits between the three countries, the U.S. Congress remained indifferent to its NAFTA partners. Section 110 of the Act generated a lot of bitter criticism from border communities that wanted U.S. legislators to separate domestic politics from the growing commercial interdependence between the three NAFTA partners and give Canadians and Mexicans a special status under the bill. Their advice carried no weight with U.S. lawmakers. The U.S. congressional view was that it possessed the competence to control and regulate the movement of people across U.S. borders and nothing in the NAFTA limited its right to do so. A tiny concession achieved by the Canadian government was to defer implementation of the Act until March 30, 2001. Now, with the passage of the Homeland Security Act, the new rules and regulations apply to Canadians as well as everyone else. Canada's NAFTA status did not merit any special consideration.

If Canada and Mexico are to develop a strategic border culture, they need to reposition themselves in North America and defend their side of the Great Northern and Southern Border. To this end there are three basic principles that should be committed to memory and then acted on.

Protecting political refugees, poverty eradication, regional development and human rights, Canada and Mexico need to build leverage, acquire voice and co-ordinate their efforts. Kissinger was prescient when he wrote that 'foreign policy is domestic policy'. If this is true for the United States, it doubly applies to Canada and Mexico, countries in which social diversity, hybridity, and multiculturalism define their respective national identities and are the strategic interests that must be nurtured and protected. Increasingly, foreign policy will have to reflect the social values of Canadian and Mexican society, rather than, as in the past, the special interests of their self-interested business elites. That is why if the NAFTA cousins expect to be a more effective actors globally, they have to connect with their publics in ways that they never did in the past.

The Stranger or the Prodigal Son?

DAVID FITZGERALD

When migrants return from the North laden with gifts for the annual patron saint fiesta, the municipal government receives them under a banner reading

David Fitzgerald, *A Nation of Emigrants: How Mexico Manages Its Migration* (Berkeley: University of California Press, 2009), 125–144, 151–152. © 2008 by the Regents of the University of California. Published by the University of California Press.

"Welcome, Hijos Ausentes." Families reunite and dollars crackle through the local economy. Yet many residents, and even many migrants, resent the cultural changes that migrants bring back with them. A 1991 cartoon in a weekly newspaper expressed a common ambivalence toward *norteños*, the migrants with extensive experience in the United States. "January is here, it's fiesta … and our norteños," reads the headline over a bird's-eye view of Arandas and a skull and crossbones on a road sign warning "ARANDAS: 15,000 NORTEÑOS." The caption reads, "And the worst part: in the U.S. they don't go out because they're afraid, and here, even their moms can't stand them. The solution? A new city for them, special schools, fines in dollars, concentration camps …?"

The supposed transgressions of migrants are amplified because they take place during the fiesta celebrating the Virgin of Guadalupe, patron of Arandas and Mexico. The fiesta is also the town's main civic event, when the government self-consciously promotes local traditions of tequila, mariachis, and *charro* horsemen. Jaliscienses pride themselves on being the most Mexican of the Mexicans, and within Jalisco, Alteños pride themselves on being the most Jalisciense and Mexican of them all. Patron saint fiestas are a celebration of the sacred as well as a celebration of the collective self. At a fiesta for the hijos ausentes in a nearby town in Los Altos, a parade float juxtaposes the illegal drugs and homelessness of Chicago with the "idyllic, tranquil, family- and religion-centred life of the home town." Foreign "impurities" introduced by migrants are on public display during the fiesta and generate open controversy.

Asking how actors in the sending community try to maintain the cultural authenticity of migrants and the hometown flips the conventional question about the assimilation of immigrants that dominates studies of international migration. The mirror image of *assimilation*, the process of groups or individuals becoming similar, is *dissimilation*, the process of becoming different. Rather than ask how U.S. institutions attempt to integrate the immigrant population, I ask how Mexican institutions try to prevent the *dis*integration of the community of origin when emigrants leave and return. Those efforts involve a delicate balance between trying to take advantage of the economic and cultural advantages of emigration while trying to prevent the seepage of undesirable foreign ideas and practices into the home community. Long periods of socialization in another state's cage create many problems—and fewer opportunities—for the state, the Church, and other actors in the community of origin. A tension develops between attempts to extend the community by including extraterritorial members, as scholars of transnationalism have emphasized, and attempts to protect the community by monitoring returnees and moderating the effects of migration, a project consistent with the classical view of state-led nationalizing. This tension is obscured by the notion of a "transnational community," which misleadingly suggests a holistic cultural unit.

In the view of Alteños, the economic rewards of migration come at a steep cultural price. Attitudes about economic impacts in Arandas and Agua Negra were generally positive among household heads in the 2003 survey I conducted. Among the migrants, 88 percent thought emigration had a positive economic impact on the community, and 77 percent of nonmigrants thought the same.

More surprising is that migrants and nonmigrants in the sample were equally likely to report that migration has had a negative impact on the community's customs and morals; 77 percent of both nonmigrants and migrants held that view. Most Arandenses share an image of who is a good member of the community and who is a transgressor. Just as nonmigrants fear the corrupting influence of American culture on their hometown, migrants fear its corrupting influence on their own children, whether they are in the United States or Mexico. Church and state have developed practices such as the hijos ausentes fiesta to celebrate the "good" migrant, while distancing themselves from migrants who violate cultural norms.

Negative views of the cultural impacts of migration in Los Altos are consistent with national surveys; in 2006, twice as many Mexicans said the cultural influence of the United States has been unfavorable for Mexico (44 percent) as said it has been favorable (21 percent). On the other hand, the level of nationalism directed against the United States is mitigated when Mexicans look northward for a model of modernity. The suspicions of Mexican elites are "often allied to a sneaking admiration" that has become more pronounced with the advent of the 1994 North American Free Trade Agreement and a generation of technocrats schooled in top U.S. universities. Widespread ambivalence toward the effects of migration to the United States reflects a broader ambivalence toward the northern neighbor in general.

With the possible exception of the clergy and a handful of literati, most Arandenses say that the economic benefits of migration to the community outweigh the cultural costs. A former migrant who spent twenty-two years working in blue-collar jobs in factories in Los Angeles before returning to Arandas to become president chief of police expressed a common view: "The cultural problem of different customs that are taken from the United States through migration and brought here—customs which maybe don't go with the culture of Arandas, and so people say, 'These noisy characters come here and bring their loud music and walk around all tattooed and this and that'—I think that doesn't have the importance that foreign exchange income has for the country, its economic development, the transformation of the towns to a much better level of living, and better dwellings for its residents."

Alteño families often depend on remittances for economic survival, or at least have grown accustomed to the material comforts that remittances offer. Seventy-eight percent of households in Agua Negra and 44 percent in Arandas include at least one migrant. The norteño is not an exotic character, but one's husband, son, nephew, or cousin. Most people know that migrants suffer on their journey despite all their bravado and stories of adventure. An Alteño adage expresses residents' two minds toward migrants who bring home dollars and arrogant attitudes, yet who must often borrow money to return to the North after the fiesta: "When they come, they strike fear, and when they leave, they strike pity."

For Arandenses to describe and explain how migrants are changed by their experiences in the United States, migrants first must be identified and monitored.

In Arandas, the clearest form of social labeling of emigrants is applied to the subset who have settled abroad for long periods, the norteños.

How do residents of Arandas, a town of forty thousand, decide who is a norteño? When asked in interviews, Arandenses usually listed the same set of cues: Young, male, urban migrants wear baggy or short pants, tattoos, earrings, and gold necklaces. Their head is shaved or they wear their hair long. Both men and woman dye their hair, the only cue Arandenses mentioned for (young) migrant women. Most Arandenses called this a *cholo* style. Labeling migrants is an inexact science: Imitators who have never left Los Altos have access to migrant styles through locally produced copies or the gifts of returnees, and migrants who avoid the cholo aesthetic do not display obvious cues. It is harder to tell a returned migrant from a nonmigrant when both sport the popular ranchero look of boots, jeans, sombrero, and buttoned shirt, though the apparent expense of these fashions and accompanying gold chains are more subtle indicators of migrant status. The behavior of migrants dressed in a ranchero or generic urban style is not as readily categorized as norteño. Consequently, the behavior of the cholos receives greater scrutiny and disproportionately influences the public sense of how migrants behave. All of my local informants expressed negative views of cholos.

The personal presentation of earlier generations of migrants was the object of similar negative reactions from a government preoccupied with sculpting the modern Mexican man while maintaining social solidarity. The Secretariat of Labor's 1946 surveys of returning braceros found that more than a third of the returnees had changed their "normal" way of dress to clothes that were "expensive, flashy, exaggerated" and "uncomfortable and inappropriate for the milieu of their origin." The study's authors argued that "this mutation in their clothing can be explained as the satisfaction of desires unsatisfied and repressed for a long time, and the desire to appear original and to distinguish themselves in their home environment and signal themselves as recent visitors from the United States."

Vehicles also telegraph signals that identify migrants. Symbols of Americana such as decal flags, U.S. license plates, English-language music pulsating from sound systems, chrome detailing, and dramatic driving styles all display migrant status.

The disorder created by returned migrants can become a policing issue. Just across the Guanajuato state line in Manuel Doblado a government billboard reads, "Welcome to your land, paisano. We invite you to respect the rules of your town." In neighboring parts of Michoacán in 1907 police opened a checkpoint at the local train station to register returnees by collecting information on their Mexican place of residence, the weapons they carried, and details of their migration to the United States. Today even the police use informal membership categorization to monitor migrants, rather than checking official identification papers.

In Arandas, police trouble with returnees does not generally include serious, sustained violence. A former municipal president who served in the 1950s said that rambunctious returnees are "a bother, but there are other, more important crimes for the government to worry about." Another former municipal president from 1990s said he ordered police to confiscate the car stereos of those who played their music too loud. The incoming police chief, a former migrant himself, launched a publicity campaign promising to crack down on people who drive aggressively and play loud music. He aimed the measures at the entire population but considered norteños the primary offenders.

Control over members' bodies is one of the goals shared by Church and state in their exercise of pastoral power. Migrants are blamed for the introduction of illegal drugs and increased consumption of alcohol. In 1946, the Secretariat of Labor found that braceros drank more alcohol upon their return than before they had left. According to a 1997 study by the government of Jalisco, in rural communities with high levels of emigration migrants were eleven times more likely than nonmigrants to have used at least one of a set of drugs including solvents, marijuana, cocaine, and heroin. And a 2003 report on the condition of migrants commissioned by the government of Jalisco warned of "the presence of mental health problems and addictions originating in the loss or alteration of their original customs and the necessity to adopt new ways of life." Jalisco has a "Go Healthy, Return Healthy" program in twenty-seven counties of high emigration to discourage drug use and other unhealthy behaviors. In Arandas, the portfolio of one of the council members includes combating drug addiction. "There is a very close relationship between the addiction of the Arandense and traveling to the United States," he said. While the overwhelming weight of the public discourse in Arandas about drugs blames outsiders in general and migrants in particular, there are exceptions. At the outset of an antidrug crusade in the 1980s sponsored by the Church with support from local government, a prominent editorial from an ex-migrant in *El Arandense* urged Arandenses to stop pointing the finger at outsiders and start recognizing their own culpability for the drug problem in Arandas.

Blaming sexually transmitted diseases on outsiders is another way for Arandenses to set themselves apart from the rest of Mexico and the United States as more Catholic and morally pure. There were twenty-two known cases of AIDS in the county of Arandas in 2003. Arandenses blame migrants for bringing back AIDS from the United States, though according to the government of Jalisco, of the nearly seven thousand cases in the state reported from 1983 to 2001, only 6 percent were people who had lived in the United States for more than six months. The county doctor blames venereal diseases such as syphilis on men who have returned from northern fleshpots, rather than the clandestine sex industry in certain roadside bars outside Arandas. Several of the local elites I interviewed, including priests and a prominent PAN politician, claimed that migrants were responsible for the introduction of homosexuality to Arandas.

Many Mexicans believe that the lack of moral discipline in private U.S. religious and family life promotes undisciplined behavior in both countries. They see migrants as cut loose from the conservative Catholicism of Los Altos and adrift in a heterogeneous religious environment where they are preyed upon by the proselytizing of Mormons, Jehovah's Witnesses, and Evangelicals, or simply lured into religious apathy by a more secular U.S. society. The loosening of family bonds generally and the absence of watchful wives in particular are also thought to promote vice and immorality among men.

Most Arandenses think that cultural dissimilation, becoming less like "us" and more like "them," is usually a bad thing. Government employees, priests, and the press monitor migrants to mitigate those cultural impacts and reinforce their pastoral power. The drugs, criminality, and disease that North Americans often blame immigrants for importing to the United States are seen in Mexico as *exports* from the United States to Mexico via emigrant carriers. On both sides of the border, the same practices are viewed as foreign pathologies. For those in the business of maintaining national and local purity within the territorially defined community, migration is a threatening conduit of cultural change.

One of the legal indicators of dissimilation is the loss of Mexican citizenship when migrants naturalize in the United States. Residents of Arandas and Agua Negra draw a distinction between migrants in general and migrants who become U.S. citizens. Many Alteños object to the transformation of Mexicans into U.S. citizens and the idea of dual nationality. The extent of this contention belies the notion that migrants and those who stay behind form part of one "transnational community." The old-fashioned nationality in a single nation-state apparently matters to many residents of source communities, who are not all enthusiastic about the possibilities of a "trans-" or "postnational" society.

The more negative views regarding migrants who nationalize in the United States are accompanied by negative attitudes toward dual nationality. Since 1998, Mexican law has allowed Mexicans by birth to hold both Mexican and foreign nationalities. Ninety-two percent of migrants and only 68 percent of nonmigrants support the right to dual nationality. A logistic regression found that nonmigrants, people without a migrant in their household, women, and Agua Negrans were significantly more likely than migrants, people with a migrant in their household, men, and people living in the city of Arandas to oppose the right to dual nationality. Dual loyalties appear more threatening to people with less direct experience with migration or the greater social diversity found in towns.

The myth of being forced to trample or spit on the Mexican flag as part of the U.S. naturalization ceremony remains ubiquitous in Mexican migrant source communities and among many immigrant Latinos in the United States. Negative attitudes toward migrants who become U.S. citizens have probably contributed to historically low naturalization rates for Mexicans in the United States, but such attitudes may be waning. The percentage of Mexican immigrants in the United States who have naturalized climbed from 15 in 1994–95 to 25 in 2000–2001. Growing public acceptance of naturalized emigrants in Mexico would likely contribute to a further rise in U.S. naturalization, especially as Mexico has legally recognized dual nationality since 1998.

Arandense intellectuals complain in public about the cultural side of denationalizing. According to editorials in the local newspapers, U.S.-style Christmas and Halloween celebrations are two of the biggest expressions of migrants' cultural degeneracy. For example, in a front-page Christmas Day editorial in 1993 headlined "Santa Claus Should Disappear," *El Arandense* decried the displacement of nativity scenes by Christmas trees and the invasion of secular, materialistic values from the United States that pollute the local religious tradition. A municipal president in the 1990s ordered the publication of material condemning Halloween as a foreign import and promoting the celebration of the authentically Mexican Day of the Dead. A 1990 editorial in *Notiarandas* took up the same crusade against Halloween, which it saw as part of the cultural "invasion" of migrants "who come to Mexico to do what they can't do in the United States, and in so doing trample on our beautiful traditions."

Doña Marina is the name that the Spanish conquistadors gave to La Malinche, an indigenous woman who betrayed her people to become the mistress of leader Hernán Cortés. *Malinchismo*, a syndrome of preferring the foreign to the authentically native, has its modern incarnation in *pochismo*, the phenomenon of people of Mexican descent born in the United States acting like gringos. Malinchismo and pochismo loom large in Mexican nationalism and are rhetorically powerful slurs used by Arandense elites during interviews. Even college-educated nonmigrants tend to see norteños' U.S.-born children in subtractive cultural terms as having "no culture" because they fall between two discrete cultural systems.

Some migrants see themselves as "taking the best from here and there" in what researchers would call an additive cultural hybridization of two systems. A former migrant who lived in California and Illinois for ten years before returning to publish *El Arandense* subscribes to the additive view of culture, but he said he was socially rejected when he returned. He blamed the negative reception on the "inferiority complex" of Arandenses who stayed behind: "If you said that you were coming from the United States, many people scorned you…. A lot of people here, for this same inferiority complex, wanted to tell you that the culture there was not appropriate for the culture here, that it was a lower culture, that it would harm them."

Linguistic shifts are another site of cultural contention. During summer vacation and the patron saint fiesta, groups of returnees can be heard speaking English in the streets of Los Altos. The lay head of the migrant ministry in Agua Negra says that when returnees speak English with each other, she and her friends tell them, "Shh, shh, you're in Mexico!" Residents complain that "mental *gabachos*" born in Mexico or the "pocho" children of Mexican origin born in the United States anglicize their Spanish pronunciation and invent hybrid neologisms such as *parquear* (to park) and *marqueta* (market). Learning English is seen as an accomplishment, and nonmigrant elites often send their children to learn English in local private classes, but "losing" Spanish is viewed as a moral failure and a rejection of being Mexican. Arandenses who have visited the United States as tourists often tell stories of interacting with people of Mexican origin there "who don't want to speak Spanish even though you can tell by looking at them" that they do speak Spanish. The folk theory is that their reticence is "because they are ashamed of their roots." Mexican visitors often fail to understand that many of the second or later generations simply don't speak proficient Spanish, and perhaps never had a facility to lose in the first place. For all the fears in the United States that immigrants and their children are not learning English fast enough, the second generation prefers to speak English, and away from the border region the third generation rarely speaks Spanish with any proficiency.

In interviews, elites frequently referred to the problems putatively caused by Mexicans in the United States as an embarrassment to Mexico. The middle and upper classes emphasize that migrants are drawn disproportionately from the ranks of people "sin cultura" (without culture)—a category that captures both the economic class and cultural status dimensions of "low-class." The distancing of Mexican elites from migrants has been a regular theme since the early twentieth century, when Mexican consular officials called on officials in Mexico to stop the emigration of poor workers because it was giving Mexico a bad image abroad. Resentment of migrants' class mobility is also a factor. The wage differential between Mexico and the United States means that people with little education who migrate to the United States and then return are often richer than professionals who never left Mexico. As one entrepreneur described his youth in Arandas in the 1970s, "I was studying and saw migrants returning. I asked myself, 'How come someone who doesn't even read or write is doing better than me?'" Professionals are frustrated by the economic success of nouveau riche migrants who return to Arandas.

Resentment of class mobility is only a partial explanation for the negative attitudes about the cultural transformations wrought by migration, however. Such negative attitudes are the norm among nonmigrants and migrants across the population. Migrants often fear the cultural shifts in their own Americanizing children. Household heads in Agua Negra were just as likely as household heads in Arandas to say they had a negative view of migration's cultural effects, even though there are no real "elites" in Agua Negra, where social stratification is limited to the division between poor farmers with their own land and even poorer day laborers. The class dimension of talk about emigration's negative effects is subsumed by culturally driven fears of destructive influences.

Many of the problems attributed to migration, and state responses attempting to manage those problems, become visible in public education. Teachers throughout the historic sending areas complain that widespread migration encourages adolescents to drop out of school and migrate themselves. In an interview with a Catholic weekly newspaper, the director of the technical secondary school in Arandas said the principal problem with the student population was the dropout rate: "Many students go to the United States. A very large number of boys come and enroll, but come December, their friends from the North come back with cash, and off they go [in January]." In the primary school in Agua Negra, the director said the students were too young to talk about their plans to migrate, but the school's population fell 20 percent between 1980 and 2003 as whole families migrated to the United States, León, and Arandas. Consequently, the Secretariat of Public Education stripped the school of one of its seven teachers. Migration also contributes to school absenteeism for the estimated 7 percent of students who join the corn harvest in November and December because their fathers left crops in their care. All ten of the educators interviewed agreed that migration was implicated in disciplinary problems at school.

The perpetuation of migrants' cultural nationality through state education in Mexico and the United States is an explicit policy of the government of Mexico and the state of Jalisco. In their 2000 Declaration of Puebla, the directors of state offices of attention to migrants aborad said their sports and cultural programs were designed to keep paisanos" away from the vices and practices alien to our values, principles, and customs." Mexican consulates have distributed thousands of Spanish-language text-books to schools in the United States, raising the hackles of U.S. nationalists for referring to the stars and stripes as "the enemy flag" and portraying the 1846–48 Mexican-American War as a disaster. According to a 2003 report, the state of Jalisco seeks to "preserve and strengthen our traditions, values, and national identity" for the benefit of 4.5 million Jaliscienses abroad. Thirteen Jalisciense teachers that year participated in an exchange program to teach in public schools in areas of Jalisciense concentration in California, Michigan, and Illinois.

On the local level, the director of the primary school in Agua Negra explained that the civic education classes are designed to inculcate patriotism. On September 16, when Mexico's independence from Spain is celebrated, schoolchildren parade through Agua Negra. "We want them to learn to be well cemented in their values here so that they don't adopt the customs of the North. In the United States, morals are more liberal than they are here," he said. When asked what values are important to inculcate in Agua Negra, he mentioned honor, solidarity, antimaterialism, family unity, and patriotic values "so they don't disown their motherland when they're in the United States."

In the minds of educators, migration is a major channel for the introduction of undesirable American culture.

Cultural representations of migrants are sometimes contradictory in rural communities, whose residents already feel unsettled by the pace of change as they become more integrated into the rest of the nation and the world. Celebrations of the "absent son" who leaves to provide for his family contrast with more ambivalent representations of the "prodigal son" who returns to his family after learning that the American dream is an illusion. The norteño can even become like Georg Simmel's "stranger," who reminds the community of what its culture is by showing what it is not. Representations of the norteño-as-stranger allow Arandenses to invert the status hierarchy by asserting the moral superiority of local traditions and ways of life against the agringado customs of the migrant. These culture wars *a la mexicana* influence outcomes as diverse as how migrants maintain ties with their hometowns and employers' hiring decisions.

For migrants, events such as the Señorita Arandas pageant and the winners' tour of Jalisco are ways to claim that migrants still are moral members of the community. Neatly coiffed young women dressed in styles reminiscent of the nineteenth century are attempting to establish an alternative schema for norteños, in contrast to the predominant cholo schema of a young man with shaved head and tattoos driving recklessly through the plaza, playing rap music and shouting out the window. The religious procession of hijos ausentes and the luncheon with mariachi music extolling the absentee and his nostalgia for Arandas are institutional venues where mainstream migrants, the Church, and the state join to display their idea of a proper moral order. The Mexican government at various levels attempts to socialize the population in Mexico and even Mexicans in the United States through educational and cultural programs that promote a sense of mexicanidad and local ties. Hometown association projects such as donating an ambulance create prestige by showing not only that migrants have wealth, but that they are using their wealth for the benefit of the community. All of these activities are important ways to maintain hometown ties.

In short, the cultural transformations wrought by migration crystallize a fundamental ambivalence about the influence of the United States and how to enjoy the fruits of modernity and economic growth without sacrificing patriotism, faith, and social solidarity. Cultural nationalists in countries of emigration are concerned with the dissimilation of emigrants and the disintegration of their communities brought on by emigration. This negotiation takes place in a broad cultural field that transcends the territorial border between the United States and Mexico, but it is hardly the open field of free-flowing people and ideas proclaimed by the globalists. Some actors in Mexico are actively intervening in that cultural landscape with attempts to repair the bars of the nation-state's cage.

FURTHER READING

Bowden, Charles. *Juárez: The Laboratory of Our Future* (1998).

———. *Murder City: Ciudad Juarez and the Global Economy's New Killing Fields* (2010).

Bowden, Charles, and Julián Cardona. *Exodus/Éxodo* (2008).

Buchanan, Patrick. *State of Emergency? The Third World Invasion and Conquest of America* (2007).

Clarkson, Stephen. *Does North America Exist? Governing the Continent After NAFTA and 9/11* (2008).

Crossing Arizona. Directed by Joseph Matthew and Dan Devivo. Rainlake Productions, 2005.

Drache, Daniel. *Borders Matter: Homeland Security and the Search for North America* (2007).

De Genova, Nicholas. *Working the Boundaries: Race, Space, and "Illegality" in Mexican Chicago* (2005).

Fink, Leon. *The Maya of Morgantown: Work and Community in the Nuevo New South* (2007).

Fitzgerald, David. *A Nation of Emigrants: How Mexico Manages Its Migration* (2009).

Hakim, Peter, and Robert Litan, eds. *The Future of North American Integration: Beyond NAFTA* (2002).

Hendricks, Tyche. *The Wind Doesn't Need a Passport: Stories from the U.S.-Mexico Borderlands* (2010).

Martinez, Ruben. *Crossing Over: A Mexican Family on the Migrant Trail* (2002).

Smith, Robert. *Mexican New York: Transnational Lives of New Immigrants* (2005).

Thorpe, Helen. *Just Like Us: The True Story of Four Mexican Girls Coming of Age in America* (2009).

Urrea, Luis Alberto. *The Devil's Highway: A True Story* (2005).

Vollman, William T. *Imperial* (2009).